Advanced 3-D Game Programming Using DirectX® 8.0

Peter Walsh

Wordware Publishing, Inc.

ISBN 1-55622-513-X
10 9 8 7 6 5 4 3 2 1
0109

DirectX is a registered trademark of Microsoft Corporation in the United States and/or other counties.
Other product names mentioned are used for identification purposes only and may be trademarks of their respective
companies.

All inquiries for volume purchases of this book should be addressed to Wordware Publishing, Inc., at
the above address. Telephone inquiries may be made by calling:

(972) 423-0090

Dedications

*To my best friends
Joanna, Carolyn, Mike, Jon, Caroline, Leslie,
Laz, Clare, Stew, and of course everyone else that
I don't have room to list!*

Peter

To my parents, Manny and Maria.

Adrian

Original edition for DirectX version 7.0 written by
Adrian Perez with Dan Royer.
Revised and updated by Peter Walsh.

Contents

Preface xv
Acknowledgments xvii
Introduction xix

Chapter 1 Windows 1
A Word about Windows 1
Hungarian Notation 2
General Windows Concepts 3
Message Handling in Windows 5
    Explaining Message Processing 5
Hello World—Windows Style 7
    Explaining the Code 9
        Registering the Application 11
        Initializing the Window 11
        WndProc—The Message Pump 15
Manipulating Window Geometry 15
Important Window Messages 17
MFC 22
Class Encapsulation 23
COM: The Component Object Model 30
References 33
For Further Reading 33

Chapter 2 DirectX—The Basic Components 35
What is DirectX? 35
Installation 36
Setting up VC++ 36
What Happened to DirectDraw?! 38
Direct3D 40
    2-D Graphics—A Primer 40
        Surfaces 44
        Complex Surfaces 46
        The IDirect3DSurface8 Interface 49
        Surface Operations 49
        Surfaces and Memory 52
        Modifying the Contents of Surfaces 52
        Drawing on Surfaces with GDI 54

The Direct3D Device Object. 54
  Windowed vs. Full-screen. 55
The Direct3D Object 55
  Creating Direct3D Surfaces. 56
  More on Direct3D Devices 57
Implementing Direct3D with cGraphicsLayer 57
  Creating the Graphics Layer 62
  Full-screen Initialization 63
  Shutting Down Direct3D 69
  Changes to cApplication. 69
Application: Direct3D Sample 70
DirectInput 73
Why Should You Use DirectInput? 73
Devices 74
  Receiving Device States 75
  Cooperative Levels 78
  Application Focus and Devices 79
The DirectInput Object. 79
  Implementing DirectInput with cInputLayer 80
  Additions to cApplication 94
DirectSound. 94
The Essentials of Sound 95
DirectSound Concepts 96
  DirectSound Buffers. 97
Sound Buffer Operations 100
  Loading WAV Files 103
Implementing DirectSound with cSoundLayer 105
  Creating the DirectSound Object 105
  Setting the Cooperative Level 106
  Grabbing the Primary Buffer. 107
The cSound Class 111
  Additions to cApplication 117
Application: DirectSound Sample 118
References 123
For Further Reading 123

Chapter 3 3-D Math Foundations 125
Points. 125
The point3 Structure 129
Basic point3 Functions. 130
  Assign. 130
  Mag and MagSquared 130
  Normalize 131
  Dist. 131
point3 Operators 132

Addition/Subtraction 132
Vector-scalar Multiplication/Division 134
Vector Equality 135
Dot Product 137
Cross Product 139
Polygons 140
Triangles 143
Strips and Fans 144
Planes 146
Defining Locality with Relation to a Plane 149
Back-face Culling 152
Clipping Lines 153
Clipping Polygons 154
Object Representations 158
Transformations 160
Matrices 161
The matrix4 Structure 172
Translation 175
Basic Rotations 175
Axis-Angle Rotation 177
The LookAt Matrix 179
Perspective Projection Matrix 181
Inverse of a Matrix 182
Collision Detection with Bounding Spheres 183
Lighting 185
Representing Color 186
Lighting Models 188
Specular Reflection 190
Light Types 191
Parallel Lights (or Directional Lights) 191
Point Lights 192
Spotlights 193
Shading Models 194
Lambert 195
Gouraud 195
Phong 196
BSP Trees 197
BSP Tree Theory 198
BSP Tree Construction 199
BSP Tree Algorithms 204
Sorted Polygon Ordering 204
Testing Locality of a Point 205
Testing Line Segments 206
BSP Tree Code 206
Wrapping It Up 217

	References	218
	For Further Reading	218
Chapter 4	**Artificial Intelligence**	**219**
	Starting Point	220
	Locomotion	220
	Steering—Basic Algorithms	221
	Chasing	221
	Evading	222
	Pattern-based AI	222
	Steering—Advanced Algorithms	223
	Potential Functions	224
	The Good	225
	The Bad	226
	Application: potentialFunc	227
	Path Following	229
	Groundwork	230
	Graph Theory Done Really, Really Quickly	232
	Using Graphs to Find Shortest Paths	235
	Application: Path Planner	237
	Motivation	241
	Non-Deterministic Finite Automata (NFAs)	241
	Genetic Algorithms	244
	Rule-Based AI	245
	Neural Networks	246
	A Basic Neuron	247
	Simple Neural Networks	249
	Training Neural Networks	251
	Using Neural Networks in Games	252
	Application: NeuralNet	252
	Some Closing Thoughts	261
	References	262
	For Further Reading	262
Chapter 5	**UDP Networking**	**263**
	Terminology	263
	Endianness	263
	Network Models	265
	Protocols	266
	Packets	267
	The Right Tool for the Job (aka "DirectPlay and why I'm not using it")	268
	Implementation 1: MTUDP	268
	Design Considerations	268
	Things that go "argh, my kidney!" in the night	268
	Mutexes	270

Threads, Monitor, and the Problem of the
try/throw/catch Construction 272
MTUDP: The Early Years 272
MTUDP::Startup() and MTUDP::Cleanup() 273
MTUDP::MTUDP() and MTUDP::~MTUDP() 275
MTUDP::StartListening(). 275
MTUDP::StartSending() 276
MTUDP::ThreadProc(). 276
MTUDP::ProcessIncomingData() 278
MTUPD::GetReliableData() 279
MTUDP::ReliableSendTo() 279
cDataPacket 279
cQueueIn. 280
cHost. 282
MTUDP::ReliableSendTo() 286
cUnreliableQueueIn 293
cUnreliableQueueOut 294
cHost::AddACKMessage() / cHost::ProcessIncomingACKs() 294
cNetClock 299
Implementation 2: Smooth Network Play 302
Geographic and Temporal Independence 302
Timing is Everything 303
Pick and Choose 304
Prediction and Extrapolation 305
Conclusion 307

Chapter 6 Beginning Direct3D—Immediate Mode. 309
Introduction to D3D. 309
The Direct3D8 Object. 310
The Direct3DDevice8 Object 310
Device Semantics 311
Device Types. 312
Hardware 312
Software 312
Reference 313
Ramp (and Other Legacy Devices). 314
Determining Device Capabilities 314
Setting Device Render States 318
Fundamental Direct3D Structures 322
D3DCOLOR. 322
D3DCOLORVALUE 322
D3DVECTOR 323
D3DMATRIX. 324
The Depth Problem (and How Direct3D Solves It) 324
W-Buffering 327

Contents

Stencil Buffers 328
Vertex Buffers 329
Texture Mapping 331
    Materials and Lights 331
        Using Lights 332
        Using Materials 336
The Geometry Pipeline 338
    Clipping and Viewports 339
Fog 340
    Vertex-based Fog 341
    Pixel-based Fog 342
    Using Fog 342
Drawing with the Device 344
    Direct3D Vertex Structures 344
        Flexible Vertex Format Flags 344
    Primitive Types 347
    The DrawPrimitive Functions 348
        DrawPrimitive 348
        DrawPrimitiveUP 349
        DrawIndexedPrimitive 349
        DrawIndexedPrimitiveUP 350
    Adding Direct3D to the Graphics Layer 350
        Direct3D Initialization 351
            Acquire an IDirect3D8 Interface 351
            Fill In the Presentation Parameters 352
            Create a Viewport and Projection Matrix 354
Further Additions to the GameLib 356
The Direct3DX Library 357
Application: D3D View 357
    The .o3d Format 357
    The cModel Class 358

Chapter 7 **Advanced 3-D Programming** **369**
Animation Using Hierarchical Objects 369
    Forward Kinematics 371
    Inverse Kinematics 373
        Application: InvKim 376
Parametric Curves and Surfaces 379
    Bezier Curves and Surfaces 380
        Bezier Concepts 380
        The Math 382
        Finding the Basis Matrix 384
        Calculating Bezier Curves 386
        Forward Differencing 387
        Drawing Curves 391

Drawing Surfaces 392
Application: Teapot 393
B-Spline Curves 399
Application: BSpline 400
Subdivision Surfaces 401
Subdivision Essentials 402
Triangles vs. Quads 404
Interpolating vs. Approximating 404
Uniform vs. Non-Uniform 404
Stationary vs. Non-Stationary 405
Modified Butterfly Method Subdivision Scheme 405
Application: SubDiv 408
Progressive Meshes 421
Progressive Mesh Basics 422
Choosing Our Edges 423
Stan Melax's Edge Selection Algorithm 424
Quadric Error Metrics 424
Implementing a Progressive Mesh Renderer 426
Radiosity 428
Radiosity Foundations 429
Progressive Radiosity 432
The Form Factor 432
Application: Radiosity 434
References 438
For Further Reading 439
Chapter 8 **Advanced Direct3D** **441**
Alpha Blending 441
The Alpha Blending Equation 442
A Note on Depth Ordering 443
Enabling Alpha Blending 443
Blending Modes 443
Texture Mapping 101 445
Fundamentals 446
Affine Versus Perspective Mapping 447
Texture Addressing 448
Wrap 448
Mirror 449
Clamp 450
Border Color 451
Texture Wrapping 451
Texture Aliasing 452
MIP Maps 454
Filtering 454
Point Sampling 455

Bilinear Filtering 456
Trilinear Filtering 456
Anisotropic Filtering 457
Textures in Direct3D 459
Texture Management. 459
Texture Loading 460
DDS Format 461
The cTexture Class 461
Activating Textures 465
Texture Mapping 202 465
Multiple Textures Per Primitive 466
Texture Transforms. 474
Effects Using Multiple Textures 475
Light Maps (a.k.a. Dark Maps) 476
Environment Maps 478
Specular Maps 484
Detail Maps. 484
Glow Maps 491
Gloss Maps 493
Other Effects. 495
Application: MultiTex 495
Pass 1: Base Map 495
Pass 2: Detail Map 497
Pass 3: Glow Map 499
Pass 4: Environment Map 502
Pass 5: Gloss Map 505
Pass 6: Cloud Map 508
Putting Them All Together 510
Using the Stencil Buffer 513
Overdraw Counter 515
Dissolves and Wipes. 516
Stencil Shadows and Stencil Mirrors 517
Validating Device Capabilities with ValidateDevice() 517
For Further Reading 519

Chapter 9 **Scene Management. 521**
The Scene Management Problem 521
Solutions to the Scene Management Problem 522
Quadtrees/Octrees 523
Portal Rendering. 524
Portal Rendering Concepts 525
Exact Portal Rendering. 532
Approximative Portal Rendering. 534
Portal Effects. 534
Mirrors 534

Translocators and Non-Euclidean Movement 537
Portal Generation 539
Precalculated Portal Rendering (PVS) . . . . 540.
Advantages/Disadvantages 541
Implementation Details 541
Application: Mobots Attack! 542
Interobject Communication 542
Network Communication 546
Code Structure 549
For Further Reading 549
Closing Thoughts 550

Appendix **An STL Primer** **551**
Templates 551
Containers 552
Iterators 554
Functors 556
STL Resources 556

Index 557

Preface

A wise man somewhere, somehow, at some point in history, may have said the best way to start a book is with an anecdote. Never to question the words of a wise man who may or may not have existed, here we go.

A long, long time ago in the distant past I was walking through a mall past a few software stores when my eyes caught a glimpse of a game that was so intriguing I had to check if what I was gazing at was genuine. The name of the game was *Wolfenstein 3D* by id Software and, sure enough, the amazing 3D graphics that streamed dreamily onto the screen (probably at about 10fps at the time!) were in fact real. And the computer had absolutely nothing special added to it.

I hastily took the game home and remained engrossed in it for hours. Later, I took a break and started wondering how it worked. Thirty minutes later, in total confusion, I proudly decided to myself that *I* would make a 3D game. I just needed to figure out how to program first! So began a lengthy journey into the mists of knowledge that I have still to complete. Because, of course, once I had the knowledge to craft *Wolfenstein*, I wanted to create *Doom*, and after that *Quake III Arena*, and so on. I have come to the conclusion over the last decade that designing games is akin to philosophy: The more you know, the less you know!

It was *Wolfenstein 3D* all those years ago, created by a few guys in Texas, that transformed the entire direction of my life, in addition to countless others around the world. With that in mind, I must tip my hat to the men of id Software and Apogee/3D realms. If it weren't for them I might have been, I hate to say it, a boring old software engineer.

The game development community is all about the sharing of knowledge. When one of us figures out a new trick, it is swiftly posted around the net for the education of others. And that is what I hope to give you with this book. A lot of the information that I wished I had in one place when I was learning is contained within this tome. I hope this book helps many more people travel from their humble beginnings of game play into the brave new world of interactive entertainment engineering.

Peter Walsh

Acknowledgments

Like Adrian says below, this book, like any other, was not just the work of one (or two or three) people; there are so many people over the years who have helped me in one way or another, and the result of all these efforts contributed to the knowledge contained in this book. I will try to thank everyone I can. The update of this book by me would not have occurred without the help of Tracy Williams, a woman who has changed my life more than once. Not only did she get me going on my first book, but she got me hooked up with Wordware for this, my second. And of course I must thank Jim Hill, Wes Beckwith, and Tim McEvoy of Wordware for being such great people to work with.

Thanks to Phil Taylor on the DirectX team at Microsoft for agreeing to do the tech check, and also to Wolfgang Engel for his technical support. Also thanks to all the guys on the Abertay University Computer Games Tech degree course.

And where would I be without my friends, who keep me sane (and hung over!) during the many months that I spent researching and writing these tomes. So thank you, Mike, Joanna, Carolyn, Laz, Stew, Caroline, Leslie, Jon, Clare, and everyone else I know.

The worst thing about writing acknowledgments is that you always forget someone who helped you until the day the book goes to print. So thank you to everyone else I forgot—please accept my apologies; my poor brain is worn out after all this work!

Peter Walsh

This book couldn't have been completed without the help and guidance of a whole lot of people. I'll try to remember them all here. First, thanks go to Wes Beckwith and Jim Hill at Wordware Publishing. They were extremely forgiving of my hectic schedule, and they helped guide me to finishing this book. I also must thank Alex Dunne for letting me write an article in 1998 for *Game Developer* magazine. If I hadn't written that article, I never would have written this book.

Everything I know about the topics in this book I learned from other people. Some of these people were mentors, others were bosses, still others were professors and teachers. Some were just cool people who took the time to sit and talk with me. I can't thank them enough. Paul Heckbert, Tom Funkhouser, Eric Petajan, Charles Boyd, Mike Toelle, Kent Griffin, David Baraff, Randy Pausch, Howie Choset, Michael Abrash, Hugues Hoppe, and Mark Stehlik: You guys rock, thank you.

Thanks to Microsoft, ATI, nVidia, id Software, and Lydia Choy for helping me with some of the images used in the text.

A lot of people helped assure the technical correctness and general sanity of this text. Ian Parberry and his class at University of North Texas were immensely helpful: Thanks, guys. Michael Krause was an indispensable help in assuring the correctness of the DirectX chapters. Bob Gaines, Mikey Wetzel, and Jason Sandlin from the DirectX team at Microsoft helped make sure Chapters 2, 6, and 8 were shipshape: Mad props to them. David Black was kind enough to look over Chapter 9 and help remove some errors and clarify a few points.

Finally I need to thank all of the people who helped me get this thing done. I know I won't be able to remember all of them, but here's a short list: Manual and Maria Perez, Katherin Peperzak, Lydia Choy (again), Mike Schuresko, Mike Breen (and the rest of the Originals), Vick Mukherjee, Patrick Nelson, Brian Sharp, and Marcin Krieger.

Adrian Perez

Introduction

I've found that the best way to get a lot of useful information down in a short amount of space is to use the tried-and-true FAQ (frequently asked questions) format. I figured if people needed answers to some questions about this book as they stood in their local bookstore trying to decide whether or not to buy it, these would be them.

Who are you? What are you doing here?

Many years ago, when I was first learning to program games, I learned almost everything I knew from the few books that were available at the time. As time went on, the number of books available on game programming increased dramatically, and reflected the growing complexity of interactive entertainment software. However, there are always holes in the library of books available, for instance on advanced development techniques using DirectX 8.0.

The contents of this book reflect some of the gems that I've discovered from the millions of books and articles that I have come across in the past, along with meetings and first-hand experience. Since a lot of the knowledge that I now have came from books, I hope that this will provide you, the reader, with a lot of useful information as you climb the game development ladder.

Why was this book written?

I've learned from a lot of amazingly brilliant people, covered a lot of difficult ground, and asked a lot of dumb questions. One thing that I've found is that the game development industry is all about sharing. If everyone shares, everyone knows more neat stuff and the net knowledge of the industry increases. This is a good thing, because then we all get to play better games. No one person could discover all the principles behind computer graphics and game programming themselves; no one can learn in a vacuum. People took the time to share what they learned with me, and now I'm taking the time to share what I've learned with you.

Who should read this book?

This book was intended specifically for people who know how to program already, but have taken only rudimentary stabs at graphics/game programming, or have never taken any stab at all. You may be a programmer in another field or a college student looking to embark on some side projects.

Who should *not* read this book?

This book was <u>not</u> designed for beginners. I'm not trying to sound aloof or anything; I'm sure a beginner will be able to trudge through this book if he or she feels up to it. However, since I'm so constrained for space, oftentimes I need to breeze past certain concepts (such as inheritance in C++). If you've never programmed before, you'll have an exceedingly difficult time with this book.

On the other hand, this book isn't really designed for professionals either. I'm sure that most people who have pushed games out the door will only find one or two chapters in this book have any material they haven't seen before.

What are the requirements for using the code?

The code was written in C++, using Microsoft Visual C++ 6.0. The .DSPs and .DSWs are provided on the CD; the .DSPs will work with versions previous to 6.0, and the .DSWs will work with 6.0 and up. If you choose to use a different compiler, getting the source code to work should be a fairly trivial task. I specifically wrote this code to use as little non-standard C++ as possible (as far as I know, the only non-standard C++ I use is nameless structures within unions).

Why use Windows? Why not use Linux?

I chose Win32 as the API environment to use because 90% of computer users currently work on Windows. Win32 is not an easy API to understand, especially after using DOS coding conventions. It isn't terribly elegant either, but I suppose it could be worse. I could choose other platforms to work on, but doing so reduces my target audience by a factor of 9 or more.

If you've never heard of Linux, Linux is an open source operating system. This means anyone can download the source to see how the system works, and anyone can join teams that work on future versions and make contributions to the operating system. The Linux community has a lot of pride for what it does, and as a result Linux is an incredibly small, fast, and stable operating system.

There are a variety of window managers available for download, some that emulate other WMs like Windows or MacOS, some that take new directions (like the ultra-simplistic Blackbox and the uber-complicated Enlightenment). Check out www.linux.org.

Why use Direct3D? Why not use OpenGL?

For those of you who have never used it, OpenGL is another graphics API. Silicon Graphics designed it in the early '90s for use on their high-end graphics workstations. It has been ported to countless platforms and operating systems. Outside of the games industry, in areas like simulation and academic research, OpenGL is the de facto standard for doing computer graphics. It is a simple, elegant, and fast API. Check out www.opengl.org for more information.

But it isn't perfect. First of all, OpenGL has a large amount of functionality in it. Making the interface so simple requires that the implementation take care of a lot of ugly details to make sure everything works correctly. Because of the way drivers are implemented, each company that makes a 3-D card has to support the entire OpenGL feature set in order to have a fully compliant OpenGL driver. These drivers are extremely difficult to implement correctly, and the performance on equal hardware can vary wildly based on driver quality. In addition, DirectX has the added advantage of being able to move quicker to accommodate new hardware features. DirectX is controlled by Microsoft (which can be a good or bad thing, depending on your view of it, while OpenGL extensions need to be deliberated by committees.

My initial hope was to have two versions of the source code, one for Windows and Direct3D, the other for Linux and OpenGL. This ended up not being possible, so I had to choose one or the other; I chose Direct3D.

Why use C++? Why not {C, ASM, Java, *}?

I had a few other language choices I was kicking around when planning this book. Although there are acolytes out there for Delphi, VB, and even C#, the only languages I seriously considered were C++, Java, and C. Java is designed by Sun Microsystems and is an inherently object-oriented language, with some high-level language features like garbage collection. C is about as low level as programming gets without dipping into assembly. It has very few if any high-level constructs and doesn't abstract anything away from the programmer.

C++ is an interesting language because it essentially sits directly between the functionality of the other two languages. C++ supports COM better than C does (this is more thoroughly discussed in Chapter 1). Also, class systems and operator overloading generally make code easier to read (although of course any good thing can and will be abused). Java, although very cool, is an interpreted language. Every year this seems to be less important: JIT compilation gets faster and more grunt work is handed off to the APIs. However, I felt C++ would be a better fit for the book. Java is still a very young language and is still going through a lot of change.

Do I need a 3-D accelerator?

That depends. Technically no, you can get by without any accelerator at all, just using Direct3D's software rasterizer. However, it's extremely slow, and far from real time for anything but trivially simple scenes. It's almost impossible to buy a computer these days without some sort of 3-D acceleration, and an accelerator capable of handling all the code in this book can be purchased for under $100.

How hardcore is the C++ in this book?

Some people see C++ as a divine blade to smite the wicked. They take control of template classes the likes of which you have never seen. They overload the iostream operators for all of their classes. They see multiple inheritance as a hellspawn of Satan himself. I see C++ as a tool. The more esoteric features of the language (such as the iostream library) I don't use at all. Less esoteric features (like multiple inheritance) I use when it makes sense. Having a coding style you stick to is invaluable. The code for this book was written over an 11-month period, plus another three for the revision, but I can pick up the code I wrote at the beginning and still grok it, because I commented and used some good conventions. If I can understand it, hopefully you can too.

What are the coding conventions used in the source?

One of the greatest books I've ever read on programming was *Code Complete* (Microsoft Press). It's a handbook on how to program well, not just how to program. Nuances like the length of variable names, design of subroutines, and length of files are covered in detail in this book; I strongly encourage anyone who wants to become a great programmer to pick it up. You may notice some of the conventions I use in this book are similar to the conventions described in *Code Complete*. Others are borrowed from the great game programmers like John Carmack, and some of them are borrowed from source in DirectX, MFC, and Win32.

I've tried really hard to make the code in this book accessible to everyone. I comment anything I think is unclear, I strive for good choice in variable names, and I try to make my code look clean while still trying to be fast. Of course, I won't please everyone. Assuredly, there are some C++ coding standards I'm probably not following correctly. There are some pieces of code that would get much faster with a little obfuscation.

If you've never used C++ before, or are new to programming, this book is going to be extremely hard to digest. A good discussion on programming essentials and the C++ language is *C++ Primer* (Lippman et al.; Addison-Wesley Publishing).

Class/structure names

MFC names its classes with a prefixed C. As an example, a class that represents the functionality of a button is called CButton. I like this fine, but due to namespace clashing, I instead prefix my own classes with a lowercase c for classes, a lowercase s for structs, a lowercase i for interfaces, and a lowercase e for enumerations (cButton or sButton).

There is one notable exception. While most classes are intended to hide functionality away and act as components, there are a few classes/structures that are intended to be instantiated as basic primitives. So for basic mathematic primitives like points and matrices, I have no prefix, and I postfix with the dimension of the primitive (2-D points are point2, 3-D points are point3, etc.). This is to allow them to have the same look and feel as their closest conceptual neighbor, float. For the same reason, all of the mathematic primitives have a lot of overloaded operators to simplify math-laden code.

Variable names

Semi-long variable names are a good thing. They make your code self-comment itself. One needs to be careful though: Make them too long, and they distract from both the code itself and the process of writing it.

I use short variables very sporadically; int i, j, k pop up a lot in my code for loops and whatnot, but besides that I strive to give meaningful names to the variables I use. Usually, this means that they have more than one word in them. The system I use specifies lowercase for the first word and initial cap for each word after that, with no underscores (an example would be int numObjects). If the last letter of a word is a capital letter, an underscore is placed to separate it from the next word (example, class cD3D_App).

A popular nomenclature for variables is Hungarian notation, which we'll touch on in Chapter 1. I'm not hardcore about it, but generally my floats are prefixed with "f," my ints with "i," and my pointers with "p" (examples: float fTimer; int iStringSize; char* pBuffer). Note that the prefix counts as the first word, making all words after it caps. (I find pBuffer much more readable than pbuffer.)

I also use prefixes to define special qualities of variables. Global variables are preceded with a "g_" (an example would be int g_hInstance); static variables are preceded with an "s_" (static float s_fTimer); and member variables of classes are preceded with an "m_" (int m_iNumElements).

Chapter 1

Windows

Before you can start exploring the world of 3-D game programming, you need a canvas to work on. Basic operations like opening and closing a program, handling rudimentary input, and painting basic primitives must be discussed before you start messing with anything too difficult. If you're familiar with the Windows API, you should breeze through this chapter; otherwise, hold on to your seat!

A Word about Windows

Windows programs are fundamentally different in almost every way from DOS programs. In traditional DOS programs, you have 100% of the processor time, 100% control over all the devices and files in the machine. You also need an intimate knowledge of all of the devices on a user's machine (you probably remember old DOS games, which almost always required you to input DMA and IRQ settings for sound cards). When a game crashed, you didn't need to worry too much about leaving things in a state for the machine to piece itself together; the user could just reboot. Some old 320x200x256 games would crash without even changing the video mode back to normal, leaving the user with a screen full of oversized text with the crash information.

In Windows, things are very different. When your application is running, it is sharing the processor with many other tasks, all running concurrently (at the same time). You can't hog control of the sound card, the video card, the hard disk, or any other system resource for that matter. The input and output is abstracted away, and you don't poll the keyboard or mess with interrupts; Windows doesn't let you do that.

This is both a good and bad thing. On one hand, Windows applications have a consistent look and feel. Unless you want to get picky, any window you create is automatically familiar to Windows users. They already know how to use menus and toolbars, so if you build your application with the basic Windows constructs, they can pick up the user interface quickly. Also, a lot of mundane GUI tasks are completely handled by the Windows API, such as displaying complex property pages, freeing us to write the interesting code.

> **Aside:** "Reinventing the wheel," or rewriting existing code, can make sense sometimes, especially when writing games. However, not on the scale of operating systems; nobody wants to re-implement the functionality of the Windows API.

On the other hand, you have to put a lot of faith into Windows and other applications. Until DirectX came around, you needed to use the default Windows drawing commands (called the GDI). While the GDI can automatically handle any bit depth and work on any monitor, it's not the speediest thing in the world. Many DOS developers swore off ever working in Windows. Pretty much the best you could do with graphics was using a device-independent bitmap which got drawn into a client window. You have to give up a lot when you write a Windows application.

However, there are a lot of things that Windows can do that would be a nightmare to code in the DOS world. You can play sound effects using a single line of code (the PlaySound function), query the time stamp counter, use a robust TCP/IP network stack, get access to virtual memory, and the list goes on. Even though you have to take a few speed hits here and there, the advantages of Windows far outweigh the disadvantages.

I'll be using the Win32 environment to write all of the applications for the book. Win32 is not a programming language; it is an application programming interface (API). In other words, it is a set of C functions that an application uses to make a Windows-compliant program. It abstracts away a lot of difficult operations like multi-tasking and protected memory, as well as providing interfaces to higher-level concepts. Supporting menus, dialog boxes, and multimedia have well-established, fairly easy-to-use library functions written for that specific task.

Windows is an extremely broad set of APIs. You can do just about anything, from playing videos to loading web pages. And for every task, there are a slew of different ways to accomplish it. There are some seriously large books devoted just to the more rudimentary concepts in Windows programming. So unfortunately, my discussion here will be rather limited. Instead of covering the tomes of knowledge required to set up dialogs with tree controls, print documents, and read/write keys in the registry, I'm going to deal with the simplest case: creating a window that can draw the world, passing input to the program, and having at least the beginnings of a pleasant relationship with the operating system.

Hungarian Notation

All of the variable names in Windows land use what is called Hungarian notation. The name came from its inventor, Charles Simonyi, a now-legendary Microsoft programmer who happened to be Hungarian.

Hungarian notation is just prefixing variables with their type. This is helpful so variables are supplied to functions in the right format and to ease the flow between program interfaces. However, it can be really confusing to people who haven't seen it before.

Table 1.1 gives some of the more common prefixes used in most of the Windows and DirectX code that you'll see in this book.

Table 1.1: Some common Hungarian notation prefixes

b (example: bActive)	Variable is a BOOL, a C precursor to the Boolean type found in C++. BOOLs can be TRUE or FALSE.
l (example: lPitch)	Variable is a long integer.
dw (example: dwWidth)	Variable is a DWORD, or unsigned long integer.
w (example: wSize)	Variable is a WORD, or unsigned short integer.
sz (example: szWindowClass)	Variable is a pointer to a string terminated by a zero (a standard C-style string).
p or lp (example: lpData)	Variable is a pointer (lp is a carryover from the far pointers of the 16-bit days; it means long pointer). A pointer-pointer is prefixed by pp or lplp, and so on.
h (example: hInstance)	Variable is a Windows handle.

General Windows Concepts

Notepad.exe is probably the best example of a simple Windows program. It allows basic text input, lets you do some basic text manipulation like searching and using the clipboard, and also lets you load, save, and print to a file. The program appears in Figure 1.1.

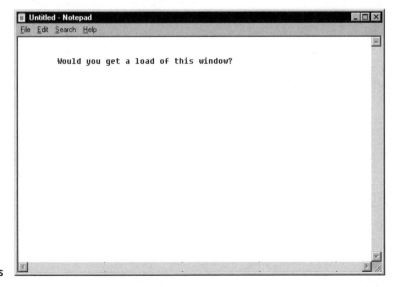

Figure 1.1:
Note-
pad.exe—
as basic as a
window gets

The windows I show you how to create will be similar to this. A window such as this is partitioned into several distinct areas. Windows manages some of them, but the rest your application manages. The partitioning looks something like Figure 1.2.

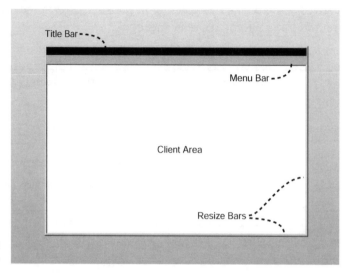

Figure 1.2:
The impor-
tant GUI
components
of a window

The main parts are:

Title Bar	This area appears in most windows. It gives the name of the window and provides access to the system buttons that allow the user to close, minimize, or maximize an application. The only real control you have over the title bar is via a few flags in the window creation process. You can make it disappear, make it appear without the system icons, or make it thinner.
Menu Bar	The menu is one of the primary forms of interaction in a GUI program. It provides a list of commands the user can execute at any one time. Windows also controls this piece of the puzzle. You create the menu and define the commands, and Windows takes care of everything else.
Resize Bars	Resize bars allow the user to modify the size of the window on screen. You have the option of turning them off during window creation if you don't want to deal with the possibility of the window resizing.
Client Area	The client area is the meat of what you deal with. Windows essentially gives you a sandbox to play with in the client area. This is where you draw your scene. Windows can draw on parts of this region too. When there are scroll bars or toolbars in the application, they are intruding in the client area, so to speak.

Message Handling in Windows

Windows also have something called *focus*. Only one window can have focus at a time. The rest appear with a different color title bar. Because of this, only one application gets to know about the keyboard state.

How does your application know this? How does it know things like when it has focus or when the user clicks on it? How does it know where its window is located on the screen? Well, Windows "tells" the application when certain events happen. Also, you can tell other windows when things happen (in this way, different windows can communicate with each other).

Hold on though... How does Windows "tell" an application anything? This can be a very foreign concept to people used to DOS, but it is paramount to the way Windows works. The trick is, Windows (and other applications) share information by sending packets of data back and forth called *messages*. The structure of a Windows message appears below:

```
typedef struct tagMSG {
    HWND    hwnd;
    UINT    message;
    WPARAM  wParam;
    LPARAM  lParam;
    DWORD   time;
    POINT   pt;
} MSG;
```

hwnd	Handle to the window that should receive the message
message	The identifier of the message. For example, the application receives a msg object when the window is resized, and the message member variable is set to the constant WM_SIZE.
wParam	Information about the message; dependent on the type of message
lParam	Additional information about the message
time	Specifies when the message was posted
pt	Mouse location when the message was posted

Explaining Message Processing

What is an HWND? It's basically just an integer, representing a handle to a window. When a Windows application wants to tell another window to do something, or wants to access a volatile system object like a file on disk, Windows doesn't actually let it fiddle with pointers or give it the opportunity to trounce on another application's memory space. Everything is done with handles to objects. It allows the app to send messages to the object, directing it to do things. A good way to think of a handle is like a bar code. That is, a handle is a unique identifier that allows you, and Windows, to differentiate between different objects such as windows, bitmaps, fonts, and so on.

Each window in Windows exists in a hierarchy and each has an identifier, or *handle*. A window handle is an integer describing a window; there can be up to 16,384 windows open simultaneously (2^{14}). When you tell Windows "I want the client rectangle for window x," Windows finds the window corresponding to handle x. It fetches the client rectangle of said window, and passes it back to the application. If the window does not exist (for example if you give a bogus window handle), then an error is returned.

Note: The Win32 API predated the current OOP frenzy in the programming world, and thus doesn't take advantage of some newer programming concepts like exception handling. Every function in Windows instead returns an error code (called an HRESULT) that tells the caller how the function did. A non-negative HRESULT means the function succeeded.

If the function returns a negative number, an error occurred. The FAILED() macro returns true if an HRESULT is negative. There are a myriad of different types of errors that can result from a function; two examples are E_FAIL (generic error) and E_NOTIMPL (the function was not implemented).

An annoying side effect of having everything return an error code is that all the calls that retrieve information need to be passed a pointer of data to fill (instead of the more logical choice of just returning the requested data).

Messages can tell a window anything from "Paint yourself" to "You have lost focus" or "User double-clicked at location <x, y>." Each time a message is sent to a window, it is added to a message queue deep inside Windows. Each window has its own associated message queue. A message queue ensures that each message gets processed in the order it gets received, even if it arrives while the application is busy processing other messages. In fact, when most Windows applications get stuck in an infinite loop or otherwise stop working, you'll notice because they'll stop processing messages, and thus don't redraw or process input.

So how does an application process messages? Windows defines a function that all programs must implement called the window procedure (or WndProc for short). When you create a window, you give Windows your WndProc function in the form of a function pointer. Then, when messages are processed, they are passed as parameters to the function, and the WndProc deals with them. So, for example, when theWndProc function gets passed a message saying "Paint yourself!" that is the signal for the window to redraw itself.

When you send a message, Windows examines the window handle you provide, using it to find out where to send the message. The message ID describes the message being sent, and the parameters to the ID are contained in the two other fields in a message, wParam and lParam. Back in the 16-bit days, wParam was a 16-bit (word sized) integer, and lParam was a 32-bit (long sized) integer, but now they're both 32 bits long. The messages wait in a queue until the application receives them.

The window procedure should return 0 for any message it processes. All messages it doesn't process should be passed to the default Windows message procedure, DefWindowProc(). Windows can start behaving erratically if DefWindowProc doesn't see all of your non-processed messages.

Hello World—Windows Style

To help explain these ideas, let me show you a minimalist Win32 program and analyze what's going on. This code was modified from the default "Hello, World" code that Visual C++ 6.0 will automatically generate for you, but some of the things were removed, leaving this one of the most stripped-down Windows programs you can write.

Listing 1.1: One of the simplest possible Windows programs

```
// This code is derived from the "Hello, World!" default Win32
// program that Visual C++ 6.0 can create for you. Excess
// things, like the menu, icon, accelerators, etc., were removed

#include <windows.h>

// Global Variables:
HINSTANCE    g_hInstance;
char         g_szTitle[]       = "Simple";
char         g_szWindowClass[] = "Simple";

// Forward code declarations
ATOM              MyRegisterClass(HINSTANCE hInstance);
BOOL              InitInstance(HINSTANCE, int);
LRESULT CALLBACK  WndProc(HWND, UINT, WPARAM, LPARAM);

int APIENTRY WinMain(HINSTANCE hInstance,
                     HINSTANCE hPrevInstance,
                     LPSTR     lpCmdLine,
                     int       nCmdShow)
{
    // Register the application to windows
    MyRegisterClass(hInstance);

    // Create the application's window
    if (!InitInstance (hInstance, nCmdShow))
        return FALSE;
```

```
        // Main message loop:
        MSG msg;
        while (GetMessage(&msg, NULL, 0, 0))
        {
            TranslateMessage(&msg);
            DispatchMessage(&msg);
        }

        return msg.wParam;
}

ATOM MyRegisterClass(HINSTANCE hInstance)
{
    WNDCLASSEX wcex;

    wcex.cbSize = sizeof(WNDCLASSEX);

    wcex.style          = CS_HREDRAW | CS_VREDRAW;
    wcex.lpfnWndProc    = (WNDPROC)WndProc;
    wcex.cbClsExtra     = 0;
    wcex.cbWndExtra     = 0;
    wcex.hInstance      = hInstance;
    wcex.hIcon          = 0;
    wcex.hCursor        = 0;
    wcex.hbrBackground  = (HBRUSH)(COLOR_WINDOW+1);
    wcex.lpszMenuName   = 0;
    wcex.lpszClassName  = g_szWindowClass;
    wcex.hIconSm        = 0;

    return RegisterClassEx(&wcex);
}

BOOL InitInstance(HINSTANCE hInstance, int nCmdShow)
{
    HWND hWnd;

    g_hInstance = hInstance; // Store instance in global variable

    hWnd = CreateWindow(g_szWindowClass, g_szTitle,
                    WS_OVERLAPPEDWINDOW, 20, 20, 500, 400,
                    NULL, NULL, hInstance, NULL);

    if (!hWnd)
    {
        return FALSE;
    }

    ShowWindow(hWnd, nCmdShow);
    UpdateWindow(hWnd);

    return TRUE;
```

```
}

LRESULT CALLBACK WndProc(HWND hWnd, UINT message,
                        WPARAM wParam, LPARAM lParam)
{
    PAINTSTRUCT ps;
    HDC hdc;
    char szHello[] = "Hello, World!";
    switch (message)
    {
        case WM_PAINT:
            hdc = BeginPaint(hWnd, &ps);
            RECT rt;
            GetClientRect(hWnd, &rt);
            DrawText(hdc, szHello, strlen(szHello), &rt, DT_CENTER);
            EndPaint(hWnd, &ps);
            break;
        case WM_DESTROY:
            PostQuitMessage(0);
            break;
        default:
            return DefWindowProc(hWnd, message, wParam, lParam);
    }
    return 0;
}
```

It's easy to get worried when you think this is one of the simplest Windows programs you can write, and it's still over 100 lines long. The good thing is that the code above is more or less common to all Windows programs. Most Windows programmers don't remember the exact order everything goes in; they just copy the working Windows initialization code from a previous application.

Explaining the Code

Every C/C++ program has its entry point in main(), where it is passed control from the operating system. In Windows, things work a little differently. There is some code that the Win32 API runs first, before letting us run. The actual stub for main() lies deep within the Win32 DLLs where you can't touch it. However, this application starts at a different point: a function called WinMain(). Windows does its setup work when your application is first run, and then calls WinMain(). This is why when you debug a Windows app "WinMain" doesn't appear at the bottom of the call stack; the internal DLL functions that called it are. WinMain is passed (in order):

■ The instance of the application (another handle, this one representing an instantiation of a running executable). Each process has a separate instance handle that uniquely identifies the process to Windows. This is different from window handles, as each application can have many windows under its control. You need to hold on to this instance, as certain Windows API calls need to know what instance is calling them.

■ The HINSTANCE of another copy of your application currently running. Back in the day, before machines had memory, Windows would have multiple instances of a running program share memory. These days each process is run in its own separate memory space, so this parameter is always NULL. It remains this way so that legacy Windows applications still work.

■ A pointer to the command line. When the user drags a file onto an executable in Explorer (not a running copy of the program), Windows runs the program with the first parameter of the command line being the file dragged on. This is an easy way to do drag-and-drop. The hard way involves OLE/COM, but let's keep OLE under a restraining order. It is useful, but at the price of being a seriously ugly piece of work.

■ A set of flags describing how the window should initially be drawn (such as fullscreen, minimized, etc.).

The conceptual flow of the function is to do the following:

Listing 1.2: Conceptual flow of the program

```
WinMain
    Register the application class with Windows
    Create the main window
    while( Someone hasn't told us to exit )
        Process any messages that Windows has sent us
```

MyRegisterClass takes the application instance and tells Windows about the application (registering it, in essence). InitInstance creates the primary window on the screen and starts it drawing. Then the code enters a while loop that remains in execution until the application quits. The function GetMessage looks at the message queue. It always returns 1 unless there is a specific system message in the queue: This is the "Hey you! Quit! Now!!" message and has the message ID WM_QUIT. If there is a message in the queue, GetMessage will remove it and fill it into the message structure, which is the "msg" variable above. Inside the while loop, you first take the message and translate it using a function called TranslateMessage.

This is a convenience function. When you receive a message saying a key has been pressed or released, you get the specific key as a virtual key code. The actual values for the IDs are arbitrary, but the namespace is what you care about: When the letter a is pressed, one of the message parameters is equivalent to the #define VK_A. Since that nomenclature is a pain to deal with if you're doing something like text input, TranslateMessage does some housekeeping, and converts the parameter from "VK_A" to "(char)'a' ". This makes processing regular text input much easier. Keys without clear ASCII equivalents, such as Page Up and Left Arrow, keep their virtual key code values (VK_PRIOR and

VK_LEFT respectively). All other messages go through the function and come out unchanged.

The second function, DispatchMessage, is the one that actually processes it. Internally, it looks up which function was registered to process messages (in MyRegisterClass) and sends the message to that function. You'll notice that the code never actually calls the window procedure. That's because Windows does it for you when you ask it to with the DispatchMessage function.

All told, this while loop is the central nervous system for any Windows program. It constantly grabs messages off the queue and processes them as fast as it can. It's so universal it actually has a special name: the *message pump*. Whenever you see a reference to a message pump in a text, or optimizing message pumps for this application or that, that's what it is in reference to.

Registering the Application

MyRegisterClass() fills a structure that contains the info Windows needs to know about your application before it can create a window, and passes it to the Win32 API. This is where you tell Windows what to make the icon for the application that appears in the taskbar (hIcon, the large version, and hIconSm, the smaller version). You can also give it the name of the menu bar if you ever decide to use one. (For now there is none, so it's set to 0.) You need to tell Windows what the application instance is (the one received in the WinMain); this is the hInstance parameter. You also tell it which function to call when it processes messages; this is the lpfnWndProc parameter. The window class has a name as well, lpszClassName, that is used to reference the class later in the CreateWindow function.

> **Warning:** A window class is completely different from a C++ class. Windows predated the popularity of the C++ language.

Initializing the Window

InitInstance creates the window and starts the drawing process. The window is created with a call to CreateWindow:

```
HWND CreateWindow(
  LPCTSTR lpClassName,
  LPCTSTR lpWindowName,
  DWORD dwStyle,
  int x,
  int y,
  int nWidth,
  int nHeight,
  HWND hWndParent,
  HMENU hMenu,
  HANDLE hInstance,
```

```
        LPVOID lpParam
    );
```

lpClassName	A null-terminated string giving the class name for the window class that was registered with RegisterClass. This defines the basic style of the window, along with which WndProc will be handling the messages (you can create more than one window class per application).
lpWindowName	The title of the window. This will appear in the title bar of the window and in the taskbar.
dwStyle	A set of flags describing the style for the window (such as having thin borders, being unresizable, and so on). For these discussions windowed applications will all use WS_OVERLAPPEDWINDOW (this is the standard-looking window, with a resizable edge, a system menu, a title bar, etc.). However, fullscreen applications will use the WS_POPUP style (no Windows features at all, not even a border; it's just a client rectangle).
x, y	The x and y location, relative to the top-left corner of the monitor (x increasing right, y increasing down), where the window should be placed.
nWidth, nHeight	The width and height of the window.
hWndParent	A window can have child windows (imagine a paint program like Paint Shop Pro, where each image file exists in its own window). If this is the case and you are creating a child window, pass the HWND of the parent window here.
hMenu	If an application has a menu (yours doesn't), pass the handle to it here.
hInstance	This is the instance of the application that was received in WinMain.
lpParam	Pointer to extra window creation data you can provide in more advanced situations (for now, just pass in NULL).

The width and height of the window that you pass to this function is the width and height for the <u>entire</u> window, not just the client area. If you want the client area to be a specific size, say 640 by 480 pixels, you need to adjust the width and height passed to account for the pixels needed for the title bar, resize bars, etc. You can do this with a function called AdjustWindowRect (discussed later in the chapter). You pass a rectangle structure filled with the desired client rectangle, and the function adjusts the rectangle to reflect the size of the window that will contain the client rectangle, based on the style you pass it (hopefully the same style passed to CreateWindow). A window created with WS_POPUP has no extra Windows UI features, so the window will go through unchanged. WS_OVERLAPPEDWINDOW has to add space on each side for the resize bar and on the top for the title bar.

If CreateWindow fails (this will happen if there are too many windows or if it receives bad inputs, such as an hInstance different from the one provided in MyRegisterClass), you shouldn't try processing any messages for the window (since there is no window!) so return false. This is handled in WinMain by exiting the application before entering the message pump. Normally, before exiting, you'd bring up some sort of pop-up alerting the user to the error, instead of just silently quitting. Otherwise, call ShowWindow, which sets the show state of the window just created (the show state was passed to as the last formal parameter in WinMain), and UpdateWindow, which sends a paint message to the window so it can draw itself.

Warning: CreateWindow calls the WndProc function several times before it exits! This can be the cause of endless headaches in getting Windows programs to work.

Before the function returns and you get the window handle back, WM_CREATE, WM_MOVE, WM_SIZE, and WM_PAINT (among others) are sent to you through the WndProc.

If you're using any components that need the HWND of a program to perform work (a good example is a DirectX window, whose surface must resize itself whenever it gets a WM_SIZE message), you need to tread very carefully so that you don't try to resize the surface before it has been initialized. One way to handle this is to record your window's HWND inside WM_CREATE, since one of the parameters that gets passed to the WndProc is the window handle to receive the message.

When something happens, how would you alert the user? Unfortunately, you no longer have the printf and getchar commands to print out error messages, so instead you have to create dialogs that present information, like the reason the program failed, to the user. Creating complex dialogs with buttons and edit boxes and whatnot are beyond the scope of this book; however, there are some basic dialogs that Windows can automatically create, such as the infamous pop-up window you see when you attempt to exit any sort of document editing software that says "Save SomeFile.x before exiting?" and has two buttons marked "Yes" and "No."

The function you use to automate the dialog creation process is called MessageBox. It is one of the most versatile and useful Windows functions. Take a look at its prototype in the following listing.

```
int MessageBox(
  HWND hWnd,
  LPCTSTR lpText,
  LPCTSTR lpCaption,
  UINT uType
);
```

hWnd	Handle to the owner of the window (this is generally the application's window handle).
lpText	Text for the inside of the message box.

lpCaption	Title of the message box.
uType	A set of flags describing the behavior of the message box. The flags are described in Table 1.2.

The function displays the dialog on the desktop, and does not return until the box is closed.

Table 1.2: A set of the common flags used with MessageBox

MB_OK	The message box has just one button marked OK. This is the default behavior.
MB_ABORTRETRYIGNORE	Three buttons appear—Abort, Retry, and Ignore.
MB_OKCANCEL	Two buttons appear—OK and Cancel.
MB_RETRYCANCEL	Two buttons appear—Retry and Cancel.
MB_YESNO	Two buttons appear—Yes and No.
MB_YESNOCANCEL	Three buttons appear—Yes, No, and Cancel.
MB_ICONEXCLAMATION, MB_ICONWARNING	An exclamation mark icon is displayed.
MB_ICONINFORMATION, MB_ICONASTERISK	An information icon (a lowercase i inscribed in a circle) is displayed.
MB_ICONQUESTION	A question mark icon is displayed.
MB_ICONSTOP, MB_ICONERROR, MB_ICONHAND	A stop sign icon is displayed.

The return value of MessageBox depends on which button was pressed. Table 1.3 gives the possible return values. Note that this is one of the rare Windows functions that does <u>not</u> return an HRESULT.

Table 1.3: Return values for MessageBox

IDABORT	The Abort button was pressed.
IDCANCEL	The Cancel button was pressed.
IDIGNORE	The Ignore button was pressed.
IDNO	The No button was pressed.
IDOK	The OK button was pressed.
IDRETRY	The Retry button was pressed.
IDYES	The Yes button was pressed.

WndProc—The Message Pump

WndProc is the window procedure. This is where everything happens in a Windows application. Since this application is so simple, it will only process two messages (more complex Windows programs will need to process dozens upon dozens of messages). The two messages that probably every Win32 application handles are WM_PAINT (sent when Windows would like the window to be redrawn) and WM_DESTROY (sent when the window is being destroyed). An important thing to note is that any message you don't process in the switch statement goes into DefWindowProc, which defines the default behavior for every Windows message. Anything not processed needs to go into DefWindowProc for the application to behave correctly.

System messages, such as the message received when the window is being created and destroyed, are sent by Windows internally. You can post messages to your own application with two functions: PostMessage and SendMessage. PostMessage adds the message to the application's message queue to be processed in the message pump. SendMessage actually calls the WndProc with the given message itself.

One extremely important point to remember when you're doing Windows programming is that you don't need to memorize any of this. Very few, if any, people know all the inputs and outputs to all of the Windows functions; usually it's looked up in MSDN, copied from another place, or filled in for you by a project wizard. So don't worry if you're barely following some of this stuff.

One thing you might notice is that for a program that just says "Hello, World!" there sure is a lot of code. Most of it exists in all Windows programs. All windows need to register themselves, they all need to create a window if they want one, and they all need a window procedure. While it may be a bit on the long side, the program does a lot. You can resize it, move it around the screen, have it become occluded by other windows, minimize, maximize, and so on. Windows users automatically take this functionality for granted, but there is a lot of code going on behind the scenes.

Manipulating Window Geometry

Since for now the application's use of Windows is so restricted, you only need to concern yourself with two basic Windows structures that are used in geometry functions: POINT and RECT.

In Windows, there are two coordinate spaces. One is the client area coordinate space. The origin (0,0) is the top-left corner of the client rectangle. Coordinates relative to the client area don't need to change when the window is moved around the screen. The other coordinate space is the desktop coordinate space. This space is absolute, and the origin is the top-left corner of the screen.

Windows uses the POINT structure to represent 2D coordinates. It has two long integers, one for the horizontal component and one for the vertical:

```
typedef struct tagPOINT {
    LONG x;
    LONG y;
} POINT;
```

Since all windows are rectangular, Windows has a structure to represent a rectangle. You'll notice that essentially the structure is two points end to end, the first describing the top-left corner of the rectangle, the other describing the bottom-right.

```
typedef struct _RECT {
    LONG left;
    LONG top;
    LONG right;
    LONG bottom;
} RECT;
```

left	Left side of the window.
top	Top of the window.
right	Right side of the window (width is right–left).
bottom	Bottom side of the window (height is bottom–top).

To get the client rectangle of a window you can use the function GetClientRect. The left and top members are always zero, and the right and bottom give you the width and height of the window.

```
BOOL GetClientRect(
    HWND hWnd,
    LPRECT lpRect
);
```

hWnd	Handle to the window you want information about.
lpRect	Pointer to a RECT structure you would like filled with the client rectangle.

Once you have the client rectangle, you often need to know what those points are relative to the desktop coordinate space. ClientToScreen, which has the following prototype, provides this functionality:

```
BOOL ClientToScreen(
    HWND hWnd,
    LPPOINT lpPoint
);
```

hWnd	Handle to the window the client point is defined in.
lpPoint	Pointer to the client point; this point is changed to screen space.

To change the rectangle you get through GetClientRect to screen space, you can use the ClientToScreen function on the bottom and right members of a rectangle. Slightly inelegant, but it works.

One thing that can mess up window construction is determining the width and height of the window. You could say you want a client rectangle that is 800 pixels by 600 pixels (or some other resolution), but you call CreateWindow giving the dimensions of the whole window, including any resize, title bar, and menu bars. Luckily, you can convert a rectangle representing the client rectangle to one representing the window dimensions using AdjustWindowRect. It pushes all of the coordinates out to accommodate the window style dwStyle, which should be the same one used in CreateWindow for it to work correctly. For non-pop-up windows, this will make the top and left coordinates negative.

```
BOOL AdjustWindowRect(
  LPRECT lpRect,
  DWORD dwStyle,
  BOOL bMenu
);
```

lpRect	Pointer to the RECT structure to be adjusted.
dwStyle	Style of the intended window, this defines how much to adjust each coordinate. For example, WS_POPUP style windows aren't adjusted at all.
bMenu	Boolean that is TRUE if the window will have a menu. If, like in this case, there is no menu then you can just pass FALSE for this parameter.

Windows has a full-featured graphics library that performs operations on a handle to a graphics device. The package is called the GDI, or Graphical Device Interface. It has functionality that allows users to draw, among other things, lines, ellipses, bitmaps, and text (I'll show you its text painting ability in a later chapter). The sample program uses it to draw the "Hello, World!" text on the screen. I'll show you more of the GDI's functions later in the book (especially in Chapter 4).

Important Window Messages

Most of the code in this book uses Windows as a jumping-off point—a way to put a window up on the screen that allows you to draw in it. I'll only be showing you a small subset of the massive list of window messages in Windows, which is a good thing since they can get pretty boring after a while. Table 1.4 describes the important messages and their parameters.

Table 1.4: Some important window messages

WM_CREATE	Sent to the application when Windows has completed creating its window but before it is drawn. This is the first time the application will see what the HWND of its window is.
WM_PAINT	Sent to the application when Windows wants the window to draw itself.
	Parameters:
	`(HDC) wParam`
	A handle to the device context for the window that you can draw in.
WM_ERASEBKGND	Called when the background of a client window should be erased. If you process this message instead of passing it to DefWindowProc, Windows will let you erase the background of the window (later, I'll show you why this can be a good thing).
	Parameters:
	`(HDC) wParam`
	A handle to the device context to draw in.
WM_DESTROY	Sent when the window is being destroyed.
WM_CLOSE	Sent when the window is being asked to close itself. This is where you can, for example, ask for confirmation before closing the window.
WM_SIZE	Sent when the window is resized. When the window is resized, the top-left location stays the same (so when you resize from the top left, both a WM_MOVE and a WM_SIZE message are sent).
	Parameters:
	`wParam`
	Resizing flag. There are other flags, but the juicy one is SIZE_MINIMIZED; it's sent when the window is minimized.
	`LOWORD(1Param)`
	New width of the client area (not total window).
	`HIWORD(1Param)`
	New height of the client area (not total window).
WM_MOVE	Sent when the window is moved.
	Parameters:
	`(int)(short)LOWORD(1Param)`
	New upper-left x coordinate of client area.
	`(int)(short)HIWORD(1Param)`
	New upper-left y coordinate of client area.

WM_QUIT	Last message the application gets; upon its receipt the application exits. You never process this message, as it actually never gets through to WndProc. Instead, it is caught in the message pump in WinMain and causes that loop to drop out and the application to subsequently exit.
WM_KEYDOWN	Received every time a key is pressed. Also received after a specified time for auto-repeats.
	Parameters:
	`(int)wParam`
	The virtual key code for the pressed key. If you call TranslateMessage on the message before processing it, if it is a key with an ASCII code equivalent (letters, numbers, punctuation marks) it will be equivalent to the actual ASCII character.
WM_KEYUP	Received when a key is released.
	Parameters:
	`(int)wParam`
	The virtual key code for the released key.
WM_MOUSEMOVE	MouseMove is a message that is received almost constantly. Each time the mouse moves in the client area of the window, the application gets notified of the new location of the mouse cursor relative to the origin of the client area.
	Parameters:
	`LOWORD(1Param)`
	The x-location of the mouse, relative to the upper-left corner of the client area.
	`HIWORD(1Param)`
	The y-location of the mouse, relative to the upper-left corner of the client area.
	`WParam`
	Key flags. This helps you tell what the keyboard state is for special clicks (such as Alt-left click, for example). Test the key flags to see if certain flags are set. The flags are:
	• MK_CONTROL: Indicates the Control key is down.
	• MK_LBUTTON: Indicates the left mouse button is down.
	• MK_MBUTTON: Indicates the middle mouse button is down.
	• MK_RBUTTON: Indicates the right mouse button is down.
	• MK_SHIFT: Indicates the Shift key is down.

WM_LBUTTONDOWN	This message is received when the user presses the left mouse button in the client area. You only receive one message when the button is pressed, as opposed to receiving them continually while the button is down.

Parameters:

LOWORD(lParam)

The x-location of the mouse, relative to the upper-left corner of the client area.

HIWORD(lParam)

The y-location of the mouse, relative to the upper-left corner of the client area.

WParam

Key flags. This helps you tell what the keyboard state is for special clicks (such as Alt-left click, for example). Test the key flags to see if certain flags are set. The flags are:

- MK_CONTROL: Indicates the Control key is down.

- MK_MBUTTON: Indicates the middle mouse button is down.

- MK_RBUTTON: Indicates the right mouse button is down.

- MK_SHIFT: Indicates the Shift key is down.

WM_MBUTTONDOWN	You receive this message when the user presses the middle mouse button in the client area. You only receive one message when the button is pressed, as opposed to receiving them continually while the button is down.

Parameters:

LOWORD(lParam)

The x-location of the mouse, relative to the upper-left corner of the client area.

HIWORD(lParam)

The y-location of the mouse, relative to the upper-left corner of the client area.

WParam

Key flags. This helps you tell what the keyboard state is for special clicks (such as Alt-left click, for example). Test the key flags to see if certain flags are set. The flags are:

- MK_CONTROL: Indicates the Control key is down.

- MK_LBUTTON: Indicates the left mouse button is down.

- MK_RBUTTON: Indicates the right mouse button is down.

- MK_SHIFT: Indicates the Shift key is down.

WM_RBUTTONDOWN	You receive this message when the user presses the right mouse button in the client area. You only receive one message when the button is pressed, as opposed to receiving them continually while the button is down.

Parameters:

`LOWORD(1Param)`

The x-location of the mouse, relative to the upper-left corner of the client area.

`HIWORD(1Param)`

The y-location of the mouse, relative to the upper-left corner of the client area.

`WParam`

Key flags. This helps you tell what the keyboard state is for special clicks (such as Alt-left click, for example). Test the key flags to see if certain flags are set. The flags are:

- MK_CONTROL: Indicates the Control key is down.
- MK_LBUTTON: Indicates the left mouse button is down.
- MK_MBUTTON: Indicates the middle mouse button is down.
- MK_SHIFT: Indicates the Shift key is down.

WM_LBUTTONUP	Received when the user releases the left mouse button in the client area.

Parameters:

The parameters are the same as for WM_LBUTTONDOWN.

WM_MBUTTONUP	Received when the user releases the middle mouse button in the client area.

Parameters:

The parameters are the same as for WM_MBUTTONDOWN.

WM_RBUTTONUP	Received when the user releases the right mouse button in the client area.

Parameters:

The parameters are the same as for WM_RBUTTONDOWN.

WM_MOUSEWHEEL	Most new mice come equipped with a z-axis control, in the form of a wheel. It can be spun forward and backward and clicked. If it is clicked, it generally sends middle mouse button messages. However, if it is spun forward or backward, the following messages are sent.

Parameters:

`(short) HIWORD(wParam)`

The amount the wheel has spun since the last message. A positive value means the wheel was spun forward (away from the user). A negative value means the wheel was spun backward (towards the user).

```
(short) LOWORD(1Param)
```

The x-location of the mouse, relative to the upper-left corner of the client area.

```
(short) HIWORD(1Param)
```

The y-location of the mouse, relative to the upper-left corner of the client area.

```
LOWORD(wParam)
```

Key flags. This helps you tell what the keyboard state is for special clicks (such as Alt-left click, for example). Test the key flags to see if certain flags are set. The flags are:

- MK_CONTROL: Indicates the Control key is down.

- MK_LBUTTON: Indicates the left mouse button is down.

- MK_MBUTTON: Indicates the middle mouse button is down.

- MK_RBUTTON: Indicates the right mouse button is down.

- MK_SHIFT: Indicates the Shift key is down.

MFC

As you have probably guessed already, programming Windows isn't the easiest thing in the world. People tend to fear difficult things, blowing them up in their mind, making them many times worse than they actually are. While it is ugly code, a lot of the stuff required to make Windows work is used in every application, and should be abstracted away. While there are many libraries on the market to do this, the predominant one is the one made by Microsoft, called MFC.

MFC, or the Microsoft Foundation Classes, is a system of classes designed to encapsulate the Win32 API. It tries to create simple ways to do the most common tasks in Windows programs. Your application derives from CWinApp, your window from CWnd, your dialogs from CDialog, etc. This makes applications much easier to write, as a lot of the muscle work required in Windows is taken care of for you. MFC is a fantastic tool for making quick and dirty front ends to existing code.

However, it isn't all peaches and cream. First of all, MFC is geared towards document view type applications (like WordPad). It has loads of code to support docking toolbars, handle modeless dialogs, and work with the GDI. Unfortunately, those things aren't of much use if all you want to do is make 3-D games.

Another inherent MFC problem is the size and speed penalties. The added functionality given by MFC comes at a price: The DLLs are fairly large, and unless they're already loaded in memory, they can hit your application in load time.

Finally, MFC isn't the perfect bedfellow for DirectX. The programming models with which both APIs are designed are different. For example, windowed Direct3D applications need to know when the window it is drawing is moved or resized. However, getting notified of such changes isn't an instant event in MFC, particularly if the DirectX window is a document window that can move relative to its parent window. These hurdles are not insurmountable; they're just kind of a pain. Most of your applications will run in full-screen mode anyway and don't need the GUI bells and whistles that MFC provides.

I wish I had more space to discuss MFC, but since it won't be in any of the code that I show, I won't be talking about it in the book. However, if you seriously start developing a 3-D game you'll need utilities to help manage your data. When the day comes that you need to build those utilities, crack open a good book on MFC and you'll have stuff up and running in no time. A few good resources are listed at the end of this chapter. One of the best books on MFC is *Professional MFC with Visual C++* by Mike Blaszczak, published by Wrox Press.

Class Encapsulation

So, now that you can create a window, I'm going to show you how to design a framework that will sit beneath the Direct3D and other game code and simplify the programming tasks needed in all of the other applications you'll be building in the book. Now that you know how to make a window, I'm going to hide that code so that you never need to look at it again.

As a first step, let's look at a list of benefits that could be gained from the encapsulation. In no particular order, it would be good if the application had:

■ The ability to control and re-implement the construction and destruction of the application object.

■ The ability to automatically create standard system objects (right now just the application window, but later on Direct3D, DirectInput, and so on), and facilities to create your own.

■ The ability to add objects that can listen to the stream of window messages arriving to the application and add customized ways to handle them.

■ A simple main loop that runs repeatedly until the application exits.

The way I'll do this is with two classes. One of them will abstract the Windows code that needs to be run; it is called cWindow. It will be used by a bigger class that is responsible for actually running the application. This class is called cApplication. Each new application that you create (with a couple of exceptions) will be subclassed from cApplication.

Whenever something goes wrong during the execution that requires the application to exit, the infrastructure is designed so that an error can be thrown. The entire application is wrapped around a Try...catch block, so any errors are caught in WinMain, and the application is shut down. A text message describing the error can be passed in the thrown exception, and the string is popped up using a message box before the application exits.

I chose to do this because it was considerably nicer than the alternative of having every single function return an error code, and having each function check the result of each function it calls. Exceptions get thrown so rarely that the added complexity that error codes add seems pretty superfluous really. With exception handling, the code is nice and clean. The error that almost all of the code in this book throws is called cGameError, and is defined in Listing 1.3.

Listing 1.3: The cGameError object and eResult enumeration

```
class cGameError
{
    string m_errorText;
public:
    cGameError( char* errorText )
    {
        DP1("***\n*** [ERROR] cGameError thrown! text: [%s]\n***\n",
            errorText );
        m_errorText = string( errorText );
    }

    const char* GetText()
    {
        return m_errorText.c_str();
    }
};

enum eResult
{
    resAllGood      = 0,       // function passed with flying colors
    resFalse        = 1,       // function worked and returns 'false'
    resFailed       = -1,      // function failed miserably
    resNotImpl      = -2,      // function has not been implemented
    resForceDWord = 0x7FFFFFFF
};
```

The window abstraction, cWindow, is fairly straightforward. MyRegisterClass is replaced with cWindow::RegisterClass, MyInitInstance is now cWindow:: InitInstance, and WndProc is now a static function cWindow::WndProc. The function is static because non-static class functions have a hidden first variable passed in (the *this* pointer) that is not compatible with the WndProc function declaration. Later on I'll define a child class for you that allows the creation of full-screen ready windows. In practice, this is the same as a normal window; the only change is that WS_POPUP is used as the window style instead of WS_OVERLAPPEDWINDOW.

The message pump that you'll come to know and love is encapsulated in two functions. HasMessages() checks the queue and sees if there are any messages waiting to be processed, returning true if there are any. Pump() processes a single message, sending it off to WndProc using TranslateMessage/DispatchMessage. When Pump receives the WM_QUIT message, which again is a notification from Windows that the application should exit, it returns resFalse.

Special care needs to be taken to handle thrown exceptions that happen during the window procedure. You see, between the execution of DispatchMessage() and WndProc(), the call stack meanders into some kernel DLL functions. If a thrown exception flies into them, bad stuff happens (anything from your program crashing to your machine crashing). To handle this, any and all exceptions are caught in the WndProc and saved in a temporary variable. When Pump finishes pumping a message, it checks the temporary variable to see if an error was thrown. If there is an error waiting, Pump rethrows the error and it rises up to WinMain.

```
class cWindow
{
protected:

    int m_width, m_height;
    HWND m_hWnd;
    std::string m_name;
    bool m_bActive;
    static cWindow* m_pGlobalWindow;

public:

    cWindow(
        int width,
        int height,
        const char* name = "Default window name" );
    ~cWindow();

    virtual LRESULT WndProc(
        HWND hWnd,
        UINT uMsg,
        WPARAM wParam,
        LPARAM lParam );

    virtual void RegisterClass( WNDCLASSEX* pWc = NULL );
    virtual void InitInstance();

    HWND GetHWnd();
    bool IsActive();
    bool HasMessages();
    eResult Pump();
    static cWindow* GetMainWindow();
};

inline cWindow* MainWindow();
```

`m_width, m_height`	Width and height of the client rectangle of the window. This is different from the width and height of the actual window.
`m_hWnd`	Handle to the window. Use the public function GetHWnd to get access to it outside the class.
`m_name`	The name of the window used to construct the window class and window.
`m_bActive`	Boolean value; TRUE if the window is active (a window is active if it is currently in the foreground).
`m_pGlobalWindow`	Static variable that points to the single instantiation of a cWindow class for an application. Initially set to NULL.
`cWindow(...)`	Constructs a window object. You can only create one instance of this object; this is verified by setting the m_pGlobalWindow object.
`~cWindow()`	The destructor destroys the window and sets the global window variable to NULL, so that it cannot be accessed any longer.
`WndProc()`	Window procedure for the class. Called by a hidden function inside Window.cpp.
`RegisterClass(...)`	Virtual function that registers the window class. This function can be overloaded in child classes to add functionality, such as a menu or different WndProc.
`InitInstance()`	Virtual function that creates the window. This function can be overloaded in child classes to add functionality, such as changing the window style.
`GetHWnd()`	Returns the window handle for this window.
`IsActive()`	Returns true if the application is active and in the foreground.
`HasMessages()`	True if the window has any messages in its message queue waiting to be processed. Uses PeekMessage with PM_NOREMOVE.
`Pump()`	Pumps the first message off the queue and dispatches it to the WndProc. Returns resAllGood, unless the message gotten off the queue was WM_QUIT, in which case it returns resFalse.
`GetMainWindow()`	Public function; used by the global function MainWindow to gain access to the only window object.
`MainWindow`	Global function that returns the single instance of the cWindow class for this program. Any piece of code can use this to query information about the window. For example, any code can get the hWnd for the window by calling MainWindow()->GetHWnd().

Finally, there is the Big Kahuna—cApplication. Child classes will generally only re-implement SceneInit and DoFrame. However, other functions can be re-implemented if added functionality, like the construction of extra system objects, is needed. The game presented at the end of the book will use several other system objects that it will need to construct.

```
class cApplication
{
```

```
protected:

    string  m_title;
    int     m_width;
    int     m_height;

    bool    m_bActive;

    static cApplication*    m_pGlobalApp;

    virtual void InitPrimaryWindow();
    virtual void InitGraphics();
    virtual void InitInput();
    virtual void InitSound();
    virtual void InitExtraSubsystems();

public:

    cApplication();
    virtual ~cApplication();

    virtual void Init();

    virtual void Run();
    virtual void DoFrame( float timeDelta );
    virtual void DoIdleFrame( float timeDelta );
    virtual void ParseCmdLine( char* cmdLine );

    virtual void SceneInit();
    virtual void SceneEnd();

    void Pause();
    void UnPause();

    static cApplication* GetApplication();

    static void KillApplication();
};

inline cApplication* Application();

HINSTANCE AppInstance();

cApplication*   CreateApplication();
```

m_title	Title for the application. Sent to the cWindow when it is constructed.
m_width, m_height	Width and height of the client area of the desired window.
m_bActive	True if the application is active and running. When the application is inactive, input isn't received and the idle frame function is called.

`m_pGlobalApp`	Static pointer to the single global instance of the application.
`InitPrimaryWindow(...)`	Virtual function to initialize the primary window for this application. If bExclusive is true, a pop-up window is created in anticipation of full-screen mode. If it is false, a regular window is made.
`InitGraphics()`	This function will be filled in Chapter 2.
`InitInput()`	This function will be filled in Chapter 2.
`InitSound()`	This function will be filled in Chapter 2.
`InitExtraSubsystems(...)`	Virtual function to initialize any additional subsystems the application wants before the scene is initialized.
`cApplication()`	Constructor; fills in default values for the member variables.
`~cApplication()`	Shuts down all of the system objects (which I'll show you in Chapter 2).
`Init()`	Initializes all of the system objects (which I'll show you in Chapter 2).
`Run()`	Main part of the application. Displays frames as fast as it can until the WM_QUIT message arrives.
`DoFrame(...)`	This function is called every frame by Run. In it, the subclassing application should perform all game logic and draw the frame. timeDelta is a floating-point value representing how much time elapsed since the last frame. This is to aid in making applications perform animations at constant speed independent of the frame rate of the machine.
`DoIdleFrame(...)`	This function is called by Run if the application is currently inactive. Most of the applications that I'll show you won't need this function, but it exists for completeness.
`ParseCmdLine(...)`	Virtual function to allow subclasses to view the command line before anything is run.
`SceneInit()`	Virtual function; overload this to perform scene-specific initialization. Called after the system objects are created.
`SceneEnd()`	Virtual function; overload to perform scene-specific shutdown code.
`Pause()`	Pause the application.
`UnPause()`	Un-pause the application.
`GetApplication()`	Public accessor function to acquire the global application pointer.
`KillApplication()`	Kills the application and invalidates the global application pointer.
`Application()`	Global inline function to simplify access to the global application pointer. Equivalent to cApplication::GetApplication().
`AppInstance()`	Global inline function to acquire the HINSTANCE of this application.
`CreateApplication()`	This global function is undefined and must be declared in all further applications. It creates an application object for the code inside GameLib to use. If an application subclasses cApplication with a class cMyApplication, CreateApplication should simply return (new cMyApplication).

The WinMain for the application is abstracted away from child applications, hidden inside the GameLib code. Just so you don't miss it, the code for it appears in Listing 1.4.

Listing 1.4: WinMain

```
int APIENTRY WinMain(HINSTANCE hInstance,
                     HINSTANCE hPrevInstance,
                     LPSTR     lpCmdLine,
                     int       nCmdShow)
{

    cApplication* pApp;

    g_hInstance = hInstance;

    try
    {
        pApp = CreateApplication();

        pApp->ParseCmdLine( lpCmdLine );

        pApp->Init();
        pApp->SceneInit();
        pApp->Run();
    }
    catch( cGameError& err )
    {
        /**
         * Knock out the graphics before displaying the dialog,
         * just to be safe.
         */
        if( Graphics() )
        {
            Graphics()->DestroyAll();
        }
        MessageBox(
            NULL,
            err.GetText(),
            "Error!",
            MB_OK|MB_ICONEXCLAMATION );
        // Clean everything up
        delete pApp;
        return 0;
    }

    delete pApp;
    return 0;
}
```

COM: The Component Object Model

Component-based software development is big business. Instead of writing one, deeply intertwined piece of software (called *monolithic* software development), a team writes a set of many smaller components that talk to one another. This ends up being an advantage because if the components are modular enough, they can be used in other projects without a lot of headache. Not only that, but the components can be updated and improved independently of each other. As long as the components talk to each other the same way, no problems arise.

To aid in component-based software design, Microsoft created a scheme called the *Component Object Model,* or COM for short. It provides a standard way for objects to communicate with other objects and expose their functionality to other objects that seek it. It is language independent, platform independent, and even machine independent (a COM object can talk to another COM object over a network connection). In this section I'll cover how COM objects are used in component-based software. As the knowledge required to construct your own COM objects is more than can be covered here, the end of the chapter lists some additional resources on COM.

A COM object is basically a block of code that implements one or more COM interfaces. (I love circular definitions like this. Look up "worrier" in the dictionary; it's defined as "someone who worries.") A COM interface is just a set of functions. Actually, it's implemented the same way that almost all C++ compilers implement virtual function tables. In C++, COM objects just inherit one or more abstract base classes, which are called COM interfaces. Other classes can get a COM object to do work by calling functions in its interfaces, but that's it. There are no other functions besides the ones in the interfaces, and no access to member variables outside of Get/Set functions existing in the interfaces.

All COM interfaces derive, either directly or indirectly, from a class called IUnknown. In technical terms, this means the first three entries in the vTable of all COM interfaces are the same three functions of IUnknown. The interface is provided in Listing 1.5.

Listing 1.5: The IUnknown interface

```
typedef struct interface
interface IUnknown
{
    virtual HRESULT QueryInterface( REFIID idd, void** ppvObject ) = 0;
    virtual ULONG AddRef( void ) = 0;
    virtual ULONG Release( void ) = 0;
};
```

AddRef and Release implement reference counting for us. COM objects are created outside of your control. They may be created with new, malloc, or a completely different memory manager. Because of this you can't simply delete the interface when you're done with it. Reference counting lets the object perform its own memory management. The reference count is the number of other pieces of code that are referencing an object. When you create a COM object, the reference count will most likely be 1, since you're the only one using it. When another piece of code in a different component wants an interface, generally you call AddRef() on the interface to tell the COM object that there is an additional piece of code using it. When a piece of code is done with an interface, it calls Release(). This decrements the reference count. When the reference count reaches 0, that means that no objects are referencing the COM object and it can safely destroy itself.

Warning: If you don't release your COM objects when you're done with them, they won't destroy themselves. This can cause annoying resource leaks in your application.

QueryInterface is the one function that makes COM work. It allows an object to request another interface from a COM object it has an interface for. You pass QueryInterface an interface ID, and a pointer to a void pointer to fill with an interface pointer if the requested interface is supported.

As an example, let's consider a car. You create the car object and get an interface pointer to an iCarIgnition interface. If you want to change the radio station, you can ask the owner of the iCarIgnition interface if it also supports the iCarRadio interface.

Listing 1.6: Querying for interfaces

```
ICarRadio* pRadio = NULL;
HRESULT hr = pIgnition->QueryInterface(
    IID_ICarRadio,
    (VOID**)&pRadio );
if( !pRadio || FAILED( hr ) )
{
    /* handle error */
}

// Now pRadio is ready to use.
```

This is the beauty of COM. The object can be improved without needing to be recompiled. If you decide to add support for a CD player in your car, all a piece of code needs to do is run QueryInterface for an iCarCDPlayer interface.

Getting COM to work like this forces two restrictions on the design of a system. First up, all interfaces are public. If you poke through the DirectX headers, you'll find the definitions for all of the DirectX interfaces. Any COM program can use any COM object, as long as it has the interface definition and the IDs for the COM interfaces.

A second, bigger restriction is that COM interfaces can never change. Once they are publicly released, they can never be modified in any way (not even fairly harmless modifications, like appending functions to the end of the interface). If this wasn't enforced, applications that used COM objects would need to be recompiled whenever an interface changed, which would defeat COM's whole purpose.

To add functionality to a COM object, you need to add new interfaces. For instance, say you wanted to extend iCarRadio to add bass and treble controls. You can't just add the functions. Instead, you have to put the new functions into a new interface, which would most likely be called iCarRadio2. Any applications that didn't need the new functionality, or ones that predated the addition of the iCarRadio2 interface, wouldn't need to worry about anything and would continue working using the iCarRadio interface. New applications could take advantage of the new functions by simply using QueryInterface to acquire an iCarRadio2 interface.

The one last big question to address is how COM objects get created. To use DirectX, you don't need to worry about a lot of the innards of COM object creation, but I'll give you a cursory overview.

You create a COM object by providing a COM object ID and an interface ID. Internally, the COM creation functions consult the registry, looking for the requested object ID. If the COM object is installed on your system, there will be a registry entry tying an object ID to a DLL. The DLL is loaded by your application, the object is constructed using a DLL-side class factory (returning an IUnknown interface), and then the interface is QueryInterface'd for the provided interface ID. If you look up the object ID for Direct3D in the registry, you'll find it sitting there, tied to ddraw.dll.

Note: The registry is a location for Windows to put all sorts of information pertaining to your machine. Versions previous to Windows 95 stored this information in .ini files.

So what are these object and interface IDs, and how are they given out? Well, all COM object creators couldn't be in constant communication, making sure the IDs they chose weren't already in use by someone else, so the creators of COM use what are called *globally unique identifiers* (GUIDs for short). These are 16-byte numbers that are guaranteed to be unique over time and space. (They're made up of an extremely large timestamp in addition to hardware factors like the ID of the network card of the machine that created it.) That way, when an interface is created, a GUID can be generated for it automatically that is guaranteed to not be in use (using a program called GUIDGEN that comes with Visual C++).

References

Petzold, Charles. *Programming Windows, The Definitive Guide to the Win32 API*. Redmond: Microsoft Press, 1998. ISBN: 157231995X.

Rogerson, Dale. *Inside COM (Programming Series)*. Redmond: Microsoft Press, 1997. ISBN: 1572313498.

For Further Reading

Petzold, Charles. *Programming Windows, The Definitive Guide to the Win32 API*. Redmond: Microsoft Press, 1998. ISBN: 157231995X.

Programming Windows is an indispensable resource to any Windows programmer. For information about the workings of the Win32 API, like dialogs, menus, and resources, look no further than this book. This is practically a required text.

Blasczak, Mike. *Professional MFC with Visual C++ 6*. Wrox Press, 1999. ISBN: 1861000154.

This is probably the most complete book on MFC ever published and is definitely equal in stature to Petzold's books for the MFC world. At 1,200 pages it's pretty long, but after reading it you will be an expert on the subject.

Richter, Jeffrey. *Advanced Windows (3rd Ed)*. Redmond: Microsoft Press, 1997. ISBN: 1572315482.

Advanced Windows continues where *Programming Windows* leaves off, delving deeper into the Win32 API. If you're hardcore about Win32 development, you'll probably want this book.

Rogerson, Dale. *Inside COM (Programming Series)*. Redmond: Microsoft Press, 1997. ISBN: 1572313498.

This book is an excellent introduction to COM programming. It takes you through the steps of how COM objects are implemented, how to create them, and how to use some more advanced COM features like aggregation.

Kruglinski, David J. et al. *Programming Microsoft Visual C++, Fifth Edition*. Redmond: Microsoft Press, 1998. ISBN: 1572318570.

This is a great introduction to MFC programming. It leads you through creating document view applications, dialog-based applications, and some of the cooler features of MFC programming. There is also a lot of information about Internet programming that most game programmers may not find terribly useful, but the MFC material is still excellent.

Chapter 2

DirectX—The Basic Components

I remember when I first started programming protected mode DOS using Watcom 10.0. My first stabs at graphics programming were extremely basic, using the provided graphics library that came with the Watcom SDK. My first graphics program did nothing more than draw a single point in the center of the screen, but let me tell you, that was one magical program. Sure, I could get the computer to do fairly uninteresting stuff like print text and read in text, but now I could actually make pictures.

Getting your first graphics program working, even if it just draws one dot on the screen, is an amazingly cool, almost religious experience. By the end of this chapter, not only will you be able to draw graphics to the screen, you'll also be able to read input and play sounds, all using the DirectX API.

What is DirectX?

Shortly after the release of Windows 95, Microsoft made a push to end DOS's reign as the primary game platform on the PC. Developers weren't swooned by the added abilities that Win32 programming gives you (a robust TCP/IP stack, multi-tasking, access to system information). They wanted the total control they had in DOS. Besides that, graphics in Windows at that time were done with WinG or even the Windows GDI. While WinG was pretty cool (and written by all-around cool guy Chris Hecker), it didn't have the feature set that games of the time needed, especially when it came to things like full-screen rendering. The GDI was designed to work on a myriad of different configurations, different resolutions, different bit depths—it was not designed to be fast.

Microsoft's answer to game developers was *The Game SDK*, which was really the first version of DirectX. Finally, developers could write fast games and still get the advantages of using the Win32 API, like multithreading support, a TCP/IP stack, and countless UI features. With version 2.0, the SDK's name was changed to DirectX. This was because Microsoft realized that game developers weren't the only people who wanted the graphics and audio acceleration provided by the SDK; developers of everything from video playback programs to presentation software wanted faster graphics.

Installation

Installing DirectX is a straightforward process. The only real decision you need to make is choosing between the retail and debug builds. The retail builds are stripped of lots of sanity checks and are also compiled to run faster. If you just plan on running other DirectX applications and not writing your own, the retail builds will be fine.

The debug builds are designed to help out coders while they're getting their DirectX applications up and running. For example, when you try to do something using DirectX and it fails, chances are the debug builds will print something to the debug window as to why it failed (which is often something easily fixed, like "dwSize parameter not set"). The tradeoff, however, is that they run slightly slower than the retail builds. I recommend that while you are learning you use the debug version of the software; it will save you many headaches later.

The other piece of software you'll most likely need to install is the latest version of your video card's drivers, if your video card predates the release of DirectX 8.0. You can pick them up off your video card manufacturer's web site or the Microsoft Windows update site. Having the newest possible versions of drivers is important, especially for recently released cards.

Setting up VC++

After you have gotten DirectX installed, you might want to take one of the samples (like boids, for instance) and try to compile it. To get it working you'll need to do a couple of things.

Visual C++ needs to know where the headers and library files for DirectX are so it can correctly compile and link your application. You only need to set this up once, since all projects use the same include and lib directories. To specify the directories, select Options from the Tools menu. In the Options dialog box, select the Directories tab. For include directories, you should enter DX 8.0 SDK Install Path\include. For lib directories, enter DX 8.0 SDK Install Path\Lib.

DX 8.0 SDK Install Path is just the directory where you installed the DirectX SDK on your hard disk.

The other trick is that the directories need to appear at the top of the list, so that they get searched first. When the compiler searches for d3d8.h, for example, it should find DX 8.0 SDK Install Path\include\d3d8.h (the 8.0 version of the header) first, and not use DEVSTUDIO\VC98\include\d3d.h (the 3.0 version of the header). Figures 2.1 and 2.2 show what the include and lib directory listings should look like.

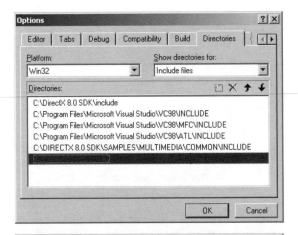

Figure 2.1:
The include directory listing

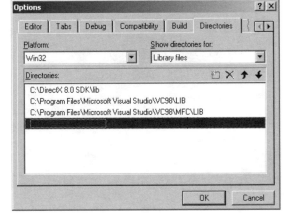

Figure 2.2:
The library directory listing

If the directories aren't set up correctly, you'll see some telltale signs in the errors the compiler produces. For example, if you get an error like this:

```
e:\book\chapter 08\gamelib\dxhelper.h(89) : error C2065: '_D3DSURFACE_DESC :
undeclared identifier
```

this means that it can't find the header with the D3DSURFACE_DESC structure, which was defined after DirectX 7.0. The headers that come with Visual C++ are from version 3.0, and the compiler is incorrectly trying to use the old versions of the headers.

The other thing you need when building a DirectX application is to have the right libraries listed for the linking step. Most of the applications you write will need the following libraries linked in:

- **winmm.lib** The windows multimedia library, which has timeGetTime
- **dxguid.lib** Has the GUIDs for all of the DirectX COM objects
- **d3d8.lib** Direct3D
- **d3dx.lib** Useful D3DX utility extensions

- **dsound.lib**   DirectSound
- **dinput8.lib**   DirectInput

Figure 2.3 shows an example of one of the Chapter 8 programs and the first few libraries it links in (it links in several more than can fit in the window).

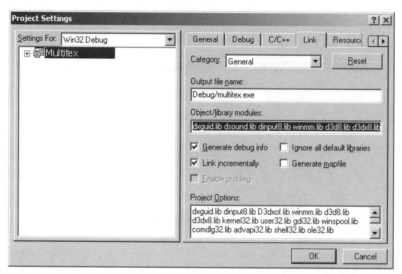

Figure 2.3:
Linking in
libraries

If you don't include the libraries correctly, you'll see errors such as these:

```
GameLib.lib(GraphicsLayer.obj) : error LNK2001: unresolved external symbol
_IID_IDirect3D8
GameLib.lib(GraphicsLayer.obj) : error LNK2001: unresolved external symbol
_IID_IDirect3DRefDevice
GameLib.lib(GraphicsLayer.obj) : error LNK2001: unresolved external symbol
_IID_IDirect3DRGBDevice
GameLib.lib(GraphicsLayer.obj) : error LNK2001: unresolved external symbol
_IID_IDirect3DHALDevice
GameLib.lib(GraphicsLayer.obj) : error LNK2001: unresolved external symbol
_IID_IDirect3DTnLHalDevice
```

Fixing this would just be a case of linking in dxguid.lib.

What Happened to DirectDraw?!

If you have any previous experience with DirectX graphics, then you will have probably heard of terms such as DirectDraw, Direct3D, Immediate Mode, and Retained Mode. If not, then don't worry; I am about to explain them in a moment. Version 8.0 of DirectX was described by Microsoft as the single most significant upgrade to DirectX since its initial release all those years ago. Version 8.0 is to DirectX what Windows 95 was to 3.11. So let me begin with a short introduction into the way things used to be, so that if you come across these terms you will know what is going on.

Graphical output on the PC can be roughly divided into two groups: 2-D and 3-D, with the latter obviously being far more complex. The implementation of DirectX graphics pretty much followed this train of thought. You had *DirectDraw*, which looked after 2-D graphics, and *Direct3D*, which looked after 3-D. Direct3D was further split into two groups—*Immediate Mode*, which provided a low-level interface to the 3-D graphics hardware that was generally considered very complex but fast. *Retained Mode* provided a higher-level, easy to use interface to the hardware, but it was bloated, inflexible, and slow.

As the development of DirectX continued, a number of patterns started to become clear:

- The development of DirectDraw had all but come to an end, except for a few new features, as of DirectX 5.0. There was just nothing left to do with it and most resources were being focused on Direct3D.

- The learning curve for DirectDraw was too steep; it was too complicated and required too many tedious steps to set up in code.

- The theoretical split between Direct3D and DirectDraw was becoming unnecessary, and it seemed to make more sense to have all the code for graphics accessible from one location.

- Direct3D Retained Mode was a complete failure with almost no commercial take-up and its support was pretty much dropped from DirectX 6.0.

- Direct3D Immediate Mode was too complicated, although it did improve significantly with the release of DirectX 5.0, and of course its successors.

To fix these issues, Microsoft took some bold steps and completely reorganized Direct3D and DirectDraw. They made the following changes:

- DirectDraw was completely removed as a separate entity and integrated entirely with Direct3D.

- Direct3D Retained Mode was ripped out and was not replaced.

- Direct3D Immediate Mode remains, but is now much more simplified, faster, and just all around more elegant.

The result of all these changes is that the graphics section of DirectX is now called DirectX Graphics, although I will be referring to it as Direct3D, since that is where all the functionality is now implemented. The setup portion of code for Direct3D has dropped from a staggering 1,000-plus lines to about 200, which is nice, although it leaves poor authors like myself with little to write about!

Don't forget that although throughout the book I'll be referring to DirectX Graphics as Direct3D, I am not necessarily talking about 3-D graphics, since Direct3D now handles the 2-D stuff as well. For instance, in the next section I talk heavily about 2-D graphics.

OK, so now that you've had your history lesson, let's look at Direct3D in a little more detail.

Direct3D

For the uninitiated, Direct3D can be really confusing. It uses a lot of paradigms you may have never seen before. It forces your code to behave nicely with other applications that can be simultaneously using system resources. Diving in to the code that makes Direct3D work will be confusing enough, so to start out I'm just going to talk about the concepts behind the code, which will hopefully make the rocky road ahead a little less painful.

Don't let anyone else tell you otherwise: Direct3D is hard. If you don't get this stuff immediately, it doesn't mean you're slow and it doesn't mean you're not ready for Windows programming; it means you're normal. DirectX wasn't designed to be easy to use. It was designed to be fast while allowing Windows to maintain some semblance of control over the system. DirectX has gotten much better in recent versions, but it still isn't a trivial thing to pick up.

Direct3D is a set of interfaces and functions that allow a Windows application to talk to the video card(s) in a machine. Only the most basic 2-D graphics functions are handled by Direct3D. There are some 2-D graphics libraries, such as the GDI, that can do things like draw rounded rectangles, ellipses, lines, thick lines, n-sided polygons, and so forth. Direct3D cannot do any of this. Any raster operations need to be developed by you, the game programmer.

What Direct3D <u>does</u> do is provide a transparent layer of communication with the hardware on the user's machine. Supported Direct3D functions, like blitting images (which I'll discuss later in the chapter), are implemented by the video card's super-fast internal hardware if the card can handle it. If no hardware is available, Direct3D will transparently emulate the hardware capabilities with hand-optimized assembly routines.

Aside: If you want raster operations like drawing lines and don't want to use Direct3D, the web is rife with shareware and freeware libraries to do this for you. Search and you shall find.

2-D Graphics—A Primer

The way your computer represents images on the screen is as a rectangle of values. Each value in this is called a *pixel*, short for *picture element*. If the image is m pixels wide and n pixels high, then there are m*n pixels in the image. Each pixel may be anywhere from 1 bit to 4 bytes in size, representing different kinds of color information. The total memory taken up by an image can generally be found as the width of the image times the height of the image times the number of bytes per pixel.

Color on computers is dealt with the same way it is drawn on monitors. Computer screens have three cathode ray tubes shining light onto the phosphorous screen dozens of times a second. The rays shine on red, green, and blue phosphors. By controlling how much red, green, and blue light hits each area of the monitor, the color that results from the phosphors changes. A white pixel, when examined very closely, is actually three smaller pixels: one red, one green, and one blue. You've probably noticed this if you've ever gotten drops of water on your monitor, which magnify what is under them. I wouldn't do this on purpose by the way—try a magnifying glass instead.

There are two main ways that color images are represented on computers. In the first, called *paletted* images, there exists a table of color values (usually with 256 entries) and an image where each pixel is a character indexing into the list. This restricts the image to having 256 unique colors. Before a few years ago, all games used 256-color images for all of their graphics, and before then even fewer colors were used (16 in high-resolution VGA, 4 in EGA and CGA). See Figure 2.4 for a diagram of what this looked like.

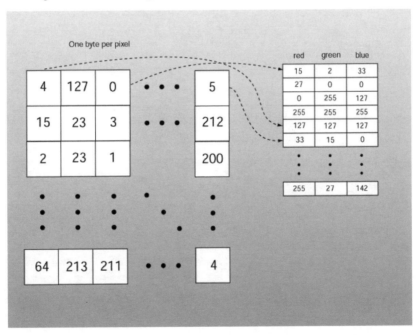

Figure 2.4: The workings of paletted images

Nowadays every PC you can buy has hardware that can render images with thousands or millions of individual colors. Rather than have an array with thousands of color entries, the images instead contain explicit color values for each pixel. A 16-bit display is named since each pixel in a 16-bit image is taken up by 16 bits (2 bytes): 5 bits of red information, 6 bits of green information, and 5 bits of blue information. Incidentally, the extra bit (and thusly twice as much color resolution) is given to green because your eyes are more sensitive to green. A 24-bit display, of course, uses 24 bits, or 3 bytes per pixel, for color information. This gives 1 byte, or 256 distinct values, for red, green, and blue. This is generally called *true color*, because 256³ (16.7 million) colors is about as much as your eyes can discern, so more color resolution really isn't necessary, at least for computer monitors.

Finally, there is 32-bit color, something seen on many of the newer graphics cards. Many 3-D accelerators keep 8 extra bits per pixel around to store transparency information, which is generally referred to as *alpha*, and thusly take up 4 bytes, or 32 bits, of storage per pixel. Rather than re-implement the display logic on 2-D displays that don't need alpha information, these 8 bits are usually just wasted.

Almost universally, all computer images have an origin located at the top-left corner of the image. The top-left corner pixel is referenced with the x,y pair (0,0). The value of x increases to the right; y increases down. This is a departure from the way people usually think of Cartesian coordinates, where the origin is usually in the lower left or center. Figure 2.5 shows the coordinate convention your images will use.

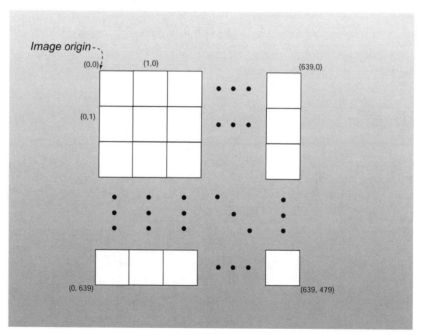

Figure 2.5: Coordinate setup of an image

Each horizontal row of pixels is called a *scan line*. The image is stored in memory by attaching each scan line from the top to the bottom end-to-end into a single large one-dimensional array. That way, accessing *pixel (x,y)* on the screen requires you to move across to the correct scan line (the scan line number is y; each scan line is *width* pixels across), and then move across the scan line to the correct pixel.

```
pixel(x,y)=width*y+x
```

There is one special image in memory that describes the pixels that the monitor will draw. Back in the DOS days, if you put the machine into 320x200x256 color mode and then set *(0xa0000) = 15, a white pixel would appear in the top-left corner of the screen (palette entry 15 is white by default). The pointer 0xa0000 pointed to the start of the 64KB block of video memory on VGA cards. A graphics application takes this block of memory and fills it with whatever it would like to show up on the screen.

There's a problem, however. The screen isn't updated instantly. It's a physical device, and thusly moves eons slower than the CPU. The actual electron gun that lights the screen is internally flying across each scan line of the monitor, reading from the screen's image data and displaying the appropriate colors on the screen. When it reaches the end of a scan line, it moves diagonally down and to the left to the start of the next scan line. When it finishes the last scan line, it moves diagonally up and to the left back to the start of the first scan line. The movement from the bottom-right to the top-left corners is called the *vertical blank* or *vertical retrace* (shown in Figure 2.6) and it takes a long time in terms of processor speed. I'm talking years here.

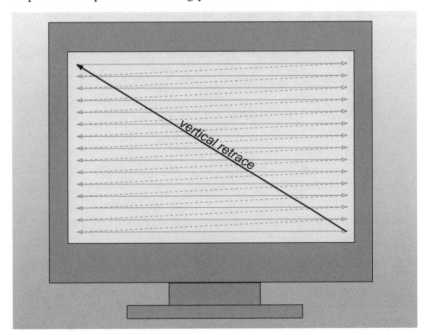

Figure 2.6:
The vertical blank

Keep this in mind when rendering your images. If you update the screen image at an arbitrary time, the electron gun may be in the middle of the screen. So for that particular frame, the top half of the screen will display the old image, and the bottom half will display the new image. That's assuming you can change the image quickly enough. If you don't, pieces of new image may be smattered all over the screen, creating a horrible, ugly mess. This effect is known as *tearing*.

Because of this, every game under the sun uses a trick called *double buffering*. The final image is composed into a secondary, off-screen buffer. Then the application waits around for the vertical blank to begin. At that point it can safely copy the image to the screen image. You can be fairly sure that the memory copy will finish before the vertical blank does, so when the electron gun starts drawing again, it's using the new image. While it's drawing the new image, you start rendering the next image into your off-screen buffer, and the cycle continues. The image you render into is called the *back buffer*.

Note: Actually, applications can go a step further and use triple or even quadruple buffering. This is useful to help smooth out jerky frame rates, but requires a lot of precious video memory (especially at high resolutions).

Surfaces

2-D images in Direct3D are wrapped by objects called *surfaces*. Internally, a surface is just a structure that manages image data as a contiguous block of memory. Because of this you see the concept of a surface being used in lots of places in DirectX to take care of different types of data, from vertex buffers to sound buffers. The structure keeps track of the vital statistics of the surface, such as its height, width, and format of the pixel. You create them using the Direct3D object, and use the IDirect3DSurface8 interface to play with them.

One of the features that surfaces implement is locking. This is because of the asynchronous (multiple things happening in parallel) nature of many video cards. Instead of having to wait for every operation to finish, you can tell the hardware to do something for you, and it will perform the task in the background while you are doing other stuff. When multiple things are accessing the same piece of memory at the same time, caution must be taken.

For example, imagine you draw an image to a surface and request Direct3D to copy the pixels to the screen (using a *blit*, or bit block transfer, which I'll discuss in a moment). The task gets queued with the other tasks the card is currently doing and will be finished eventually. However, without memory protection, you could quickly copy another image onto the bits of the surface before the blit gets executed. When the card got around to performing the blit, it would be blitting a different image!

This is a horrible problem. Depending on how much load was on the video card (and whether or not it operates asynchronously; some cards do not), sometimes the surface will be replaced before it is copied, sometimes it won't, sometimes it may even be in the process of being replaced when the card gets to it.

For this reason, you do not have continual access to the raw bits of data that make up your image at all times. DirectX uses a fairly common concurrency paradigm called a *lock*. When you acquire a lock to a surface, you have exclusive access to it until you are finished with it. If you request a lock on a surface and another piece of code is using it, you won't be able to get it until the other process releases its lock on the surface. When you successfully complete a lock, you are given a pointer to the raw bits, which you may modify to your delight, while being confident that no other programs will mess with your memory. In the previous example, Direct3D would lock the surface when you requested the blit and unlock it once the blit had completed. If you tried to mangle the bits of the image, your code would not be able to get a pointer to the image data (one of the things you receive when you engage a lock) until the lock had been released by Direct3D.

Surfaces, along with having the raw bits to image data, contain a lot of information about the pixels they contain. The width, height, format of the pixel, type of surface, etc., are stored in the surface. There is another important variable that a surface contains that I should mention, called the *pitch*. Some hardware devices require that image rows begin aligned to 4-pixel boundaries, or 10-pixel boundaries, or any other possible value. If you tried to make an image with an odd width, the card would not be able to handle it. Because of this, Direct3D uses the concept of a pitch in addition to the width. The pitch of an image is similar to the width; however, it may be a bit bigger to accommodate the way the display adapter works. The address of the pixel directly below the top-left corner of a Direct3D surface is not surface_width * bytes_per_pixel.

Rather, it is pixel * surface_pitch. The surface pitch is <u>always</u> measured in bytes; it doesn't vary in relation to the number of bits per pixel. See Figure 2.7.

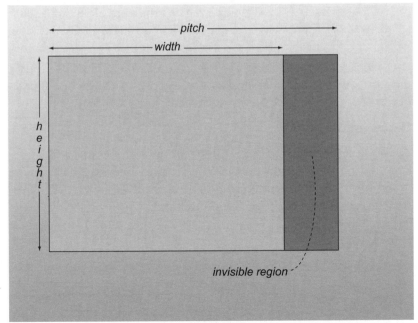

Figure 2.7:
The extra issue of dealing with image pitch

Note: This is very important so don't forget it: The pitch of a surface is always measured in bytes and has nothing to do with the number of bits per pixel you are currently working with.

Complex Surfaces

Surfaces can be attached to other surfaces in something called a *chain* of surfaces. This paradigm is used to represent MIP maps, cubic environment maps (both discussed in Chapter 8), and flipping chains.

Flipping chains allow an easier way for the hardware to implement double buffering if two (or more) surfaces exist in the chain. One of them is actually the screen image, the pixels the electron gun will use to display the image on the monitor. The other is the back buffer, the buffer you render the scene into. When you're done rendering, you can flip the surfaces, which will actually swap the addresses of the buffers internally on the video card. Then, the back buffer becomes the screen image, and the screen image becomes the back buffer. The next time the application starts rendering a frame, it will be rendering into what once was the screen image, while what once was the back buffer is currently being drawn to the screen by the monitor.

Warning: If you're counting on the results from the previous frame when rendering the current frame, be wary. The bits you get when you're using double buffering with a flipping chain isn't the state of the frame buffer at the end of the previous frame; it's the frame buffer from two frames ago!

Direct3D has a special name for the screen image. Since it's pretty much the most important surface an application can have (it's the one that shows off all of the other surfaces), it is known as the *primary surface*.

Describing Surfaces

When you create surfaces or request information about surfaces, the capabilities and vital statistics for the surface are inscribed in a structure called the surface description. The surface description is represented by the D3DSURFACE_DESC structure, and has the following definition:

```
typedef struct _D3DSURFACE_DESC {
    D3DFORMAT           Format;
    D3DRESOURCETYPE     Type;
    DWORD               Usage;
    D3DPOOL             Pool;
    UINT                Size;
    D3DMULTISAMPLE_TYPE MultiSampleType;
    UINT                Width;
    UINT                Height;
} D3DSURFACE_DESC;
```

Table 2.1: The D3DSURFACE_DESC structure

Format	A member of the D3DFORMAT enumeration identifying the format for the surface that you want to use. This can be set to any of the following values, although you don't have to worry about most of them for now. I have bolded the most important flags that you will probably come across.

- D3DFMT_UNKNOWN—The surface format is not known.
- **D3DFMT_R8G8B8**—Standard 24-bit RGB (red, green, blue) format
- **D3DFMT_A8R8G8B8**—Standard 32-bit ARGB (alpha, red, green, blue) format
- D3DFMT_X8R8G8B8—32-bit RGB format
- **D3DFMT_R5G6B5**—Standard 16-bit RGB format
- D3DFMT_X1R5G5B5—15-bit RGB format
- D3DFMT_A1R5G5B5—16-bit ARGB format
- D3DFMT_A4R4G4B4—16-bit ARGB format
- D3DFMT_R3G3B2—8-bit RGB format
- D3DFMT_A8—8-bit alpha-only surface
- D3DFMT_A8R3G3B2—16-bit ARGB format
- D3DFMT_X4R4G4B4—16-bit RGB format
- D3DFMT_A8P8—16-bit AP surface format (8 bits alpha, 8 bits palette)
- **D3DFMT_P8**—8-bit palettized surface
- D3DFMT_L8—8-bit luminance-only surface
- D3DFMT_A8L8—16-bit AL surface (8 bits alpha, 8 bits luminance)
- D3DFMT_A4L4—8-bit AL surface (4 bits alpha, 4 bits luminance)
- D3DFMT_V8U8—16-bit bump map format
- D3DFMT_L6V5U5—16-bit bump map surface with luminance
- D3DFMT_X8L8V8U8—32-bit bump map surface with luminance (8 bits each)
- D3DFMT_Q8W8V8U8—32-bit bump map surface
- D3DFMT_V16U16—32-bit bump map only surface format
- D3DFMT_W11V11U10—32-bit bump map only surface format
- D3DFMT_UYVY—PC98 compatible UYVY format
- D3DFMT_YUY2—PC98 compatible YUY2 format
- D3DFMT_DXT1—DXT1 compressed surface
- D3DFMT_DXT2—DXT2 compressed surface
- D3DFMT_DXT3—DXT3 compressed surface
- D3DFMT_DXT4—DXT4 compressed surface

- D3DFMT_DXT5—DXT5 compressed surface
- D3DFMT_D16_LOCKABLE—16-bit lockable depth buffer
- D3DFMT_D32—32-bit depth buffer
- D3DFMT_D15S1—16-bit depth buffer with a 1-bit stencil buffer
- D3DFMT_D24S8—32-bit depth buffer with an 8-bit stencil buffer
- **D3DFMT_D16**—Standard 16-bit depth buffer
- D3DFMT_D24X8—24-bit depth buffer on a 32-bit surface
- D3DFMT_D24X4S4—32-bit depth buffer with a 4-bit stencil buffer
- D3DFMT_VERTEXDATA—The surface contains vertex buffer data
- D3DFMT_INDEX16—The surface contains 16-bit index buffer data
- D3DFMT_INDEX32—The surface contains 32-bit index buffer data

Type	A member of the D3DRESOURCETYPE enumeration, identifying the type of surface. The possible values for Type are listed below. Again, don't worry too much about what they mean just yet—I'll cover everything important throughout the book. For now just specify the D3DRTYPE_SURFACE identifier.

- **D3DRTYPE_SURFACE**—The object you are creating will be a surface.
- D3DRTYPE_VOLUME—The object you are creating will be a volume.
- D3DRTYPE_TEXTURE—The object will be a standard texture.
- D3DRTYPE_VOLUMETEXTURE—The object will be a volume texture.
- D3DRTYPE_CUBETEXTURE—The object will be a cubic texture.
- D3DRTYPE_VERTEXBUFFER—The object will be a vertex buffer.
- D3DRTYPE_INDEXBUFFER—The object will be an index buffer.

Usage	This specifies how the surface will be used. If you are creating an off-screen surface to hold an image, set this to NULL. If the surface will be used as a render target (e.g., a back buffer), specify D3DUSAGE_RENDERTARGET. Or, if you want to create a depth or stencil buffer, which I'll cover in later chapters, specify D3DUSAGE_DEPTHSTENCIL.
Pool	A member of the D3DPOOL enumeration identifying where in memory you want the new surface to reside. The possible values for the D3DPOOL enumeration are shown below, but you will almost always want to specify D3DPOOL_MANAGED for this variable, since Direct3D will look after all the complicated, behind the scenes work of keeping the texture in the correct place.

D3DPOOL_DEFAULT—Direct3D will automatically place the surface in the memory (system, video, AGP, etc.) that is best suited to hold it.

D3DPOOL_MANAGED—The surface will be copied into video memory as it is needed automatically and is backed up by system memory so the image is unaffected by device loss, which I will talk about shortly.

	D3DPOOL_SYSTEMMEM—The surface will reside in system memory, which is usually not accessible by the display adapter.
Size	The size of the surface in bytes
MultiSampleType	Member of the D3DMULTISAMPLE_TYPE enumeration identifying the number of multisample levels that the device supports. Just assume this to be D3DMULTISAMPLE_NONE for now.
Width	The width, in pixels, of the surface
Height	The height, in pixels, of the surface

Don't worry, I'm not expecting you to get this yet. At the moment I am throwing a lot of information at you. The important thing to do is to keep your head above the mud and keep reading. So now that you've seen how surfaces are described let's look at an actual Direct3D surface.

The IDirect3DSurface8 Interface

A Direct3D surface is represented with a COM interface. Since more and more features have been added through the different versions of DirectX, new COM interfaces have been made (remember that you can never change COM interfaces once they're published). The current version of the Direct3D surface interface is called IDirect3DSurface8. Unlike previous versions of this interface, which used to be called IDirectDrawSurface7, IDirect3DSurface8 has only eight member functions; they are listed in Table 2.1.

Table 2.2: IDirect3DSurface8 methods

GetDevice	Gets a pointer to the device that was used to create this surface.
GetContainer	Gets a pointer to a parent texture if one exists.
GetDesc	Retrieves a D3DSURFACE_DESC structure, which is filled with information describing the surface.
LockRect	The all-important function that is used to lock a surface so that you can access it. The function gets you a D3DLOCKED_RECT structure, which contains the pitch of the surface as well as a pointer to the start of the image data.
UnlockRect	Unlocks a previously locked surface.
FreePrivateData	Frees any memory used to hold extra information with the surface that programmer has set.
GetPrivateData	Gets the private data that may have been attached to this surface.
SetPrivateData	Attaches private data to the surface.

Surface Operations

These days Direct3D only has a few facilities to help you play with surfaces. The main one is blitting. Blit (or bit block transfer) is the short name for physically copying the contents of one image on top of another image. The 2-D games of yore focused intently on blitting; games lived and died by the speed of their blitting engine. When you saw Mario running about the screen, you were actually looking at two small square images, one representing the head and shoulders and one representing the body, that were copied onto the screen, one on top of the other, to look like an Italian plumber doing his best to fulfill his archaic gender role and save Princess Toadstool.

Back in the pre-Direct3D days, people generally did blitting by themselves, without the help of Windows. In the simplest case (no scaling, no transparency), it was just a matter of doing some memcpy's to overwrite a section of one surface's contents with a section of another's. However, in the brave new world of hardware accelerated video cards, this is not the best thing to do. Most (if not all) modern video cards support many basic 2-D operations (like blitting) in hardware, making them orders of magnitude faster than the fastest memcpy you could ever write. In order to transparently use whatever hardware is currently supported on the machine, you tell Direct3D what you want to do, and Direct3D translates your commands to whatever hardware is available. If no hardware acceleration is available, Direct3D does all the work itself, using heavily optimized code, which is just as good if not better than anything you or I would be able to write.

While 2-D games may employ blits all over the place, calling hundreds or thousands of them per frame, 3-D applications don't really need them. You'll just be using blitting in a couple of places, oftentimes making only one blit per frame. Because of this I'm not going to go into the myriad of effects, specializations, optimizations, and so forth that deal with image blitting.

Warning: Direct3D cannot blit between two surfaces that have different pixel formats, according to the spec. The one exception is compressed textures, which are not covered in this text anyway. However, there are some new tools with Direct3D 8.0 which allow you to get around this problem easily.

In the past blitting was an integral part of surfaces. There used to be an actual function called IDirectDrawSurface7::Blt(). However, for some reason or another, an incredible amount of functionality was removed from surfaces during the unification of Direct3D and DirectDraw, and the blitting technology is now implemented in functions external to the object. It seems like a step backwards from object orientation, but I'm sure Microsoft had their reasons.

These days if you want to copy one surface to another you use the DirectX utility function D3DXLoadSurfaceFromSurface(), which I have prototyped for you below:

```
HRESULT D3DXLoadSurfaceFromSurface(
  LPDIRECT3DSURFACE8 pDestSurface,
```

```
    CONST PALETTEENTRY* pDestPalette,
    CONST RECT* pDestRect,
    LPDIRECT3DSURFACE8 pSrcSurface,
    CONST PALETTEENTRY* pSrcPalette,
    CONST RECT* pSrcRect,
    DWORD Filter,
    D3DCOLOR ColorKey
);
```

The term *loading* is the new Microsoft word-of-the-future for filling a surface with data. As you will see later you can also load a surface from a file, from a memory resource, or from just about anywhere. Okay, now let's take a moment to look at the function. Don't get too overwhelmed with it just yet—it is much simpler than it seems. The parameters are shown in Table 2.3.

Table 2.3: The parameters to D3DXLoadSurfaceFromSurface()

pDestSurface	Pointer to the destination IDirect3DSurface8 surface, which will be filled with the new image.
pDestPalette	This can hold a pointer to a PALETTEENTRY palette for the destination surface if the surface is palettized. However, these days palettized surfaces are rare so you will probably just want to go ahead and set this to NULL.
pDestRect	This parameter takes the address of a destination rectangle within the surface that you want to fill with the source image. Depending on flags specified in the Filter parameter the image will either be cropped or scaled to fit this rectangle. If you want to use the entire surface as the destination then you can specify NULL for this parameter.
pSrcSurface	Takes the address of the source IDirect3DSurface8 surface that you want to copy.
pSrcPalette	Similarly to the pDestPalette parameter, this parameter takes the address of the palette for the source surface if it is palettized. You will usually set this parameter to NULL.
pSrcRect	This is the address of a RECT rectangle that contains the dimensions of the area within the source surface that you want to copy. If you want to copy the entire source surface then set this parameter to NULL.
Filter	This is an interesting parameter that you can set to change the way that the image is copied if the dimensions of the destination rectangle do not match the source. I have listed the important flags in the following:
D3DX_FILTER_NONE	No filter will be applied and the image will be cropped (have its edges chopped off) to make it fit the destination rectangle.
D3DX_FILTER_POINT	A point filter will be applied to scale the source image to fit the destination. Point filtering is very fast but results in a blocky image.
D3DX_FILTER_LINEAR	A linear filter is used to scale the image. Linear filtering is slightly slower than point filtering, although the results, which are smoothly scaled, are orders of magnitude better.

D3DX_FILTER_TRIANGLE	This is the highest quality, and slowest, of the scaling filters. The performance tradeoff generally does not justify its use over linear filtering—the results are often indistinguishable.
ColorKey	A D3DCOLOR value, which specifes the color that you want to be used as a colorkey. Unfortunately this is not a proper implementation of color keying; instead the pixels within the source image that match the color key are just turned to black on the destination image. If you want true color key support, I'm afraid you are going to have to program it yourself.

Don't worry about this too much just yet—all the pieces of the puzzle will fall into place in your mind as you progress though the book.

You will probably use D3DXLoadSurfaceFromSurface() as your primary tool when copying surfaces. There is, however, one exception, and that is when you are copying from an off-screen back surface onto the primary surface, which I will cover shortly.

Surfaces and Memory

Surfaces can exist in system RAM or in the video card's memory. Where you should put the surface depends on what you want to do with it. Blits between system RAM and video RAM are slow because the data needs to be transferred over the system bus. The bus usually runs at a lower clock rate than the system RAM or the video card, causing both of them to sit around waiting for the bits to be sent.

In general, surfaces that get blitted on top of each other should be in the same region of memory if at all possible. For example, say you are composing a scene with hundreds of blitted images like in a complex 2-D game. Since you probably won't be able to fit all of the surfaces in video memory, you need to plan to have at least a few of them in system memory. The blind algorithm would be to blit each of the surfaces onto the back buffer. The surfaces in video memory would blit much faster, because they not only don't need to go over the bus, they can be blitted by the 2-D hardware. Conversely, the system memory surfaces can hurt the application greatly.

Modifying the Contents of Surfaces

Applications that wish to perform their own raster functions on surfaces, such as plotting pixels or drawing triangles with custom rasterizers, must first lock the surface before being able to modify the pixels of the image.

> ***Warning:*** To prevent other programs from modifying a locked surface,
> Direct3D may acquire a win16mutex. This can cause problems if you try
> to, for example, step through code between lock/unlock calls using a
> debugger like Visual C++. Luckily, these problems only crop up on
> Win9x; Win2K uses the NT kernel and therefore isn't affected by this
> problem. With DirectX 8.0 now fully integrated into Win2K I suggest that
> you use that platform for your development. Not only is it a better sys-
> tem, but you can usually recover from crashed programs easily and
> without restarting your PC.

To lock a surface you use the IDirect3DSurface8::Lock() function, which I have
prototyped in the following:

```
HRESULT LockRect(
    D3DLOCKED_RECT* pLockedRect,
    CONST RECT* pRect,
    DWORD Flags
);
```

Table 2.4: LockRect parameters

pLockedRect	A pointer to a D3DLOCKED_RECT structure, which will be filled with information about the locked surface. The D3DLOCKED_RECT structure has the following members:
	
	`typedef struct _D3DLOCKED_RECT {`
	`        INT                Pitch;`
	`        void*              pBits;`
	`} D3DLOCKED_RECT;`

Pitch	The pitch, in bytes, of the locked surface.
pBits	A pointer to the start of the surface's image data.
pRect	Takes the address of a RECT structure that is filled with the dimensions within the surface that you want to lock. If you want to lock the entire surface, set this parameter to NULL.
Flags	This can be set to flags that change the behavior of the surface in rare situations. Usually you will just set this parameter to NULL. If you want more information on the other flags, see *DirectX 8.0 C++ Documentation/DirectX Graphics/Direct3D C++ Reference/Interfaces/IDirect3DSurface8/IDirect3DSurface8::LockRect* in the online documentation.

Since locking a surface causes most of the critical components of Windows to
start getting into a traffic jam, I cannot overstate the importance of unlocking a
surface when you are done with it. If you do not, Windows will grind to a halt
and eventually stall. To unlock a surface, use the function
IDirect3DSurface8::UnlockRect, which looks like this:

```
HRESULT UnlockRect();
```

As you can see, it does not take any parameters. Call this function as soon as you are finished updating the contents of the surface.

Drawing on Surfaces with GDI

In past versions of DirectX it was incredibly easy to use the Windows GDI to draw onto a Direct3D surface. However, rather inexplicably, Microsoft has removed all interoperability between surfaces and the GDI. So unless you want to manually program your own routines to copy GDI data to Direct3D surfaces, you are kind of stuck. I'm not going to go into this in this book because Microsoft no longer recommends using the GDI with Direct3D, but in one of my other books, *The Zen of Direct3D Game Programming*, I provide detailed coverage on how to achieve this with DirectX 8.0. See the "For Further Reading" section at the end of this chapter for more information.

Anyway, it is so complicated that you would be better off just rewriting your own optimized rectangle, line, or circle functions than resorting to the monstrously slow GDI.

The Direct3D Device Object

The Direct3D device object provides a line of communication between your software and the video card in the host machine. Typically, since only one video card exists in a machine, you only have to concern yourself with one device object. However, in the case of a machine with a separate add-in 3-D card (such as the 3DFX Voodoo or Voodoo2), or a machine with multiple monitors, there can be multiple Direct3D device objects to choose from. In this case you may have to be careful which object you create. For example, if the user had a 3DFX card and you wrongly chose the primary Direct3D object instead of the object corresponding to the 3DFX card, you wouldn't be able to access its 3-D capabilities. This is due to the fact that when you build Direct3D code in Chapter 6, it is built on top of Direct3D. However, these days this is not so much of an issue since there are almost no separate add-in cards left on the market. Instead, 3D functionality is built right into the primary display adapter. If you have one of these older cards, it is probably time that you went out and purchased a new one, especially if you are interested in development.

The Direct3D object lets you do things that you could never do with only the standard Windows API. For example, you can change the bit depth and the resolution of the display to any mode the card supports. You can ask the object for a list of available resolutions and select from among them.

The Direct3D device object is created by the Direct3D object, which I will show you shortly.

Windowed vs. Full-screen

The two main modes of operation of Direct3D are windowed rendering and full-screen rendering. In windowed rendering, your application draws its graphics to the client rectangle of a regular old window, sharing space with other running applications. When your window is resized, you need to take care to resize your internal structures to adapt to the new size. The same applies when the window is moved around the screen. In addition, windowed rendering makes use of a Direct3D concept called a *clipper*. A clipper object keeps track of any windows that are on top of your window, so that when you draw your surface to the screen only the pixels that actually belong to the application's client rectangle are drawn. Luckily the process of handling clipping is completely handled by Direct3D, so you never have to touch it.

Figure 2.8 shows the kind of issue I'm talking about. If you just drew arbitrarily to the client rectangle, you would overwrite the top-left part of the Notepad application floating over the window.

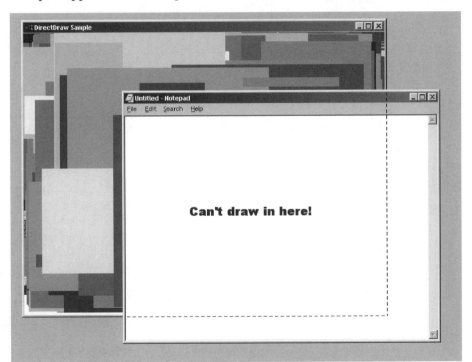

Figure 2.8:
We can't draw wherever we want to!

The Direct3D Object

The IDirect3D8 interface is the first interface that you will interact with when you are using DirectX Graphics. It does basically nothing except for creating the Direct3D device object, which I talked about previously. It is the device that is used to interact with the graphics hardware. Well, I kind of lied; IDirect3D8 does have some functionality but to tell you the truth in all the time I have used

Direct3D 8.0, I have rarely used any of its functionality since most of it is replicated in the device object anyway.

IDirect3D8 is created with the Direct3DCreate8() function, which I will show you shortly. Now, before I bring all this stuff together, let me take a moment to show you how to create surfaces.

Creating Direct3D Surfaces

Creating surfaces used to be a total pain before version 8.0 came out. You had to fill out massive annoying structures that contained an unbelievable amount of entries and substructures. Couple that with poor, badly structured documentation, and it was no wonder that so many people found the learning curve for DirectX Graphics so steep.

Luckily these days all that is gone and all you have to do is make a simple call to a function called IDirect3DDevice::CreateImageSurface().

```
HRESULT CreateImageSurface(
  UINT Width,
  UINT Height,
  D3DFORMAT Format,
  IDirect3DSurface8** ppSurface
);
```

Table 2.5: CreateImageSurface parameters

Width	The width that you want the new surface to be, in pixels.
Height	The height that you want the new surface to be, in pixels.
Format	A member of the D3DFORMAT enumerated type, specifying the format for the surface. You can see the full list of possible values for this parameter earlier in the chapter in Table 2.1. However, you will usually want to set this to D3DFMT_A8R8G8B8 for 32-bit surfaces. For more information, see *DirectX 8.0 C++ Documentation/DirectX Graphics/Direct3D C++ Reference/Enumerated Types/D3DFORMAT* in the online documentation.
ppSurface	Takes the address of a pointer that will be filled with the address of the newly created surface.

So if you wanted to create a simple 32-bit ARGB, 640x480 surface you could use the following code:

Listing 2.1: Creating a new image surface

```
HRESULT r = 0;
LPDIRECT3DSURFACE8 pSurface = 0;

r = g_pDevice->CreateImageSurface( 640, 480, D3DFMT_A8R8G8B8, &pSurface );
if( FAILED( r ) )
{
  // Error
```

```
}

// Success!
```

When you are finished with a surface that uses a large amount of resources, don't forget to release it using the IDirect3DSurface8::Release() function, like this:

```
pSurface->Release();
pSurface = 0;
```

More on Direct3D Devices

There are two pieces of code running in Direct3D applications. The first is the extremely thin layer that takes requests to blit surfaces, for example, and converts those into hardware instructions for the video card to perform. This thin layer that wraps the hardware, abstracting it away, is called the *hardware abstraction layer* (HAL).

In the event that a desired effect in Direct3D is not supported by the HAL, usually it is handled by a larger piece of code that emulates what the hardware would do, actually performing the work with the CPU. This layer is called the *hardware emulation layer* (HEL). The HEL can be considerably slower than the HAL, both because it isn't asynchronous and because it needs to use the CPU to do its dirty work, which isn't specialized for graphics operations.

Any piece of hardware that can accelerate 3-D graphics will support the subset of Direct3D (which, essentially, is just surface blits and filled blits). If you plan on using more esoteric features, you should check the device capabilities. This can be done usingIDirect3DDevice8::GetDeviceCaps(). There isn't space to cover the function or the structure of capability bits it fills up because it is literally massive. However, if you are feeling motivated you can check this bad boy out in *DirectX 8.0 C++ Documentation/DirectX Graphics/Direct3D C++ Reference/Interfaces/IDirect3DDevice8/IDirect3DDevice8::GetDeviceCaps* in the online documentation.

Implementing Direct3D with cGraphicsLayer

To implement Direct3D I'm going to create a class called cGraphicsLayer. Like cApplication, it is a class that can only have one instance. In creating this class, there are several abilities that it should possess:

- Initialization of full-screen Direct3D should be automatic.
- It should be easy to get access to the Direct3D objects if need be, but that need should arise as rarely as possible.
- You should be able to initialize Direct3D with the primary display adapter.

Let's dive into the code. First, have a look at the header file DxHelper.h, which helps simplify some of the programming tasks.

Listing 2.2: DxHelper.h

```
/******************************************************************
 *          Advanced 3D Game Programming using DirectX 8.0
 * * * * * * * * * * * * * * * * * * * * * * * * * * * * * * * *
 *    Title: DxHelper.h
 *     Desc: Direct3D helper classes
 *           constructors take care of a lot of grunt work
 * copyright (c) 2001 by Peter A Walsh and Adrian Perez
 * See license.txt for modification and distribution information
 ******************************************************************/

#ifndef _DXHELPER_H
#define _DXHELPER_H

#include <memory.h>

/**
 * This class takes care of the annoying gruntwork
 * of having to zero-out and set the size parameter
 * of our Windows and DirectX structures.
 */
template <class T>
struct sAutoZero : public T
{
  sAutoZero()
  {
      memset( this, 0, sizeof(T) );
      dwSize = sizeof(T);
  }
};

/**
 * The Right Way to release our COM interfaces.
 * If they're still valid, release them, then
 * invalidate them.
 */
template <class T>
inline void SafeRelease( T& iface )
{
  if( iface )
  {
      iface->Release();
      iface = NULL;
  }
}
```

```
#endif // _DXHELPER_H
```

The interface for the graphics layer appears in GraphicsLayer.h, which is given in Listing 2.3.

Listing 2.3: GraphicsLayer.h

```
/******************************************************************
 *         Advanced 3D Game Programming using DirectX 8.0
 * * * * * * * * * * * * * * * * * * * * * * * * * * * * * * *
 *    Title: GraphicsLayer.h
 *     Desc: Declaration of a layer abstracting Direct3D
 * (C) 2001 by Peter A Walsh and Adrian Perez
 * See license.txt for modification and distribution information
 ******************************************************************/

#ifndef _GRAPHICSLAYER_H
#define _GRAPHICSLAYER_H

#include <list>
#include <string>
using std::string;
using std::list;

#include <d3d8.h>
#include "GameTypes.h"
#include "DxHelper.h"

class cApplication;

class cGraphicsLayer
{
protected:

  HWND            m_hWnd;          // The handle to the window
  LPDIRECT3D8     m_pD3D;          // The IDirect3D8 interface
  LPDIRECT3DDEVICE8    m_pDevice;  // The IDirect3DDevice8 interface
  LPDIRECT3DSURFACE8 m_pBackSurf;  // Pointer to the back buffer

  RECT            m_rcScreenRect;  // The dimensions of the screen

  cGraphicsLayer( HWND hWnd );              // Constructor
  static cGraphicsLayer* m_pGlobalGLayer;   // Pointer to the main global gfx
object

public:

  void DestroyAll();
  ~cGraphicsLayer();
```

```
/**
 * Initialization calls.
 */
void InitD3DFullScreen( GUID* pGuid, int width, int height, int bpp );

/**
 * This function uses Direct3DX to write text to the back buffer.
 * Its much faster than using the GDI
 */
void DrawTextString( int x, int y, DWORD color, const char * str );

//================------------------------- Accessor functions
// Gets a pointer to the IDirect3D8
LPDIRECT3D8 GetD3D()
{
    return m_pD3D;
}

// Gets a pointer to the device
LPDIRECT3DDEVICE8 GetDevice()
{
    return m_pDevice;
}

// Gets a pointer to the back buffer
LPDIRECT3DSURFACE8 GetBackBuffer()
{
    return m_pBackSurf;
}

// Gets the screen width
int Width() const
{
    return m_rcScreenRect.right;
}

// Gets the screen height
int Height() const
{
    return m_rcScreenRect.bottom;
}

// Presents the back buffer to the primary surface
void Flip();

// Gets a pointer to the main gfx object
static cGraphicsLayer* GetGraphics()
{
    return m_pGlobalGLayer;
}
```

```
    // Initializes this object
    static void Create(
         HWND hWnd, // handle to the window
    short width, short height, // width and height
    NULL ); // use the primary display adapter
};

inline cGraphicsLayer* Graphics()
{
  return cGraphicsLayer::GetGraphics();
}



#endif //_GRAPHICSLAYER_H
```

GraphicsLayer.cpp is rather involved and long, so I'll show it to you step by step. There are a few functions that don't deal with initialization, which I'll list here. The first is a helper function used to draw text onto a Direct3D surface (such as the back buffer). It uses the D3DX utility COM object ID3DXFont to display the text.

Listing 2.4: cGraphicsLayer::DrawTextString

```
void cGraphicsLayer::DrawTextString( int x, int y, DWORD color, const char *
                                      str )
{

  HRESULT r = 0;

  if( !m_pBackSurf )
       return;

  // Get a handle for the font to use
  HFONT hFont = (HFONT)GetStockObject( SYSTEM_FONT );

  LPD3DXFONT pFont = 0;
  // Create the D3DX Font
  r = D3DXCreateFont( m_pDevice, hFont, &pFont );
  if( FAILED( r ) )
       return;

  // Rectangle where the text will be located
  RECT TextRect = { x, y, 0, 0 };

  // Inform font it is about to be used
  pFont->Begin();

  // Calculate the rectangle the text will occupy
  pFont->DrawText( str, -1, &TextRect, DT_CALCRECT, 0 );
```

```
// Output the text, left aligned
pFont->DrawText( str, -1, &TextRect, DT_LEFT, color );

// Finish up drawing
pFont->End();

// Release the font
pFont->Release();

}
```

The other function not covered by the initialization code is Flip(). It is called when you are finished rendering the frame to the back buffer. Flipping is accomplished with a call to IDirect3DDevice8::Present(), which takes no parameters.

Listing 2.5: cGraphicsLayer::Flip

```
void cGraphicsLayer::Flip()
{

HRESULT r = 0;

// Make sure the device has been created.
assert( m_pDevice );

// Blit the back buffer to the primary surface
r = m_pDevice->Present( NULL, NULL, NULL, NULL );
if( FAILED( r ) )
{
    OutputDebugString( "Flipping Failed!\n" );
}

}
```

Creating the Graphics Layer

In a moment I'm going to dive into the code that initializes Direct3D for full-screen rendering. The way the code actually gets called is in cApplication::Init-Graphics. That code calls the static function cGraphicsLayer::Create, which appears in the following listing.

Listing 2.6: cGraphicsLayer::Create

```
void cGraphicsLayer::Create(
  HWND hWnd,
  short width, short height,
  GUID* pGuid )
{
```

```
      new cGraphicsLayer( hWnd ); // construct the object.

      // Init Direct3D and the device for fullscreen operation
      Graphics()->InitD3DFullScreen( pGuid, width, height, 32 );
    }
```

Now that you know how the initialization code will be called, let's dive in and see how it works.

Full-screen Initialization

Initializing Direct3D for full-screen mode is easier than windowed mode. The set and order of things to do is fairly consistent, so it's easy to hide it away into an initialization function. I'll go through the process step by step.

Step 1: Create the Direct3D object.

The first step in Direct3D initialization is to create an instance of the Direct3D object and acquire an interface to it. Instead of using the standard COM construction technique, which is a total pain, you can use a pleasantly wrapped-up function called Direct3DCreate8():

```
      IDirect3D8* Direct3DCreate8( UINT SDKVersion );
```

Table 2.6: Direct3DCreate8 parameters

SDKVersion	An identifier specifying the version of Direct3D that you are using. You should always specify D3D_SDK_VERSION for this parameter, which automatically contains the correct version.

Listing 2.7: Sample code to create the Direct3D interface

```
// Create the Direct3D object
m_pD3D = Direct3DCreate8( D3D_SDK_VERSION );
if( !m_pD3D )
{
  // Handle fatal error
  }
```

Step 2: Set the present parameters.

The new word for moving the contents of the back buffer to the primary surface is *present*. So when you are done messing with the back buffer and want to display it, you present it to the primary surface. Keep that in your head because it pops up a lot in this section. The first thing you need to do when initializing Direct3D is to fill in what are called the present parameters. This is basically just a structure that contains information about the size and bit depth of the back buffer and primary surface, which is important because in version 8.0, Direct3D manages these two surfaces for you. The structure looks like this:

```
typedef struct _D3DPRESENT_PARAMETERS_ {
        UINT                    BackBufferWidth;
        UINT                    BackBufferHeight;
        D3DFORMAT               BackBufferFormat;
        UINT                    BackBufferCount;

        D3DMULTISAMPLE_TYPE     MultiSampleType;

        D3DSWAPEFFECT           SwapEffect;
        HWND                    hDeviceWindow;
        BOOL                    Windowed;
        BOOL                    EnableAutoDepthStencil;
        D3DFORMAT               AutoDepthStencilFormat;
        DWORD                   Flags;

        UINT                    FullScreen_RefreshRateInHz;
        UINT                    FullScreen_PresentationInterval;

} D3DPRESENT_PARAMETERS;
```

Table 2.7: D3DPRESENT_PARAMETERS structure members

`BackBufferWidth`	Width of the back buffer, in pixels.
`BackBufferHeight`	Height of the back buffer, in pixels.
`BackBufferFormat`	A D3DFORMAT enumeration member specifying the format for the back buffer, which can be any of the flags in Table 2.1. You will usually set this to D3DFMT_A8R8G8B8 for 32-bit surfaces or D3DFMT_R5G6R5 for 16-bit surfaces.
`BackBufferCount`	The number of back buffers that you want to associate with the primary surface. You normally want this to be 1.
`MultiSampleType`	A member of the D3DMULTISAMPLE_TYPE enumeration, specifying the type of multisampling, if any, that you want to use. Just set this parameter to D3DMULTISAMPLE_NONE.
`SwapEffect`	A D3DSWAPEFFECT enumeration member specifying the semantics that you want to use when presenting the back buffer to the primary surface. You will normally set this to D3DSWAPEFFECT_COPY.
`hDeviceWindow`	A handle to the window that you want to use as the rendering target.
`Windowed`	A Boolean value specifying whether the application runs in full-screen or windowed mode. Specify FALSE for full-screen operation.

EnableAutoDepthStencil	A Boolean value specifying whether you want Direct3D to manage the depth and/or stencil buffer for you. This is usually a good thing so you should specify TRUE.
AutoDepthStencilFormat	Takes a member of the D3DFORMAT enumeration that specifies the format of the depth buffer that you want Direct3D to manage. D3DFMT_16 is a good choice; it creates a 16-bit depth buffer for you.
Flags	Set this to its only possible value, D3DPRESENTFLAG_LOCK-ABLEBACKBUFFER. If you will not be messing with the back buffer, set this to 0 for a slight performance improvement.
FullScreen_RefreshRateInHz	The refresh rate that you want the monitor to run at. Set this to D3DPRESENT_RATE_DEFAULT to allow Direct3D to use what it thinks is the best rate.
FullScreen_PresentationInterval	Specifies how quickly you want the back buffer to be presented to the primary surface. Specify D3DPRESENT_INTERVAL_IM-MEDIATE to allow the process to complete as quickly as possible.

It is not as hard as it looks since most of the entries can be set to default values that you never have to look at again. Have a look at the code snippet below as an example of how to fill in the structure to create a standard, full-screen, 640x480, 32-bit application:

Listing 2.8: Filling in the D3DPRESENT_PARAMETERS structure

```
// Structure to hold the creation parameters for the device
D3DPRESENT_PARAMETERS d3dpp;
ZeroMemory( &d3dpp, sizeof( d3dpp ) );

// The width and height for the initial back buffer
d3dpp.BackBufferWidth       = 640;
d3dpp.BackBufferHeight      = 480;
// The surface will have a depth of 32 bits
d3dpp.BackBufferFormat      = D3DFMT_A8R8G8B8;
// Only have one back buffer associated with the primary surface
d3dpp.BackBufferCount       = 1;
// No multisampling
d3dpp.MultiSampleType       = D3DMULTISAMPLE_NONE;
// Copy the back buffer to the primary surface normally
d3dpp.SwapEffect            = D3DSWAPEFFECT_COPY;
// The handle to the window to render in to
d3dpp.hDeviceWindow         = m_hWnd;
// Full-screen operation
d3dpp.Windowed              = FALSE;
// Let Direct3D look after the depth buffer
d3dpp.EnableAutoDepthStencil = TRUE;
// Set the depth buffer depth to 16 bits
```

```
d3dpp.AutoDepthStencilFormat              = D3DFMT_D16;
// Use the default refresh rate
d3dpp.FullScreen_RefreshRateInHz          = D3DPRESENT_RATE_DEFAULT;
// Update the screen as soon as possible
d3dpp.FullScreen_PresentationInterval     = D3DPRESENT_INTERVAL_IMMEDIATE;
// Allow the back buffer to be locked
d3dpp.Flags                          = D3DPRESENTFLAG_LOCKABLE_BACKBUFFER;
```

And that's it. After the structure is filled in it is very simple to create the device, which I am just about to show you.

Step 3: Create the device.

The Direct3D rendering device is created with a call to IDirect3DDevice8:: CreateDevice(). Recall that the device is Direct3D lingo for the COM object that communicates your rendering requests to the actual physical display adapter in your PC. The function is prototyped in the following:

```
HRESULT CreateDevice(
  UINT Adapter,
  D3DDEVTYPE DeviceType,
  HWND hFocusWindow,
  DWORD BehaviorFlags,
  D3DPRESENT_PARAMETERS* pPresentationParameters,
  IDirect3DDevice8** ppReturnedDeviceInterface
);
```

Table 2.8: CreateDevice parameters

Adapter	Integer identifying which display device you want to render with. Specify 0 to use the primary display adapter.
DeviceType	A D3DDEVTYPE enumeration member specifying the type of device that you want to create. Use D3DDEVTYPE_HAL for a hardware accelerated device, D3DDEVTYPE_SW for a software device, or D3DDEVTYPE_REF for a reference device. You'll almost always want to go with a hardware device. Only use reference devices for debugging; they contain all possible hardware features emulated in software, but they are extremely slow.
hFocusWindow	Handle to the window that you want to use as the default rendering target. This should match the handle that you specified in the present parameters structure.
BehaviorFlags	Takes flags that define the behavior of the device; most of these are superfluous and you will probably want to stick with just D3DCREATE_SOFTWARE_VERTEXPROCESSING. If you have a newfangled hardware transform and lighting card you can specify D3DCREATE_HARDWARE_VERTEXPROCESSING.
pPresentationParameters	Address of the D3DPRESENT_PARAMETERS structure that you filled with information about the device.

ppReturnedDeviceInterface	Address of a pointer that will be filled with the address of the newly created device.

So if you were going to create a standard hardware accelerated device with software vertex processing you could use the following code:

Listing 2.9: Creating the device

```
// Create the device using hardware acceleration if available
  r = m_pD3D->CreateDevice( D3DADAPTER_DEFAULT, D3DDEVTYPE_HAL,
                  m_hWnd, D3DCREATE_SOFTWARE_VERTEXPROCESSING,
                  &d3dpp, &m_pDevice );
  if( FAILED( r ) )
  {
      // Handle fatal error
  }
```

In previous versions of DirectX you had to program a million other things like creating clippers, setting the cooperative level, setting the screen resolution, and on and on. These days you are lucky because Direct3D does it all for you. That one call to CreateDevice() handles all the grunt work and you can pretty much start rendering as soon as it is created. However, before I start getting ahead of myself, let me show you a function I created that automates this whole process.

Step 4: Put it together.

Now that you know what you need to do, you can write a full-screen initialization routine. It takes as input a GUID to use for the device, a width, a height, and a depth, and then it does the rest. The GUID can be set to NULL to use the primary display device.

Listing 2.10: Direct3D full-screen initialization in cGraphicsLayer

```
void cGraphicsLayer::InitD3DFullScreen(GUID* pGuid, int width,
                                       int height, int bpp )
{

  HRESULT r = 0;

  // Create the Direct3D object
  m_pD3D = Direct3DCreate8( D3D_SDK_VERSION );
  if( !m_pD3D )
  {
      throw cGameError( "Could not create IDirect3D8" );
  }

  // Structure to hold the creation parameters for the device
  D3DPRESENT_PARAMETERS d3dpp;
```

```
ZeroMemory( &d3dpp, sizeof( d3dpp ) );

// The width and height for the initial back buffer
d3dpp.BackBufferWidth              = width;
d3dpp.BackBufferHeight             = height;

// Set the flags for bit depth - only supports 16, 24, and 32 bit formats
if( bpp == 16 )
     d3dpp.BackBufferFormat        = D3DFMT_R5G6B5;
else if( bpp == 24 )
     d3dpp.BackBufferFormat        = D3DFMT_X8R8G8B8;
else if( bpp == 32 )
     d3dpp.BackBufferFormat        = D3DFMT_A8R8G8B8;
else
{

     OutputDebugString( "Invalid surface format - defaulting to 32bit" );
     d3dpp.BackBufferFormat        = D3DFMT_A8R8G8B8;
}


// Only have one back buffer associated with the primary surface
d3dpp.BackBufferCount              = 1;
// No multisampling
d3dpp.MultiSampleType              = D3DMULTISAMPLE_NONE;
// Copy the back buffer to the primary surface normally
d3dpp.SwapEffect                   = D3DSWAPEFFECT_COPY;
// The handle to the window to render in to
d3dpp.hDeviceWindow                = m_hWnd;
// Fullscreen operation
d3dpp.Windowed                     = FALSE;
// Let Direct3D look after the depth buffer
d3dpp.EnableAutoDepthStencil       = TRUE;
// Set the depth buffer depth to 16 bits
d3dpp.AutoDepthStencilFormat       = D3DFMT_D16;
// Use the default refresh rate
d3dpp.FullScreen_RefreshRateInHz   = D3DPRESENT_RATE_DEFAULT;
// Update the screen as soon as possible (don't wait for vsync)
d3dpp.FullScreen_PresentationInterval = D3DPRESENT_INTERVAL_IMMEDIATE;
// Allow the back buffer to be locked
d3dpp.Flags                        = D3DPRESENTFLAG_LOCKABLE_BACKBUFFER;

// Create the device using hardware acceleration if available
r = m_pD3D->CreateDevice( D3DADAPTER_DEFAULT, D3DDEVTYPE_HAL, m_hWnd,
                          D3DCREATE_SOFTWARE_VERTEXPROCESSING,
                          &d3dpp, &m_pDevice );
if( FAILED( r ) )
{
     throw cGameError( "Could not create IDirect3DDevice8" );
}


// Keep a copy of the screen dimensions
```

```
m_rcScreenRect.left        = m_rcScreenRect.top = 0;
m_rcScreenRect.right       = width;
m_rcScreenRect.bottom      = height;

// Get a copy of the pointer to the back buffer
m_pDevice->GetBackBuffer( 0, D3DBACKBUFFER_TYPE_MONO, &m_pBackSurf );


}
```

Shutting Down Direct3D

After the application has finished its rendering, it must properly shut down Direct3D before terminating the application. This is just a matter of releasing the back buffer, Direct3D device interface, and finally the IDirect3D8 interface. By the way, you should always try to release the interfaces to COM objects in the opposite order of the way they were created.

The code to shut down Direct3D appears in cGraphicsLayer::DestroyAll. The destructor calls DestroyAll, but other modules may call it if need be.

Listing 2.11: cGraphicsLayer::DestroyAll

```
void cGraphicsLayer::DestroyAll()
{

        SafeRelease( m_pBackSurf );
        SafeRelease( m_pDevice );

        SafeRelease( m_pD3D );

        /**
         * Prevent any further access to the graphics class
         */
        m_pGlobalGLayer = NULL;
}
```

Changes to cApplication

A new member variable was added to cApplication class to modify the behavior of the graphics layer when it is initialized. The new variable is given in Listing 2.12.

Listing 2.12: New member variables added to cApplication

```
int     m_bpp;                        // Desired depth (may not be possible)
```

m_bpp is set to be 32 bits by default in the constructor—you can change this if you find it necessary.

Using the members in cApplication, cApplication::InitGraphics sets up the graphics subsystem. At the end of the function you can see the cGraphicsLayer:: Create function I discussed earlier. At the moment it just sets up Direct3D with the call to cGraphicsLayer::Create, but if you needed to do any other graphics initialization you could put the code here, away from the Direct3D messiness.

Listing 2.13: Graphics initialization code

```
void cApplication::InitGraphics()
{

  cGraphicsLayer::Create(
      MainWindow()->GetHWnd(),
      m_width, m_height,
      NULL );
}
```

Application: Direct3D Sample

To give an idea of how you might use the graphics layer in a regular application, I'll go through a bare-bones Direct3D application, with just 2D graphics for now. In every frame, it fills the screen with pseudo-random pixels, and then uses a color blit to copy a filled rectangle to the screen. It also flashes text around random locations.

Warning: Almost all of the sample applications in this book depend on the GameLib library (and the Math3d library, which I'll show you in Chapter 3). To make them compile correctly, make sure that the dependencies are set up correctly (this can be checked by selecting the Project|Dependencies menu option). GameLib, for this sample and any others that use it, should be listed as a dependency of your project.

Since the program is so short, I'll include all of the source code for it. This appears in Listing 2.14.

Listing 2.14: DDSample.cpp

```
/*******************************************************************
 *        Advanced 3D Game Programming using DirectX 8.0
 * * * * * * * * * * * * * * * * * * * * * * * * * * * * * * * * * *
 *    Title: DDSample.cpp
 *     Desc: Sample application for Direct3D
 *
 * copyright (c) 2001 by Peter A Walsh and Adrian Perez
 * See license.txt for modification and distribution information
```

```
                ****************************************************************/

                #include "stdafx.h"

                #include <string>
                using namespace std;

                class cD3DSampleApp : public cApplication
                {

                public:

                  //=================================== cApplication

                  virtual void DoFrame( float timeDelta );

                  cD3DSampleApp() :
                       cApplication()
                  {
                       m_title = string( "Direct3D Sample" );
                  }
                };

                cApplication* CreateApplication()
                {
                  return new cD3DSampleApp();
                }

                void cD3DSampleApp::DoFrame( float timeDelta )
                {

                  HRESULT hr;
                  if( !Graphics() ) return;

                  // Clear the previous contents of the back buffer
                  Graphics()->GetDevice()->Clear( 0, 0, D3DCLEAR_TARGET | D3DCLEAR_ZBUFFER,
                                              D3DCOLOR_XRGB( 0,0,0), 1.0f, 0 );

                  // Structure to hold information about the locked back buffer
                  D3DLOCKED_RECT  LockedRect;

                  // Get a local pointer to the back buffer
                  LPDIRECT3DSURFACE8 pBackSurf = Graphics()->GetBackBuffer();

                  // Lock the back buffer
                  pBackSurf->LockRect( &LockedRect, NULL, NULL );

                  // Get a pointer to the back buffer
                  DWORD* pData = (DWORD*)LockedRect.pBits;
                  // Convert the pitch to work with 32 bit (4 byte) surfaces
```

```
        int Pitch32 = LockedRect.Pitch / 4;

        int x, y;      // Holds the location of the random pixel
        DWORD Color;   // Holds the color of the pixels and rectangles

        // ------------- PART 1: Draw 10,000 randomly colored pixels
        for( int i = 0 ; i < 10000 ; i++ )
        {
            // Get a random location for the pixel
            x = rand()%639;
            y = rand()%479;

            // Get a random color for the pixel
            Color = D3DCOLOR_XRGB( rand()%255, rand()%255, rand()%255 );

            // Set the pixel at x,y to the color
            pData[ Pitch32 * y + x ] = Color;
        }

        // ------------- PART 2: Draw 10 random rectangles

        RECT Rect; // Structure to hold the dimensions of the rectangles
        for( int j = 0 ; j < 10 ; j++ )
        {
            // Create a random sized rectangle
            SetRect( &Rect, rand()%639, rand()%479,
                            rand()%639, rand()%479 );

            // Get a random rectangle color
            Color = D3DCOLOR_XRGB( rand()%255, rand()%255, rand()%255 );

            // Draw the rectangle (i.e., clear a rectangle to a color)
            Graphics()->GetDevice()->Clear( 1, (D3DRECT*)&Rect, D3DCLEAR_TARGET,
                                            Color, 1.0f, 0 );
        }

        // Unlock the back surface. Very important to do this!
        pBackSurf->UnlockRect();
        pBackSurf = 0;

        // ------------- PART 3: Output text to the back surface
        // Tell Direct3D we are about to start rendering through Direct3D
        Graphics()->GetDevice()->BeginScene();

        // Output green text at a random location
        Graphics()->DrawTextString( rand()%640, rand()%480,
                D3DCOLOR_XRGB( 0, 255, 0 ), "Advanced Direct3D 8.0" );

        // Tell Direct3D we are finished rendering
        Graphics()->GetDevice()->EndScene();
```

```
// Present the back buffer to the primary surface to make it visible
Graphics()->Flip();

}
```

DirectInput

DirectInput was created by Microsoft to provide a direct way to communicate with the input devices that exist on users' systems. It supplies the ability to enumerate all the devices connected to a machine, and even enumerate the capabilities of a particular device. You can take any input device under the sun; as long as it has a DirectInput driver written for it, your application can talk to it.

There are a lot of nifty features in DirectInput like force feedback, but I don't have much space to discuss it. This DirectInput discussion will be limited to just mouse and keyboard usage. However, once you understand the concepts that make DirectInput work, getting more complex things done with it won't be difficult.

Why Should You Use DirectInput?

The Win32 API has a full set of window messages that can inform you when keys are pressed, when the mouse moves, etc. There is even rudimentary support for joysticks. Why would you use DirectInput at all?

Well, there are several reasons:

■ The Win32 API was not designed for games, or speed.

■ Joystick support under Win32 is flaky at best. Supporting complex joysticks with several axes, 8 to 10 buttons, a point of view hat, etc., just can't be done on Win32.

■ The mouse support is limited to three buttons, two axes, and the mouse wheel if one is present. Many mice on the market today have four, five, or even more buttons.

■ The keyboard support in Win32 was designed for keyboard entry applications. There is a lot of functionality to handle automatically repeating keys, conversion from key codes to ASCII characters, etc., that a game just doesn't need.

■ The Win32 keyboard handling code captures some keys for you (like Alt) that require special message processing to handle correctly.

■ Message processing isn't the fastest thing in the world. Applications get flooded with mouse message requests, and since you can't render a frame until the message queue is empty, this can slow down the application.

Devices

A DirectInput device represents a physical object that can give input to the computer. The keyboard, the mouse, and any joysticks/joypads are examples of devices. You talk to devices through a COM interface, just like with Direct3D. The interface name in DirectX 8.0 is IDirectInputDevice8.

Devices are composed of a set of *objects*, each one defining a button, axis, POV hat, etc. A device can enumerate the objects it contains using IDirectInputDevice8::EnumObjects. This is only really useful for joysticks, as keyboards and mice have a standard set of objects.

An object is described by a structure called DIDEVICEOBJECTINSTANCE. The set of DirectInput functionality that I'm going to show you doesn't require you to understand the workings of this structure, but I'll give you a peek at it anyway. The structure has, among other things, a GUID that describes the type of object. The current set of object types appears in Table 2.9. More may appear in the future, as people create newer and better object types.

Table 2.9: The current set of object type GUIDs

GUID_XAxis	An axis representing movement in the x-axis (for example, left-to-right movement on a mouse).
GUID_YAxis	An axis representing movement in the y-axis (for example, up-to-down movement on a mouse).
GUID_ZAxis	An axis representing movement in the z-axis (for example, the mouse wheel on newer models).
GUID_RxAxis	An axis representing rotation relative to the x-axis.
GUID_RyAxis	An axis representing rotation relative to the y-axis.
GUID_RzAxis	An axis representing rotation relative to the z-axis.
GUID_Slider	A slider axis (for example, the throttle slider that appears on some joysticks).
GUID_Button	A button (on a mouse or joystick).
GUID_Key	A key (on a keyboard).
GUID_POV	A POV hat that appears on some joysticks.
GUID_Unknown	An unknown type of device.

When an application requests the current state of the device, the information needs to be transmitted in some meaningful way. Just getting a list of bytes wouldn't provide enough information, and forcing applications to use a standard communication method wouldn't elegantly solve the problem for all the different types of devices on the market. Because of this, DirectInput lets the application dictate to the device how it wishes to receive its data. If you only want one or two buttons on a joystick, you don't need to request all of the data from the joystick, which may have dozens of buttons. Among other things, the application can decide if any axes on the device should be absolute (centered around a neutral origin, like a joystick axis) or relative (freely moving, like a mouse axis). When a device is created, you must call IDirectInputDevice8::Set-DataFormat.

```
HRESULT IDirectInputDevice8::SetDataFormat(
    LPCDIDATAFORMAT lpdf
);
```

lpdf   A pointer to a DIDATAFORMAT structure that defines the format of the data received from the device.

There are some defined constants that you can use:

- c_dfDIKeyboard

Standard keyboard structure. An array of 256 characters, one for each key.

- c_dfDIMouse

Standard mouse structure. Three axes and four buttons. Corresponds to the DIMOUSESTATE structure.

- c_dfDIMouse2

Extended mouse structure. Three axes and eight buttons. Corresponds to the DIMOUSESTATE2 structure.

- c_dfDIJoystick

Standard joystick. Three positional axes, three rotation axes, two sliders, a POV hat, and 32 buttons. Corresponds to the DIJOYSTATE structure.

- c_dfDIJoystick2

Extended capability joystick. Refers to the SDK documentation for the truly massive data format definition. Corresponds to the DIJOYSTATE2 structure.

Receiving Device States

There are two ways to receive data from a device: *immediate* data access and *buffered* data access. This code only uses immediate data access, but buffered data access is not without its merits. Buffered data access is useful for when you absolutely need to get every input event that happens. If a key is quickly pressed and released between immediate device state requests, you will miss it since the state changes aren't queued. If the application is running at any reasonable frame rate, however, this won't be a problem. Immediate data access is used to find the current state of the device at some point in time. If buttons were pressed and released between when you ask, you don't see them. You ask for the device state using IDirectInputDevice8::GetDeviceState:

```
HRESULT IDirectInputDevice8::GetDeviceState(
    DWORD cbData,
    LPVOID lpvData
);
```

cbData	Size, in bytes, of the data structure being passed in with lpvData.
lpvData	Pointer to a buffer to fill with the device state. The format of the data depends on the format you defined using SetDataFormat.

For mouse devices, if you set the data format to c_dfDIMouse, the parameters to GetDeviceData should be sizeof(DIMOUSESTATE) and the address of a valid DIMOUSESTATE structure. After the function completes, if it is successful, the structure will be filled with the data from the mouse.

```
typedef struct DIMOUSESTATE {
    LONG lX;
    LONG lY;
    LONG lZ;
    BYTE rgbButtons[4];
} DIMOUSESTATE, *LPDIMOUSESTATE;
```

lX	X-axis of movement. Relative movement; if the axis hasn't moved since the last time you checked this will be 0.
lY	Y-axis of movement. Relative movement; if the axis hasn't moved since the last time you checked this will be 0.
lZ	Z-axis (mouse wheel) movement. Relative movement; if the axis hasn't moved since the last time it was checked this will be 0.
rgbButtons	A set of bytes, one for each of four mouse buttons. To support a mouse with more buttons, use the DIMOUSESTATE2 structure.

As for the keyboard data, all you do is pass in a 256-element array of characters. Each character represents a certain key. You can index into the array to find a certain key using the DirectInput key constants. There is a constant for every possible key on a keyboard. Table 2.10 has a list of the common ones. Some of the more esoteric ones, like the ones for Japanese keyboards and web keyboards, are not included for the sake of brevity. See the SDK documentation for a complete list at *DirectX 8.0 C++ Documentation/DirectInput/DirectInput C++ Reference/Device Constants/Keyboard Device Constants*.

Table 2.5: The common DirectInput keyboard constants

DIK_A … DIK_Z	A through Z keys
DIK_0 … DIK_9	0 through 9 keys
DIK_F1 … DIK_F15	F1 through F15 keys, if they exist
DIK_NUMPAD0 … DIK_NUMPAD9	Number pad keys. The keys are the same regardless of whether or not Num Lock is on.
DIK_ESCAPE	Esc key
DIK_MINUS	– key on the top row

DIK_EQUALS	= key on the top row
DIK_BACK	Backspace key
DIK_TAB	Tab key
DIK_LBRACKET	[(left bracket) key
DIK_RBRACKET	] (right bracket) key
DIK_RETURN	Return key
DIK_LCONTROL	Left-side Ctrl key
DIK_SEMICOLON	; key
DIK_APOSTROPHE	' (apostrophe) key
DIK_GRAVE	` (grave accent) key; usually the same as the tilde (~) key
DIK_LSHIFT	Left-side Shift key
DIK_BACKSLASH	\ (backslash) key
DIK_COMMA	, (comma) key
DIK_PERIOD	. (period) key
DIK_SLASH	/ (forward slash) key
DIK_RSHIFT	Right-side Shift key
DIK_MULTIPLY	* key on numeric pad
DIK_LMENU	Left-side Alt key
DIK_SPACE	Spacebar
DIK_CAPITAL	Caps Lock key
DIK_NUMLOCK	Num Lock key
DIK_SCROLL	Scroll Lock key
DIK_SUBTRACT	− sign on keypad
DIK_ADD	+ sign on keypad
DIK_DECIMAL	. sign on keypad
DIK_NUMPADENTER	Enter on keypad
DIK_RCONTROL	Right-side Ctrl key
DIK_DIVIDE	/ sign on keypad
DIK_SYSRQ	SysRq (same as PrtScrn) key
DIK_RMENU	Right-side Alt key
DIK_PAUSE	Pause key
DIK_HOME	Home key (if there is a set separate from the keypad)
DIK_UP	Up arrow
DIK_PRIOR	PgUp key (if there is a set separate from the keypad)
DIK_LEFT	Left arrow

DIK_RIGHT	Right arrow
DIK_END	End key (if there is a set separate from the keypad)
DIK_DOWN	Down arrow
DIK_NEXT	PgDn key (if there is a set separate from the keypad)
DIK_INSERT	Insert key (if there is a set separate from the keypad)
DIK_DELETE	Delete key (if there is a set separate from the keypad)
DIK_LWIN	Left-side Windows key
DIK_RWIN	Right-side Windows key
DIK_APPS	Application key

Cooperative Levels

DirectInput devices have a concept of a cooperative level, since they are shared by all applications using the system. Setting the cooperative level is the first thing that you should do upon successful creation of a DirectInputDevice8 interface. The call to set the cooperative level is:

```
HRESULT IDirectInputDevice8::SetCooperativeLevel(
  HWND hwnd,
  DWORD dwFlags
);
```

hwnd	Handle to the window of the application that created the object.
dwFlags	A set of flags describing the cooperative level desired. Can be a combination of the following:

- DISCL_BACKGROUND

When this flag is set, the application may acquire the device at any time, even if it is not the currently active application.

- DISCL_EXCLUSIVE

Application requests exclusive access to the input device. This prevents other applications from simultaneously using the device (for example, Windows itself). If the mouse device is set to exclusive mode, Windows stops sending mouse messages and the cursor disappears.

- DISCL_FOREGROUND

When this flag is set, the device is automatically unacquired when the window moves to the background. It can only be reacquired when the application moves to the foreground.

- DISCL_NONEXCLUSIVE

Application requests non-exclusive access to the input device. This way it doesn't interfere with the other applications that are simultaneously using the device (for example, Windows itself).

- DISCL_NOWINKEY

Disables the use of the windows key. This prevents the user from accidentally being knocked out of an exclusive application by pressing the windows key.

All devices must set either DISCL_FOREGROUND or DISCL_BACKGROUND (but not both), as well as either DISCL_EXCLUSIVE or DISCL_NONEXCLUSIVE (but not both).

Application Focus and Devices

If you ever can't get the device state from a device, chances are access to it has been lost. For example, when the application doesn't have focus you can't grab the state of the keyboard. The application class will automatically detect when it loses focus and stop the input code from polling the devices until focus is regained. When you get focus, you need to reacquire the device before you can start requesting its state. That is done using the parameter-free function IDirectInputDevice8::Acquire(). You'll see Acquire scattered throughout the input code for both the keyboard and the mouse.

The DirectInput Object

The DirectInput object (which has the interface IDirectInputDevice8) doesn't have a clear tie to a physical device as the Direct3D device object did. It is useful, however; you need it to enumerate available devices, and to create them.

To create the DirectInput object, you use the global function DirectInput8Create, which wraps up all the necessary COM work.

```
HRESULT WINAPI DirectInput8Create(
  HINSTANCE hinst,
  DWORD dwVersion,
  REFIID riidltf,
  LPVOID* ppvOut,
  LPUNKNOWN punkOuter
);
```

hinst	Handle to the instance of the application that is creating the DirectInput.
dwVersion	The version number of the DirectInput object that you want to create. You should specify DIRECTINPUT_VERSION for this parameter.
riidltf	An identifier for the interface you want to create. Specify IID_IDirectInput8 for this parameter and you won't go wrong.
ppvOut	Address of a pointer that will receive the address of the newly created interface.
punkOuter	Used for COM aggregation—just specify NULL.

Once you have the DirectInput interface, you can use it to enumerate and create devices. Device creation is done using IDirectInput8:: CreateDevice.

Implementing DirectInput with cInputLayer

Due to the small subset of the total DirectInput functionality I'm showing you, the code to handle DirectInput is very simple. Adding support for simple joysticks wouldn't be too much harder, but implementing a robust system that could enumerate device objects and assign tasks to each of them would take considerably more work than I have space to apply.

The way the code works is the input layer constructs and holds onto a mouse object and a keyboard object (cMouse and cKeyboard, respectively). Both the mouse and the keyboard can have *listeners*, or classes that are notified when events happen. To make a class a listener, two things must happen. First, the class must implement the iKeyboardReceiver interface (for keyboards) and/or the iMouseReceiver interface (for mouse devices). Second, it must tell the keyboard or mouse to make itself a receiver. This can be done by calling cKeyboard::SetReceiver() or cMouse::SetReceiver(). Just pass in the address of the class that wishes to become a receiver. Here are the interfaces:

Listing 2.15: Input communication interfaces

```
/**
 * Any object that implements this interface can receive input
 * from the keyboard.
 */
struct iKeyboardReceiver
{
    virtual void KeyUp( int key ) = 0;
    virtual void KeyDown( int key ) = 0;
};

/**
 * Any object that implements this interface can receive input
 * from the mouse.
 */
struct iMouseReceiver
{
    virtual void MouseMoved( int dx, int dy ) = 0;
    virtual void MouseButtonUp( int button ) = 0;
    virtual void MouseButtonDown( int button ) = 0;
};
```

The input layer is another system object, and like the others can only have one instance. This condition is validated in the constructor. The input layer appears in Listings 2.16 (header) and 2.17 (source).

Listing 2.16: InputLayer.h

```
/**********************************************************************
 *          Advanced 3D Game Programming using DirectX 8.0
 * * * * * * * * * * * * * * * * * * * * * * * * * * * * * * * * * * *
```

```
*    Title: InputLayer.h
*     Desc: Manages DirectInput
*           Currently only has support for keyboard/mouse
* copyright (c) 2001 by Peter A Walsh and Adrian Perez
* See license.txt for modification and distribution information
****************************************************************/

#ifndef _INPUTLAYER_H
#define _INPUTLAYER_H

#include <dinput.h>
#include "Keyboard.h"
#include "Mouse.h"

class cInputLayer
{
    cKeyboard*      m_pKeyboard;
    cMouse*         m_pMouse;

    // The DI8 object
    LPDIRECTINPUT8  m_pDI;

    static cInputLayer* m_pGlobalILayer;

    cInputLayer(
        HINSTANCE hInst,
        HWND hWnd,
        bool bExclusive,
        bool bUseKeyboard = true,
        bool bUseMouse = true );

public:

    virtual ~cInputLayer();

    cKeyboard* GetKeyboard()
    {
        return m_pKeyboard;
    }

    cMouse* GetMouse()
    {
        return m_pMouse;
    }

    void UpdateDevices();

    static cInputLayer* GetInput()
    {
        return m_pGlobalILayer;
```

```
        }

        LPDIRECTINPUT8 GetDInput()
        {
            return m_pDI;
        }

        void SetFocus();  // called when the app gains focus
        void KillFocus(); // called when the app must release focus

        static void Create(
            HINSTANCE hInst,
            HWND hWnd,
            bool bExclusive,
            bool bUseKeyboard = true,
            bool bUseMouse = true )
        {
            // everything is taken care of in the constructor
            new cInputLayer(
                hInst,
                hWnd,
                bExclusive,
                bUseKeyboard,
                bUseMouse );
        }
};

inline cInputLayer* Input()
{
  return cInputLayer::GetInput();
}


#endif //_INPUTLAYER_H
```

Listing 2.17: InputLayer.cpp

```
/*****************************************************************
 *         Advanced 3D Game Programming using DirectX 8.0
 * * * * * * * * * * * * * * * * * * * * * * * * * * * * * * * * *
 *    Title: InputLayer.cpp
 *     Desc: Manages DirectInput
 *           Currently has support for keyboard/mouse
 * copyright (c) 2001 by Peter A Walsh and Adrian Perez
 * See license.txt for modification and distribution information
 *****************************************************************/

#include "stdafx.h"
#include "InputLayer.h"
#include "Keyboard.h"
#include "Mouse.h"
```

```
#include "Application.h"
#include "Window.h"

cInputLayer* cInputLayer::m_pGlobalILayer = NULL;

cInputLayer::cInputLayer(
 HINSTANCE hInst,
 HWND hWnd,
 bool bExclusive,
 bool bUseKeyboard,
 bool bUseMouse )
{

 m_pKeyboard = NULL;
 m_pMouse = NULL;

 if( m_pGlobalILayer )
 {
     throw cGameError("cInputLayer already initialized!\n");
 }
 m_pGlobalILayer = this;

 HRESULT hr;

 /**
  * Create the DI8 object
  */

 hr = DirectInput8Create( hInst, DIRECTINPUT_VERSION,
                          IID_IDirectInput8, (void**)&m_pDI, NULL );
   if( FAILED(hr) )
 {
     throw cGameError("DirectInput8 object could not be created\n");
 }

 try
 {
     if( bUseKeyboard )
     {
         m_pKeyboard = new cKeyboard( hWnd );
     }
     if( bUseMouse )
     {
         m_pMouse = new cMouse( hWnd, bExclusive );
     }
 }
 catch( ... )
 {
     SafeRelease( m_pDI );
     throw;
```

```
          }

     }


     cInputLayer::~cInputLayer()
     {
      if( m_pDI )
      {
           if( m_pKeyboard )
           {
                delete m_pKeyboard; // this does all the de-init.
           }

           if( m_pMouse )
           {
                delete m_pMouse;    // this does all the de-init.
           }
           SafeRelease( m_pDI );
      }
      m_pGlobalILayer = NULL;
     }

     void cInputLayer::UpdateDevices()
     {
      if( m_pKeyboard )
      {
           m_pKeyboard->Update();
      }
      if( m_pMouse )
      {
           m_pMouse->Update();
      }
     }


     void cInputLayer::SetFocus()
     {
      if( m_pKeyboard )
      {
           m_pKeyboard->ClearTable();
      }
      if( m_pMouse )
      {
           m_pMouse->Acquire();
      }
     }


     void cInputLayer::KillFocus()
     {
```

```
    if( m_pKeyboard )
    {
         m_pKeyboard->ClearTable();
    }
    if( m_pMouse )
    {
         m_pMouse->UnAcquire();
    }
}
```

The Keyboard object pretty much wraps around the IDirectInputDevice8 interface, while providing the listener interface for an easy way for classes to listen to keys that get pressed. If you don't want to use listeners, just call the Poll method on the keyboard object to find the state of a certain key at the last checked time.

Listing 2.18: Keyboard.h

```
/****************************************************************
 *          Advanced 3D Game Programming using DirectX 8.0
 * * * * * * * * * * * * * * * * * * * * * * * * * * * * * * * *
 *    Title: Keyboard.h
 *      Desc: Wrapper of a DirectInput keyboard object
 *
 * copyright (c) 2001 by Peter A Walsh and Adrian Perez
 * See license.txt for modification and distribution information
 ****************************************************************/

#ifndef _KEYBOARD_H
#define _KEYBOARD_H

#include <memory.h>
#include <dinput.h>

class cInputLayer;

/**
 * Any object that implements this interface can receive input
 * from the keyboard.
 */
struct iKeyboardReceiver
{
 virtual void KeyUp( int key ){};
 virtual void KeyDown( int key ){};
};


class cKeyboard
{
 // The DInput device used to encapsulate the keyboard
```

```
        LPDIRECTINPUTDEVICE8 m_pDevice;

    char                m_keyState[256];

    iKeyboardReceiver*  m_pTarget;
public:

    void ClearTable()
    {
        memset( m_keyState, 0, sizeof(char)*256 );
    }

    cKeyboard( HWND hWnd );
    ~cKeyboard();

    // Poll to see if a certain key is down
    bool Poll( int key );

    // Use this to establish a KeyboardReceiver as the current input focus
    void SetReceiver( iKeyboardReceiver* pTarget );

    eResult Update();
};

#endif //_KEYBOARD_H
```

Listing 2.19: Keyboard.cpp

```
/******************************************************************
 *          Advanced 3D Game Programming using DirectX 8.0
 * * * * * * * * * * * * * * * * * * * * * * * * * * * * * * * * *
 *    Title: Keyboard.cpp
 *     Desc: Wrapper of a DirectInput keyboard object
 *
 * copyright (c) 2001 by Peter A Walsh and Adrian Perez
 * See license.txt for modification and distribution information
 ******************************************************************/

#include "stdafx.h"
#include "InputLayer.h"
#include "window.h"

#include <stack>
using namespace std;

#include "Keyboard.h"


cKeyboard::cKeyboard( HWND hWnd )
```

```
{
 m_pTarget = NULL;

 HRESULT hr;

/**
 * Get the DInput interface pointer
 */
LPDIRECTINPUT8 pDI = Input()->GetDInput();

/**
 * Create the keyboard device
 *
      */
hr = Input()->GetDInput()->CreateDevice( GUID_SysKeyboard, &m_pDevice,
                                          NULL );
    if( FAILED(hr) )
    {
     throw cGameError("Keyboard could not be created\n");
    }

/**
 * Set the keyboard data format
 */
    hr = m_pDevice->SetDataFormat(&c_dfDIKeyboard);
    if( FAILED(hr) )
    {
    SafeRelease( m_pDevice );
        throw cGameError("Keyboard could not be created\n");
    }

/**
 * Set the cooperative level
 */
    hr = m_pDevice->SetCooperativeLevel(
    hWnd,
    DISCL_FOREGROUND | DISCL_NONEXCLUSIVE);
    if( FAILED(hr) )
    {
    SafeRelease( m_pDevice );
        throw cGameError("Keyboard coop level could not be changed\n");
    }

 memset( m_keyState, 0, 256*sizeof(bool) );
}

cKeyboard::~cKeyboard()
{
 if( m_pDevice )
 {
     m_pDevice->Unacquire();
```

```
            SafeRelease( m_pDevice );
    }
}




void cKeyboard::SetReceiver( iKeyboardReceiver* pTarget )
{
 // Set the new target.
 m_pTarget = pTarget;
}




bool cKeyboard::Poll( int key )
{
 // stuff goes in here.
 if( m_keyState[key] & 0x80 )
        return true;
 return false;
}




eResult cKeyboard::Update()
{
 char     newState[256];
        HRESULT  hr;

        hr = m_pDevice->Poll();
        hr = m_pDevice->GetDeviceState(sizeof(newState),(LPVOID)&newState);

        if( FAILED(hr) )
        {
        hr = m_pDevice->Acquire();
        if( FAILED( hr ) )
        {
            return resFailed;
        }

      hr = m_pDevice->Poll();
      hr = m_pDevice->GetDeviceState(sizeof(newState),(LPVOID)&newState);
       if( FAILED( hr ) )
       {
            return resFailed;
       }
       }


   if( m_pTarget )
   {
        int i;
        for( i=0; i< 256; i++ )
```

```
        {
            if( m_keyState[i] != newState[i] )
            {
                // Something happened to this key since last checked
                if( !(newState[i] & 0x80) )
                {
                    // It was Released
                    m_pTarget->KeyUp( i );
                }
                else
                {
                    // Do nothing; it was just pressed, it'll get a keydown
                    // in a bit, and we don't want to send the signal to
                    // the input target twice
                }
            }

            // copy the state over (we could do a memcpy at the end, but this
            // will have better cache performance)
            m_keyState[i] = newState[i];

            if( Poll( i ) )
            {
                // It was pressed
                m_pTarget->KeyDown( i );
            }
        }
    }
    else
    {
        // copy the new states over.
        memcpy( m_keyState, newState, 256 );
    }

    return resAllGood;
}
```

The mouse object is almost identical in function to the keyboard object. The code behind the mouse is in Listings 2.20 (header) and 2.21 (source).

Listing 2.20: Mouse.h

```
/****************************************************************
 *          Advanced 3D Game Programming using DirectX 8.0
 * * * * * * * * * * * * * * * * * * * * * * * * * * * * * * * * *
 *   Title: Mouse.h
 *    Desc: Wrapper of a DirectInput mouse object
 *
 * copyright (c) 2001 by Peter A Walsh and Adrian Perez
 * See license.txt for modification and distribution information
```

```
    **********************************************************/

#ifndef _MOUSE_H
#define _MOUSE_H

#include <dinput.h>

/**
 * Any object that implements this interface can receive input
 * from the mouse.
 */
struct iMouseReceiver
{
 virtual void MouseMoved( int dx, int dy ){};
 virtual void MouseButtonUp( int button ){};
 virtual void MouseButtonDown( int button ){};
};


class cMouse
{
  LPDIRECTINPUTDEVICE8        m_pDevice;

  DIMOUSESTATE               m_lastState;

  iMouseReceiver*            m_pTarget;

public:

  cMouse( HWND hWnd, bool bExclusive );
  ~cMouse();

  /**
   * Use this to establish a MouseReceiver as the current
   * input focus
   */
  void SetReceiver( iMouseReceiver* pTarget );

  eResult Update();

  eResult Acquire();
  void UnAcquire();
};

#endif // _MOUSE_H
```

Listing 2.21: Mouse.cpp

```
/*******************************************************************
 *          Advanced 3D Game Programming using DirectX 8.0
 * * * * * * * * * * * * * * * * * * * * * * * * * * * * * * *
 *    Title: Mouse.cpp
 *     Desc: Wrapper of a DirectInput mouse object
 *
 * copyright (c) 2001 by Peter A Walsh and Adrian Perez
 * See license.txt for modification and distribution information
 *******************************************************************/

#include "stdafx.h"
#include "InputLayer.h"
#include "Window.h"

#include "Mouse.h"

cMouse::cMouse(  HWND hWnd, bool bExclusive )
{
 m_pTarget = NULL;

 HRESULT hr;

 /**
  * Create the device
  *
  */
 hr = Input()->GetDInput()->CreateDevice( GUID_SysMouse,
                                          &m_pDevice, NULL );
 if( FAILED( hr ))
 {
      throw cGameError("[cMouse::Init]: Couldn't create the device!\n");
 }

 /**
  * Set the data format
  */
 hr = m_pDevice->SetDataFormat(&c_dfDIMouse);
 if( FAILED( hr ))
 {
      SafeRelease( m_pDevice );
      throw cGameError("[cMouse::Init]: SetDataFormat failed\n");
 }

 /**
  * Set the cooperative level
  */
 if( bExclusive )
 {
```

```
                        hr = m_pDevice->SetCooperativeLevel( hWnd, DISCL_EXCLUSIVE |
                                            DISCL_NOWINKEY | DISCL_FOREGROUND );
    }
    else
    {
        hr = m_pDevice->SetCooperativeLevel( hWnd, DISCL_NONEXCLUSIVE |
                                        DISCL_FOREGROUND);
    }

    if( FAILED( hr ))
    {
        SafeRelease( m_pDevice );
        throw cGameError("[cMouse::Init]: SetCooperativeLevel failed\n");
    }


  m_lastState.lX = 0;
  m_lastState.lY = 0;
  m_lastState.lZ = 0;
  m_lastState.rgbButtons[0] = 0;
  m_lastState.rgbButtons[1] = 0;
  m_lastState.rgbButtons[2] = 0;
  m_lastState.rgbButtons[3] = 0;
}

cMouse::~cMouse()
{
 if( m_pDevice )
 {
        m_pDevice->Unacquire();
        SafeRelease( m_pDevice );
 }
}


void cMouse::SetReceiver( iMouseReceiver* pTarget )
{
 m_pTarget = pTarget;
}


eResult cMouse::Update()
{
 DIMOUSESTATE currState;
    HRESULT  hr;

    hr = m_pDevice->Poll();
    hr = m_pDevice->GetDeviceState( sizeof(DIMOUSESTATE),
                                    (void*)&currState );

        if( FAILED(hr) )
```

```
        {
        hr = m_pDevice->Acquire();
        if( FAILED( hr ) )
        {
              return resFailed;
        }

      hr = m_pDevice->Poll();
      hr = m_pDevice->GetDeviceState( sizeof(DIMOUSESTATE),
                                      (void*)&currState );

        if( FAILED( hr ) )
        {
              return resFailed;
        }
        }
if( m_pTarget )
{
        int dx = currState.lX;
        int dy = currState.lY;
        if( dx || dy )
        {
              m_pTarget->MouseMoved( dx, dy );
        }
        if( currState.rgbButtons[0] & 0x80 )
        {
              // the button got pressed.
              m_pTarget->MouseButtonDown( 0 );
        }
        if( currState.rgbButtons[1] & 0x80 )
        {
              // the button got pressed.
              m_pTarget->MouseButtonDown( 1 );
        }
        if( currState.rgbButtons[2] & 0x80 )
        {
              // the button got pressed.
              m_pTarget->MouseButtonDown( 2 );
        }
        if( !(currState.rgbButtons[0] & 0x80) && (m_lastState.rgbButtons[0]
                                                  & 0x80) )

        {
              // the button got released.
              m_pTarget->MouseButtonUp( 0 );
        }
        if( !(currState.rgbButtons[1] & 0x80) && (m_lastState.rgbButtons[1]
                                                  & 0x80) )

        {
              // the button got released.
              m_pTarget->MouseButtonUp( 1 );
        }
```

```
                  if( !(currState.rgbButtons[2] & 0x80) && (m_lastState.rgbButtons[2]
                                                                    & 0x80) )
              {
                      // the button got released.
                      m_pTarget->MouseButtonUp( 2 );
              }
          }
          m_lastState = currState;
          return resAllGood;
      }


      eResult cMouse::Acquire()
      {
        HRESULT hr = m_pDevice->Acquire();
        if( FAILED(hr) )
        {
              return resFailed;
        }
        return resAllGood;
      }


      void cMouse::UnAcquire()
      {
        m_pDevice->Unacquire();
      }
```

Additions to cApplication

The only addition to cApplication is the InitInput call. It initializes both the key-board and the mouse. The method can be overloaded if this behavior isn't what you want. The code is in Listing 2.22.

Listing 2.22: cApplication::InitInput

```
cInputLayer::Create( AppInstance(),
MainWindow()->GetHWnd(), NULL, true, true );
```

DirectSound

There was a time when computers didn't come with sound cards. Sound cards were add-ons that people bought and installed manually. I clearly remember the first time I played *Wolfenstein 3D* on a sound card-enabled machine; after that I ran out and bought one. Sound can totally change the experience of electronic entertainment. Instead of just associating visual images with a virtual experience, adding sound to an application makes it still more immersive, especially if the sound effects are well made.

Before the great move to Windows, using sound was a tricky process for programmers. Usually it involved licensing an expensive and complex third-party sound library that could interface with the different types of sound cards on the market. These libraries could cost hundreds or thousands of dollars. With the advent of DirectSound, the need for these libraries has all but disappeared. DirectSound is an API that can play sound on any Windows-capable sound card (which is, basically, all of them). It has advanced features for more advanced cards, like 3-D sound effects.

While the Win32 API has some limited sound-playing functionality, it's not something that is practical for most games. Sounds can't be mixed together, signal processing is nonexistent, and it isn't the fastest thing in the world.

As of DirectX 6.1, there was a new component to DirectX called DirectMusic that allows applications to dynamically improvise music for games. There's enough stuff in DirectMusic to justify a very large chapter if not a whole book, so I'm not going to touch it with a ten-foot pole.

The Essentials of Sound

Sound itself is a wave of kinetic energy caused by the motion of an object. The wave travels through matter at a speed dependent on the type of matter and temperature (very quickly through solids; through air at 24° C (75° F) it moves at about 1240 kph (775 mph)). Sound waves have energy, so they can cause objects to move; when they hit a solid object, some of the sound is transmitted through the object, some is absorbed, and some is reflected back (the reflecting back is known as echo). When the waves hit an object, they make it vibrate. When the vibrating object is your eardrum, electric signals go to your brain and it hears the sound.

The waves are sinusoidal in nature, and they have an *amplitude* and a *frequency*. The amplitude defines how loud the sound is, and is usually measured in decibels (dB). The frequency is how many different wave oscillations fit into one second, measured in hertz (Hz). The frequency of a sound defines what its pitch is; lower-pitched sounds resonate less than higher-pitched sounds. The A above middle C has a wave that resonates 440 times a second, so it has a frequency of 440 Hz.

Sound is additive; that is, if two sounds are going through the air together, they both apply their energy to the air molecules around them. When the crests of the sound waves match up, their result is a louder sound, while if opposite crests match up, they cancel each other out. The more things there are creating sound in a room, the more sound there generally is in the room.

On a computer, sound is represented as a stream of discrete samples. Each sample is usually an 8-bit or 16-bit integer, representing the amplitude of the sample. With 16 bits the amplitude can be better approximated, since there is a range of about 65,000 values, instead of only 256 found in 8 bits. Successive samples are played, and when enough samples are put together, they approximate the continuous sound curve well enough that the human ear can't tell the difference. In order to approximate it well, the sampling rate (number of samples every second) is much higher than the frequency of most audible sounds—for CD-quality sound, 44.1 thousand samples per second are used to approximate the waveform. See Figure 2.9 for what this looks like. The figure shows an extremely magnified waveform; the amount of signal shown would probably account for a few hundredths of a second of sound.

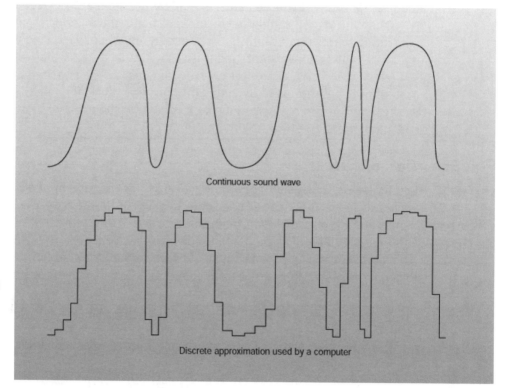

Continuous sound wave

Discrete approximation used by a computer

Figure 2-9: Continuous waveforms, and a computer's approximation

DirectSound Concepts

DirectSound centers around a set of interfaces that perform all the work you need to do. The DirectSound interfaces are summed up in Table 2.11. Due to space constraints, I'm only going to scrape the surface of DirectSound, to the point of being able to play sounds. My rationale for this choice is that there are a dozen other books on the market that cover this topic in detail, and there is too much other material to cover. The "For Further Reading" section at the end of this chapter lists some additional resources if you're interested in the more advanced concepts of DirectSound.

Table 2.11: The main DirectSound interfaces

IDirectSound8	Used in determining capabilities of the sound card and creating buffers for playback.
IDirectSoundBuffer8	A buffer of data used to hold onto the data for a playable sound.
IDirectSound3DBuffer8	A buffer used to contain a 3-D sound. Has additional information like distance, position, projection cones, and so forth.
IDirectSound3DListener8	An object used to represent a 3-D listener. Depending on the location and direction of the listener in 3-D space, 3-D buffers sound different.
IDirectSoundCapture8	Interface used to create capture buffers.
IDirectSoundCaptureBuffer8	Buffer used to hold sound data recorded from a device such as a microphone.
IDirectSoundNotify8	Object that can be used to notify an application when a sound has finished playing.
IKsPropertySet8	An interface used by sound card manufacturers to add special abilities to their driver without needing to extend the spec. This isn't covered in this text.

DirectSound Buffers

DirectSound buffers are your main tools in DirectSound. They are akin to the surfaces used in Direct3D in more ways than one. They even operate in a similar way. Just like surfaces, in order to access their data you need to lock them and then unlock them when you're finished. This is for the same reason as in Direct3D: The DirectSound driver can operate asynchronously from the user application, so care must be taken that no application is reading data when another is reading from it, or vice versa.

There are two kinds of buffers in DirectSound: primary buffers and secondary buffers. The primary buffer (there is only one of them) represents the sound that is currently playing on the card. There is a secondary buffer for each sound effect an application wants to play. Secondary sound buffers are mixed together into the primary buffer and play out the speakers. Using the mixer is how you get multiple sound effects to play at once; DirectSound has a well-optimized piece of code that can mix a bunch of secondary sound buffers together, and many sound cards can perform this operation in hardware automatically.

One main difference between Direct3D surfaces and DirectSound buffers is that buffers are conceptually circular. When a sound effect is playing, the play marker loops around to the beginning of the buffer when it reaches the end, unless you tell it to do otherwise. The play marker is a conceptual marker in the buffer that represents where sound data is being retrieved.

Just like surfaces, buffers are created by filling out a description of what you want in the buffer. The structure used to describe a DirectSound buffer is called DSBUFFERDESC:

```
typedef struct {
    DWORD           dwSize;
    DWORD           dwFlags;
    DWORD           dwBufferBytes;
    DWORD           dwReserved;
    LPWAVEFORMATEX  lpwfxFormat;
    GUID            guid3DAlgorithm;
} DSBUFFERDESC, *LPDSBUFFERDESC;
```

dwSize	Size of the structure; set this to sizeof(DSBUFFERDESC).
dwFlags	Flags that describe the capabilities or desired capabilities of the surface. Can be one or more of the following:

- DSBCAPS_CTRL3D

The buffer requires 3-D control. It may be a primary or secondary buffer.

- DSBCAPS_CTRLFREQUENCY

The buffer requires the ability to control its frequency.

- DSBCAPS_CTRLPAN

The buffer requires the ability to control panning.

- DSBCAPS_CTRLPOSITIONNOTIFY

The buffer requires position notification. This feature is not discussed in this text.

- DSBCAPS_CTRLVOLUME

The buffer requires the ability to control its volume.

- DSBCAPS_GETCURRENTPOSITION2

Any calls to GetCurrentPosition() should use the new behavior of putting the read position where it is actually reading. The old behavior put it right behind the write position. The old behavior was also only on emulated DirectSound devices.

- DSBCAPS_GLOBALFOCUS

Like DSBCAPS_STICKYFOCUS, except the buffer can also be heard when other DirectSound applications have focus. The exception is applications that request exclusive access to the sound cards. All other global sounds will be muted when those applications have focus.

- DSBCAPS_LOCDEFER

The buffer can be assigned to either hardware or software playback, depending on the mood of the driver. This flag must be set if the voice management features in version 8.0 are to be used.

- DSBCAPS_LOCHARDWARE

Forces the buffer to be mixed in hardware. The application must make sure there is a mixing channel available for the buffer. If there isn't enough memory on the card, or the card doesn't support hardware mixing, calling CreateSoundBuffer will fail.

- DSBCAPS_LOCSOFTWARE

Forces the buffer to be mixed in software.

- DSBCAPS_MUTE3DATMAXDISTANCE

This flag applies to 3-D sound buffers, which are not discussed in this text.

- DSBCAPS_PRIMARYBUFFER

Indicates that the buffer is the single and only primary buffer for the sound card. A secondary buffer is created if this flag is not set.

- DSBCAPS_STATIC

Informs the driver that the buffer will be filled once and played many times. This makes the driver more likely to put the buffer in hardware memory.

- DSBCAPS_STICKYFOCUS

Changes the focus behavior of a sound buffer. Buffers created with sticky focus aren't muted when the user switches to a non-DirectSound application. This is useful for applications like TV cards, where the user wants to hear what is happening while using another application. However, if the user switches to another DirectSound application, all sound effects are muted.

dwBufferBytes	Size of the buffer, in bytes. When you create the primary surface, this parameter should be set to zero.
dwReserved	Reserved for use by DirectSound; don't use.
lpwfxFormat	Pointer to a WAVEFORMATEX structure describing the format of the wave data in the buffer. This is analogous to the pixel formats describing the format of the pixels in Direct3Dsurfaces.
guid3DAlgorithm	GUID that defines the two-speaker virtualization algorithm to be used for software rendering. This GUID is ignored unless the buffer needs 3-D control (set by the DSBCAPS_CTRL3D flag). See the documentation for a listing of the available GUIDs for this parameter.

The lpwfxFormat member of the sound buffer description is a pointer to a WAVEFORMATEX structure. The reason why there's no DS prefixing the structure is because it isn't a DirectSound structure, but instead is one used intrinsically by Windows for its sound playback work.

```
typedef struct {
    WORD  wFormatTag;
    WORD  nChannels;
    DWORD nSamplesPerSec;
    DWORD nAvgBytesPerSec;
    WORD  nBlockAlign;
    WORD  wBitsPerSample;
    WORD  cbSize;
} WAVEFORMATEX;
```

wFormatTag	A tag describing the content of the sound data. If the data is compressed, this tag will correspond to the particular method that was used to compress it. For non-compressed data, this will be set to the constant WAVE_FORMAT_PCM.
nChannels	The number of separate audio channels for the sound data. For monaural sound there is one channel; for stereo sound there are two.
nSamplesPerSec	The number of samples per second. For CD-quality audio this is about 44,000; for radio quality it is about 22,000.
nAvgBytesPerSec	The required data throughput to play the sound. This is here so you can deal with compressed sound files.
nBlockAlign	Block alignment in bytes. Essentially this is the amount of data for one sample. If you had two channels of audio and 16 bits (2 bytes) per sample, this would be 2*2 = 4.
wBitsPerSample	The number of bits for each discrete sample. This is generally either 8 or 16.
cbSize	The size of any extra info that is appended to the structure. This is only used by compressed sound formats.

Sound Buffer Operations

Once you have created a buffer and filled it with the appropriate data, you would, of course, like to play it. The Play() method on the buffer interface plays a sound buffer on the primary surface. The sound can be stopped by calling the Stop() method, which takes no parameters.

```
HRESULT IDirectSoundBuffer8::Play(
  DWORD dwReserved1,
  DWORD dwPriority,
  DWORD dwFlags
);

HRESULT IDirectSoundBuffer8::Stop();
```

dwReserved1	Reserved parameter; must be set to 0.
dwPriority	The priority of the sound. This is used by the sound manager in the event that it needs to evict a playing sound (it evicts the one with the lowest priority). The valid range is anywhere from 0x0 to 0xFFFFFFFF. 0 has the lowest priority. This value shouldn't be used if the surface wasn't created with the LOC_DEFER flag, and should be left as 0.
dwFlags	A set of flags describing the method's behavior. They are:
	• DSBPLAY_LOOPING
	Whenever the end of the buffer is reached, DirectSound wraps to the beginning of the buffer and continues playing it. This is useful for sounds like engine hums. The sound effect continues playing until it is explicitly shut off using Stop().
	• DSBPLAY_LOCHARDWARE

This flag only affects surfaces created with the DSBCAPS_LOCDEFER flag. It forces the buffer to be played in the hardware. If there aren't any voices available and no TERMINATEBY_* flags are set, Play() will fail. This flag shouldn't be used with DSBPLAY_LOCSOFTWARE.

- DSBPLAY_LOCSOFTWARE

This flag only affects surfaces created with the DSBCAPS_LOCDEFER flag. It forces the buffer to be played in software. If there aren't any voices available and no TERMINATEBY_* flags are set, Play() will fail. This flag shouldn't be used with DSBPLAY_LOCHARDWARE. If neither LOCSOFTWARE or LOCHARDWARE is specified, the location for playback will be decided by the sound driver, depending on the available resources.

- DSBPLAY_TERMINATEBY_TIME

Setting this flag enables the buffer to steal resources from another buffer. The driver is forced to play the buffer in hardware. If no hardware voices are available, the driver chooses a buffer to remove, choosing the buffer that has the least amount of time left to play. The only candidate buffers for removal are ones created with the DSBCAPS_LOCDEFER flag.

- DSBPLAY_TERMINATEBY_DISTANCE

This flag is only relevant to 3-D buffers, which are not discussed in this text.

- DSBPLAY_TERMINATEBY_PRIORITY

Setting this flag enables the buffer to steal resources from another buffer. The driver is forced to play the buffer in hardware. If no hardware voices are available, the driver chooses a buffer to remove, choosing the buffer that has the lowest priority. The only candidate buffers for removal are ones created with the DSBCAPS_LOCDEFER flag.

Unfortunately, there is only one play marker per sound buffer, so you can't play the same sound twice at the same time. However, the code I'll show you can clone the sound effect into a new buffer and play the new effect, so you can have multiple sounds of the same type playing at the same time. To implement this, however, you need to know if the sound buffer is playing at any point in time. You can do this using the GetStatus method on the sound buffer interface:

```
HRESULT IDirectSoundBuffer8::GetStatus(
  LPDWORD lpdwStatus
);
```

lpdwStatus   Pointer to a DWORD that will be filled with the status of the sound buffer. If the function succeeds, the DWORD can check to see if any of the following flags are set:

- DSBSTATUS_BUFFERLOST

The sound buffer was lost. Before it can be played or locked, it must be restored using the Restore() method on the DirectSoundBuffer. Restore takes no parameters, and reallocates the required memory for a DirectSound buffer.

- DSBSTATUS_LOOPING

The buffer is playing and also looping. It won't stop until the Stop() method is called on it.

- DSBSTATUS_PLAYING

The buffer is currently playing. The buffer is stopped if this flag isn't set.

- DSBSTATUS_LOCSOFTWARE

The buffer is playing from system RAM. This flag is only meaningful for buffers that were created with the DSBCAPS_LOCDEFER flag.

- DSBSTATUS_LOCHARDWARE

The buffer is playing on the sound card's memory. This flag is only meaningful for buffers that were created with the DSBCAPS_LOCDEFER flag.

- DSBSTATUS_TERMINATED

The buffer was terminated by the sound logic.

To play a buffer with anything meaningful in it, you're going to need to fill it with something. Unfortunately, DirectSound doesn't have the ability to automatically load WAV files, so you have to do it yourself. When you load the file and get the data, you put it into the sound buffer by locking it and getting a pointer to the buffer to write into. This is done using the Lock() method on the sound buffer interface.

```
HRESULT IDirectSoundBuffer8::Lock(
    DWORD dwWriteCursor,
    DWORD dwWriteBytes,
    LPVOID lplpvAudioPtr1,
    LPDWORD lpdwAudioBytes1,
    LPVOID lplpvAudioPtr2,
    LPDWORD lpdwAudioBytes2,
    DWORD dwFlags
);
```

dwWriteCursor	Offset from the start of the buffer (in bytes) to where the lock should begin.
dwWriteBytes	Number of bytes that should be locked. Remember that sound buffers are circular, conceptually. If more bytes are requested than are left in the file, the lock continues at the beginning of the buffer (and the *Audio*2 variables get filled).
lplpvAudioPtr1	Pointer to be filled with the requested data pointer of the lock.

lpdwAudioBytes1	Pointer to be filled with the number of bytes of the first data block. This may or may not be the same as dwWriteBytes, depending on whether or not the lock wrapped to the beginning of the sound buffer.
lplpvAudioPtr2	Pointer to be filled with the secondary data pointer of the lock. This member is only set if the memory requested in the lock wrapped to the beginning of the buffer (it will be set to the beginning of the buffer). If the lock did not require a wrap, this pointer will be set to NULL.
lpdwAudioBytes2	Pointer to be filled with the number of bytes of the second data block. If the lock required a wrap, this will be the number of bytes left over after the wrap around.
dwFlags	A set of flags modifying the behavior of the lock method: • DSBLOCK_FROMWRITECURSOR Locks from the current write cursor in the buffer. This feature is not discussed in this text. • DSBLOCK_ENTIREBUFFER Locks the entire sound buffer. The dwWriteBytes parameter is ignored, and can be set to zero.

To unlock a sound buffer after filling it, just call the Unlock() method on it. This allows other concurrent tasks on the machine, like the sound hardware, to access the sound buffer's data bits.

```
HRESULT IDirectSoundBuffer8::Unlock(
    LPVOID lpvAudioPtr1,
    DWORD dwAudioBytes1,
    LPVOID lpvAudioPtr2,
    DWORD dwAudioBytes2
);
```

lpvAudioPtr1	Pointer to the first block of data to unlock. This must be the same value that was given by Lock().
dwAudioBytes1	Length of the first block of data to unlock. This must be the same value that was given by Lock().
lpvAudioPtr2	Pointer to the second block of data to unlock. This must be the same value that was given by Lock().
dwAudioBytes2	Length of the second block of data to unlock. This must be the same value that was given by Lock().

Loading WAV Files

Call me a wuss, but I try to avoid reinventing any wheels I can. One I distinctly do not want to reinvent is the WAV-file-loading wheel. The DirectX SDK comes with code to load a WAV file and create a DirectSound buffer, and I'm going to use it verbatim here. Rather than list the source code for it, which is pretty confusing, I'm just going to list the interface for it. You'll see how this fits into the code later.

Listing 2.23: WavRead.h, the Microsoft-provided interface for the Wave Sound Reader object

```
//-----------------------------------------------------------------------------
// File: WavRead.h
//
// Desc: Support for loading and playing Wave files using DirectSound sound
//       buffers.
//
// Copyright (c) 1999 Microsoft Corp. All rights reserved.
//-----------------------------------------------------------------------------
#ifndef WAVE_READ_H
#define WAVE_READ_H


#include <mmreg.h>
#include <mmsystem.h>



//-----------------------------------------------------------------------------
// Name: class CWaveSoundRead
// Desc: A class to read in sound data from a Wave file
//-----------------------------------------------------------------------------
class CWaveSoundRead
{
public:
    WAVEFORMATEX* m_pwfx;        // Pointer to WAVEFORMATEX structure
    HMMIO         m_hmmioIn;     // MM I/O handle for the WAVE
    MMCKINFO      m_ckIn;        // Multimedia RIFF chunk
    MMCKINFO      m_ckInRiff;    // Use in opening a WAVE file

public:
    CWaveSoundRead();
    ~CWaveSoundRead();

    HRESULT Open( CHAR* strFilename );
    HRESULT Reset();
    HRESULT Read( UINT nSizeToRead, BYTE* pbData, UINT* pnSizeRead );
    HRESULT Close();

};

#endif WAVE_READ_H
```

Implementing DirectSound with cSoundLayer

The final system layer I'm going to implement in this chapter is the sound layer. The class is called cSoundLayer, and has the same restrictions as the graphics and input layers (most notably only one instance of the class may exist in any application).

Creating the sound layer is simple enough. The sound layer has the same interface for creation that the graphics and input layers did: a static Create() method that took care of the initialization hassles. The Create method for the sound layer is simple enough, and it appears in Listing 2.24.

Listing 2.24: cSoundLayer::Create

```
static void cSoundLayer::Create( HWND hWnd )
{
    new cSoundLayer( hWnd );
}
```

The code that lies inside the cSoundLayer constructor is what I'll dissect next in the step-by-step process of setting up DirectSound.

Creating the DirectSound Object

The first step in initializing DirectSound is to actually acquire the interface pointer to the IDirectSound8 object. To do this, you call the function DirectSoundCreate8.

```
HRESULT WINAPI DirectSoundCreate8(
  LPCGUID lpcGuid,
  LPDIRECTSOUND8 * ppDS,
  LPUNKNOWN  pUnkOuter
);
```

lpcGuid	A pointer to a GUID that describes the device you wish to create. While you can enumerate all of the sound devices with DirectSoundEnumerate, generally there is only one sound card on a machine. To get the default device (which is what you want, usually), set this to NULL.
ppDS	A pointer to an LPDIRECTSOUND8 interface pointer that will be filled with a valid interface pointer if the function succeeds.
pUnkOuter	Used for COM aggregation; leave this as NULL.

Sample code to create the sound interface appears in Listing 2.25.

Listing 2.25: Sample code to create a DirectSound object

```
LPDIRECTSOUND8 m_pDSound = 0;

// Create IDirectSound using the primary sound device
hr = DirectSoundCreate8( NULL, &m_pDSound, NULL );
if( FAILED( hr ) )
{
  // Handle critical error
}
```

Setting the Cooperative Level

After you acquire the interface pointer, the next step is to declare how coopera-tive you intend on being. Just like DirectInput, this is done using the SetCooperativeLevel command.

```
HRESULT IDirectSound8::SetCooperativeLevel(
  HWND hwnd,
  DWORD dwLevel
);
```

hwnd	Handle to the window to be associated with the DirectSound object. This should be the primary window.
dwLevel	One of the following flags, describing the desired cooperative level.

- DSSCL_EXCLUSIVE

Grab exclusive control of the sound device. When the application has focus, it is the only audible application.

- DSSCL_NORMAL

Smoothest, yet most restrictive cooperative level. The primary format cannot be changed. This is the cooperative level the sound layer uses.

- DSSCL_PRIORITY

Like DDSCL_NORMAL except the primary format may be changed.

- DSSCL_WRITEPRIMARY

This is the highest possible priority for an application to have. It can't play any secondary buffers, and it has the ability to manually mangle the bits of the primary buffer. Only for the extremely hardcore.

This code will be changing the primary format of the sound buffer, so I'll go ahead and set this to DSSCL_PRIORITY. Sample code to do this appears in List-ing 2.26.

Listing 2.26: Sample code to set up the cooperative level of DirectSound

```
// pDSound is a valid LPDIRECTSOUND8 object.
HRESULT hr = pDSound->SetCooperativeLevel( hWnd, DSSCL_PRIORITY );
if( FAILED( hr ) )
{
    /* handle error */
}
```

Grabbing the Primary Buffer

Since the sound layer sets the cooperative level's priority, it can do some crazy things like change the format of the primary buffer. Generally it's best to set the primary buffer to the same format that all of your secondary buffers will be in; this makes the mixer's job easier, as it doesn't have to resample any sound effects to be able to mix them into the primary buffer. You can imagine what would happen if you tried to play a 22KHz sound effect in a 44KHz buffer without resampling: You would run out of samples twice as soon as you would expect, and the sound effect would have sort of a chipmunkish quality to it.

To change the format of the primary buffer, you just need to grab it using CreateSoundBuffer, fill out a new format description, and set it using the SetFormat() method on the primary buffer. Listing 2.27 has code that sets the primary format to 22KHz, 16-bit stereo.

Listing 2.27: Sample code to change the format of the primary buffer

```
// pDSound is a valid LPDIRECTSOUND object.
LPDIRECTSOUNDBUFFER pDSBPrimary = NULL;

sAutoZero<DSBUFFERDESC> dsbd;
dsbd.dwFlags       = DSBCAPS_PRIMARYBUFFER;
dsbd.dwBufferBytes = 0;
dsbd.lpwfxFormat   = NULL;

HRESULT hr = pDSound->CreateSoundBuffer( &dsbd, &pDSBPrimary, NULL );
if( FAILED( hr ) )
{
    /* handle error */
}

// Set primary buffer format to 22kHz and 16-bit output.
WAVEFORMATEX wfx;
ZeroMemory( &wfx, sizeof(WAVEFORMATEX) );
wfx.wFormatTag     = WAVE_FORMAT_PCM;
wfx.nChannels      = 2;
wfx.nSamplesPerSec = 22050;
wfx.wBitsPerSample = 16;
wfx.nBlockAlign    = wfx.wBitsPerSample / 8 * wfx.nChannels;
```

```
wfx.nAvgBytesPerSec = wfx.nSamplesPerSec * wfx.nBlockAlign;

HRESULT hr = hr = pDSBPrimary->SetFormat(&wfx)
if( FAILED( ) )
{
    throw cGameError( "SetFormat (DS) failed!" );
}

SafeRelease( pDSBPrimary );
```

With all the code in place, you can actually write the sound layer class. The header appears in Listing 2.28, and the source code is in Listing 2.29.

Listing 2.28: SoundLayer.h

```
/*******************************************************************
 *          Advanced 3D Game Programming using DirectX 8.0
 * * * * * * * * * * * * * * * * * * * * * * * * * * * * * * * *
 *    Title: SoundLayer.h
 *     Desc: Wrapper for DirectSound
 *           Based off of the SDK samples
 * copyright (c) 2001 by Peter A Walsh and Adrian Perez
 * See license.txt for modification and distribution information
 *******************************************************************/

#ifndef _SOUNDLAYER_H
#define _SOUNDLAYER_H

#include <dsound.h>
#include "GameErrors.h"              // Added by ClassView

class cSound;

class cSoundLayer
{

  LPDIRECTSOUND8      m_pDSound;
  LPDIRECTSOUNDBUFFER8 m_pPrimary;    // primary mixer

  static cSoundLayer*  m_pGlobalSLayer;

  cSoundLayer( HWND hWnd );

public:
 virtual ~cSoundLayer();

 static cSoundLayer* GetSound()
 {
      return m_pGlobalSLayer;
```

```
}

LPDIRECTSOUND8 GetDSound()
{
    return m_pDSound;
}

static void Create( HWND hWnd )
{
    new cSoundLayer( hWnd );
}
};

inline cSoundLayer* Sound()
{
  return cSoundLayer::GetSound();
}

#endif //_SOUNDLAYER_H
```

Listing 2.29: SoundLayer.cpp

```
/******************************************************************
 *          Advanced 3D Game Programming using DirectX 8.0
 * * * * * * * * * * * * * * * * * * * * * * * * * * * * * * *
 *    Title: SoundLayer.cpp
 *     Desc: DirectSound wrapper, based off of the SDK samples
 *
 * (C) 2001 by Peter A Walsh and Adrian Perez
 * See license.txt for modification and distribution information
 ******************************************************************/

#include "stdafx.h"

#include "SoundLayer.h"
#include "Sound.h"

cSoundLayer* cSoundLayer::m_pGlobalSLayer = NULL;

cSoundLayer::cSoundLayer( HWND hWnd )
{
  m_pDSound = NULL;
  m_pPrimary = NULL;

  if( m_pGlobalSLayer )
  {
      throw cGameError( "cSoundLayer already initialized!" );
  }
  m_pGlobalSLayer = this;
```

```
        HRESULT            hr;
        LPDIRECTSOUNDBUFFER pDSBPrimary = NULL;


        // Create IDirectSound using the primary sound device
    hr = DirectSoundCreate8( NULL, &m_pDSound, NULL );
        if( FAILED( hr ) )
    {
            throw cGameError( "DirectSoundCreate failed!" );
    }


        // Set coop level to DSSCL_PRIORITY
    hr = m_pDSound->SetCooperativeLevel( hWnd, DSSCL_PRIORITY );
        if( FAILED( hr ) )
    {
            throw cGameError( "SetCooperativeLevel (DS) failed!" );
    }


        // Get the primary buffer
    sAutoZero<DSBUFFERDESC> dsbd;
        dsbd.dwFlags      = DSBCAPS_PRIMARYBUFFER;
        dsbd.dwBufferBytes = 0;
        dsbd.lpwfxFormat   = NULL;

    hr = m_pDSound->CreateSoundBuffer( &dsbd, &pDSBPrimary, NULL );
        if( FAILED( hr ) )
    {
            throw cGameError( "CreateSoundBuffer (DS) failed!" );
    }


        // Set primary buffer format to 22kHz and 16-bit output.
        WAVEFORMATEX wfx;
        ZeroMemory( &wfx, sizeof(WAVEFORMATEX) );
        wfx.wFormatTag      = WAVE_FORMAT_PCM;
        wfx.nChannels       = 2;
        wfx.nSamplesPerSec  = 22050;
        wfx.wBitsPerSample  = 16;
        wfx.nBlockAlign     = wfx.wBitsPerSample / 8 * wfx.nChannels;
        wfx.nAvgBytesPerSec = wfx.nSamplesPerSec * wfx.nBlockAlign;

        if( FAILED( hr = pDSBPrimary->SetFormat(&wfx) ) )
    {
            throw cGameError( "SetFormat (DS) failed!" );
    }


        SafeRelease( pDSBPrimary );
}

cSoundLayer::~cSoundLayer()
{
 SafeRelease( m_pPrimary );
```

```
        SafeRelease( m_pDSound );
        m_pGlobalSLayer = NULL;
}
```

The cSound Class

To help facilitate the creation and playback of secondary buffers, I constructed an encapsulation class called cSound. A cSound object can be constructed either from a filename or from another cSound object. The copy constructor uses a ref-counting map so that all cSounds based on the same WAV file use the same CWaveSoundRead object. The overhead of the map could have been avoided if the CWaveSoundRead code was changed to accommodate the needed functionality, but I felt it was better to leave the code unchanged from the DirectX SDK.

Without any further ado, let's just dive into the code. The details of how this code works isn't terribly interesting, so I'll just let the code speak for itself.

Listing 2.30: Sound.h

```
/****************************************************************
 *          Advanced 3D Game Programming using DirectX 8.0
 * * * * * * * * * * * * * * * * * * * * * * * * * * * * * * *
 *    Title: Sound.h
 *     Desc: Class wrapper for a WAV sound.  Uses the supplied
 *           DirectX code to read WAV files
 * copyright (c) 2001 by Peter A Walsh and Adrian Perez
 * See license.txt for modification and distribution information
 ****************************************************************/

#ifndef _SOUND_H
#define _SOUND_H

#include <map>

#include "SoundLayer.h"
#include "Wavread.h"

class cSound
{
  CWaveSoundRead*          m_pWaveSoundRead;
  LPDIRECTSOUNDBUFFER8     m_pBuffer;
  int                      m_bufferSize;

  /**
   * Multiple sounds that use the same
   * file shouldn't re-read it, they should
   * share the CWSR object.  This map
   * implements rudimentary reference counting.
   * I would have just changed CWaveSoundRead,
   * but I wanted to keep it unchanged from the
```

```
         * samples.
         */
        static std::map< CWaveSoundRead*, int > m_waveMap;

        void Init();

public:
        cSound( char* filename );
        cSound( cSound& in );
        cSound& operator=( const cSound &in );

        virtual ~cSound();

        void Restore();
        void Fill();
        void Play( bool bLoop = false );

        bool IsPlaying();

};

#endif //_SOUND_H
```

Listing 2.31: Sound.cpp

```
/************************************************************************
 *          Advanced 3D Game Programming using DirectX 8.0
 * * * * * * * * * * * * * * * * * * * * * * * * * * * * * *
 *    Title: Sound.cpp
 *     Desc: Class wrapper for a WAV sound.  Uses the supplied
 *           DirectX code to read WAV files
 * copyright (c) 2001 by Peter A Walsh and Adrian Perez
 * See license.txt for modification and distribution information
 ************************************************************************/

#include "stdafx.h"

#include "WavRead.h"
#include "Sound.h"

using std::map;

map< CWaveSoundRead*, int > cSound::m_waveMap;

cSound::cSound( char* filename )
{
 m_pWaveSoundRead = NULL;
 m_pBuffer = NULL;

        // Create a new wave file class
```

```
                m_pWaveSoundRead = new CWaveSoundRead();
                m_waveMap[ m_pWaveSoundRead ] = 1;

                // Load the wave file
                if( FAILED( m_pWaveSoundRead->Open( filename ) ) )
                {
                        throw cGameError("couldn't open file!");
                }

        Init();
        Fill();
}

cSound::cSound( cSound& in )
{
        m_pWaveSoundRead = in.m_pWaveSoundRead;
        m_waveMap[ m_pWaveSoundRead ]++;
        Init();
        Fill();
}

cSound& cSound::operator=( const cSound &in )
{
        /**
         * Destroy the old object
         */
        int count = --m_waveMap[ m_pWaveSoundRead ];
        if( !count )
        {
                delete m_pWaveSoundRead;
        }
        SafeRelease( m_pBuffer );

        /**
         * Clone the incoming one
         */
        m_pWaveSoundRead = in.m_pWaveSoundRead;
        m_waveMap[ m_pWaveSoundRead ]++;

        Init();
        Fill();

        return *this;
}


cSound::~cSound()
{
        int count = m_waveMap[ m_pWaveSoundRead ];
        if( count == 1 )
        {
```

```
            delete m_pWaveSoundRead;
    }
    else
    {
        m_waveMap[ m_pWaveSoundRead ] = count - 1;
    }

    SafeRelease( m_pBuffer );
}

void cSound::Init()
{
 /**
  * Set up the DirectSound surface. the size of the sound file
  * and the format of the data can be retrieved from the wave
  * sound object.  Besides that, we only set the STATIC flag,
  * so that the driver isn't restricted in setting up the
  * buffer.
  */
 sAutoZero<DSBUFFERDESC> dsbd;
    dsbd.dwFlags       = DSBCAPS_STATIC;
    dsbd.dwBufferBytes = m_pWaveSoundRead->m_ckIn.cksize;
    dsbd.lpwfxFormat   = m_pWaveSoundRead->m_pwfx;

    HRESULT hr;

 // Temporary pointer to old DirectSound interface
 LPDIRECTSOUNDBUFFER pTempBuffer = 0;

 // Create the sound buffer
 hr = Sound()->GetDSound()->CreateSoundBuffer( &dsbd, &pTempBuffer, NULL );
    if( FAILED( hr ) )
    {
        throw cGameError("CreateSoundBuffer failed!");
    }

 // Upgrade the sound buffer to version 8
 pTempBuffer->QueryInterface( IID_IDirectSoundBuffer8, (void**)&m_pBuffer );
 if( FAILED( hr ) )
    {
        throw cGameError("SoundBuffer query to 8 failed!");
    }

 // Release the temporary old buffer
 pTempBuffer->Release();

 /**
  * Remember how big the buffer is
  */
    m_bufferSize = dsbd.dwBufferBytes;
```

```
      }


void cSound::Restore()
{
        HRESULT hr;

        if( NULL == m_pBuffer )
    {
        return;
    }

        DWORD dwStatus;
        if( FAILED( hr = m_pBuffer->GetStatus( &dwStatus ) ) )
    {
        throw cGameError( "couldn't get buffer status" );
    }

        if( dwStatus & DSBSTATUS_BUFFERLOST )
        {
        /**
         * Chances are, we got here because the app /just/
         * started, and DirectSound hasn't given us any
         * control yet.  Just spin until we can restore
         * the buffer
         */
         do
         {
             hr = m_pBuffer->Restore();
             if( hr == DSERR_BUFFERLOST )
                 Sleep( 10 );
         }
         while( hr = m_pBuffer->Restore() );

        /**
         * The buffer was restored.  Fill 'er up.
         */
         Fill();
    }
}


void cSound::Fill()
{
    HRESULT hr;
    uchar*  pbWavData; // Pointer to actual wav data
    uint    cbWavSize; // Size of data
    void*   pbData  = NULL;
    void*   pbData2 = NULL;
    ulong   dwLength;
```

```
    ulong   dwLength2;

/**
 * How big the wav file is
 */
    uint nWaveFileSize = m_pWaveSoundRead->m_ckIn.cksize;

/**
 * Allocate enough data to hold the wav file data
 */
    pbWavData = new uchar[ nWaveFileSize ];
    if( NULL == pbWavData )
{
    delete [] pbWavData;
        throw cGameError("Out of memory!");
}

hr = m_pWaveSoundRead->Read(
    nWaveFileSize,
        pbWavData,
        &cbWavSize );
    if( FAILED( hr ) )
{
    delete [] pbWavData;
        throw cGameError("m_pWaveSoundRead->Read failed");
}

/**
 * Reset the file to the beginning
 */
    m_pWaveSoundRead->Reset();

    /**
 * Lock the buffer so we can copy the data over
 */
hr = m_pBuffer->Lock(
    0, m_bufferSize, &pbData, &dwLength,
        &pbData2, &dwLength2, OL );
    if( FAILED( hr ) )
{
    delete [] pbWavData;
        throw cGameError("m_pBuffer->Lock failed");
}

/**
 * Copy said data over, unlocking afterwards
 */
    memcpy( pbData, pbWavData, m_bufferSize );
    m_pBuffer->Unlock( pbData, m_bufferSize, NULL, 0 );
```

```
/**
 * We're done with the wav data memory.
 */
    delete [] pbWavData;
}
```

```
bool cSound::IsPlaying()
{
    DWORD dwStatus = 0;

    m_pBuffer->GetStatus( &dwStatus );

    if( dwStatus & DSBSTATUS_PLAYING )
        return true;
    else
        return false;
}
```

```
void cSound::Play( bool bLoop )
{
 HRESULT hr;
      if( NULL == m_pBuffer )
        return;

      // Restore the buffers if they are lost
      Restore();

      // Play buffer
      DWORD dwLooped = bLoop ? DSBPLAY_LOOPING : OL;
      if( FAILED( hr = m_pBuffer->Play( 0, 0, dwLooped ) ) )
 {
      throw cGameError("m_pBuffer->Play failed");
 }
}
```

Additions to cApplication

The only addition to cApplication is the InitSound call, which initializes the sound layer. After the call completes you can freely create cSound objects and play them. If this is not the behavior you would like in your application, the function is overloadable. The code is in Listing 2.32.

Listing 2.32: cApplication::InitSound

```
void cApplication::InitSound()
{
    cSoundLayer::Create( MainWindow()->GetHWnd() );
}
```

Application: DirectSound Sample

While Adrian (the co-author of the DirectX 7.0 version of this book) was in college, he tried to be well-rounded. As part of that effort, he participated in extracurricular activities that actually had nothing to do with programming. One of them was an a cappella group in which he sang bass. One of his jobs in the group was to take care of some of the vocal percussion.

You see, since a cappella music can't have any sort of accompaniment, any percussion needs to be done with the human voice. This has spawned an entire subculture of vocal percussionists, each trying to make that perfect snare sound or cymbal crash using only their mouths. The DirectSound sample for this chapter was created using Adrian's unique vocal abilities.

When you load the file DSSAMPLE from the companion CD, you're presented with a small window that lists six different vocal percussion sounds. The keys 1 through 6 play each of the sounds, and you can press multiple keys simultaneously to play multiple sounds.

You'll note that I didn't show you a DirectInput sample, because I figured it would be better to roll DirectSound and DirectInput into one sample. DirectInput is used to capture the keystrokes. With some practice you can get a pretty swank beat going. The code behind the sample appears in Listing 2.33.

Listing 2.33: The vocal percussion DirectSound sample app

```
/******************************************************************
 *          Advanced 3D Game Programming using DirectX 8.0
 * * * * * * * * * * * * * * * * * * * * * * * * * * * * * * * *
 *    Title: DSSample.cpp
 *     Desc: DirectSound Sample app
 *
 * (C) 2001 by Peter A Walsh and Adrian Perez
 * See license.txt for modification and distribution information
 ******************************************************************/

#include "stdafx.h"

#include <vector>
#include <string>
using namespace std;
```

```
class cDSSampleApp : public cApplication, public iKeyboardReceiver
{
 vector< cSound* > m_sounds[6];
 string m_names[6];

 int m_states[6]; // states of the keys 1-6

public:

 void PlaySound( int num );

 //==========------------------------- cApplication

 virtual void DoFrame( float timeDelta );
 virtual void SceneInit();

 cDSSampleApp() :
      cApplication()
 {
      m_title = string( "DirectSound Sample" );
      m_width = 320;
      m_height = 200;

      for( int i=0; i<6; i++ ) m_states[i] = 0;
 }

 ~cDSSampleApp()
 {
      for( int i=0; i<6; i++ )
      {
           for( int i2=0; i2< m_sounds[i].size(); i2++ )
           {
                delete m_sounds[i][i2];
           }
      }
 }

 virtual void KeyUp( int key );
 virtual void KeyDown( int key );

};


cApplication* CreateApplication()
{
 return new cDSSampleApp();
}
```

```
void DestroyApplication( cApplication* pApp )
{
 delete pApp;
}


void cDSSampleApp::SceneInit()
{
 m_names[0] = string("media\\keg.wav");
 m_names[1] = string("media\\crash1.wav");
 m_names[2] = string("media\crash2.wav");
 m_names[3] = string("media\\bass.wav");
 m_names[4] = string("media\\snare.wav");
 m_names[5] = string("media\\hihat.wav");

 Input()->GetKeyboard()->SetReceiver( this );

 for( int i=0; i<6; i++ )
 {
     m_sounds[i].push_back( new cSound( (char*)m_names[i].c_str() ) );
 }
}


void cDSSampleApp::PlaySound( int num )
{
 /**
  * iterate through the vector, looking
  * for a sound that isn't currently playing.
  */
 vector<cSound*>::iterator iter;
 for( iter = m_sounds[num].begin(); iter != m_sounds[num].end(); iter++ )
 {
     if( !(*iter)->IsPlaying() )
     {
         (*iter)->Play();
         return;
     }
 }

 /**
  * A sound wasn't found.  Create a new one.
  */
 DP("spawning a new sound\n");

 cSound* pNew = new cSound( *m_sounds[num][0] );
 m_sounds[num].push_back( pNew );
 m_sounds[num][ m_sounds[num].size() - 1 ]->Play();
}
```

```
void cDSSampleApp::DoFrame( float timeDelta )
{
  // Clear the previous contents of the back buffer
  Graphics()->GetDevice()->Clear( 0, 0, D3DCLEAR_TARGET | D3DCLEAR_ZBUFFER,
                                  D3DCOLOR_XRGB( 0,0,200), 1.0f, 0 );

  // Set up the strings
  string help;
  help += "DirectSound Sample application\n";
  help += "Vocal Percussion with Adrian Perez\n";
  help += "  [1]: Keg drum\n";
  help += "  [2]: Crash 1\n";
  help += "  [3]: Crash 2\n";
  help += "  [4]: Bass drum\n";
  help += "  [5]: Snare drum\n";
  help += "  [6]: Hi-Hat\n";

  // Tell Direct3D we are about to start rendering
  Graphics()->GetDevice()->BeginScene();

  // Output the text
  Graphics()->DrawTextString( 1, 1, D3DCOLOR_XRGB( 0, 255, 0), help.c_str() );

  // Tell Direct3D we are done rendering
  Graphics()->GetDevice()->EndScene();

  // Present the back buffer to the primary surface
  Graphics()->Flip();
}


void cDSSampleApp::KeyDown( int key )
{
  switch( key )
  {
  case DIK_1:
      if( !m_states[0] )
      {
          m_states[0] = 1;
          PlaySound(0);
      }
      break;
  case DIK_2:
      if( !m_states[1] )
      {
          m_states[1] = 1;
          PlaySound(1);
      }
      break;
  case DIK_3:
      if( !m_states[2] )
```

```
            {
                 m_states[2] = 1;
                 PlaySound(2);
            }
            break;
      case DIK_4:
            if( !m_states[3] )
            {
                 m_states[3] = 1;
                 PlaySound(3);
            }
            break;
      case DIK_5:
            if( !m_states[4] )
            {
                 m_states[4] = 1;
                 PlaySound(4);
            }
            break;
      case DIK_6:
            if( !m_states[5] )
            {
                 m_states[5] = 1;
                 PlaySound(5);
            }
            break;
   }
}

void cDSSampleApp::KeyUp( int key )
{
 switch( key )
 {
 case DIK_1:
      m_states[0] = 0;
      break;
 case DIK_2:
      m_states[1] = 0;
      break;
 case DIK_3:
      m_states[2] = 0;
      break;
 case DIK_4:
      m_states[3] = 0;
      break;
 case DIK_5:
      m_states[4] = 0;
      break;
 case DIK_6:
      m_states[5] = 0;
      break;
```

```
    }
}
```

References

Bargen, Bradley, and Terence Peter Donnelly. *Inside DirectX (Microsoft Programming Series)*. Redmond: Microsoft Press, 1998. ISBN: 1572316969.

For Further Reading

Lamothe, Andre. *Tricks of the Windows Game Programming Gurus: Fundamentals of 2-D and 3-D Game Programming*. MacMillan Publishing Company, 1999. ISBN: 0672313618.

While the title is a bit deceiving (the text doesn't cover 3-D graphics, as it is part one of a two-volume set), this book has good information about DirectX programming, including covering 3-D sound effects and DirectMusic, as well as a lot of DirectDraw material. The material is also getting a little out of date; it only covers DirectX 5.0/6.0.

Walsh, Peter. *The Zen of Direct3D Game Programming*. Prima Publishing, 2001. ISBN: 0761534296.

Call me a punk for plugging my own book, but it contains an incredible amount of information on Direct3D that I didn't go into here so that I could explore other topics. This tome covers just about everything you could ever possibly want to know about the GDI, GDI interaction with Direct3D, and Direct3D itself. The entire book is devoted to the exploration of graphical techniques with DirectX 8.0 and Win32.

Chapter 3

3-D Math Foundations

When you really get down to it, using 3-D graphics is an exercise in math. Some of the math can be intensely interesting; some of it can be quite banal. It all depends on the eye of the beholder. Love it or hate it, however, you still have to learn it. A solid foundation in math is a requirement if you want to be a successful 3-D coder. Don't worry, though; I'll try to keep this chapter as interesting as possible.

Points

Let's start with the most basic of basic primitives: the 3-D *point*, or *vector*. Points are paramount in 3-D graphics. The vertices of objects, the objects' locations and directions, and their velocities/forces are all described with 3-D points. Three-dimensional objects have width, height, and depth, which are represented with the shorthand components x (width), y (height), and z (depth). Points and vectors, when used in equations, are referred to as *vector quantities*, while regular numbers are referred to as *scalar quantities*. In the text I'll refer to 3-D vectors with lowercase, boldface letters (examples would be **v** and **p**). The three components are written separated by commas like this: $<x,y,z>$. They are also represented as a single row matrix (or, equivalently, a transposed single column matrix). If you're unfamiliar with the concept of matrices, have patience: I'll get there soon. At the right is an example of how points are represented using matrix notation:

$$\mathbf{v} = [\mathbf{v}_x \quad \mathbf{v}_y \quad \mathbf{v}_z]$$

and

$$\mathbf{v} = \begin{bmatrix} \mathbf{v}_x \\ \mathbf{v}_y \\ \mathbf{v}_z \end{bmatrix}^T$$

Note: In the text I use the terms "point" and "vector" interchangeably. They loosely mean the same thing. A point is a location in 3-D space, and a vector is a line that goes from the origin to a location in 3-D space. For all the math that I'm discussing in this text, they can be used interchangeably.

Here are a few examples of three-dimensional points. It's difficult to represent the dimensions on paper, so please be tolerant of the illustrations used in this book.

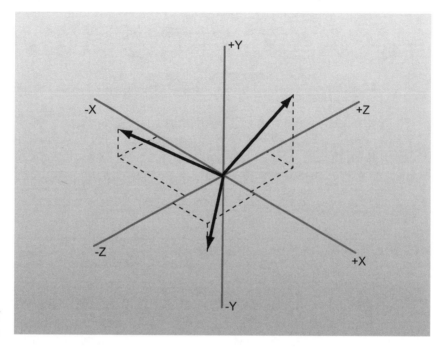

Figure 3.1:
Examples of
3-D vectors

3-D points are graphed in a way analogous to the 2-D Cartesian coordinate system. There are three principal axes stretching off into infinity in both directions. These are the x, y, and z axes. They meet at the *origin*, a specific point that represents the center of the current coordinate system (typically you have several coordinate systems to worry about, but I'll leave this until later). The coordinates of the origin are, of course, <0,0,0>.

Which way do the axes point? In some systems (for example, some 3-D modelers like 3-D Studio), x increases to the right, y increases forward (into the page), and z increases up. These directions are all dependent on the orientation of the viewer of the scene. My choice of axes direction is the one used in most 3-D games: x increases to the right, y increases up, and z increases forward, into the monitor.

Note: This text uses a left-handed coordinate space, where x increases to the right, y increases up, and z increases forward (into the screen). In right-handed coordinate systems (like that of Foley et al.), z increases coming out of the screen.

A point always exists some distance away from the origin of the coordinate space; this quantity is called the *magnitude* of the vector (or, more intuitively, the *length* of the vector). To compute the magnitude of vectors in 2-D, you use the Pythagorean theorem:

$$\text{magnitude} = \sqrt{x^2 + y^2}$$

Luckily, the Pythagorean theorem extends into 3-D to measure the length of 3-D vectors by simply adding the extra z component into the equation. You can see that the 2-D Pythagorean equation is simply a special case of the 3-D equation where the z-distance from the origin is zero.

There is a shorthand notation used to denote the magnitude of a vector when used in more complex equations. The notation is the vector surrounded on both sides by double vertical lines. The equation for vector length, given a vector **v** with components x, y, and z is:

$$\|\mathbf{v}\| = \sqrt{x^2 + y^2 + z^2}$$

A special type of vector is one that has a length of 1. This type of vector has a term associated with it: *unit vector*. Each unit vector touches a point on what is called the *unit sphere*, a conceptual sphere with radius 1, situated at the origin.

It's often the case that you want a unit-length version of a given vector. For example, the unit-length version **n** of a given vector **m** would be:

$$\mathbf{n} = \frac{\mathbf{m}}{\|\mathbf{m}\|}$$

For sanity's sake, however, I'll introduce some shorthand notation. The same equation can be represented by putting a bar over **m** to signify the unit-length version:

$$\mathbf{n} = \overline{\mathbf{m}}$$

There are three specific unit vectors that represent the directions along the three primary axes: **i** <1,0,0>, **j** <0,1,0>, and **k** <0,0,1>.

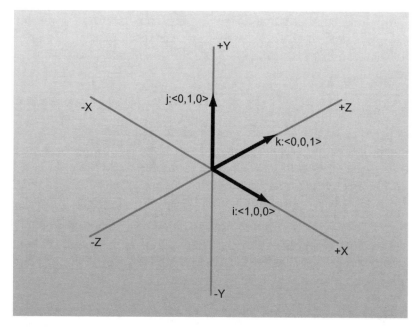

Figure 3.2:
The i, j, and k vectors

Many physics texts use the **i**, **j**, and **k** vectors as primitives to describe other 3-D vectors, so it is worth mentioning it here. Any point in 3-D can be represented as a linear combination of the **i**, **j**, and **k** vectors. You can define any vector as a sum of the scalar components with the three principal vectors. For example, if you had the 3-D vector **a** = <3,5,2>, you could represent it like this:

a = 3**i** + 5**j** + 2**k**

This trait will become more important later on, when I discuss matrices and the spaces they represent.

Aside: While it isn't really pertinent to the level of expertise you need to reach in this text, the concept of a linear combination is important when talking about spaces and transformations.

Given *n* vectors $\mathbf{b}_0..\mathbf{b}_{n-1}$, any vector **v** is a linear combination of the set of the vectors if the following equation can be satisfied:

$$\mathbf{v} = k_0\mathbf{b}_0 + k_1\mathbf{b}_1 + \cdots + k_{n-1}\mathbf{b}_{n-1}$$

where $k_0..k_{n-1}$ are scalars.

That is, if you want to get to **v**, you can start at the origin and walk along any or all of the vectors some amount and reach **v**.

You can say the set of **b** vectors is linearly independent if no single **b** vector is a linear combination of the others.

The point3 Structure

It is always useful to design a class to encapsulate a generic 3-D point. The class name I use is point3. Unlike most of the other classes you have seen so far, the intent of the point3 structure is to act as a mathematical primitive like float or int. The post-fixed 3 denotes the dimension of the point. I'll also define 2-D and 4-D versions of points, which are named point2 and point4, respectively.

Listing 3.1: The point3 structure (defined in point3.h)

```
struct point3
{
    union
    {
        struct
        {
            float x,y,z;      // 3 real components of the vector
        };
        float v[3];           // Array access useful in for loops
    };

    // Default constructor
    point3(){}

    // Construct a point with 3 given inputs
    point3( float X, float Y, float Z ) :
        x(X), y(Y), z(Z)
    {
    }
    // ... more will go in here.
};
```

This class uses a union in conjunction with a nameless struct. If you've never encountered unions before, a union is used to name components that share memory. So, in the above code, the y variable and the v[1] variable represent the same piece of memory; when one of them changes, both of them change. A nameless struct is used to let you define the x, y, and z components as one atomic unit (since I don't want them to each be referring to the same piece of memory). This way you can use the familiar x,y,z notation for most of the code, but maintain the ability to index into an array for iteration.

Aside: The non-default constructor uses initialization lists. C++ classes should use these whenever possible. They clarify the intent of the code to the compiler, which lets it do its job better (it has a better chance to inline the code, and the code will end up being considerably more efficient, especially for complex structures).

Finally, you may wonder why I'm choosing floats (32 bits/4 bytes) instead of doubles (64 bits/8 bytes) or long doubles (80 bits/10 bytes). Well, I could just implement the point as a template class, but there are too many other interactions with other classes to complicate the code that much. Using it as a template in a way defeats the concept of using the point as a generic primitive, especially since there is a space of only three types I would use.

Doubles and long doubles are slower than floats, about twice as slow for things like divides (19 versus 39 cycles), and on top of that they require twice the space. The added precision really isn't important unless you really need a wide range of precision. Within a few years worlds will be big enough and model resolution will be fine enough that you may need to employ larger floating-point resolutions to get the job done. Until then I'd suggest sticking with traditional floats.

Basic point3 Functions

The point3 structure is pretty lame right now. All it can do is construct structures! To spice it up, I'm going to add some member functions to help perform some basic operations on 3-D points, and explain what they are used for.

Assign

Setting a point to a certain value is a common task. It could be done explicitly in three lines, setting the x, y, and z values separately. However, for simplicity's sake, it's easier to set them all at once, with a single function call. This is also better than just creating a new variable on the stack with a point3 constructor; it's more efficient to reuse stack variables whenever possible. The code to do this appears in Listing 3.2.

Listing 3.2: point3::Assign

```
// Reassign a point without making a temporary structure
inline void point3::Assign( float X, float Y, float Z )
{
    x=X;
    y=Y;

    z=Z;
}
```

Mag and MagSquared

The function Mag uses the 3-D version of the Pythagorean theorem mentioned previously to calculate the length of the point structure (the distance from the point to the origin). The code appears in Listing 3.3.

Listing 3.3: point3::Mag

```
inline float point3::Mag() const
{
    return (float)sqrt( x*x + y*y + z*z );
}
```

Sometimes you want the squared distance (for example, when calculating the attenuation factor for a point-source light). Rather than computing the expensive square root and squaring it, you can avoid the cost and simply make an extra function to do it for you, which appears in Listing 3.4.

Listing 3.4: point3::MagSquared

```
inline float point3::MagSquared() const
{
    return ( x*x + y*y + z*z );
}
```

Normalize

Normalize takes a point structure and makes it a unit-length vector pointing in the same direction. The code appears in Listing 3.5.

Listing 3.5: point3::Normalize

```
inline void point3::Normalize()
{
    float foo=1/Mag();
    x*=foo;
    y*=foo;
    z*=foo;
}
```

Dist

Dist is a static function that calculates the distance between two point structures. Conceptually it finds the vector that connects them (which is the vector **b**–**a**) and computes its length. The code appears in Listing 3.6.

Listing 3.6: point3::Dist

```
inline static float point3::Dist( const point3 &a, const point3 &b )
{
    point3 distVec( b.x - a.x, b.y - a.y, b.z - a.z );
    return distVec.Mag();
}
```

point3 Operators

Now that there is a basic primitive I can use, like other primitives (e.g., int or float), I need some way to operate on the data. Since vectors can be added, subtracted, and multiplied (sort of), just like scalars, it would be cool to have an easy way to perform these operations. Operator overloading to the rescue! C++ lets you modify/define the behavior of operators on classes.

Addition/Subtraction

Vector addition and subtraction are useful in moving points around in 3-D. Conceptually adding a vector to another moves the location of the first vector in the direction of the second. Figure 3.3 shows what the result of vector addition look like, and Figure 3.4 shows the result of vector subtraction.

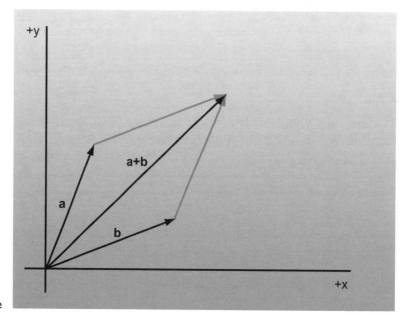

Figure 3.3:
Vector addition example

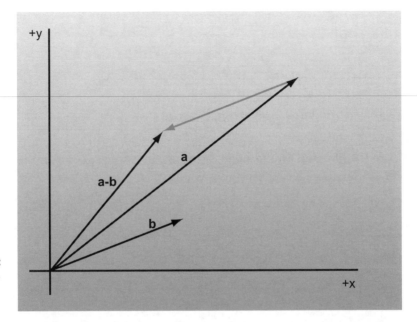

Figure 3.4:
Vector subtraction example

In many respects, vector addition/subtraction is incredibly similar to the scalar addition that I'm sure you know and love. For example, if you wanted to find the average location of a set of vectors, you simply add them together and divide the result by the number of vectors added, the same averaging formula used for scalars.

The code for adding/subtracting vectors is equally similar to their scalar cousins: Simply add (or subtract) each component together separately. I'll give the + and – operators; in the code you'll find the += and –= operators, which I'm leaving out for the sake of brevity.

Listing 3.7: Addition and subtraction operators for point3

```
inline point3 operator+(point3 const &a, point3 const &b)
{
    return point3
    (
        a.x+b.x,
        a.y+b.y,
        a.z+b.z
    );
};

inline point3 operator-(point3 const &a, point3 const &b)
{
    return point3
    (
        a.x-b.x,
```

```
            a.y-b.y,
            a.z-b.z
      );
};
```

Vector-scalar Multiplication/Division

Often, you may want to increase or decrease the length of a vector, while making sure it still points in the same direction. In essence, you want to scale the vector by a scalar. Figure 3.5 shows what scaling vectors looks like.

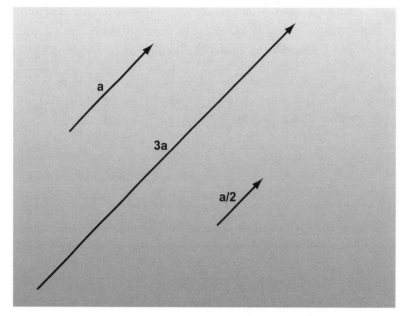

Figure 3.5: Multiplying/ dividing vectors by scalars

Doing this in code is easy enough; just multiply (or divide) each component in the vector by the provided scalar. Listing 3.8 has the * and / operators; the *= and /= operators are defined in the header. Note that I defined two multiplicative operators; one for vector * scalar and another for scalar * vector.

Listing 3.8: Scalar multiplication/division operators for point3

```
inline point3 operator*(point3 const &a, float const &b)
{
    return point3
    (
        a.x*b,
        a.y*b,
        a.z*b
    );
};
```

```
inline point3 operator*(float  const &a, point3 const &b)
{
    return point3
    (
        a*b.x,
        a*b.y,
        a*b.z
    );
};

inline point3 operator/(point3 const &a, float const &b)
{
    float inv = 1.f / b; // Cache the division.
    return point3
    (
        a.x*inv,
        a.y*inv,
        a.z*inv
    );
};
```

Vector Equality

Often, you want to know if two points represent the same location in 3-D. You can use this to see if two polygons share an edge, or if two triangles are the same, for example. I'll overload the equality operator (==) to do this.

This one, at first glance, would be a no-brainer; just compare to see if the x, y, and z values match up. However, the answer is not as simple as that. This is one of many points where an important line in the sand must be drawn, a line between the wonderful land of theory and the painful land of reality.

In Theory, there is infinite precision for scalar values. The decimal value of 1/3 has a string of 3s that never ends. When you multiply two scalar numbers together, the solution is exactly the correct one. When comparing two floating-point numbers, you know (with infinite precision) whether or not the numbers are equal. When multiplying an extremely large number by an extremely small one, the result is exactly what was expected. Everything is nice, in Theory. However, right now real estate is pretty expensive over there, so you and I are going have to stay here, in Reality.

In Reality, floating pointers do not have infinite precision. Floats (32 bits) and doubles (64 bits) can only encode so much precision (around 5 and 15 base 10 places, respectively). They do not multiply nicely. If you multiply an extremely large number and an extremely small number, the solution is not the solution you might expect, due to the lack of precision. Finally, they do not handle equality too well. Due to all the imprecision floating around, two different paths of calculation that should result in the same answer can yield subtly different, although technically equal, numbers.

Note: Look on the web for programming horror stories, and you'll see that countless problems in computer programming come from assuming that floating- or fixed-point numbers will have enough precision for what you need.

So, how is this little issue fixed? In practice, the problem really can't be fixed, but it is possible to hack out a solution that works well enough. Epsilon values provide the answer. (You'll see them covered throughout the book; epsilons are used all over the place to correct for numerical imprecision.) What you do is make each point have a certain, extremely small mass, going out in each direction a value epsilon. For instance, I will be using an epsilon of 10^{-3}, or 0.001. That way, in order to see if two points are equal (or, in this case, equal enough), you test to see if the difference between them is less than or equal to epsilon. If this case is satisfied for all three coordinates, then it can safely be said the two points are equal.

Note: In case you haven't picked it up yet, getting a solution to a problem that is not necessarily correct but good enough is one of the mantras of graphics programming. There is never enough time to calculate everything the hard way; the more corners you can cut without people being able to tell, the more of an edge you'll have over your competition.

In code, this becomes:

Listing 3.9: point3 equality operator

```
// above somewhere: #define EPSILON 0.001
inline bool operator==(point3 const &a, point3 const &b)
{
    if( fabs(a.x-b.x)<EPSILON )
    {
        if( fabs(a.y-b.y)<EPSILON )
        {
            if( fabs(a.z-b.z)<EPSILON )
            {
                return true; // We passed
            }
        }
    }
    return false; // The points were not equal enough
};
```

Dot Product

The dot product (mathematically represented with the symbol •) is one of the most important operations in 3-D graphics. It is used everywhere. Everything from transformation to clipping to BSP tree traversal uses the dot product.

The mathematical definition for the dot product is this:

$$\mathbf{u} \bullet \mathbf{v} = \|\mathbf{u}\| \times \|\mathbf{v}\| \times \cos(\theta)$$

In this equation, **u** and **v** represent two vectors in 3-D. The $\|\mathbf{u}\|$ and $\|\mathbf{v}\|$ represent the lengths of the vectors, and theta (θ) represents the angle between the vectors. As you can see from the equation, the result of the dot product equation is a scalar, not a vector.

Conceptually, the dot product describes the relation between two vectors in scalar form. If one of the vectors is normalized, the dot product represents the length of the shadow that the other vector would cast, as shown in Figure 3.6.

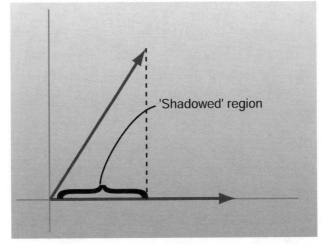

'Shadowed' region

Figure 3.6: The conceptual "shadow" the dot product produces

This particular trait is used in clipping.

Using the equation given above, you can rearrange the terms to provide a way to find the angle theta between two vectors:

$$\cos(\theta) = \frac{\mathbf{u} \bullet \mathbf{v}}{\|\mathbf{u}\| \times \|\mathbf{v}\|}$$

This works out very conveniently if both vectors are unit-length; two square roots (to find the vector lengths) and a division drop out of the equation and you get:

$$\theta = \cos^{-1}(\mathbf{u} \bullet \mathbf{v}) \qquad \text{(if } \mathbf{u} \text{ and } \mathbf{v} \text{ are unit-length)}$$

How does this work? This seems like a rather arbitrary trait for the dot product to have. Well, for some insight, think back to your trigonometry days. My trigonometry professor had a little pneumonic device to help remember the basic rules of trigonometry called "SOHCAHTOA". The middle three letters say that cosine is equal to the adjacent edge divided by the hypotenuse of a right triangle or:

$$\cos(\theta) = \frac{adjacent}{hypotenuse}$$

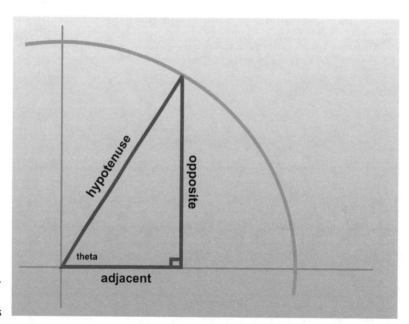

Figure 3.7:
Visual definitions of the cosine terms

Now, on a unit circle, the hypotenuse will be length 1, so that drops out of the equation. You're left with $\cos(\theta) =$ adjacent edge. Think of the adjacent edge as the shadow of the hypotenuse onto the x-axis:

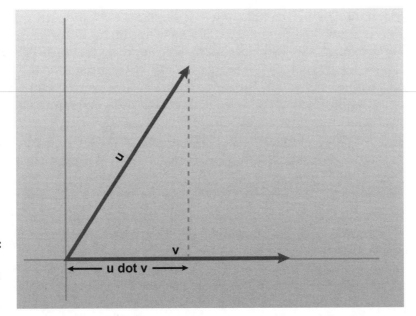

Figure 3.8: The analog to cosine in the vector world

So if, for the sake of this example, **v** is a unit vector going out along the x-axis, and **u** is a unit vector of the hypotenuse, then **u•v** will give the length of the shadow of **u** onto **v**, which is equivalent to the adjacent edge in the right triangle, and therefore $\cos(\theta)$.

The actual code behind the dot product is much simpler than the equations above, devoid of square roots, divides, and cosines (which is great, since the dot product is computed so often!). The dot product is achieved by summing the piecewise multiplication of each of the components. To implement dot products, I'm going to overload the multiplication operator *. It seems almost mysterious how three multiplications and two additions can make the same result that you get from the complex equation above, but don't look a gift horse in the mouth, as they say.

Listing 3.10: Dot product operator

```
inline float operator*(point3 const &a, point3 const &b)
{
    return a.x*b.x + a.y*b.y + a.z*b.z;
}
```

Cross Product

Another operation that can be performed between two vectors is called the cross product. It's represented mathematically with the symbol ×. The formula for computing the cross product is shown at the right:

$$\mathbf{a} \times \mathbf{b} = \begin{bmatrix} \mathbf{a}_y \mathbf{b}_z - \mathbf{a}_x \mathbf{b}_y \\ \mathbf{a}_z \mathbf{b}_x - \mathbf{a}_x \mathbf{b}_y \\ \mathbf{a}_x \mathbf{b}_y - \mathbf{a}_x \mathbf{b}_y \end{bmatrix}^T$$

The operation returns a vector, not a scalar like the dot product. The vector it returns is mutually orthogonal to both input vectors. A vector mutually orthogonal to two others means that it is perpendicular to both of them. The resultant vector from a cross product is perpendicular (or orthogonal) to both of the input vectors. Once I start discussing planes you'll see how useful they can be. For most applications of the cross product, you want the result to be unit-length.

> **Warning:** If the two input vectors in a cross-product operation are parallel, the result of the operation is undefined (as there are an infinite number of vectors that are perpendicular to one vector).

An important note is that the cross product operation is not commutative. That is, **a** cross **b** is <u>not</u> the same as **b** cross **a**. They are very similar, however, as one points in the opposite direction of the other.

Implementation time. Since the * operator is already used for the dot product, something else needs to be picked instead. The choice of operator is fairly arbitrary, but following the example of a former professor of mine named David Baraff (who's now working at Pixar), I use the XOR operator ^. The code, while not the most intuitive thing in the world, follows the equations stated above.

Listing 3.11: Cross product operator

```
inline point3 operator^(point3 const &a, point3 const &b)
{
    return point3
    (
        (a.y*b.z-a.z*b.y),
        (a.z*b.x-a.x*b.z),
        (a.x*b.y-a.y*b.x)
    );
}
```

The full code that defines all the behavior for points in 3-D is found on the companion CD in the code directory for this chapter in point3.h and point3.cpp. Also included are point4.h and point4.cpp, which define four-dimensional points (you'll see these later for quaternion rotations and parametric surfaces).

Polygons

The polygon is the bread and butter of computer graphics. Rendered images would be pretty bland if you didn't have the polygon. While there are other primitives used in computer graphics (implicit surfaces, for example), just about every personal computer on the market today has hardware in it to accelerate the drawing of polygons (well, triangles actually ... but same difference), so the polygon is king.

All of the polygons dealt with here are convex. Convex polygons have no dents or pits, i.e., no internal obtuse angles. A convex polygon is much easier to rasterize, easier to clip, easier to cull, and the list goes on. While you could deal with concave polygons, the code to manage them and draw them is harder than in the convex case. It's much easier to represent concave polygons with two or more convex polygons.

Polygons (or triangles, which I'll discuss next) describe the boundary representation of an object (academic and CAD texts often use the term *b-rep* to mean this). A b-rep is simply a set of polygons that exactly define the boundary surface of an object. If the object is a cube, the b-rep is the six square polygons that make up each face.

Below are four examples of polygons. Two are convex, and two are not.

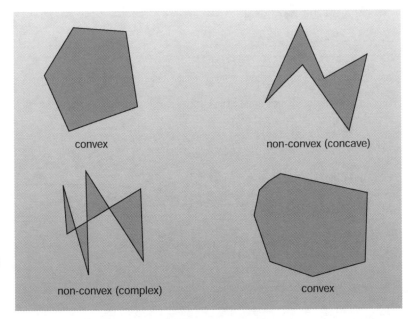

convex

non-convex (concave)

non-convex (complex)

convex

Figure 3.9: Different types of polygons

For now, I'll implement polygons with a template class. This is because I don't want to have to re-implement the class for holding indices or point data (I'll discuss what this means later). While polygons could be implemented with a fully dynamic array, like an STL vector, I chose to limit the functionality for the sake of speed. Each polygon is created with a maximum number of possible elements it can contain. For most applications, a number like 8 or 10 will suffice. In addition to this, there is the number of actual elements in the polygon. This number should never be greater than the maximum number of elements. Let's take a look at the polygon class. Listing 3.12 has the code for it.

Listing 3.12: The polygon template struct, defined in polygon.h

```
template <class type>
struct polygon
{
    int nElem; // number of elements in the polygon
    int maxElem;

    type *pList;

    polygon()
    {
        nElem = 0;
        maxElem = 0;
        pList = NULL;
    }

    polygon( int maxSize )
    {
        maxElem = maxSize;
        pList = new type[maxSize];
    }

    polygon( const polygon &in )
    {
        CloneData( in );
    }

    ~polygon()
    {
        DestroyData();
    }

    void CloneData( const polygon &in )
    {
        if( !in.pList )
            return;

        pList = new type[in.maxElem];
        maxElem = in.maxElem;
        nElem = in.nElem;
        for( int i=0; i<in.nElem; i++ )
        {
            pList[i] = in.pList[i];
        }
    }

    void DestroyData( )
    {
        delete[] pList;
        pList = NULL;
```

```
        }

    polygon& operator=( const polygon<type> &in )
    {
        if( &in != this )
        {
            DestroyData();

            CloneData( in );
        }

        return *this;
    }
};
```

Triangles

Triangles are to 3-D graphics what pixels are to 2-D graphics. Every PC hardware accelerator under the sun uses triangles as the fundamental drawing primitive (well … scan line aligned trapezoids actually, but that's a hardware implementation issue). When you draw a polygon, hardware devices really draw a fan of triangles. Triangles "flesh out" a 3-D object, connecting them together to form a skin or mesh that defines the boundary surface of an object. Triangles, like polygons, generally have an orientation associated with them, to help in normal calculations. All of the code in this book uses the convention that you are located in front of a triangle if the ordering of the vertices goes clockwise around the triangle. Figure 3.10 shows what a clockwise ordered triangle would look like.

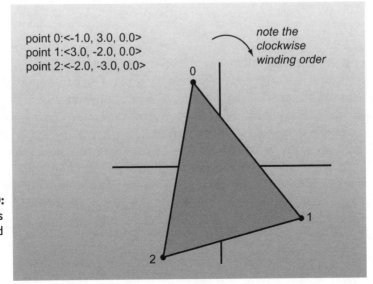

point 0:<-1.0, 3.0, 0.0>
point 1:<3.0, -2.0, 0.0>
point 2:<-2.0, -3.0, 0.0>

note the clockwise winding order

Figure 3.10: Three points in space, and the triangle connecting them

When defining a mesh of triangles that define the boundary of a solid, you set it up so that all of the triangles along the skin are ordered clockwise when viewed from the outside.

It is impossible to see triangles that face away from you (you can find this out by computing the triangle's plane normal and performing a dot product with a vector from the camera location to a location on the plane).

On to the code. To help facilitate using the multiple types, I'll implement triangles using templates. The code is fairly simple; it uses triangles as a container class, so I only define constructors and keep the access public so accessors are not needed.

Listing 3.13: The tri template struct

```
template <class type>
struct tri
{

    type v[3]; // Array access useful in for loops

    tri()
    {
        // nothing
    }

    tri( type v0, type v1, type v2 )
    {
        v[0] = v0;
        v[1] = v1;
        v[2] = v2;
    }
};
```

Strips and Fans

Lists of triangles are generally represented in one of three ways. The first is an explicit list or array of triangles, where every three elements represent a new triangle. However, there are two additional representations, designed to save bandwidth while sending triangles to dedicated hardware to draw them. They are called *triangle strips* and *triangle fans*.

Triangle fans, conceptually, look like the folding fans you see in Asian souvenir shops. They are a list of triangles that all share a common point. The first three elements indicate the first triangle. Then each new element is combined with the first element and the current last element to form a new triangle. Note that an N-sided polygon can be represented efficiently using a triangle fan. Figure 3.11 illustrates what I'm talking about.

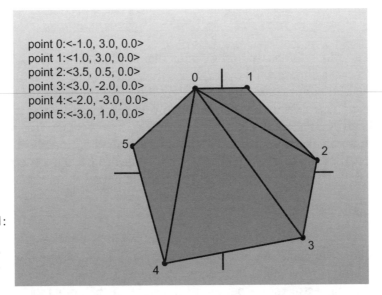

Figure 3.11:
A list of
points com-
posing a tri-
angle fan

Triangles in a triangle strip, instead of sharing a common element with all other triangles like a fan, only share elements with the triangle immediately preceding them. The first three elements define the first triangle. Then each subsequent element is combined with the two elements before it, in clockwise order, to create a new triangle. See Figure 3.12 for an explanation of strips.

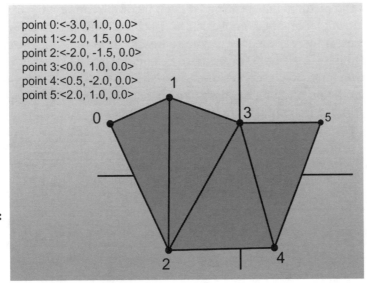

Figure 3.12:
A list of
points com-
posing a tri-
angle strip

Planes

The next primitive to discuss is the plane. Planes are to 3-D what lines are in 2-D; they're n–1 dimensional hyperplanes that can help you accomplish various tasks. Planes are defined as infinitely large, infinitely thin slices of space, like big pieces of paper. Triangles that make up your model each exist in their own plane. When you have a plane that represents a slice of 3-D space, you can perform operations like classification of points and polygons and clipping.

So how do you represent planes? Well it is best to build a structure from the equation that defines a plane in 3-D. The implicit equation for a plane is:

$$ax + by + cz + d = 0$$

What do these numbers represent? The triplet $<a,b,c>$ represents what is called the normal of the plane. A *normal* is a unit vector that, conceptually speaking, sticks directly out of a plane. A stronger mathematical definition would be that the normal is a vector that is perpendicular to all of the points that lie in the plane.

The d component in the equation represents the distance from the plane to the origin. The distance is computed by tracing a line towards the plane until you hit it. Finally the triplet $<x,y,z>$ is any point that satisfies the equation. The set of all points $<x,y,z>$ that solve the equation is exactly all the points that lie in the plane.

All of the pictures I'm showing you will be of the top-down variety, and the 3-D planes will be on edge, appearing as 2-D lines. This makes figure drawing much easier; if there is an easy way to represent infinite 3-D planes in 2-D, I sure don't know it. (If only Q was here, he could tell me.)

Following are two examples of planes. The first has the normal pointing away from the origin, which causes d to be negative (try some sample values for yourself if this doesn't make sense). The second has the normal pointing towards the origin, so d is positive. Of course, if the plane goes through the origin, d is zero (the distance from the plane to the origin is zero). Figure 3.13 and Figure 3.14 provide some insight into this relation.

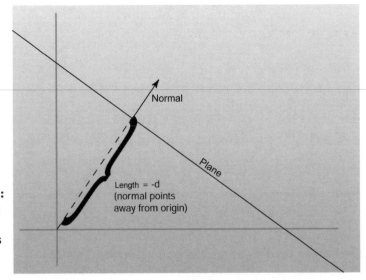

Figure 3.13:
d is negative
when the
normal faces
towards the
origin

Normal

Plane

Length = -d
(normal points
away from origin)

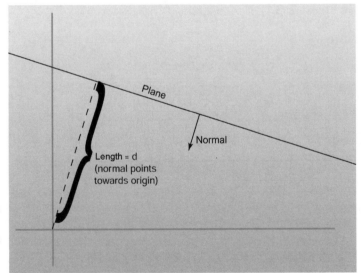

Figure 3.14:
d is positive
when it faces
away from
the origin

Plane

Normal

Length = d
(normal points
towards origin)

It's important to notice that technically the normal $<a,b,c>$ does not have to be unit-length for it to have a valid plane equation. But since things end up nicer if the normal is unit-length, all of the normals in this text are unit-length.

The basic plane3 structure is defined in Listing 3.14.

Listing 3.14: The plane3 structure

```
struct plane3 {

    point3 n; // Normal of the plane
    float d;  // Distance along the normal to the origin
```

```
        plane3( float nX, float nY, float nZ, float D) :
            n( nX, nY, nZ ), d( D )
        {
            // All done.
        }
        plane3( const point3& N, float D) :
            n( N ), d( D )
        {
            // All done.
        }

        // Construct a plane from three 3-D points
        plane3( const point3& a, const point3& b, const point3& c);

        // Construct a plane from a normal direction and
        // a point on the plane
        plane3( const point3& norm, const point3& loc);

        // Construct a plane from a polygon
        plane3( const polygon<point3>& poly );

        plane3()
        {
            // Do nothing
        }

        // Flip the orientation of the plane
        void Flip();
};
```

Constructing a plane given three points that lie in the plane is a simple task. You just perform a cross product between the two vectors made up by the three points (<point 2 – point 0> and <point 1 – point 0>) to find a normal for the plane. After generating the normal and making it unit length, finding the *d* value for the plane is just a matter of storing the negative dot product of the normal with any of the points. This holds because it essentially solves the plane equation above for *d*. Of course plugging a point in the plane equation will make it equal 0, and this constructor has three of them. Listing 3.15 has the code to construct a plane from three points.

Listing 3.15: Constructing a plane from three points on the plane

```
inline plane3::plane3(
    const point3& a,
    const point3& b,
    const point3& c )
{
    n = (b-a)^(c-a);
    n.Normalize();
```

```
        d = -(n*a);
    }
```

If you already have a normal, and also have a point on the plane, the first step can be skipped. See Listing 3.16.

Listing 3.16: Constructing a plane from a normal and a point on the plane

```
inline plane3::plane3( const point3& norm, const point3& loc) :
    n( norm ), d( -(norm*loc) )
{
    // all done
}
```

Finally, constructing a plane given a polygon of point3 elements is just a matter of taking three of the points and using the constructor given above. Listing 3.17 shows what I'm talking about.

Listing 3.17: Constructing a plane given a polygon<point3> structure

```
inline plane3::plane3( const polygon<point3>& poly )
{
    point3 a = poly.pList[0];
    point3 b = poly.pList[1];
    point3 c = poly.pList[2];

    n = (b-a)^(c-a);
    n.Normalize();
    d = -(n*a);
}
```

This brings up an important point. If you have an *n*-sided polygon, nothing discussed up to this point is forcing all of the points to be coplanar. Problems can crop up if some of the points in the polygon aren't coplanar. For example, when I discuss back-face culling in a moment, you may misidentify what is actually behind the polygon, since there won't be a plane that clearly defines what is in front of and what is behind the plane. That is one of the advantages of using triangles to represent geometry—three points define a plane exactly.

Defining Locality with Relation to a Plane

One of the most important operations planes let you perform is defining the location of a point with respect to a plane. If you drop a point into the equation, it can be classified into three cases: in front of the plane, in back of the plane, or coplanar with the plane. Front is defined as the side of the plane the normal sticks out of.

Here, once again, precision will rear its ugly head. Instead of doing things the theoretical way, having the planes infinitely thin, I'm going to give them a certain thickness of (you guessed it) epsilon.

How do you orient a point in relation to a plane? Well, simply plug x, y, and z into the equation, and see what you get on the right side. If you get zero (or a number close enough to zero by plus or minus epsilon), then the point satisfied the equation and lies on the plane. Points like this can be called coplanar. If the number is greater than zero, then you know that you would have to travel farther along the origin following the path of the normal than you would need to go to reach the plane, so the point must be in front of the plane. If the number is negative, it must be behind the plane. Note that the first three terms of the equation simplify to the dot product of the input vector and the plane normal. Figure 3.15 has a visual representation of this operation, and Listing 3.18 has the code for it.

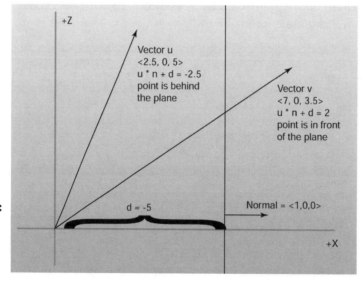

Figure 3.15: Classifying points with respect to a plane

Listing 3.18: plane3::TestPoint

```
// Defines the three possible locations of a point in
// relation to a plane
enum ePointLoc
{
    ptFront,
    ptBack,
    ptCoplanar
};

// we're inlining this because we do it constantly
inline ePointLoc plane3::TestPoint( point3 const &point ) const
{
```

```
        float dp = (point * n) + d;

        if(dp > EPSILON)
        {
            return ptFront;
        }
        if(dp < -EPSILON )
        {
            return ptBack;
        }
        return ptCoplanar; // it was between EP and -EP
}
```

Once you have code to classify a point, classifying other primitives, like polygons, becomes pretty trivial, as shown in Listing 3.19. The one issue is there are now four possible definition states when the element being tested isn't infinitesimally small. The element may be entirely in front of the plane, entirely in back, or perfectly coplanar. It may also be partially in front and partially in back. I'll refer to this state as *splitting* the plane. It's just a term; the element isn't actually splitting anything.

Listing 3.19: Polygon classification code

```
// Defines the four possible locations of a point list in
// relation to a plane. A point list is a more general
// example of a polygon.
enum ePListLoc
{
    plistFront,
    plistBack,
    plistSplit,
    plistCoplanar
};

ePListLoc plane3::TestPList( point3 *list, int num ) const
{
    bool allfront=true, allback=true;

    ePointLoc res;

    for( int i=0; i<num; i++ )
    {
        res = TestPoint( list[i] );

        if( res == ptBack )
        {
            allfront = false;
        }
        else if( res == ptFront )
        {
```

```
            allback = false;
        }
    }
    if( allfront && !allback )
    {
        // All the points were either in front or coplanar
        return plistFront;
    }
    else if( !allfront && allback )
    {
        // All the points were either in back or coplanar
        return plistBack;
    }
    else if( !allfront && !allback )
    {
        // Some were in front, some were in back
        return plistSplit;
    }
    // All were coplanar
    return plistCoplanar;
}
```

Back-face Culling

Now that you know how to define a point with respect to a plane, you can perform back-face culling, one of the most fundamental optimization techniques of 3-D graphics.

Let's suppose you have a triangle whose elements are ordered in such a fashion that when viewing the triangle from the front, the elements appear in clockwise order. Back-face culling allows you to take triangles defined with this method and use the plane equation to discard triangles that are facing away. Conceptually, any closed mesh, a cube for example, will have some triangles facing you and some facing away. You know for a fact that you'll never be able to see a polygon that faces away from you; they are always hidden by triangles facing towards you. This, of course, doesn't hold if you're allowed to view the cube from its inside, but this shouldn't be allowed to happen if you want to really optimize your engine.

Rather than perform the work necessary to draw all of the triangles on the screen, you can use the plane equation to find out if a triangle is facing towards the camera, and discard it if it is not. How is this achieved? Given the three points of the triangle, you can define a plane that the triangle sits in. Since you know the elements of the triangle are listed in clockwise order, you also know that if you pass the elements in order to the plane constructor, the normal to the plane will be on the front side of the triangle. If you then think of the location of the camera as a point, all you need to do is perform a point-plane test. If the point of the camera is in front of the plane, then the triangle is visible and should be drawn.

There's an optimization to be had. Since you know three points that lie in the plane (the three points of the triangle) you only need to hold onto the normal of the plane, not the entire plane equation. To perform the back-face cull, just subtract one of the triangle's points from the camera location, and perform a dot product with the resultant vector and the normal. If the result of the dot product is greater than zero, then the view point was in front of the triangle. Figure 3.16 can help explain the point.

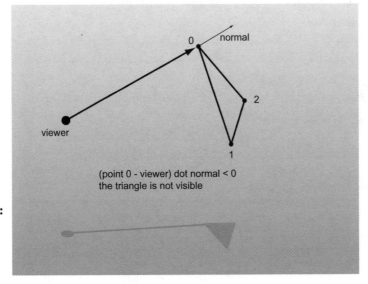

Figure 3.16:
A visual example of back-face culling

In practice, 3-D accelerators can actually perform back-face culling by themselves, so as the triangle rates of cards increase, the amount of manual back-face culling that is performed has steadily decreased. However, the information is useful for custom 3-D engines that don't plan on using the facilities of Direct3D.

Clipping Lines

One thing that you'll need is the ability to take two points (**a** and **b**) that are on different sides of a plane defining a line segment, and find the point making the intersection of the line with the plane.

This is easy enough to do. Think of this parametrically. Point **a** can be thought of as the point at time 0 and point **b** as the line at point a at time 1, and the point of intersection is somewhere between there, the number you want to find.

Take the dot product of **a** and **b**. Using them and the inverse of the plane's *d* parameter, you can find the scale value (which is a value between 0 and 1 that defines the parametric location of the particle when it intersects the plane). Armed with that, you just use the scale value, plugging it into the linear parametric equation to find the intersection location. Figure 3.17 shows this happening visually, and Listing 3.20 has the code.

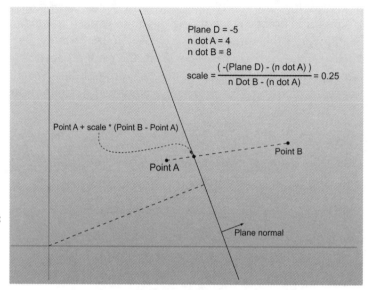

Figure 3.17:
Finding the
intersection
of a plane
and a line

Listing 3.20: plane3::Split

```
inline const point3 plane3::Split( const point3 &a, const point3 &b ) const
{
    float aDot = (a * n);
    float bDot = (b * n);

    float scale = ( -d - aDot ) / ( bDot - aDot );

    return a + (scale * (b - a));
}
```

Clipping Polygons

With the ability to clip lines, you can now also clip polygons. Clipping polygons against planes is a common operation. You take a plane and a polygon, and want to get a polygon in return that represents only the part of the input polygon that sits in front of the plane. Conceptually, you can think of the plane slicing off the part of the polygon that is behind it.

Clipping polygons is used principally in clipping. If a polygon is sitting in a position such that when it was drawn it would be partially on screen and partially off screen, you want to clip the polygon such that you only draw the part of the polygon that would be sitting on the screen. Trying to draw primitives that aren't in the view can wreak havoc in many programs. Figure 3.18 shows the dilemma.

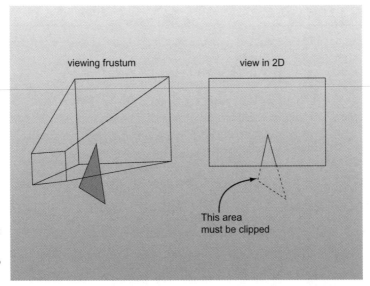

Figure 3.18:
A polygon that needs to be clipped

To implement polygon clipping, I'll use the Sutherland-Hodgeman polygon clipping algorithm, discussed in section 3.14.1 of *Computer Graphics: Principles and Practice, Second Edition in C* by James Foley et al.

The algorithm is fairly straightforward. In a clockwise fashion, you wind all the way around the polygon, considering each adjacent pair of points. If the first point is on the front side of the plane (found using a plane to point classification call), you add it to the end of the outgoing polygon (it starts out empty). If the first and second vertices are on different sides, find the split point, and add that to the list. While it may not intuitively seem obvious, the algorithm does work. The visual steps of it working appear in Figure 3.19. Listing 3.21 has code to perform the task. The function returns true if the clipped polygon is not degenerate (has three or more vertices).

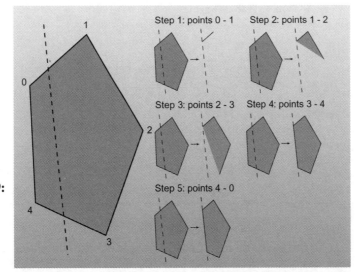

Figure 3.19:
Clipping using the Sutherland-Hodgeman algorithm

Listing 3.21: plane3::Clip

```cpp
bool plane3::Clip( const polygon<point3> &in, polygon<point3> *out ) const
{
    // Make sure our pointer to the out polygon is valid
    assert( out );
    // Make sure we're not passed a degenerate polygon
    assert( in.nElem > 2 );

    int thisInd=in.nElem-1;
    int nextInd=0;

    ePointLoc thisRes = TestPoint( in.pList[thisInd] );
    ePointLoc nextRes;

    out->nElem = 0;

    for( nextInd=0; nextInd<in.nElem; nextInd++ )
    {

        nextRes = TestPoint( in.pList[nextInd] );

        if( thisRes == ptFront || thisRes == ptCoplanar )
        {
            // Add the point
            out->pList[out->nElem++] = in.pList[thisInd];
        }

        if( ( thisRes == ptBack && nextRes == ptFront ) ||
            ( thisRes == ptFront && nextRes == ptBack ) )
        {
            // Add the split point
            out->pList[out->nElem++] = Split(
                in.pList[thisInd],
                in.pList[nextInd] );
        }

        thisInd = nextInd;

        thisRes = nextRes;
    }
    if( out->nElem >= 3 )
    {
        return true;
    }
    return false;
}
```

If you have code to take a polygon and clip off the area behind a plane, then creating a function to save the area behind the plane into an additional polygon isn't too hard. The operation takes a polygon that has elements lying on both sides of a plane and splits it into two distinct pieces, one completely in front of and one completely behind the plane. The BSP code at the end of this chapter uses polygon splitting. The algorithm to do this follows directly from the clipping code, and the code is very similar.

Listing 3.22: plane3::Split

```
bool plane3::Split( polygon<point3> const &in, polygon<point3> *pFront,
                    polygon<point3> *pBack ) const
{

    // Make sure our pointer to the out polygon is valid
    assert( pFront );
    // Make sure our pointer to the out polygon is valid
    assert( pBack );
    // Make sure we're not passed a degenerate polygon
    assert( in.nElem > 2 );

    // Start with curr as the last vertex and next as 0.
    pFront->nElem = 0;
    pBack->nElem = 0;

    int thisInd=in.nElem-1;
    int nextInd=0;

    ePointLoc thisRes = TestPoint( in.pList[thisInd] );
    ePointLoc nextRes;

    for( nextInd=0; nextInd<in.nElem; nextInd++) {

        nextRes = TestPoint( in.pList[nextInd] );

        if( thisRes == ptFront )
        {
            // Add the point to the front
            pFront->pList[pFront->nElem++] = in.pList[thisInd];
        }

        if( thisRes == ptBack )
        {
            // Add the point to the back
            pBack->pList[pBack->nElem++] = in.pList[thisInd];
        }

        if( thisRes == ptCoplanar )
        {
            // Add the point to both
            pFront->pList[pFront->nElem++] = in.pList[thisInd];
            pBack->pList[pBack->nElem++] = in.pList[thisInd];
```

```
        }

        if( ( thisRes == ptBack && nextRes == ptFront ) ||
            ( thisRes == ptFront && nextRes == ptBack ) )
        {
            // Add the split point to both
            point3 split = Split(
                in.pList[thisInd],
                in.pList[nextInd] );
            pFront->pList[pFront->nElem++] = split;
            pBack->pList[pBack->nElem++] = split;
        }

        thisInd = nextInd;
        thisRes = nextRes;
    }
    if( pFront->nElem > 2 && pBack->nElem > 2 )
    {
        // Nothing ended up degenerate
        return true;
    }
    return false;
}
```

Object Representations

Now that you have polygons and triangles, you can build objects. An *object* is just a boundary representation (and a few other traits, like materials, textures, and transformation matrices). Representing the boundary representations of objects is one of the ways that differentiate the myriad of 3-D engines out there. There are many different ways to represent polygon data, each with its own advantages and disadvantages.

A big concern is that triangles and polygons need more information than just position if anything interesting is going to be drawn. Typically, the points that make up the triangle faces of an object are called *vertices*, to differentiate them from points or vectors. Vertices can have many different types of data in them besides position, from normal information for smooth shading, to texture coordinates for texture mapping, to diffuse and specular color information. I'll visit this point in Chapter 6 when I start showing you how to make 3-D objects, but for right now keep in mind that the models will be more complex than just a list of points connecting a bunch of triangles.

A naïve first approach to representing an object would be to explicitly list each triangle as a triplet of vertices. This method is bad for several reasons. The big reason is that generally the objects are made up of a closed mesh of triangles. They meet up and touch each other; each vertex is the meeting point of two or more triangles. While a cube actually has only eight vertices, this method would need three distinct vertices for each of the 12 triangles, a total of 36 vertices. Any amount of work to do per-vertex would have to be done four times more than if you had a representation with only eight vertices. Because of this downfall, this method isn't used terribly often.

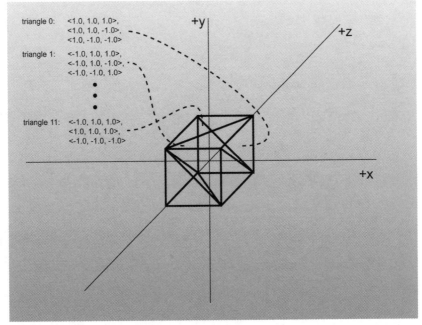

Figure 3.20: Example of an object made up of distinct triangles

However, it isn't without its advantages. For example, if the triangles are all distinct entities, you can do some neat effects, such as having the triangles fly off in separate directions when the object explodes (the game *MDK* did a good job with this; at the end of each level the world broke up into its component triangles and flew up into the sky).

Another big advantage that this method has is it allows triangles that share vertex locations to have different color/texture/normal information. For example, if you have the eight-vertex cube, where each vertex had a position and a color, all the triangles that share each corner have the same color information for that corner. If you want each face of the cube to have a different color, you can use explicit vertices for each triangle.

Note: A better way to do this would be to only have explicit copies of the color information and just use one vector. However, this style of object representation doesn't work well with Direct3D.

If you don't need distinct information for each triangle, there is a much better way to represent the objects. There are two lists: one list of vertices representing all of the vertices in the object and one list of triangles, where each triangle is a triplet of integers, not points. The integers represent indices into the vertex list.

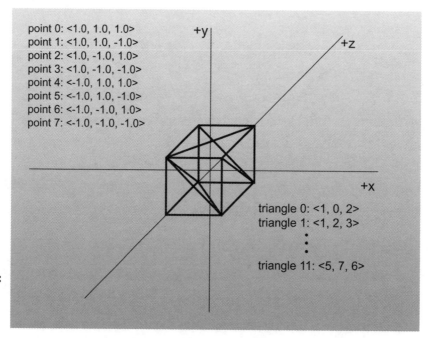

point 0: <1.0, 1.0, 1.0>
point 1: <1.0, 1.0, -1.0>
point 2: <1.0, -1.0, 1.0>
point 3: <1.0, -1.0, -1.0>
point 4: <-1.0, 1.0, 1.0>
point 5: <-1.0, 1.0, -1.0>
point 6: <-1.0, -1.0, 1.0>
point 7: <-1.0, -1.0, -1.0>

triangle 0: <1, 0, 2>
triangle 1: <1, 2, 3>
.
.
.
triangle 11: <5, 7, 6>

Figure 3.21:
Index-based object definition

This is the method used by many 3-D applications, and the method most preferred by Direct3D. In Chapter 6, I'll create a format to represent objects of this type, and provide code both to load objects from disk and draw them.

These aren't the only two horses in town. In Chapter 7, I'll talk about objects where vertices need to know adjacency information (that is, which other vertices are connected to it by triangle edges). There are even more esoteric systems, like the quad-edge data structure, whose data structures barely resemble objects at all, essentially being a pure graph of nodes and edges (nodes represent vertices; triangles are represented by loops in the graph).

Transformations

Now that there are objects in the world, it would be good to be able to move them around the scene: animate them, spin them, and so forth. To do this you need to define a set of transformations that act upon the points in the objects. I'll start out simple: translation.

To move an object by a given vector **p**, all you need to do is add **p** to each of the points in the object. The translation transformation can be defined by a vector **p** as T(**p**). The translation transformation is inverted easily. The transformation T⁻¹(**p**) that undoes T(**p**) is just T(−**p**), in essence subtracting **p** from each point in the object.

Unfortunately, translation isn't terribly interesting. It is also important to be able to rotate the objects around arbitrary points and axes as well as translating them. The next thing to do is add rotation transformations. Before doing that, however, I need to talk a little about matrices.

Matrices

A matrix is really just a shorthand way to write a set of simultaneous equations. For example, let's say you're trying to solve x, y, and z that satisfy the following three equations:

$$3x - 8y + 12z = 0$$
$$15x + 14y - 2z = 0$$
$$32x + 0.5y - z = 0$$

First, put all the coefficients of the equations into an *n* by *m* box called a *matrix*, where *n* (the vertical dimension) is the number of equations and *m* (the horizontal dimension) is the number of coefficients:

$$
\begin{matrix} 3x - 8y + 12z \\ 15x + 14y - 2z \\ 32x + 0.5y - z \end{matrix} \Rightarrow
\begin{bmatrix} 3 & -8 & 12 \\ 15 & 14 & -2 \\ 32 & 0.5 & 1 \end{bmatrix}
$$

Here's a 3x4 matrix:

$$
\begin{bmatrix}
a_{11} & a_{12} & a_{13} & a_{14} \\
a_{21} & a_{22} & a_{23} & a_{24} \\
a_{31} & a_{32} & a_{33} & a_{34}
\end{bmatrix}
$$

The subscript notation used above is how to reference individual elements of a matrix. The first component is the row number, and the second component is the column number.

Matrices can be added together simply by adding each component. However, the matrices must be the same size to be able to add them (you couldn't, for example, add a 3x3 and a 2x2 matrix together).

$$
\begin{bmatrix} a_{11} & a_{12} \\ a_{21} & a_{22} \end{bmatrix} +
\begin{bmatrix} b_{11} & b_{12} \\ b_{21} & b_{22} \end{bmatrix} =
\begin{bmatrix} a_{11} + b_{11} & a_{12} + b_{12} \\ a_{21} + b_{21} & a_{22} + b_{22} \end{bmatrix}
$$

Multiplying matrices together is a bit more involved. To find **AB**=**C**, each component c_{ij} of the resultant matrix is found by computing the dot product of the ith row of **A** with the jth column of **B**. The rules for matrix sizes are different than that in addition. If **A** is m by n and **B** is o by p, the multiplication is only valid if $n = o$, and the dimension of the resultant matrix is m by p. Note that multiplication only is valid if the row length of matrix **A** is the same as the column length of matrix **B**.

$$\begin{bmatrix} a_{11} & a_{12} \\ a_{21} & a_{22} \end{bmatrix} \begin{bmatrix} b_{11} & b_{12} \\ b_{21} & b_{22} \end{bmatrix} = \begin{bmatrix} a_{11}b_{11} + a_{12}b_{21} & a_{11}b_{12} + a_{12}b_{22} \\ a_{21}b_{11} + a_{22}b_{21} & a_{21}b_{12} + a_{22}b_{22} \end{bmatrix}$$

Another example (3x3 times 3x1 yields 3x1):

$$\begin{bmatrix} a_{11} & a_{12} & a_{13} \\ a_{21} & a_{22} & a_{23} \\ a_{31} & a_{32} & a_{33} \end{bmatrix} \begin{bmatrix} b_{11} \\ b_{21} \\ b_{31} \end{bmatrix} = \begin{bmatrix} a_{11}b_{11} + a_{12}b_{21} + a_{13}b_{31} \\ a_{21}b_{11} + a_{22}b_{21} + a_{23}b_{31} \\ a_{31}b_{11} + a_{32}b_{21} + a_{33}b_{31} \end{bmatrix}$$

This way it is easy to represent the problem above of trying to solve a matrix equation. If you multiply out the matrices below into three simultaneous equations, you'll get the same three above.

$$\begin{bmatrix} 3 & -8 & 12 \\ 15 & 14 & -2 \\ 32 & 0.5 & 1 \end{bmatrix} \begin{bmatrix} x \\ y \\ z \end{bmatrix} = \begin{bmatrix} 0 \\ 0 \\ 0 \end{bmatrix}$$

Warning: Note that multiplication is not commutative. That is, **AB** is not the same as **BA**.

Matrix multiplication has an identity value, just like scalar multiplication (which has an identity of 1). The identity is only defined for square matrices, however. It is defined as a zeroed-out matrix with ones running down the diagonal. Here is the 3x3 identity matrix $\mathbf{I}_3$:

$$\mathbf{I}_3 = \begin{bmatrix} 1 & 0 & 0 \\ 0 & 1 & 0 \\ 0 & 0 & 1 \end{bmatrix}$$

Matrix multiplication also has the law of associativity going for it. That means that as long as you preserve left-to-right order, you can multiply matrix pairs together in any order:

$$ABCD = A(BC)D = (AB)(CD) = (((AB)C)D)$$

This will come into play later; right now just keep it in the back of your head.

What does all this have to do with anything? Very good question. Matrices can be used to represent transformations, specifically rotations. You can represent rotations with 3x3 matrices and points as 1x3 matrices, multiplying them together to get transformed vertices.

$$\mathbf{vA = v'}$$

$$\begin{bmatrix} x & y & z \end{bmatrix} \begin{bmatrix} a_{11} & a_{12} & a_{13} \\ a_{21} & a_{22} & a_{23} \\ a_{31} & a_{32} & a_{33} \end{bmatrix} = \begin{bmatrix} x' & y' & z' \end{bmatrix}$$

There are three standard matrices to facilitate rotations about the x, y, and z axes by some angle theta. They are:

$$R_x(\theta) = \begin{bmatrix} 1 & 0 & 0 \\ 0 & \cos(\theta) & \sin(\theta) \\ 0 & -\sin(\theta) & \cos(\theta) \end{bmatrix}$$

$$R_y(\theta) = \begin{bmatrix} \cos(\theta) & 0 & -\sin(\theta) \\ 0 & 1 & 0 \\ \sin(\theta) & 0 & \cos(\theta) \end{bmatrix}$$

$$R_z(\theta) = \begin{bmatrix} \cos(\theta) & \sin(\theta) & 0 \\ -\sin(\theta) & \cos(\theta) & 0 \\ 0 & 0 & 1 \end{bmatrix}$$

To show this happening, let's manually rotate the point <2,0,0> 45 degrees clockwise about the z axis.

$$v' = R_z(45)v$$

$$v' = \begin{bmatrix} 0.707 & 0.707 & 0 \\ -0.707 & 0.707 & 0 \\ 0 & 0 & 1 \end{bmatrix} \times \begin{bmatrix} 2 \\ 0 \\ 0 \end{bmatrix}$$

$$v' = \begin{bmatrix} 2 \times 0.707 + 0 \times 0.707 + 0 \times 0 \\ 2 \times -0.707 + 0 \times 0.707 + 0 \times 0 \\ 2 \times 0 + 0 \times 0 + 0 \times 0 \end{bmatrix}$$

$$v' = \begin{bmatrix} 1.414 \\ -1.414 \\ 0 \end{bmatrix}$$

Now you can take an object and apply a sequence of transformations to it to make it do whatever you want. All you need to do is figure out the sequence of transformations needed, and then apply the sequence to each of the points in the model.

As an example, let's say you want to rotate an object sitting at a certain point p around its z axis. You would perform the following sequence of transformations to achieve this:

$$v = vT(-p)$$

$$v = vR_z\left(\frac{\pi}{2}\right)$$

$$v = vT(p)$$

The first transformation moves a point such that it is situated about the world origin instead of being situated about the point p. The next one rotates it (remember, you can only rotate about the origin, not arbitrary points in space). Finally, after the point is rotated, you want to move it back so that it is situated about p. The final translation accomplishes this.

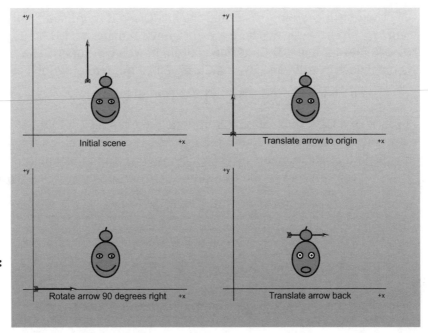

Figure 3.22:
Visualizing compound transformations

Notice the difference between a rotation followed by a translation and a translation followed by a rotation.

You would be set now, except for one small problem: Doing things this way is kind of slow. There may be dozens of transformations to perform on an object, and if the object has thousands of points, that is dozens of thousands of transformations that need to be trudged through.

The nice thing about matrices is that they can be concatenated together before they are multiplied by points. If there are two rotations, A and B, you know from the associativity law:

$$\mathbf{v}' = (\mathbf{v}\mathbf{A})\mathbf{B} \Rightarrow \mathbf{v}' = \mathbf{v}(\mathbf{A}\mathbf{B})$$

So before multiplying each of the points by both rotation transformations, you multiply them together into one matrix that represents both rotations, and just multiply the points by the new matrix. If you could also represent translations as matrices, you could concatenate the entire string of matrices together into one big matrix, cutting down on the transformation work quite a bit.

There's a problem: 3x3 matrices can't encode translation. A translation is just an addition by another vector, and because of the semantics of matrix multiplication, you just can't make a 3x3 matrix that adds a vector to an input one.

The way the graphics, robotics, mathematics, and physics communities have solved this problem is to introduce a fourth component to the vectors and an added dimension to the matrices, making them 4x4.

The fourth coordinate is called the *homogenous coordinate*, and is represented with the letter w. There are an infinite number of 4-D homogenous coordinates for any 3-D Cartesian coordinate you can supply. The space of homogenous coordinates given a Cartesian coordinate is defined as this:

$$\begin{bmatrix} x & y & z \end{bmatrix} \Rightarrow \begin{bmatrix} bx & by & bz & b \end{bmatrix} \qquad \text{(for all b != 0)}$$

To reclaim a Cartesian coordinate from a homogenous coordinate, just make sure the w component is 1, and then get the x, y, and z values. If w isn't 1, then divide all four components by w (removing the b from the equation).

Now you can change the translation transformation to a 4x4 matrix:

$$T(\mathbf{p}) = \begin{bmatrix} 1 & 0 & 0 & 0 \\ 0 & 1 & 0 & 0 \\ 0 & 0 & 1 & 0 \\ \mathbf{p}_x & \mathbf{p}_y & \mathbf{p}_z & 1 \end{bmatrix}$$

Note that multiplication by this matrix has the desired behavior:

$$\begin{bmatrix} x & y & z & 1 \end{bmatrix} \begin{bmatrix} 1 & 0 & 0 & 0 \\ 0 & 1 & 0 & 0 \\ 0 & 0 & 1 & 0 \\ \mathbf{p}_x & \mathbf{p}_y & \mathbf{p}_z & 1 \end{bmatrix} = \begin{bmatrix} x + \mathbf{p}_x & y + \mathbf{p}_y & z + \mathbf{p}_z & 1 \end{bmatrix}$$

The identity and rotation matrices change too, to reflect the added dimension:

$$\mathbf{I}_4 = \begin{bmatrix} 1 & 0 & 0 & 0 \\ 0 & 1 & 0 & 0 \\ 0 & 0 & 1 & 0 \\ 0 & 0 & 0 & 1 \end{bmatrix}$$

$$R_x(\theta) = \begin{bmatrix} 1 & 0 & 0 & 0 \\ 0 & \cos(\theta) & \sin(\theta) & 0 \\ 0 & -\sin(\theta) & \cos(\theta) & 0 \\ 0 & 0 & 0 & 1 \end{bmatrix}$$

$$R_y(\theta) = \begin{bmatrix} \cos(\theta) & 0 & -\sin(\theta) & 0 \\ 0 & 1 & 0 & 0 \\ \sin(\theta) & 0 & \cos(\theta) & 0 \\ 0 & 0 & 0 & 1 \end{bmatrix}$$

$$R_z(\theta) = \begin{bmatrix} \cos(\theta) & \sin(\theta) & 0 & 0 \\ -\sin(\theta) & \cos(\theta) & 0 & 0 \\ 0 & 0 & 1 & 0 \\ 0 & 0 & 0 & 1 \end{bmatrix}$$

Now that know how to represent all of the transformations with matrices, you can concatenate them together, saving a load of time and space. This also changes the way you might think about transformations. Each object defines all of its points with respect to a local coordinate system, with the origin representing the center of rotation for the object. Each object also has a matrix, which transforms the points from the local origin to some location in the world. When the object is moved, the matrix can be manipulated to move the points to a different location in the world.

To understand what is going on here, you need to modify the way you perceive matrix transformations. Rather than translate or rotate, they actually become maps from one coordinate space to another. The object is defined in one coordinate space (which is generally called the object's *local coordinate space*), and the object's matrix maps all of the points to a new location in another coordinate space, which is generally the coordinate space for the entire world (generally called the *world coordinate space*).

A nice feature of matrices is that it's easy to see where the matrix that transforms from object space to world space is sitting in the world. If you look at the data the right way, you can actually see where the object axes get mapped into the world space.

Consider four vectors, called **n**, **o**, **a**, and **p**. The **p** vector represents the location of the object coordinate space with relation to the world origin. The **n**, **o**, and **a** vectors represent the orientation of the **i**, **j**, and **k** vectors, respectively.

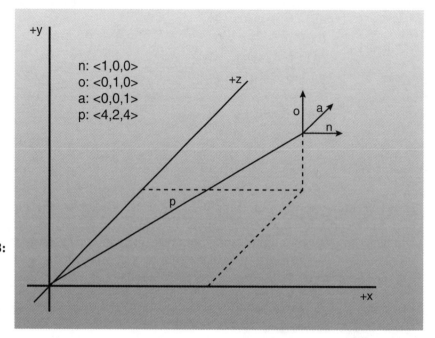

Figure 3.23:
The n, o, a, and p vectors for a transformation

You can get and set these vectors right in the matrix, as they are sitting there in plain sight:

$$\begin{bmatrix} n_x & n_y & n_z & 0 \\ o_x & o_y & o_z & 0 \\ a_x & a_y & a_z & 0 \\ p_x & p_y & p_z & 1 \end{bmatrix}$$

This system of matrix concatenations is how almost all 3-D applications perform their transformations. There are four spaces that points can live in: object space, world space, and two new spaces: view space and screen space.

View space defines how images on the screen are displayed. Think of it as a camera. If you move the camera around the scene, the view will change. You see what is in front of the camera (in front is defined as positive z).

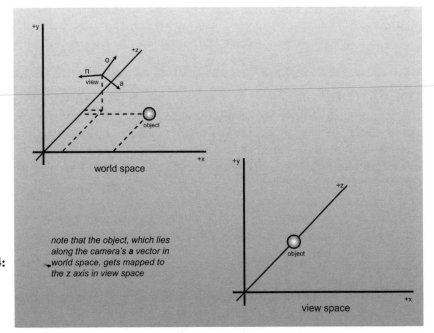

Figure 3.24: Mapping from world space to view space

The transformation here is different than the one used to move from object space to world space. Now, while the camera is defined with the same **n**, **o**, **a**, and **p** vectors as defined with the other transforms, the matrix itself is different.

In fact, the view matrix is the inversion of what the object matrix for that position and orientation would be. This is because you're performing a backward transformation: taking points once they're in world space and putting them into a local coordinate space.

As long as you compose the transformations of just rotations and translations (and reflections, by the way, but that comes into play much later in the book), computing the inverse of a transformation is easy. Otherwise, computing an inverse is considerably more difficult and may not even be possible. The inverse of a transformation matrix is given below.

$$
\begin{bmatrix}
n_x & n_y & n_z & 0 \\
o_x & o_y & o_z & 0 \\
a_x & a_y & a_z & 0 \\
p_x & p_y & p_z & 1
\end{bmatrix}^{-1}
=
\begin{bmatrix}
n_x & o_x & a_x & 0 \\
n_y & o_y & a_y & 0 \\
n_z & o_z & a_z & 0 \\
-(p \bullet n) & -(p \bullet o) & -(p \bullet a) & 1
\end{bmatrix}
$$

Warning: This formula for inversion is not universal for all matrices. In fact, the only matrices that can be inverted this way are ones composed exclusively of rotations, reflections, and translations.

There is a final transformation that the points must go through in the transformation process. This transformation maps 3-D points defined with respect to the view origin (in view space) and turns them into 2-D points that can be drawn on the display. After transforming and clipping the polygons that make up the scene such that they are visible on the screen, the final step is to move them into 2-D coordinates, since in order to actually draw things on the screen you need to have absolute x,y coordinates on the screen to draw.

The way this used to be done was without matrices, just as an explicit projection calculation. The point $<x,y,z>$ would be mapped to $<x',y'>$ using the following equations:

$$x' = scale\frac{x}{z} + xCenter$$

$$y' = height - (scale\frac{y}{z} + yCenter)$$

where xCenter and yCenter were half of the width and height of the screen, respectively. These days more complex equations are used, especially since there is now the need to make provisions for z-buffering. While you want x and y to still behave the same way, you don't want to use a value as arbitrary as scale.

Instead, a better value to use in the calculation of the projection matrix is the horizontal field of view (fov). The horizontal fov will be hardcoded, and the code chooses a vertical field of view that will keep the aspect ratio of the screen. This makes sense: You couldn't get away with using the same field of view for both horizontal and vertical directions unless the screen was square; it would end up looking vertically squished.

Finally, you also want to scale the z values appropriately. In Chapter 6, I'll teach you about z-buffering, but for right now just make note of an important feature: They let you clip out certain values of z-range. Given the two variables z_{near} and z_{far}, nothing in front of z_{near} will be drawn, nor will anything behind z_{far}. To make the z-buffer work swimmingly on all ranges of z_{near} and z_{far}, you need to scale the valid z values to the range of 0.0 to 1.0.

For purposes of continuity, I'll use the same projection matrix definition that Direct3D recommends in the documentation. First, let's define some values. You initially start with the width and height of the viewport and the horizontal field of view.

$$aspect = \frac{height}{width}$$

$$w = aspect \frac{\cos(fov)}{\sin(fov)}$$

$$h = \frac{\cos(fov)}{\sin(fov)}$$

$$q = \frac{z_{far}}{z_{far} - z_{near}}$$

With these parameters, the following projection matrix can be made:

$$\begin{bmatrix} w & 0 & 0 & 0 \\ 0 & h & 0 & 0 \\ 0 & 0 & q & 1 \\ 0 & 0 & -q(z_{near}) & 0 \end{bmatrix}$$

Just for a sanity check, check out the result of this matrix multiplication:

$$\begin{bmatrix} x & y & z & 1 \end{bmatrix} \begin{bmatrix} w & 0 & 0 & 0 \\ 0 & h & 0 & 0 \\ 0 & 0 & q & 1 \\ 0 & 0 & -q(z_{near}) & 0 \end{bmatrix} = \begin{bmatrix} wx & hy & qz - q(z_{near}) & z \end{bmatrix}$$

Hmm… this is almost the result wanted, but there is more work to be done. Remember that in order to extract the Cartesian (x,y,z) coordinates from the vector, the homogenous w component must be 1.0. Since, after the multiplication, it's set to z, (which can be any value) all four components need to be divided by w to normalize it. This gives the following Cartesian coordinate:

$$\begin{bmatrix} \frac{wx}{z} & \frac{hy}{z} & q\left(1 - \frac{(z_{near})}{z}\right) & 1 \end{bmatrix}$$

As you can see, this is exactly what was wanted. The width and height are still scaled by values as in the above equation and they are still divided by z. The visible x and y pixels are mapped to $[-1,1]$, so before rasterization Direct3D multiplies and adds the number by xCenter or yCenter. This, in essence, maps the coordinates from $[-1,1]$ to $[0,width]$ and $[0,height]$.

With this last piece of the puzzle, it is now possible to create the entire transformation pipeline. When you want to render a scene, you set up a world matrix (to transform an object's local coordinate points into world space), a view matrix (to transform world coordinate points into a space relative to the viewer), and a projection matrix (to take those viewer-relative points and project them onto a 2-D surface so that they can be drawn on the screen). You then multiply the world, view, and projection matrices together (in that order) to get a total matrix that transforms points from object-space to screen-space.

$$\mathbf{v}_{world} = \mathbf{v}_{local}\mathbf{M}_{world}$$

$$\mathbf{v}_{view} = \mathbf{v}_{world}\mathbf{M}_{view}$$

$$\mathbf{v}_{screen} = \mathbf{v}_{view}\mathbf{M}_{projection}$$

$$\mathbf{v}_{screen} = \mathbf{v}_{local}\left(\mathbf{M}_{world}\mathbf{M}_{view}\mathbf{M}_{projection}\right)$$

> **Warning:** OpenGL uses a different matrix convention (where vectors are column vectors, not row vectors, and all matrices are transposed). If you're used to OpenGL, the equation above will seem backward to what you're used to. This is the convention that Direct3D uses, so to avoid confusion, it's what is used here.

To draw a triangle, for example, you would take its local-space points defining its three corners and multiply them by the transformation matrix. Then you have to remember to divide through by the *w* component and voilá! The points are now in screen space and can be filled in using a 2-D raster algorithm. Drawing multiple objects is a snap, too. For each object in the scene all you need to do is change the world matrix and reconstruct the total transformation matrix.

The matrix4 Structure

Now that all the groundwork has been laid out to handle transformations, let's actually write some code. The struct is called matrix4, because it represents 4-D homogenous transformations. Hypothetically, if you wanted to just create rotation matrices, you could do so with a class called matrix3. The definition of matrix4 appears in Listing 3.23.

Listing 3.23: The matrix4 structure

```
struct matrix4
{

    /**
     * we're using m[y][x] as our notation.
     */
```

```
union
{
    struct
    {
        float    _11, _12, _13, _14;
        float    _21, _22, _23, _24;
        float    _31, _32, _33, _34;
        float    _41, _42, _43, _44;
    };
    float    m[4][4];
};

// justification for a function this ugly:
// provides an easy way to initialize static matrix variables
// like base matrices for bezier curves and the identity
matrix4(float IN_11, float IN_12, float IN_13, float IN_14,
        float IN_21, float IN_22, float IN_23, float IN_24,
        float IN_31, float IN_32, float IN_33, float IN_34,
        float IN_41, float IN_42, float IN_43, float IN_44)
{
    _11 = IN_11; _12 = IN_12; _13 = IN_13; _14 = IN_14;
    _21 = IN_21; _22 = IN_22; _23 = IN_23; _24 = IN_24;
    _31 = IN_31; _32 = IN_32; _33 = IN_33; _34 = IN_34;
    _41 = IN_41; _42 = IN_42; _43 = IN_43; _44 = IN_44;
}

matrix4()
{
    // Do nothing.
}

static const matrix4 Identity;
};
```

The code contains three main ways to multiply matrices. Two 4x4 matrices can be multiplied together; this is useful for concatenating matrices. A point4 structure can be multiplied by a matrix4 structure; the result is the application of the transformation to the 4-D point. Finally, a specialization for multiplying point3 structures and matrix4 structures exists to apply a non-projection transformation to a point3 structure. The matrix4*matrix4 operator creates a temporary structure to hold the result, and isn't terribly fast. Matrix multiplications aren't performed often enough for this to be much of a concern, however.

> **Warning:** If you plan on doing a lot of matrix multiplications per object or even per triangle, you won't want to use the operator. Use the provided MatMult function; it's faster.

Listing 3.24: Matrix multiplication routines

```
matrix4 operator*(matrix4 const &a, matrix4 const &b)
{
    matrix4 out;       // temporary matrix4 for storing result
    for (int j = 0; j < 4; j++)       // transform by columns first
        for (int i = 0; i < 4; i++)   // then by rows
            out.m[i][j] = a.m[i][0] * b.m[0][j] +
                          a.m[i][1] * b.m[1][j] +
                          a.m[i][2] * b.m[2][j] +
                          a.m[i][3] * b.m[3][j];
    return out;
};

inline const point4 operator*( const matrix4 &a, const point4 &b)
{
    return point4(
        b.x*a._11 + b.y*a._21 + b.z*a._31 + b.w*a._41,
        b.x*a._12 + b.y*a._22 + b.z*a._32 + b.w*a._42,
        b.x*a._13 + b.y*a._23 + b.z*a._33 + b.w*a._43,
        b.x*a._14 + b.y*a._24 + b.z*a._34 + b.w*a._44
    );
};

inline const point4 operator*( const point4 &a, const matrix4 &b)
{
    return b*a;
};

inline const point3 operator*( const matrix4 &a, const point3 &b)
{
    return point3(
        b.x*a._11 + b.y*a._21 + b.z*a._31 + a._41,
        b.x*a._12 + b.y*a._22 + b.z*a._32 + a._42,
        b.x*a._13 + b.y*a._23 + b.z*a._33 + a._43
    );
};

inline const point3 operator*( const point3 &a, const matrix4 &b)
{
    return b*a;
};
```

There are two ways to create each type of matrix transformation. One performs on an existing matrix4 structure (it doesn't create a temporary matrix4 structure, which is slow). The function for a transformation *x* is void matrix4::To*x*. The other is a static function designed to help write cleaner looking code, not for speed. The format for these functions is static matrix4 matrix4::*x*.

Translation

Here again is the matrix for the translation transformation by a given point **p**:

$$
\begin{bmatrix}
1 & 0 & 0 & 0 \\
0 & 1 & 0 & 0 \\
0 & 0 & 1 & 0 \\
p_x & p_y & p_z & 1
\end{bmatrix}
$$

The code to create this type of transformation matrix appears in Listing 3.25.

Listing 3.25: Code to create a translation transformation

```
void matrix4::ToTranslation( const point3& p )
{
    MakeIdent();
    _41 = p.x;
    _42 = p.y;
    _43 = p.z;
}

matrix4 matrix4::Translation( const point3& p )
{
    matrix4 out;
    out.ToTranslation( p );
    return out;
}
```

Basic Rotations

The matrices used to rotate around the three principal axes, again, are:

$$
R_x(\theta) =
\begin{bmatrix}
1 & 0 & 0 & 0 \\
0 & \cos(\theta) & \sin(\theta) & 0 \\
0 & -\sin(\theta) & \cos(\theta) & 0 \\
0 & 0 & 0 & 1
\end{bmatrix}
$$

$$
R_y(\theta) =
\begin{bmatrix}
\cos(\theta) & 0 & -\sin(\theta) & 0 \\
0 & 1 & 0 & 0 \\
\sin(\theta) & 0 & \cos(\theta) & 0 \\
0 & 0 & 0 & 1
\end{bmatrix}
$$

$$
R_z(\theta) =
\begin{bmatrix}
\cos(\theta) & \sin(\theta) & 0 & 0 \\
-\sin(\theta) & \cos(\theta) & 0 & 0 \\
0 & 0 & 1 & 0 \\
0 & 0 & 0 & 1
\end{bmatrix}
$$

The code to set up Euler rotation matrices appears in Listing 3.26.

Listing 3.26: Code to create Euler rotation transformations

```
void matrix4::ToXRot( float theta )
{
    float c = (float) cos(theta);
    float s = (float) sin(theta);
    MakeIdent();
    _22 = c;
    _23 = s;
    _32 = -s;
    _33 = c;
}

matrix4 matrix4::XRot( float theta )
{
    matrix4 out;
    out.ToXRot( theta );
    return out;
}


//==========------------------------

void matrix4::ToYRot( float theta )
{
    float c = (float) cos(theta);
    float s = (float) sin(theta);
    MakeIdent();
    _11 = c;
    _13 = -s;
    _31 = s;
    _33 = c;
}

matrix4 matrix4::YRot( float theta )
{
    matrix4 out;
    out.ToYRot( theta );
    return out;
}


//==========------------------------

void matrix4::ToZRot( float theta )
{
    float c = (float) cos(theta);
    float s = (float) sin(theta);
    MakeIdent();
    _11 = c;
    _12 = s;
```

```
    _21 = -s;
    _22 = c;
}

matrix4 matrix4::ZRot( float theta )
{
    matrix4 out;
    out.ToZRot( theta );
    return out;
}
```

Axis-Angle Rotation

While there isn't enough space to provide a derivation of the axis-angle rotation matrix, that doesn't stop it from being cool. Axis-angle rotations are the most useful matrix-based rotation (I say matrix-based because quaternions are faster and more flexible than matrix rotations; see *Real-Time Rendering* by Tomas Moller and Eric Haines for a good discussion on them).

There are a few problems with using just Euler rotation matrices (the x-rotation, y-rotation, z-rotation matrices you've seen thus far). For starters, there really is no standard way to combine them together.

Imagine that you want to rotate an object around all three axes by three angles. In which order should the matrices be multiplied together? Should the x-rotation come first? The z-rotation? Since no answer is technically correct, usually people pick the one convention that works best and stick with it.

A worse problem is that of *gimbal lock*. To explain, look at how rotation matrices are put together. There are really two ways to use rotation matrices. Method 1 is to keep track of the current yaw, pitch, and roll rotations, and build a rotation matrix every frame. Method 2 uses the rotation matrix from the last frame, by just rotating it a small amount to represent any rotation that happened since the last frame.

The second method, while it doesn't suffer from gimbal lock, suffers from other things, namely the fact that all that matrix multiplication brings up some numerical imprecision issues. The **i**, **j**, and **k** vectors of your matrix gradually become non-unit length and not mutually perpendicular. This is a bad thing. While there are ways to fix it that are pretty standard (renormalizing the vectors, using cross-products to assure orthogonality), I can't discuss them much here.

Gimbal lock pops up when you're using the first method detailed above. Imagine that you perform a yaw rotation first, then pitch, then roll. Also, say that the yaw and pitch rotations are both a quarter-turn (this could come up quite easily in a game like *Descent*). So imagine you perform the first rotation, which takes you from pointing forward to pointing up. The second rotation spins you around the y axis 90 degrees, so you're still facing up but your up direction is now to the right, not backward.

Now comes the lock. When you go to do the roll rotation, which way will it turn you? About the z axis, of course. However, given any roll value, you can reach the same final rotation just by changing yaw or pitch. So essentially, you have lost a degree of freedom. This, as you would expect, is bad.

Axis-angle rotations fix both of these problems by doing rotations much more intuitively. You provide an axis that you want to rotate around and an angle amount to rotate around that axis. Simple. The actual matrix to do it, which appears below, isn't quite as simple, unfortunately. For sanity's sake, just treat it as a black box. See *Real-Time Rendering* (Moller and Haines) for a derivation of how this matrix is constructed.

$$\begin{bmatrix} xx(1-\cos(\theta))+\cos(\theta) & yx(1-\cos(\theta))+z\sin(\theta) & xz(1-\cos(\theta))-y\sin(\theta) & 0 \\ xy(1-\cos(\theta))-z\sin(\theta) & yy(1-\cos(\theta))+\cos(\theta) & yz(1-\cos(\theta))+x\sin(\theta) & 0 \\ xz(1-\cos(\theta))+y\sin(\theta) & yz(1-\cos(\theta))-x\sin(\theta) & zz(1-\cos(\theta))+\cos(\theta) & 0 \\ 0 & 0 & 0 & 1 \end{bmatrix}$$

Code to create an axis-angle matrix transformation appears in Listing 3.27.

Listing 3.27: Axis-angle matrix transformation code

```
void matrix4::ToAxisAngle( const point3& inAxis, float angle )
{
    point3 axis = inAxis.Normalized();
    float s = (float)sin( angle );
    float c = (float)cos( angle );
    float x = axis.x, y = axis.y, z = axis.z;

    _11 = x*x*(1-c)+c;
    _21 = x*y*(1-c)-(z*s);
    _31 = x*z*(1-c)+(y*s);
    _41 = 0;
    _12 = y*x*(1-c)+(z*s);
    _22 = y*y*(1-c)+c;
    _32 = y*z*(1-c)-(x*s);
    _42 = 0;
    _13 = z*x*(1-c)-(y*s);
    _23 = z*y*(1-c)+(x*s);
    _33 = z*z*(1-c)+c;
    _43 = 0;
    _14 = 0;
    _24 = 0;
    _34 = 0;
    _44 = 1;

}
```

```
matrix4 matrix4::AxisAngle( const point3& axis, float angle )
{
    matrix4 out;
    out.ToAxisAngle( axis, angle );
    return out;
}
```

The LookAt Matrix

I discussed before that the first three components of the first three rows (the **n**, **o**, and **a** vectors) make up the three principal axes (**i**, **j**, and **k**) of the coordinate space that the matrix represents. I am going to use this to make a matrix that represents a transformation of an object looking a particular direction. This is useful in many cases, and is most often used in controlling the camera. Usually, there is a place where the camera is and a place you want the camera to focus on. You can accomplish this using an inverted LookAt matrix (you need to invert it because the camera transformation brings points from world space to view space, not the other way around, like object matrices).

There is one restriction the LookAt matrix has. It always assumes that there is a constant up vector, and the camera orients itself to that, so there is no tilt. For the code to work, the camera cannot be looking in the same direction that the up vector points. This is because a cross product is performed with the view vector and the up vector, and if they're the same thing the behavior of the cross product is undefined. In games like *Quake III: Arena*, you can look almost straight up, but there is some infinitesimally small epsilon that prevents you from looking in the exact direction.

Three vectors are passed into the function: a location for the matrix to be, a target to look at, and the up vector (the third parameter will default to **j** <0,1,0> so you don't need to always enter it). The transformation vector for the matrix is simply the location. The **a** vector is the normalized vector representing the target minus the location (or a vector that is the direction you want the object to look in). To find the **n** vector, simply take the normalized cross product of the up vector and the direction vector. (This is why they can't be the same vector; the cross product would return garbage.) Finally, you can get the **o** vector by taking the cross product of the **n** and **a** vectors already found.

I'll show you two versions of this transformation, one to compute the matrix for an object to world transformation, and one that computes the inverse automatically. Use ObjectLookAt to make object matrices that look in certain directions, and CameraLookAt to make cameras that look in certain directions.

Listing 3.28: LookAt matrix generation code

```
void matrix4::ToObjectLookAt(
    const point3& loc,
    const point3& lookAt,
    const point3& inUp )
{

    point3 viewVec = lookAt - loc;
    float mag = viewVec.Mag();
    viewVec /= mag;

    float fDot = inUp * viewVec;
    point3 upVec = inUp - fDot * viewVec;
    upVec.Normalize();

    point3 rightVec = upVec ^ viewVec;

    // The first three rows contains the basis
    // vectors used to rotate the view to point at the lookat point
    _11 = rightVec.x;    _21 = upVec.x;    _31 = viewVec.x;
    _12 = rightVec.y;    _22 = upVec.y;    _32 = viewVec.y;
    _13 = rightVec.z;    _23 = upVec.z;    _33 = viewVec.z;

    // Do the translation values
    _41 = loc.x;
    _42 = loc.y;
    _43 = loc.z;

    _14 = 0;
    _24 = 0;
    _34 = 0;
    _44 = 1;

}

matrix4 matrix4::ObjectLookAt(
    const point3& loc,
    const point3& lookAt,
    const point3& inUp )
{
    matrix4 out;
    out.ToObjectLookAt( loc, lookAt, inUp );
    return out;
}

//================================-----------
```

```
void matrix4::ToCameraLookAt(
    const point3& loc,
    const point3& lookAt,
    const point3& inUp )
{
    point3 viewVec = lookAt - loc;
    float mag = viewVec.Mag();
    viewVec /= mag;

    float fDot = inUp * viewVec;
    point3 upVec = inUp - fDot * viewVec;
    upVec.Normalize();

    point3 rightVec = upVec ^ viewVec;

    // The first three columns contain the basis
    // vectors used to rotate the view to point
    // at the lookat point
    _11 = rightVec.x;    _12 = upVec.x;    _13 = viewVec.x;
    _21 = rightVec.y;    _22 = upVec.y;    _23 = viewVec.y;
    _31 = rightVec.z;    _32 = upVec.z;    _33 = viewVec.z;

    // Do the translation values
    _41 = - (loc * rightVec);
    _42 = - (loc * upVec);
    _43 = - (loc * viewVec);

    _14 = 0;
    _24 = 0;
    _34 = 0;
    _44 = 1;
}

matrix4 matrix4::CameraLookAt(
    const point3& loc,
    const point3& lookAt,
    const point3& inUp )
{
    matrix4 out;
    out.ToCameraLookAt( loc, lookAt, inUp );
    return out;
}
```

Perspective Projection Matrix

Creating a perspective projection matrix will be handled by the graphics layer when I add Direct3D to it in Chapter 6, using the matrix discussed earlier in the chapter.

Inverse of a Matrix

Again, the inverse of a matrix composed solely of translations, rotations, and reflections (scales such as <1,1,–1> that flip sign but don't change the length) can be computed easily. The inverse matrix looks like this:

$$
\begin{bmatrix}
n_x & n_y & n_z & 0 \\
o_x & o_y & o_z & 0 \\
a_x & a_y & a_z & 0 \\
p_x & p_y & p_z & 1
\end{bmatrix}^{-1}
=
\begin{bmatrix}
n_x & o_x & a_x & 0 \\
n_y & o_y & a_y & 0 \\
n_z & o_z & a_z & 0 \\
-(p \bullet n) & -(p \bullet o) & -(p \bullet a) & 1
\end{bmatrix}
$$

Code to perform inversion appears in Listing 3.29.

Listing 3.29: Matrix inversion code

```
void matrix4::ToInverse( const matrix4& in )
{

        // first transpose the rotation matrix
        _11 = in._11;
        _12 = in._21;
        _13 = in._31;
        _21 = in._12;
        _22 = in._22;
        _23 = in._32;
        _31 = in._13;
        _32 = in._23;
        _33 = in._33;

        // fix right column
        _14 = 0;
        _24 = 0;
        _34 = 0;
        _44 = 1;

        // now get the new translation vector
        point3 temp = in.GetLoc();

        _41 = -(temp.x * in._11 + temp.y * in._12 + temp.z * in._13);
        _42 = -(temp.x * in._21 + temp.y * in._22 + temp.z * in._23);
        _43 = -(temp.x * in._31 + temp.y * in._32 + temp.z * in._33);

}

matrix4 matrix4::Inverse( const matrix4& in )
{
```

```
        matrix4 out;
        out.ToInverse( in );
        return out;
    }
```

Collision Detection with Bounding Spheres

Up until now, when I talked about moving 3-D objects around, I did so completely oblivious to wherever they may be moving. But suppose there is a sphere slowly moving through the scene. During its journey it collides into another object (for the sake of simplicity, say another sphere). You generally want the reaction that results from the collision to be at least partially similar to what happens in the real world.

In the real world, depending on the mass of the spheres, the amount of force they absorb, the air resistance in the scene, and a slew of other factors, they will physically react to each other the moment they collide. If they were rubber balls, they may bounce off of each other. If the spheres were instead made of crazy glue, they would not bounce at all, but would become inextricably attached to each other. Physics simulation aside, you most certainly do not want to allow any object to blindly fly through another object (unless, of course, that is the effect you're trying to achieve, such as an apparition object like the ghosts in Mario Brothers games).

Correctly dealing with collisions is beyond the scope of this book. There are some references listed at the end of the chapter if you're interested in reading up on the topic of correctly handling collisions.

All I'm going to discuss here is just getting a rough idea of when a collision has occurred. Most of the time, games only have the horsepower to do very quick and dirty collision detection. Games generally use *bounding boxes* or *bounding spheres* to accomplish this; I'm going to talk about bounding spheres. They try to simplify complex graphics tasks like occlusion and collision detection.

The general idea is that instead of performing tests against possibly thousands of polygons in an object, you can simply hold on to a sphere that approximates the object, and just test against that. Testing a plane or point against a bounding sphere is a simple process, requiring only a subtraction and a vector comparison. When the results you need are approximate, using bounding objects can speed things up nicely. This gives up the ability to get exact results. Fire up just about any game and try to just miss an object with a shot. Chances are (if you're not playing something with great collision detection like *MDK*, *Goldeneye*, or *House of the Dead*) you'll hit your target anyway. Most of the time you don't even notice, so giving up exact results isn't a tremendous loss.

Even if you do need exact results, you can still use bounding objects. They allow you to perform trivial rejection. An example is in collision detection. Typically, to calculate collision detection exactly is an expensive process (it can be as bad as $O(mn)$, where m and n are the number of polygons in each object). If you have multiple objects in the scene, you need to perform collision tests between all of them, a total of $O(n^2)$ operations where n is the number of objects. This is prohibitive with a large amount of complex objects. Bounding object tests are much more manageable, typically being $O(1)$ per test.

To implement bounding spheres, I'll create a structure called bSphere3. It can be constructed from a location and a list of points (the location of the object, the object's points) or from an explicit location and radius check. Checking if two spheres intersect is a matter of calling bSphere3::Intersect with both spheres. It returns true if they intersect each other. This is only a baby step that can be taken towards good physics, mind you, but baby steps beat doing nothing!

Listing 3.30: Bounding sphere structure

```
struct bSphere3
{
    float m_radius;
    point3 m_loc;

    bSphere3(){}

    bSphere3( float radius, point3 loc ) :
        m_radius( radius ), m_loc( loc )
    {
    }

    bSphere3( point3 loc, int nVerts, point3* pList )
    {
        m_loc = loc;
        m_radius = 0.f;
        float currRad;
        for( int i=0; i< nVerts; i++ )
        {
            currRad = pList[i].Mag();
            if( currRad > m_radius )
            {
                m_radius = currRad;
            }
        }
    }

    template< class iter >
    bSphere3( point3 loc, iter& begin, iter& end )
    {
```

```
        iter i = begin;
        m_loc = loc;
        m_radius = 0.f;
        float currRad;
        while( i != end )
        {
            currRad = (*i).Mag();
            if( currRad > m_radius )
            {
                m_radius = currRad;
            }
            i++;
        }
    }

    static bool Intersect( bSphere3& a, bSphere3& b )
    {
        // avoid a square root by squaring both sides of the equation
        float magSqrd =
            (a.m_radius + b.m_radius) *
            (a.m_radius + b.m_radius);
        if( (b.m_loc - a.m_loc).MagSquared() > magSqrd )
        {
            return false;
        }
        return true;
    }
};
```

Some additional operators are defined in bSphere3.h, and plane-sphere classification code is in plane3.h as well. See the companion CD.

Lighting

Lighting your scenes is essentially a prerequisite if you want them to look realistic. Lighting is a fairly slow and complex system, especially when modeling light correctly (this doesn't happen too often). Later in the book I'll discuss some advanced lighting schemes, specifically radiosity. Advanced lighting models typically are done as a preprocessing step, as they can take several hours or even days for complex scenes. For real-time graphics you need simpler lighting models that approximate correct lighting. I'll discuss two points in this section: how to acquire the amount of light hitting a point in 3-D and how to shade a triangle with those three points.

Representing Color

Before you can go about giving color to anything in a scene, you need to know how to represent color! Usually you use the same red, green, and blue channels discussed in Chapter 2, but for this there will also be a fourth component called *alpha*. The alpha component stores transparency information about a surface. It's discussed more in detail in Chapter 8, but for right now let's plan ahead. There will be two structures to ease the color duties: color3 and color4. They both use floating-point values for their components; color3 has red, green, and blue, while color4 has the additional fourth component of alpha in there.

Colors aren't like points—they have a fixed range. Each component can be anywhere between 0.0 and 1.0 (zero contribution of the channel or complete contribution). If performing operations on colors, such as adding them together, the components may rise above 1.0 or below 0.0. Before trying to use a color, for example feeding it to Direct3D, it needs to be saturated. That is what the Sat() function does. The conversions to unsigned longs will be used in Chapter 6, when the colors start to get plugged into Direct3D.

The code for color4 appears in Listing 3.31. Some code, like the color3 structure, operators, and the constant color values, has been omitted for brevity.

Listing 3.31: The color4 structure

```
struct color4
{
    union {
        struct
        {
            float r, g, b, a; // Red, Green, and Blue color data
        };
        float c[4];
    };

    color4(){}

    color4( float inR, float inG, float inB, float inA ) :
        r( inR ), g( inG ), b( inB ), a( inA )
    {
    }

    color4( const color3& in, float alpha = 1.f )
    {
        r = in.r;
        g = in.g;
        b = in.b;
        a = alpha;
    }

    color4( unsigned long color )
    {
```

```
    b = (float)(color&255) / 255.f;
    color >>= 8;
    g = (float)(color&255) / 255.f;
    color >>= 8;
    r = (float)(color&255) / 255.f;
    color >>= 8;
    a = (float)(color&255) / 255.f;
}


void Assign( float inR, float inG, float inB, float inA )
{
    r = inR;
    g = inG;
    b = inB;
    a = inA;
}

unsigned long MakeDWord()
{
    unsigned long iA = (int)(a * 255.f ) << 24;
    unsigned long iR = (int)(r * 255.f ) << 16;
    unsigned long iG = (int)(g * 255.f ) << 8;
    unsigned long iB = (int)(b * 255.f );
    return iA | iR | iG | iB;
}

unsigned long MakeDWordSafe()
{
    color4 temp = *this;
    temp.Sat();
    return temp.MakeDWord();
}

// if any of the values are >1, cap them.
void Sat()
{
    if( r > 1 )
        r = 1.f;
    if( g > 1 )
        g = 1.f;
    if( b > 1 )
        b = 1.f;
    if( a > 1 )
        a = 1.f;
    if( r < 0.f )
        r = 0.f;
    if( g < 0.f )
        g = 0.f;
    if( b < 0.f )
        b = 0.f;
```

```
        if( a < 0.f )
            a = 0.f;
    }

    color4& operator += ( const color4& in );
    color4& operator -= ( const color4& in );
    color4& operator *= ( const color4& in );
    color4& operator /= ( const color4& in );
    color4& operator *= ( const float& in );
    color4& operator /= ( const float& in );

    // some basic colors.
    static const color4 Black;
    static const color4 Gray;
    static const color4 White;
    static const color4 Red;
    static const color4 Green;
    static const color4 Blue;
    static const color4 Magenta;
    static const color4 Cyan;
    static const color4 Yellow;

};
```

Lighting Models

Lighting an object correctly is an extremely difficult process. Even today, it's still an area of research in academia. There are applications on the market that cost tens of thousands of dollars to perform renderings of scenes that have extremely accurate lighting. These renderings can take inordinate amounts of time to compute, sometimes on the order of several hours or even days for extremely complex images.

Never one to do difficult things, Direct3D and OpenGL graphics programmers use approximations of correct lighting models to get fast but good looking lighting models. While the images invariably end up looking computer generated, they can be done in real time. True photo realism needs to have incredibly accurate lighting, as human eyes are very sensitive to lighting in a scene. All the kinds of light are cubby-holed into four essential types:

■ **Ambient light**—Ambient light can be thought of as the average light in a scene. It is light that is equally transmitted to all points on all surfaces the same amount. Ambient lighting is a horrible hack—an attempt to impersonate the diffuse reflection that is better approximated by radiosity (covered in Chapter 7), but it works well enough for many applications. The difference between ambient light and ambient reflection is that ambient reflection is how much a surface reflects ambient light.

- **Diffuse light**—Diffuse light is light that hits a surface and reflects off equally in all directions. Surfaces that only reflect diffuse light appear lit the same amount, no matter how the camera views it. If modeling chalk or velvet, for example, only diffuse light would be reflected.

- **Specular light**—Specular light is light that only reflects off a surface in a particular direction. This causes a shiny spot on the surface, which is called a *specular highlight*. The highlight is dependent on both the location of the light and the location of the viewer. For example, imagine picking up an apple. The shiny spot on the apple is a good example of a specular highlight. As you move your head, the highlight moves around the surface (which is an indication that it's dependent on the viewing angle).

- **Emissive light**—Emissive light is energy that actually comes off of a surface. A light bulb, for example, looks very bright, because it has emissive light. Emissive light does not contribute to other objects in the scene. It is not a light itself; it just modifies the appearance of the surface.

Ambient and diffuse lights have easier equations, so I'll give those first. If the model doesn't reflect specular light at all, you can use the following equation to light each vertex of the object. This is the same diffuse and ambient lighting equation that Direct3D uses (given in the Microsoft DirectX 8.0 SDK documentation). The equation sums all of the lights in the scene.

$$D_v = I_a S_a + S_e + \sum_i A_i \left(R_{di} S_d L_{di} + S_a L_{ai} \right)$$

Table 3.1: Terms in the ambient/diffuse/emissive lighting equation for a surface

D_v	Final color for the surface.
I_a	Ambient light for the entire scene.
S_a	Ambient color for the surface.
S_e	Emitted color of the surface.
A_i	Attenuation for light i. This value depends on the kind of light you have, but essentially means how much of the total energy from the light hits an object.
R_{di}	Diffuse reflection factor for light i. This is usually the inverse of the dot product between the vertex normal and the direction in which the light is coming. That way, normals that are facing directly to the light receive more than normals that are turned away from it (of course, if the reflectance factor is less than zero, no diffuse light hits the object). Figure 3.25 shows the calculation visually.
S_d	Diffuse color for the surface.
L_{di}	Diffuse light emitted by light i.
L_{ai}	Ambient light emitted by light i.

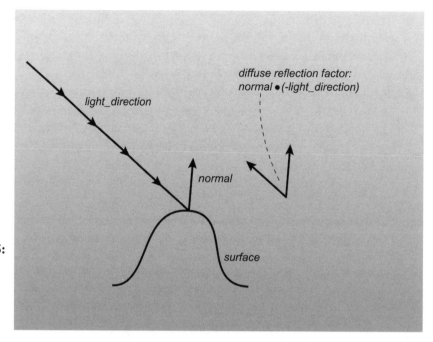

Figure 3.25:
Computa-
tion of the
diffuse
reflection
factor

The surfaces in the above equation will end up being vertices of the 3-D models once D3D is up and running. The surface reflectance components are usually defined with material structures defined in Chapter 6.

Specular Reflection

Specular reflections are more complex than ambient, emissive, or diffuse reflections, requiring more computation to use. Many old applications don't use specular reflections because of the overhead involved, or they'll do something like approximate them with an environment map. However, as accelerators are getting faster (especially since newer accelerators, such as the GeForce 3, can perform lighting in hardware) specular lighting is increasingly being used to add more realism to scenes.

To find the amount of specular color to attribute to a given vector with a given light, you use the following equations (taken from the Microsoft DirectX 8.0 SDK documentation):

$$\mathbf{v} = \overline{\mathbf{P}_c - \mathbf{P}_v}$$

$$\mathbf{h} = \overline{\mathbf{v} - \mathbf{l}_d}$$
$$R_s = \left(\mathbf{n} \bullet \mathbf{h}\right)^p$$
$$S_s = C_s A R_s L_s$$

The meanings of the variables are given in Table 3.2.

Table 3.2: Meanings of the specular reflection variables

p_c	Location of the camera.
p_v	Location of the surface.
l_d	Direction of the light.
h	The "halfway" vector. Think of this as the vector bisecting the angle made by the light direction and the viewer direction. The closer this is to the normal, the brighter the surface should be. The normal-halfway angle relation is handled by the dot product.
n	The normal of the surface.
R_s	Specular reflectance. This is, in essence, the intensity of the specular reflection. When the point you're computing lies directly on a highlight, it will be 1.0; when it isn't in a highlight at all, it'll be 0.
p	The "power" of the surface. The higher this number, the sharper the specular highlight. A value of 1 doesn't look much different than diffuse lighting, but using a value of 15 or 20 gives a nice sharp highlight.
S_s	The color being computed (this is what you want).
C_s	Specular color of the surface. That is, if white specular light was hitting the surface, this is the specular color you would see.
A	Attenuation of the light (how much of the total energy leaving the light actually hits the surface).
L_s	Specular color of the light.

Note that this only solves for one light; you need to solve the same equation for each light, summing up the results as you go.

Light Types

Now that you have a way to find the light hitting a surface, you're going to need some lights! There are three types of lights I am going to discuss, which happen to be the same three light types supported by Direct3D.

Parallel Lights (or Directional Lights)

Parallel lights cheat a little bit. They represent light that comes from an infinitely far away light source. Because of this, all of the light rays that reach the object are parallel (hence the name). The canonical use of parallel lights is to simulate the sun. While it's not infinitely far away, 93 million miles is good enough!

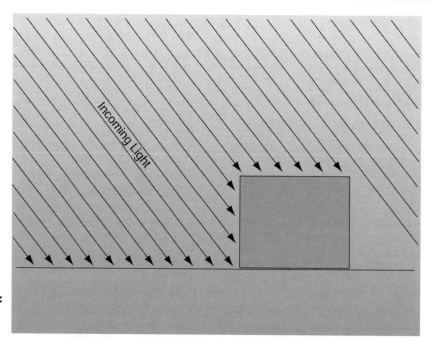

Figure 3.26:
Parallel light
sources

The great thing about parallel lights is that a lot of the ugly math goes away. The attenuation factor is always 1 (for point/spotlights, it generally involves divisions if not square roots). The incoming light vector for calculation of the diffuse reflection factor is the same for all considered points, whereas point lights and spotlights involve vector subtractions and a normalization per vertex.

Typically, lighting is the kind of effect that is sacrificed for processing speed. Parallel light sources are the easiest and therefore fastest to process. If you can't afford to do the nicer point lights or spotlights, falling back to parallel lights can keep your frame rates at reasonable levels.

Point Lights

One step better than directional lights are point lights. They represent infinitesimally small points that emit light. Light scatters out equally in all directions. Depending on how much effort you're willing to expend on the light, you can have the intensity fall off based on the inverse squared distance from the light, which is how real lights work.

$$\text{attenuation\_factor} = \frac{k}{\left|\text{surface\_location} - \text{light\_location}\right|^2}$$

The light direction is different for each surface location (otherwise the point light would look just like a directional light). The equation for it is:

$$light\_direction = \frac{surface\_location - light\_location}{|surface\_location - light\_location|}$$

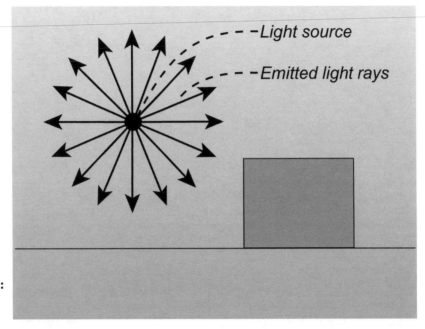

Figure 3.27:
Point light
sources

Spotlights

Spotlights are the most expensive type of light I discuss in this text, and should be avoided if possible. They model a spotlight not unlike the type you would see in a theatrical production. They are point lights, but light only leaves the point in a particular direction, spreading out based on the aperture of the light.

Spotlights have two angles associated with them. One is the internal cone whose angle is generally referred to as theta (θ). Points within the internal cone receive all of the light of the spotlight; the attenuation is the same as it would be if point lights were used. There is also an angle that defines the outer cone; the angle is referred to as phi (ϕ). Points outside the outer cone receive no light. Points outside the inner cone but inside the outer cone receive light, usually a linear fall-off based on how close it is to the inner cone.

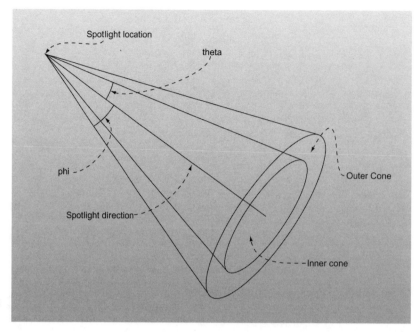

Figure 3.28:
A spotlight

If you think all of this sounds mathematically expensive, you're right. Direct3D implements lighting for you, so you won't need to worry about the math behind spotlights, but rest assured that they're extremely expensive and can slow down your application a great deal. Then again, they do provide an incredible amount of atmosphere when used correctly, so you will have to figure out a line between performance and aesthetics.

Shading Models

Once you've found lighting information, you need to know how to draw the triangles with the supplied information. There are currently only two real ways to do this, and a third that should become a hardware feature at some point (hopefully). Here is a polygon mesh of a sphere, which I'll use to explain the shading models:

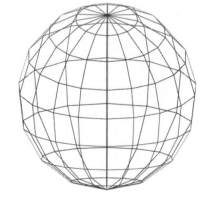

Figure 3.29:
Wireframe
view of our
polygon
mesh

Lambert

Triangles that use Lambertian shading are painted with one solid color instead of using a gradient. Typically each triangle is lit using that triangle's normal. The resulting object looks very angular and sharp. Lambertian shading was used mostly back when computers weren't fast enough to do Gouraud shading in real time. To light a triangle, you compute the lighting equations using the triangle's normal and any of the three vertices of the triangle.

Figure 3.30: Flat shaded view of our polygon mesh

Gouraud

Gouraud (pronounced gore-row) shading is the current de facto shading standard in accelerated 3-D hardware. Instead of specifying one color to use for the entire triangle, each vertex has its own separate color. The color values are linearly interpolated across the triangle, creating a smooth transition between the vertex color values. To calculate the lighting for a vertex, you use the position of the vertex and a vertex normal.

Of course, it's a little hard to correctly define a normal for a vertex. What people do instead is average the normals of all the polygons that share a certain vertex, using that as the vertex normal. When the object is drawn, the lighting color is found for each vertex (rather than each polygon), and then the colors are linearly interpolated across the object. This creates a slick and smooth look, like the one in Figure 3.31.

Figure 3.31:
Gouraud
shaded view
of our poly-
gon mesh

One problem with Gouraud shading is that the triangles' intensities can never be greater than the intensities at the edges. So if there is a spotlight shining directly into the center of a large triangle, Gouraud shading will interpolate the intensities at the three dark corners, resulting in an incorrectly dark triangle.

> **Aside:** The internal highlighting problem usually isn't that bad. If there are enough triangles in the model, the interpolation done by Gouraud shading is usually good enough. If you really want internal highlights but only have Gouraud shading, you can subdivide the triangle into smaller pieces.

Phong

Phong shading is the most realistic shading model I'm going to talk about, and also the most computationally expensive. It tries to solve several problems that arise when you use Gouraud shading. If you're looking for something more realistic, Foley discusses nicer shading models like Tarrence-Sparrow, but they aren't real time (at least not right now).

First of all, Gouraud shading uses a linear gradient. Many objects in real life have sharp highlights, such as the shiny spot on an apple. This is difficult to handle with pure Gouraud shading. The way Phong does this is by interpolating the normal across the triangle face, not the color value, and the lighting equation is solved individually for each pixel.

Phong shading currently isn't supported by any hardware cards, since interpolating normal values is considerably more difficult than interpolating color or texture information (a square root and a division are needed per pixel). However, it ends up not being much of a problem. Triangle rates are going through the roof, so you can afford to just subdivide triangles with internal highlights, and use Gouraud shading across the sub-triangles. The smaller triangles get, the less obvious the problems with Gouraud are.

A solution that many systems use is to use the more complex Phong lighting equations to shade the vertices of triangles, then use Gouraud shading to interpolate the values along them. With small enough triangles, this looks just as good as Phong, but is available in hardware now, whereas true Phong in hardware may be several years off.

Figure 3.32: Phong shaded view of a polygon mesh

BSP Trees

If all you want to do is just draw lists of polygons and be done with it, then you now have enough knowledge at your disposal. However, there is a lot more to 3-D game programming that you must concern yourself with. Hard problems abound, and finding an elegant way to solve the problems is half the challenge of graphics programming (actually implementing said solution is the other half).

A lot of the hard graphics problems, such as precise collision detection or ray-object intersection, boil down to a question of spatial relationship. You need to know where objects (defined with a boundary representation of polygons) exist in relation to the other objects around them.

You can, of course, find this explicitly if you'd like, but this leads to a lot of complex and slow algorithms. For example, say you're trying to see if a ray going through space is hitting any of a list of polygons. The slow way to do it would be to explicitly test each and every polygon against the ray. Polygon-ray intersection is not a trivial operation, so if there are a few thousand polygons, the speed of the algorithm can quickly grind to a halt.

A spatial relationship of polygons can help a lot. If you were able to say, "The ray didn't hit this polygon, but the entire ray is completely in front of the plane the polygon lies in," then you wouldn't need to test anything that sat behind the first polygon. BSP trees, as you shall soon see, are one of the most useful ways to partition space.

> *Aside* I implemented a ray-tracer a while back using two algorithms. One was a brute-force, test-every-polygon-against-every-ray nightmare; the other used BSP trees. The first algorithm took about 90 minutes to render a single frame with about 15K triangles in it. With BSP trees, the rendering time went down to about 45 seconds. Saying BSP trees make a big difference is quite an understatement.

It all started when Henry Fuchs and Zvi Kedem, both professors at the University of Texas at Dallas, found a bright young recent grad working at Texas Instruments named Bruce Naylor. They talked him into becoming a graduate student in their graphics department, and he started doing work on computational geometry. Fuchs was a sort of bright, energetic type, and Kedem contained that spark that few other theoretical computer scientists have: He was able to take theory and apply it to practical problems. Out of this triumvirate came two SIGGRAPH papers, and Naylor's Ph.D. thesis, which gave birth to BSP trees (see the FAQ in the "References" section).

BSP Tree Theory

BSP trees are a specialization of binary trees, one of the most basic constructs of computer science. A *BSP tree* represents a region of space (the tree can have any number of nodes, including just one). The tree is made up of *nodes* (having exactly two children) and *leaves* (having exactly zero children). A node represents a partitioning of the space that the tree it is a part of represents. The partitioning creates two new spaces, one in front of the node and one in back of the node.

In 2-D applications, such as *Doom* (which used BSP trees to represent the worlds the fearless space marine navigated), the top-level tree represents the entire 2-D world. The root node, which contains in it a line equation, defines a partitioning of the world into two pieces, one in front of the line and one in back of it. Each of these pieces is represented by a subtree, itself a BSP tree. The node also contained a line segment that was part of the line equation used in the partitioning. The line segment, with other information like the height and texture ID, became a wall in the world. Subtrees are leaves if and only if the space that they represent has no other walls in it. If it did, the wall would be used to partition the space yet again.

In 3-D applications, things are pretty much the same. The space is partitioned with 3-D planes, which contain polygons within them. The plane at each node slices its region into two hunks, one that is further subdivided by its front child node, and the other further subdivided by its back child node.

The recursion downward stops when a space cannot be partitioned any further. For now, this happens when there are no polygons inside of it. At this point, a leaf is created, and it represents a uniform, convex region of space.

There are two primary ways to do BSP trees. In the first method (called *node-based BSP trees*), nodes contain both polygons and the planes used to partition. Leaves are empty. In the other method (called *leaf-based* or *leafy BSP trees*), nodes only contain planes. Leaves contain all of the polygons that form the boundary of that convex space. I'm only going to talk about node-based BSP trees, but leaf-based BSPs are useful, for example in computing the potentially visible set (PVS) of a scene.

BSP trees are most useful when the set of polygons used to construct the tree represents the boundary-representation of an object. The object has a conceptual inside made of solid matter, an outside of empty space surrounding it, and polygons that meet in the middle. Luckily this is how I am representing the objects anyway. When the tree is complete, each leaf represents either solid or empty space. This will prove to be extremely useful, as you shall see in a moment.

BSP Tree Construction

The algorithm to create a node-based BSP tree is simple and recursive. It is fairly time consuming, however, enough so that generally the set of polygons used to construct the BSP tree remains static. This is the case for most of the worlds that players navigate in 3-D games, so games such as *Quake* consist of a static BSP tree (representing a world) and a set of objects (health boxes, ammo boxes, players, enemies, doors, etc.) that can move around in the world.

I'll go through the tree construction process step by step. Pseudocode for the algorithm appears in Listing 3.32.

Listing 3.32: Pseudocode for BSP construction

```
struct node
    polygon poly
    plane   part_plane
    ptr     front
    ptr     back
    vector< polygon > coplanar_polygons

struct leaf
    bool solid

leaf Make_Leaf( bool solid )
    leaf out = new leaf
    out.solid = solid
    return out

polygon Get_Splitting_Polygon( vector< polygon > input_list )
    polygon out = polygon that satisfies some hueristic
    remove out from input_list
    return out
```

```
node Make_Node( vector< polygon > input_list )
    vector< polygon > front_list, back_list
    node out = new node
    chosen_polygon = Get_Splitting_Polygon( input_list )
    out.part_plane = Make_Plane_From_Polygon( chosen_polygon )
    out.poly = chosen_polygon
    for( each polygon curr in input_list )
        switch( out.part_plane.Classify_Polygon( curr ) )
            case front
                add curr to front_list
            case back
                add curr to back_list
            case coplanar
                add curr to node.coplanar_polygons
            case split
                split curr into front and back polygons
                add front to front_list
                add back to back_list
    if( front_list is empty )
        out.front = Make_Leaf( false )
    else
        out.front = Make_Node( front_list )
    if( back_list is empty )
        out.back = Make_Leaf( true )
    else
        out.back = Make_Node( back_list )
    return out

node Make_BSP_Tree( vector< polygon > input_list )
    return Make_Node( input_list )
```

Let's step through a sample 2-D tree to show what is going on. The initial case will be a relatively small data set with four edges defining a closed region surrounded by empty space. Figure 3.33 shows the initial case, with the polygons on the left and a list on the right that will be processed. Each of the segments also has its plane normal visible; note that they all point out of the solid region.

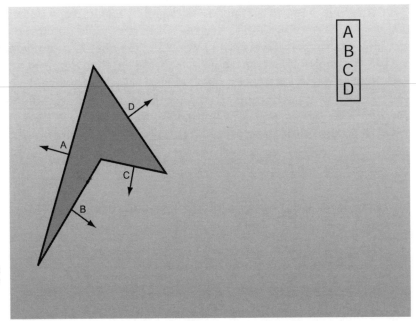

Figure 3.33:
Initial case of
the BSP
construction

To create the root node, segment A is used. Segments B, C, and D are all behind segment A, so they all go in the back list. The front list is empty, so the front child is made a leaf representing empty space corresponding to the entire subspace in front of segment A. The back list isn't empty, so it must be recursed, processing the subspace behind segment A. The result of the first partition appears in Figure 3.34.

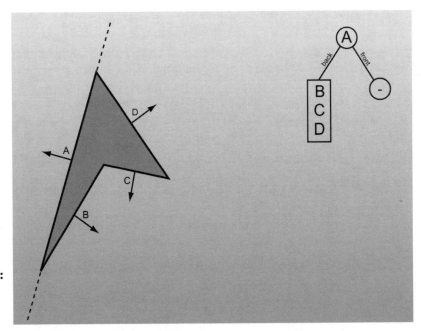

Figure 3.34:
Result after
the first
partitioning

Once recursion into the root node's back child is complete, a polygon to partition with must once again be selected. While real-world applications probably wouldn't choose it, to diversify the example I'm going to use segment B. Segment C is completely in front, but segment D is partially in front and partially in back. It is split into two pieces, one completely in front (which I'll call D_F) and one completely in back (called D_B). After the classification, both the front list and the back list have polygons in them, so they must be recursed with each. Figure 3.35 shows the progress up to this point.

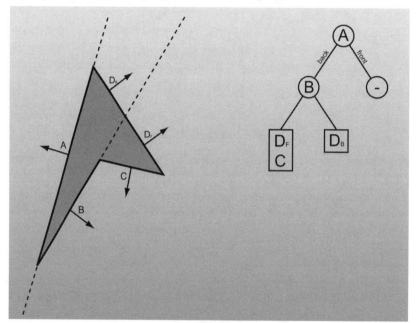

Figure 3.35: Result after the second partitioning

Note: Notice the dashed line for segment B. It doesn't intrude into the space in front of segment A, because it is only partitioning the subspace behind A. This is a very important point you'll need to assimilate if you want to understand BSP trees fully.

I'll partition the front side of the node, the one with a list of D_F and C. I'll use D_F as the partitioning polygon. C is the only polygon to classify, and it's completely behind D_F. The front list is empty, so I create an empty space leaf. This brings the progress up to Figure 3.36.

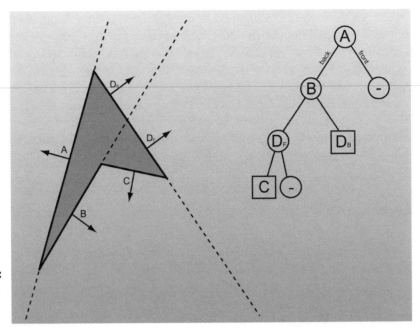

Figure 3.36:
Result of the third partitioning

Now there are two nodes left to process, C and D_B. For the sake of brevity, I'll consolidate them into one step. They both have no other polygons to classify once the only polygon in each list is selected to be the partitioner. This creates two child leaf nodes, one in back of the polygon representing solid space (represented with a plus sign) and one in front representing empty space (represented with a minus sign). This results in the final BSP tree, which appears below. I put small dashed lines from each of the leaf nodes to the subspace they represent.

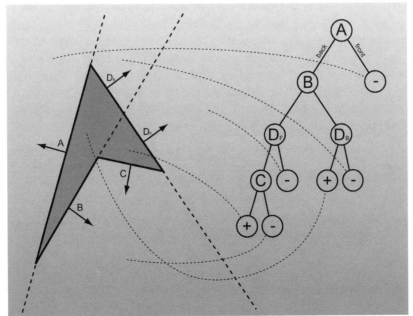

Figure 3.37:
The final BSP tree

One piece that's left out of the equation is how you take the list of polygons during each step and choose the polygon to use as the partitioner. There are two heuristics you can try to satisfy: Choose the polygon that causes the least amount of splits, or choose the polygon that most evenly divides the set. One problem, however, is that you can have a ton of polygons in the data set, especially at the top levels of the tree. In Foley's *Computer Graphics* it mentions that after you check about 10% of the polygons, the best candidate found thus far is so similar to the ideal one that it's not worth checking any more. This code will use a strict least-split heuristic, checking the first 10% of the polygon data (or the whole set if it's below some threshold).

BSP Tree Algorithms

Now that you've covered enough ground to create a BSP tree, hopefully a few algorithms will be at your disposal to perform operations on them. A few of the algorithms work in all polygon configurations, but generally they're suited for BSP trees that represent the boundary representation of an object.

Sorted Polygon Ordering

One of the first uses of BSP trees was to get a list of polygons sorted by distance from a given viewpoint. This was used back before hardware z-buffers, when polygons needed to be drawn in back-to-front order to be rendered correctly. It's still useful, however; z-buffer rendering goes faster if you reject early (so rendering front-to-back can be an advantage), and alpha-blended polygons need to be rendered back-to-front to be rendered correctly.

The fundamental concept behind the algorithm is that if you have a certain plane in the scene dividing it into two pieces, and you are on one side of the plane, then nothing behind the plane can occlude anything in front of the plane. Armed with this rule, all you need to do is traverse the tree. At each node, you check to see which side the camera is on. If it's in front, then you add all the polygons behind the plane (by traversing into the back node), then all the polygons in the plane (the partitioning polygon and any coplanar polygons), and finally the polygons in front of the plane (by traversing into the front node). The opposite applies if it is in back. Leaves just return automatically.

> **Note:** If you don't want to draw polygons facing away, you can automatically discard the node polygon if the camera point is behind the node plane. The coplanar polygons you can check, unless you keep two lists of coplanar polygons—one facing in the same direction as the partitioning polygons and one facing the opposite way.

The algorithm to do this is fairly simple and recursive. Pseudocode for it appears in Listing 3.33.

Listing 3.33: Pseudocode to sort a polygon list based on distance

```
void node::GetSortedPolyList(
    list< polygon3 >* pList,
    point& camera )
{
    switch( node.part_plane.Classify_Point( camera ) )
    {
    case front
        back. GetSortedPolyList( pList, camera );
        add all node polygons to pList
        front. GetSortedPolyList( pList, camera );
    case back
        front. GetSortedPolyList( pList, camera );
        add all node polygons to pList
        back. GetSortedPolyList( pList, camera );
    case coplanar
        // order doesn't matter
        front. GetSortedPolyList( pList, camera );
        back. GetSortedPolyList( pList, camera );
    }
}

void leaf:: GetSortedPolyList(
    list< polygon3 >* pList,
    point& camera )
{
    return;
}
```

Testing Locality of a Point

A really great use of BSP trees is testing the locality of points. Given a point and a tree, you can tell whether the point is sitting in a solid leaf or not. This is useful for collision detection, among other things.

The algorithm to do it is amazingly simple. At each branch of the tree, you test the point against the plane. If it's in front, you drop it down the front branch; if it's in back, you drop it down the back branch. If the point is coplanar with the polygon, you can pick either one. Whenever you land in a leaf, you have found the region of space that the point is sitting in. If the leaf is tagged as being solid, then the point is sitting in solid space; otherwise it's not. Pseudocode for this algorithm appears in Listing 3.34.

Listing 3.34: Pseudocode to define the locality of a point

```
bool node::TestPoint(
    point& pt )
{
    switch( node.part_plane.Classify_Point( pt ) )
    {
    case front
        return front.TestPoint( pt );
    case back
        return back.TestPoint( pt );
    case coplanar
        // Let's drop down the back tree
        return back.TestPoint( pt );
    }
}

bool leaf::TestPoint(
    point& pt )
{
    if( solid )
        return true;
    return false;
}
```

Testing Line Segments

While there are many other algorithms for use with BSP trees (see the FAQ listed under "References" at the end of this chapter), the last one I'll discuss lets you test a line segment against a tree. The algorithm returns true if there is a clear line of sight between both endpoints of the line, and false otherwise. Another way to think of it is to say that the algorithm returns true if and only if the line segment only sits in non-solid leaves.

Like all the other algorithms I've discussed, this is a conceptually simple and elegant algorithm. Starting at the root, you compare the line segment to the plane at a node. If the line segment is completely in front, you drop it down the front side. If it's completely in back, you drop it down the back side. If the line segment is on both sides of the plane, you divide it into two pieces (one in front of the plane and one in back) and recurse with both of them. If any piece of segment ever lands in a solid cell, then you know there is no line of sight, and you return false.

Source code to do this appears in the following BSP tree source code.

BSP Tree Code

Listings 3.35 and 3.36 have the header and source code for the BSP class. I'll be using it in Chapter 7 to find the form factor in the radiosity simulator. The main difference between this code and the pseudocode given above is this code uses the same node structure to represent both nodes and leaves. This made the code simpler but is an inefficient use of space (leaves only need a single word defining them as solid; here a lot more than that is used).

Listing 3.35: BspTree.h

```
/***********************************************************
 *          Advanced 3-D Game Programming using DirectX 8.0
 * * * * * * * * * * * * * * * * * * * * * * * * * * * * * *
 *    Title: BspTree.h
 *     Desc: BSP tree code, node-based construction, 3-D only
 *           uses dynamic polygons
 * copyright (c) 2001 by Peter A Walsh and Adrian Perez
 * See license.txt for modification and distribution information
 ***********************************************************/

#ifndef _BSPTREE_H
#define _BSPTREE_H

#include <point3.h>
#include <polygon.h>
#include <plane3.h>

#include <vector>
using std::vector;

const float percentageToCheck = .1f; // 10%

/**
 * This code expects the set of polygons we're giving it to be
 * closed, forming a continuous skin.  If it's not, weird things
 * may happen.
 */
class cBspTree
{
public:

    // construction/destruction
    cBspTree();
    ~cBspTree();

    // we need to handle copying
    cBspTree( const cBspTree &in );
    cBspTree& operator=( const cBspTree &in );

    // add a polygon to the tree
    void AddPolygon( const polygon<point3>& in );
    void AddPolygonList( vector< polygon<point3> >& in );
```

```
        void TraverseTree(
            vector< polygon<point3>* >* polyList,
            const point3& loc );

        bool LineOfSight( const point3& a, const point3& b );

protected:

private:

    class cNode
    {

        cNode*      m_pFront;        // pointer to front subtree
        cNode*      m_pBack;         // pointer to back subtree

        polygon<point3> m_poly;
        plane3      m_plane;
        bool        m_bIsLeaf;
        bool        m_bIsSolid;

        vector< polygon<point3> >   m_coplanarList;

        static int BestIndex( vector< polygon<point3> >& polyList );

    public:
        cNode( bool bIsSolid );                      // leaf constructor
        cNode( const polygon<point3>& in );          // node constructor
        cNode( vector< polygon<point3> >& in );      // node constructor
        ~cNode();

        // we need to handle copying
        cNode( const cNode &in );
        cNode& operator=( const cNode &in );

        void AddPolygon( const polygon<point3>& in );

        void TraverseTree(
            vector< polygon<point3>* >* polyList,
            const point3& loc );

        bool IsLeaf()
        {
            return m_bIsLeaf;
        }

        bool LineOfSight( const point3& a, const point3& b );
    };
```

```
            cNode* m_pHead; // root node of the tree

    };


    inline cBspTree::cBspTree( const cBspTree &in )
    {
        // clone the tree
        if( in.m_pHead )
            m_pHead = new cNode( *in.m_pHead );
        else
            m_pHead = NULL;
    }

    inline cBspTree& cBspTree::operator=( const cBspTree &in )
    {
        if( &in != this )
        {
            // delete the tree if we have one already
            if( m_pHead )
                delete m_pHead;

            // clone the tree
            if( in.m_pHead )
                m_pHead = new cNode( *in.m_pHead );
            else
                m_pHead = NULL;
        }

        return *this;
    }


    inline cBspTree::cNode::cNode( const cNode &in )
    {
        m_poly = in.m_poly;
        m_plane = in.m_plane;
        m_bIsLeaf = in.m_bIsLeaf;
        m_bIsSolid = in.m_bIsSolid;

        // clone the trees
        m_pFront = NULL;
        if( in.m_pFront )
            m_pFront = new cNode( *in.m_pFront );

        m_pBack = NULL;
        if( in.m_pBack )
            m_pBack = new cNode( *in.m_pBack );
    }
```

```
inline cBspTree::cNode& cBspTree::cNode::operator=( const cNode &in )
{
    if( &in != this )
    {
        // delete the subtrees if we have them already
        if( m_pFront )
            delete m_pFront;
        if( m_pBack )
            delete m_pBack;

        // copy all the data over
        m_poly = in.m_poly;
        m_plane = in.m_plane;
        m_bIsLeaf = in.m_bIsLeaf;
        m_bIsSolid = in.m_bIsSolid;

        // clone the trees
        m_pFront = NULL;
        if( in.m_pFront )
            m_pFront = new cNode( *in.m_pFront );

        m_pBack = NULL;
        if( in.m_pBack )
            m_pBack = new cNode( *in.m_pBack );
    }
    return *this;
}


#endif //_BSPTREE_H
```

Listing 3.36: BspTree.cpp

```
/*******************************************************************
 *          Advanced 3-D Game Programming using DirectX 8.0
 * * * * * * * * * * * * * * * * * * * * * * * * * * * * * * * * *
 *    Title: BspTree.cpp
 *     Desc: BSP tree code, node-based construction, 3-D only
 *            uses dynamic polygons
 * copyright (c) 2001 by Peter A Walsh and Adrian Perez
 * See license.txt for modification and distribution information
 *******************************************************************/

#include <template.h>
#include <BspTree.h>


cBspTree::cBspTree()
{
}
```

```
cBspTree::~cBspTree()
{
    // destroy the tree
}
```

```
void cBspTree::AddPolygon( const polygon<point3>& in )
{
    if( !m_pHead )
    {
        // if there's no tree, make a new one
        m_pHead = new cNode( in );
    }
    else
    {
        // otherwise add it to the tree
        m_pHead->AddPolygon( in );
    }
}
```

```
void cBspTree::AddPolygonList( vector< polygon<point3> >& in )
{
    if( !m_pHead )
    {
        // if there's no tree, make a new one
        m_pHead = new cNode( in );
    }
    else
    {
        /**
         * Adding a list of polygons to
         * an existing tree is unimplemented
         * (exercise to the reader)
         */
        assert( false );
    }
}
```

```
void cBspTree::TraverseTree(
    vector<polygon<point3>*>* polyList,
    const point3& loc )
{
    if( m_pHead )
    {
        // drop it down
        m_pHead->TraverseTree( polyList, loc );
    }
}
```

```
bool cBspTree::LineOfSight( const point3& a, const point3& b )
{
    assert( m_pHead ); // make sure there is a tree to test against

    return m_pHead->LineOfSight( a, b );
}


cBspTree::cNode::~cNode()
{
    delete m_pFront;
    delete m_pBack;
}


cBspTree::cNode::cNode( bool bIsSolid )
: m_bIsLeaf( true )
, m_bIsSolid( bIsSolid )
, m_pFront( NULL )
, m_pBack( NULL )
{
    // all done.
}

cBspTree::cNode::cNode( const polygon<point3>& in )
: m_bIsLeaf( false )
, m_poly( in )
, m_plane( in )
, m_pFront( new cNode( false ) )
, m_pBack( new cNode( true ) )
{
    // all done.
}

cBspTree::cNode::cNode( vector< polygon<point3> >& in )
: m_bIsLeaf( false )
{
    // if the list is empty, we're bombing out.
    assert( in.size() );

    // get the best index to use as a splitting plane
    int bestIndex = BestIndex( in );

    // we could remove the index from the vector, but that's slow.
    // instead we'll just kind of ignore it during the next phase.
    // remove the best index
    polygon<point3> splitPoly = in[bestIndex];

    m_plane = plane3( splitPoly );
    m_poly = splitPoly;
```

```
    // take the rest of the polygons and divide them.
    vector< polygon<point3> > frontList, backList;

    int i;
    for( i=0; i<in.size(); i++ )
    {
        // ignore the polygon if it's the one
        // we're using as the splitting plane
        if( i == bestIndex ) continue;

        // test the polygon against this node.
        pListLoc res = m_plane.TestPoly( in[i] );

        polygon<point3> front, back; // used in PLIST_SPLIT

        switch( res )
        {
        case PLIST_FRONT:
            // drop down the front
            frontList.push_back( in[i] );
            break;
        case PLIST_BACK:
            // drop down the back
            backList.push_back( in[i] );
            break;
        case PLIST_SPLIT:
            // split the polygon, drop the halves down.
            m_plane.Split( in[i], &front, &back );
            frontList.push_back( front );
            backList.push_back( back );
            break;
        case PLIST_COPLANAR:
            // add the polygon to this node's list
            m_coplanarList.push_back( in[i] );
            break;
        }
    }

    // we're done processing the polygon list. Deal with them.
    if( frontList.size() )
    {
        m_pFront = new cNode( frontList );
    }
    else
    {
        m_pFront = new cNode( false );
    }
    if( backList.size() )
    {
        m_pBack = new cNode( backList );
    }
```

```
        else
        {
            m_pBack = new cNode( true );
        }

    }

    void cBspTree::cNode::AddPolygon( const polygon<point3>& in )
    {
        if( m_bIsLeaf )
        {
            // reinitialize ourselves as a node
            *this = cNode( in );
        }
        else
        {
            // test the polygon against this node.
            pListLoc res = this->m_plane.TestPoly( in );

            polygon<point3> front, back; // used in PLIST_SPLIT
            switch( res )
            {
            case PLIST_FRONT:
                // drop down the front
                m_pFront->AddPolygon( in );
                break;
            case PLIST_BACK:
                // drop down the back
                m_pBack->AddPolygon( in );
                break;
            case PLIST_SPLIT:
                // split the polygon, drop the halves down.
                m_plane.Split( in, &front, &back );
                m_pFront->AddPolygon( front );
                m_pBack->AddPolygon( back );
                break;
            case PLIST_COPLANAR:
                // add the polygon to this node's list
                m_coplanarList.push_back( in );
                break;
            }
        }
    }

    void cBspTree::cNode::TraverseTree( vector< polygon<point3>* >* polyList,
    const point3& loc )
    {
        if( m_bIsLeaf )
        {
            // do nothing.
        }
```

```
        else
        {
            // test the loc against the current node
            pointLoc res = m_plane.TestPoint( loc );

            int i;
            switch( res )
            {
            case POINT_FRONT:
                // get back, us, front
                m_pBack->TraverseTree( polyList, loc );
                polyList->push_back( &m_poly ); // the poly at this node
                for( i=0; i<m_coplanarList.size(); i++ )
                {
                    polyList->push_back( &m_coplanarList[i] );
                }
                m_pFront->TraverseTree( polyList, loc );
                break;

            case POINT_BACK:
                // get front, us, back
                m_pFront->TraverseTree( polyList, loc );
                polyList->push_back( &m_poly ); // the poly at this node
                for( i=0; i<m_coplanarList.size(); i++ )
                {
                    polyList->push_back( &m_coplanarList[i] );
                }
                m_pBack->TraverseTree( polyList, loc );
                break;

            case POINT_COPLANAR:
                // get front, back, us
                m_pFront->TraverseTree( polyList, loc );
                m_pBack->TraverseTree( polyList, loc );
                polyList->push_back( &m_poly ); // the poly at this node
                for( i=0; i<m_coplanarList.size(); i++ )
                {
                    polyList->push_back( &m_coplanarList[i] );
                }
                break;

            }
        }
}

int cBspTree::cNode::BestIndex( vector< polygon<point3> >& polyList )
{
    /**
     * The current hueristic is blind least-split
     */
    // run through the list, searching for the best one.
```

```
                // the highest polygon we'll bother testing (10% of total)
                int maxCheck;
                maxCheck = (int)(polyList.size() * percentageToCheck);
                if( !maxCheck ) maxCheck = 1;

                int i, i2;
                int bestSplits = 100000;
                int bestIndex = -1;
                int currSplits;
                plane3 currPlane;
                for( i=0; i<maxCheck; i++ )
                {
                    currSplits = 0;
                    currPlane = plane3( polyList[i] );
                    pListLoc res;

                    for( i2=0; i2< polyList.size(); i2++ )
                    {
                        if( i == i2 ) continue;

                        res = currPlane.TestPoly( polyList[i2] );
                        if( res == PLIST_SPLIT )
                            currSplits++;
                    }
                    if( currSplits < bestSplits )
                    {
                        bestSplits = currSplits;
                        bestIndex = i;
                    }
                }
                assert( bestIndex >= 0 );
                return bestIndex;
        }


        bool cBspTree::cNode::LineOfSight( const point3& a, const point3& b )
        {
            if( m_bIsLeaf )
            {
                // if we land in a solid node, then there is no line of sight
                return !m_bIsSolid;
            }

            pointLoc aLoc = m_plane.TestPoint( a );
            pointLoc bLoc = m_plane.TestPoint( b );

            point3 split;

            if( aLoc == POINT_COPLANAR && bLoc == POINT_COPLANAR )
            {
                // for sake of something better to do, be conservative
```

```
        //return false;
        return m_pFront->LineOfSight( a, b );
    }

    if( aLoc == POINT_FRONT && bLoc == POINT_BACK )
    {
        //split, then return the logical 'or' of both sides
        split = m_plane.Split( a, b );

        return m_pFront->LineOfSight( a, split )
            && m_pBack->LineOfSight( b, split );

    }

    if( aLoc == POINT_BACK && bLoc == POINT_FRONT )
    {
        // split, then return the logical 'or' of both sides
        split = m_plane.Split( a, b );

        return m_pFront->LineOfSight( b, split )
            && m_pBack->LineOfSight( a, split );
    }

    // the other == POINT_COLPLANAR or POINT_FRONT
    if( aLoc == POINT_FRONT || bLoc == POINT_FRONT )
    {
        // drop down the front
        return m_pFront->LineOfSight( a, b );
    }

    else // they're both on the back side
    {
        // drop down the front
        return m_pBack->LineOfSight( a, b );
    }

    return true;
}
```

Wrapping It Up

Most of the code discussed in this chapter is on the CD in one library, called
math3d.lib. The rest of it (most notably the transformation, clipping, and lighting pipeline) won't be implemented by you; that's being left wholly to Direct3D.
There aren't any sample applications for this chapter because you won't be able
to draw any primitives until Chapter 6. The directory for this chapter on the CD
contains more complete, more commented versions of the code discussed in this

chapter. I didn't want to fill this chapter with too much source code, so a lot was stripped for size considerations.

References

Foley, James D. et al. *Computer Graphics: Principles and Practice, Second Edition in C*. Addison-Wesley Publishing Co. ISBN: 0201848406.

Moller, Tomas, and Eric Haines. *Real-Time Rendering*. A K Peters Ltd., 1999. ISBN: 1568811012.

BSP Tree Frequently Asked Questions (FAQ). Available at http://reality.sgi .com/bspfaq/index.shtml.

DirectX 8.0 SDK documentation. Microsoft 2000. Available at http://msdn .microsoft.com/directx.

For Further Reading

Moller, Tomas, and Eric Haines. *Real-Time Rendering*. A K Peters Ltd., 1999. ISBN: 1568811012.

This book is indispensable. Buy it now, if you haven't already. Much more detail on many of the topics in this chapter than I had space to allot. Well written and well put together.

Baraff, David, and Andrew Witkin. *Physically Based Modeling: Principles and Practice*. Available at http://www.cs.cmu.edu/~baraff/sigcourse/index.html.

Notes from a course taught at SIGGRAPH 97. An excellent tutorial to get your feet wet in the world of physically based modeling.

Chapter 4
Artificial Intelligence

Some of my earliest memories are of my dad bouncing me on his knee, playing computer games on our 8088. I was fascinated with computers, despite the fact that we only had two games for the machine: a game where a donkey ran down the road avoiding cars, and an app that used the PC speaker to crudely simulate a piano. One of my first phrases was "Dunkee n musik," a jumbled group of syllables I would yelp when I wanted to play the games.

Right around then was when I saw my first AI application. The title escapes me (I believe it may have been just *Animal*), but the premise was simple enough. The object of the game was for the computer to guess an animal you were thinking about. It would ask a series of yes/no questions that would narrow down the possible choices (examples would be "does your animal fly?" or "does your animal have four legs?"), and when it was sure, it would tell you what it thought your animal was. The neat thing was, if it didn't guess your animal, it would ask you for a question that differentiated the two animals, something your animal had that the other didn't. From then on, the program would be able to guess your animal! It could learn!

This impressed my young mind to no end. After some formal training in programming, I've come to accept that it's a fairly trivial program: The application keeps an internal binary tree with a question at each branch and an animal at each leaf. It descends down the tree asking the question at each branch and taking the appropriate direction. If it reaches a leaf and the animal stored there isn't yours, it creates a new branch, adds your question, and puts your animal and the animal previously in the leaf in two new leaves.

How the program worked, however, really isn't that important. The trick is, it <u>seemed</u> intelligent to me. Game programmers need to aim for this. While academia argues for the next 50 years over whether or not human-level intelligence is possible with computers, game developers need only be concerned with tricking humans into thinking what they're playing against is intelligent. And luckily (for both developers and academia), humans aren't that smart.

This is, of course, not as easy as it sounds. Video games are ripe with pretty stupid computer opponents. Early first-person shooters had enemies that walked towards the player in a zigzag pattern, never walking directly towards their target, shooting intermittently. Bad guys in other games would sometimes walk into a corner looking for you, determined that they would eventually find you even though you were several rooms away. Fighting games are even worse. The AI governing computer opponents can become extremely repetitive (so that every time you jump towards the opponent, they execute the same move). I can't promise to teach you everything you need to know to make the next *Reaper Bot*; that would be the topic of an entire book all its own. By the end of this chapter, however, you should be able to write an AI that can at least challenge you and maybe even surprise you!

Starting Point

Most AI problems that programmers face fall into three groups. At the lowest level is the problem of physical movement—how to move the unit, how to turn, how to walk, etc. This group is sometimes called *locomotion*, or *motor skills*. Moving up one level is a higher-level view of unit movement, where the unit has to decide how to get from point A to point B, avoiding obstacles and/or other units. This group is called *steering*, or *task generation*. Finally, at the highest level, the meatiest part of AI, is the actual thinking. Any cockroach can turn in a circle and do its best to avoid basic obstacles (like a human's foot). That does not make the cockroach intelligent. The third and highest stage is where the unit decides what to do and uses its ability to move around and plan directions to carry out its wishes. This highest level is called *motivation*, or *action steering*.

Locomotion

Locomotion, depending on how you look at it, is either trivial or trivially complex. An animation-based system can handle locomotion pretty easily, move forward one unit, and use the next frame of animation in the walk cycle. Every game on the market uses something similar to this to handle AI locomotion.

However, that isn't the whole story. When you walk up stairs, you need a stair walking animation; when you descend down a hill, you naturally lean back to retain your balance. The angle you lean back is dependent on the angle of the hill. The amount you dig your feet into the ice is dependent on how slippery the ice is and how sure your footing needs to be before you proceed. Animation systems robust enough to handle cases like this require a lot of special casing and scripting; most animation systems use the same walk animation for all cases. I always found it kind of disappointing when the guards in the surface level of *Goldeneye* could simply walk up 8-foot tall, 70 degree banks of snow.

A branch of control theory attempts to solve this with *physical controllers*. You can actually teach an AI how to stand, and tell it how to retain its balance, how to walk around, jump, anything. This gives the AI incredible control, as the algorithms can handle any realistic terrain, any conditions. Many people agree that the future of locomotion in games is physical controllers.

However, physical controllers aren't easy. At all. For these purposes, it's total overkill. As Moore's law inevitably marches forward, there will eventually be enough processing power to devote the cycles to letting each creature figure out how to run towards their target. When this happens games will be one huge step closer to looking like real life. Until then, however, I'm not going to touch that topic with a ten-foot pole. As interesting as it can be, I don't have the space to give it justice. Chris Hecker wrote a good primer on this topic in the April 1999 issue of *Game Developer* magazine.

Steering—Basic Algorithms

Even games with little or no AI at all need to implement some form of steering. Steering allows entities to navigate around the world they exist in. Without it, enemies would just sit there with a rather blank look in their eyes. There are a slew of extremely basic steering algorithms that I'll touch upon, and a couple of slightly more advanced ones that I'll dig into a little deeper.

Chasing

The first AI that most people implement is the ruthless, unthinking, unrelenting Terminator AI. The creature never thinks about rest, about getting health or ammo, about attacking other targets, or even walking around obstacles: It just picks a target and moves towards it each frame relentlessly. The code to handle this sort of AI is trivial. Each frame, the creature takes the position of its target, generates a vector to it, and moves along the vector a fixed amount (the amount is the speed of the creature). Pseudocode to handle this type of AI is in Listing 4-1.

Listing 4.1: The Terminator manifested

```
void cCreature::Chase( cObject* target )
{
    // Find the locations of the creature and its target.
    point3 creatureLoc = m_loc;
    point3 targetLoc = target->GetLoc();

    // Generate a direction vector between the objects
    point3 direction = targetLoc - creatureLoc;

    // Normalize the direction (make it unit-length)
    direction.Normalize();

    // move our object along the direction vector some fixed amount
    m_loc += direction * m_speed;
}
```

Evading

The inverse of a chasing algorithm is what I could probably get away with calling rabbit AI, but I'll leave it at evading. Each frame, you move directly away from a target as fast as you can (although in this case the target would most likely be a predator).

Listing 4.2: John Connor, perhaps?

```
void cCreature::Evade( cObject* target )
{
    // Find the locations of the creature and its target.
    point3 creatureLoc = m_loc;
    point3 targetLoc = target->GetLoc();

    // Generate a direction vector between the objects
    point3 direction = targetLoc - creatureLoc;

    // Normalize the direction (make it unit-length)
    direction.Normalize();

    // move our object away from the target by multiplying
    // by a negative speed
    m_loc += direction * -m_speed;
}
```

Pattern-based AI

The final ultra-simple AI algorithm I'm going to discuss is pattern-based AI. If you have ever played the classic *Space Invaders*, you're familiar with this AI algorithm. Aliens take turns dive-bombing the player, with every type of alien attacking in one uniform way. The way it attacks is called a *pattern*. At each point in time, each creature in the simulation is following some sort of pattern.

The motivation engine (in this case, usually a random number generator) decides from a fixed set of patterns to perform. Each pattern encodes a series of movements to be carried out each frame. Following the *Space Invaders* theme, examples of pattern-based AI would be moving back and forth, diving, and diving while shooting. Anyone who has played the game has noticed that each unit type dives towards the player the same way, oblivious to where the player is. When the baddies aren't diving, they all slide back and forth in the same exact way. They're all following the same set of patterns.

The algorithm to run a pattern-based AI creature is straightforward. I'll define a pattern to be an array of points that define direction vectors for each frame of the pattern. Since the arrays can be of any length, I also keep track of the length of the array. Then during the AI simulation step the creature moves itself by the amount in the current index of the array. When it reaches the end of an array, it randomly selects a new pattern. Let's examine some pseudocode to handle pattern-based AI.

Listing 4.3: Pattern-based AI

```
struct sPattern
{
    int patternLength;
    point3 *pattern; // array of length patternLength
};

sPattern g_patterns[ NUM_PATTERNS ];

void cCreature::FollowPattern()
{
    // pattFrame is the current frame of the pattern
    // pattNum is the current pattern we're using.

    if( pattFrame >= g_patterns[ pattNum ].patternLength )
    {
        // new pattern
        pattNum = rand()%NUM_PATTERNS;
        pattFrame = 0;
    }

    // follow our current pattern.
    m_loc += g_patterns[pattNum].pattern[pattFrame++];
}
```

Pattern-based AI can be specialized into what is known as *scripted* AI. When a certain state is reached, the motivation engine can run a certain scripted steering pattern. For example, an important state would be your player entering a room with a bad guy in it. This could cause the creature to follow a specialized animation just for that one game situation. The bad guy could run and trip an alarm, dive out of bed towards his bludgeoning weapon of choice, or anything else you can dream up.

Steering—Advanced Algorithms

In case you haven't figured it out yet, the basic steering algorithms provided so far are terrible! They merely provide the creature with an ability to move. Moving in a pattern, moving directly towards an opponent, or fleeing directly away from it is only slightly more believable than picking a random direction to move every frame! No one will ever mistake your basic cretins for intelligent creatures. Real creatures don't follow patterns. Moving directly towards or directly away from you makes them an easy target. A prime example of how this would fail is illustrated in Figure 4-1.

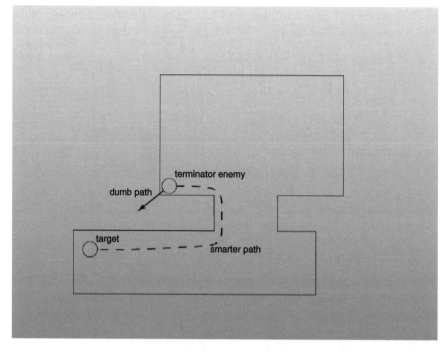

Figure 4.1:
Chasing
directly
towards a
target
wouldn't be
too smart in
many cases

How can you make the creatures appear more intelligent? It would be cool to give them the ability to navigate through an environment, avoiding obstacles. If the top-level motivation AI decides that it needs health or ammo, or needs to head to a certain location, the task of getting there intelligently should be handed off to the steering engine. Two general algorithms for achieving this are what I'll discuss next.

Potential Functions

Luckily for game programmers, a lot of the hard problems in steering and autonomous navigation for AI creatures have already been solved by the robotics community. Getting an autonomous unit, like a Mars rover, to plan a path and execute it in a foreign environment is a problem that countless researchers and academics have spent years trying to solve. One of the ways they have come up with to let a robot (or a creature in the game) wander through an unknown scene is to use what are called *potential functions*.

Imagine a scene filled with obstacles, say tree trunks in a forest. There is a path from the start to the goal and no tricky situations (like a U-shaped wall of trees, which ends up being a real problem as you'll see in a moment). The unit should be able to reach the goal; all it needs to do is not run into any trees. Any time it gets close to a tree, logically, it should adjust its direction vector so it moves away from the tree. The amount it wants to move away from the tree should be a function based on the distance from the obstacle; that is, if it is right next to the obstacle, it will want to avoid it more than if it is half a mile away from it. Figure 4.2 shows an example of this. It will obviously want to try to avoid obstacle 1 more than it tries to avoid obstacle 2, since obstacle 2 is so much farther away.

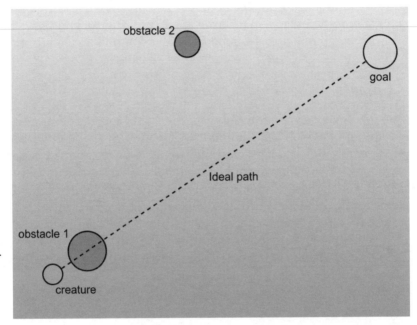

Figure 4.2: Some obstacles should be avoided more than others

This statement can be turned into an equation. Initially the direction is the normalized vector leading to the goal (or the goal location minus the current location). Then, for each obstacle, you find the normalized vector that moves directly away from it. Then multiply it by a constant, and divide it by the squared distance from the obstacle. When finished, you have a vector that the object should use as a direction vector (it should be normalized, however).

$$\text{direction} = \overline{\text{goal}_{loc} - \text{curr}_{loc}} + \sum_{n} \left(\overline{\text{curr}_{loc} - \text{obst}^n_{loc}} \times \frac{k}{\left\| \text{curr}_{loc} - \text{obst}^n_{loc} \right\|^2} \right)$$

Generally the obstacles (and the object navigating) have some radius associated with them, so the last term in the equation can be adjusted to use the distance between the spheres, instead of the distance between the spheres' centers.

The Good

Potential functions work great in sparse areas with physical obstacles, particularly outdoor scenes. You can reach a goal on the other side of a map avoiding trees, rocks, and houses beautifully and with little computational effort. A quick and easy optimization is to only consider the objects that are within some reasonable distance from you, say 50 feet; that way you don't need to test against every object in the world (which could have hundreds or thousands of objects in it).

One great advantage of potential functions is that the obstacles themselves can move around. You can use potential functions to model the movement of a squad of units across a map for example. They can avoid obstacles in the scene (using potential functions or more complex path finding algorithms like A*), and then avoid each other using potential functions.

The Bad

Potential functions are not a silver bullet for all problems, however. As intelligent as units can look being autonomously navigated with this method, they're still incredibly stupid. Mathematically, think of the potential functions as descending into a valley towards a goal, with the obstacles appearing as hills that roll past. If there is a miniature valley that is descended into, there is no way of getting out of it, since the only way to move is downward. This miniature valley can appear all over the place; if two obstacles are too close to each other, you won't be able to pass between them, and if obstacles are organized to form a barrier, like a wall or specifically a U-shaped obstacle, you're totally screwed. Figure 4.3 gives an example of this.

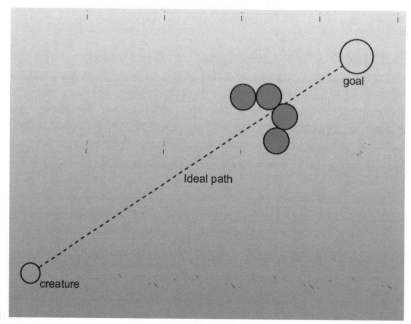

Figure 4.3: Potential functions alone cannot get to the goal in this configuration

Application: potentialFunc

To help explain the ideas described above, I wrote a small test app to show off potential functions. You can use the z, x, and c keys to make large, medium, and small obstacles under the mouse, respectively. The Space key releases a creature under the mouse that heads to the goal, which appears as a green circle. Since the GDI is so slow, I decided against clearing the window every frame, so the creatures leave trails as they move around. For most cases, the creatures (more than one can be created at once) reach their goal well, as evidenced in the following picture:

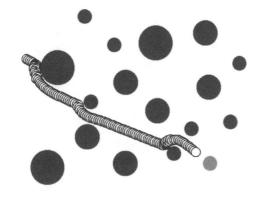

Figure 4.4: Potential functions doing their job

However, they don't work all the time, as evidenced by this picture:

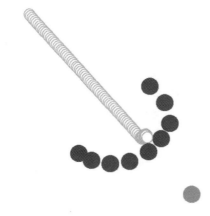

Figure 4.5: Potential functions failing spectacularly

You'll notice that inside the code I sum the potential forces for the objects and move a bit ten times each frame. If I only moved once, I would need to move a fairly large amount to have the speed of the creature be anything interesting. However, when the deltas are that large, the result is some ugly numerical stability problems (characterized by a jittering when the creature gets very close to an obstacle). Sampling multiple times each frame fixes the problem.

The GDI isn't useful for writing 3-D games, so I'm covering it very minimally in this book. However, for doing something like a potential function application it turns out to be quite useful. While I'm providing no explanations of how GDI works, armed with this code and the Win32 SDK documentation, figuring it out on your own won't be terribly difficult. There are references at the end of Chapter 2 if you want some more information on the GDI.

The code uses two main classes, cCreature (an entity that tries to reach the goal) and cObstacle (something obstructing the path to the goal). The code keeps vectors of all of the creatures and objects in the scene. Each frame, each member of the creature vector gets processed, during which it examines the list of obstacles. A nice extension to the program would be for creatures to also avoid other creatures; currently they blindly run all over each other.

The code for this application is mostly GUI and drawing code, and the important function is cCreature::Process. It is called every frame, and it performs the potential function equation listed above to find the new location. After each creature gets processed, the entire scene gets drawn. Rather than list all of the code for the program, I'll just give this one function.

Listing 4.4: The main function of note, cCreature::Process

```
bool cCreature::Process()
{
    point3 goalVec = g_goalLoc - m_loc;

    if( goalVec.Length() < g_creatureSpeed )
        return false; // we reached the goal, destroy ourselves

    point3 dirVec = goalVec / goalVec.Length();

    float k = .1f;

    // for each obstacle
    for( int i=0; i<g_obstacles.size(); i++ )
    {
        // find the vector between the creature and the obstacle
        point3 obstacleVec = m_loc - g_obstacles[i].m_loc;

        // compute the length, subtracting object radii to find
        // the distance between the spheres,
        // not the sphere centers
        float dist = obstacleVec.Length() -
            g_obstacles[i].m_rad - m_rad;

        // this is the vector pointing away from the obstacle
        obstacleVec.Normalize();

        dirVec += obstacleVec * ( k / (dist * dist) );
```

```
    }
    dirVec.Normalize();

    m_loc += g_creatureSpeed * dirVec;
    return true; // we should continue processing
}
```

Path Following

Path following is the process of making an agent look intelligent by having it proceed to its destination using a logical path. The term "path following" is really only half of the picture. Following a path once you're given it is fairly easy. The tricky part is generating a logical path to a target. This is called *path planning*.

Before it is possible create a logical path it must be defined. For example, if a creature's desired destination (handed to it from the motivation code) is on the other side of a steep ravine, a logical path would probably be to walk to the nearest bridge, cross the ravine, then walk to the target. If there were a steep mountain separating it from its target, the most logical path would be to walk around the mountain, instead of whipping out climbing gear.

A slightly more precise definition of a logical path is *the path of least resistance*. Resistance can be defined as one of a million possible things, from a lava pit to a strong enemy to a brick wall. In an example of a world with no environmental hazards, enemies, cliffs, or whatnot, the path of least resistance is the shortest one, as shown in Figure 4.6.

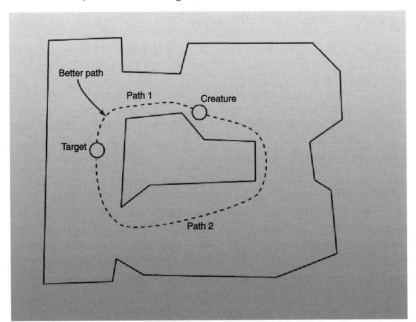

Figure 4.6: Choosing paths based on length alone

Other worlds are not so constant. Resistance factors can be worked into algorithms to account for something like a room that has the chance of being filled with lava (like the main area of DM2 in *Quake*). Even if traveling through the lava room is the shortest of all possible paths using sheer distance, the most logical path is to avoid the lava room if it made sense. Luckily, once the path finding algorithm is set up, modifying it to support other kinds of cost besides distance is a fairly trivial task. If other factors are taken into account, the chosen path may be different. See Figure 4.7.

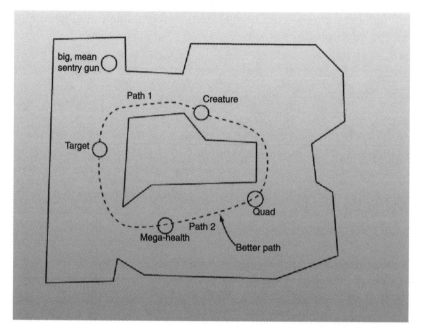

Figure 4.7: Choosing paths based on other criterion

Groundwork

While there are algorithms for path planning in just about every sort of environment, I'm going to focus on path planning in networked convex polyhedral cells. Path planning for something like a 2-D map (like those seen in *Starcraft*) is better planned with algorithms like A*.

A convex cell will be defined as a region of passable space that a creature can wander through, such as a room or hallway. Convex polyhedrons follow the same rules for convexity as the polygons. For a polygon (2-D) or a polyhedron (3-D) to be convex, any ray that is traced between any two points in the cell cannot leave the cell. Intuitively, the cell cannot have any dents or depressions in it; there isn't any part of the cell that sticks inward. Concavity is a very important trait for what is being done here. At any point inside the polyhedron, exiting the polyhedron at any location is possible and there is no need to worry about bumping into walls. Terminator logic can be used from before until the edge of the polyhedron is reached.

The polyhedrons, when all laid out, become the world. They do not intersect with each other. They meet up such that there is exactly one convex polygon joining any two cells. This invisible boundary polygon is a special type of polygon called a *portal*. Portals are the doorways connecting rooms, and are passable regions themselves. If you enter and exit cells from portals, and you know a cell is convex, then you also know that any ray traveled between two portals will not be obstructed by the walls of the cell (although it may run against a wall). Until objects are introduced into the world, if the paths are followed exactly, there is no need to perform collision tests.

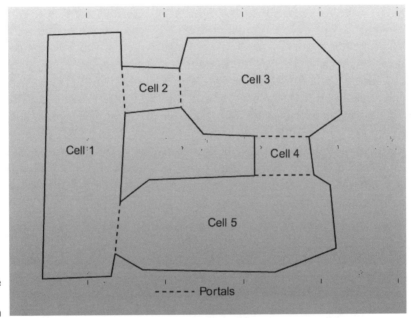

Figure 4.8:
Cells and the portals connecting them

I'll touch upon this spatial definition later in the book when I discuss hidden surface removal algorithms; portal rendering uses this same paradigm to accelerate hidden surface removal tasks.

The big question that remains is how do you move around this map? To accomplish finding the shortest path between two arbitrary locations on the map (the location of the creature and a location the user chooses), I'm going to build a directed, weighted graph and use Dijkstra's algorithm to find the shortest edge traversal of the graph.

If that last sentence didn't make a whole lot of sense, read on. People who are already familiar with Dijkstra's algorithm and/or directed, weighted graphs can skip to the next section.

Graph Theory Done Really, Really Quickly

The need to find the shortest path in graphs shows up everywhere in computer programming. Graphs can be used to solve a large variety of problems, from finding a good path to send packets through on a network of computers, to planning airline trips, to generating door-to-door directions using map software.

A *weighted, directed graph* is a set of *nodes* connected to each other by a set of *edges*. Nodes contain locations, states you would like to reach, machines, anything of interest. Edges are bridges from one node to another (The two nodes being connected can be the same node, although for these purposes that isn't terribly useful.) Each edge has a value that describes the cost to travel across the edge, and is unidirectional. To travel from one node to another and back, two edges are needed: one to take you from the first node to the second, and one that goes from the second node to the first.

Dijkstra's algorithm allows you to take a graph with positive weights on each edge and a starting location and find the shortest path to all of the other nodes (if they are reachable at all). In this algorithm each node has two pieces of data associated with it: a "parent" node and a "best cost" value. Initially, all of the parent values for all of the nodes are set to invalid values, and the best cost values are set to infinity. The start node's best cost is set to zero, and all of the nodes are put into a priority queue that always removes the element with the lowest cost. Figure 4.9 shows the initial case.

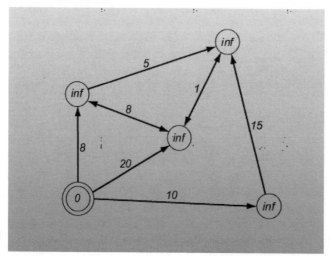

Figure 4.9: Our initial case for the shortest path computation

Note: Notice that the example graphs I'm using seem to have bidirectional edges (edges with arrows on both sides). These are just meant as shorthand for two unidirectional edges with the same cost in both directions. In the successive images, gray circles are visited nodes and dashed lines are parent links.

Iteratively remove the node with the lowest best cost from the queue. Then look at each of its edges. If the current best cost for the destination node for any of the edges is greater than the current node's cost plus the edges' cost, then there is a better path to the destination node. Then update the cost of the destination node and the parent node information, pointing them to the current node. Pseudocode for the algorithm appears in Listing 4.5.

Listing 4.5: Pseudocode for Dijkstra's algorithm

```
struct node
    vector< edge > edges
    node parent
    real cost

struct edge
    node dest
    real cost

while( priority_queue is not empty )
    node curr = priority_queue.pop
    for( all edges leaving curr )
        if( edge.dest.cost > curr.cost + edge.cost )
            edge.dest.cost = curr.cost + edge.cost
            edge.dest.parent = curr
```

Let me step through the algorithm so I can show you what happens. In the first iteration, I take the starting node off the priority queue (since it's best cost is zero and the rest are all set to infinity). All of the destination nodes are currently at infinity, so they get updated, as shown in Figure 4.10.

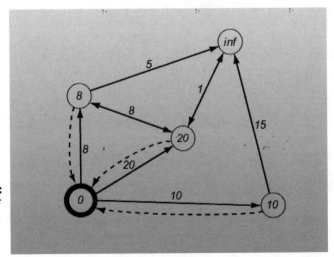

Figure 4.10: Aftermath of the first step of Dijkstra's algorithm

Then it all has to be done again. The new node you pull off the priority queue is the top-left node, with a best cost of 8. It updates the top-right node and the center node, as shown in Figure 4.11.

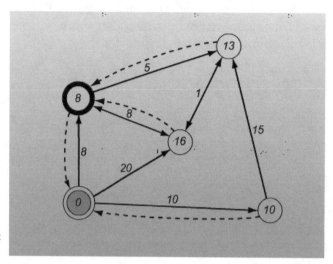

Figure 4.11:
Step 2

The next node to come off the queue is the bottom-right one, with a value of 10. Its only destination node, the top right one, already has a best cost of 13, which is less than 15 (10 + the cost of the edge – 15). Thus, the top-right node doesn't get updated, as shown in Figure 4.12.

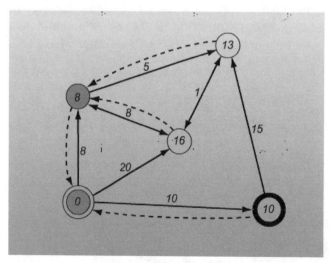

Figure 4.12:
Step 3

Next is the top-right node. It updates the center node, giving it a new best cost of 14, producing Figure 4.13.

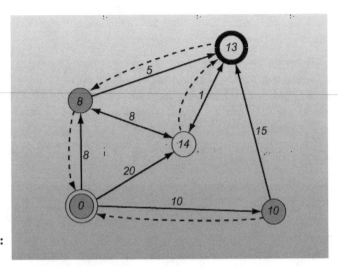

Figure 4.13:
Step 4

Finally, the center node is visited. It doesn't update anything. This empties the priority queue, giving the final graph, which appears in Figure 4.14.

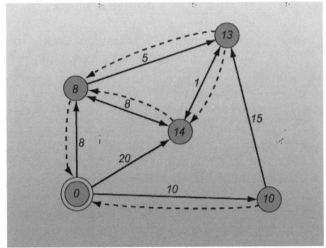

Figure 4.14:
The graph
with the final
parent-
pointers and
costs

Using Graphs to Find Shortest Paths

Now, armed with Dijkstra's algorithm, you can take a point and find the shortest path and shortest distance to all other visitable nodes on the graph. But one question remains: How is the graph to traverse generated? As it turns out, this is a simple, automatic process, thanks to the spatial data structure.

First, the kind of behavior that you wish the creature to have needs to be established. When a creature's target exists in the same convex cell the creature is in, the path is simple: Go directly towards the object using something like the Terminator AI I discussed at the beginning of the chapter. There is no need to worry about colliding with walls since the definition of convexity assures that it is possible to just march directly towards the target.

> **Warning:** I'm ignoring the fact that the objects take up a certain amount of space, so the total set of the creature's visitable points is slightly smaller than the total set of points in the convex cell. For the purposes of what I'm doing here, this is a tolerable problem, but a more robust application would need to take this fact into account.

So first there needs to be a way to tell which cell an object is in. Luckily, this is easy to do. Each polygon in a cell has a plane associated with it. All of the planes are defined such that the normal points into the cell. Simply controlling the winding order of the polygons created does this. Also known is that each point can be classified whether it is in front of or in back of a plane; I covered this in Chapter 3. For a point to be inside a cell, it must be in front of all of the planes that make up the boundary of the cell.

It may seem mildly counterintuitive to have the normals sticking in towards the center of the object rather than outwards (like in Chapter 3), but remember that they're never going to be considered for drawing from the outside. The cells are areas of empty space surrounded by solid matter. You draw from the inside, and the normals point towards you when the polygons are visible, so the normals should point inside.

Now you can easily find out the cell in which both the source and destination locations are. If they are in the same cell, you're done (marching towards the target). If not, more work needs to be done. You need to generate a path that goes from the source cell to the destination cell. To do this, you put nodes inside each portal, and throw edges back and forth between all the portals in a cell. An implementation detail is that a node in a portal is actually held by both of the cells on either side of the portal. Once the network of nodes is set up, building the edges is fairly easy. Add two edges (one each way) between each of the nodes in each cell. You have to be careful, as really intricate worlds with lots of portals and lots of nodes have to be carefully constructed so as not to overload the graph. (Naturally, the more edges in the graph, the longer Dijkstra's algorithm will take to finish its task.)

You may be wondering why I'm bothering with directed edges. The effect of having two directed edges, going in opposite directions, would be the same as having one bi-directed edge, and you would only have half the edges in the graph. In this 2-D example there is little reason to have unidirectional edges. But in 3-D everything changes. If, for example, the cell on the other side of the portal has a floor 20 feet below the other cell, you can't use the same behavior you use in the 2-D example, especially when incorporating physical properties like gravity. In this case, you would want to let the creature walk off the ledge and fall 20 feet, but since the creature wouldn't be able to turn around and miraculously leap 20 feet into the air into the cell above, you don't want an edge that would tell you to do so.

Here is where you can start to see a very important fact about AI. Although a creature seems intelligent now (well... more intelligent than the basic algorithms at the beginning of the chapter would allow), it's following a very standard algorithm to pursue its target. It has no idea what gravity is, and it has no idea that it can't leap 20 feet. The intelligence in this example doesn't come from the algorithm itself, but rather it comes from the implementation, specifically the way the graph is laid out. If it is done poorly (for example, putting in an edge that told the creature to move forward even though the door was 20 feet above it), the creature will follow the same algorithm it always does, but will look much less intelligent (walking against a wall repeatedly, hoping to magically cross through the doorway 20 feet above it).

Application: Path Planner

The second application for this chapter is a fully functioning path planner and executor. The code loads a world description off the disk, and builds an internal graph to navigate with. When the user clicks somewhere in the map, the little creature internally finds the shortest path to that location and then moves there.

Parsing the world isn't terribly hard; the data is listed in ASCII format (and was entered manually, yuck!). The first line of the file has one number, providing the number of cells. Following, separated by blank lines, are that many cells. Each cell has one line of header (containing the number of vertices, number of edges, number of portals, and number of items). Items were never implemented for this demo, but they wouldn't be too hard to stick in. It would be nice to be able to put health in the world and tell the creature "go get health!" and have it go get it.

Points are described with two floating-point coordinates, edges with two indices, and portals with two indices and a third index corresponding to the cell on the other side of the doorway. Listing 4.6 has a sample cell from the world file you'll be using.

Listing 4.6: Sample snippet from the cell description file

```
17

6 5 1 0
-8.0 8.0
-4.0 8.0
-4.0 4.0
-5.5 4.0
-6.5 4.0
-8.0 4.0
0 1
1 2
```

```
2 3
4 5
5 0
3 4 8

... more cells
```

Building the graph is a little trickier. The way it works is that each pair of door-ways (remember, each conceptual doorway has a doorway structure leading out of both of the cells touching it) holds onto a node situated in the center of the doorway. Each cell connects all of its doorway nodes together with dual edges—one going in each direction.

When the user clicks on a location, first the code makes sure that the user clicked inside the boundary of one of the cells. If it did not, the click is ignored. Only approximate boundary testing is used (using two-dimensional bounding boxes); more work would need to be done to do more exact hit testing (this is left as an exercise for the reader).

When the user clicks inside a cell, then the fun starts. Barring the trivial case (the creature and clicked location are in the same cell), a node is created inside the cell and edges are thrown out to all of the doorway nodes. Then Dijkstra's algorithm is used to find the shortest path to the node. The shortest path is inserted into a structure called sPath that is essentially just a stack of nodes. While the creature is following a path, it peeks at the top of the stack. If it is close enough to it within some epsilon, the node is popped off the stack and the next one is chosen. When the stack is empty, the creature has reached its destination.

The application uses the GDI for all the graphics, making it fairly slow. Also, the graph searching algorithm uses linear searches to find the cheapest node while it's constructing the shortest path. To put it bluntly, I'm leaving a lot of room for improvement. (What fun would it be if I did all the work for you?) A screen shot from the path planner appears in Figure 4.15. The creature appears as a red circle.

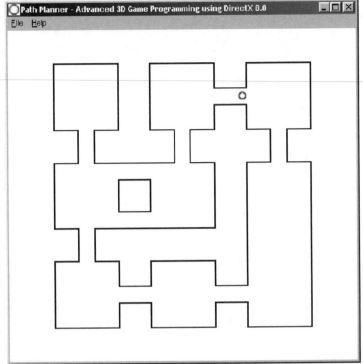

Figure 4.15:
Screen shot from the path planner

Listing 4.7 gives the code used to find the shortest path in the graph. There is plenty of other source code to wander through in this project, but this seemed like the most interesting part.

Listing 4.7: The graph searching code for the path planner

```
cNode* cWorld::FindCheapestNode()
{
    // ideally, we would implement a slightly more advanced
    // data structure to hold the nodes, like a heap.
    // since our levels are so simple, we can deal with a
    // linear algorithm.

    float fBestCost = REALLY_BIG;
    cNode* pOut = NULL;
    for( int i=0; i<m_nodeList.size(); i++ )
    {
        if( !m_nodeList[i]->m_bVisited )
        {
            if( m_nodeList[i]->m_fCost < fBestCost )
            {
                // new cheapest node
                fBestCost = m_nodeList[i]->m_fCost;
                pOut = m_nodeList[i];
            }
        }
```

```
            }
        }

        // if we haven't found a node yet, something is
        // wrong with the graph.
        assert( pOut );

        return pOut;
}

void cNode::Relax()
{
    this->m_bVisited = true;

    for( int i=0; i<m_edgeList.size(); i++ )
    {
        cEdge* pCurr = m_edgeList[i];
        if( pCurr->m_fWeight + this->m_fCost < pCurr->m_pTo->m_fCost )
        {
            // relax the 'to' node
            pCurr->m_pTo->m_pPrev = this;
            pCurr->m_pTo->m_fCost = pCurr->m_fWeight + this->m_fCost;
        }
    }
}

void cWorld::ShortestPath( sPath* pPath, cNode *pTo, cNode* pFrom )
{
    // easy out.
    if( pTo == pFrom ) return;

    InitShortestPath();

    pFrom->m_fCost = 0.f;

    bool bDone = false;
    cNode* pCurr;
    while( 1 )
    {
        pCurr = FindCheapestNode();
        if( !pCurr )
            return; // no path can be found.
        if( pCurr == pTo )
            break; // We found the shortest path

        pCurr->Relax(); // relax this node
    }

    // now we construct the path.

    // empty the path first.
```

```
        while( !pPath->m_nodeStack.empty() ) pPath->m_nodeStack.pop();

        pCurr = pTo;
        while( pCurr != pFrom )
        {
            pPath->m_nodeStack.push( pCurr );
            pCurr = pCurr->m_pPrev;
        }
    }
```

Motivation

The final area of AI I'll be discussing is the motivation of a creature. I feel it's the most interesting facet of AI. The job of the motivation engine is to decide, at a very high level, what the creature should be doing. Examples of high-level states would be "get health" or "attack nearest player." Once you have decided on a behavior, you create a set of tasks for the steering engine to accomplish. Using the "get health" example, the motivation engine would look through an internal map of the world for the closest health, and then direct the locomotion engine to find the shortest path to it and execute the path. I'll show you a few high-level motivation concepts.

Non-Deterministic Finite Automata (NFAs)

NFAs are popular in simpler artificial intelligence systems (and not only in AI; NFAs are used everywhere). If, for example, you've ever used a search program like grep (a UNIX searching command), you've used NFAs. They're a classical piece of theoretic computer science, an extension of Deterministic Finite Automata (DFAs).

How do they work? In the classic sense, you have a set of nodes connected with edges. One node (or more) is the start node and one (or more) is the end node. At any point in time, there is a set of active nodes. You send a string of data into an NFA. Each piece is processed individually.

The processing goes as follows: Each active node receives the current piece of data. It makes itself inactive, and compares the data to each of its edges. If any of its outgoing edges match the input data, they turn their destination node on. There is a special type of edge called an *epsilon edge*, which turns its destination on regardless of the input.

When all of the data has been processed, you look at the list of active nodes. If any of the end nodes are active, then that means the string of data passed. You construct the NFA to accept certain types of strings, and can quickly run a string through an NFA to test it.

Here are a few examples to help make the definition more concrete. Both of the examples are fairly simple NFAs just to show the concepts being explained.

Let's say there is an alphabet with exactly two values, A and B. The first example, Figure 4.16, is an NFA that accepts only the string ABB and nothing else.

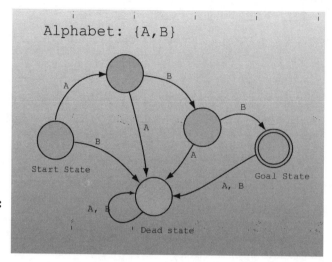

Figure 4.16:
NFA that
accepts the
string ABB

The second example, Figure 4.17, shows an NFA that accepts the string A*B, where A* means any number of As, including zero.

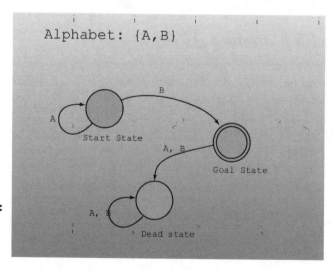

Figure 4.17:
NFA that
accepts the
string A*B

How is this useful for game programming? If you encode the environment that the creature exists in into a string that you feed into an NFA, you can allow it to process its scene and decide what to do. You could have one goal state for each of the possible behaviors (that is, one for "attack enemy," one for "get health," and other high-level behaviors). As an example, one of the entries in the array of NFA data could represent how much ammo the character has. Let's say there are three possible states: {Plenty of ammo, Ammo, Little or no ammo}. The edge that corresponded to "Plenty of ammo" would lead to a section of the NFA that would contain aggressive end states, while the "Little or no ammo" edges would lead to a section of the NFA that would most likely have the creature decide that it needed to get some ammo. The next piece of data would describe a different aspect of the universe the creature existed in, and the NFA would have branches ready to accept it.

Table 4.1 contains some examples of states that could be encoded in the string of data for the NFA.

Table 4.1: Some example states that could be encoded into an NFA

Proximity to nearest opponent	Very near; Average distance; Very far.
	If the nearest opponent is very far, the edge could lead to states that encourage the collection of items.
Health	Plenty of health; Adequate health; Dangerous health.
	If the creature has dangerously low health and the opponent was very near, a kamikaze attack would probably be in order. If the nearest enemy was very far away, it should consider getting some health.
Environment	Tight and close; Medium; Expansive.
	A state like this would determine which weapon to use. For example, explosive weapons like a rocket launcher shouldn't be used in tight and close areas.
Enemy health	Plenty of health; Adequate health; Dangerous health.
	The health of the nearest enemy determines the attacking pattern of the creature. Even if the creature has moderate to low health, it should try for the kill if the enemy has dangerous health.
Enemy altitude	Above; Equal; Below.
	It's advantageous in most games to be on higher ground than your opponent, especially in games with rocket launcher splash damage. If the creature is below its nearest opponent and the opponent is nearby, it might consider retreating to higher ground before attacking.

One way to implement NFAs would be to have a function pointer in each end state that got executed after the NFA was processed if the end state succeeded.

The only problem with NFAs is that it's extremely difficult to encode fuzzy decisions. For example, it would be better if the creature's health was represented with a floating-point value, so there would be a nearly continuous range of responses based on health. I'll show you how to use neural networks to do this. However, NFA-based AI can be more than adequate for many games. If your NFA's behavior is too simple, you generally only need to extend the NFA, adding more behaviors and more states.

Genetic Algorithms

While not directly a motivation concept, genetic algorithms (or GAs) can be used to tweak other motivation engines. They try to imitate nature to solve problems. Typically, when you're trying to solve a problem that has a fuzzy solution (like, for example, the skill of an AI opponent), it's very hard to tweak the numbers to get the best answer.

One way to solve a problem like this is to attack it the way nature does. In nature (according to Darwin, anyway) animals do everything they can to survive long enough to produce offspring. Typically, the only members of a species that survive long enough to procreate are the most superior of their immediate peers. In a pride of lions, only one male impregnates all of the females. All of the other male lions vie for control of the pride, so that their genes get carried on.

Added to this system, occasionally, is a bit of mutation. An offspring is the combination of the genes of the two parents, but it may be different from either of the parents by themselves. Occasionally, an animal will be born with bigger teeth, sharper claws, longer legs, or in Simpsonian cases, a third eye. The change might give that particular offspring an advantage over its peers. If it does, that offspring is more likely than the other animals to carry on its genes, and thus, over time, the species improves.

That's nice and all, but what does that have to do with software development? A lot, frankly. What if you could codify the parameters of a problem into genes? You could randomly create a set of animals, each with their own genes. They are set loose, they wreak havoc, and a superior pair of genes is found. Then you combine these two genes, sprinkle some random perturbations in, and repeat the process with the new offspring and another bunch of random creatures.

For example, you could define the behavior of all the creatures in terms of a set of scalar values. Values that define how timid a creature is when it's damaged, how prone it is to change its current goal, how accurate its shots are when it is moving backward, and so forth. Correctly determining the best set of parameters for each of the creatures can prove difficult. Things get worse when you consider other types of variables, like the weapon the creature is using and the type of enemy it's up against.

Genetic algorithms to the rescue! Initially, you create a slew of creatures with a bunch of random values for each of the parameters, and put them into a virtual battleground, having them duke it out until only two creatures remain. Those two creatures mate, combining their genes and sprinkling in a bit of mutation to create a whole new set of creatures, and the cycle repeats.

The behavior that genetic algorithms exhibit is called *hill climbing*. You can think of a creature's idealness as a function of n variables. The graph for this function would have many relative maximums and one absolute maximum. In the case where there were only two variables, you would see a graph with a bunch of hills (where the two parameters made a formidable opponent), a bunch of valleys (where the parameters made a bad opponent), and an absolute maximum (the top of the tallest mountain: the best possible creature).

For each iteration, the creature that will survive will hopefully be the one that was the highest on the graph. Then the iteration continues, with a small mutation (you can think of this as sampling the area immediately around the creature). The winner of the next round will be a little bit better than its parent as it climbs the hill. When the children stop getting better, you know you have reached the top of a hill, a relative maximum.

How do you know if you reached the absolute maximum, the tallest hill on the graph? It's extremely hard to do. If you increase the amount of mutation, you increase the area you sample around the creature, so you're more likely to happen to hit a point along the slope of the tallest mountain. However, the more you increase the sampling area, the less likely you are to birth a creature further up the mountain, so the function takes much longer to converge.

Rule-Based AI

The world of reality is governed by a set of rules, rules that control everything from the rising and setting of the sun to the way cars work. The AI algorithms discussed up to this point aren't aware of any rules, so they would have a lot of difficulty knowing how to start a car, for example.

Rule-based AI can help alleviate this problem. You define a set of rules that govern how things work in the world. The creature can analyze the set of rules to decide what to do. For example, let's say that a creature needs health. It knows that there is health in a certain room, but to get into the room the creature must open the door, which can only be done from a security station console. One way to implement this would be to hardcode the knowledge into the creature. It would run to the security station, open the door, run through it, and grab the health.

However, a generic solution has a lot of advantages. The behavior it can exhibit isn't limited to just opening security doors. Anything you can describe with a set of rules is something it can figure out. See Listing 4.8 for a subset of the rules for a certain world.

Listing 4.8: Some rules for an example world

```
IF [Health_Room == Visitable]
    THEN [Health == Gettable]
IF [Security_Door == Door_Open]
    THEN [Health_Room == Visitable]
IF [Today == Sunday]
    THEN [Tacos == 0.49]
IF [Creature_Health < 0.25]
    THEN [Creature_State = FindGettableHealth]
IF [Creature_Position NEAR Security_Console]
    THEN [Security_Console_Usable]
```

```
IF [Security_Console_Usable] AND [Security_Door != Door_Open]
   THEN [Creature_Use(Security_Console)]
IF [Security_Console_Used]
   THEN [Security_Door == Door_Open]
IF [Creature_Move_To(Security_Console)]
   THEN [Creature_Position NEAR Security_Console]
```

Half the challenge in setting up rule-based systems is to come up with an efficient way to encode the rules. The other half is actually creating the rules. Luckily a lot of the rules, like the Creature_Move_To rule at the end of the list, can be automatically generated.

How does the creature figure out what to do, given these rules? It has a goal in mind: getting health. It looks in the rules, and finds the goal it wants, [Health == Gettable]. It then needs to satisfy the condition for that goal to be true, that is [Health_Room == Visitable]. The creature can query the game engine and ask it if the health room is visitable. When the creature finds out that it is not, it has a new goal: making the health room visitable.

Searching the rules again, it finds that [Health_Room == Visitable] if [Security_Door == Door_Open]. Once again, it sees that the security door is not open, so it analyzes the rule set again, looking for a way to satisfy the condition.

This process continues until the creature reaches the rule saying that if it moves to the security console, it will be near the security console. Finally, a command that it can do! It then uses path planning to get to the security console, presses the button to open the security door, moves to the health room, and picks up the health.

AI like this can be amazingly neat. Nowhere do you tell how to get the health. It actually figured out how to do it all by itself. If you could encode all the rules necessary to do anything in a particular world, then the AI would be able to figure out how to accomplish whatever goals it wanted. The only tricky thing is encoding this information in an efficient way. And if you think that's tricky, try getting the creature to develop its own rules as it goes along. If you can get that, your AI will always be learning, always improving.

Neural Networks

One of the huge areas of research in AI is in neural networks (NNs). They take a very fundamental approach to the problem of artificial intelligence by trying to closely simulate intelligence, in the physical sense.

Years of research have gone into studying how the brain actually works (it's mystifying that evolution managed to design an intelligence capable of analyzing itself). Researchers have discovered the basic building blocks of the brain, and have found that, at a biological level, it is just a really, really (REALLY) dense graph. On the order of billions or trillions of nodes, and each node is connected to thousands of others.

The difference between the brain and other types of graphs is that the brain is extremely connected. Thinking of several concepts brings up several other concepts, simply through the fact that the nodes are connected. As an example, think for a moment about an object that is leafy, green, and crunchy. You most likely thought about several things, maybe celery or vegetable. That's because there is a strong connection between the leafy part of your brain, and things that are leafy. When the leafy neuron fires, it sends its signal to all the nodes it's connected to. The same goes for green and crunchy. Since, when you think of those things, they all fire and all send signals to nodes, some nodes receive enough energy to fire themselves, such as the celery node.

Now, I'm not going to attempt to model the brain itself, but you can learn from it and build your own network of electronic neurons. Graphs that simulate brain activity in this way are generally called *neural networks*.

Neural networks are still a very active area of research. In the last year or so, a team was able to use a new type of neural network to understand garbled human speech better than humans can! One of the big advantages of neural networks is that they can be trained to remember their past actions. You can teach them, giving them an input and then telling them the correct output. Do this enough times and the network can learn what the correct answer is.

However, that is a big piece of pie to bite down on. Instead, I'm going to delve into a higher-level discussion of neural networks, by explaining how they work sans training, and providing code for you to play with.

A Basic Neuron

Think of a generic neuron in your brain as consisting of three biological parts: an *axon*, *dendrites*, and a *soma*. The processing unit is the soma. It takes input coming from the dendrites and outputs to the axon. The axon, in turn, is connected to the dendrites of other neurons, passing the signals on. These processes are all handled with chemicals in real neurons; a soma that fires is, in essence, sending a chemical down its axon that will meet up with other dendrites, sending the fired message to other neurons. Figure 4.18 shows what a real neuron looks like.

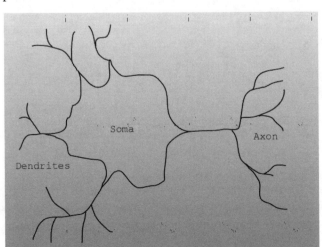

Figure 4.18:
A biological neuron

The digital version is very similar. There is a network of nodes connected by edges. When a node is processed, it takes all of the signals on the incoming edges and adds them together. One of these edges is a special bias or memory edge, which is just an edge that is always on. This value can change to modify the behavior of the network (the higher the bias value, the more likely the neuron is to fire). If the summation of the inputting nodes is above the threshold (usually 1.0), then the node sends a fire signal to each of its outgoing edges. The fire signal is not the result of the addition, as that may be much more than 1.0. It is always 1.0. Each edge also has a bias that can scale the signal being passed it higher or lower. Because of this, the input that arrives at a neuron can be just about any value, not just 1.0 (firing neurons) or 0 (non-firing neurons). They may be anywhere; if the edge bias was 5.0, for example, the neuron would receive 5.0 or 0, depending on whether the neuron attached to it fired or not. Using a bias on the edges can also make a fired neuron have a dampened effect on other neurons.

The equation for the output of a neuron can be formalized as follows:

$$x = b(B) + \sum_n \text{bias}_n(\text{node}_n)$$

$$\text{out} = \begin{cases} 1.0 & \text{if } x > 1.0 \\ 0.0 & \text{otherwise} \end{cases}$$

where you sum over the inputs n (the bias of the edge, multiplied by the output of the neuron attached to it) plus the weight of the bias node times the bias edge weight.

Other types of responses to the inputs are possible; some systems use a Sigmoid exponential function like the one below. A continuous function such as this makes it easier to train certain types of networks (back propagation networks, for example), but for these purposes the all-or-nothing response will do the job.

$$x = b(B) + \sum_n \text{bias}_n(\text{node}_n)$$

$$\text{out} = \frac{1.0}{1.0 + e^{-x}}$$

One of the capabilities of the brain is the ability to imagine things given a few inputs. Imagine you hear the phrases "vegetable," "orange," and "eaten by rabbits." Your mind's eye conjures up an image of carrots. Imagine your neural network's inputs are these words, and your outputs are names of different objects. When you hear the word "orange," somewhere in your network (and your brain) an "orange" neuron fires. It sends a fire signal to objects you have associated with the word "orange" (for example: carrots, oranges, orange crayons, an orange shirt). That signal alone probably won't be enough for any particular one of those other neurons to fire; they need other signals to help bring the total over the threshold. If you then hear another phrase, such as "eaten by rabbits," the "eaten by rabbits" neuron will fire off a signal to all the nodes associated with that word (for example: carrots, lettuce, boisterous English crusaders). Those two signals may be enough to have the neuron fire, sending an output of carrots. Figure 4.19 abstractly shows what is happening.

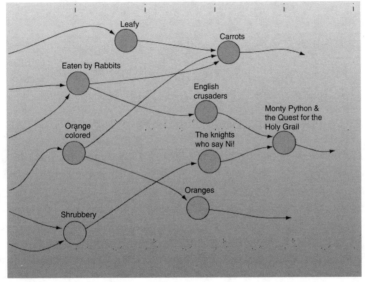

Figure 4.19:
A subsection of a hypothetical neural network

Simple Neural Networks

Neural networks are Turing-complete; that is, they can be used to perform any calculation that computers can do, given enough nodes and enough edges. Given that you can construct any processor using nothing but NAND gates, this doesn't seem like too ridiculous a conjecture. Let's look at some simpler neural networks before trying to tackle anything more complex.

AND

Binary logic seems like a good place to start. As a first stab at a neural net, let's try to design a neural net that can perform a binary AND. The network appears in Figure 4.20.

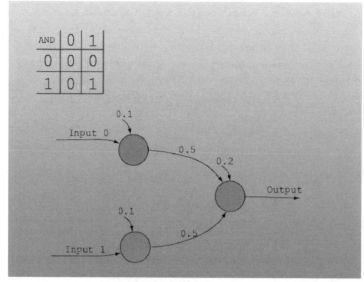

Figure 4.20:
A neural network that can perform a binary AND function

Note that the input nodes have a bias of 0.1. This is to help fuzzify the numbers a bit. You could make the network strict if you'd like (setting the bias to 0.0), but for many applications 0.9 is close enough to 1.0 to count as being 1.0.

OR

Binary OR is similar to AND; the middle edges just have a higher weight so that either one of them can activate the output node. The net appears in Figure 4.21.

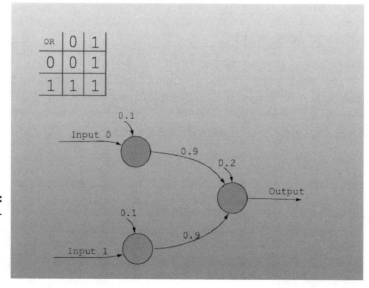

Figure 4.21:
A neural network that can perform a binary OR function

XOR

Handling XOR requires a bit more thought. Three nodes alone can't possibly handle XOR; you need to make another layer to the network. A semi-intuitive reasoning behind the workings of Figure 4.22: The top internal node will only be activated if both input nodes fire. The bottom one will fire if either of the input nodes fires. If both internal nodes fire, that means that both input nodes fired (a case you should not accept), which is correctly handled by having a large negative weight for the edge leading from the top internal node to the output node.

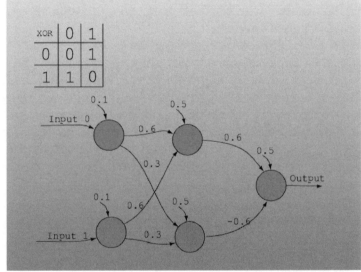

Figure 4.22: A neural network that can perform a binary XOR function

Training Neural Networks

While it's outside the scope of this book, it's important to know one of the most important and interesting features about neural nets: They can be trained. Suppose you create a neural net to solve a certain problem (or put another way, to give a certain output given a set of inputs). You can initially seed the network with random values for all of the edge biases, and then have the network learn. Neural nets can be trained or can learn autonomously. An autonomously learning neural net would be, for example, an AI that was trying to escape from a maze. As it moves, it learns more information, but it has no way to check its answer as it goes along. These types of networks learn much slower than trained networks. Trained neural networks on the other hand have a cheat sheet; that is, they know the solution to each problem. They run an input and check their output against the correct answer. If it is wrong, the network modifies some of the weights so that it gets the correct answer the next time.

Using Neural Networks in Games

Using a neural network to decide the high-level action to perform in lieu of NFAs has a lot of advantages. For example, the solutions are often much fuzzier. Reaching a certain state isn't as black and white as achieving a certain value in the string of inputs; it's the sum of a set of factors that all contribute to the behavior.

As an example, let's say that you have a state that, when reached, causes your creature to flee its current location in search of health. You may want to do this in many cases. One example would be if there was a strong enemy nearby. Another would be if there was a mildly strong enemy nearby and the main character is low on health. You can probably conjure up a dozen other cases that would justify turning tail and fleeing.

While it's possible to codify all of these cases separately into an NFA, it's rather tedious. It's better to have all of the input states (proximity of nearest enemy, strength of nearest enemy, health, ammo, etc.) become inputs into the neural network. Then you could just have an output node that, when fired, caused the creature to run for health. This way, the behavior emerges from the millions of different combinations for inputs. If enough factors contribute to the turn-and-flee state to make it fire, it will sum over the threshold and fire.

A neural network that does this is exactly what I'm going to show you how to write.

Application: NeuralNet

The NeuralNet sample application is a command-line application to show off a neural network simulator. The network is loaded off disk from a description file; input values for the network are requested from the user, then the network is run and the output appears on the console. I'll also build a sample network that simulates a simple creature AI. An example running of the network appears in Listing 4.9. In this example, the creature has low health, plenty of ammo, and an enemy nearby. The network decides to select the state [Flee_Enemy_Towards_Health]. If this code were to be used in a game, state-setting functions would be called in lieu of printing out the names of the output states.

Listing 4.9: Sample output of the neural net simulator

```
Advanced 3-D Game Programming using DirectX 8.0
-----------------------------------------------

Neural Net Simulator

Using nn description file [creature.nn]


Neural Net Inputs:
```

```
------------------
Ammo (0..1)
1 - Ammo (0..1)
Proximity to enemy (0..1)
1 - Proximity to enemy (0..1)
Health (0..1)
1 - Health (0..1)

Enter Inputs:
-------------
Enter floating point input for [Ammo (0..1)]
1.0
```

The NeuralNet description file (*.nn) details the network that the application will run. Each line that isn't a comment starts with a keyword describing the data contained in the line. The keywords appear in Table 4.2.

Table 4.2: Neural net description keywords

NN_BEGIN	Defines the beginning of the neural network. Always the first line of the file. First token is the number of layers in the neural network. The input layer counts as one, and so does the output layer.
NN_END	Defines the ending of the neural network description.
NEURON	Declares a neuron. The first token is the name of the neuron, and the second is the bias of the neuron.
INPUT	Declares an input. The first token is the name of the neuron to receive the input, and the second token (enclosed in quotes) is the user-friendly name for the input. The list of inputs is iterated for user inputs prior to running the simulation.
DEFAULTOUT	The default output of the neural network. Only token is the text of the default output.
OUTPUT	Declares an output. The first token is the name of the neuron, the second is the text to print if the neuron fires, and the third is the bias of the neuron.
EDGE	Declares an edge. The first token is the name of the source node, the second token is the name of the destination node, and the third token is the floating-point weight of the edge.

The order in which the neurons appear in the file is pivotally important. They are appended to an STL vector as they are loaded in, and the vector is traversed when the network is run. Therefore, they should appear ordered in the file as they would appear left to right in the diagrams presented thus far (the input nodes at the beginning, the internal nodes in the middle, the output nodes at the end).

Listing 4.10 shows the sample network description creature.nn. This is a simplistic creature AI that can attack, flee, and find items it needs. The network is simple enough that it's easy to see that adding more states wouldn't be too hard a task. It's important to note that this network is designed to have its inputs range from –1 to 1 (so having health input as 0 means the creature has about 50% health).

Listing 4.10: creature.nn

```
# First line starts the NN loading and gives the # of layers.
NN_BEGIN 2
#
# NEURON x y z
# x = layer number
# y = node name
# z = node bias
NEURON 0 health 0.0
NEURON 0 healthInv 0.0
NEURON 0 ammo 0.0
NEURON 0 ammoInv 0.0
NEURON 0 enemy 0.0
NEURON 0 enemyInv 0.0
NEURON 1 findHealth 0.2
NEURON 1 findAmmo 0.2
NEURON 1 attackEnemy 0.5
NEURON 1 fleeToHealth 0.5
NEURON 1 fleeToAmmo 0.5
#
# DEFAULTOUT "string"
# string = the default output
DEFAULTOUT "Chill out"
#
# EDGE x y z
# x = source neuron
# y = dest neuron
# z = edge weight
#
EDGE health attackEnemy 0.5
EDGE ammo attackEnemy 0.5
EDGE enemy attackEnemy 0.5
EDGE healthInv attackEnemy -0.5
EDGE ammoInv attackEnemy -0.5
EDGE enemyInv attackEnemy -0.6
#
EDGE healthInv findHealth 0.6
EDGE enemyInv findHealth 0.6
#
EDGE ammoInv findAmmo 0.6
EDGE enemyInv findAmmo 0.6
#
EDGE healthInv fleeToHealth 0.8
EDGE enemy fleeToHealth 0.5
#
```

```
EDGE ammoInv fleeToAmmo 0.8
EDGE enemy fleeToAmmo 0.5
#
# INPUT/OUTPUT x "y"
# x = node for input/output
# y = fancy name for the input/output
INPUT health "Health (0..1)"
INPUT healthInv "1 - Health (0..1)"
INPUT ammo "Ammo (0..1)"
INPUT ammoInv "1 - Ammo (0..1)"
INPUT enemy "Proximity to enemy (0..1)"
INPUT enemyInv "1 - Proximity to enemy (0..1)"
OUTPUT findHealth "Find Health"
OUTPUT findAmmo "Find Ammo"
OUTPUT attackEnemy "Attack Nearest Enemy"
OUTPUT fleeToHealth "Flee Enemy Towards Health"
OUTPUT fleeToAmmo "Flee Enemy Towards Ammo"
#
NN_END
```

The source code for the neural network simulator appears in Listings 4.11 and 4.12.

Listing 4.11: NeuralNet.h

```
/*******************************************************************
 *          Advanced 3-D Game Programming using DirectX 8.0
 * * * * * * * * * * * * * * * * * * * * * * * * * * * * * * * *
 *    Title: NeuralNet.h
 *     Desc: code to run a neural network
 *
 * copyright (c) 2001 by Peter A Walsh and Adrian Perez
 * See license.txt for modification and distribution information
 *******************************************************************/

#ifndef _NEURALNET_H
#define _NEURALNET_H

#include <string>
#include <vector>
#include <map>

using namespace std;

#include "file.h"

class cNeuralNet
{
protected:
    class cNode;
```

```
        class cEdge;

public:
    string GetOutput();

    void SendInput( const char* inputName, float amt );

    void Load( cFile& file );
    void Run();
    void Clear();
    cNeuralNet();
    virtual ~cNeuralNet();

    void ListInputs();
    void GetInputs();

protected:


    cNode* FindNode( const char* name );

    class cNode
    {
    public:
        void Init( const char* name, float weight );

        void Clear();
        virtual void Run();

        void AddOutEdge( cNode* target, float edgeWeight );
        void SendInput( float in );

        const char* GetName() const;
        float GetTotal() const;
    protected:

        // Computes the output function given the total.
        virtual float CalcOutput();

        string  m_name;
        float   m_weight; // initial bias in either direction
        float   m_total;  // total of the summed inputs
        vector< cEdge > m_outEdges;

    };

    class cEdge
    {
        cNode*  m_pSrc;
        cNode*  m_pDest;
        float   m_weight;
```

```
        public:

            cEdge( cNode* pSrc, cNode* pDst, float weight );

            void Fire( float amount );
        };
        friend class cNode;

        vector< vector< cNode* > > m_nodes;

        // maps the names of output nodes to output strings.
        map< string, string > m_inputs;
        map< string, string > m_outputs;

        string m_defaultOutput;
};

inline const char* cNeuralNet::cNode::GetName() const
{
    return m_name.c_str();
}

inline float cNeuralNet::cNode::GetTotal() const
{
    return m_total;
}

#endif // _NEURALNET_H
```

Some code is omitted from Listing 4.12 for brevity, including the routines to get input and the routine to load the file.

Listing 4.12: NeuralNet.cpp

```
/******************************************************************
 *          Advanced 3-D Game Programming using DirectX 8.0
 * * * * * * * * * * * * * * * * * * * * * * * * * * * * * * * * *
 *    Title: NeuralNet.cpp
 *      Desc: Code to load and run a neural net.
 *
 * copyright (c) 2001 by Peter A Walsh and Adrian Perez
 * See license.txt for modification and distribution information
 ******************************************************************/

using namespace std;

int main(int argc, char* argv[])
{
    // Sorry, I don't do cout.
    printf( "Advanced 3-D Game Programming using DirectX 8.0\n" );
```

```
        printf( "-------------------------------------------------\n\n" );
        printf( "Neural Net Simulator\n\n");

        if( argc != 2 )
        {
            printf("Usage: neuralnet filename.nn\n");
            return 0;
        }

        printf("Using nn description file [%s]\n\n", argv[1] );

        cNeuralNet nn;
        cFile nnFile;
        nnFile.Open( argv[1] );
        nn.Load( nnFile );
        nnFile.Close();

        int done = 0;
        while( !done )
        {
            // Clear the totals
            nn.Clear();

            // List the inputs for the net from the user
            nn.ListInputs();

            // Get the inputs for the net from the user
            nn.GetInputs();

            // Run the net
            nn.Run();

            // Get the net's output.
            string output = nn.GetOutput();

            printf("\nNeural Net output was [%s]\n", output.c_str() );
            printf("\nRun Again? (y/n)\n");
            char buff[80];
            gets( buff );

            if( !(buff[0] == 'y' || buff[0] == 'Y') )
            {
                done = 1;
            }
        }
        return 0;
}

cNeuralNet::cNeuralNet()
{
    // no work needs to be done.
```

```
    }

cNeuralNet::~cNeuralNet()
{
    // delete all of the nodes. each node will get its outgoing edges
    int numLayers = m_nodes.size();
    for( int i=0; i<numLayers; i++ )
    {
        int layerSize = m_nodes[i].size();
        for( int j=0; j<layerSize; j++ )
        {
            delete m_nodes[i][j];
        }
    }
}

cNeuralNet::cNode* cNeuralNet::FindNode( const char *name)
{
    cNode* pCurr;

    // Search for the node.
    int numLayers = m_nodes.size();
    for( int i=0; i<numLayers; i++ )
    {
        int layerSize = m_nodes[i].size();
        for( int j=0; j<layerSize; j++ )
        {
            pCurr = m_nodes[i][j];
            if( 0 == strcmp( pCurr->GetName(), name ) )
                return pCurr;
        }
    }

    // didn't contain the node (bad)
    printf( "ERROR IN NEURAL NET FILE!\n");
    printf( "Tried to look for node named [%s]\n", name );
    printf( "but couldn't find it!\n");
    exit(0);
    return NULL;
}

void cNeuralNet::Clear()
{
    // Call clear on each of the networks.
    cNode* pCurr;

    int numLayers = m_nodes.size();
    for( int i=0; i<numLayers; i++ )
    {
        int layerSize = m_nodes[i].size();
        for( int j=0; j<layerSize; j++ )
```

```
        {
            pCurr = m_nodes[i][j];
            pCurr->Clear();
        }
    }
}

void cNeuralNet::Run()
{
    // Run each layer, running each node in each layer.
    int numLayers = m_nodes.size();
    for( int i=0; i<numLayers; i++ )
    {
        int layerSize = m_nodes[i].size();
        for( int j=0; j<layerSize; j++ )
        {
            m_nodes[i][j]->Run();
        }
    }
}

void cNeuralNet::SendInput( const char *inputTarget, float amt)
{
    // Find the node that we're sending the input to, and send it.
    FindNode( inputTarget )->SendInput( amt );
}

void cNeuralNet::cNode::Clear()
{
    // initial total is set to the bias
    m_total = m_weight;
}

void cNeuralNet::cNode::Run()
{
    // Compute the transfer function
    float output = CalcOutput();

    // Send it to each of our children
    cEdge* pCurr;
    int size = m_outEdges.size();
    for( int i=0; i< size; i++ )
    {
        m_outEdges[i].Fire( output );
    }
}

void cNeuralNet::cNode::Init( const char *name, float weight)
{
    m_name = string( name );
```

```
        m_weight = weight;
    }

    float cNeuralNet::cNode::CalcOutput()
    {
        // This can use an exponential-type function
        // but for simplicity's sake we're just doing
        // flat yes/no.
        if( m_total >= 1.0f )
            return 1.0f;
        else
            return 0.f;
    }

    void cNeuralNet::cNode::SendInput(float in)
    {
        // just add the input to the total for the network.
        m_total += in;
    }

    void cNeuralNet::cNode::AddOutEdge(cNode *target, float edgeWeight)
    {
        // Create an edge structure
        m_outEdges.push_back( cEdge( this, target, edgeWeight) );
    }


    cNeuralNet::cEdge::cEdge( cNode *pSrc, cNode *pDest, float weight)
    : m_pSrc( pSrc )
    , m_pDest( pDest )
    , m_weight( weight)
    {
        // all done.
    }

    void cNeuralNet::cEdge::Fire( float amount )
    {
        // Send the signal, multiplied by the weight,
        // to the destination node.
        m_pDest->SendInput( amount * m_weight );
    }
```

Some Closing Thoughts

Creating a successful AI engine needs the combined effort of a bunch of different concepts and ideas. Neural networks alone can't do much, but combine them with path planning and you can create a formidable opponent. Use genetic algorithms to evolve the neural networks (well, actually just the bias weights for the neural networks) and you can breed an army of formidable opponents, each one different in its own way. It's a truly exciting facet of game programming, and you're only cheating yourself if you don't investigate the topic further.

References

Rao, Dr. Valluro, and Hayagriva Rao. *C++ Neural Networks and Fuzzy Logic*. IDG Books Worldwide, 1995. ISBN: 1558515526.

LaMothe, Andre. "Neural Netware." Available at http://www.xgames3d.com/ articles/netware/areadnet.htm.

Rogers, Joey. *Object-Oriented Neural Networks in C++*. Morgan Kaufmann Publishers, 1996. ISBN: 0125931158.

For Further Reading

If you can get your hands on them, the course notes from the Game Developers Conference is full of great articles about game-style AI. I strongly recommend checking that out.

LaMothe, Andre. *Tricks of the Windows Game Programming Gurus: Fundamentals of 2D and 3D Game Programming*. MacMillan Publishing Company, 1999. ISBN: 0672313618.

LaMothe has a nice discussion of fuzzy logic in his book, a topic that goes hand in hand with neural networks.

Chapter 5

UDP Networking

Doom. Quake III: Arena. Duke Nukem'. Unreal Tournament. It seems like every game released these days is written to be played on the Internet. It's the wave of the future—the world is becoming a global village and there's a dire need to kill everyone in town. But writing a game and writing a game that can be played over the Internet are two very different things. Far too many games have died in their infancy because programmers assumed it would be a simple matter of adding in network code when everything else was done. Nothing could be further from the truth. In this chapter, I'm going to show you the basics of setting up a network game and reducing the amount of lag, and then investigate some possible optimizations.

Terminology

First, you need to know some basic terminology.

Endianness

There are a few major problems with the Internet. First, it's completely unorganized; second, data sent over the Internet has a good chance of never reaching its destination. It's important to understand some of what is going on inside the Internet in order to overcome these problems.

The reason the Internet is so unorganized is that it is still evolving. Different operating systems, different hardware—it can be a real headache. By far one of the furthest reaching differences is that of *endianness*. When a computer CPU has to store information that takes up more than 1 byte, most types of CPUs will store the bytes in order from smallest to largest. This is known as *big endian*. However, some machines do it a little differently. Suppose you have a whole number that takes up 2 bytes. In a *little endian* system, the bytes are stored with bits 0-7 representing the values 2^0-2^7 and bits 8-15 representing values 2^8-2^{15}. But the CPU in a big endian system stores the same value the other way around with bits 0-7 representing values 2^8-2^{15} and bits 8-15 representing values 2^0-2^7.

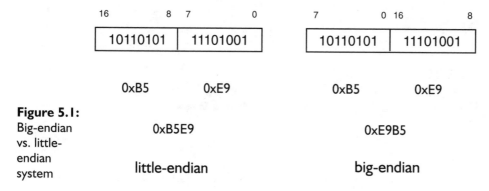

Figure 5.1:
Big-endian
vs. little-
endian
system

This means that when you want to send data over the Internet you have to make sure that your numbers are in the default endianness of the Internet, and when you receive information you have to be sure to switch back to your computer's default endianness.

Another effect of such an unorganized system is that a system of addresses had to be created so as to tell one machine from another. Known as a *host address* or *IP address*, they take the form *nnn.nnn.nnn.nnn*, where *nnn* is a whole number between 0 and 255, inclusive. This would imply that there can't be more than 4 billion machines on the Internet simultaneously but in practice the limit is quite a bit lower. The reason is that there are three types of networks called class A, class B, and class C. Each class uses a certain range of possible IP addresses, severely limiting the total possible combinations. For example, class C networks use IP addresses in the range 192.0.0.*x* through 223.255.255.*x*. Class C networks use the first three bits to identify the network as class C, which leaves 21 bits for identifying a computer on the network. The value 2^{21} is a total of 2,097,152 possible addresses; as of 2000, over 55% of those have been assigned to computers that are always online. But it gets worse—class B networks have a total of 16,384 combinations and class A networks only have 128. Fortunately, new legislation is changing all that. For more information check out the American Registry for Internet Numbers (www.arin.net).

But enough segue! There are two kinds of addresses: For those machines that are always on the Internet there are static addresses that never change. For those computers that have dial-up connections or that aren't regularly on the Internet there are dynamic addresses that are different each time the computer connects.

With all the phone numbers, bank accounts, combination locks, secret passwords, and shoe sizes, there isn't much room left over in most people's memories for a collection of IP addresses. So in order to make things a little more user friendly, *host names* were introduced. A host name such as www.flipcode.com or www.gamedev.net represents the four-number address. If the IP address changes, the host name keeps working. A host name has to be resolved back into the IP address before it can be used to make a connection attempt. In order to resolve a host name, the computer trying to resolve must already know the address of a *Domain Name Server* (DNS). It contacts the DNS and sends the host name. The DNS server responds by returning the numeric IP address of the host.

With so many programs running on so many different computers around the globe, there has to be a way to separate communication into different "channels," much like separate phone lines or TV stations. Inside any Winsock-compliant computer are 65,534 imaginary *ports* to which data can be sent. Some recognized protocols have default ports—HTTP uses port 80 and FTP uses port 21 (more on protocols in a moment). Any program can send data to any port, but if there's no one listening the data will be ignored, and if the listening program doesn't understand the data then things could get ugly. In order to listen or transmit data to a port, both machines must begin by initializing Winsock, a standard library of methods for accessing network firmware/hardware. Winsock is based in part on UNIX sockets so most methods can be used on either type of operating system without need for rewriting. Once Winsock has been initialized, the two machines must each create a *socket* handle and associate that socket with a port. Having successfully completed socket association, all that remains to do is transfer data and then clean up when you're done. But your problems are just beginning. Once you've finished all the fundamental communication code there should only be one thing on your mind: speed, speed, and more speed.

Network Models

In order to make games run smoothly some kind of order has to be imposed on the Internet; some clearly defined way of making sure that every player in the game sees as close to the same thing as possible. The first thought that leaps to mind is "connect every machine to every other machine!" This is known as a peer-to-peer configuration and it sounds like a good configuration. In fact it was used in some of the first networked games. However, as the number of players rise, this peer-to-peer model quickly becomes impractical. Consider a game with four players. Each player must have three connections to other players for a total of six connections. Each player also has to send the same data three times. Hmm. Dubious. Now consider the same game with six players. Each player has to send the same data out five times and there are a total of 15 connections. In an eight-player game there are 28 connections. Try it yourself—the equation is

$$\frac{P \times (P-1)}{2}$$ where P is the number of players.

Another method might be to arrange all the players in a ring, with each player connected to two other machines. This sounds a bit better because there are only (P + 1) connections and each player only has to send data once, clockwise around the ring. My computer tells your computer, your computer tells her computer, and so on around the ring until it comes back to me at which point I do nothing. But consider the amount of time it takes to send information from one computer to another. Even if a computer sends data in both directions at once it will still take too long for data to travel halfway around the ring. Things can become pretty complicated if one of the player's computers suddenly crashes or leaves the game—all the data that it had received but not yet transmitted to the next machine in the ring suddenly vanishes, leaving some machines with one version of the game and some with another.

Figure 5.2:
Peer to peer, ring, and client/server network configurations

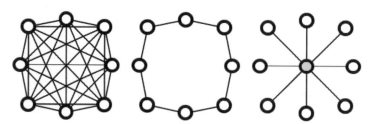

The most popular design is a *client/server* configuration, which might look like a star because every player is connected to a powerful central computer. This central computer is the server and it makes sure everyone is synchronized and experiencing the same thing. There are, at most, P connections in a client/server configuration and the clients only have to send data once. The server does the bulk of the work, sending out the same data, at most, P times. This method ensures the smallest possible time difference between any two clients but can be quite taxing on the server, so much so that some computers are *dedicated servers* that do nothing but keep games running for other people.

Protocols

Once you've decided on which model you're going to use (I reach out with my mind powers and see that you have chosen client/server...) there comes the decision of what protocol. Protocols are accepted standard languages that computers use to transmit data back and forth. Most protocol information does not have to be set up by the programmer (phew) but is required for making sure that data reaches its intended destination. At the core, most protocols consist of basically the same thing. The following is a list of some of the more commonly used protocols and a brief description of each.

■ *Internet Protocol* (IP) is one of the simplest protocols available. Programmers use protocols built on top of IP in order to transmit data.

■ *User Datagram Protocol* (UDP) adds the barest minimum of features to IP. It's just enough to transmit data and it does the job very fast. However, UDP data is unreliable, meaning that if you send data through UDP, some of it may not reach the destination machine and even if it does it may not arrive in the order that it was sent. For real-time games this is the protocol of choice and the one I will be covering in this chapter.

- *Transmission Control Protocol* (TCP) is also built on top of IP and adds a lot of stability to network data transmission at the expense of speed. If you want reliable data transmission, this is the protocol for you. It is best suited for turn-based games that don't have to worry about speed so much as making sure the right information reaches its destination. This is not to say it can't be used for real-time games—*NetStorm* (an Activision title) uses TCP/IP. However, it is my considered opinion that the amount of data being transmitted in *NetStorm* is far lower than in, say, *Unreal Tournament*.

- *Internet Control Messsage Protocol* (ICMP) is built on top of IP and provides a way to return error messages. ICMP is at the heart of every Ping utility. Its features are duplicated in so many other protocols that sometimes its features are mistaken as being a part of IP.

Packets

Any data you transmit is broken into packets, blocks of data of a maximum size. Each packet is then prefixed with a header block containing information such as host address, host port, the amount of time the packet has been traveling through the Internet, and whatever else the selected protocol requires. A UDP packet's maximum size is 4096 bytes. If it doesn't seem like much, you're right. But remember, most dial-up connections have trouble reaching 10 kilobytes per second, and you're going to be transmitting a lot of information both ways. When a packet is sent out into the Internet, it must first travel to one of the servers that forms the backbone of the Internet. Up until that point the packet is traveling in a straight line and there's no confusion. However, the moment the packet reaches the first server on the backbone it starts to follow a new set of rules. Each computer with more than one connection has a series of weights associated with each connection to another computer. These weights determine which computer should receive the most traffic. If these weights should change, the packets from your computer could take a much longer route than necessary and in some cases never even reach their destination. The real drawback is that it means packets may not arrive at their destination in any particular order. It could also be that every copy of the packet takes a scenic route, dies of old age, and the machine you were trying to send to never gets the packet at all.

In this case I'm willing to sacrifice a little reliability in exchange for the increased speed, but sometimes there are messages being sent to the server that must get through. For that reason I'll show you how to set up a reliable, ordered communication system for the few, the proud, the brave: the UDP packets.

The Right Tool for the Job (aka "DirectPlay and why I'm not using it")

I've heard a lot of programmers lambaste Windows. In fact, they hate anything Microsoft. Now, I'm no MS groupie, but what is it? Don't they provide good products? Is there something wrong with providing so many things in an SDK? Still, sometimes I can see their point of view. For example, I've never heard of anyone even trying to use DirectPlay's data encryption features. I'm not saying that Winsock is perfect either, but it's a much lower-level API, which means I can custom tailor each application and thereby gain a better understanding of the inner workings.

Implementation 1: MTUDP

Design Considerations

Since this is a tutorial, I'm only going to develop for the Windows platform. This means that I don't have to be very careful about endianness. I've also chosen to use UDP because it's the fastest way to communicate and makes the most sense in a real-time game. I'm also going to design with the client/server (star) configuration in mind, because it is the most scalable and the most robust.

Things that go "argh, my kidney!" in the night

In all the online tutorials that I've read about creating multiplayer networked games, there's always one detail that's left out and that detail is about the same size and level of danger as an out-of-control 18-wheel truck. The problem is multithreading.

Consider for a moment a simple single-thread game: In your main loop you read in from the keyboard, move things in the world, and then draw to the screen. So it would seem reasonable that in a network game you would read in from the keyboard, read in from the Internet, move things, send messages back out to the Internet, and then draw to the screen. Sadly, this is not the case. Oh sure, you can write a game to work like this (I learned the hard way), but it won't work the way you expect it to. Why? Let's say your computer can draw 20 frames per second. That means that most of 50ms is being spent drawing, which means that nearly 50ms go by between any two checks for new data from the Internet. So what? Anyone who's ever played a network game will tell you that 50ms can mean the difference between life and death. So when you send a message to another computer, that message could be waiting to be read for nearly 50ms and the reply could be waiting in your machine's hardware for an extra 50ms for an extra round trip time of 100ms!

Worse still is the realization that if you stay with a single-threaded app, there's nothing you can do to solve the problem; nothing will make that delay go away. Yes, it would be shorter if the frame rate were higher. But just try to tell people they can't play unless their frame rate is high enough—I bet good money they tar and feather you.

The solution is, of course, to write a multithreaded app. I'll admit the first time I had to write one I was pretty spooked. I thought it was going to be a huge pain. Please believe me when I say that as long as you write clean, careful code, you can get it right the first time and you won't have to debug a multithreaded app. And since everything you do from here on in will depend on that multithreading, let's start the MTUDP (multithreaded UDP) class there. First of all, be sure that you tell the compiler you're not designing a single-threaded app. In MSVC 6.0 the option to change is in Project|Settings|C/C++| Code Generation|Use Runtime Library.

Windows multithreading is, from what I hear, completely insane in its design. Fortunately, it's also really easy to get started. CreateThread() is a standard Windows function and, while I won't go into much detail about its inner working here (you have MSDN; look it up!) I will say that I call it as follows:

```
void cThread::Begin()
{
  d_threadHandle = CreateThread( NULL,
                                 0,
                                 (LPTHREAD_START_ROUTINE)gsThreadProc,
                                 this,
                                 0,
                                 (LPDWORD)&d_threadID );
  if( d_threadHandle == NULL )
    throw cError( "cThread() - Thread creation failed." );
  d_bIsRunning = true;
}
```

As you can tell, I've encapsulated all my thread stuff into a single class. This gives me a nice place to store d_threadHandle so I can kill the thread later, and it means I can use cThread as a base class for, oh, say, MTUDP and I can reuse the cThread class in all my other applications without making any changes to it.

CreateThread() takes six parameters, the most important of which are parameters 3 and 4, gsThreadProc and this. *this* is a pointer to the instance of cThread and will be sent to gsThreadProc. This is crucial because gsThreadProc cannot be a class function because Windows doesn't like that. Instead, gsThreadProc is defined at the very beginning of cThread.cpp as follows:

```
static DWORD WINAPI cThreadProc( cThread *pThis )
{
  return pThis->ThreadProc();
}
```

I don't know about you, but I think that's pretty sneaky. It also happens to work! Back in the cThread class ThreadProc is a virtual function that returns zero immediately. ThreadProc can return anything you like, but I've always liked to return zero when there is no problem and use every other number as an error code.

Sooner or later you're going to want to stop the thread. Again, this is pretty straightforward.

```
void cThread::End()
{
  if( d_threadHandle != NULL )
  {
    d_bIsRunning = false;
    WaitForSingleObject( d_threadHandle, INFINITE );
    CloseHandle( d_threadHandle );
    d_threadHandle = NULL;
  }
}
```

The function cThread::End() is set up in such a way that you can't stop a thread more than once, but the real beauty is hidden. Notice d_bIsRunning? Well, you can use it for more than just telling the other threads that you're still working. Let's look at a simple version of a derived class's ThreadProc().

```
DWORD MTUDP::ThreadProc()
{
  while( d_bIsRunning == true )
  {
    // Read and process network data here.
  }
  return 0;
}
```

This means that the moment d_bIsRunning is set to false, the thread will quit. Of course, we could get the thread to quit any time—if it detected an error, for example. This is an easy way for one thread to have start/stop control on another thread. In fact, if you didn't set d_bIsRunning to false the first thread would stop running forever while it waited for WaitForSingleObject(d_thread-Handle, INFINITE). This is because d_threadHandle functions like a *mutex*.

Mutexes

Mutexes are crucial in multithreading because they protect data that is in a critical section. For example, let's say you have a linked list of information. One thread is adding to the linked list and the other thread is removing. What would happen if the two tried to access the linked list at the same time? There's a chance that one thread could walk through the linked list and then step off into "funny RAM" (some undefined location in RAM that is potentially dangerous to modify) because the other thread hadn't finished working with the linked list pointers.

Fortunately, C++ lets you set up a really nice little class to monitor these critical sections and make sure every thread plays nice.

```
class cMonitor
{
protected:

  HANDLE d_mutex;

public:
  cMonitor();
  virtual ~cMonitor();

  void MutexOn() const;
  void MutexOff() const;
};
```

Again, this class is used as a base class for every class that has a critical section. In fact, I defined cThread as class cThread : public cMonitor. The four cMonitor functions are also very interesting.

```
cMonitor::cMonitor()
{
  // This mutex will help the two threads share their toys.
  d_mutex = CreateMutex( NULL, false, NULL );
  if( d_mutex == NULL )
    throw cError( "cMonitor() - Mutex creation failed." );
}

cMonitor::~cMonitor()
{
  if( d_mutex != NULL )
  {
    CloseHandle( d_mutex );
    d_mutex = NULL;
  }
}
```

cMonitor will create a new mutex and clean up after itself.

```
void cMonitor::MutexOn() const
{
  WaitForSingleObject( d_mutex, INFINITE );
}


void cMonitor::MutexOff() const
{
  ReleaseMutex( d_mutex );  // To be safe...
}
```

Once again you see that WaitForSingleObject() will stall a thread forever if necessary. The big difference between this and d_threadHandle is that d_threadHandle was released by Windows. Here, control is left up to a thread. If WaitForSingleObject() is called, the thread will gain control of a mutex and every other thread will have to wait until that same thread calls ReleaseMutex() before they get a turn, and it's first come, first serve. This means you have to be very careful with how you handle your mutexes—if you don't match every WaitFor... with a ReleaseMutex(), threads will hang forever and you will soon find yourself turning your computer off to reboot it. I suppose I could have written a version of MutexOn() that would wait *n* milliseconds and return an error code but I haven't found a need for it yet.

Threads, Monitor, and the Problem of the try/throw/catch Construction

Try/throw/catch is a wonderful construction that can simplify your debugging. Unfortunately, it doesn't work very well inside other threads. Actually, it works, but it might surprise you. The following would work, but would not catch anything thrown by the other thread.

```
// somewhere inside thread #1
  try
  {
    cThreadDerived myNewThread;

    mNewThread.Begin();

    // Do other stuff.
  }
  catch( cError &err )
  {
    // No error would be reported.
  }
}

// somewhere inside cThreadDerived::ThreadProc()
  throw cError( "Gack!" );
```

The solution is to put an extra try/catch inside the ThreadProc of cThreadDerived and then store the error somewhere for the other thread to read it, or process it right there and then.

MTUDP: *The Early Years*

You've seen the multithreading class and you've got a way to protect the critical sections. So here's how it's going to work: The main thread can read and send data with MTUDP whenever it can get the mutex. The rest of the time it can render, check the keyboard, play music, etc. MTUDP, meanwhile, will be constantly rechecking the network to see if there is data to be read in from the Internet and processing any that arrives.

Now you can start getting down to business!

```
class MTUDP : public cThread
{
protected:
  SOCKET          d_listenSocket,
                  d_sendSocket;
  unsigned short  d_localListenPort,
                  d_foreignListenPort;
  bool            d_bStarted,
                  d_bListening,
                  d_bSending;
  // A list of all the data packets that have arrived.

public:
  MTUDP();
  virtual ~MTUDP();

  virtual ThreadProc();

  void            Startup( unsigned short localListenPort,
                           unsigned short ForeignListenPort );
  void            Cleanup();
  void            StartListening();
  void            StartSending();
  void            StopListening();
  void            StopSending();
  unsigned short GetReliableData( char * const pBuffer,
                                  unsigned short maxLen );
  void            ReliableSendTo( const char * const pStr, unsigned short len );
};
```

Startup() and Cleanup() are the bookends of the class and are required to initialize and tidy up. StartListening() and StartSending() will create the d_listenSocket and d_sendSocket, respectively. One or more of these has to be called before ReliableSendTo() or GetReliableData() will do anything.

MTUDP::Startup() and MTUDP::Cleanup()

```
void MTUDP::Startup( unsigned short localListenPort,
                     unsigned short foreignListenPort )
{
  Cleanup();  // just in case somebody messed up out there...

  WSAData wsaData;
  int     error;

  error = WSAStartup( MAKEWORD( 2, 2 ), &wsaData );
```

```
      if( error == SOCKET_ERROR )
      {
        char errorBuffer[ 100 ];

        error = WSAGetLastError();
        if( error == WSAVERNOTSUPPORTED )
        {
          sprintf( errorBuffer,
  "MTUDP::Startup() - WSAStartup() error.\nRequested v2.2, found only v%d.%d.",
            LOBYTE( wsaData.wVersion ), HIBYTE( wsaData.wVersion ) );
          WSACleanup();
        }
        else
          sprintf( errorBuffer, "MTUDP::Startup() - WSAStartup() error %d",
            WSAGetLastError() );

        throw cError( errorBuffer );
      }

    d_localListenPort = localListenPort;
    d_foreignListenPort = foreignListenPort;
    d_bytesTransfered = 0;
    d_bStarted = true;
  }
```

Really the only mystery here is WSAStartup(). It takes two parameters: a word that describes what version of Winsock you'd like to use and a pointer to an instance of WSAData which will contain all kinds of useful information regarding this machine's Winsock capabilities. I admire the way the Winsock programmers handle errors—just about everything will return SOCKET_ERROR, at which point you can call WSAGetLastError() to find out more information. The two variables passed to Startup (d_localListenPort and d_foreignListenPort) will be used a little later.

```
  void MTUDP::Cleanup()
  {
    if( d_bStarted == false )
      return;

    d_bStarted = false;

    StopListening();
    StopSending();

    // Clean up all data waiting to be read

    WSACleanup();
  }
```

An important note: WSAStartup() causes a DLL to be loaded, so be sure to match every call to WSAStartup() with exactly <u>one</u> call to WSACleanup().

MTUDP::MTUDP() and MTUDP::~MTUDP()

All programming (and, as I've learned, all attempts to explain things to people) should follow the "method of least surprise." MTUDP's creation and destruction methods prove we've been able to stick to that rule.

At this point all the creation method does is initialize d_bStarted to false and the destruction method calls Cleanup().

MTUDP::StartListening()

Now we get to put d_localListenPort to use.

```
void MTUDP::StartListening()
{
  if( d_bListening == true ||
      d_bStarted == false )
    return;

  d_bListening = true;
```

Nothing special yet; this just prevents you from calling StartListening() twice.

```
d_listenSocket = socket( AF_INET, SOCK_DGRAM, 0 );
if( d_listenSocket == INVALID_SOCKET )
  // throw an error here.
```

Socket() is a Winsock method that creates a socket. The three parameters are the address family, the socket type, and the protocol type (which modifies the socket type). The only parameter here you should ever mess with is SOCK_DGRAM, which could be changed to SOCK_STREAM if you wanted to work in TCP/IP.

```
SOCKADDR_IN localAddr;
int        result;

memset( &localAddr, 0, sizeof( SOCKADDR_IN ) );
localAddr.sin_family = AF_INET;
localAddr.sin_addr.s_addr = htonl( INADDR_ANY );
localAddr.sin_port = htons( d_localListenPort );

result = bind( d_listenSocket,
               (sockaddr *)&localAddr,
               sizeof( SOCKADDR_IN ) );
if( result == SOCKET_ERROR )
{
  closesocket( d_listenSocket );
  // throw another error.
}
```

Bind() takes three parameters—the port number on which to open the new listening socket, some information about the type of socket (in the form of a

SOCKADDR or SOCKADDR_IN structure), and the size of parameter 2. Every time you Bind() a socket you have to make sin_family equal to the same thing as the socket's address family. Since this is a listening socket, you want it to be on port d_localListenPort so that's what sin_port is set to. The last parameter, sin_addr.s_addr, is the address you would be sending data to. The listen socket will never send any data so set it to INADDR_ANY. Lastly, if the Bind() fails, be sure to close the socket. There's only one step left!

```
    // We're go for go!
    cThread::Begin();
}
```

MTUDP::StartSending()

The start of StartSending() is the same old deal—check that a send socket has not been opened (d_bSending == false) and create the send socket (which looks exactly the same as it did in StartListening()). The only significant change comes in the call to bind().

```
    SOCKADDR_IN localAddr;
    int         result;

    memset( &localAddr, 0, sizeof( SOCKADDR_IN ) );
    localAddr.sin_family = AF_INET;
    localAddr.sin_addr.s_addr = htonl( INADDR_ANY );
    localAddr.sin_port = htons( 0 );

    result = bind( d_sendSocket, (sockaddr *)&localAddr, sizeof( SOCKADDR_IN )
);
    if( result == SOCKET_ERROR )
        // close the socket and throw an error.
```

I don't care what port the send socket is bound to, so sin_port is set to zero. Even though data is being sent, because UDP is being used, the sin_addr.s_addr is once again set to INADDR_ANY. This would have to change if you wanted to use TCP/IP, because once you open a TCP/IP socket it can only send to one address until it is closed or forced to change.

At the end of StartSending() you do not call cThread::Begin(). Thanks to the cThread class it wouldn't have an effect, so make sure to call StartListen() before StartSending(). Another good reason to call StartListening() first is because there's a very small chance that the random port Winsock binds your send socket to is the same port you want to use for listening.

MTUDP::ThreadProc()

Now to the real meat and potatoes. I'll explain the whole thing at the end.

```
DWORD MTUDP::ThreadProc()
{
```

```
if( d_bListening == false )
  return 0;  // Quit already?!  It can happen...

char             inBuffer[ MAX_UDPBUFFERSIZE ];
timeval          waitTimeStr;
SOCKADDR_IN      fromAddr;
int              fromLen;
unsigned short   result;
FD_SET           set;

try
{
  while( d_bListening == true )
  {
    // Listen to see if there is data waiting to be read.
    FD_ZERO( &set );
    FD_SET( d_listenSocket, &set );

    waitTimeStr.tv_sec = 0;    // Wait 0 seconds
    waitTimeStr.tv_usec = 0;   // Wait 0 microseconds (1/(1*10^6) seconds)

    // Select tells us if there is data to be read.
    result = select( FD_SETSIZE, &set, NULL, NULL, &waitTimeStr );
    if( result == 0 )
      continue;
    if( result == SOCKET_ERROR )
      // throw an error.

    // Recvfrom gets the data and puts it in inBuffer.
    fromLen = sizeof( SOCKADDR );
    result = recvfrom( d_listenSocket,
                       inBuffer,
                       MAX_UDPBUFFERSIZE,
                       0,
                       (SOCKADDR *)&fromAddr,
                       &fromLen );
    if( result == 0 )
      continue;
    if( result == SOCKET_ERROR )
      // throw an error.

    // Put the received data in a mutex-protected queue here.
    ProcessIncomingData( inBuffer,
                         result,
                         ntohl( fromAddr.sin_addr.s_addr ),
                         GetTickCount() );
  }  // while
}  // try
catch( cError &err )
{
  // do something with err.d_text so that the
```

```
        // other thread knows this thread borked.
    }

    // Returns 1 if the close was not graceful.

    return d_bListening == true;
}
```

It may seem a little weird to put a check for d_bListening at the start of the thread proc. I added it because there is a short delay between when you call Begin() and when ThreadProc() is actually called, and even if you clean up properly when you're going to quit, it can make your debug output look a little funny.

MAX_UDPBUFFERSIZE is equal to the maximum size of a UDP packet, 4096 bytes. I seriously doubt you will ever send a UDP block this big, but it never hurts to play it safe. As you can see, try/catch/throw is here, just like I said. The next step is the while loop, which begins with a call to Select(). Select() will check any number of sockets to see if there is data waiting to be read, check if one of the sockets can send data, and/or check if an error occurred on one of the sockets. Select() can be made to wait for a state change as long as you want, but I set waitTimeStr to 0 milliseconds so that it would poll the sockets and return immediately. That way it's a little more thread friendly.

Some of you may have some experience with Winsock and are probably wondering why I didn't use something called "asynchronous event notification." Two reasons: First, it takes a lot of effort to get set up and then clean up again. Second, it makes MTUDP dependent on a window handle, which makes it dependent on the speed at which WndProc() messages can be parsed, and it would make MTUDP even more dependent on Windows functions, something we'd like to avoid, if possible.

The next steps only happen if there is data to be read. Recvfrom() will read in data from a given socket and return the number of bytes read, but no more than the MAX_UDPBUFFERSIZE limit. Recvfrom() will also supply some information on where the data came from in the fromAddr structure.

If some data was successfully read in to inBuffer, the final step in the while loop is called. This is a new MTUDP function called ProcessIncomingData().

MTUDP::ProcessIncomingData()

Well, I'm sorry to say that, for now, ProcessIncomingData() is virtually empty. However, it is the first opportunity to see mutexes in action.

```
void MTUDP::ProcessIncomingData( char * const pData,
                                 unsigned short length,
                                 DWORD address,
                                 DWORD receiveTime )
{
    cMonitor::MutexOn();
```

```
                    // Add the data to our list of received packets.
                    cMonitor::MutexOff();
                }
```

MTUPD::GetReliableData()

GetReliableData() is one of the few methods that can be called by another thread. Because it also messes with the list of received packets mutexes have to be used again.

```
unsigned short MTUDP::GetReliableData( char * const pBuffer,
                                        unsigned short maxLen )
{
  if( pBuffer == NULL )
    throw cError( "MTUPD::GetReliableData() - Invalid parameters." );

  if( maxLen == 0 )
    return 0;

  cMonitor::MutexOn();
  // take one of the received packets off the list.
  cMonitor::MutexOff();
  // fill pBuffer with the contents of the packet.
  // return the size of the packet we just read in.
}
```

TA DA! You've now got everything required to asynchronously read data from the Internet while the other thread renders, reads input, picks its nose, gives your hard drive a wedgie, you name it; it's coded. Of course, it doesn't really tell you who sent the information, and it's a long way from being reliable.

MTUDP::ReliableSendTo()

It's a good thing that I left this for the end because some of the code to get ReliableSendTo() working will help with reliable communications. In music circles this next bit would be called a bridge—the melody changes, maybe even enters a new key, but it gets you where you need to go.

cDataPacket

You've probably had all sorts of ideas on how to store the incoming data packets. I'm going to describe my data packet format, which may be a little puzzling at first. Trust me, by the end it will all make perfect sense.

```
// this file is eventually inherited everywhere else, so this seemed
// like a good place to define it.
#define MAX_UDPBUFFERSIZE   4096

class cDataPacket
{
```

```
public:
  char            d_data[ MAX_UDPBUFFERSIZE ];
  unsigned short  d_length,
                  d_timesSent;
  DWORD           d_id,
                  d_firstTime,
                  d_lastTime;

  cDataPacket();
  virtual ~cDataPacket();

  void Init( DWORD time,
             DWORD id,
             unsigned short len,
             const char * const pData );

  cDataPacket &operator=( const cDataPacket &otherPacket );
};
```

As always, it follows the K.I.S.S. (keep it simple, stupid) principle. Init sets
d_firstTime and d_lastTime to time, d_id to id, and d_length to len, and copies
len bytes from pData into d_data. The = operator copies one packet into
another.

cQueueIn

CQueueIn stores all the data packets in a nice, neat, orderly manner. In fact it
keeps two lists—one for data packets that are in order and one for the rest
(which are as ordered as can be, given that some may be missing from the list).

```
class cQueueIn : public cMonitor
{
protected:
  list<cDataPacket *> d_packetsOrdered;
  list<cDataPacket *> d_packetsUnordered;
  DWORD               d_currentPacketID,
                      d_count;   // number of packets added to this queue.

public:
  cQueueIn();
  virtual ~cQueueIn();

  void          Clear();
  void          AddPacket( DWORD packetID,
                           const char * const pData,
                           unsigned short len,
                           DWORD receiveTime );
  cDataPacket   *GetPacket();
  bool          UnorderedPacketIsQueued( DWORD packetID );
  DWORD         GetHighestID();
  inline DWORD  GetCurrentID();   // returns d_currentPacketID.
```

```
    inline DWORD  GetCount();        // returns d_count.
};
```

d_currentPacketID is equal to the highest ordered packet id plus 1. Clear()
removes all packets from all lists. GetPacket() removes the first packet in the
d_packetsOrdered list (if any) and returns it. UnorderedPacketIsQueued()
informs the caller if the packet is in the d_packetsUnordered list and returns
true if packetID < d_currentPacketID. GetHighestID() returns the highest unor-
dered packet id plus 1 (or d_currentPacketID if d_packetsUnordered is empty).
In fact, the only tricky part in this whole class is AddPacket().

```
void cQueueIn::AddPacket( DWORD packetID,
                          const char * const pData,
                          unsigned short len,
                          DWORD receiveTime )
{
  if( pData == NULL ||
      len == 0 ||
      d_currentPacketID > packetID )
    return;

  // Create the packet.
  cDataPacket *pPacket;

  pPacket = new cDataPacket;
  if( pPacket == NULL )
    throw cError( "cQueueIn::AddPacket() - insufficient memory." );

  pPacket->Init( receiveTime, packetID, len, pData );


  // Add the packet to the queues.
  cMonitor::MutexOn();

  if( d_currentPacketID == pPacket->d_id )
  {
    // This packet is the next ordered packet.  Add it to the ordered list
    // and then move all unordered that can be moved to the ordered list.
    d_packetsOrdered.push_back( pPacket );
    d_currentPacketID++;
    d_count++;

    pPacket = *d_packetsUnordered.begin();
    while( d_packetsUnordered.empty() == false &&
           d_currentPacketID == pPacket->d_id )
    {
      d_packetsUnordered.pop_front();
      d_packetsOrdered.push_back( pPacket );
      d_currentPacketID++;
      pPacket = *d_packetsUnordered.begin();
    }
```

```
      }
      else  // d_currentPacketID < pPacket->d_id
      {
        // Out of order.  Sort into the list.
        list<cDataPacket *>::iterator iPacket;
        bool                          bExists;

        bExists = false;

        for( iPacket = d_packetsUnordered.begin();
             iPacket != d_packetsUnordered.end(); ++iPacket )
        {
          // Already in list - get out now!
          if( (*iPacket)->d_id == pPacket->d_id )
          {
            bExists = true;
            break;
          }
          if( (*iPacket)->d_id > pPacket->d_id )
            break;
        }

        if( bExists == true )
          delete pPacket;
        else
        {
          // We've gone 1 past the spot where pPacket belongs. Back up and insert.
          d_packetsUnordered.insert( iPacket, pPacket );
          d_count++;
        }
      }
    }

    cMonitor::MutexOff();
  }
```

Now I could stop right here, add an instance of cQueueIn to MTUDP and there would be almost everything needed for reliable communications, but that's not why I went off on this tangent. There is still no way of sending data to another computer and also no way of telling who the data came from.

cHost

Yes, this is another new class. Don't worry, there's only four more, but they won't be mentioned for quite some time. (I'm only telling you that to fill you with anticipation and dread in the same way Stephen King would start a chapter with "three weeks before the church steeple blew up" or Hitchcock would show you the ticking bomb hidden under a restaurant table. It's a spooky story and an education! More BANG! (aah!) for your buck.) The cHost class doesn't contain much yet, but it will be expanded later.

```
class cHost : public cMonitor
{
  DWORD             d_address;
  unsigned short    d_port;
  cQueueIn          d_inQueue;

public:
  cHost();
  virtual ~cHost();

  unsigned short ProcessIncomingReliable( char * const pBuffer, unsigned
                                          short len, DWORD receiveTime );
  void           SetPort( unsigned short port );
  bool           SetAddress( const char * const pAddress );
  bool           SetAddress( DWORD address );
  DWORD          GetAddress();   // returns d_address.
  unsigned short GetPort();      // returns d_port.

  cQueueIn       &GetInQueue();  // returns d_inQueue.
};
```

There are only two big mysteries here: SetAddress() and
ProcessIncomingReliable().

```
bool cHost::SetAddress( const char * const pAddress )
{
  if( pAddress == NULL )
    return true;

  IN_ADDR *pAddr;
  HOSTENT *pHe;

  pHe = gethostbyname( pAddress );
  if( pHe == NULL )
    return true;

  pAddr = (in_addr *)pHe->h_addr_list[ 0 ];
  d_address = ntohl( pAddr->s_addr );

  return false;
}
```

The other SetAddress assumes you've already done the work, so it just sets
d_address equal to address and returns.

As I said before, the cHost you're working with is a really simple version of
the full cHost class. Even ProcessIncomingReliable(), which I'm about to show,
is a simple version of the full ProcessIncomingReliable().

```
unsigned short cHost::ProcessIncomingReliable( char * const pBuffer,
                                               unsigned short maxLen,
                                               DWORD receiveTime )
```

```
{
  DWORD             packetID;
  char              *readPtr;
  unsigned short    length;

  readPtr = pBuffer;
  memcpy( &packetID, readPtr, sizeof( DWORD ) );
  readPtr += sizeof( DWORD );
  memcpy( &length, readPtr, sizeof( unsigned short ) );
  readPtr += sizeof( unsigned short );

  // If this message is a packet, queue the data
  // to be dealt with by the application later.
  d_inQueue.AddPacket( packetID, (char *)readPtr, length, receiveTime );
  readPtr += length;

  // d_inQueue::d_count will be used here at a much much later date.

  return readPtr - pBuffer;
}
```

This might seem like overkill, but it will make the program a lot more robust and net-friendly in the near future.

Things are now going to start building on the layers that came before. To start with, MTUDP is going to store a list<> containing all the instances of cHost, so the definition of MTUDP has to be expanded.

```
// Used by classes that call MTUDP, rather than have MTUDP return a pointer.
typedef DWORD    HOSTHANDLE;

class MTUDP : public cThread
{
private:
  // purely internal shortcuts.
  typedef map<HOSTHANDLE, cHost *> HOSTMAP;
  typedef list<cHost *>            HOSTLIST;

protected:
  HOSTLIST          d_hosts;
  HOSTMAP           d_hostMap;
  HOSTHANDLE        d_lastHandleID;

public:
  HOSTHANDLE        HostCreate( const char * const pAddress,
                                 unsigned short port );
  HOSTHANDLE        HostCreate( DWORD address, unsigned short port );
  void              HostDestroy( HOSTHANDLE hostID );
  unsigned short    HostGetPort( HOSTHANDLE hostID );
  DWORD             HostGetAddress( HOSTHANDLE hostID );
```

So what exactly did I do here? Well, MTUDP returns a unique HOSTHANDLE for each host so that no one can do anything silly (like try to delete a host). It also means that because MTUDP has to be called for everything involving hosts, MTUDP can protect d_hostMap and d_hosts with the cThread::cMonitor.

Now, it may surprise you to know that MTUDP creates hosts at times other than when some outside class calls HostCreate(). In fact, this is a perfect time to also show you just what's going to happen to cHost::QueueIn() by revisiting MTUDP::ProcessIncomingData().

```
void MTUDP::ProcessIncomingData( char * const pData, unsigned short length,
                                 DWORD address, DWORD receiveTime )
{
  // Find the host that sent this data.
  cHost              *pHost;
  HOSTLIST::iterator iHost;

  cMonitor::MutexOn();
  // search d_hosts to find a host with the same address.
  if( iHost == d_hosts.end() )
  {
    // Host not found!  Must be someone new sending data to this computer.
    DWORD hostID;

    hostID = HostCreate( address, d_foreignListenPort );
    if( hostID == 0 )
      // turn mutex off and throw an error, the host creation failed.
    pHost = d_hostMap[ hostID ];
  }
  else
    pHost = *iHost;

  assert( pHost != NULL );

  // This next part will get more complicated later.
  pHost->ProcessIncomingReliable( pData, length, receiveTime );
}
```

Of course, that means you now have a list of hosts. Each host might contain some new data that arrived from the Internet, so you're going to have to tell the other thread about it somehow. That means you're going to have to make changes to MTUDP::GetReliableData().

```
unsigned short MTUDP::GetReliableData( char * const pBuffer,
                                       unsigned short maxLen,
                                       HOSTHANDLE * const pHostID )
{
  if( pBuffer == NULL ||
      pHostID == NULL )
    throw cError( "MTUPD::GetReliableData() - Invalid parameters." );
```

```
          if( maxLen == 0 )
            return 0;

      cDataPacket           *pPacket;
      HOSTLIST::iterator iHost;

      pPacket = NULL;

      cMonitor::MutexOn();

      // Is there any queued, ordered data?
      for( iHost = d_hosts.begin(); iHost != d_hosts.end(); ++iHost )
      {
        pPacket = (*iHost)->GetInQueue().GetPacket();
        if( pPacket != NULL )
          break;
      }

      cMonitor::MutexOff();

      unsigned short length;

      length = 0;

      if( pPacket != NULL )
      {
        length = pPacket->d_length > maxLen ? maxLen : pPacket->d_length;
        memcpy( pBuffer, pPacket->d_data, length );

        delete pPacket;

        *pHostID = (*iHost)->GetAddress();
      }

    return length;
  }
```

See how I deal with pPacket copying into pBuffer after I release the mutex? This
is an opportunity to reinforce a very important point: <u>Hold on to a mutex for as
little time as possible.</u> A perfect example: Before I had a monitor class my network class had one mutex. Naturally, it was being held by one thread or another
for vast periods of time (20ms!), and it was creating the same delay effect as
when I was only using one thread. Boy, was my face black and blue (mostly
from hitting it against my desk in frustration).

MTUDP::ReliableSendTo()

Finally! Code first, explanation later.

```
void MTUDP::ReliableSendTo( const char * const pStr, unsigned short length,
                            HOSTHANDLE hostID )
{
  if( d_bSending == false )
    throw cError( "MTUDP::ReliableSendTo() - Sending not initialized!" );

  cHost *pHost;

  cMonitor::MutexOn();

  pHost = d_hostMap[ hostID ];
  if( pHost == NULL )
    throw cError( "MTUDP::ReliableSendTo() - Invalid parameters." );

  char             outBuffer[ MAX_UDPBUFFERSIZE ];
  unsigned short   count;
  DWORD            packetID;

  count = 0;
  memset( outBuffer, 0, MAX_UDPBUFFERSIZE );


  // Attach the message data.
  packetID = pHost->GetOutQueue().GetCurrentID();
  if( pStr )
  {
    // Flag indicating this block is a message.
    outBuffer[ count ] = MTUDPMSGTYPE_RELIABLE;
    count++;

    memcpy( &outBuffer[ count ], &packetID, sizeof( DWORD ) );
    count += sizeof( DWORD );
    memcpy( &outBuffer[ count ], &length, sizeof( unsigned short ) );
    count += sizeof( unsigned short );
    memcpy( &outBuffer[ count ], pStr, length );
    count += length;
  }


  // Attach the previous message, just to ensure that it gets there.
  cDataPacket secondPacket;

  if( pHost->GetOutQueue().GetPreviousPacket( packetID, &secondPacket )
      == true )
  {
    // Flag indicating this block is a message.
    outBuffer[ count ] = MTUDPMSGTYPE_RELIABLE;
    count++;

    // Append the message
    memcpy( &outBuffer[ count ], &secondPacket.d_id, sizeof( DWORD ) );
```

```
            count += sizeof( DWORD );
            memcpy( &outBuffer[ count ],
                    &secondPacket.d_length,
                    sizeof( unsigned short ) );
            count += sizeof( unsigned short );
            memcpy( &outBuffer[ count ], secondPacket.d_data, secondPacket.d_length );
            count += secondPacket.d_length;
        }


    #if defined( _DEBUG_DROPTEST ) && _DEBUG_DROPTEST > 1
        if( rand() % _DEBUG_DROPTEST != _DEBUG_DROPTEST - 1 )
        {
    #endif
            // Send
            SOCKADDR_IN     remoteAddr;
            unsigned short  result;

            memset( &remoteAddr, 0, sizeof( SOCKADDR_IN ) );
            remoteAddr.sin_family = AF_INET;
            remoteAddr.sin_addr.s_addr = htonl( pHost->GetAddress() );
            remoteAddr.sin_port = htons( pHost->GetPort() );

            // Send the data.
            result = sendto( d_sendSocket,
                             outBuffer,
                             count,
                             0,
                             (SOCKADDR *)&remoteAddr,
                             sizeof( SOCKADDR ) );
            if( result < count )
                // turn off the mutex and throw an error - could not send all data.
            if( result == SOCKET_ERROR )
                // turn off the mutex and throw an error - sendto() failed.

    #if defined( _DEBUG_DROPTEST )
        }
    #endif

        if( pStr )
            pHost->GetOutQueue().AddPacket( pStr, length );

        cMonitor::MutexOff();
    }
```

Since I've covered most of this before, there are only four new and interesting
things.

The first is _DEBUG_DROPTEST. This function will cause a random packet
to not be sent, which is equivalent to playing on a really bad network. If your
game can still play on a LAN with a _DEBUG_DROPTEST as high as four, then

you have done a really good job, because that's more than you would ever see in a real game.

The second new thing is sendto(). I think any logically minded person can look at the bind() code, look at the clearly named variables, and understand how sendto() works.

It may surprise you to see that the mutex is held for so long, directly contradicting what I said earlier. As you can see, pHost is still being used on the next-to-last line of the program, so the mutex <u>has</u> to be held in case the other thread calls MTUDP::HostDestroy(). Of course, the only reason it has to be held so long is because of HostDestroy().

The third new thing is MTUDPMSGTYPE_RELIABLE. I'll get to that a little later.

The last and most important new item is cHost::GetOutQueue(). Just like its counterpart, GetOutQueue provides access to an instance of cQueueOut, which is remarkably similar (but not identical) to cQueueIn.

```
class cQueueOut : public cMonitor
{
protected:
  list<cDataPacket *> d_packets;
  DWORD               d_currentPacketID,
                      d_count;  // number of packets added to this queue.

public:
  cQueueOut();
  virtual ~cQueueOut();

  void          Clear();
  void          AddPacket( const char * const pData, unsigned short len );
  void          RemovePacket( DWORD packetID );
  bool          GetPacketForResend( DWORD waitTime, cDataPacket *pPacket );
  bool          GetPreviousPacket( DWORD packetID, cDataPacket *pPacket );
  cDataPacket  *BorrowPacket( DWORD packetID );
  void          ReturnPacket();
  DWORD         GetLowestID();
  bool          IsEmpty();

  inline DWORD GetCurrentID();  // returns d_currentPacketID.
  inline DWORD GetCount();      // returns d_count.
};
```

There are several crucial differences between cQueueIn and cQueueOut: d_currentPacketID is the ID of the last packet sent/added to the queue; GetLowestID() returns the ID of the first packet in the list (which, incidentally, would also be the packet that has been in the list the longest); AddPacket() just adds a packet to the far end of the list and assigns it the next d_currentPacketID; and RemovePacket() removes the packet with d_id == packetID.

The four new functions are GetPacketForResend(), GetPreviousPacket(), BorrowPacket(), and ReturnPacket(), of which the first two require a brief overview and the last two require a big warning. GetPacketForResend() checks if there are any packets that were last sent more than waitTime milliseconds ago. If there are, it copies that packet to pPacket and updates the original packet's d_lastTime. This way, if you know the ping to some other computer, then you know how long to wait before you can assume the packet was dropped. GetPreviousPacket() is far simpler; it returns the packet that was sent just before the packet with d_id == packetID. This is used by ReliableSendTo() to "piggyback" an old packet with a new one in the hopes that it will reduce the number of resends caused by packet drops.

BorrowPacket() and ReturnPacket() are evil incarnate. I say this because they really, really bend the unwritten mutex rule: Lock and release a mutex in the same function. I know I should have gotten rid of them, but when you see how they are used in the code (later), I hope you'll agree it was the most straightforward implementation. I put it to you as a challenge to remove them. Never more shall I mention the functions-that-cannot-be-named().

Now, about that MTUDPMSGTYPE_RELIABLE: The longer I think about MTUDPMSGTYPE_RELIABLE, the more I think I should have given an edited version of ReliableSendTo() and then gone back and introduced it later. But then a little voice says, "Hey! That's why they put ADVANCED on the cover!" The point of MTUDPMSGTYPE_RELIABLE is that it is an identifier that would be read by ProcessIncomingData(). When ProcessIncomingData() sees MTUDPMSGTYPE_RELIABLE, it would call pHost->ProcessIncomingReliable(). The benefit of doing things this way is that it means I can send other stuff in the same message and piggyback it just like I did with the old messages and GetPreviousPacket(). In fact, I could send a message that had all kinds of data and no MTUDPMSGTYPE_RELIABLE (madness! utter madness!). Of course, in order to be able to process these different message types I'd better make some improvements, the first of which is to define all the different types.

```
enum eMTUDPMsgType
{
    MTUDPMSGTYPE_ACKS        = 0,
    MTUDPMSGTYPE_RELIABLE    = 1,
    MTUDPMSGTYPE_UNRELIABLE  = 2,
    MTUDPMSGTYPE_CLOCK       = 3,
    MTUDPMSGTYPE_NUMMESSAGES = 4,
};
```

I defined this enum in MTUDP.cpp because it's a completely internal matter that no other class should be messing with.

Although you're not going to work with most of these types (just yet) here's a brief overview of what they're for:

■ MTUDPMSGTYPE_CLOCK is for a really cool clock I'm going to add later. "I'm sorry, did you say cool?" Well, okay, it's not cool in a *Pulp Fiction/Fight*

Club kind of cool, but it is pretty neat when you consider that the clock will read almost exactly the same value on all clients and the server. This is a critical feature of real-time games because it makes sure that you can say "this thing happened at this time" and everyone can correctly duplicate the effect.

■ MTUDPMSGTYPE_UNRELIABLE is an unreliable message. When a computer sends an unreliable message it doesn't expect any kind of confirmation because it isn't very concerned if the message doesn't reach the intended destination. A good example of this would be the update messages in a game—if you're sending 20 messages a second, a packet drop here and a packet drop there is no reason to have a nervous breakdown. That's part of the reason we made _DEBUG_DROPTEST in the first place!

■ MTUDPMSGTYPE_ACKS is vital to reliable message transmission. If my computer sends a reliable message to your computer, I need to get a message back saying "yes, I got that message!" If I don't get that message, then I have to resend it after a certain amount of time (hence GetPacketForResend()).

Now, before I start implementing the stuff associated with eMTUDPMsgType, let me go back and improve MTUDP::ProcessIncomingData().

```
assert( pHost != NULL );

// Process the header for this packet.
bool           bMessageArrived;
unsigned char  code;
char           *ptr;

bMessageArrived = false;
ptr = pData;

while( ptr < pData + length )
{
  code = *ptr;
  ptr++;

  switch( code )
  {
    case MTUDPMSGTYPE_ACKS:
      // Process any ACKs in the packet.
      ptr += pHost->ProcessIncomingACKs( ptr,
                                         pData + length - ptr,
                                         receiveTime );
      break;
    case MTUDPMSGTYPE_RELIABLE:
      bMessageArrived = true;
      // Process reliable message in the packet.
```

```
                    ptr += pHost->ProcessIncomingReliable( ptr,
                                                           pData + length - ptr,
                                                           receiveTime );
                  break;
                case MTUDPMSGTYPE_UNRELIABLE:
                  // Process UNreliable message in the packet.
                  ptr += pHost->ProcessIncomingUnreliable( ptr,
                                                             pData + length - ptr,
                                                             receiveTime );
                  break;
                case MTUDPMSGTYPE_CLOCK:
                  ptr += ProcessIncomingClockData( ptr,
                                                   pData + length - ptr,
                                                   pHost,
                                                   receiveTime );
                  break;
                default:
                  // turn mutex off, throw an error.  something VERY BAD has happened,
                  // probably a write to bad memory (such as to an uninitialized
                  // pointer).
                  break;
            }
        }

    cMonitor::MutexOff();


    if( bMessageArrived == true )
    {
      // Send an ACK immediately. If this machine is the
      // server, also send a timestamp of the server clock.
      ReliableSendTo( NULL, 0, pHost->GetAddress() );
    }
}
```

So ProcessIncomingData() reads in the message type, then sends the remaining data off to be processed. It repeats this until there's no data left to be processed. At the end, if a new message arrived, it calls ReliableSendTo() again. Why? Because I'm going to make more improvements to it!

```
// some code we've seen before
memset( outBuffer, 0, MAX_UDPBUFFERSIZE );


// Attach the ACKs.
if( pHost->GetInQueue().GetCount() != 0 )
{
  // Flag indicating this block is a set of ACKs.
  outBuffer[ count ] = MTUDPMSGTYPE_ACKS;
  count++;
```

```
        count += pHost->AddACKMessage( &outBuffer[ count ], MAX_UDPBUFFERSIZE );
      }

      count += AddClockData( &outBuffer[ count ],
                             MAX_UDPBUFFERSIZE - count,
                             pHost );
```

// some code we've seen before.

So now it is sending clock data, ACK messages, and as many as two reliable packets in every message sent out. Unfortunately, there are now a number of outstanding issues:

■ ProcessIncomingUnreliable() is all well and good, but how do you send unreliable data?

■ How do cHost::AddACKMessage() and cHost::ProcessingIncomingACKs() work?

■ Ok, so I ACK the messages. But you said I should only resend packets if I haven't received an ACK within a few milliseconds of the ping to that computer. So how do I calculate ping?

■ How do AddClockData() and ProcessIncomingClockData() work?

Unfortunately, most of those questions have answers that overlap, so I apologize in advance if things get a little confusing.

Remember how I said there were four more classes to be defined? The class cQueueOut was one and here come two more.

cUnreliableQueueIn

```
      class cUnreliableQueueIn : public cMonitor
      {
        list<cDataPacket *> d_packets;
        DWORD               d_currentPacketID;

      public:
        cUnreliableQueueIn();
        virtual ~cUnreliableQueueIn();

        void      Clear();
        void      AddPacket( DWORD packetID,
                             const char * const pData,
                             unsigned short len,
                             DWORD receiveTime );
        cDataPacket *GetPacket();
      };
```

cUnreliableQueueOut

```
class cUnreliableQueueOut : public cMonitor
{
  list<cDataPacket *> d_packets;
  DWORD               d_currentPacketID;
  unsigned char       d_maxPackets,
                      d_numPackets;

public:
  cUnreliableQueueOut();
  virtual ~cUnreliableQueueOut();

  void  Clear();
  void  AddPacket( const char * const pData, unsigned short len );
  bool  GetPreviousPacket( DWORD packetID, cDataPacket *pPacket );
  void  SetMaxPackets( unsigned char maxPackets );

  inline DWORD GetCurrentID();  // returns d_currentPacketID.
};
```

They certainly share a lot of traits with their reliable counterparts. The two differences are that I don't want to hang on to a huge number of outgoing packets, and I only have to sort incoming packets into one list. In fact, my unreliable packet sorting is really lazy—if the packets don't arrive in the right order, the packet with the lower ID gets deleted. As you can see, cQueueOut has a function called SetMaxPackets() so you can control how many packets are queued. Frankly, you'd only ever set it to 0, 1, or 2.

Now that that's been explained, let's look at MTUDP::UnreliableSendTo(). UnreliableSendTo() is almost identical to ReliableSendTo(). The only two differences are that unreliable queues are used instead of the reliable ones and the previous packet (if any) is put into the outBuffer first, followed by the new packet. This is done so that if packet N is dropped, when packet N arrives with packet N+1, my lazy packet queuing won't destroy packet N.

cHost::AddACKMessage() / cHost::ProcessIncomingACKs()

Aside from these two functions, there's a few other things that have to be added to cHost with regard to ACKs.

```
#define ACK_MAXPERMSG          256
#define ACK_BUFFERLENGTH       48

class cHost : public cMonitor
{
protected:
  // A buffer of the latest ACK message for this host
  char            d_ackBuffer[ ACK_BUFFERLENGTH ];
```

```
        unsigned short  d_ackLength;  // amount of the buffer actually used.

        void ACKPacket( DWORD packetID, DWORD receiveTime );

    public:
        unsigned short  ProcessIncomingACKs( char * const pBuffer,
                                             unsigned short len,
                                             DWORD receiveTime );
        unsigned short  AddACKMessage( char * const pBuffer, unsigned short
                                       maxLen );
    }
```

The idea here is that I'll probably be sending more ACKs than receiving packets, so it only makes sense to save time by generating the ACK message when required and then using a cut and paste. In fact, that's what AddACKMessage() does—it copies d_ackLength bytes of d_ackBuffer into pBuffer. The actual ACK message is generated at the end of cHost::ProcessIncomingReliable(). Now you'll finally learn what cQueueIn::d_count, cQueueIn::GetHighestID(), cQueueIn::GetCurrentID(), and cQueueIn:: UnorderedPacketIsQueued() are for.

```
    // some code we've seen before.
    d_inQueue.AddPacket( packetID, (char *)readPtr, length, receiveTime );
    readPtr += length;

    // Should we build an ACK message?
    if( d_inQueue.GetCount() == 0 )
      return ( readPtr - pBuffer );

    // Build the new ACK message.
    DWORD          lowest, highest, ackID;
    unsigned char mask, *ptr;

    lowest = d_inQueue.GetCurrentID();
    highest = d_inQueue.GetHighestID();

    // Cap the highest so as not to overflow the ACK buffer
    // (or spend too much time building ACK messages).
    if( highest > lowest + ACK_MAXPERMSG )
      highest = lowest + ACK_MAXPERMSG;

    ptr = (unsigned char *)d_ackBuffer;
    // Send the base packet ID, which is the
    // ID of the last ordered packet received.
    memcpy( ptr, &lowest, sizeof( DWORD ) );
    ptr += sizeof( DWORD );
    // Add the number of additional ACKs.
    *ptr = highest - lowest;
    ptr++;


    ackID = lowest;
```

```
    mask = 0x80;

    while( ackID < highest )
    {
      if( mask == 0 )
      {
        mask = 0x80;
        ptr++;
      }

      // Is there a packet with id 'i' ?
      if( d_inQueue.UnorderedPacketIsQueued( ackID ) == true )
        *ptr |= mask;      // There is
      else
        *ptr &= ~mask;     // There isn't

      mask >>= 1;
      ackID++;
    }

    // Record the amount of the ackBuffer used.
    d_ackLength = ( ptr - (unsigned char *)d_ackBuffer ) + ( mask != 0 );

    // return the number of bytes read from
    return readPtr - pBuffer;
  }
```

For those of you who don't dream in binary (wimps), here's how it works. First of all, you know the number of reliable packets that have arrived in the correct order. So telling the other computer about all the packets that have arrived since last time that are below that number is just a waste of bandwidth. For the rest of the packets, I could have sent the IDs of every packet that has been received (or not received), but think about it: Each ID requires 4 bytes, so storing, say, 64 IDs would take 256 bytes! Fortunately, I can show you a handy trick:

```
// pretend ackBuffer is actually 48 * 8 BITS long instead of 48 BYTES.
for( j = 0; j < highest - lowest; j++ )
{
  if( d_inQueue.UnorderedPacketIsQueued( j + lowest ) == true )
    ackBuffer[ j ] == 1;
  else
    ackBuffer[ j ] == 0;
}
```

Even if you used a whole character to store a 1 or a 0 you'd still be using one-fourth the amount of space. As it is, you could store those original 64 IDs in 8 bytes, eight times less than originally planned.

The next important step is cHost::ProcessIncomingACKs(). I think you get the idea—read in the first DWORD and ACK every packet with a lower ID that's still in d_queueOut. Then go one bit at a time through the rest of the ACKs (if any) and if a bit is 1, ACK the corresponding packet. So I guess the only thing left to show is how to calculate the ping using the ACK information.

```
void cHost::ACKPacket( DWORD packetID, DWORD receiveTime )
{
  cDataPacket *pPacket;

  pPacket = d_outQueue.BorrowPacket( packetID );
  if( pPacket == NULL )
    return;  // the mutex was not locked.

  DWORD time;

  time = receiveTime - pPacket->d_firstTime;
  d_outQueue.ReturnPacket();

  unsigned int i;

  if( pPacket->d_timesSent == 1 )
  {
    for( i = 0; i < PING_RECORDLENGTH - 1; i++ )
      d_pingLink[ i ] = d_pingLink[ i + 1 ];
    d_pingLink[ i ] = time;
  }
  for( i = 0; i < PING_RECORDLENGTH - 1; i++ )
    d_pingTrans[ i ] = d_pingTrans[ i + 1 ];
  d_pingTrans[ i ] = time;

  d_outQueue.RemovePacket( packetID );
}
```

In classic Hollywood style, I've finally finished one thing just as I open the door and introduce something else. If you take a good look at cHost::ACKPacket() you'll notice the only line that actually does anything to ACK the packet is the last one! Everything else helps with the next outstanding issue: ping calculation.

There are two kinds of ping: link latency ping and transmission latency ping. *Link ping* is the shortest possible time it takes a message to go from one computer and back, the kind of ping you would get from using a ping utility (open a DOS box, type "ping [some address]" and see for yourself). *Transmission latency ping* is the time it takes two programs to respond to each other. In this case, it's the average time that it takes a reliably sent packet to be ACKed, including all the attempts to resend it.

In order to calculate ping for each cHost, the following has to be added:

```
#define PING_RECORDLENGTH      64
#define PING_DEFAULTVALLINK    150
#define PING_DEFAULTVALTRANS   200

class cHost : public cMonitor
{
```

```
protected:
  // Ping records
  DWORD d_pingLink[ PING_RECORDLENGTH ],
        d_pingTrans[ PING_RECORDLENGTH ];

public:
  float GetAverageLinkPing( float percent );
  float GetAverageTransPing( float percent );
}
```

As packets come in and are ACKed their round trip time is calculated and stored in the appropriate ping record (as previously described). Of course, the two ping records need to be initialized and that's what PING_DEFAULTVALLINK and PING_DEFAULTVALTRANS are for. This is done only once, when cHost is created. Picking good initial values is important for those first few seconds before a lot of messages have been transmitted back and forth. Too high or too low and GetAverage...Ping() will be wrong, which could temporarily mess things up.

Since both average ping calculators are the same (only using different lists), I'll only show the first, GetAverageLinkPing(). Remember how in the cThread class I showed you a little cheat with cThreadProc()? I'm going to do something like that again.

```
// This is defined at the start of cHost.cpp for qsort.
static int sSortPing( const void *arg1, const void *arg2 )
{
  if( *(DWORD *)arg1 < *(DWORD *)arg2 )
    return -1;
  if( *(DWORD *)arg1 > *(DWORD *)arg2 )
    return 1;
  return 0;
}


float cHost::GetAverageLinkPing( float bestPercentage )
{
  if( bestPercentage <= 0.0f ||
      bestPercentage > 100.0f )
    bestPercentage = 100.0f;

  DWORD pings[ PING_RECORDLENGTH ];
  float sum, worstFloat;
  int   worst, i;

  // Recalculate the ping list
  memcpy( pings, &d_pingLink, PING_RECORDLENGTH * sizeof( DWORD ) );
  qsort( pings, PING_RECORDLENGTH, sizeof( DWORD ), sSortPing );

  // Average the first bestPercentage / 100.
  worstFloat = (float)PING_RECORDLENGTH * bestPercentage / 100.0f;
  worst = (int)worstFloat + ( ( worstFloat - (int)worstFloat ) != 0 );
```

```
    sum = 0.0f;
    for( i = 0; i < worst; i++ )
      sum += pings[ i ];

    return sum / (float)worst;
  }
```

The beauty of this seemingly overcomplicated system is that you can get an average of the best *n* percent of the pings. Want an average ping that ignores the three or four worst cases? Get the best 80%. Want super accurate best times? Get 30% or less. In fact, those super accurate link ping times will be vital when I answer the fourth question: How do AddClockData() and ProcessIncomingClockData() work?

cNetClock

There's only one class left to define and here it is.

```
class cNetClock : public cMonitor
{
protected:
  struct cTimePair
  {
  public:
    DWORD d_actual,  // The actual time as reported by GetTickCount()
          d_clock;   // The clock time as determined by the server.
  };

  cTimePair d_start,     // The first time set by the server.
            d_lastUpdate; // the last updated time set by the server.
  bool      d_bInitialized; // first time has been received.

public:
  cNetClock();
  virtual ~cNetClock();

  void  Init();
  void  Synchronize( DWORD serverTime,
                     DWORD packetSendTime,
                     DWORD packetACKTime,
                     float ping );
  DWORD GetTime() const;
  DWORD TranslateTime( DWORD time ) const;
};
```

The class cTimePair consists of two values: d_actual (which is the time returned by the local clock) and d_clock (which is the estimated server clock time). The value d_start is the clock value the first time it is calculated and d_lastUpdate is the most recent clock value. Why keep both? Although I haven't written it here in the book, I was running an experiment to see if you could determine the rate at which the local clock and the server clock would drift apart and then compensate for that drift.

Anyhow, about the other methods. GetTime() returns the current server clock time. TranslateTime will take a local time value and convert it to server clock time. Init() will set up the initial values and that just leaves Synchronize().

```
void cNetClock::Synchronize( DWORD serverTime,
                             DWORD packetSendTime,
                             DWORD packetACKTime,
                             float ping )
{
  cMonitor::MutexOn();

  DWORD dt;

  dt = packetACKTime - packetSendTime;

  if( dt > 10000 )
    // this synch attempt is too old.  release mutex and return now.

  if( d_bInitialized == true )
  {
    // if the packet ACK time was too long OR the clock is close enough
    // then do not update the clock.
    if( abs( serverTime + ( dt / 2 ) - GetTime() ) <= 5 )
      // the clock is already very synched.  release mutex and return now.

    d_lastUpdate.d_actual = packetACKTime;
    d_lastUpdate.d_clock = serverTime + (DWORD)( ping / 2 );
    d_ratio = (double)( d_lastUpdate.d_clock - d_start.d_clock ) /
              (double)( d_lastUpdate.d_actual - d_start.d_actual );
  }
  else  // d_bInitialized == false
  {
    d_lastUpdate.d_actual = packetACKTime;
    d_lastUpdate.d_clock = serverTime + ( dt / 2 );
    d_start.d_actual = d_lastUpdate.d_actual;
    d_start.d_clock = d_lastUpdate.d_clock;
    d_bInitialized = true;
  }

  cMonitor::MutexOff();
}
```

As you can see, Synchronize() requires three values: serverTime, packetSend-Time, and packetACKTime. Two of the values seem to make good sense—the time a packet was sent out and the time that packet was ACKed. But how does serverTime fit into the picture? For that I have to add more code to MTUDP.

```
class MTUDP : public cThread
{
protected:
  bool      d_bIsServerOn,
            d_bIsClientOn;
  cNetClock d_clock;

    unsigned short  AddClockData( char * const pData,
                                  unsigned short maxLen,
                                  cHost * const pHost );
    unsigned short  ProcessIncomingClockData( char * const pData,
                                  unsigned short len,
                                  cHost * const pHost,
                                  DWORD receiveTime );

public:
  void  StartServer();
  void  StopServer();
  void  StartClient();
  void  StopClient();

  // GetClock returns d_clock and returns a const ptr so
  // that no one can call Synchronize and screw things up.
  inline const cNetClock &GetClock();
}
```

All the client/server stuff you see here is required for the clock and only for the clock. In essence, what it does is tell MTUDP who is in charge and has the final say about what the clock should read. When a client calls AddClockData() it sends the current time local to that client, not the server time according to the client. When the server receives a clock time from a client it stores that time in cHost. When a message is going to be sent back to the client, the server sends the last clock time it got from the client and the current server time. When the client gets a clock update from the server it now has three values: the time the message was originally sent (packetSendTime), the server time when a response was given (serverTime), and the current local time (packetACKTime). Based on these three values the current server time should be approximately cNetClock::d_lastUpdate.d_clock = serverTime + (packetACKTime – packetSendTime) / 2.

Of course, you'd only do this if the total round trip was extremely close to the actual ping time because it's the only way to minimize the difference between client net clock time and server net clock time.

As I said, the last client time has to be stored in cHost. That means one final addition to cHost.

```
class cHost : public cMonitor
{
protected:
  // For clock synchronization
  DWORD d_lastClockTime;
  bool  d_bClockTimeSet;
public:
  DWORD GetLastClockTime();                // self explanatory.
  void  SetLastClockTime( DWORD time );    // self explanatory.

  inline bool  WasClockTimeSet();          // returns d_bClockTimeSet.
}
```

And that appears to be that. In just about 35 pages I've showed you how to set up all the harder parts of network game programming. In the next section I'll show you how to use the MTUDP class to achieve first-rate, super-smooth game play.

Implementation 2: Smooth Network Play

Fortunately, this section is a lot shorter. Unfortunately, this section has no code because the solution for any one game probably wouldn't work for another game.

Geographic and Temporal Independence

Although in this book I am going to write a real-time, networked game it is important to note the other types of network games and how they affect the inner workings. The major differences can be categorized in two ways: the time separation and the player separation, more formally referred to as geographic independence and temporal independence.

Geographic independence means separation between players. A best-case example would be a two-player *Tetris* game where the players' game boards are displayed side by side. There doesn't have to be a lot of accuracy because the two will never interact. A worst-case example would be a crowded room in *Quake*—everybody's shooting, everybody's moving, and it's very hard to keep everybody nicely synched. This is why in a heavy firefight the latency climbs; the server has to send out a lot more information to a lot more people.

Temporal independence is the separation between events. A best-case example would be a turn-based game such as chess. I can't move a piece until you've moved a piece and I can take as long as I want to think about the next move, so there's plenty of time to make sure that each player sees exactly the same thing. Again, the worst-case scenario is *Quake*—everybody's moving as fast as they can, and if you don't keep up then you lag and die.

It's important when designing your game to take the types of independence into consideration because it can greatly alter the way you code the inner workings. In a chess game I would only use MTUDP::ReliableSendTo(), because every move has to be told to the other player and it doesn't matter how long it takes until he gets the packet; he'll believe I'm still thinking about my move. In a *Tetris* game I might use ReliableSendTo() to tell the other player what new piece has appeared at the top of the well, where the pieces land, and other important messages like "the other player has lost." The in-between part while the player is twisting and turning isn't really all that important, so maybe I would send that information using MTUDP::UnreliableSendTo(). That way they look like they're doing something and I can still guarantee that the final version of each player's well is correctly imitated on the other player's computer.

Real-time games, however, are a far more complicated story. The login and logout are, of course, sent with Reliable...(). But so are any name, model, team, color, shoe size, decal changes, votes, chat messages—the list goes on and on. In a game, however, updates about the player's position are sent 20 times a second and they are sent unreliably. Why? At 20 times a second a player can do a lot of fancy dancin' and it will be (reasonably) duplicated on the other computers. But because there are so many updates being sent, you don't really care if one or two get lost—it's no reason to throw yourself off a bridge. If, however, you were sending all the updates with Reliable...(), the slightest hiccup in the network would start a chain reaction of backlogged reliable messages that would very quickly ruin the game.

While all these updates are being sent unreliably, important events like shooting a rocket, colliding with another player, opening a door, or a player death are all sent reliably. The reason for this is because a rocket blast could kill somebody, and if you don't get the message, you would still see them standing there. Another possibility is that you don't know the rocket was fired, so you'd be walking along and suddenly ("argh!") you'd die for no reason.

Timing is Everything

The next challenge you'll face is a simple problem with a complicated solution. The client and the server are sending messages to each other at roughly 50 millisecond intervals. Unfortunately, tests will show that over most connections the receiver will get a "burst" of packets followed by a period of silence followed by another burst. This means you definitely cannot assume that packets arrive exactly 50ms apart—you can't even begin to assume when they were first sent. (If you were trying, cut it out!)

The solution comes from our synchronized network clock.

```
cGame::SendUpdate()
{
  if( time to send another update )
  {
    update.SetTime( d_MTUDPInstance.GetClock().GetTime() );
    update.SetPlayerData( pPlayer->ID(), pPlayer->Pos(), pPlayer->Vel() );
    d_MTUDPInstance.UnreliableSendTo( update.Buffer(),
```

```
                                             update.BufferLength(),
                                             someHostID );
      }
   }

   cGame::ProcessIncomingUpdate( anUpdate )
   {
     currentTime = d_MTUDPInstance.GetClock().GetTime();
     eventTime = anUpdate.GetTime();

     updatePos = anUpdate.GetPos();
     updateVel = anUpdate.GetVelocity();

     newPos = updatePos + updateVel * ( currentTime - eventTime );
     pPlayer[ playerID ].SetPos( newPos );
   }
```

The above case would only work if people moved in a straight line. Since most games don't, you also have to take into account their turning speed, physics, whether they are jumping, etc.

In case it wasn't clear yet, let me make it perfectly crystal: <u>Latency is public enemy #1</u>. Of course, getting players to appear isn't the only problem.

Pick and Choose

Reducing the amount of data is another important aspect of network programming. The question to keep in mind when determining what to send is: "What is the bare minimum I have to send to keep the other computer(s) up to date?" For example, in a game like Quake there are a lot of ambient noises. Water flowing, lava burbling, moaning voices, wind, and so on. Not one of these effects is an instruction from the server. Why? Because none of these sounds are critical to keeping the game going. In fact, none of the sounds are. Not that it makes any difference because you can get all your "play this sound" type messages for free.

Every time a sound is played, it's because something happened. When something happens, it has to be duplicated on every computer. This means that every sound event is implicit in some other kind of event. If your computer gets a message saying "a door opened," then your machine knows it has to open the door and play the door open sound.

Another good question to keep in mind is "how can I send the same information with less data?" A perfect example is the ACK system. Remember how I used 1 bit per packet and ended up using one-eighth the amount of data? Then consider what happens if, instead of saying "player x is turning left and moving forward" you use 1-bit flags. It only takes 2 bits to indicate left, right, or no turning and the same goes for walking forward/back or left/right. A few more 1-bit flags that mean things like "I am shooting," "I am reloading," or "I am shaving my bikini zone," and you've got everything you need to duplicate the events of one computer on another. Another good example of reducing data comes in the form of a parametric movement. Take a rocket, for example. It flies in a nice straight line, so you only have to send the message "a rocket has been fired from pos X with vel Y at time Z" and the other computer can calculate its trajectory from there.

Prediction and Extrapolation

Of course, it's not just as simple as processing the messages as they arrive. The game has to keep moving things around whether or not it's getting messages from the other computer(s) for as long as it can. That means that everything in the game has to be predictable: All players of type Y carrying gun X move at a speed Z. Without constants like that, the game on one machine would quickly become different from that on other machines and everything would get very annoying. But there's more to it, and that "more" is a latency related problem.

> **Note:** This is one of the few places where things start to differ between the client and server, so please bear with me.

The server isn't just the final authority on the clock time, it's also the final authority on every single player movement or world event (such as doors and elevators). That means it also has to shoulder a big burden. Imagine that there's a latency of 100 milliseconds between client and server. On the server, a player gets hit with a rocket and dies. The server builds a message and sends it to the client. From the time the server sent the message until the client gets the message the two games are not synchronized. It may not sound like much but it's the culmination of all these little things that make a great game terrible—or fantastic, if they're solved. In this case, the server could try predicting to see where everyone and everything will be *n* milliseconds from now and send messages that say things like "if this player gets hit by that rocket he'll die." The client will get the message just in time and no one will be the wiser. In order to predict where everyone will be *n* milliseconds from now, the server must first extrapolate the players' current position based on the last update sent from the clients. In other words, the server uses the last update from a client and moves the player based on that information every frame. It then uses this new position to predict where the player is <u>going to be</u> and then it can tell clients "player X will be at position Y at time Z." In order to make the game run its smoothest for all clients the amount of time to predict ahead should be equal to half the client's transmission ping. Of course, this means recalculating the predictions for every player, but it's a small price to pay for super-smooth game play.

The clients, on the other hand, should be getting the "player X will be at position Y at time Z" just about the same moment the clock reaches time Z. You would think that the client could just start extrapolating based on that info, right? Wrong. Although both the clients and the server are showing almost exactly the same thing, the clients have one small problem, illustrated in this example: If a client shoots at a moving target, that target will not be there by the time the message gets to the server. Woe! Sufferance! What to do? Well, the answer is to <u>predict</u> where everything will be *n* milliseconds from now. What is *n*? If you guessed half the transmission ping, you guessed right.

You're probably wondering why one is called prediction and the other is extrapolation. When the server is extrapolating, it's using old data to find the current player positions. When a client is predicting, it's using current data to extrapolate future player positions.

Using cHost::GetAverageTransPing(50.0f) to get half the transmission ping is not the answer. Using cHost::GetAverageTransPing(80.0f)/2 would work a lot better. Why? By taking 80 percent of the transmission pings you can ignore a few of the worst cases where a packet was dropped (maybe even dropped twice!), and since ping is the round trip time you have to divide it by two.

Although predicting helps to get the messages to the server on time, it doesn't help to solve the last problem—what happens if a prediction is wrong? The players on screen would "teleport" to new locations without crossing the intermediate distance. It could also mean that a client thinks someone got hit by a rocket when in fact on the server he dodged at just the last second.

The rocket-dodging problem is the easier problem to solve so I'll tackle it first. Because the server has the final say in everything, the client should perform collision detection as it always would: Let the rocket blow up, spill some blood pixels around the room, and then do nothing to the player until it got a message from the server saying "player X has definitely been hit and player X's new health is Y." Until that message is received, all the animations performed around/with the player should be as non-interfering and superficial as a sound effect. All of which raises an important point: Both the client and the server perform collision detection, but it's the server that decides who lives and who dies.

As for the teleport issue, well, it's a bit trickier. Let's say you are watching somebody whose predicted position is (0,0) and they are running (1,0). Suddenly your client gets an update that says the player's <u>new</u> predicted position is (2,0) running (0,1). Instead of teleporting that player and suddenly turning him, why not interpolate the difference? By that I mean the player would very (very) quickly move from (0,0) to somewhere around (2,0.1) and make a fast turn to the left. Naturally, this can only be done if the updates come within, say, 75 milliseconds of each other. Anything more and you'd have to teleport the players or they might start clipping through walls.

And last but not least, there are times when a real network can suddenly go nuts and lag for as much as 30 seconds. In cases where the last message from a computer was more than two seconds ago, I would freeze all motion and try to get the other machine talking again. If the computer does eventually respond, the best solution for the server would be to send a special update saying where everything is in the game right now and let the client start predicting from scratch. If there's still no response after 15 seconds I would disconnect that other computer from the game (or disconnect myself, if I'm a client).

Conclusion

In this chapter I've divulged almost everything I know about multithreading and network game programming. Well, except for my biggest secrets! There's only two things left to make note of.

First, if MTUDP::ProcessIncomingData() is screaming its head off because there's an invalid message type (i.e., the byte read does not equal one of the eMTUDPMsgType) then it means that somewhere in the rest of your program you are writing to funny memory such as writing beyond the bounds of an array or trying to do something funny with an uninitialized pointer.

Second, do not try to add network support to a game that has already been written because it will drive you insane. Try it this way—when most people start writing an engine, they begin with some graphics, then add keyboard or mouse support because graphics are more important and without graphics, keyboard and mouse are useless. The network controls a lot of things about how the graphics will appear, which means that the network is more important than the graphics! A perfect example of how not to write a game vis-à-vis networking is the game included on the companion CD. As I am writing these words we are still incorporating networking into the graphics framework and it is a huge pain.

I didn't mean to end on such a sour note so let me just say I am sure you will have endless fun with the network topics I have discussed here as long as you incorporate them from the beginning!

Chapter 6

Beginning Direct3D—Immediate Mode

I remember when I was but a lad and went through the rite of passage of learning to ride a bicycle. It wasn't pretty. At first, I was simply terrified of getting near the thing. I figured my own two feet were enough. Personally, I felt the added speed and features of a bike weren't worth the learning curve. I would straddle my bicycle, only to have it violently buck me over its shoulders like some vicious bull at a rodeo. The balance I needed, the speed control, the turning-while-braking—it was all almost too much. Every ten minutes, I would burst into my house, looking for my mom so she could bandage up my newly skinned knees. It took awhile, but eventually the vicious spirit of the bike was broken and I was able to ride around. Once I got used to it, I wondered why it took me so long to get the hang of it. Once I got over the hump of the learning curve, the rest was smooth sailing.

And with that, I delve into something quite similar to learning to ride a bicycle. Something that initially is hard to grasp, something that may scrape your knees a few times (maybe as deep as the arteries), but something that is worth learning and, once you get used to it, pretty painless: Direct3D programming.

Introduction to D3D

There are two major interfaces that are all-important in Direct3D: the Direct3D object and the Direct3D device. You came across both of these peripherally in Chapter 2. The Direct3D object is communicated with through the IDirect3D8 interface. It handles creation of the Direct3D device and vertex buffers (which I'll talk about later), enumeration of devices and z-buffer formats, and eviction of managed textures. You essentially create it during initialization, use it a couple of times, then pretty much forget about it.

The Direct3D device, on the other hand, will become the center of your 3-D universe. Just about all of the work you do in Direct3D goes through the device. It represents a specific pipeline to do 3-D work in. Each card has several different kinds of pipelines available. If the card supports accelerated rasterization, then it will have a device that takes advantage of those capabilities. It also has devices that completely render in software. I'll discuss all of the different device types in a moment.

> **Note:** This is the first time I've had to really worry about the concept of rasterization, so it makes sense to at least define the term. *Rasterization* is the process of taking a graphics primitive (such as a triangle) and actually rendering it pixel by pixel to the screen. It's an extremely complex (and interesting) facet of computer graphics programming; you're missing out if you've never tried to write your own texture mapper from scratch!

You'll use the device for everything: setting textures, setting render states (which control the state of the device), drawing triangles, setting up the transformation matrices, etc. It is your mode of communication with the hardware on the user's machine. You'll use it constantly. Learn the interface, and love it.

Many of the concepts I talked about in Chapter 3 will come back in full effect here. It's no coincidence that the same types of lights I discussed are the same ones Direct3D supports. In order to grasp the practical concepts of Direct3D, I needed to first show you the essentials of 3-D programming. With that in your back pocket you can start exploring the concepts that drive Direct3D programming.

The Direct3D8 Object

The Direct3D object is the way you can talk to the 3-D capabilities of the video card, asking it what kinds of devices it supports (whether or not it has hardware acceleration, etc.), or requesting interfaces to a particular type of device.

To get a IDirect3D8 pointer, all you need to do is call Direct3DCreate8(). I covered this back in Chapter 2.

The Direct3DDevice8 Object

All of the real work in Direct3D is pushed through the Direct3D device. In earlier versions of Direct3D, the D3DDevice interface was actually implemented by the same object that implemented IDirectDrawSurface. In recent versions, it has become its own object. It transparently abstracts the pipeline that is used to draw primitives on the screen.

If, for example, you have a card that has hardware support for rasterization, the device object takes rasterization calls you make and translates them into something the card can understand. When hardware acceleration for a particular task does not exist, Direct3D does its best to support it in software (although, for several reasons, this isn't feasible for some effects).

This gives you a very powerful tool. You can write code once and have it work on all machines, regardless of what kind of accelerated hardware they have installed (even if they have none at all!). This is a far cry from the way games used to be written, with developers pouring months of work into hand-optimized texture mapping routines and geometry engines, and supporting each 3-D accelerator individually.

> **Aside:** If you've ever played the old game *Forsaken*, you know what the old way was like—the game had a separate executable for each hardware accelerator that was out at the time: almost a dozen exe files!

It's not as perfect as you would like, however. Direct3D's software rasterizer (which must be used when no hardware is available on a machine) is designed to work as a general case for all types of applications. As such it isn't as fast as those hand-optimized texture mappers that are designed for a specific case (like vertical or horizontal lines of constant-Z that were prevalent in 2-D games like *Doom*). However, with each passing month more and more users have accelerators in their machines; it's almost impossible to buy a computer today without some sort of 3-D accelerator in it. For the ability to run seamlessly on dozens of hardware devices, some control must be relinquished. This is a difficult thing for many programmers (myself included!) to do. Also, not all 3-D cards out there are guaranteed to support the entire feature set of Direct3D. You must look at the capability bits of our 3-D card to make sure what we want to do can be done at all.

There is an even uglier problem. The drivers that interface to hardware cards are exceedingly complex, and in the constant efforts of all card manufacturers to get a one-up on benchmarks, stability and feature completeness are often pushed aside. As a result, the set of features that the cap bits describe is often a superset of the actual ability features that the card can handle. For example, most consumer level hardware out today can draw multiple textures at the same time (a feature called *multitexturing*). They can also all generally do tri-linear MIP map interpolation. However, many of them can't do both things at the same time. You can deal with this (and I'll show you how in Chapter 8), but it is still a headache. However, today these problems have really diminished with the consolidation and progression of the 3D accelerator market. The main manufacturers ATI, Matrox, and nVidia and a few others pump millions of dollars into their cards. Enough other problems have been solved so that they can now focus on quality assurance instead of just performance.

Device Semantics

Most Direct3D applications create exactly one device and use it the entire time the application runs. Some applications may try to create more than one device, but this is only useful in fairly esoteric cases (for example, using a second device to render a pick buffer for use in something like a level editor). Using multiple Direct3D devices under DirectX 8.0 can be a performance hit (it wasn't in previous versions), so in this text I'll just be using one.

Devices are conceptually connected to exactly one surface, where primitives are rendered. This surface is generally called the *frame buffer*. In most cases, the frame buffer is the back buffer in a page flipping (full-screen) or blitting (windowed) application. This is a regular LPDIRECT3DSURFACE8.

Device Types

The capabilities of people's machines can be wide and varied. Some people may not have any 3-D hardware (although this is rare) at all but want to play games anyway. Some may have hardware but not hardware that supports transformation and lighting, only 2-D rasterization of triangles in screen space. Others may have one of the newer types of cards that support transformation and lighting on the hardware. There is a final, extremely small slice of the pie: developers or hardware engineers who would like to know what their code would look like on an ideal piece of hardware, while viewing it at an extremely reduced frame rate. Because of this, Direct3D has built in several different types of devices to do rendering. The three currently supported device types are hardware, software, and reference.

Hardware

The HAL (or hardware abstraction layer) means that D3D's purpose is to perform transformation and lighting and supply the 3-D card in a user's machine with screen-space triangles to draw. Optionally, of course, users could manually transform and light their triangles and hand them to the card. The difference between HAL and TnLHal (the transform and lighting enabled hardware abstraction layer) is that when using the HAL, Direct3D assumes that the card is only capable of drawing transformed, lit triangles, and makes sure that is the only type of triangle it gets.

If there is not a hardware accelerator in a user's machine, attempting to create a HAL device will fail. If this happens, you should create a software device. Unless something is truly, truly wrong with the user's machine (for example, if DirectX 8.0 isn't installed), creating an RGB device won't fail.

To try to create a HAL device, you call IDirect3D8::CreateDevice with D3DDEVTYPE_HAL as the second parameter. This step will be discussed in the "Direct3D Initialization" section later in this chapter.

Software

The software device is used to emulate hardware acceleration when none exists on a user's machine. Creating a software device involves passing in D3DDEV-TYPE_SW as the second parameter in the call to IDirect3D8::CreateDevice.

Don't confuse the software device with what used to be a software device in Direct3D. In the past a software device was a piece of Direct3D code, known as the HEL (or hardware emulation layer) that was used to render graphics when no hardware acceleration was present. However, in the DirectX 8.0 implementation, a software device can also be an external pluggable piece of software that you must provide. Have a look in the DirectX documentation for more information, since this is a very advanced topic.

Interestingly enough, it isn't always the case that software is slower than the hardware installed on your machine. In truly extreme cases (for example, a really old accelerator like an S3 Virge running on a P3-800), a software renderer may be faster than the hardware renderer. That is a sad, sad state of affairs indeed. If you come across a PC like this it is time to don your missionary boots and spread the word of the new happy world of upgrading.

Reference

The reference rasterizer (or RefRast for short) is designed for developers and engineers who want to check the correctness of their code. Sometimes correct D3D code will not work. This could be because the cards' drivers are not working correctly, or because the hardware doesn't support the desired effect. To allow you to check your code and make sure it would work on an ideal piece of hardware—one that supported all of Direct3D's features (such a card currently does not exist)—you can try to create a RefRast device.

RefRast is also used by hardware manufacturers to ensure that their hardware performs correctly. The Voodoo Graphics chipset by 3DFX, for example, draws triangles that appear brighter than other cards. RefRast was created so that engineers making cards could ensure that the output of their hardware looked correct (that is, looked like the output of RefRast).

In practice, using RefRast for anything other than testing purposes is almost ludicrous. It is designed to have perfectly correct output. Most of the speed-up tricks that can be used do not apply to the reference rasterizer (though many of them exist in the RGB device). Do not be surprised if your application takes a second or more to render each frame. It is so slow, in fact, that it is not supported by D3D by default. In order to allow RefRast devices to be created (passing in D3DDEVTYPE_REF as the first parameter to IDirect3D8::CreateDevice), you must check a box in the Direct3D property page. See Figure 6.1.

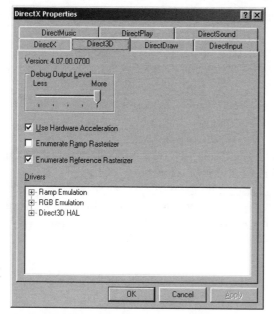

Figure 6.1:
The DirectX
Properties
page

Ramp (and Other Legacy Devices)

Older books on D3D discuss other device types, specifically Ramp and MMX.
These two device types are not supported in Direct3D 8.0. If you wish to access
them, you must use a previous version of the Direct3D interfaces (5.0, for example). The MMX device was a different type of software accelerator that was
specifically optimized for MMX machines. MMX (and Katmai/3DNow) support
is now intrinsically supported in the software device. The Ramp device was used
for drawing 3-D graphics in 256-color displays. In this day and age of high-color
and true-color displays, 256-color graphics are about as useful as a lead life
jacket. The Ramp device was dropped a few versions ago.

Determining Device Capabilities

Once you go through the process of creating the Direct3D device object, you
need to know what it can do. Since all hardware devices are different, you can't
assume that it can do whatever you want. Direct3D has a structure called a
Device Capabilities structure (D3DCAPS8). It is a very comprehensive description of exactly what the card can and cannot do. However, the features
described in the device description may be a superset of the actual features, as
some features on some cards cannot be used simultaneously (such as the
multitexture/tri-linear example given before). Note that I'm not covering every
facet of the device for the sake of brevity; refer to the SDK documentation for
more information.

```
typedef struct _D3DCAPS8 {
    D3DDEVTYPE          DeviceType;
```

```
UINT                    AdapterOrdinal;

DWORD                   Caps;
DWORD                   Caps2;
DWORD                   Caps3;
DWORD                   PresentationIntervals;

DWORD                   CursorCaps;

DWORD                   DevCaps;

DWORD                   PrimitiveMiscCaps;
DWORD                   RasterCaps;
DWORD                   ZCmpCaps;
DWORD                   SrcBlendCaps;
DWORD                   DestBlendCaps;
DWORD                   AlphaCmpCaps;
DWORD                   ShadeCaps;
DWORD                   TextureCaps;
DWORD                   TextureFilterCaps;
DWORD                   CubeTextureFilterCaps;
DWORD                   VolumeTextureFilterCaps;
DWORD                   TextureAddressCaps;
DWORD                   VolumeTextureAddressCaps;

DWORD                   LineCaps;

DWORD                   MaxTextureWidth, MaxTextureHeight;
DWORD                   MaxVolumeExtent;

DWORD                   MaxTextureRepeat;
DWORD                   MaxTextureAspectRatio;
DWORD                   MaxAnisotropy;
float                   MaxVertexW;

float                   GuardBandLeft;
float                   GuardBandTop;
float                   GuardBandRight;
float                   GuardBandBottom;

float                   ExtentsAdjust;
DWORD                   StencilCaps;

DWORD                   FVFCaps;
DWORD                   TextureOpCaps;
DWORD                   MaxTextureBlendStages;
DWORD                   MaxSimultaneousTextures;

DWORD                   VertexProcessingCaps;
DWORD                   MaxActiveLights;
DWORD                   MaxUserClipPlanes;
```

```
        DWORD               MaxVertexBlendMatrices;
        DWORD               MaxVertexBlendMatrixIndex;

        float               MaxPointSize;

        DWORD               MaxPrimitiveCount;
        DWORD               MaxVertexIndex;
        DWORD               MaxStreams;
        DWORD               MaxStreamStride;

        DWORD               VertexShaderVersion;
        DWORD               MaxVertexShaderConst;

        DWORD               PixelShaderVersion;
        float               MaxPixelShaderValue;
} D3DCAPS8;
```

Device Type	A D3DDEVTYPE enumeration member identifying the type of device.
AdapterOrdinal	A number identifying which adapter is encapsulated by this device.
Caps	Flags indicating the capabilities of the driver
Caps2	Flags indicating the capabilities of the driver
Caps3	Flags indicating the capabilities of the driver
PresentationIntervals	Flags identifying which swap intervals the device supports
CursorCaps	Flags identifying the available mouse cursor capabilities.
DevCaps	Flags identifying device capabilities
PrimitiveMiscCaps	General primitive capabilities
RasterCaps	Raster drawing capabilities
ZCmpCaps	Z-buffer comparison capabilities
SrcBlendCaps	Source blending capabilities
DestBlendCaps	Destination blending capabilities
AlphaCmpCaps	Alpha comparison capabilities
ShadeCaps	Shading capabilities
TextureCaps	Texture mapping capabilities
TextureFilterCaps	Texture filtering capabilities
CubeTextureFilterCaps	Cubic texturing capabilities
VolumeTextureFilterCaps	Volumetric texturing capabilities
TextureAddressCaps	Texture addressing capabilities
VolumeTextureAddressCaps	Volumetric texturing capabilities
LineCaps	Line drawing capabilities

MaxTextureWidth and MaxTextureHeight	The maximum width and height of textures that the device supports
MaxVolumeExtent	Maximum volume extent
MaxTextureRepeat	Maximum texture repeats
MaxTextureAspectRatio	Maximum texture aspect ration; usually a power of 2
MaxAnisotrophy	Maximum valid value for the D3DTSS_MAXANISOTROPHY texture-stage state
MaxVertexW	Maximum depth that the device supports for W buffers
GuardBandLeft, GuardBandRight, GuardBandTop, and GuardBandBottom	Screen space coordinates of the guard band clipping region
ExtentsAdjust	Number of pixels to adjust extents to compensate anti-aliasing kernels
StencilCaps	Stencil buffer capabilities
FVFCaps	Flexible vertex format capabilities
TextureOpCaps	Texture operations capabilities
MaxTextureBlendStages	Maximum supported texture blend stages
MaxSimultaneousTextures	Maximum number of textures that can be bound to the texture blending stages
VertexProcessingCaps	Vertex processing capabilities
MaxActiveLights	Maximum number of active lights
MaxUserClipPlanes	Maximum number of user-defined clipping planes
MaxVertexBlendMatrices	Maximum number of matrices the device can use to blend vertices
MaxVertexBlendMatrixIndex	The maximum matrix that can be indexed into using per-vertex indices
MaxPointSize	The maximum size for a point primitive; equals 1.0 if unsupported
MaxPrimitiveCount	Maximum number of primitives for each draw primitive call
MaxVertexIndex	Maximum size of indices for hardware vertex processing
MaxStreams	Maximum number of concurrent streams for IDirect3DDevice8::SetStreamSource()
MaxStreamStride	Maximum stride for IDirect3DDevice8::SetStreamSource()
VertexShaderVersion	The vertex shader version employed by the device
MaxVertexShaderConst	Maximum number of vertex shader constants
PixelShaderVersion	The pixel shader version employed by the device
MaxPixelShaderValue	Maximum value for the pixel shader arithmetic component

That is just a cursory overview of the structure; a full explanation would be truly massive. You won't be using it much though, so don't worry. However, if you want the real deal, check out *DirectX 8.0 Documentation/DirectX Graphics/Direct3D C++ Reference/Structures/D3DCAPS8.*

Setting Device Render States

The Direct3D device is a state machine. This means that when you change the workings of the device by adding a texture stage, modifying the lighting, etc., you're changing the state of the device. The changes you make remain until you change them again, regardless of your current location in the code. This can end up saving you a lot of work. If you want to draw an alpha-blended object, you change the state of the device to handle drawing it, draw the object, and then change the state to what you draw next. This is much better than having to explicitly fiddle with drawing styles every time you want to draw a triangle, both in code simplicity and code speed: less instructions have to be sent to the card.

As an example, Direct3D can automatically back-face cull primitives for us. There is a render state that defines how Direct3D culls primitives (it can either cull clockwise triangles, counter-clockwise triangles, or neither). When you change the render state to not cull anything, for example, every primitive you draw until you change the state again is not back-face culled.

Depending on the hardware your application is running on, state changes, especially a lot of them, can have adverse effects on system performance. One of the most important optimization steps you can learn about Direct3D is batching your primitives according to the type of state they have. If *n* number of the triangles in your scene use a certain set of render states, you should try to set the render states once, and then draw all *n* of them together. This is improved from blindly iterating through the list of primitives, setting the appropriate render states for each one. Changing the texture is an especially important render state you should try to avoid as much as possible. If multiple triangles in your scene are rendered with the same texture, draw them all in a bunch.

A while back a Microsoft intern friend of mine wrote a DLL wrapper to re-interpret glide calls as Direct3D calls. (Don't try this at home; since then 3DFX has put a clause in its EULA forbidding such things.) He couldn't understand why cards that were about as capable as a Voodoo2 at the time couldn't match the frame rates of a Voodoo2 in games like the glide version of *Unreal Tournament*. After some experimentation, he found the answer: excessive state changes. State changes on most cards are actually fairly expensive and should be grouped together if at all possible (for example, instead of drawing all of the polygons in your scene in arbitrary order, a smart application should group them by the textures they use so the active texture doesn't need to be changed that often). On a 3DFX card, however, state changes are practically free. The *Unreal* engine, when it drew its world, wasn't batching its state changes at all; in fact it was doing about eight state changes <u>per polygon</u>!

Direct3D states are set using the SetRenderState function:

```
HRESULT IDirect3DDevice8::SetRenderState(
  D3DRENDERSTATETYPE State,
  DWORD Value
);
```

State	A member of the D3DRENDERSTATETYPE enumeration describing the render state of which we would like to set the state.
Value	A DWORD that contains the desired state for the supplied render state.

and retrieved using the GetRenderState function:

```
HRESULT IDirect3DDevice7::GetRenderState(
  D3DRENDERSTATETYPE State,
  LPDWORD pValue
);
```

State	A member of the D3DRENDERSTATETYPE enumeration describing the render state of which we would like to get the state.
pValue	A pointer to a DWORD that should be filled with the current state of the supplied render state.

There is a long list of render states that allow you to modify the behavior of the lighting engine, the z-buffering state, alpha blending states, and so forth. See the SDK documentation for further information on particular states.

Table 6.1: Direct3D render states

D3DRS_ZENABLE	Depth buffering state defined with a member of the D3DZBUFFERTYPE enumeration
D3DRS_FILLMODE	The fill mode; specified with the D3DFILLMODE enumeration
D3DRS_SHADEMODE	The shade mode; specified with the D3DSHADEMODE enumeration
D3DRS_LINEPATTERN	A D3DLINEPATTERN structure specifying the line pattern
D3DRS_ZWRITEENABLE	TRUE if you want access to the depth buffer
D3DRS_ALPHATESTENABLE	TRUE to enable alpha testing
D3DRS_LASTPIXEL	FALSE to enable drawing the last pixel in a line or triangle
D3DRS_SRCBLEND	A member of the D3DBLEND enumeration specifying the source blend mode
D3DRS_DESTBLEND	A member of the D3DBLEND enumeration specifying the destination blend mode
D3DRS_CULLMODE	A member of the D3DCULL enumeration specifying the cull mode
D3DRS_ZFUNC	A D3DCMPFUNC enumeration member identifying the depth buffer comparison function

D3DRS_ALPHAREF	A reference value to compare alpha values against
D3DRS_ALPHAFUNC	A D3DCMPFUNC enumeration member identifying the alpha comparison function
D3DRS_DITHERENABLE	TRUE to enable dithering
D3DRS_ALPHABLENDENABLE	TRUE to enable alpha blended transparency
D3DRS_FOGENABLE	TRUE to enable fog
D3DRS_SPECULARENABLE	TRUE to enable specular highlights
D3DRS_ZVISIBLE	Not implemented
D3DRS_FOGCOLOR	A D3DCOLOR specifying the fog color
D3DRS_FOGTABLEMODE	A D3DFOGMODE enumeration identifying the fog type
D3DRS_FOGSTART	The depth where fog effects start
D3DRS_FOGEND	The depth where fog effects end
D3DRS_FOGDENSITY	The fog density ranging from 0.0 through 1.0
D3DRS_EDGEANTIALIAS	TRUE to antialias lines forming the convex outline of objects
D3DRS_ZBIAS	Value 0 to 16 that causes physically coplanar polygons to appear separate
D3DRS_RANGEFOGENABLE	TRUE to enable range-based fog
D3DRS_STENCILENABLE	TRUE to enable stencil buffering
D3DRS_STENCILFAIL	Stencil operation to execute if the stencil test fails
D3DRS_STENCILZFAIL	Stencil operation to execute if the stencil test passes but the z test fails
D3DRS_STENCILPASS	Stencil operation to execute if the stencil test passes
D3DRS_STENCILFUNC	The comparison function to use for stenciling
D3DRS_STENCILREF	Integer reference for the stencil test
D3DRS_STENCILMASK	Mask to apply to the reference value for stenciling
D3DRS_STENCILWRITEMASK	Write mask to apply when stenciling
D3DRS_TEXTUREFACTOR	Color used for multiple texture blending
D3DRS_WRAP0 to D3DRS_WRAP7	Texture wrapping behavior for multiple sets of texture coordinates
D3DRS_CLIPPING	TRUE to enable primitive clipping
D3DRS_LIGHTING	TRUE to enable lighting
D3DRS_AMBIENT	A D3DCOLOR specifying the ambient light color
D3DRS_FOGVERTEXMODE	The fog formula to use for vertex fog
D3DRS_COLORVERTEX	TRUE to enable per vertex coloring
D3DRS_LOCALVIEWER	TRUE to enable camera-relative specular highlights
D3DRS_NORMALIZENORMALS	TRUE to enable automatic normalization of vertex normals

D3DRS_DIFFUSEMATERIALSOURCE	Diffuse color source for lighting calculations
D3DRS_SPECULARMATERIALSOURCE	Specular color source for lighting calculations
D3DRS_AMBIENTMATERIALSOURCE	Ambient color source for light calculations
D3DRS_EMISSIVEMATERIALSOURCE	Emissive color source for light calculations
D3DRS_VERTEXBLEND	Number of vertices to use to perform vertex blending
D3DRS_CLIPENABLE	Enables or disables user-defined clip planes
D3DRS_SOFTWAREVERTEXPROCESSING	TRUE to use software vertex processing; see documentation for details
D3DRS_POINTSIZE	Float value indicating the size to use for point primitives
D3DRS_MULTISAMPLEANTIALIAS	BOOL value controlling how samples are computed when multisampling
D3DRS_MULTISAMPLEMASK	The mask to use as an accumulation buffer when multisampling
D3DRS_PATCHEDGESTYLE	Sets whether to use float style tessellation. Specified with a member of the D3DPATCHEDGESTYLE enumeration.
D3DRS_PATCHSEGMENTS	Sets the number of segments when using patches
D3DRS_DEBUGMONITORTOKEN	A member of the D3DDEBUGMONITORTOKENS enumeration specifying a token for the debug monitor
D3DRS_INDEXEDVERTEXBLENDENABLE	TRUE to enable vertex blending
D3DRS_COLORWRITEENABLE	UINT value that can enable a per-channel write for the render target color buffer.

Yes, it is big. And it is ugly; but don't worry—it will all make perfect sense soon.

Stencil buffer, z-buffer, and alpha blending can have a comparison function set for them. The possible values for their states are members of the D3DCMPFUNC enumeration:

Table 6.2: Values for the D3DCMPFUNC enumeration

D3DCMP_NEVER	Always fails the test.
D3DCMP_LESS	Passes if the tested pixel is less than the current pixel.
D3DCMP_EQUAL	Passes if the tested pixel is equal to the current pixel.
D3DCMP_LESSEQUAL	Passes if the tested pixel is less than or equal to the current pixel.
D3DCMP_GREATER	Passes if the tested pixel is greater than the current pixel.
D3DCMP_NOTEQUAL	Passes if the tested pixel is not equal to the current pixel.
D3DCMP_GREATEREQUAL	Passes if the tested pixel is greater than or equal to the current pixel.
D3DCMP_ALWAYS	Always passes the test.

Fundamental Direct3D Structures

Direct3D has some basic structures to encapsulate vertices, vectors, colors, and matrices. However, they aren't quite as easy to use as the structures I defined in Chapter 3 (at least I think so). Luckily, the structures I showed you in Chapter 3 are compatible with the Direct3D ones, so you can use simple static casts to convert them. For completeness, I'll briefly discuss these structures here.

D3DCOLOR

Most colors in Direct3D are represented with D3DCOLOR structures. They are defined thusly:

```
typedef DWORD D3DCOLOR, D3DCOLOR, *LPD3DCOLOR;
```

They represent color the same way it is held in a 32-bit frame buffer—with a DWORD (which itself is a typedef of unsigned long). The first (lowest order) 8 bits represent blue, the second 8 bits represent green, the third 8 bits represent red, and the last (highest order) 8 bits represent alpha. Two convenience macros are defined that let you convert floating-point color values into DWORDS. The code to do this is already inside color3 and color4 I created in Chapter 3.

There are two useful macros used to create DWORD colors using Direct3D. They are:

Listing 6.1: D3DCOLOR conversion macros

```
// convert an r,g,b triple into a DWORD
D3DCOLOR_XRGB(r,g,b) \
    ((D3DCOLOR)(((&0xff)<<24)|(((r)&0xff)<<16)|(((g)&0xff)<<8)|((b)&0xff)))

// convert an r,g,b,a quad into a DWORD
D3DCOLOR_ARGB(a,r,g,b) \
    ((D3DCOLOR)((((a)&0xff)<<24)|(((r)&0xff)<<16)|(((g)&0xff)<<8)|((b)&0xff)))
```

There isn't a structure in our library to represent this structure, but that's okay. All of the color manipulation in this book is just done in floating point, and converted to DWORD with the conversion functions color3::MakeDWord() and color4::MakeDWord() provided in the library.

D3DCOLORVALUE

When extra resolution for color information is needed, you can opt to use floating points. Using floats to represent color also has the added advantage that you can deal with saturation more elegantly. If DWORDs saturate (that is, they go past the highest value for each color), they simply roll over back to the lowest value. Floats can go above the highest value, but you must remember to clamp them down to the valid color range before attempting to use them, or the behavior can get weird.

D3D's structure to handle floating-point color values is called D3DCOLORVALUE. It is defined as:

Listing 6.2: The D3DCOLORVALUE structure

```
typedef struct _D3DCOLORVALUE {
    union {
        D3DVALUE r;
        D3DVALUE dvR;
    };
    union {
        D3DVALUE g;
        D3DVALUE dvG;
    };
    union {
        D3DVALUE b;
        D3DVALUE dvB;
    };
    union {
        D3DVALUE a;
        D3DVALUE dvA;
    };
} D3DCOLORVALUE;
```

This structure is equivalent to the color4 structure. The library has an added method to automatically cast a color4 pointer to a D3DCOLORVALUE pointer when the need arises. Color3s, when they want to look like a D3DCOLORVALUE, can't just mangle the pointer, as there is an extra float on the end (for alpha) that is missing in that structure. You can, however, change the color3 into a color4 first, using an alpha of 1.0.

D3DVECTOR

The D3DVECTOR structure defines a point in 3-D, just like our point3 structure. Again, the structures are equivalent, so a conversion between them is painless.

Listing 6.3: The D3DVECTOR structure

```
typedef struct _D3DVECTOR {
    union {
        D3DVALUE x;
        D3DVALUE dvX;
    };
    union {
        D3DVALUE y;
        D3DVALUE dvY;
    };
```

```
    union {
        D3DVALUE z;
        D3DVALUE dvZ;
    };
} D3DVECTOR, *LPD3DVECTOR;
```

D3DMATRIX

The D3DMATRIX structure defines a 4x4 matrix. You may notice we used similar variable layout when I created the matrix4 structure. You can use a C-style cast to convert a matrix4 pointer to a D3DMATRIX pointer, as they are laid out in memory the same way.

Listing 6.4: The D3DMATRIX structure.

```
typedef struct _D3DMATRIX {
    D3DVALUE _11, _12, _13, _14;
    D3DVALUE _21, _22, _23, _24;
    D3DVALUE _31, _32, _33, _34;
    D3DVALUE _41, _42, _43, _44;
} D3DMATRIX, *LPD3DMATRIX;
```

The Depth Problem (and How Direct3D Solves It)

Often in computer graphics, you run into the problem of determining which pixels of each triangle are visible to the viewer. A drawing algorithm typically acts in the same way as a painter. When you draw a triangle on the screen, the device draws it right over everything else that's there, like painting one on a canvas. This presents an immediate problem: The image can appear incorrect if you draw polygons out of order. Imagine what a picture would look like if a painter placed birds and clouds on the canvas first, then painted the blue sky on top of it, covering everything he had already drawn! Figure 6.2 shows what I am talking about.

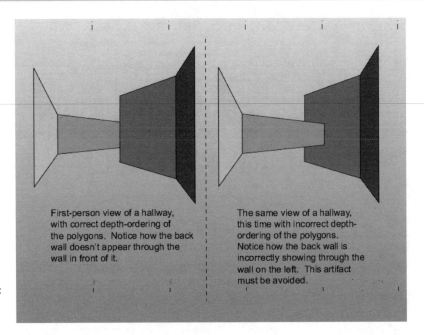

First-person view of a hallway, with correct depth-ordering of the polygons. Notice how the back wall doesn't appear through the wall in front of it.

The same view of a hallway, this time with incorrect depth-ordering of the polygons. Notice how the back wall is incorrectly showing through the wall on the left. This artifact must be avoided.

Figure 6.2:
The depth problem

The old way to solve this problem, before there was readily available hardware to solve the problem for you, was to implement the painter's algorithm. In it, you draw the world the same way a painter would: Draw the farthest things first, the nearest things last. This way, your image ends up being drawn correctly. If it doesn't seem intuitive, just think of how painters create paintings. First, they draw the farthest things away (sky, mountains, whatnot). As the paint dries they paint on top of what they had previously, adding elements in the foreground.

There are a few problems with this algorithm. First of all, it doesn't always work. You have to sort your polygons based on depth, but unless the polygons are parallel with the view plane, how do you determine the depth of the entire polygon? You could use the nearest vertex, the farthest, or the average of all the vertices, but these all have cases that won't work. There are some other cases, like triangles that intersect each other, that cannot possibly be drawn correctly with the painter's algorithm. Some triangle configurations are also unrenderable using the painter's algorithm (see Figure 6.3). Finally, you need to actually have an ordered list of polygons to draw. That involves a lot of sorting, which can become prohibitive as the triangle count increases. Most naïve sorting algorithms are $O(n^2)$, and while the fastest ones approach $O(n \lg n)$, this still will kill you if you have thousands of triangles visible on the screen at once.

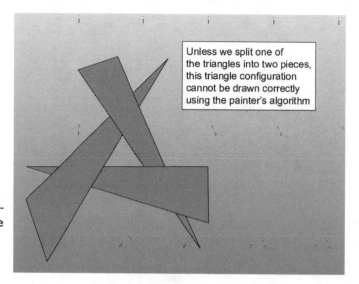

Unless we split one of the triangles into two pieces, this triangle configuration cannot be drawn correctly using the painter's algorithm

Figure 6.3: Some sadistic polygon sorting problems can't be solved without splitting polygons.

Isn't there a better way to handle finding the nearest triangle at each pixel? As usual in computer science, there's an extremely simple but inefficient brute force way to attack the problem. The brute force way ends up being the one that most cards use. Some cards, like the NEC Power VR and PowerVR2, do not, but they are old cards. Pretty much every other card on the market these days do. The method is called *z-buffering*.

The z-buffer is a second image buffer you keep in addition to the frame buffer. The z-buffer holds a single number that represents the distance at every pixel (measured with the z component, since you're looking down the z-axis with the coordinate system). Each pixel in the z-buffer holds a z-value of the closest pixel drawn up to that point. Note that you don't use the Pythagorean distance in the z-buffer, just the raw z-value of the pixels.

Before drawing, you initialize the buffer to an extremely far away value. When you draw a triangle, you iterate not only color information, but also the depth (distance, along the z-axis from the camera) of the current pixel you want to draw. When you go to draw, you check the iterated depth against the value currently in the depth buffer. If the current depth is closer than the buffer depth, it means the pixel is in front of the pixel already in the frame buffer. So you can update the frame buffer with the color value and update the depth buffer with the new depth. If the iterated depth is farther away than the z-buffer depth, that means the pixel already in the frame buffer is closer than the one you're trying to draw, so you do nothing. That way, you never draw a pixel that is obscured by something already in the scene. See Figure 6.4 to see how the frame buffer changes as you rasterize a triangle.

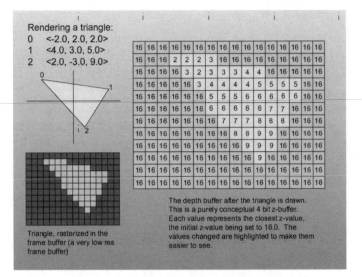

Figure 6.4: Our buffers after rasterizing a triangle

Z-buffering is not a perfect solution. First of all, you don't have infinite resolution to represent depth (again, numerical imprecision comes up to haunt us). The problem is that the precision of z-buffers doesn't vary linearly with z (because z doesn't vary linearly in screen space). Because of this, a lot of the precision (like 90% of it) is used up in the front 10% of the scene. The end result is artifacts tend to show up, especially in primitives drawn far away from the viewer. *Quake* players may remember camping beside the mega-health outside in the pent courtyard in DM3. Sometimes people hiding in the enclave on the opposite side of the courtyard would appear through the wall obscuring them. This was caused by a lack of z-buffer precision in the *Quake* software rasterizer. This can be fixed by having a higher-resolution z-buffer (24 bits, for example). Going any higher than 24 bits is really a waste; going to 32 bits means there are 4 billion possible depth values between your near and far plane, which is way too much. This is why the top 8 bits of a 32-bit depth buffer are usually used for stencil information (this is covered in Chapter 8).

Another problem with z-buffering is the speed of the algorithm. You need to perform a comparison per-pixel per-triangle. This would be prohibitive, but thankfully the card does this automatically for you, generally at no speed loss. Thanks to the silicon, you don't have to worry about the rendering order of the triangles (until, of course, you start doing stuff like alpha blending, but that comes later...). Actually the main reason anyone uses the z-buffer algorithm is that brute force algorithms tend to be extremely easy to implement in hardware.

W-Buffering

Some cards have a crafty way of getting around the resolution problems of fixed-point numbers. Instead of using fixed-point values, they use floating-point values. Floating-point z-buffers are generally called w-buffers, because they use the w component of the 4-D vector instead of z. You'll remember that when performing the perspective projection, the w component can become a value other than 1, so you must divide all four components by it to renormalize it. With most projection matrices, the w component actually ends up being the z value for the scene, so you get the perspective divide many of you may be used to if you did graphics coding back in the day. W-buffering is totally a hardware side issue. It uses the same type of memory as a z-buffer; it's just how the card will interpret the values. If the card supports it, you merely need to turn it on to get its benefits.

What are its benefits? W-buffering is implemented with the reciprocal homogenous value which boils down to 1/z in most projection matrices. One-over-z, unlike z, <u>does</u> vary linearly in screen space. The precision of the z-buffer is spread out over the entire range of z-values. Because of this, far away primitives are less susceptible to artifacts, but the trade-off is that primitives close to the viewer may have some minor artifacts.

> ***Warning:*** W-buffers can get flaky if the ratio of the far plane over the near plane is too high (too high is a relative term, but a ratio of between 200 and 500 should work just fine).

You can check for w-buffer support on a device by checking one of the raster caps bits, and turn it on using a render state:

Listing 6.5: W-buffer detection and selection code

```
// how to check for w-buffer support
// g_pDevice is a valid LPDIRECT3DDEVICE8 object

D3DCAPS8 DevCaps;

g_pDevice->GetDeviceCaps( &DevCaps );

if( DevCaps.RasterCaps | D3DPRASTERCAPS_WBUFFER )
{
  g_pDevice->SetRenderState( D3DRS_ZENABLE, D3DZB_USEW );
}
```

Stencil Buffers

Stencil buffers have risen to fame recently, as there are now a plethora of accelerators that support them. Originally they existed solely on high-end SGI machines costing barrels of money, but finally they have entered the consumer market.

Stencils are used all over the place in the "real world." For example, when people paint arrows and letters on the street, they lay large pieces of metal on the ground, then spray a whole lot of paint on them. The stencil constrains where the paint can go, so that you get a nice arrow on the ground without having to painstakingly paint each edge.

Stencil buffers work in a similar way. You can use them to constrain drawing to a particular region and to record how many times a particular region has been written to. They can even be used to render dynamic shadows really quickly. We'll discuss them more in Chapter 8, but for right now just keep them in mind. Know that typically they come in 1- and 8-bit varieties, and that they share bits with the depth buffer (in a 32-bit z-buffer, you can set up 24 bits are for z, 8 are for stencil).

Vertex Buffers

DirectX 6.0 was the first version of the SDK to include vertex buffers. The circular definition is that they are buffers filled with vertices, but this is actually about as good a definition as you'll need. Instead of creating a surface with image data or sound data, this is a surface with vertex data. Like any other surface, it must be locked to gain access and unlocked when you relinquish said access. These vertices may be at any stage of the pipeline (transformed, untransformed, lit, unlit). You can draw them using special draw primitive commands that specifically make use of the vertex buffer.

Vertex buffers have two primary uses. First, they accelerate the rendering of static geometry: You create a vertex buffer to hold the geometry for an object, fill it once, and draw the set of vertices every frame. You can use the vertex buffer to optimize the vertex data for the particular device, so it can draw it as fast as possible. The other use for vertex buffers is to provide a high-bandwidth stream of data so you can feed the graphics cards primitives as fast as you can.

Vertex buffers also make it easier for the hardware to reuse vertex data. For example, let's say you're drawing an object with multiple textures on it, or with multiple states for one section or another. Instead of having to separately transform, light, and clip all of the vertices in the object for each texture, you can run the entire geometry pipeline on the vertex buffer once, then draw groups of vertices as you like. There is also a big advantage to vertex buffers on hardware transformation and lighting cards. You can place the vertices into memory on the card once, and then draw them as many times as you like. The subdivision surface sample application discussed in Chapter 7 makes use of vertex buffers, if you want to see a piece of code that takes advantage of this nifty feature.

Creating vertex buffers is very simple; it is done with a call to IDirect3DDevice8::CreateVertexBuffer().

```
HRESULT CreateVertexBuffer(
  UINT Length,
  DWORD Usage,
  DWORD FVF,
  D3DPOOL Pool,
  IDirect3DVertexBuffer8** ppVertexBuffer
);
```

Length	The size of the vertex buffer, in bytes
Usage	Flags specifying the usage of the buffer. You will usually set this to D3DUSAGE_WRITEONLY since you hardly ever read from these buffers.
FVF	A combination of flexible vertex format (FVF) flags identifying the types of vertices that you want to use. I will discuss these shortly.
Pool	A member of the D3DPOOL enumeration identifying how you want the buffer to be managed in memory. You will generally use the D3DPOOL_DEFAULT flag, which allows Direct3D to place it in the most appropriate memory.
ppVertexBuffer	The address of a pointer that will be filled with the address of the newly created vertex buffer.

Once you create a vertex buffer, it must be filled with vertex data. To fill the vertex buffer you must first lock it, using the Lock method on the newly created vertex buffer interface:

```
HRESULT IDirect3DVertexBuffer8::Lock(
  UINT OffsetToLock,
  UINT SizeToLock,
  BYTE** ppbData,
  DWORD Flags
);
```

OffsetToLock	The offset into the buffer that you want to lock
SizeToLock	The size of the vertex buffer, in bytes, that you want to lock. Specify 0 to lock the entire buffer.
ppbData	The address of a pointer that will be filled with a pointer to the locked vertex data
Flags	A combination of zero or more of the following flags, which indicate how the memory should be locked. You normally set this parameter to NULL.
	• D3DLOCK_DISCARD—The application is going to overwrite the entire vertex buffer.
	• D3DLOCK_NOOVERWRITE—This can lead to performance enhancements if you are only appending data in the buffer.
	• D3DLOCK_NOSYSLOCK—Cause a critical section lock not to be held for the duration of the lock.
	• D3DLOCK_READONLY—The application will not write to the buffer.

If the lock succeeds you receive a pointer to the vertex data. You can then freely fill in the vertex buffer with all the vertex data you wish to render with. When you're finished, call Unlock, just like a surface. It takes no parameters.

You must use vertex buffers to draw primitives, such as triangles, lines, and so on. In the past you could just draw primitives with calls to certain functions, but these days you <u>must</u> package your rendering data into vertex buffers before rendering them with DrawPrimitive or DrawIndexedPrimitive. Well, I kind of lied—you can use the DrawPrimitiveUP or DrawIndexedPrimitiveUP functions to render raw vertices from memory, and I'll show you these in action shortly.

To render vertex buffers you must attach them to something that is called a rendering stream. Once the vertex buffer is attached, you can then call one of the DrawPrimitive functions, and it will render whatever is attached to the rendering stream. You attach a vertex buffer to a rendering stream with the function SetStreamSource, which has the following definition:

```
HRESULT SetStreamSource(
  UINT StreamNumber,
  IDirect3DVertexBuffer8* pStreamData,
  UINT Stride
);
```

Stream Number	The stream number that you want to attach the vertex buffer to. This will usually be set to 0 to indicate stream zero.
pStreamData	A pointer to the vertex buffer that you want to attach to the rendering stream.
Stride	The distance between each of the vertices in the buffer. In other words, you can just do a sizeof() to figure out the size of your vertex structure.

Texture Mapping

Texture mapping is pretty much the feature that adds the most wow power to a 3-D application. It's also one of the most complex and varied features Direct3D has. Since there is so much to it, I'll save most of the discussion for Chapter 8, and just try to get the basics here.

Materials and Lights

Back in the old school of Direct3D 6.0 and previous versions, using lights and materials was a tedious process. Ref-counted COM interfaces were used to represent lights and materials, which led to much confusion and obfuscation. It wasn't a really big deal, though; before 7.0 and the advent of hardware accelerated transformation and lighting, nobody really used the lighting pipeline anyway.

With 7.0, Microsoft decided to clean up the interfaces used to handle materials and lighting, since at long last it seemed that people might actually use them. Lights and materials are represented with regular C-style structures (not even Win32 style structures; you don't need to set a dwSize variable!) and you use a much simpler interface to initialize and activate lights.

Using Lights

In any given scene you have one material and *n* lights (the number of lights allowable by the device is listed in the device description but is usually in the tens of thousands). Since you can have many more initialized lights in a scene than activated lights, it's best to create all of the lights at application startup. As you render the world, you activate and deactivate lights as you wish, for example, picking the three or four closest lights to the camera for use in rendering. Of course, the fewer lights you use, and the simpler those lights are, the faster everything goes. Directional lights are the fastest, followed by point source lights and spotlights at a distant third. On hardware T&L cards, however, the first few lights are free regardless of complexity.

Lights are abstracted by a structure called the D3DLIGHT8 structure. It is defined as follows:

```
typedef struct _D3DLIGHT8 {
    D3DLIGHTTYPE    Type;
    D3DCOLORVALUE   Diffuse;
    D3DCOLORVALUE   Specular;
    D3DCOLORVALUE   Ambient;
    D3DVECTOR       Position;
    D3DVECTOR       Direction;
    float           Range;
    float           Falloff;
    float           Attenuation0;
    float           Attenuation1;
    float           Attenuation2;
    float           Theta;
    float           Phi;
} D3DLIGHT8;
```

Type	Defines the type of light the structure represents. The D3DLIGHTTYPE enumeration supports three values. The values are D3DLIGHT_POINT (for point-source lights), D3DLIGHT_SPOT (for spotlights), and D3DLIGHT_DIRECTIONAL (for directional lights).
Diffuse	A D3DCOLORVALUE that represents the diffuse light emitted by the light object.
Specular	A D3DCOLORVALUE that represents the specular light emitted by the light object.
Ambient	A D3DCOLORVALUE that represents the ambient light emitted by the light object.
Position	A D3DVECTOR that represents the position of the light. This only applies for point source lights and spotlights; for directional lights this value is ignored.

Direction	A D3DVECTOR that represents the direction that the light is pointing. Since point source lights are omni-directional, this value does not apply to them, but it does apply to spotlights and directional lights. The value doesn't need to be normalized, but it does need to have a non-zero length for the light to function correctly.
Range	A float that represents the farthest distance an object can be to be influenced by the light. If a vertex is any farther away, this light will not be considered in the lighting calculations. As this only works for lights that have a defined position, it does not apply to directional lights.
Falloff	A float that represents how much of an intensity difference exists between a spotlight's inner cone and outer cone. Programs can be hit significantly by using this value, especially if no dedicated lighting hardware exists in the machine, so if spotlights are used, this value is typically set to 1.0.
Attenuation0	The constant falloff based on distance for the light. This value does not apply to directional lights.
Attenuation1	The linear falloff based on distance for the light. This value does not apply to directional lights. Most applications can get by with just linear falloff, but quadratic fall-off is the most physically correct.
Attenuation2	The quadratic falloff based on distance for the light. This value does not apply to directional lights.
Theta	A float (in radians) that represents the angle between the direction and the edge of the inner cone of a spotlight (points inside the inner cone of a spotlight are fully lit). Only applies to spotlights.
Phi	A float (in radians) that represents the angle between the direction and the edge of the outer cone of a spotlight (points outside the inner cone of a spotlight are not lit). Only applies to spotlights.

D3D Lighting Semantics

Lights can be set, activated, or disabled through the Direct3D device. The device can handle a certain number of simultaneously active lights (the number can be found in the MaxActiveLights member of the D3DCAPS8 structure). You set the values for a light using the D3DDevice function SetLight:

```
HRESULT IDirect3DDevice8::SetLight(
  DWORD Index,
  LPD3DLIGHT8 pLight
);
```

Index	The index of the light you would like to change. (Direct3D keeps an internal list of lights; setting two lights to the same index will cause the second to overwrite the values of the first.)
pLight	A pointer to a D3DLIGHT8 structure you have filled up to define a light in the scene.

After you have set up the light, you might think you were all set. This is not the case! After you initialize the light structures, you need to explicitly turn each of them on. Why is this? The expected use of D3D lighting is to initialize all of your lights at application startup, turn on the visible ones when you want to use them, and turn them off when you stop. In order to enable or disable individual lights that you have initialized with SetLight, you must call LightEnable:

```
HRESULT IDirect3DDevice8::LightEnable(
    DWORD LightIndex,
    BOOL bEnable
);
```

LightIndex	The index of the light you would like to change. (Direct3D keeps an internal list of lights; setting two lights to the same index will cause the second to overwrite the values of the first.)
bEnable	If this value is non-zero, the light in question is enabled. If this value is zero, it is disabled.

What happens if you try to enable a light that you have not initialized? There is a default light structure that Direct3D uses, which is a white directional light pointing out into your scene in the +Z direction.

The sLight Helper Class

To help facilitate the use of lights in Direct3D, I wrote a helper class to automatically construct lights based on the constructor used. The class is called sLight, and the class definition appears in Listing 6.6.

Listing 6.6: The sLight structure

```
/**
 * sLight helps the D3DLIGHT8 structure.
 * The static constructors make it possible to
 * automatically create certain light types
 */
struct sLight : public D3DLIGHT8
{
  sLight()
  {
      // do nothing
  }

  static sLight Directional(
      const point3& dir,
      const color3& diff = color3::White,
      const color3& spec = color3::Black,
      const color3& amb = color3::Black )
  {
      sLight out;
```

```
        memset(out, 0, sizeof(D3DLIGHT8));
        out.Type = D3DLIGHT_DIRECTIONAL;

        out.Direction = *(D3DVECTOR*)&dir;

        out.Diffuse = *(D3DCOLORVALUE*)&diff;
        out.Specular = *(D3DCOLORVALUE*)&spec;
        out.Ambient = *(D3DCOLORVALUE*)&amb;
        return out;
}

static sLight PointSource(
        const point3& loc,
        const color3& diff = color3::White,
        const color3& spec = color3::Black,
        const color3& amb = color3::Black )
{
        sLight out;
        memset(out, 0, sizeof(D3DLIGHT8));
        out.Type = D3DLIGHT_POINT;

        out.Range = D3DLIGHT_RANGE_MAX;

        out.Attenuation0 = 0.f;
        out.Attenuation1 = 1.f;
        out.Attenuation2 = 0.f;

        out.Position = *(D3DVECTOR*)&loc;

        out.Diffuse = *(D3DCOLORVALUE*)&diff;
        out.Specular = *(D3DCOLORVALUE*)&spec;
        out.Ambient = *(D3DCOLORVALUE*)&amb;
        return out;
}

static sLight Spot(
        const point3& loc,
        const point3& dir,
        float theta, float phi,
        const color3& diff = color3::White,
        const color3& spec = color3::Black,
        const color3& amb = color3::Black )
{
        sLight out;
        memset(out, 0, sizeof(D3DLIGHT8));
        out.Type = D3DLIGHT_SPOT;

        out.Range = D3DLIGHT_RANGE_MAX;

        out.Attenuation0 = 0.f;
        out.Attenuation1 = 1.f;
```

```
                    out.Attenuation2 = 0.f;

                    out.Theta = theta;
                    out.Phi = phi;
                    out.Position = *(D3DVECTOR*)&loc;
                    out.Direction = *(D3DVECTOR*)&dir;

                    out.Diffuse = *(D3DCOLORVALUE*)&diff;
                    out.Specular = *(D3DCOLORVALUE*)&spec;
                    out.Ambient = *(D3DCOLORVALUE*)&amb;
                    return out;
            }

            operator D3DLIGHT8*()
            {
                    return this;
            }
            operator const D3DLIGHT8*() const
            {
                    return (const D3DLIGHT8* )this;
            }
        };
```

By the way, just as a footnote for the above. See the D3DLIGHT_RANGE_MAX identifier? That used to be defined in previous versions of DirectX, but these days it has disappeared for some reason. If you want to use it you must define it yourself like this:

```
#define D3DLIGHT_RANGE_MAX      ((float)sqrt(FLT_MAX))
```

Using Materials

Materials, also discussed in Chapter 3, help us define the look of an object. Using different material parameters, you can make a surface look shiny (like an apple), matte (like chalk), emissive (like a light), and anywhere in between.

```
typedef struct _D3DMATERIAL8 {
        D3DCOLORVALUE   Diffuse;
        D3DCOLORVALUE   Ambient;
        D3DCOLORVALUE   Specular;
        D3DCOLORVALUE   Emissive;
        float           Power;
} D3DMATERIAL8;
```

Diffuse	Diffuse color reflectance for the material.
Ambient	Ambient color reflectance for the material.
Specular	Specular color reflectance for the material.
Emissive	Emissive color for the material.

Power	Power used in the lighting equations. Floating-point number 1.0 will give very soft highlights, where values of 20-40 will only look correct on highly tessellated models, as the highlights will be extremely small.

D3D Material Semantics

Direct3D materials have two functions to play with: one to set the current material and one to retrieve it. Again, there is only one material for scenes in this book, which is why I don't have an index variable like the lighting functions. You can set the material using SetMaterial:

```
HRESULT IDirect3DDevice8::SetMaterial(
  D3DMATERIAL8* pMaterial
);
```

pMaterial	Pointer to a material structure filled with what the current material should become.

And retrieve the material with GetMaterial:

```
HRESULT IDirect3DDevice8::GetMaterial(
  D3DMATERIAL8* pMaterial
);
```

pMaterial	Pointer to a material structure to be filled with what the current material is.

The sMaterial Helper Class

As with the sLight helper class discussed previously, the library has a class to help initialize materials, with a constructor to automate the creation process for you.

Listing 6.7: The sMaterial structure

```
struct sMaterial : public D3DMATERIAL8
{

  sMaterial(
      float pow,
      color4 diff = color4( 1.f, 1.f, 1.f, 1.f ),
      color4 spec = color4( 1.f, 1.f, 1.f, 1.f ),
      color4 amb = color4( 1.f, 1.f, 1.f, 1.f ),
      color4 emit = color4( 0.f, 0.f, 0.f, 0.f ) )
  {
      ZeroMemory( this, sizeof(D3DMATERIAL8) );

      /**
       * We could make an operator for this, but
       * putting d3d.h everywhere kills compile time.
```

```
        */
    Diffuse = *(D3DCOLORVALUE*)&diff;
    Ambient = *(D3DCOLORVALUE*)&amb;
    Specular = *(D3DCOLORVALUE*)&spec;
    Emissive = *(D3DCOLORVALUE*)&emit;
    Power = pow;
}

operator D3DMATERIAL8*()
{
    return this;
}
operator const D3DMATERIAL8*() const
{
    return (const D3DMATERIAL8* )this;
}
};
```

The Geometry Pipeline

Direct3D has an extremely robust, extremely fast software geometry pipeline, when a hardware one is not available. The only argument against using it is that it turns part of your program into a black box. If there is a nifty optimization you can pull off because of the way your scene works (for example, if you can get perspective projection for a terrain scene using only adds), you should consider implementing the pipeline yourself.

In order to use the geometry pipeline, all you need to do is specify matrices you would like Direct3D to use when it performs transformations. All of Direct3D's internal matrices start out as the identity matrix. The main matrices you want to worry about right now are the world, view, and projection matrices. The world matrix transforms local coordinate space points to world space; the view matrix transforms world coordinate space points to view space; the projection matrix projects view-space points into screen-space. This was covered in Chapter 3.

Transformation matrices are changed using two methods on the device interface: GetTransform and SetTransform.

```
HRESULT IDirect3DDevice8::GetTransform(
    D3DTRANSFORMSTATETYPE State,
    D3DMATRIX* pMatrix
);
HRESULT IDirect3DDevice8::SetTransform(
    D3DTRANSFORMSTATETYPE State,
    D3DMATRIX* pMatrix
);
```

State	A member of the D3DTRANSFORMSTATETYPE enumeration describing which Direct3D matrix the call is in reference to. The members are given below.
pMatrix	Pointer to the matrix being used.

D3DTRANSFORMSTATETYPE has the following members:

Table 6.3: Members of the D3DTRANSFORMSTATETYPE enumeration

D3DTS_WORLD	Primary world matrix transformation. Transforms from object space to world space.
D3DTS_VIEW	View matrix transformation. Transforms from world space to view space.
D3DTS_PROJECTION	Projection matrix transformation. Transforms from view space to screen space.
D3DTS_TEXTURE0D3DTS_TEXTURE7	Texture transformation matrices.

Some internal housekeeping is done when matrices are changed, especially the first three. At the very least, Direct3D needs to perform two matrix multiplications to concatenate the world, view, and projection matrices together whenever one of them is changed. Excessive transformation changes (excessive being tens of thousands a frame) can slow down performance and should be avoided. An application should only need to change the view matrix once per frame (if the camera moves), and the world matrix once per object drawn.

Clipping and Viewports

Direct3D, in addition to the transformation pipeline, can clip your primitives for you, so only the parts that are actually within the dimensions of the frustum get used. In order for Direct3D to know what frustum to clip to, you need to define a viewport, which describes which part of the frame buffer you want to render to. While you can make it a subset of our total surface if you like, generally you want to set up the viewport so it renders to the entire surface.

The viewport structure is called D3DVIEWPORT8 and is defined as follows:

```
typedef struct _D3DVIEWPORT8{
    DWORD      X;
    DWORD      Y;
    DWORD      Width;
    DWORD      Height;
    D3DVALUE   MinZ;
    D3DVALUE   MaxZ;
} D3DVIEWPORT8;
```

X, Y	The x and y coordinates of the top-left corner of the viewport. If you want to use the entire surface, set these parameters to 0.

Width, Height	The width and height of the viewport. If you want to use the entire surface, set these parameters to the width and height of the drawing surface.
MinZ, MaxZ	The range of z values you want your application to draw. These numbers aren't the same ones you use when we make the projection matrix; almost universally you should set these to 0.0 and 1.0.

The viewport functions are similar to the material functions; one to set the viewport...

```
HRESULT IDirect3DDevice8::SetViewport(
  CONST D3DVIEWPORT8* pViewport
);
```

pViewport	Pointer to a viewport structure filled with what the current viewport should become.

... and one to retrieve it.

```
HRESULT IDirect3DDevice8::GetViewport(
  D3DVIEWPORT8* pViewport
);
```

pViewport	Pointer to a viewport structure to be filled with what the current viewport is.

I decided against making a wrapper class for the viewport, since it's only touched in one piece of code, so the abstraction seemed unnecessary.

Fog

Fog in games is one of those double-edged swords. On one hand, there are games like *Goldeneye* for the N64, which used tinted fog to add ambience to the levels (I was blown away the first time I saw the satellite dish eerily emerge from the gray fog in the surface level). On the other hand, there are games like *Turok: Dinosaur Hunter*; it had an impenetrable fog layer 20 feet away from the player because there wasn't enough of a triangle budget to draw any further.

Whether you're using it to add mood or using it to add speed, Direct3D has all the fog functionality you could possibly want. It supports two different fog interfaces: pixel-based fog and vertex-based fog. *Pixel fog* (or *table fog*) is implemented in the Direct3D driver and is a per-pixel operation; it's implemented in hardware on most HAL devices. *Vertex fog*, on the other hand, is part of the D3D lighting engine, and is computed by the Direct3D lighting engine and passed to the rasterization engine. On TnLHal devices, it's hardware accelerated, but in software it is dependent on the main processor to do the grunt work and it can get a bit slow.

They both work with the same concept in mind. As the distance of a primitive increases, a fog color is applied, until some faraway distance at which point it is completely shrouded in fog. This tries to imitate atmospheric interference, where particles of dust and pollen in the air can gradually color distant objects. If you've ever been driving in the mountains you know this effect; the farther back a mountain is, the more the atmosphere around it tints it.

The way fog acts on vertices can be summed up with an equation:

$$\text{fog intensity } f = \text{fog function(distance)}$$

$$\text{color}_{\text{final}} = f \times \text{color}_{\text{curr}} + \left(1 - f\right) \times \text{color}_{\text{fog}}$$

> **Warning:** The fog engine uses the projection matrix for the scene to find the range of depth values to use in the lighting equations. Even if you're not using the projection matrix (performing your own transformations), a w-friendly projection matrix must be set for fog to work.

Vertex-based Fog

Vertex-based fog is performed by the D3D lighting engine. Thus, it can only be calculated for unlit, untransformed vertices. If you perform your own lighting or transform your own vertices, you can only use pixel fog. The lighting engine calculates the fog value for each vertex of each primitive. Then the fog intensity is linearly interpolated across the primitive, like Gouraud color.

Due to speed constraints, only one fog mode, linear fog, is supported for vertex-based fog. This means that the fog color increases linearly as the distance increases. Pixel fog can handle more esoteric blending rates, such as logarithmic fog.

Offsetting this shortcoming is the fact that vertex-based fog can be eye-relative if the need arises. Usually fog is calculated based on the incorrect distance function of the z-value of the vertex in view space. While this is correct for vertices directly in front of the camera, when they are off to the side, they actually receive less fog than they should.

This can cause really nasty artifacts. Consider Figure 6.5. As the camera rotates, Object 2 moves out of the fog and into visible space. This, of course, is incorrect. Ideally, the distance used to compute fog should be the actual Pythagorean distance I showed you in Chapter 3. This calculation involves two multiplications and a square root per vertex, however, and can slow down a lot for scenes with a high number of primitives.

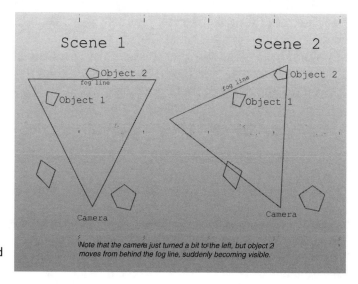

Figure 6.5:
Problems
with z-based
fog

Pixel-based Fog

Pixel-based fog is performed by the rasterizer as opposed to the lighting engine. It's also called table-based fog because typically the fog color is generated using a look-up table of fog intensities for certain distances.

Because pixel fog uses a look-up table, you're not constrained to having fog vary based on distance. You can use two additional fog modes: D3DFOG_EXP, which varies fog intensity exponentially based on distance, and D3DFOG_EXP2, which varies fog intensity exponentially based on the squared distance. You can also define the density of the fog, which helps define how much distance is required before the object disappears. The SDK documentation has a good chart displaying the different falloff methods in a chart listed under *DirectX 8.0 C++ Documentation/DirectX Graphics/Using DirectX Graphics/Techniques and Special Effects/Fog/Fog Formulas*.

Using Fog

Fog in Direct3D is controlled completely by render states. There are a slew of them, each controlling one particular facet of the fog pipeline.

Table 6.4: Fog render states

D3DRS_FOGENABLE	Set to TRUE to turn on fog blending. Setting the rest of these modes is pointless unless you actually turn fog on! (default = FALSE)
D3DRS_FOGCOLOR	A D3DCOLOR that represents the color of the fog. The alpha component is ignored. This color is the color of the atmosphere. As objects move farther back they will blend more and more into the fog color, eventually disappearing entirely.

D3DRS_FOGTABLEMODE	Fog mode to use for pixel-based fog (or table fog). Must be a member of the D3DFOGMODE enumeration, presented below. (default = D3DFOG_NONE)

D3DRS_FOGSTART	The starting point for the fog effect in linear fog modes. For vertex fog, this number is the distance value in world space. For pixel fog, the value can be in world space (for eye-relative fog) or device space [0.0,1.0] (for z-relative fog). The number is given in floating point, so it must be cast to a DWORD like so:
	
	`float start = 0.0f;      // or some other value`
	`* ((DWORD*) (&start)))`

D3DRS_FOGEND	The end point for the fog effect in linear fog modes. For vertex fog, this number is the distance value in world space. For pixel fog, the value can be in world space (for eye-relative fog) or device space [0.0,1.0] (for z-relative fog). The number is given in floating point, so it must be cast to a DWORD like so:
	
	`float end = 1.0f;      // or some other value`
	`*((DWORD*) (&end)))`

D3DRS_FOGDENSITY	The fog density used in the two exponential fog modes. The number is given in floating point, so it must be cast to a DWORD like so:
	
	`float density = 1.0f;    // or some other value`
	`*((DWORD*) (&density)))`
	
	(default = 1.0)

D3DRS_RANGEFOGENABLE	Setting this state to TRUE enables range-based fog. The fog value is found based on the distance from the eye point, not the z-value in view space. This is physically correct but computationally expensive. Also, range-based fog only works for D3DVERTEX primitives. Vertices that are lit or transformed and lit are assumed to have their fog component already computed. A value of FALSE means the system uses z-based fog. (default = FALSE)
D3DRS_FOGVERTEXMODE	Fog mode to use for vertex-based fog. Must be a member of the D3DFOGMODE enumeration, presented below. (default = D3DFOG_NONE)

There are four fog modes for the FOGVERTEXMODE and FOGTABLEMODE render states. They are described by the D3DFOGMODE enumeration.

Table 6.5: Members of the D3DFOGMODE enumeration

D3DFOG_NONE	No fog effect is used.
D3DFOG_EXP	The effect of the fog increases exponentially with distance. The amount of fog color applied relates to distance with the formula: $$\text{fog intensity} = \frac{1}{e^{\text{distance} \times \text{fog density}}}$$

D3DFOG_EXP2	The effect of the fog increases exponentially with the square of the distance. The amount of fog color applied relates to distance with the formula:
	$$\text{fog intensity} = \frac{1}{e^{(\text{distance} \times \text{fog density})^2}}$$
D3DFOG_LINEAR	The effect of the fog varies linearly with the distance's relation between the fog start point and fog end point. This is the only mode supported by vertex fog. The amount of fog color applied relates to distance with the formula:
	$$\text{fog intensity} = \frac{\text{fog}_{end} - \text{distance}}{\text{fog}_{end} - \text{fog}_{start}}$$

Drawing with the Device

Once you have set up the states of the device to your liking, turned on the fog, made your vertex buffers, and set up the lighting, you need to actually draw some triangles!

The Draw*Primitive* interface has existed since Direct3D 5.0 to let applications draw line strips, triangle fans, point lists, and so on. Before DirectX 5.0, 3-D applications needed to use what were called *execute buffers*. They provided a way to batch rendering commands into buffers so that the software rasterizer could execute them as quickly as possible. The interface was a total pain to use, however. Thank your lucky stars that execute buffers were dropped a few versions ago. No, really; get down and start thanking the gods!

Direct3D Vertex Structures

When you want to draw primitives, you can't just give an x, y, and z location. Direct3D needs to know more information, such as texture mapping coordinates, diffuse/specular color information, and/or normal information. Prior to Direct3D 6.0, you had to use one of three predefined structures, D3DVERTEX, D3DLVERTEX, or D3DTLVERTEX. However, now there are no set structures that you can use for your vertices; instead you must use what is called the flexible vertex format.

Flexible Vertex Format Flags

Since DirectX 6.0, applications have been able to define their own vertex structures. You can define extra sets of texture coordinates, define just diffuse data instead of both diffuse and specular (saving 4 bytes of storage per vertex), and even define geometry blending factors.

This is accomplished by filling a bit vector with flexible vertex format flags (FVF), and passing the bit vector to the device when you render. If a particular flag is set, that means that the vertex contains that info. The values must appear in a certain order, for example, position data is always the first value in a vertex (and must be included). The flags, in the order they must appear in the vertex, are shown in Table 6.6.

Table 6.6: The set of flexible vertex format flags

D3DFVF_XYZ	This flag means you include the position of the point you wish to draw. The value must be untransformed. The location is stored as a triplet of floats representing x, y, and z locations. Cannot be used with the D3DFVF_XYZRHW flag.
D3DFVF_XYZRHW	This flag means you are including the location of a transformed vertex. This means the x and y components are in screen space, the z component is the distance from the view plane, and an additional float called RHW holds the reciprocal homogeneous w coordinate. This is incompatible with the D3DFVF_NORMAL flag.
D3DFVF_XYZBx (x = {1..5})	Vertices can be transformed certain amounts by certain matrices to help make smooth transitions in joints with bone-based animation. These flags describe how many beta values (32-bit floats) each vertex has. Each beta value is a weight, multiplied by its corresponding world space matrix. See Chapter 7 for a discussion of geometry blending.
D3DFVF_NORMAL	If this flag is set, the vertex contains normal information. The data is stored as three floats, representing the x, y, and z components of the normal. Cannot be used with the D3DFVF_XYZRHW flag.
D3DFVF_DIFFUSE	32-bit integer (DWORD) representing the diffuse color of the vertex, in RGBA form. You can use this in conjunction with the D3DFVF_NORMAL flag to define a diffuse color per-vertex, instead of using the current material.
D3DFVF_SPECULAR	32-bit integer (DWORD) representing the specular color of the vertex, in RGBA form. You can use this in conjunction with the D3DFVF_NORMAL flag to define a specular color per-vertex, instead of using the current material.
D3DFVF_TEXx (x = {1..8})	The number of texture coordinates in this vertex. Note that the flags are not sequential. Each pair of texture coordinates is represented with two 32-bit floats, the first representing the horizontal u component and the second representing the vertical v component. Texture mapping is discussed at length in Chapter 8.
D3DFVF_TEXCOORDSIZEx (x = {1..4})	This actually isn't a flag; it's a macro. It is used to define the dimension for each set of texture coordinates. The macro D3DFVF_TEXCOORD-SIZEx(y) means that the yth set of texture coordinates are x-dimensional. The default for all sets is two-dimensional, so unless you're getting esoteric you don't need to muck around with this macro.

Predefined Flag Macros

There are a few predefined macros that help you when you're using the supplied D3D vertex structures (vertex, lit vertex, and transformed and lit vertex). They are:

■ D3DFVF_VERTEX

Flags that correspond with the D3DVERTEX structure.

■ D3DFVF_LVERTEX

Flags that correspond with the D3DLVERTEX structure.

■ D3DFVF_TLVERTEX

Flags that correspond with the D3DTLVERTEX structure.

Before rendering with Direct3D you <u>must</u> tell it what kind of vertices you are rendering, or else Direct3D will crash. What you are actually doing is setting up what is called a vertex shader, which controls how your polygons are rendered onto the screen. You set the vertex shader with a call to SetVertexShader, which has the following definition:

```
HRESULT SetVertexShader(
  DWORD Handle
);
```

Handle	A handle to the vertex shader that you want to create. This can also be a combination of FVF flags describing the vertices you are rendering.

So for instance, say you have a vertex that has a position, normal, and color. To use it, you would make the following call:

```
m_pDevice->SetVertexShader( D3DFVF_XYZ | D3DFVF_NORMAL | D3DFVF_DIFFUSE );
```

Now you are ready to go ahead and render the vertex buffer. If you find the debug output from Direct3D keeps giving you errors about not having a valid vertex shader, this is probably what your problem is.

Examples

Most of the vertex types you'll encounter in this book are one of the ones defined above. However, there are some cases (the multitexture application in Chapter 8 is a big example) where you may wish to roll your own vertices. I'll show you two examples.

In the first (shown in Listing 6.8), I'm building a simple three-pass multitexture application. The lighting is not used at all, but the transformation engine is. Also, specular coordinate data is not needed.

Listing 6.8: A vertex with three sets of texture coordinates

```
#include <point3.h>
#include <gametypes.h>            // ulong

struct texCoord2 { float m_u, m_v; };

struct mtVertex
{
    point3 m_loc;                 // Position
    ulong m_diff;                 // Color
```

```
    texCoord2 m_tex[3];          // Texture coordinates

    static ulong m_fvfFlags;     // Flags
};

ulong mtVertex::m_fvfFlags = D3DFVF_XYZ | D3DFVF_DIFFUSE | D3DFVF_TEX3;
```

The other example is about as hardcore as you're ever likely to see a vertex get. It not only uses the transformation and lighting engines, it also defines its own diffuse and specular vertex colors in addition to the lit color values. On top of that, it has two sets of texture coordinates, the first two-dimensional and the second three-dimensional.

Listing 6.9: Vertex with multidimensional texture coordinate sets

```
#include <point3.h>
#include <gametypes.h>           // ulong

struct texCoord2 { float m_u, m_v; };
struct texCoord3 { float m_u, m_v, m_w; };

struct mtVertex
{
    point3 m_loc;                // Position
    point3 m_norm;               // Normal
    ulong m_diff;                // Color (Diffuse)
    ulong m_spec;                // Color (Specular)
    texCoord2 m_tex1;
    texCoord3 m_tex2;

    static ulong m_fvfFlags;
};

ulong mtVertex::m_fvfFlags =
    D3DFVF_XYZ |
    D3DFVF_NORMAL |
    D3DFVF_DIFFUSE |
    D3DFVF_SPECULAR |
    D3DFVF_TEXCOORDSIZE2(0) |     // set 0 is 2-dimensional
    D3DFVF_TEXCOORDSIZE3(1);      // set 1 is 3-dimensional
```

Primitive Types

When drawing primitives using the D3D device, you need to inform the device what type of primitive you would like it to draw. Currently, Direct3D can draw three types of primitives: points, lines, and triangles.

D3DPT_POINTLIST	The data being handed to the driver is a list of points. The Direct3D device draws one pixel for each vertex handed to it.
D3DPT_LINELIST	The data being handed to the driver is a list of lines. The number of vertices provided to the device must be even. If *n* vertices are passed in, *n*/2 lines are drawn. For example, the third line D3D draws is from the fourth to the fifth vertex.
D3DPT_LINESTRIP	Direct3D draws a continuous strip of lines. Each vertex besides the first becomes the endpoint of a line, with a beginning of the vertex before it.
D3DPT_TRIANGLELIST	Direct3D draws a list of distinct triangles. Each three vertices are rendered as a triangle. Of course, the number of vertices supplied to the DrawPrim functions must be a multiple of three.
D3DPT_TRIANGLESTRIP	Direct3D draws a triangle strip, each vertex after the first two defining the third point of a triangle. See Chapter 3 for a discussion of triangle strips.
D3DPT_TRIANGLEFAN	Direct3D draws a triangle fan, each vertex after the first two defining the third point of a triangle. See Chapter 3 for a discussion of triangle fans.

The DrawPrimitive Functions

There are four total functions to draw primitives for us. They are all very similar and once you've mastered one, you've pretty much mastered them all. Let's take a look at each of them.

DrawPrimitive

DrawPrimitive is the most basic primitive drawing function. It simply takes the current vertex buffer that is attached to a rendering stream and renders it. It doesn't use any indexed information, and therefore isn't as efficient for drawing triangle meshes as DrawIndexedPrimitive for most applications. The one exception is drawing triangle strips and fans. On some cards (such as the GeForce), the cache coherency goes way up and using DrawPrimitive is actually faster than DrawIndexedPrimitive.

```
HRESULT DrawPrimitive(
            D3DPRIMITIVETYPE PrimitiveType,
            UINT StartVertex,
            UINT PrimitiveCount
    );
```

PrimitiveType	The type of primitive you would like the device to draw for you.
StartVertex	Index of the first vertex you want to load; usually set this to 0.
PrimitiveCount	The number of primitives to render.

DrawPrimitiveUP

DrawPrimitiveUP is very similar to the regular DrawPrimitive except that it does not require you to package your vertices in buffers. Instead it takes a pointer to vertex data that exists somewhere in memory and uses that as the rendering stream. UP, by the way, stands for *user pointer*. The function has this definition:

```
HRESULT DrawPrimitiveUP(
                D3DPRIMITIVETYPE PrimitiveType,
                UINT PrimitiveCount,
                CONST void* pVertexStreamZeroData,
                UINT VertexStreamZeroStride
        );
```

PrimitiveType	The type of primitive you would like the device to draw for you.
PrimitiveCount	The number of primitives you want to render.
pVertexStreamZeroData	A pointer to the vertex data that the device will use as rendering stream 0.
VertexStreamZeroStride	The stride between each vertex, in bytes. Usually this will be 0.

DrawIndexedPrimitive

DrawIndexedPrimitive accepts two buffers: an array of vertices and an array of indices. The entire list of vertices is transformed, and then the primitives are drawn using the list of indices.

> **Warning:**   Each time DrawIndexedPrimitive is called, the entire list of vertices is transformed, regardless of whether or not they actually end up being used in the list of indices. Thus, for efficiency reasons, DrawIndexedPrimitive shouldn't be called multiple times for the same buffer. If this type of behavior is required, consider putting the vertices in a vertex buffer and transforming them just once using the ProcessVertices method on the vertex buffer interface.

```
HRESULT DrawIndexedPrimitive(
                D3DPRIMITIVETYPE Type,
                UINT MinIndex,
                UINT NumVertices,
                UINT StartIndex,
                UINT PrimitiveCount
        );
```

Type	The type of primitive you would like the device to draw for you.
MinIndex	The lowest vertex that will be used for this call.
NumVertices	The number of vertices that will be used for this call.

StartIndex	The location in the array to start reading vertices
PrimitiveCount	The number of primitives that will be rendered.

DrawIndexedPrimitiveUP

DrawIndexedPrimitiveUP is to DrawIndexedPrimitive what DrawPrimitiveUP was to DrawPrimitive. Basically it operates in exactly the same way as DrawIndexedPrimitive, except that it uses vertex data at a particular memory location instead of requiring it to be packaged into a vertex buffer and attached to a rendering stream. It has this definition:

```
HRESULT DrawIndexedPrimitiveUP(
            D3DPRIMITIVETYPE PrimitiveType,
            UINT MinIndex,
            UINT NumVertices,
            UINT PrimitiveCount,
            CONST void* pIndexData,
            D3DFORMAT IndexDataFormat,
            CONST void* pVertexStreamZeroData,
            UINT VertexStreamZeroStride
    );
```

PrimitiveType	The type of primitive you would like the device to draw for you.
MinIndex	The minimum vertex index that will be used for a vertex in this call.
NumVertices	The number of vertices to be used for this call.
PrimitiveCount	The number of primitives that you want to render.
pIndexData	A pointer to the index data.
IndexDataFormat	This can be set to either D3DFMT_INDEX16 or D3DFMT_INDEX32, depending on whether you are using 16- or 32-bit indices. You will usually use 16-bit indices.
pVertexStreamZeroData	A pointer to the vertex data.
VertexStreamZeroStride	The stride (distance between each vertex, in bytes) for the vertices; this will almost always be 0.

Adding Direct3D to the Graphics Layer

Now that you know enough Direct3D to get up and running, let's add Direct3D support to the graphics layer in the game library. I'll be adding more than initialization code this time around, as there are some convenience functions to help and also new native matrix types.

Direct3D Initialization

Getting Direct3D initialized used to be a tricky process, but these days it is much more straightforward, conceptually. In fact, in Chapter 2, I showed you almost everything you need to know, although I'll admit I glossed over the more complex 3D topics a little. Don't worry; I'll cover them here. For the updates there will be some changes to the class system in Chapter 2. There are a few new steps to perform, such as initializing view and projection matrices, and so on.

The particular feature set an application would like may not necessarily be the same for all applications. For example, some apps may choose not to use a z-buffer to avoid the added memory overhead on low-memory cards. To facilitate the various options a user application might like, the graphics layer's Direct3D initialization call accepts a set of flags that modify the path the initialization steps go through. The flags are:

Table 6.7: The set of graphics layer flags

GLF_ZBUFFER	The application is requesting that a z-buffer is created.
GLF_HIRESZBUFFER	The application is requesting that a high-resolution (24- or 32-bit) z-buffer is created.
GLF_STENCIL	The application is requesting stencil bits in addition to depth information in the z-buffer.
GLF_FORCEREFERENCE	The application is demanding a reference device. If one of these cannot be created, the initialization phase fails.
GLF_FORCEHARDWARE	The application is demanding a hardware (HAL) device. If one of these cannot be created, the initialization phase fails.
GLF_FORCESOFTWARE	The application is demanding a software device. If one of these cannot be created, the initialization phase fails.
GLF_FORCE16BIT	The application is forcing 16-bit rendering.

I'll take a step-by-step look at how Direct3D is initialized within the graphics layer. Some of this you have already seen in Chapter 2 but for consistency I'll show you it again, since it is pretty relevant.

Acquire an IDirect3D8 Interface

Getting an IDirect3D8 interface pointer is the simplest task to do. All you need to do is ask the Direct 3-D interface pointer. This is done using Direct3DCreate8. For a discussion on how COM works, see Chapter 1.

Listing 6.10: Acquiring a Direct3D8 interface pointer

```
// Create the Direct3D interface
m_pD3D = Direct3DCreate8( D3D_SDK_VERSION );
if( !m_pD3D )
```

```
    {
    throw cGameError( "Could not create IDirect3D8" );
    }
```

Fill In the Presentation Parameters

I'm going to run through a lot of this because you have seen it before. However, it has changed somewhat, so pay attention to the updates. If you need a refresher, refer back to Chapter 2. The first part of the D3DPRESENT_PARAMETERS structure deals with the format of the back buffer. Check out the following code:

```
// Structure to hold the creation parameters for the device
D3DPRESENT_PARAMETERS d3dpp;
ZeroMemory( &d3dpp, sizeof( d3dpp ) );

// The width and height for the initial back buffer
d3dpp.BackBufferWidth          = width;
d3dpp.BackBufferHeight         = height;

// Set the flags for the bit depth - only supports 16-, 24-, and 32-bit
formats
if( bpp == 16 )
  d3dpp.BackBufferFormat        = D3DFMT_R5G6B5;
else if( bpp == 24 )
  d3dpp.BackBufferFormat        = D3DFMT_R8G8B8;
else if( bpp == 32 )
  d3dpp.BackBufferFormat        = D3DFMT_A8R8G8B8;
else
{
  OutputDebugString( "Invalid surface format - defaulting to 32bit" );
  d3dpp.BackBufferFormat        = D3DFMT_A8R8G8B8;
}

// Only have one back buffer associated with the primary surface
d3dpp.BackBufferCount          = 1;
// No multisampling
d3dpp.MultiSampleType          = D3DMULTISAMPLE_NONE;
// Copy the back buffer to the primary surface normally
d3dpp.SwapEffect               = D3DSWAPEFFECT_COPY;
// The handle to the window to render in to
d3dpp.hDeviceWindow            = m_hWnd;
// Fullscreen operation
d3dpp.Windowed                 = FALSE;
```

Notice how the bit depth format is set with flags by comparing the bit depth passed as an integer. That code is quite straightforward. Now check out the following code, which implements some of the flags that I was talking about previously to set up the depth and stencil buffer.

```
// If a depth buffer was requested
if( flags & (GLF_ZBUFFER|GLF_HIRESZBUFFER) )
{
 // Tell Direct3D we want a depth buffer
 d3dpp.EnableAutoDepthStencil          = TRUE;


 if( flags & (GLF_HIRESZBUFFER) )
 {

     if( flags & (GLF_STENCIL) )
         // 24-bit depth buffer and 8-bit stencil
         d3dpp.AutoDepthStencilFormat = D3DFMT_D24S8;
     else
         // 32-bit depth buffer and no stencil
         d3dpp.AutoDepthStencilFormat = D3DFMT_D32;
 }
 else
 {

     if( flags & (GLF_STENCIL) )
         // 15-bit depth buffer and 1-bit stencil
         d3dpp.AutoDepthStencilFormat = D3DFMT_D15S1;
     else
         // 16-bit depth buffer and no stencil
         d3dpp.AutoDepthStencilFormat = D3DFMT_D16;
 }

}
else
{
 // No depth buffer or stencil
 d3dpp.EnableAutoDepthStencil = FALSE;
}
```

That is also pretty straightforward; so I'll let the code speak for itself. Finally, just before I actually create the device there is another snippet of code that I want to show that has changed from Chapter 2:

```
// Use the default refresh rate
d3dpp.FullScreen_RefreshRateInHz= D3DPRESENT_RATE_DEFAULT;
// Update the screen as soon as possible (don't wait for vsync)
d3dpp.FullScreen_PresentationInterval = D3DPRESENT_INTERVAL_IMMEDIATE;
// Allow the back buffer to be locked
d3dpp.Flags                           = D3DPRESENTFLAG_LOCKABLE_BACKBUFFER;

// Hardware device by default
D3DDEVTYPE DeviceType = D3DDEVTYPE_HAL;

if( flags & (GLF_FORCEHARDWARE) )
 DeviceType = D3DDEVTYPE_HAL;
else if( flags & (GLF_FORCESOFTWARE) )
```

```
         DeviceType = D3DDEVTYPE_SW;
     else if( flags & (GLF_FORCEREFERENCE) )
         DeviceType = D3DDEVTYPE_REF;
```

Notice how you now have the option of forcing a certain type of device to be created by passing a flag to the InitD3DFullScreen. After all of that structure filling it is simple to create the device with a call to, you guessed it, CreateDevice. The function call looks like this:

```
// Create the device using hardware acceleration if available
r = m_pD3D->CreateDevice( Ordinal, DeviceType, m_hWnd,
                             D3DCREATE_SOFTWARE_VERTEXPROCESSING,
                             &d3dpp, &m_pDevice );
if( FAILED( r ) )
{
  throw cGameError( "Could not create IDirect3DDevice8" );
}
```

And that's it—you now have a fully 3D capable device set up and ready to render. If you have had previous experience with DirectX, particularly prior to version 5.0, you will be trying to pick your jaw off the floor out of surprise at how easy it is to create. In this last section (about two pages) is everything that used to take over a thousand lines of code to set up. Just smile and nod.

Create a Viewport and Projection Matrix

Creating the viewport is one of the more monotonous tasks in Direct3D initialization. The graphics layer is assuming that all applications will want the entire viewport as visible. If this is not the case, user applications will have to create a viewport themselves.

The code that the graphics layer uses to set up the viewport is straightforward. The z-range from 0.0 to 1.0 is used, and the bounds of the screen are used as the viewport boundaries.

Listing 6.11: Viewport creation code

```
void cGraphicsLayer::MakeViewport()
{
  HRESULT hr;
  if( !m_pDevice )
  {
       DP("[cGraphicsLayer::MakeViewport]: no device\n");
       return;
  }

       DWORD dwRenderWidth  = m_rcScreenRect.right;
       DWORD dwRenderHeight = m_rcScreenRect.bottom;
       D3DVIEWPORT8 vp = { 0, 0, dwRenderWidth, dwRenderHeight, 0.0f, 1.0f };

       hr = m_pDevice->SetViewport( &vp );
```

```
        if( FAILED( hr ) )
            throw cGameError("viewport setting failed.");
}
```

The projection matrix your application gives Direct3D is dependent on the dimensions of your frame buffer, so it is created when you create the viewport. It just uses the same projection matrix discussed in Chapter 3, which uses the recommended projection matrix from the SDK documentation.

Listing 6.12: Projection matrix construction code

```
eResult cGraphicsLayer::MakeProjectionMatrix()
{
  D3DMATRIX mat;

  DWORD width, height;
  width = m_rcScreenRect.right;
  height = m_rcScreenRect.bottom;

  float fAspect = ((float)height) / width;

  if( fabs(m_far-m_near) < 0.01f )
        return resFailed;
      if( fabs(sin(m_fov/2)) < 0.01f )
        return resFailed;

  float w = fAspect * (float)( cos(m_fov/2)/sin(m_fov/2) );
  float h =   1.0f  * (float)( cos(m_fov/2)/sin(m_fov/2) );
  float Q = m_far / ( m_far - m_near );

      ZeroMemory( &mat, sizeof(D3DMATRIX) );
      mat._11 = w;
      mat._22 = h;
      mat._33 = Q;
      mat._34 = 1.0f;
      mat._43 = -Q*m_near;

  m_pDevice->SetTransform( D3DTS_PROJECTION, &mat );

      return resAllGood;
}
```

Further Additions to the GameLib

To handle the addition of Direct3D to the GameLib, some changes and additions needed to be made.

The cGraphicsLayer class got a host of new functions added to it. Their names and functions are summed up in Table 6.8.

Table 6.8: New functions in cGraphicsLayer

`void BeginScene();`	Wraps IDirect3DDevice8::BeginScene.
`void EndScene();`	Wraps IDirect3DDevice8::EndScene.

`void SetProjectionData(`
    `float inFov,`
    `float inNear,`
    `float inFar );`
	Sets the three important projection parameters (field of view, near z plane distance, far z plane distance). By default these values are PI/2, 1.0, and 1000.0, respectively.

`void GetProjectionData(`
    `float* inFov,`
    `float* inNear,`
    `float* inFar );`
	Gets the three important projection parameters (field of view, near z plane distance, far z plane distance). By default these values are PI/2, 1.0, and 1000.0, respectively.

`eResult MakeProjectionMatrix();`	Rebuilds the projection matrix using the currently set values for field of view, near plane, and far plane. The projection matrix is identical to the one described in Chapter 3.
`void GetProjectionMatrix(` `matrix4* pMat );`	Gets the currently set projection matrix from the D3D device.
`void SetProjectionMatrix(` `const matrix4& mat );`	Sets the current projection matrix to the supplied matrix. Provided for completeness, the projection matrix should be set with SetProjectionData and MakeProjectionMatrix.
`void GetViewMatrix(` `matrix4* pMat );`	Gets the currently set view matrix from the D3D device.
`void SetViewMatrix(` `const matrix4& mat );`	Sets the current view matrix to the supplied matrix.
`void GetWorldMatrix(` `matrix4* pMat );`	Gets the currently set world matrix from the D3D device.
`void SetWorldMatrix(` `const matrix4& mat );`	Sets the current world matrix to the supplied matrix.
`LPDIRECT3DDEVICE8 GetDevice();`	Gets the Direct3D device interface.
`LPDIRECT3D8 GetD3D();`	Gets the Direct3D interface.

`void Clear(`
    `bool bClearFrame,`
    `bool bClearZ,`
    `DWORD frameColor,`
    `float zValue );`
	Clears the back buffer, and the z-buffer if needed, to the provided color and value.

The Direct3DX Library

One of the biggest complaints people made about Direct3D in the past was its complexity. The initialization procedure, loading texture correctly from disk, and many other tasks proved to be remarkably difficult. However, version 8.0 has gone a long way to improve this state of affairs.

Microsoft's answer to this was two-fold. First, Direct3D 8.0 is considerably easier to use and manage than previous versions. Lights, materials, and viewports used to be interfaces that needed to be AddRef'd and Released. All told, Direct3D 8.0 has a lot of elegance compared to previous versions, and is rapidly approaching the design elegance of OpenGL (yuck).

The second, more interesting answer to the complaints about D3D's complexity is the Direct3DX library (D3DX for short). It attempts to take care of most of the grunt work by providing things like macros, mathematical functions, COM objects, and many other useful bits and pieces that makes DirectX a nicer place to live. I'm not going to give you an exhaustive look at the D3DX library, since it so large, but I really suggest you take a look at *DirectX 8.0 C++ Documentation/DirectX Graphics/Direct3DX C++ Reference* in the documentation. You may be surprised at what you find.

D3DX is extremely useful. If you only want to test a certain feature, or if you want to check to see what a texture looks like under certain conditions, D3DX is a godsend. It is also <u>very</u> fast, and will help you to not reinvent too many wheels as you go.

D3DX, while extremely useful for prototyping, is not something I will be using much for this code, since it hides away a lot of the functionality that I'm teaching you.

Application: D3D View

The sample application for this chapter is an object viewer. It loads object files from disk and displays the object spinning around the scene. Before you can draw the spinning object, you of course need a way to load it.

There are a myriad of different object formats out there. OBJ, 3DS, DXF, ASC, and PLG files are available on the net or easy to construct. However, they're all either extremely hard to parse or not fully featured enough. Rather than trudge through a parser for one of these data types, I'm going to circumvent a lot of headache and create our own format. The web is rife with parsers for any of these other formats, so if you want to parse it you won't have to reinvent the wheel.

The .o3d Format

The name for the object format will be .o3d (object 3-D format). It's an ASCII file, which makes it easy to edit manually if the need arises. The object is designed for regular D3DVERTEX objects, which have no color information but may have normal or texture information. Listing 6.13 has the o3d file for a simple tetrahedron model.

Listing 6.13: Tetrahedron model

```
Tetrahedron 3 1 4 4
-1.0 -1.0 -1.0
1.0 1.0 -1.0
-1.0 1.0 1.0
1.0 -1.0 1.0
2 3 4
1 4 3
1 3 2
1 2 4
```

The first line of the file is the header. It has five fields, separated by spaces. They are, in order:

■ The name for the object (spaces within the name are not allowed).

■ The number of fields per vertex. This can be three (just position), five (three position and two texture), six (three position and three normal), or eight (three position, three normal, and two texture).

■ The offset for the indices. Some index lists are 0-based, some are 1-based. This offset is subtracted from each of the indices on load. Since the indices in the tetrahedron list start at 1, the offset is 1 (since index 1 will actually be element 0 internally).

■ The number of vertices in the model.

■ The number of triangles in the model.

After the header line, there is one line for each of the vertices. Each line has n fields separated by spaces (where n is the number of fields per vertex). The first three fields are always position.

After the list of vertices, there is a list of triangles. Each triangle is defined with three indices separated by spaces. Each index has the offset (defined in the header) subtracted from it.

The cModel Class

To load o3d models, I'm going to create a class that represents a model. It has one constructor that takes a filename on disk. The constructor opens the file, parses it, and extracts the vertex and triangle information. It takes the information and fills up two vectors. If the file it loads does not have normal information defined for it, the class uses face averaging to automatically generate normals for the object.

Face averaging is used often to find normals for vertices that make a model appear rounded when Gouraud shading is used on it. The normals for each of the faces are computed, and the normal is added to each of the face's vertices. When all of the faces have contributed their normals, the vertex normals are normalized. This, in essence, makes each vertex normal the average of the normals of the faces around it. This gives the model a smooth look.

The cModel class can automatically draw an object, given a matrix to use for the world matrix. It uses DrawIndexedPrimitive to draw the entire model in one fell swoop. There are also a few accessor functions; future classes that load models will use cModel to load the file for them, and just extract the vertex and triangle information for themselves.

Listing 6.14: cModel, a simple drawable 3-D object

```
#define FVF_TYPE ( D3DFVF_XYZ | D3DFVF_NORMAL | D3DFVF_DIFFUSE | D3DFVF_TEX1 )

class cModel
{
    typedef tri<unsigned short> sTri;

    vector< sTri >    m_tris;

    vector< sVertex >  m_verts;

    string            m_name;

public:

    cModel( const char* filename );

    float GenRadius();
    void Scale( float amt );

    void Draw( const matrix4& mat );

    //==========------------------------ Access functions.

    int NumVerts(){ return m_verts.size(); }
    int NumTris(){ return m_tris.size(); }
    const char* Name(){ return m_name.c_str(); }

    /**
     * Some other classes may end up using cModel
     * to assist in their file parsing.  Because of this
     * give them a way to get at the vertex and triangle
     * data.
     */
    sVertex* VertData(){ return &m_verts[0]; }
    sTri* TriData(){ return &m_tris[0]; }
```

```
    };


cModel::cModel( const char* filename )
{
    int i;

    cFile file;
    file.Open( filename );

    queue<string> m_tokens;

    file.TokenizeNextNCLine( &m_tokens, '#' );

    // first token is the name.
    m_name = m_tokens.front();
    m_tokens.pop();

    // next is the # of fields in the vertex info
    int nVertexFields = atoi( m_tokens.front().c_str() );
    m_tokens.pop();


    // next is the triangle offset
    int offset = atoi( m_tokens.front().c_str() );
    m_tokens.pop();

    // next is the # of vertices
    int nVerts = atoi( m_tokens.front().c_str() );
    m_tokens.pop();

    // next is the # of triangles
    int nTris = atoi( m_tokens.front().c_str() );
    m_tokens.pop();

    // Reserve space in the vector for all the verts.
    // This will speed up all the additions, since only
    // one resize will be done.
    m_verts.reserve( nVerts );
    for( i=0; i<nVerts; i++ )
    {
        m_tokens.empty();
        file.TokenizeNextNCLine( &m_tokens, '#' );

        sVertex curr;

        // Vertex data is guaranteed
        curr.loc.x = atof( m_tokens.front().c_str() );
        m_tokens.pop();
        curr.loc.y = atof( m_tokens.front().c_str() );
        m_tokens.pop();
```

```
        curr.loc.z = atof( m_tokens.front().c_str() );
        m_tokens.pop();

        // Load normal data if nfields is 6 or 8
        if( nVertexFields == 6 || nVertexFields == 8 )
        {
            curr.norm.x = atof( m_tokens.front().c_str() );
            m_tokens.pop();
            curr.norm.y = atof( m_tokens.front().c_str() );
            m_tokens.pop();
            curr.norm.z = atof( m_tokens.front().c_str() );
            m_tokens.pop();
        }
        else
        {
            curr.norm.Assign( 0, 0, 0 );
        }

        // Load texture data if nfields is 5 or 8
        if( nVertexFields == 5 || nVertexFields == 8 )
        {
            curr.u = atof( m_tokens.front().c_str() );
            m_tokens.pop();
            curr.v = atof( m_tokens.front().c_str() );
            m_tokens.pop();
        }
        else
        {
            curr.u = 0.f;
            curr.v = 0.f;
        }

        m_verts.push_back( curr );
    }

    // Reserve space in the vector for all the verts.
    // This will speed up all the additions, since only
    // one resize will be done.
    m_tris.reserve( nTris );
    for( i=0; i<nTris; i++ )
    {
        m_tokens.empty();
        file.TokenizeNextNCLine( &m_tokens, '#' );

        sTri tri;

        // vertex data is guaranteed
        tri.v[0] = atoi( m_tokens.front().c_str() ) - offset;
        m_tokens.pop();
        tri.v[1] = atoi( m_tokens.front().c_str() ) - offset;
        m_tokens.pop();
```

```
            tri.v[2] = atoi( m_tokens.front().c_str() ) - offset;
            m_tokens.pop();

            m_tris.push_back( tri );
        }

        if( nVertexFields == 3 || nVertexFields == 5 )
        {
            // Normals weren't provided.  Generate our own.

            // First set all the normals to zero.
            for( i=0; i<nVerts; i++ )
            {
                m_verts[i].norm.Assign( 0,0,0 );
            }

            // Then go through and add each triangle's normal
            // to each of its verts.
            for( i=0; i<nTris; i++ )
            {
                plane3 plane(
                    m_verts[ m_tris[i].v[0] ].loc,
                    m_verts[ m_tris[i].v[1] ].loc,
                    m_verts[ m_tris[i].v[2] ].loc );

                m_verts[ m_tris[i].v[0] ].norm += plane.n;
                m_verts[ m_tris[i].v[1] ].norm += plane.n;
                m_verts[ m_tris[i].v[2] ].norm += plane.n;
            }

            // Finally normalize all of the normals
            for( i=0; i<nVerts; i++ )
            {
                m_verts[i].norm.Normalize();
            }
        }
    }


void cModel::Scale( float amt )
{
    int size = m_verts.size();
    for( int i=0; i<size; i++ )
    {
        m_verts[i].loc *= amt;
    }
}


void cModel::Draw( const matrix4& mat )
{
```

```
    Graphics()->SetWorldMatrix( mat );

    Graphics()->GetDevice()->SetVertexShader( FVF_TYPE );

    Graphics()->GetDevice()->DrawIndexedPrimitiveUP(
        D3DPT_TRIANGLELIST,
        0,
        m_verts.size(),
        m_tris.size(),
        &m_tris[0],
        D3DFMT_INDEX16,
        &m_verts[0],
        sizeof( vertex ) );
}


float cModel::GenRadius()
{
    float best = 0.f;
    int size = m_verts.size();
    for( int i=0; i<size; i++ )
    {
        float curr = m_verts[i].loc.Mag();
        if( curr > best )
            best = curr;
    }
    return best;
}
```

Now that you have a way to load models, a program just needs to be wrapped around it. That is what the D3DSample program does. It takes a filename in the constructor, loads it, creates three colored directional lights, and spins the object around in front of the camera. There is no user input for this program; it's just there to look pretty. See Figure 6.6 for a screen shot of D3DSample in action.

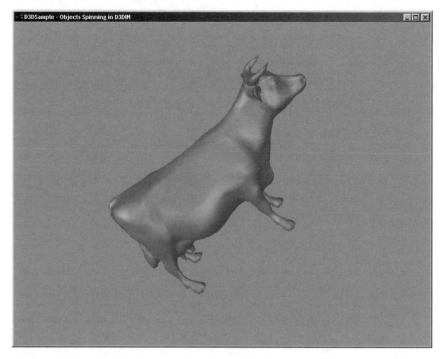

Figure 6.6:
Screen shot from D3DSample

The code for D3DSample appears in Listing 6.15. There are a few models in the Chapter 06\BIN\Media folder on the companion CD so you can mess around with it if you want to see what other models look like. I highly recommend the rabbit.

Listing 6.15: D3DSample.cpp

```
/*****************************************************************
 *          Advanced 3D Game Programming using DirectX 8.0
 * * * * * * * * * * * * * * * * * * * * * * * * * * * * * * * *
 *    Title: D3DSample.cpp
 *     Desc: An extremely simple D3D app, using the framework
 *           we have made
 * (C) 2001 by Peter A Walsh and Adrian Perez
 * See license.txt for modification and distribution information
 *****************************************************************/

#include "stdafx.h"

class cD3DSampleApp : public cApplication
{

public:

  string m_filename;
  cModel* m_pModel;
```

```
            void InitLights();

            //==========-------------------------- cApplication

            virtual void DoFrame( float timeDelta );
            virtual void SceneInit();

            virtual void SceneEnd()
            {
                delete m_pModel;
            }

            cD3DSampleApp() :
                cApplication()
            {
                m_title = string( "D3DSample - Objects Spinning in D3D" );
                m_pModel = NULL;
                m_filename = "..\\BIN\\Media\\Cow.o3d";
            }
        };

        cApplication* CreateApplication()
        {
         return new cD3DSampleApp();
        }

        void DestroyApplication( cApplication* pApp )
        {
         delete pApp;
        }

        void cD3DSampleApp::SceneInit()
        {
         /**
          * We're making the FOV less than 90 degrees.
          * this is so the object doesn't warp as much
          * when we're really close to it.
          */
         Graphics()->SetProjectionData( PI/4.f, 0.5f, 10.f );
         Graphics()->MakeProjectionMatrix();

         /**
          * initialize our scene
          */
         LPDIRECT3DDEVICE8 pDevice = Graphics()->GetDevice();

         pDevice->SetRenderState(D3DRS_CULLMODE, D3DCULL_CCW);
         pDevice->SetRenderState(D3DRS_LIGHTING, TRUE);
         pDevice->SetRenderState(D3DRS_DITHERENABLE, TRUE);
```

```
pDevice->SetRenderState(D3DRS_SPECULARENABLE, TRUE);
pDevice->SetRenderState(D3DRS_AMBIENT, 0x404040);

/**
 * initialize the camera
 */
Graphics()->SetViewMatrix( matrix4::Identity );

/**
 * Create a model with the given filename,
 * and resize it so it fits inside a unit sphere.
 */
m_pModel = new cModel( m_filename.c_str() );
m_pModel->Scale( 1.f / m_pModel->GenRadius() );

InitLights();
}


void cD3DSampleApp::InitLights()
{
  LPDIRECT3DDEVICE8 pDevice = Graphics()->GetDevice();

    sLight light;

  // Light 0
  light = sLight::Directional(
      point3(0,-4,2).Normalized(),
      0.5f * color3::White + 0.2f * color3::Red,
      0.7f * color3::White + 0.2f * color3::Red,
      0.2f * color3::White + 0.2f * color3::Red);

    // Set the light
    pDevice->SetLight( 0, &light );
  pDevice->LightEnable(0, TRUE);

  // Light 1
  light = sLight::Directional(
      point3(3,1,1).Normalized(),
      0.5f * color3::White + 0.2f * color3::Green,
      0.7f * color3::White + 0.2f * color3::Green,
      0.2f * color3::White + 0.2f * color3::Green);

    // Set the light
    pDevice->SetLight( 1, &light );
  pDevice->LightEnable(1, TRUE);

  // Light 2
  light = sLight::Directional(
      point3(-3,3,5).Normalized(),
      0.5f * color3::White + 0.2f * color3::Blue,
```

```
                    0.7f * color3::White + 0.2f * color3::Blue,
                    0.2f * color3::White + 0.2f * color3::Blue);

        // Set the light
        pDevice->SetLight( 2, &light );
    pDevice->LightEnable(2, TRUE);

        sMaterial mat(
            16.f,
            color3(0.5f,0.5f,0.5f),
            color3(0.7f,0.7f,0.7f),
            color3(0.1f,0.1f,0.1f) );

        pDevice->SetMaterial(&mat);
}


void cD3DSampleApp::DoFrame( float timeDelta )
{
 /**
  * update the time
  */
 static float rotAmt = 0.f;
 rotAmt += timeDelta;

 /**
  * then, draw the frame.
  */
 LPDIRECT3DDEVICE8 pDevice = Graphics()->GetDevice();
 if( pDevice )
 {
        Graphics()->Clear( true, true, 0x000000, 1.f );

        Graphics()->BeginScene();

        /**
         * Build a simple matrix for the object,
         * just spin around all three axes.
         */
        matrix4 mat;
        mat.MakeIdent();
        mat.Rotate( rotAmt, 1.1f * rotAmt, 1.4f * rotAmt );
        mat.Place( point3(0,0,3.f) );
        Graphics()->SetWorldMatrix( mat );

        /**
         * Here is where we actually draw our object
         */
        m_pModel->Draw( mat );
```

```
        Graphics()->EndScene();

        /**
         * flip the buffer.
         */
        Graphics()->Flip();
    }
}
```

Chapter 7

Advanced 3-D Programming

This is my favorite chapter in the book. Nothing but sweet, pure, uncut 3-D graphics. We're going to take a whirlwind tour of some more advanced topics in 3-D programming. Among other things we'll cover inverse kinematics, subdivision surfaces, and radiosity lighting. This is the most interesting and exciting part of graphics programming—experimenting with cool technology and trying to get it to work well enough to make it into a project. Sometimes it works and sometimes it doesn't, but hit or miss, it's still mind-numbingly fun. One thing I'm not going to cover is the Direct3D support for pixel and vertex shaders, since at the moment there is very little hardware support for them. However, I think the rest of the information in this chapter will keep you pretty occupied!

Animation Using Hierarchical Objects

I wish there were more space to devote to animating our objects, but unfortunately there isn't. Animation is a rich topic, from key frame animation to motion capture to rotoscoping. I'll just be able to give a sweeping discussion about a few techniques used in animation, then talk about hierarchical objects.

Back in the 2-D days, animation was done using *sprites*. Sprites are just bunches of pixels that represent images on the screen. A set of animation frames would be shown in rapid succession to give the illusion of motion. The same technique is used in animated films to give life to their characters.

In 3-D, the landscape is much more varied. Some systems use simple extensions from their 2-D counterparts. Some games have a complete set of vertex positions for each frame of each animation. This made it very similar to 2-D games, just replacing pixels with vertices. Newer games move a step further, using interpolation to smoothly morph between frames. This way the playback speed looks good independent of the recording speed; an animation recorded at 10 fps still looks smooth on a 60 fps display.

While systems like this can be very fast (you have to compute, at most, a linear interpolation per vertex), they have a slew of disadvantages. The primary disadvantage is that you must explicitly store each frame of animation in memory. If you have a model with 500 vertices, at 24 bytes (3 floats) per vertex, that's 12 kilobytes of memory needed per frame. If you have several hundred frames of animation, suddenly you're faced with around a megabyte of storage per animated object. In practice, if you have many different types of objects in your world, the memory requirements become prohibitive.

> **Note:** The memory requirements for each character model in *Quake III: Arena* were so high that the game almost had an eleventh-hour switch over to hierarchical models.

Explicitly placing each vertex in a model each frame isn't the only solution. It is lathered in redundancy. The topology of the models remains about the same. Outside of the bending and flexing that occurs at model joints, the relative locations of the vertices in relation to each other stays pretty similar.

The way humans and other animals move isn't defined by the skin moving around. Your bones are rigid bodies connected by joints that can only bend in certain directions. The muscles in your body are connected to the bones through tendons and ligaments, and the skin sits on top of the muscles. Therefore, the position of your skin is a function of the position of your bones.

This structural paradigm is emulated by bone-based animation. A model is defined once in a neutral position, with a set of bones underlying the structure of the model. All of the vertices in the forearm region of the model are conceptually bound to the forearm bone, and so forth. Instead of explicitly listing a set of vertices per frame for your animation, all this system needs is the orientation of each bone in relation to its parent bone. Typically, the root node is the hip of the model, so that the world matrix for the object corresponds to the position of the hip, and the world transformations for each of the other joints are derived from it.

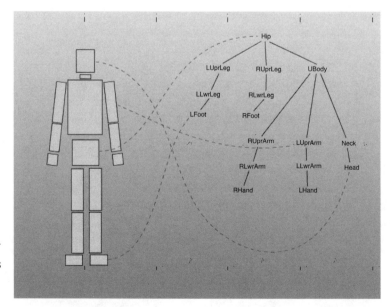

Figure 7.1:
Building a hierarchy of rigid objects to make a humanoid

With these orientations you can figure out the layout of each bone of the model, and you use the same transformation matrices. Figuring out the positions of bones, given the angles of the joints, is called *forward kinematics*.

Forward Kinematics

Understanding the way transformations are concatenated is pivotal to understanding forward kinematics. See Chapter 3 for a discussion on this topic if you're rusty on it.

Let's say we're dealing with the simple case of a 2-D two-linkage system, an upper arm and a lower arm, with shoulder and elbow joints. We'll define the vertices of the upper arm with a local origin of the shoulder, the vertices sticking out along the x-axis. The lower arm is defined in the same manner, just using the elbow as the local origin. There is a special point in the upper arm that defines where the elbow joint is situated. There is also a point that defines where the shoulder joint is situated relative to the world origin.

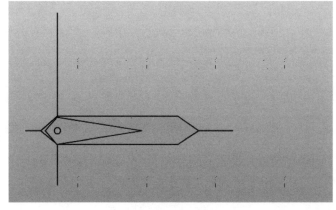

Figure 7.2:
The untransformed upper and lower arm segments

The first task is to transform the points of the upper arm. What you want to do is rotate each of the points about the shoulder axis by the shoulder angle θ_1, and then translate them so that they are situated relative to the origin. So the transformation becomes:

upper-arm transformation = $R_Z(\theta_1)T(\text{shoulder\_location})$

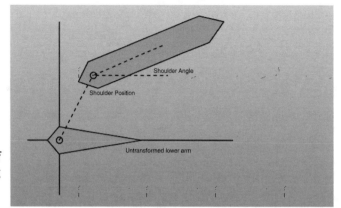

Figure 7.3:
The result of transforming just the shoulder

Transforming the elbow points is more difficult. Not only are they dependent on the elbow angle θ_2, they also depend on the position and angle of their parent, the upper arm and shoulder joint.

We can subdivide the problem to make it easier. If we can transform the elbow points to orient them relative to the origin of the shoulder, then we can just add to that the transformation for the shoulder, to take them to world space. This transformation becomes:

lower-arm transformation $= R_Z(\theta_2)T(\text{elbow\_location})\ R_Z(\theta_1)T(\text{shoulder\_location})$

or

lower-arm transformation $= R_Z(\theta_2)T(\text{elbow\_location})$ upper-arm transformation

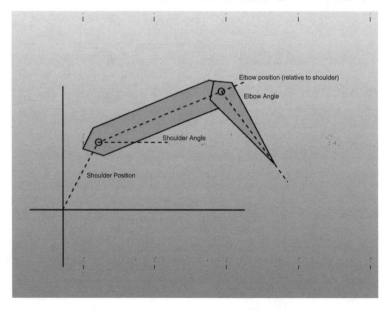

Figure 7.4:
The fully transformed arm

This system makes at least some intuitive sense. Imagine we have some point on the lower arm, initially in object space. The rotation by θ_2 rotates the point about the elbow joint, and the translation moves the point such that the elbow is sticking out to the right of the origin. At this point we have the shoulder joint at the origin, the upper arm sticking out to the right, a jointed elbow, and then our point somewhere on the lower arm. The next transformation we apply is the rotation by θ_1, which rotates everything we have up to this point (the lower arm and upper arm) by the shoulder angle. Finally, we apply the transformation to place the shoulder somewhere in the world a little more meaningful than the world space origin.

This system fits into a clean recursive algorithm very well. At each stage of the hierarchy, we compute the transformation that transforms the current joint to the space of the joint above it in the hierarchy, appending it to the front of the current world matrix, and recursing with each of the children. Pseudocode to do this appears in Listing 7.1.

Listing 7.1: Pseudocode to draw hierarchical models

```
struct hierNode
{
    vert_and_triangle_Data m_data;
    vector< hierNode* children > m_children;
    matrix4 m_matrix;

    void Draw( matrix4 parentMatrix )
    {
        matrix4 curr = m_matrix * parentMatrix;

        // draws the triangles of this node using the provided matrix
        m_data->Draw( curr );
        for( int i=0; i<m_children.size(); i++ )
        {
            m_children[i]->Draw( curr );
        }
    }
};
```

Inverse Kinematics

Forward kinematics takes a set of joint angles and finds the position of the end effector. The inverse of the problem, finding the set of joint angles required to place the end effector in a desired position, is called *inverse kinematics*.

IK is useful in a lot of applications. An example would be having autonomous agents helping the player in a game. During the course of the game, the situation may arise that the autonomous helper needs to press a button, pull a lever, or perform some other action. When this is done without IK, each type of button must be hand-animated by an artist so the agent hits the button accurately. With IK this becomes much easier. The agent just needs to move close enough to it, and find the angles for the shoulder, elbow, and hand to put the pointer finger at the location of the button.

Inverse kinematics is a hard problem, especially when you start solving harder cases. It all boils down to degrees of freedom. In all but the simplest case (being a single angular joint and a singular prismatic joint) there are multiple possible solutions for an inverse kinematics system. Take, for example, a shoulder-elbow linkage: two links with two angular joints (shoulder and elbow) and an end effector at the hand. If there is any bend in the arm at all, then there are two possible solutions for the linkage, as evidenced by Figure 7.5.

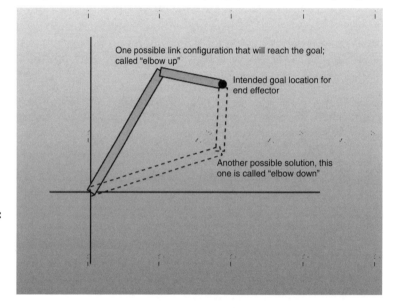

Figure 7.5: The two joint solutions for a given end effector

These two possible solutions are commonly referred to as elbow up and elbow down. While for this case it's fairly easy to determine the two-elbow configurations, it only gets worse. If you had a three-segment linkage, for example, there are potentially an infinite number of solutions to the problem.

Aside: Howie Choset, a professor at Carnegie Mellon, does research on snake robots. One of them is a six-segment linkage, and each joint has three degrees of freedom. The set of inverse kinematics solutions for a linkage like this has about ∞^{18} solutions!

There are two ways to go about solving an IK problem. One way is to do it algebraically: The forward kinematics equation gets inverted, the system is solved, and the solution is found. The other way is geometrically: Trigonometric identities and other geometric theorems are used to solve the problem. Often for more complex IK systems, a combination of both methods needs to be used.

Algebraic manipulation will get you so far towards the solution, then you take what you've gotten thus far and feed it into a geometric solution to get a little further, and so on.

To introduce you to IK, let's solve a simple system: two segments, each with a pivot joint with one degree of freedom. This corresponds closely to a human arm. The base joint is the shoulder, the second joint is the elbow, and the end effector is the wrist. It's a 2-D problem, but applying the solution in 3-D isn't hard. Ian Davis, a CMU alum currently at Activision, used this type of IK problem to implement autonomous agents in a game. The agents could wander around and help the player. When they wanted to press a button, they moved to the button such that a plane was formed with the arm and button, and then the 2-D IK solution was found in the plane.

Being able to solve the two-joint system is also useful in solving slightly more complex systems. If we want to have a third segment (a hand, pivoting at the wrist), there are an infinite amount of solutions for most positions that the pointer finger can be in. However, if we force the hand to be at a particular angle, the problem decomposes into solving a two-segment problem (given the length of the hand and the angle it should be in, the position of the wrist can be found relative to the end effector, and then the wrist, elbow, and shoulder form a solvable two-segment problem).

The two things we'll need to solve the IK problem are two laws of geometry, the law of cosines and the law of sines. They are given in Figure 7.6.

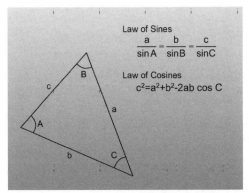

Figure 7.6: The law of sines and the law of cosines

To formally state the problem, we are given as input the lengths of two arm segments L_1 and L_2, and the desired x,y position of the end effector. We wish to find a valid set of theta angles for the shoulder and elbow joints. The problem configuration appears in Figure 7.7.

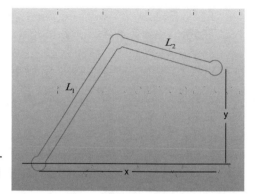

Figure 7.7:
The IK problem we wish to solve

We'll be using a bunch of variables to solve the IK problem. They are given in Figure 7.8.

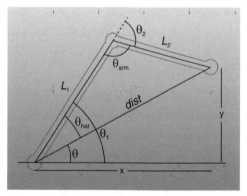

Figure 7.8:
The IK problem with the variables we'll use to solve it

Here is what we do to solve the IK problem, step by step:

1. Find *dist*, using the Pythagorean theorem.

2. Find θ, using the arc-tangent ($\theta = \tan^{-1}(y/x)$).

3. Find θ_{hat} using the law of cosines (A=*dist*, B= L_1, C=L_2).

4. We can now find the shoulder angle θ_1 by subtracting θ_{hat} from θ.

5. θ_{arm} can be found using the law of cosines as well (A=L_2, B= L_1, C=*dist*).

6. The elbow angle, θ_2, is just PI-θ_{arm}.

Application: InvKim

To show off inverse kinematics, I wrote a simple application called InvKim that solves the two-linkage problem. One of the things that it needs to do is bound the end effector position to the range of possible solutions that can be reached by the arm. The mouse controls a little icon that the end effector always moves towards. You'll notice that the end effector moves at a constant velocity, and the theta angles change to accommodate its movement. When the pointer is in a position that the arm cannot reach, it tries its best to get there, pointing towards its desired goal.

Listing 7.2: Snippets from InvKim

```
void cIKApp::DrawLinkage(){
    /**
     * Use the lengths and theta information
     * to compute the forward dynamics of
     * the arm, and draw it.
     */
    sLitVertex box[4];
    sLitVertex joint[20];
    matrix4 rot1, trans1;
    matrix4 rot2, trans2;

    /**
     * create a half circle to give our links rounded edges
     */
    point3 halfCircle[10];
    int i;
    for( i=0; i<10; i++ )
    {
        float theta = (float)i*PI/9.f;
        halfCircle[i] = point3(
            0.85f * sin( theta ),
            0.85f * cos( theta ),
            0.f );
    }

    rot1.ToZRot( m_theta1 );
    trans1.ToTranslation( point3( m_l1,0, 0 ) );

    rot2.ToZRot( m_theta2 );

    LPDIRECT3DDEVICE7 pDevice = Graphics()->GetDevice();

    /**
     * Make and draw the upper arm
     */
    matrix4 shoulderMat = rot1;
    for( i=0; i<10; i++ )
    {
        point3 temp = halfCircle[i];
        temp.x = -temp.x;
        joint[i] = sLitVertex( shoulderMat*temp, 0xFF8080 );
        joint[19-i] = sLitVertex( shoulderMat*
            (halfCircle[i] + point3( m_l1, 0, 0 )), 0x80FF80 );
    }
```

```
        pDevice->DrawPrimitive(
            D3DPT_TRIANGLEFAN, D3DFVF_LVERTEX, joint, 20, 0 );

        /**
         * Make and draw the lower arm
         */
        matrix4 elbowMat = rot2 * trans1 * rot1;
        for( i=0; i<10; i++ )
        {
            point3 temp = halfCircle[i];
            temp.x = -temp.x;
            joint[i] = sLitVertex( elbowMat * temp, 0x80FF80 );
            joint[19-i] = sLitVertex( elbowMat *
                (halfCircle[i] + point3( m_l2, 0, 0.f )), 0x8080FF );
        }
        pDevice->DrawPrimitive(
            D3DPT_TRIANGLEFAN, D3DFVF_LVERTEX, joint, 20, 0 );

        /**
         * Draw a diamond where the mouse is
         */
        matrix4 mouseTrans;
        mouseTrans.ToTranslation( m_mouse );
        box[0] = sLitVertex( point3(0.5f,0.f,0.f)*mouseTrans, 0x808080 );
        box[1] = sLitVertex( point3(0.f,-0.5f,0.f)*mouseTrans, 0x808080 );
        box[2] = sLitVertex( point3(-0.5f,0.f,0.f)*mouseTrans, 0x808080 );
        box[3] = sLitVertex( point3(0.f,0.5f,0.f)*mouseTrans, 0x808080 );

        pDevice->DrawPrimitive(
            D3DPT_TRIANGLEFAN, D3DFVF_LVERTEX, box, 4, 0 );
}

void cIKApp::FindJointAngles( float x, float y )
{
    float minD = (float)fabs(m_l1 - m_l2 );
    float maxD = m_l1 + m_l2;

    float L1 = m_l1;
    float L2 = m_l2;

    /**
     * Find the standard theta and distance
     */
    float dist = (float)sqrt(x*x+y*y);
    float theta = (float)atan2(y,x);

    /**
     * Snap the distance to values we can reach
     */
    Snap( dist, minD + EPSILON, maxD - EPSILON );
```

```
/**
 * Adjust the x and y to match the new distance
 */
x = (float)cos(theta)*dist;
y = (float)sin(theta)*dist;

/**
 * Find thetaHat using the law of cosines
 */

float thetaHat = (float)acos((L2*L2-L1*L1-dist*dist)/(-2*dist*L1));

/**
 * theta - thetaHat is theta 1
 */
m_theta1 = theta - thetaHat;

/**
 * Use the law of cosines to get thetaArm
 */
float thetaArm = (float)acos((dist*dist-L1*L1-L2*L2 )/(-2*L2*L1));

/**
 * With thetaArm we can easily find theta2
 */
m_theta2 = PI-thetaArm;

}
```

Parametric Curves and Surfaces

Something you may have noticed up to this point is that most of the objects we have been dealing with have been a little on the angular side. We can clearly see the vertices, triangles, and edges that define the boundaries. Objects in the real world, especially organic objects like humans, don't have such sharp definitions. They are curvy to some extent, a trait that is difficult to represent with generic triangle meshes. We can define mathematical entities that allow us to smoothly generate curves (called *splines*) and surfaces (called *patches*). We'll discuss two styles of curves: cubic Bezier and cubic b-spline curves.

Aside: The term spline comes from way, way back, when ships were built from wood. The process of bending planks with weights so they could build the hulls of boats is not unlike the math behind curves.

Bezier Curves and Surfaces

A cubic Bezier curve defines a parametric equation that produces a position in space from a given time parameter. They can have different degrees, but there are only two that are widely used: quadric and cubic. Quadric curves only use three control points, while cubic curves use four. We'll be covering cubic Bezier curves, but deriving the math for quadric curves won't be difficult once we're through.

Bezier Concepts

Cubic Bezier curves are defined by four points in space. These are called the *control points* of the curve. To avoid confusion, generally lines are drawn between the points to define which way they connect to each other. Figure 7.9 shows an example of four control points that define a Bezier curve.

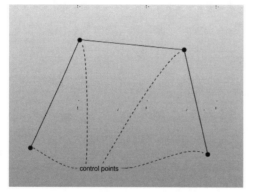

Figure 7.9:
Four points
defining a
control poly-
gon for a
Bezier curve

The actual curve is computed using these four control points, by solving an equation with a given t parameter between 0 and 1. At $t=0$, the returned point is sitting at the first control point. At $t=1$, the point is sitting at the last control point. The tangent of the curve (the direction at which the particle moves) at $t=0$ is parallel to the line connecting the first and second control points. For $t=1$, the tangent is parallel to the line connecting the third and fourth control points. The time in the middle the particle traces a smooth path between these two directions/locations, making a curve that looks like the one in Figure 7.10.

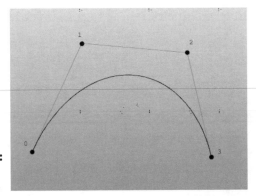

Figure 7.10:
Sample
Bezier curve

With just four points, it's hard to represent too intricate a curve. In order to have anything interesting, we have to combine them to form larger, more complex curves. True-type fonts are defined this way, as a set of Bezier curves. However, they are defined as a set of quadric curves, which are easier to rasterize.

But how do we join them? How do we know that the curviness will continue from one curve to the next? This brings up the concept of *continuity*. Bezier curves can meet together in several ways.

The first type of continuity is called C^0. In this, the last control point of one curve is in the same position as the first control point of the next curve. Because of this, the particle will go from one curve to the other without a jump. However, we'll remember from before that the direction of the particle is defined by the positions and distances of the vectors between the first/second and third/fourth control points. If the third and fourth control points of one curve are not colinear with the second control point of the next curve, there will be a sharp discontinuity, as shown as Figure 7.11.

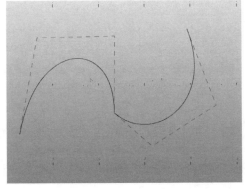

Figure 7.11:
Two curves
meeting with
C^0 continuity

We can fix this by achieving C^1 continuity. In it, the second control point of the second curve is colinear with the last two points of the previous curve, but not the same distance from the first control point that the third control point of the previous curve is. Curves with C[1] continuity appear smooth, but aren't fair, as shown in Figure 7.12.

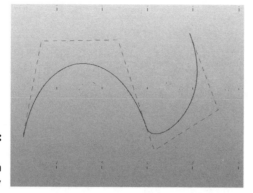

Figure 7.12:
Two curves
meeting with
C[1] continuity

To make our curves seem totally smooth, we must go for C[2] continuity. To do this, the distance between the third and fourth control points of one curve must be the same direction and same distance apart as the first and second control points of the next one. This puts serious constraints on how we can model our Bezier surfaces, however. The restrictions we have to impose give us an extremely fair, extremely smooth looking joint connecting the two curve segments, as shown in Figure 7.13.

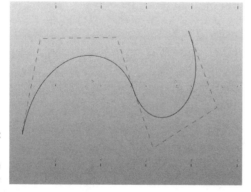

Figure 7.13:
Two curves
meeting with
C[2] continuity

The Math

Everyone put on your math caps; here comes the fun part. We'll define Bezier curve of degree *n* parametrically, as a function of *t*. We can think of *t* being the time during the particles' travel. The *t* variable varies from 0.0 to 1.0 for each Bezier curve.

$$\mathbf{q}(t) = \sum_{i=0}^{n} \mathbf{p}_i B_{i,n}(t) \qquad 0 \le t \le 1$$

where $B_{i,n}(t)$ is the *Bernstein polynomial*:

$$B_{i,n}(t) = \binom{n}{i}(1-t)^{n-i}t^i$$

$$B_{i,n}(t) = \frac{n!}{i!(n-i)!}(1-t)^{n-i}t^i$$

The vector $\mathbf{p}_i$ is control point i.

Let's work out the equations for our cubic ($n = 3$) curves. To help with the flow of the derivation we're going to do, we'll expand each equation so it's in the form of $ax^3 + bx^2 + cx + d$.

$$B_{0,3}(t) = \frac{3!}{0!(3)!}(1-t)^3 t^0$$

$$= (1-t)^3$$

$$= (1-t)(1-2t+t^2)$$

$$= (1-2t+t^2)-(t-2t^2+t^3)$$

$$= -t^3 + 3t^2 - 3t + 1$$

$$B_{1,3}(t) = \frac{3!}{1!(2)!}(1-t)^2 t^1$$

$$= 3t(1-t)^2$$

$$= 3t(1-2t+t^2)$$

$$= 3t^3 - 6t^2 + 3t$$

$$B_{2,3}(t) = \frac{3!}{2!(1)!}(1-t)^1 t^2$$

$$= 3t^2(1-t)$$

$$= 3t(1-2t+t^2)$$

$$= -3t^3 + 3t^2$$

$$B_{3,3}(t) = \frac{3!}{3!(0)!}(1-t)^0 t^3$$

$$= t^3$$

Putting everything together, we get:

$$\mathbf{q}(t) = \mathbf{p}_0 B_{0,3}(t) + \mathbf{p}_1 B_{1,3}(t) + \mathbf{p}_2 B_{2,3}(t) + \mathbf{p}_3 B_{3,3}(t)$$

$$\mathbf{q}(t) = \mathbf{p}_0(1-t)^3 + \mathbf{p}_1 3t(1-t)^2 + \mathbf{p}_2 3t^2(1-t) + \mathbf{p}_3 t^3$$

The equation can be solved using vector mathematics, or we can extract the x, y, and z components of each control point and solve the curve position for that component independently of the other two.

Some insight as to how this equation generates a curve for us comes when we graph the equation. The graph of the four Bernstein blending functions appears in Figure 7.14.

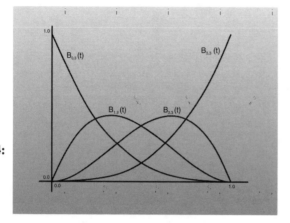

Figure 7.14:
A graph of the four blending functions

Note that at $t=0$ we are only influenced by the first control point (the Bernstein for the others evaluates to 0). This agrees with the observation that at $t=0$ our curve is sitting on top of the first control point. The same is true for the last point at $t=1$. Also note that the second and third points never get to contribute completely to the curve (their graphs never reach 1.0), which explains why we don't intersect with the middle two control points (unless our control points are all collinear, of course).

Finding the Basis Matrix

The equation presented previously to find Bezier curve points is a bit clunky, and doesn't fit well into the 3-D framework we've set up thus far. Luckily, we can decompose the equation into matrix-vector math, as we'll soon see.

Let us consider each coordinate separately, performing the equations for x, y, and z separately. So when we write p_0, for example, we're referring to one particular coordinate of the first control vector. If we think about the control points as a vector, we can rewrite the equation as a dot product of two 4-D vectors:

$$\mathbf{q}_x(t) = \begin{bmatrix} p_{0x} \\ p_{1x} \\ p_{2x} \\ p_{3x} \end{bmatrix}^T \cdot \begin{bmatrix} (1-t)^3 \\ 3t(1-t)^2 \\ 3t^2(1-t) \\ t^3 \end{bmatrix}^T$$

Note that the equations for y and z are identical, just swapping the correspond-ing components. We'll exclude the component subscripts for the rest of the equations, but keep them in mind. Now, each term in the second vector is one of the Bernstein terms. Let's fill in their full forms that we figured out above. (I took the liberty of adding a few choice zero terms, to help the logic flow of where we're taking this.)

$$\mathbf{q}(t) = \begin{bmatrix} p_0 \\ p_1 \\ p_2 \\ p_3 \end{bmatrix}^T \bullet \begin{bmatrix} -t^3 + 3t^2 - 3t + 1 \\ 3t^3 - 6t^2 + 3t + 0(1) \\ -3t^3 + 3t^2 + 0t + 0(1) \\ t^3 + 0t^2 + 0t + 0(1) \end{bmatrix}^T$$

Hmmm … well, this is interesting. We have a lot of like terms here. As it turns out, we can represent the right term as the result of the multiplication of a 4x4 matrix and the vector $<t^3, t^2, t, 1>$.

$$\mathbf{q}(t) = \begin{bmatrix} p_0 \\ p_1 \\ p_2 \\ p_3 \end{bmatrix}^T \bullet \left(\begin{bmatrix} t^3 \\ t^2 \\ t \\ 1 \end{bmatrix}^T \times \begin{bmatrix} -1 & 3 & -3 & 1 \\ 3 & -6 & 3 & 0 \\ -3 & 3 & 0 & 0 \\ 1 & 0 & 0 & 0 \end{bmatrix} \right)$$

Note: If you don't follow the jump, go to Chapter 3 to see how we multiply 4x4 and 1x4 matrices together. Try working it out on paper so you see what is happening.

If you've followed up to this point, pat yourself on the back. We just derived M_B, the basis matrix for Bezier curves:

$$M_B = \begin{bmatrix} -1 & 3 & -3 & 1 \\ 3 & -6 & 3 & 0 \\ -3 & 3 & 0 & 0 \\ 1 & 0 & 0 & 0 \end{bmatrix}$$

Now we're golden: We can find any point p(t) on a Bezier curve. For each com-ponent (x, y, and z), we multiply together a vector of those components from the four control points, the vector $<t^3, t^2, t, 1>$, and the basis matrix M_B. We per-form the 1-D computation for all three axes independently.

Calculating Bezier Curves

So this begs the question of how we render our Bezier curves. Well, the way it's typically done is stepping across the curve a discrete amount of steps, calculating the point along the curve at that point, and then drawing a small line between each pair of lines. So our curves are not perfectly curvy (unless we calculate an infinite amount of points between $t=0$ and $t=1$, which is a bit on the impossible side). However, we're always bound to some resolution below which we don't really care about. In printing, it's the dots-per-inch of the printer, and in video it's the resolution of the monitor. So if we calculate the curve such that each sub-line is less than one pixel long, it will appear exactly as the limit curve would, and has much more feasible memory and computational constraints.

Here's the code to do it.

Listing 7.3: The cSlowBezierIterator class

```
matrix4 cBezierPatch::m_basisMatrix = matrix4(
    -1.0f,  3.0f, -3.0f,  1.0f,
     3.0f, -6.0f,  3.0f,  0.0f,

    -3.0f,  3.0f,  0.0f,  0.0f,
     1.0f,  0.0f,  0.0f,  0.0f
);

class cBezierSlowIterator
{
    int     m_i;            // our current step in the iteration
    int     m_nSteps;       // the number of steps
    point4  m_p[3];         // for x, y, and z
    point3  m_cPts[4];

    point3  m_Q;            // Current position
public:
    cBezierSlowIterator(
        int nSteps, point3 p1, point3 p2, point3 p3, point3 p4 )
    {
        m_cPts[0] = p1;
        m_cPts[1] = p2;
        m_cPts[2] = p3;
        m_cPts[3] = p4;

        m_nSteps = nSteps;
        m_p[0].Assign( p1.x, p2.x, p3.x, p4.x );
        m_p[1].Assign( p1.y, p2.y, p3.y, p4.y );
        m_p[2].Assign( p1.z, p2.z, p3.z, p4.z );
    }

    void Start() {
        m_i = 0;
```

```
        }

        bool Done() {
            return !(m_i<m_nSteps);
        }

        point3& GetCurr() {
            return m_Q;
        }

        operator point3&() {
            return m_Q;
        }

        void CalcNext() {
            float t = (float)m_i / m_nSteps;
            point4 tVec( t*t*t, t*t, t, 1 );
            point4 pVec;

            m_Q.x = m_p[0] * (tVec * cBezierPatch::m_basisMatrix);
            m_Q.y = m_p[1] * (tVec * cBezierPatch::m_basisMatrix);
            m_Q.z = m_p[2] * (tVec * cBezierPatch::m_basisMatrix);
            m_i++;
        }
};
```

That code is written for readability; it's terribly slow and it isn't anything any-one would use in production-quality code. Let's write it for speed!

Forward Differencing

When we're computing a linear function (say, color across a polygon) we never try finding the result of the function at each point explicitly like this:

```
int numSteps = 50;
for( int i=0; i<numSteps; i++ )
{
    outColor[i] = FindColor(i);
}
```

Instead, we find the correct value at the first pixel (or point or whatever), and find out how much it will change during each step (this is called a *delta*). Then when we go across, we simply add the delta to the output, like so:

```
int numSteps = 50;
color curr = FindColor(0);
color delta = FindDelta( numSteps );
for( int i=0; i<numSteps; i++ )
{
    outColor[i] = curr;
```

```
        curr += delta;
    }
```

If FindColor() is an expensive function, we end up speeding up our code a whole lot, because we're replacing it with just an addition.

The reason this particular code works is because the function we're interpolating is linear. The graph of the function is a straight line. So if we can compute the slope of the line, we can increment our y by the slope whenever we increment x, and thus we compute $f(x+1)$ in terms of $f(x)$ instead of doing it explicitly.

What about Bezier curves? The delta we would add to the position during each iteration of finding p(t) isn't constant, because it's a cubic function. The first derivative of the curve formed by the Bezier curve isn't a straight line (neither is the second derivative, for that matter). To solve this problem, we'll use *forward differencing.*

We can define our Bezier equation to be just a regular cubic function (or the dot product of two 4-D vectors), like so:

$$\mathbf{q}_x(t) = at^3 + bt^2 + ct + d$$
$$\mathbf{q}_x(t) = \mathbf{t} \bullet \mathbf{c}$$
$$\mathbf{t} = \begin{bmatrix} t^3 & t^2 & t & 1 \end{bmatrix}^T$$
$$\mathbf{c} = \begin{bmatrix} a & b & c & d \end{bmatrix}^T$$
$$\mathbf{c} = \mathbf{M}_B \begin{bmatrix} \mathbf{p}_{0x} & \mathbf{p}_{1x} & \mathbf{p}_{2x} & \mathbf{p}_{3x} \end{bmatrix}^T$$

Note that in the above we only define $\mathbf{q}_x$; $\mathbf{q}_y$ and $\mathbf{q}_z$ would be essentially identical. For the remainder of the equations we're going to just abstractly deal with some function $\mathbf{q}(t)$ (in code, we'll need to do the work for each component).

Let's define the forward difference as $\Delta\mathbf{q}(t)$. The forward difference is defined such that when we add it to $\mathbf{q}(t)$, we get the next point in the iteration (the point we get after we increment t by the small inter-step delta value d. That is...

$$\mathbf{q}(t+\delta) = \mathbf{q}(t) + \Delta\mathbf{q}(t)$$

So now we just need to find $\Delta\mathbf{q}(t)$. Don't forget that d is a constant, based on the number we wish to tessellate ($\delta=1/\text{size}$). Let's get the math down:

$$\Delta\mathbf{q}(t) = \mathbf{q}(t+\delta) - \mathbf{q}(t)$$
$$\Delta\mathbf{q}(t) = a(t+\delta)^3 + b(t+\delta)^2 + c(t+\delta) + d - \left(at^3 + bt^2 + ct + d\right)$$
$$\Delta\mathbf{q}(t) = 3at^2\delta + t\left(3a\delta^2 + 2b\delta\right) + a\delta^3 + b\delta^2 + c\delta$$

Unfortunately, $\Delta\mathbf{q}(t)$ is a function of t, so we would need to calculate it explicitly each iteration. All we've done is add extra work. However, $\Delta\mathbf{q}(t)$ is a quadratic equation where $\mathbf{q}(t)$ was cubic, so we've improved a bit. Let's calculate the forward difference of $\Delta\mathbf{q}(t)$ (that is, $\Delta^2\mathbf{q}(t)$).

$$\Delta^2\mathbf{q}(t) = \Delta\mathbf{q}(t+\delta) - \Delta\mathbf{q}(t)$$
$$\Delta^2\mathbf{q}(t) = 3a(t+\delta)^2\delta + (t+\delta)(3a\delta^2 + 2b\delta) + a\delta^3 + b\delta^2 + c\delta -$$
$$\left(3at^2\delta + t(3a\delta^2 + 2b\delta) + a\delta^3 + b\delta^2 + c\delta\right)$$
$$\Delta^2\mathbf{q}(t) = 6at\delta^2 + 6a\delta^3 + 2b\delta^2$$

We're almost there. While $\Delta^2\mathbf{q}(t)$ still is a function of t, this time it's just a linear equation. We just need to do this one more time and calculate $\Delta^3\mathbf{q}(t)$:

$$\Delta^3\mathbf{q}(t) = \Delta^2\mathbf{q}(t+\delta) - \Delta^2\mathbf{q}(t)$$
$$\Delta^3\mathbf{q}(t) = 6a(t+\delta)\delta^2 + 6a\delta^3 + 2b\delta^2 - \left(6at\delta^2 + 6a\delta^3 + 2b\delta^2\right)$$
$$\Delta^3\mathbf{q}(t) = 6a\delta^3$$

Eureka! A constant! If you don't share my exuberance, hold on. Let's suppose that at some point along the curve we know $\mathbf{q}(t)$, $\Delta\mathbf{q}(t)$, $\Delta^2\mathbf{q}(t)$, and $\Delta^3\mathbf{q}(t)$. This will hold true at the initial case when $t=0$: We can explicitly compute all four variables. To arrive at the next step in the iteration, we just do:

$$\mathbf{q}(t+\delta) = \mathbf{q}(t) + \Delta\mathbf{q}(t)$$
$$\Delta\mathbf{q}(t+\delta) = \Delta\mathbf{q}(t) + \Delta^2\mathbf{q}(t)$$
$$\Delta^2\mathbf{q}(t+\delta) = \Delta^2\mathbf{q}(t) + \Delta^3\mathbf{q}(t)$$

As you can see, it's just a bunch of additions. All we need to do is keep track of everything. Suddenly, we only need to do hard work during setup; calculating n points is next to free.

The cFwdDiffIterator Class

The cFwdDiffIterator class implements the equations listed above to perform forward differencing. Compare and contrast the equations and the code until they make sense. The code appears in Listing 7.4.

Listing 7.4: Forward difference iterator class

```
class cFwdDiffIterator
{
    int    m_i;       // our current step in the iteration
    int    m_nSteps;  // the number of steps

    point3 m_p[4];    // The 4 control points

    point3 m_Q;       // the point at the current iteration location
```

```
            point3  m_dQ;       // First derivative (initially at zero)
            point3  m_ddQ;      // Second derivative (initially at zero)
            point3  m_dddQ;     // Triple derivative (constant)

    public:
        cFwdDiffIterator()
        {
            // Do nothing
        }
        cFwdDiffIterator(
            int nSteps,

            point3 p1,
            point3 p2,
            point3 p3,
            point3 p4 )
        {
            m_nSteps = nSteps;
            m_p[0] = p1;
            m_p[1] = p2;
            m_p[2] = p3;
            m_p[3] = p4;
        }

        void Start()
        {
            m_i = 0;

            float d = 1.f/(m_nSteps-1);
            float d2 = d*d; // d^2
            float d3 = d*d2;// d^3

            point4 px( m_p[0].x, m_p[1].x, m_p[2].x, m_p[3].x );
            point4 py( m_p[0].y, m_p[1].y, m_p[2].y, m_p[3].y );
            point4 pz( m_p[0].z, m_p[1].z, m_p[2].z, m_p[3].z );

            point4 cVec[3]; // <a, b, c, d> for x, y, and z.
            cVec[0] = px * cBezierPatch::m_basisMatrix;
            cVec[1] = py * cBezierPatch::m_basisMatrix;
            cVec[2] = pz * cBezierPatch::m_basisMatrix;

            m_Q = m_p[0];

            // Do the work for each component
            int i = 3;
            while (i-)
            {
                // remember that t=0 here so many of the terms
                // in the text drop out.
                float a = cVec[i].v[0];
                float b = cVec[i].v[1];
```

```
        float c = cVec[i].v[2];
        // luckily d isn't used, which
        // would clash with the other d.

        m_dQ.v[i] = a * d3 + b * d2 + c * d;
        m_ddQ.v[i] = 6 * a * d3 + 2 * b * d2;
        m_dddQ.v[i] = 6 * a * d3;
    }
}

bool Done()
{
    return !(m_i<m_nSteps);
}

point3& GetCurr()
{
    return m_Q;
}

operator point3&()
{
    return m_Q;
}

void CalcNext()
{
    // Just a bunch of additions.   YES!!
    m_Q += m_dQ;
    m_dQ += m_ddQ;
    m_ddQ += m_dddQ;

    m_i++;
}
};
```

Drawing Curves

Armed with our fast forward difference iterator, drawing curves isn't difficult at all. All we need to do is step across the Bezier curve, sample the curve point at however many locations desired, and draw the data, either as a point list or a line strip. Listing 7.5 shows what this would look like.

Listing 7.5: Sample code to draw a Bezier curve

```
void DrawCurve(
    const point3& c1,
    const point3& c2,
    const point3& c3,
    const point3& c4 )
```

```
{
    LPDIRECT3DDEVICE7 pDevice = Graphics()->GetDevice();
    // we can tessellate to any level of detail we want, but for the
    // sake of example let's generate 50 points (49 line segments)
    sLitVertex v[50];
    cFwdDiffIterator iter( 50, c1, c2, c3, c4 );
    int curr = 0;
    for( iter.Start(); !iter.Done(); iter.CalcNext() )
    {
        v[curr++] = sLitVertex( iter.GetCurr(), 0x00FFFFFF );

    }

    pDevice->DrawPrimitive(
        D3DPT_LINESTRIP,
        D3DFVF_LVERTEX,
        v,
        50,
        0 );
}
```

Drawing Surfaces

While curves are swell and all, what we really want to do is draw curved surfaces. Luckily, we're not far away from being able to do that. Instead of four control points, we're going to have 16. We define a 4x4 grid of points that will form a 3-D surface, called a *patch*. A simple patch appears in Figure 7.15.

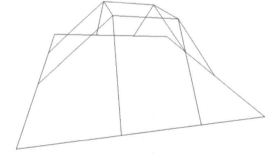

Figure 7.15:
A control net for a simple patch

So instead of the function $q(t)$ we had before, now we have a new function $q(s,t)$ that gives the point along the surface for the two inputs ([0,1],[0,1]). The four corners of our patch are (0,0), (1,0), (1,1), and (0,1). In practice, it would be possible to just iterate across the entire surface with two for loops, calculating the point using the two-dimensional function. However, we can exploit the code we wrote for calculating curves.

We can think of the patch as a series of n curves put side to side to give the impression of a surface. If we step evenly along all n curves m times, we will create an m x n grid of point values. We can use the same forward differencing code we wrote before to step m times along each of these n curves. All we need is the four control points that define each of the n curves.

No problem. We can think of the 16 control points as four sets of control points describing four vertical curves. We simultaneously step n times along each of these four curves. Each of the n iterated points is a control point for a horizontal curve. We take the four iterated points from the four curves and use that to create a horizontal curve, which we iterate across n times. We use our forward differencing code here, too. An image of a Bezier patch appears in Figure 7.16.

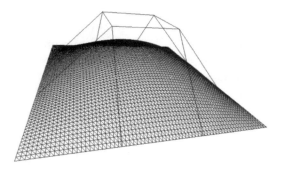

Figure 7.16: The control net, with the tessellated mesh

Application: Teapot

The application for this section is a viewer to display objects composed of Bezier surfaces. A Bezier object (represented by the class cBezierObject) holds on to a bunch of separate Bezier patches. To show off the code, we'll use the canonical Bezier patch surface: the Utah Teapot.

The teapot is used in graphics so often it's transcended to the point of being a basic geometric primitive (in both 3-D Studio and Direct3D). It's a set of 28 patches that define an object that looks like a teapot. Figure 7.17 shows what the control nets for the patches looks like, and Figure 7.18 shows the tessellated Bezier patches.

Figure 7.17:
Control nets
for the
Bezier
patches of
the teapot
model

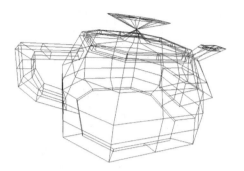

Figure 7.18: Tessellated teapot model

The Bezier patches are loaded from an ASCII .bez file. The first line gives the number of patches, and then each patch is listed on four lines (four control points per line). Each patch is separated by a line of white space.

One thing we haven't discussed yet is how to generate normals for our patches. We need to define a vertex normal for each vertex in the grid if we want it to be lit correctly. One way to do it would be to compute them the same way as for regular polygonal surfaces (that is, find normals for each of the triangles, and average the normals of all the triangles that share a vertex, making that the vertex normal). This won't work however; at least not completely. The normals of the edges will be biased inward a little (since they don't have the triangles of adjacent patches contributing to the average). This will cause our patches to not meet up correctly, causing a visual seam where adjacent normals are different.

A better way to calculate Bezier patch normals is to generate them explicitly from the definition of the curve. When we compute the Bezier function using the t-vector $<t^3,t^2,t,1>$ we compute the position along the curve. If we instead use the first derivative of the Bezier function we will get the tangent at each point instead of the position. To compute the derivative we just use a different t-vector, where each component is the derivative of the component in the regular t-vector. This gives us the vector $<3t^2,2t,1,0>$.

To do this I threw together a quick and dirty iterator class (called cTangentIterator) that uses the slow matrix multiplication method to calculate the tangent vectors. Converting the iterator to use forward differencing would not be hard, and is left as an exercise for the reader.

We step across the patch one way and find the position and u-tangent vector. We then step across the perpendicular direction, calculating the v-tangent vectors. Then we cross product the two tangent vectors to get a vector perpendicular to both of them (which is the normal we want). We use the position and normal to build the vertex list. Then when we draw, it's just one DrawIndexedPrimitive call. There's too much code in the project to list here, so I'll just put in the interesting parts.

Listing 7.6: Notable code from the teapot program

```
void cBezierPatch::Init( int size )
{
    delete [] m_vertList;
    delete [] m_triList;
    delete [] m_uTangList;
    delete [] m_vTangList;

    m_size = size;

    // allocate our lists
    m_vertList = new sVertex[ size * size ];

    m_triList = new sTri[ (size-1) * (size-1) * 2 ];

    m_uTangList = new point3[ size * size ];
    m_vTangList = new point3[ size * size ];

    Tesselate();
}


/**
 * Fill in the grid of values (all the dynamic arrays
 * have been initialized already).  The grid is of
 * size mxn where m = n = m_size
 */
void cBezierPatch::Tesselate()
{
    int u, v; // patch-space coordinates.
    point3 p1,p2,p3,p4;

    /**
     * These are the four curves that will define the
     * control points for the rest of the curves
     */
    cFwdDiffIterator mainCurve1;
    cFwdDiffIterator mainCurve2;
    cFwdDiffIterator mainCurve3;
    cFwdDiffIterator mainCurve4;

    int nSteps = m_size;
    mainCurve1 = cFwdDiffIterator( nSteps, m_ctrlPoints[0],
        m_ctrlPoints[4], m_ctrlPoints[8], m_ctrlPoints[12] );
    mainCurve2 = cFwdDiffIterator( nSteps, m_ctrlPoints[1],
        m_ctrlPoints[5], m_ctrlPoints[9], m_ctrlPoints[13] );
    mainCurve3 = cFwdDiffIterator( nSteps, m_ctrlPoints[2],
        m_ctrlPoints[6], m_ctrlPoints[10], m_ctrlPoints[14] );
```

```
mainCurve4 = cFwdDiffIterator( nSteps, m_ctrlPoints[3],
    m_ctrlPoints[7], m_ctrlPoints[11], m_ctrlPoints[15] );

mainCurve1.Start();
mainCurve2.Start();
mainCurve3.Start();
mainCurve4.Start();

for(v=0;v<m_size;v++)
{
    /**
     * Generate our four control points for this curve
     */
    p1 = mainCurve1.GetCurr();
    p2 = mainCurve2.GetCurr();
    p3 = mainCurve3.GetCurr();
    p4 = mainCurve4.GetCurr();

    /**
     * Now step along the curve filling in the data
     */
    cTangentIterator tanIter( nSteps, p1, p2, p3, p4 );
    tanIter.Start();
    cFwdDiffIterator iter( nSteps, p1, p2, p3, p4 );
    u = 0;
    for(
        iter.Start(); !iter.Done(); iter.CalcNext(), u++ )
    {
        m_vertList[m_size*v+u].loc = iter.GetCurr();

        // We're piggybacking our u-direction
        // tangent vector calculation here.
        m_uTangList[m_size*v+u] = tanIter.GetCurr();
        tanIter.CalcNext();
    }

    mainCurve1.CalcNext();
    mainCurve2.CalcNext();
    mainCurve3.CalcNext();
    mainCurve4.CalcNext();
}

/**
 * Since we can't generate the v-tangents in the same run as
 * the u-tangents (we need to go in the opposite direction),
 * we have to go through the process again, but this time in the
 * perpendicular direction we went the first time
 */
mainCurve1 = cFwdDiffIterator( nSteps, m_ctrlPoints[0],
    m_ctrlPoints[1], m_ctrlPoints[2], m_ctrlPoints[3] );
mainCurve2 = cFwdDiffIterator( nSteps, m_ctrlPoints[4],
```

```
        m_ctrlPoints[5], m_ctrlPoints[6], m_ctrlPoints[7] );
mainCurve3 = cFwdDiffIterator( nSteps, m_ctrlPoints[8],
    m_ctrlPoints[9], m_ctrlPoints[10], m_ctrlPoints[11] );
mainCurve4 = cFwdDiffIterator( nSteps, m_ctrlPoints[12],
    m_ctrlPoints[13], m_ctrlPoints[14], m_ctrlPoints[15] );
```

```
mainCurve1.Start();
mainCurve2.Start();
mainCurve3.Start();
mainCurve4.Start();

for(v=0;v<m_size;v++)
{
    // create a horizontal Bezier curve by
    // calc'ing points along the 4 vertical ones

    p1 = mainCurve1.GetCurr();
    p2 = mainCurve2.GetCurr();
    p3 = mainCurve3.GetCurr();
    p4 = mainCurve4.GetCurr();

    cTangentIterator iter( nSteps, p1, p2, p3, p4 );
    u = 0;
    for( iter.Start(); !iter.Done(); iter.CalcNext(), u++ )
    {
        // We don't get the location because all we
        // want here is the v-tangents
        m_vTangList[m_size*u+v] = iter.GetCurr();
    }

    mainCurve1.CalcNext();
    mainCurve2.CalcNext();
    mainCurve3.CalcNext();
    mainCurve4.CalcNext();
}

int offset;
for(v=0;v<m_size;v++)
{
    // tesselate across the horizontal Bezier
    for(u=0;u<m_size;u++)
    {
        offset = m_size*v+u;

        point3 norm;
        norm = m_vTangList[offset] ^ m_uTangList[offset];
        norm.Normalize();

        m_vertList[offset].norm = norm;
        m_vertList[offset].u = 0;
        m_vertList[offset].v = 0;
```

```
        }
    }

    memset( m_triList, 0, sizeof( sTri ) * (m_size-1) * (m_size-1) );

    // use an incremented pointer to the triangle list
    sTri* pCurrTri = m_triList;

    // build the tri list
    for( v=0; v< (m_size-1); v++ )
    {
        for( u=0; u< (m_size-1); u++ )
        {
            // tesselating square [u,v]

            // 0, 1, 2
            pCurrTri->v[0] = m_size*(v+0) + (u+0);
            pCurrTri->v[1] = m_size*(v+0) + (u+1);
            pCurrTri->v[2] = m_size*(v+1) + (u+1);
            pCurrTri++;

            // 2, 3, 0
            pCurrTri->v[0] = m_size*(v+1) + (u+1);
            pCurrTri->v[1] = m_size*(v+1) + (u+0);
            pCurrTri->v[2] = m_size*(v+0) + (u+0);
            pCurrTri++;

        }
    }
}

void cBezierPatch::Draw( bool bDrawNet )
{
    // hard code the control mesh lines
    static short netIndices[] = {
        0, 1, 1, 2, 2, 3, 4, 5, 5, 6, 6, 7,
        8, 9, 9, 10, 10, 11, 12, 13, 13, 14, 14, 15,
        0, 4, 4, 8, 8, 12, 1, 5, 5, 9, 9, 13,
        2, 6, 6, 10, 10, 14, 3, 7, 7, 11, 11, 15 };

    if( bDrawNet )
    {
        sLitVertex v[16];
        for( int i=0; i<16; i++ )
        {
            v[i] = sLitVertex( m_ctrlPoints[i], 0 );
        }
        Graphics()->GetDevice()->DrawIndexedPrimitive(
            D3DPT_LINELIST, D3DFVF_VERTEX,
            v, 16,
            (LPWORD)netIndices, 48, 0 );
```

```
    }

    Graphics()->GetDevice()->DrawIndexedPrimitive(
        D3DPT_TRIANGLELIST, D3DFVF_VERTEX,
        m_vertList, m_size*m_size,
        (LPWORD)m_triList, 6*(m_size-1)*(m_size-1), 0 );

}
```

B-Spline Curves

There are a myriad of other types of parametric curves and surfaces; we could not even hope to cover them all. They each have their own advantages and disadvantages, and they're each suited to particular types of applications. To help get a better idea of the kinds of curves we can do, we'll quickly cover one more type of curve before moving on to subdivision surfaces: b-splines.

Uniform, rational b-splines are quite different from Bezier curves. Rather than have a set of distinct curves, each one made up of four control points, a b-spline is made up of any number of control points (well... any number greater than four). They are C^2 continuous, but they are not interpolative (they don't pass through their control points).

Given a particular control point $\mathbf{p}_i$, we iterate from $t=0$ to $t=1$. The iteration uses the four control points ($\mathbf{p}_i$, $\mathbf{p}_{i+1}$, $\mathbf{p}_{i+2}$, $\mathbf{p}_{i+3}$). The curve it steps out sits between $\mathbf{p}_{i+1}$ and $\mathbf{p}_{i+2}$, but note that the curve itself probably won't actually go through those points. Figure 7.19 may help you understand this.

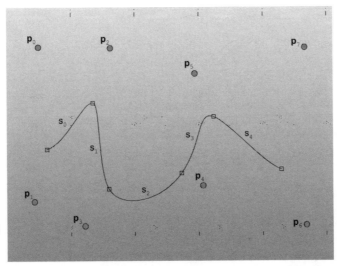

Figure 7.19: Sample b-spline

Each section of the curve (denoted by s_0, s_1, etc.) is traced out by the four control points around it. Segment s_0 is traced out by $\mathbf{p}_0$–$\mathbf{p}_3$, segment s1 by $\mathbf{p}_1$–$\mathbf{p}_4$, and so on. To compute a point along a b-spline, we use the following equation:

$$
\mathbf{q}(t) = \begin{bmatrix} t^3 \\ t^2 \\ t \\ 1 \end{bmatrix}^T \frac{1}{6} \begin{bmatrix} -1 & 3 & -3 & 1 \\ 3 & -6 & 3 & 0 \\ -3 & 0 & 3 & 0 \\ 1 & 4 & 1 & 0 \end{bmatrix} \begin{bmatrix} \mathbf{P}_i \\ \mathbf{P}_{i+1} \\ \mathbf{P}_{i+2} \\ \mathbf{P}_{i+3} \end{bmatrix}
$$

The main reason I'm including b-spline curves in this chapter is just to show you that once you've learned one style of parametric curve, you've pretty much learned them all. They almost all use the same style of equation; it's just a matter of choosing the kind of curve you want and plugging it into your code.

Application: BSpline

Just for fun, I threw together a simple application to show off b-splines. It draws a set of six splines spinning around in space, whose tails fade off to blackness. The code running the splines is pretty rudimentary; it's just there to hopefully spark an idea in your head to use them for something more complex. As simple as the code is, it can be pretty mesmerizing, and I feel it's one of the more visually pleasing sample applications in this book. Listing 7.7 has a small sample from the source; it's the code used to calculate points along the b-spline curve.

Listing 7.7: B-spline calculation code

```
/**
 * The b-spline basis matrix
 */
matrix4 cBSpline::m_baseMatrix = matrix4(
    -1,  3, -3,  1,
     3, -6,  3,  0,
    -3,  0,  3,  0,
     1,  4,  1,  0);

point3 cBSpline::Calc( float t, int i0 )
{
    assert(i0+3 < m_ctrlPoints.size() );
    assert(t>=0.f && t<=1.f );
    point4 tVec( t*t*t, t*t, t, 1 );

    point4 xVec(
        m_ctrlPoints[i0].x,
        m_ctrlPoints[i0+1].x,
        m_ctrlPoints[i0+2].x,
        m_ctrlPoints[i0+3].x );
    point4 yVec(
        m_ctrlPoints[i0].y,
        m_ctrlPoints[i0+1].y,
        m_ctrlPoints[i0+2].y,
        m_ctrlPoints[i0+3].y );
```

```
        point4 zVec(
            m_ctrlPoints[i0].z,
            m_ctrlPoints[i0+1].z,
            m_ctrlPoints[i0+2].z,
            m_ctrlPoints[i0+3].z );

        return point3(
            tVec *  (1.f/6) * m_baseMatrix * xVec,
            tVec *  (1.f/6) * m_baseMatrix * yVec,
            tVec *  (1.f/6) * m_baseMatrix * zVec );
    }


    point3 cBSpline::CalcAbs( float t )
    {
        // the T we get isn't right, fix it.
        t *= m_ctrlPoints.size() - 3;
        int vert = (int)(floor(t));
        t -= (float)floor(t);
        return Calc( t, vert );
    }
```

Subdivision Surfaces

Parametric surfaces, while really cool, are not without their problems. The main problem is in order to have smoothness, it's usually necessary to keep the valence at patch corners equal to 2 or 4. (That is, at any patch corner there is either one more or three more patches also touching that corner.) Otherwise, the patches don't meet up correctly and there's a seam in the surface. This can be fixed by using degenerate patches (patches that are really triangles); however, getting some things to look right (like the meeting point of a handle and a mug) can prove downright maddening.

Subdivision surfaces try to get around this restriction by attacking the problem of creating smooth surfaces a different way. They use a discrete operation that takes a given mesh and subdivides it. If the resultant mesh is subdivided again and again, eventually the surface reaches the *limit surface*. Most subdivision schemes have a limit surface that has C¹ continuity, which is generally all we need for games. You don't need to go all the way to the limit surface, however; each time you subdivide your surface looks smoother and smoother.

Subdivision surfaces have gotten a lot of press in the computer graphics community. Mostly this is because they're fairly straightforward to code, easy to use by artists, and very very cool looking. The first mainstream media to use subdivision surfaces was *Geri's Game*, a short by Pixar. The piece won, among other things, an Academy Award for Best Animated Short.

Subdivision Essentials

To begin the discussion of subdivision curves and surfaces, we'll consider a simple 2-D case: subdividing a curve. Once we learn how to subdivide that, we can start experimenting with surfaces. Our lowest resolution curve, the control curve, appears in Figure 7.20.

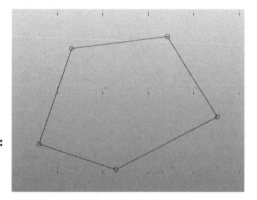

Figure 7.20:
A simple
four-seg-
ment loop

Luckily for us, this is a closed loop, so for our first baby steps we don't need to trip over boundary cases. Let's define an operation that we can perform on our curve and call it an edge split. It takes some particular edge from $\mathbf{p}_n$ to $\mathbf{p}_{n+1}$. The edge is subdivided into two new edges. The location of the new internal point (we'll call it $\mathbf{p}_{n+0.5}$) depends on the neighborhood of points around it. We want to position the new internal point such that it fits on the curve defined by the points around it.

The formula we'll define to calculate $\mathbf{p}_{n+0.5}$ is the following:

$$\mathbf{p}_{n+0.5} = -\frac{1}{16}\mathbf{p}_{n-1} + \frac{9}{16}\mathbf{p}_n + \frac{9}{16}\mathbf{p}_{n+1} - \frac{1}{16}\mathbf{p}_{n+2}$$

This equation, after some reflection, seems pretty intuitive. Most of the position of the new point is an average of the two points adjacent to it. Then, to perturb it a little, we move it away from the points one hop from it on either side by a small amount. Note that the set of constant values (called the *mask*) all add up to 1.

If we apply the equation to each of the edges in the control curve, we get a new curve. We'll call this curve the level 1 curve. It rears its not-so-ugly head in Figure 7.21.

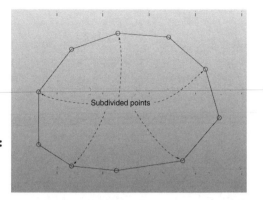

Figure 7.21:
The loop
after one
subdivision

You'll notice that after the subdivision step, we doubled the number of edges in our loop, and our loop got a tiny bit smoother. If we apply it again (shown in Figure 7.22), it gets still smoother.

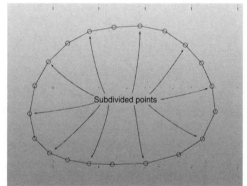

Figure 7.22:
The loop
after two
subdivisions

It's fairly easy to see that eventually this little fella will be about as smooth as we can possibly deal with. How smooth we go depends on the application. If we were Pixar, and we were making the new animated short "Geri's Curve," we could afford to subdivide it such that all of our line segments are half a pixel wide. Any smoother than that is truly excessive, and even taking it to that level is infeasible for current generation real-time 3-D graphics.

Handling surfaces is just as easy. You start out with a control mesh (in some cases this is just a regular triangular model) and each subdivision creates a more tessellated mesh. The beauty is you can decide how much to subdivide based on how much hardware is available to do the work. If someone picks up your game eight years from now, your code could automatically take advantage of the multi-quadrillion triangle rate and subdivide your curves and surfaces from here to kingdom come.

This is the driving idea behind all subdivision surface schemes: They all derive their identity from small little differences. Let's take a look at some of the differences before we decide upon a method to implement.

Triangles vs. Quads

One of the most obvious differences between subdivision schemes is the type of primitive they operate on. Some schemes, such as Catmull-Clark subdivision, operate with control meshes of quadrilaterals. Others, like butterfly subdivision, instead work with triangle meshes.

Using a subdivision mesh based on triangles has a lot of advantages over quadrilateral methods. First of all, most modeling programs can easily create meshes built out of triangles. Making one exclusively out of quadrilaterals can be considerably more difficult, and has a lot of the same problems that arise from attempting to build complex objects out of Bezier patches. Also, being able to use triangle meshes is a big plus because you may be adding subdivision surfaces to an existing project that uses regular triangle models; you won't need to do any work converting your existing media over to a subdividing system.

Interpolating vs. Approximating

After we've decided what primitive our subdivision meshes should be based on, we need to decide if the method we want to implement should be *interpolating* or *approximating*. They define how the new control mesh is reached from the original.

With approximating subdivision, the limit mesh is actually never reached by the vertices, unless the surface is subdivided an infinite amount of times. Each time a subdivision is performed, the old mesh is completely thrown away and a new mesh is created that is a bit closer to the limit curve. As subdivisions continue, the surface moves closer and closer to the limit surface, looking more and more like it. This has a few side effects. The primary one is that the initial control mesh tends not to look much like the limit surface at all. Modifying the initial mesh to get the desired result in the limit mesh isn't easy. However, for giving up a bit of intuitive control, you generally get a much nicer-looking mesh. The mesh tends to look nicer and have fewer strange-looking subdivided areas.

Interpolating subdivision, on the other hand, always adds vertices right on the limit surface. The initial control mesh is on the limit surface, each new batch of vertices and triangles we add is on the limit surface, and so on. Essentially the subdivision just interpolates new points on the limit surface, making the surface look smoother and smoother but not too different. You can anticipate what the limit curve will look like when you're examining an interpolating subdivision scheme.

Uniform vs. Non-Uniform

Uniform schemes define a single unified way to divide an edge. No matter what type of edge you have or whatever valence the endpoints have, the same scheme is used to subdivide it. Non-uniform methods tailor themselves to different cases, oftentimes specializing to take care of irregularities in the surface. For example, the modified butterfly scheme (which we'll discuss at length shortly) is non-uniform, since it uses three different ways to subdivide edges based on the types of vertices at the endpoints.

Stationary vs. Non-Stationary

This consideration is similar to the uniform/non-uniform one. When a scheme is stationary, the same scheme is used at each subdivision level. Non-stationary methods may use one method for the first subdivision, then switch to another once the surface is looking moderately smooth.

Modified Butterfly Method Subdivision Scheme

The butterfly subdivision scheme was first birthed in 1990 by Dyn, Gregory, and Levin. It handled certain types of surfaces beautifully, but it had a lot of visual discontinuities in certain situations that made it somewhat undesirable. In 1996, Zorin, Schröder, and Sweldens extended the butterfly subdivision scheme to better handle irregular cases, creating the modified butterfly method subdivision scheme. This is the method we're going to focus on for several reasons. First, it's interpolative, so our limit mesh looks a lot like our initial mesh. Second, it works on triangle meshes, which means we can take existing code and drop in subdivision surfaces pretty easily. Finally, it's visually pleasing and easy to code. What more could you want?

To subdivide our mesh, we take each edge and subdivide it into two pieces, forming four new triangles from each original triangle. This is preferred because our subdivided triangles will have a similar shape to their parent triangle (unlike, for example, creating a split location in the center of the triangle and throwing edges to the corners of the triangle). Figure 7.23 shows what a subdivision step looks like.

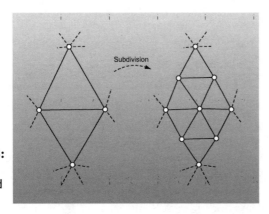

Figure 7.23: Subdividing edges to add triangles

The equation we use to subdivide an edge depends on the valence of its end-points. The valence of a vertex in this context is defined as the number of other vertices the vertex is adjacent to. There are three possible cases that we have to handle.

The first case is when both vertices of a particular edge have a valence=6. We use a mask on the neighborhood of vertices around the edge. This mask is where the modified butterfly scheme gets its name, because it looks sort of like a butterfly. It appears in Figure 7.24.

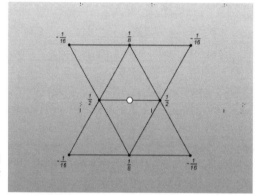

Figure 7.24:
The butterfly mask

The modified butterfly scheme added two points and a tension parameter that lets you control the sharpness of the limit surface. Since this scheme complicates the code, I chose to go with a universal w-value of 0.0 instead (which resolves to the above Figure 7.24). The modified butterfly mask appears in Figure 7.25.

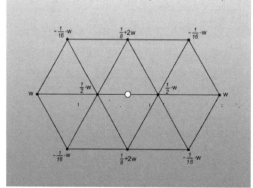

Figure 7.25:
The modified butterfly mask

To compute the location of the subdivided edge vertex (the white circle in both images), we step around the neighborhood of vertices and sum them (multiplying each vector by the weight dictated by the mask). You'll notice that all the weights sum up to 1.0. This is good; it means our subdivided point will be in the right neighborhood compared to the rest of the vertices. You can imagine if the sum was much larger the subdivided vertex would be much farther away from the origin than any of the vertices used to create it, which would be incorrect.

When only one of our vertices is regular (i.e., has a valence = 6), we compute the subdivided location using the irregular vertex, otherwise known as a k-vertex. This is where the modified butterfly algorithm shines over the original butterfly algorithm (which handled k-vertices very poorly). An example appears in Figure 7.26. The right vertex has a valence of 6, and the left vertex has a valence of 9, so we use the left vertex to compute the location for the new vertex (indicated by the white circle).

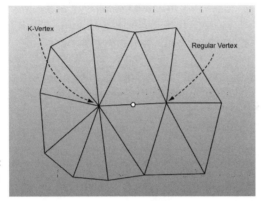

Figure 7.26: Example of a k-vertex

The general case for a k-vertex has us step around the vertex, weighting the neighbors using a mask determined by the valence of the k-vertex. Figure 7.27 shows the generic k-vertex and how we name the vertices. Note that the k-vertex itself has a weight of ¾, in all cases.

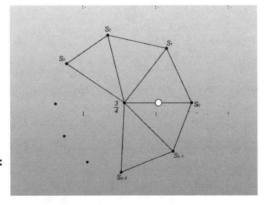

Figure 7.27: Generic k-vertex

There are three cases to deal with: k=3, k=4, and k=5. The masks for each of them are:

$$s_0 = \frac{5}{12}, s_{1,2} = -\frac{1}{12} \qquad \text{for } k = 3$$

$$s_0 = \frac{3}{8}, s_2 = -\frac{1}{8}, s_{1,3} = 0 \qquad \text{for } k = 4$$

$$s_i = \frac{1}{k}\left(\frac{1}{4} + \cos\frac{2i\pi}{k} + \frac{1}{2}\cos\frac{4i\pi}{k}\right) \text{ for } k \geq 5 \text{ (k != 6)}$$

Using this method to compute the new vertex location may seem unintuitive at first. Zorin justifies the weights he chose in his.

The third and final case we need to worry about is when both endpoints of the current edge are k-vertices. When this occurs we compute the k-vertex for both endpoints using the above weights, and average the results together.

Note that we are assuming that our input triangle mesh is closed boundary representation (doesn't have any holes in it). The paper describing the modified butterfly scheme discusses ways to handle holes in the model (with excellent results) but the code we'll write next won't be able to handle holes in the model so we won't discuss it.

Using these schema for computing our subdivided locations results in an extremely fair looking surface. Figure 7.28 shows how an octahedron looks as it is repeatedly subdivided. The application we will make next was used to create this image.

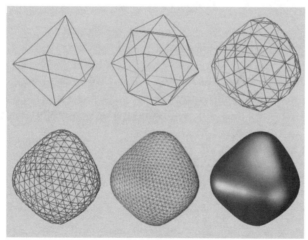

Figure 7.28:
A subdivided
octagon
model.

Levels 0 (8 triangles) through
4 (2048 triangles) are shown.
Finally, level 4 mesh is shown
in filled mode.

Application: SubDiv

The SubDiv application implements the modified butterfly subdivision scheme we just discussed. It loads an .o3d file and displays it interactively, giving the user the option of subdividing the model whenever they wish.

The model data is represented with an adjacency graph. Each triangle structure holds pointers to the three vertices it is composed of. Each vertex structure has STL vectors that contain pointers to edge structures (one edge for each vertex it's connected to) and triangle structures. The lists are unsorted (which requires linear searching; fixing this to order the edges in clockwise winding order, for example, is left as an exercise for the reader).

Listing 7.8 gives the header definitions (and many of the functions) for the vertex, edge, and triangle structures. These classes are all defined inside the subdivision surface class (cSubDivSurf).

Listing 7.8: Vertex, edge, and triangle structures

```
/**
 * Subdivision Surface vertex (name 'sVertex' is used in D3D code)
 */
struct sVert
{
    /**
     * These two arrays describe the adjacency information
     * for a vertex. Each vertex knows who all of its neighboring
     * edges and triangles are. an important note is that these
     * lists aren't sorted.  We need to search through the list
     * when we need to get a specific adjacent triangle.
     * This is, of course, inefficient.  Consider sorted insertion
     * an exercise to the reader.
     */
    std::vector< sTriangle* >   m_triList;
    std::vector< sEdge* >       m_edgeList;

    /**
     * position/normal information for the vertex
     */
    sVertex m_vert;

    /**
     * Each Vertex knows its position in the array it lies in.
     * This helps when we're constructing the arrays of
     * subdivided data.
     */
    int     m_index;

    void AddEdge( sEdge* pEdge )
    {
        assert( 0 == std::count(
            m_edgeList.begin(),
            m_edgeList.end(),
            pEdge ) );
        m_edgeList.push_back( pEdge );
    }

    void AddTri( sTriangle* pTri )
    {
        assert( 0 == std::count(
            m_triList.begin(),
            m_triList.end(),
            pTri ) );
        m_triList.push_back( pTri );
```

```
        }

        /**
         * Valence == How many other vertices are connected to this one
         * which said another way is how many edges the vert has.
         */
        int Valence()
        {
            return m_edgeList.size();
        }

        sVert() :
            m_triList( 0 ),
            m_edgeList( 0 )
        {
        }

        /**
         * Given a Vertex that we know we are attached to, this function
         * searches the list of adjacent edges looking for the one that
         * contains the input vertex.  Asserts if there is no edge for
         * that vertex.
         */
        sEdge*  GetEdge( sVert* pOther )
        {
            for( int i=0; i<m_edgeList.size(); i++ )
            {
                if( m_edgeList[i]->Contains( pOther ) )
                    return m_edgeList[i];
            }
            assert(false); // didn't have it!
            return NULL;
        }
};

/**
 * Edge structure that connects two vertices in a SubSurf
 */
struct sEdge
{
    sVert*  m_v[2];

    /**
     * When we perform the subdivision calculations on all the edges
     * the result is held in this newVLoc strucure.  Never has any
     * connectivity information, just location and color.
     */
    sVert       m_newVLoc;


    /**
```

```
 * true == one of the edges' vertices is the inputted vertex
 */
bool Contains( sVert* pVert )
{
    return (m_v[0] == pVert) || m_v[1] == pVert;
}


/**
 * retval = the other vertex than the inputted one
 */
sVert* Other( sVert* pVert )
{
    return (m_v[0] == pVert) ? m_v[1] : m_v[0];
}

void Init( sVert* v0, sVert* v1 )
{
    m_v[0] = v0;
    m_v[1] = v1;

    /**
     * Note that the edge notifies both of its vertices that it's
     * connected to them.
     */
    m_v[0]->AddEdge( this );
    m_v[1]->AddEdge( this );
}

/**
 * This function takes into consideration the two triangles that
 * share this edge.  It returns the third vertex of the first
 * triangle it finds that is not equal to 'notThisOne'.  So if
 * want one, notThisOne is passed as NULL.  If we want the other
 * one, we pass the result of the first execution.
 */
sVert* GetOtherVert( sVert* v0, sVert* v1, sVert* notThisOne )
{
    sTriangle* pTri;
    for( int i=0; i<v0->m_triList.size(); i++ )
    {
        pTri = v0->m_triList[i];
        if( pTri->Contains( v0 ) && pTri->Contains( v1 ) )
        {
            if( pTri->Other( v0, v1 ) != notThisOne )
                return pTri->Other( v0, v1 );
        }
    }
    // when we support boundary edges, we shouldn't assert
    assert(false);
    return NULL;
```

```
        }

        /**
         * Calculate the K-Vertex location of 'prim' vertex.  For triangles
         * of valence !=6
         */
        point3 CalcKVert( int prim, int sec );

        /**
         * Calculate the location of the subdivided point using the
         * butterfly method.
         * for edges with both vertices of valence == 6
         */
        point3 CalcButterfly();
    };

/**
 * Subdivision surface triangle
 */
struct sTriangle
{
    /**
     * The three vertices of this triangle
     */
    sVert*  m_v[3];
    point3  m_normal;

    void Init( sVert* v0, sVert* v1, sVert* v2 )
    {
        m_v[0] = v0;
        m_v[1] = v1;
        m_v[2] = v2;

        /**
         * Note that the triangle notifies all 3 of its vertices
         * that it's connected to them.
         */
        m_v[0]->AddTri( this );
        m_v[1]->AddTri( this );
        m_v[2]->AddTri( this );
    }

    /**
     * true == the triangle contains the inputted vertex
     */
    bool Contains( sVert* pVert )
    {
        return pVert == m_v[0] || pVert == m_v[1] || pVert == m_v[2];
    }
```

```
/**
 * retval = the third vertex (first and second are inputted).
 * asserts out if inputted values aren't part of the triangle
 */
sVert* Other( sVert* v1, sVert* v2 )
{
    assert( Contains( v1 ) && Contains( v2 ) );
    for( int i=0; i<3; i++ )
    {
        if( m_v[i] != v1 && m_v[i] != v2 )
            return m_v[i];
    }
    assert(false); // something bad happened;
    return NULL;
}
};
```

The interesting part of the application is when the model is subdivided. Since we use vertex buffers to hold the subdivided data, we have an upper bound of 2^{16}, or 65,536, vertices. Listing 7.9 gives the code that gets called when the user subdivides the model.

Listing 7.9: The code to handle subdivision

```
result cSubDivSurf::Subdivide()
{
    /**
     * We know how many components our subdivided model will have,
     * calc them
     */
    int nNewEdges = 2*m_nEdges + 3*m_nTris;
    int nNewVerts = m_nVerts + m_nEdges;
    int nNewTris = 4*m_nTris;

    /**
     * If the model will have too many triangles
     * (d3d can only handle 2^16), return
     */
    if( nNewVerts >= 65536 )
    {
        return res_False;
    }

    /**
     * Find the location of the new vertices.  Most of the hard work
     * is done here.
     */
    GenNewVertLocs();
```

```
    int i;

    // the vertices on the 3 edges (order: 0..1, 1..2, 2..0)
    sVert* inner[3];

    // Allocate space for the subdivided data
    sVert* pNewVerts = new sVert[ nNewVerts ];
    sEdge* pNewEdges = new sEdge[ nNewEdges ];
    sTriangle* pNewTris = new sTriangle[ nNewTris ];

    //=================------------------------
    Step 1: Fill vertex list

    // First batch - the original vertices
    for( i=0; i<m_nVerts; i++ )
    {
        pNewVerts[i].m_index = i;
        pNewVerts[i].m_vert = m_pVList[i].m_vert;
    }
    // Second batch - vertices from each edge
    for( i=0; i<m_nEdges; i++ )
    {
        pNewVerts[m_nVerts + i].m_index = m_nVerts + i;
        pNewVerts[m_nVerts + i].m_vert = m_pEList[i].m_newVLoc.m_vert;
    }

    //=================------------------------
    Step 2: Fill edge list

    int currEdge = 0;
    // First batch - the 2 edges that are spawned by each original edge
    for( i=0; i<m_nEdges; i++ )
    {
        pNewEdges[currEdge++].Init(
            &pNewVerts[m_pEList[i].m_v[0]->m_index],
            &pNewVerts[m_pEList[i].m_newVLoc.m_index] );
        pNewEdges[currEdge++].Init(
            &pNewVerts[m_pEList[i].m_v[1]->m_index],
            &pNewVerts[m_pEList[i].m_newVLoc.m_index] );
    }
    // Second batch - the 3 inner edges spawned by each original tri
    for( i=0; i<m_nTris; i++ )
    {
        // find the inner 3 vertices of this triangle
        // ( the new vertex of each of the triangles' edges )
        inner[0] = &m_pTList[i].m_v[0]->GetEdge(
            m_pTList[i].m_v[1] )->m_newVLoc;
        inner[1] = &m_pTList[i].m_v[1]->GetEdge(
            m_pTList[i].m_v[2] )->m_newVLoc;
        inner[2] = &m_pTList[i].m_v[2]->GetEdge(
```

```
                         m_pTList[i].m_v[0] )->m_newVLoc;

          pNewEdges[currEdge++].Init(
              &pNewVerts[inner[0]->m_index],
              &pNewVerts[inner[1]->m_index] );
          pNewEdges[currEdge++].Init(
              &pNewVerts[inner[1]->m_index],
              &pNewVerts[inner[2]->m_index] );
          pNewEdges[currEdge++].Init(
              &pNewVerts[inner[2]->m_index],
              &pNewVerts[inner[0]->m_index] );
     }



     //=================================--------------
     Step 3: Fill triangle list

     int currTri = 0;
     for( i=0; i<m_nTris; i++ )
     {
          // find the inner vertices
          inner[0] = &m_pTList[i].m_v[0]->GetEdge(
              m_pTList[i].m_v[1] )->m_newVLoc;
          inner[1] = &m_pTList[i].m_v[1]->GetEdge(
              m_pTList[i].m_v[2] )->m_newVLoc;
          inner[2] = &m_pTList[i].m_v[2]->GetEdge(
              m_pTList[i].m_v[0] )->m_newVLoc;

          // 0, inner0, inner2
          pNewTris[currTri++].Init(
              &pNewVerts[m_pTList[i].m_v[0]->m_index],
              &pNewVerts[inner[0]->m_index],
              &pNewVerts[inner[2]->m_index] );

          // 1, inner1, inner0
          pNewTris[currTri++].Init(
              &pNewVerts[m_pTList[i].m_v[1]->m_index],
              &pNewVerts[inner[1]->m_index],
              &pNewVerts[inner[0]->m_index] );

          // 2, inner2, inner1
          pNewTris[currTri++].Init(
              &pNewVerts[m_pTList[i].m_v[2]->m_index],
              &pNewVerts[inner[2]->m_index],
              &pNewVerts[inner[1]->m_index] );

          // inner0, inner1, inner2
          pNewTris[currTri++].Init(
              &pNewVerts[inner[0]->m_index],
              &pNewVerts[inner[1]->m_index],
              &pNewVerts[inner[2]->m_index] );
```

```
        }

        //=======-----------------------------
        Step 4: Housekeeping

        // Swap out the old data sets for the new ones.

        delete [] m_pVList;
        delete [] m_pEList;
        delete [] m_pTList;

        m_nVerts = nNewVerts;
        m_nEdges = nNewEdges;
        m_nTris = nNewTris;

        m_pVList = pNewVerts;
        m_pEList = pNewEdges;
        m_pTList = pNewTris;

        // Calculate the vertex normals of the new mesh
        // using face normal averaging
        CalcNormals();

        //=======-----------------------------
        Step 5: Make arrays so we can send the triangles in one batch

        delete [] m_d3dTriList;
        if( m_pVertexBuffer )
            m_pVertexBuffer->Release();
        m_pVertexBuffer = NULL;

        GenD3DData();

        return res_AllGood;
    }


/**
 * This is where the meat of the subdivision work is done.
 * Depending on the valence of the two endpoints of each edge,
 * the code will generate the new edge value
 */
void cSubDivSurf::GenNewVertLocs()
{
    for( int i=0; i<m_nEdges; i++ )
    {
        int val0 = m_pEList[i].m_v[0]->Valence();
        int val1 = m_pEList[i].m_v[1]->Valence();

        point3 loc;
```

```
        /**
         * CASE 1: both vertices are of valence == 6
         * Use the butterfly scheme
         */
        if( val0 == 6 && val1 == 6 )
        {
            loc = m_pEList[i].CalcButterfly();
        }

        /**
         * CASE 2: one of the vertices are of valence == 6
         * Calculate the k-vertex for the non-6 vertex
         */
        else if( val0 == 6 && val1 != 6 )
        {
            loc = m_pEList[i].CalcKVert(1,0);
        }

        else if( val0 != 6 && val1 == 6 )
        {
            loc = m_pEList[i].CalcKVert(0,1);
        }

        /**
         * CASE 3: neither of the vertices are of valence == 6
         * Calculate the k-vertex for each of them, and average
         * the result
         */
        else
        {
            loc = ( m_pEList[i].CalcKVert(1,0) +
                    m_pEList[i].CalcKVert(0,1) ) / 2.f;
        }

        m_pEList[i].m_newVLoc.m_vert = sVertex(
            loc , point3::Zero );

        /**
         * Assign the new vertex an index (this is useful later,
         * when we start throwing vertex pointers around.  We
         * could have implemented everything with indices, but
         * the code would be much harder to read.  An extra dword
         * per vertex is a small price to pay.)
         */
        m_pEList[i].m_newVLoc.m_index = i + m_nVerts;
    }
}


point3 cSubDivSurf::sEdge::CalcButterfly()
{
```

```
        point3 out = point3::Zero;

        sVert* other[2];
        other[0] = GetOtherVert( m_v[0], m_v[1], NULL );
        other[1] = GetOtherVert( m_v[0], m_v[1], other[0] );

        // two main ones
        out += (1.f/2.f) * m_v[0]->m_vert.loc;
        out += (1.f/2.f) * m_v[1]->m_vert.loc;

        // top/bottom ones
        out += (1.f/8.f) * other[0]->m_vert.loc;
        out += (1.f/8.f) * other[1]->m_vert.loc;

        // outside 4 verts
        out += (-1.f/16.f) *
            GetOtherVert( other[0], m_v[0], m_v[1] )->m_vert.loc;
        out += (-1.f/16.f) *
            GetOtherVert( other[0], m_v[1], m_v[0] )->m_vert.loc;
        out += (-1.f/16.f) *
            GetOtherVert( other[1], m_v[0], m_v[1] )->m_vert.loc;
        out += (-1.f/16.f) *
            GetOtherVert( other[1], m_v[1], m_v[0] )->m_vert.loc;

        return out;
}

point3 cSubDivSurf::sEdge::CalcKVert(int prim, int sec)
{
    int valence = m_v[prim]->Valence();

    point3 out = point3::Zero;

    out += (3.f / 4.f) * m_v[prim]->m_vert.loc;

    if( valence < 3 )
        assert( false );

    else if( valence == 3 )
    {
        for( int i=0; i<m_v[prim]->m_edgeList.size(); i++ )
        {
            sVert* pOther =
                m_v[prim]->m_edgeList[i]->Other( m_v[prim] );
            if( pOther == m_v[sec] )
                out += (5.f/12.f) * pOther->m_vert.loc;
            else
                out += (-1.f/12.f) * pOther->m_vert.loc;
        }
    }
```

```
        else if( valence == 4 )
        {
            out += (3.f/8.f) * m_v[sec]->m_vert.loc;

            sVert* pTemp = GetOtherVert( m_v[0], m_v[1], NULL );
            // get the one after it
            sVert* pOther = GetOtherVert( m_v[prim], pTemp, m_v[sec] );

            out += (-1.f/8.f) * pOther->m_vert.loc;
        }

        else // valence >= 5
        {
            sVert* pCurr = m_v[sec];
            sVert* pLast = NULL;
            sVert* pTemp;
            for( int i=0; i< valence; i++ )
            {
                float weight =
                    ((1.f/4.f) +
                    (float)cos( 2 * PI * (float)i / (float)valence ) +
                    (1.f/2.f) * (float)cos(4*PI*(float)i/(float)valence))
                    / (float)valence;

                out += weight * pCurr->m_vert.loc;

                pTemp = GetOtherVert( m_v[prim], pCurr, pLast );
                pLast = pCurr;
                pCurr = pTemp;
            }
        }
    }
    return out;
}

void cSubDivSurf::GenD3DData()
{
    /**
     * Create a vertex buffer
     */
    D3DVERTEXBUFFERDESC vbdesc;
    ZeroMemory(&vbdesc, sizeof(D3DVERTEXBUFFERDESC));
    vbdesc.dwSize= sizeof(D3DVERTEXBUFFERDESC);
    vbdesc.dwCaps        = 0L;
    vbdesc.dwFVF         = D3DFVF_VERTEX;
    vbdesc.dwNumVertices = m_nVerts;

    // If this isn't a TnLHal device, make sure the
    // vertex buffer uses system memory.
    if( IsEqualIID(
        Graphics()->GetDesc().deviceGUID,
        IID_IDirect3DTnLHalDevice ) )
```

```
    {
        vbdesc.dwCaps |= DDSCAPS_VIDEOMEMORY;
    }
    else
    {
        vbdesc.dwCaps |= DDSCAPS_SYSTEMMEMORY;
    }

    // Create a clipping-capable vertex buffer.
    HRESULT hr;
    hr = Graphics()->GetD3D()->CreateVertexBuffer(
        &vbdesc,
        &m_pVertexBuffer,
        NULL);
    if( FAILED( hr ))
    {
        throw cGameError("Vertex Buffer creation failed!\n");
    }

    m_d3dTriList = new sTri[ m_nTris ];

    sVertex* pVert;
    hr = m_pVertexBuffer->Lock(
        DDLOCK_WRITEONLY,
        (void**)&pVert,
        NULL );
    if( FAILED( hr ))
    {
        throw cGameError("VB Lock failed\n");
    }

    int i;

    for( i=0; i<m_nVerts; i++ )
    {
        *pVert++ = m_pVList[i].m_vert;
    }
    m_pVertexBuffer->Unlock();
    m_pVertexBuffer->Optimize( Graphics()->GetDevice(),0 );
    for( i=0; i<m_nTris; i++ )
    {
        m_d3dTriList[i].v[0] = m_pTList[i].m_v[0]->m_index;
        m_d3dTriList[i].v[1] = m_pTList[i].m_v[1]->m_index;
        m_d3dTriList[i].v[2] = m_pTList[i].m_v[2]->m_index;
    }
}
```

Progressive Meshes

The final multiresolution system we are going to discuss is progressive meshes. They're rapidly gaining favor in the game community; many games use them as a way to keep scene detail at a constant level.

Oftentimes when we're playing a 3-D game, many of our objects will appear off in the distance. For example, if we're building a combat flight simulator, bogies will appear miles away before we engage them. When an object is this far away, it will appear to be only a few pixels on the screen.

We could simply opt not to draw an object if it is this far away. However, this can lead to a discontinuity of experience for the user. He or she will suddenly remember they're playing a video game, and that should be avoided at all costs. If we have a model with thousands of triangles in it to represent our enemy aircraft, we're going to waste a lot of time transforming and lighting vertices when we'll end up with just a blob of a few pixels. Drawing several incoming bogie blobs may max out our triangle budget for the frame, and our frame rate will drop. This will hurt the user experience just as much if not more than not drawing the object in the first place.

Even when the object is moderately close, if most of the triangles are smaller than one pixel big, we're wasting effort on drawing our models. If we used, instead, a lower resolution version of the mesh to use at farther distances, the visual output would be about the same, but we would save a lot of time in model processing.

This is the problem progressive meshes try to solve. They allow us to arbitrarily scale the polygon resolution of a mesh from its max all the way down to two triangles. When our model is extremely far away, we draw the lowest resolution model we can. Then, as it approaches the camera, we slowly add detail polygon by polygon, so the user always will be seeing a nearly ideal image at a much faster frame rate. Moving between detail levels on a triangle-by-triangle basis is much less noticeable than switching between a handful of models at different resolutions. We can even morph our triangle-by-triangle transitions using what are called geomorphs, making them even less noticeable.

Progressive meshes can also help us when we have multiple close objects on the screen. If we used just the distance criterion discussed above to set polygon resolution, we could easily have the case where there are multiple dense objects close to the camera. We would have to draw them all at a high resolution, and we would hit our polygon budget and our frame rate would drop out. In this extreme situation, we can suffer some visual quality loss and turn down the polygon count of our objects. In general, when a user is playing an intense game, he or she won't notice that the meshes are lower resolution. Users will, however, immediately notice a frame rate reduction.

One thing progressive meshes can't do is add detail to a model. Unlike the other two multiresolution surface methods we have discussed, progressive meshes can only vary the detail in a model from its original polygon count down to two polygons.

Progressive meshes were originally described in a 1996 SIGGRAPH paper by Hugues Hoppe (see "References" at the end of the chapter). Since then a lot of neat things have happened with them. Hoppe has applied them to view-dependent level-of-detail and terrain rendering. They were added to Direct3D Retained Mode. Recently, Hoppe extended research done by Michael Garland and Paul Heckbert, using quadric error metrics to encode normal, color, and texture information. We'll be covering some of the basics of quadric error metrics, and Hoppe's web site has downloadable versions of all his papers. The URL is listed at the end of the chapter.

Progressive Mesh Basics

How do progressive meshes work? They center around an operation called an *edge collapse*. Conceptually, it takes two vertices that share an edge and merges them. This destroys the edge that was shared and the two triangles that shared the edge.

The cool thing about edge collapse is that it only affects a small neighborhood of vertices, edges, and triangles. We can save the state of those entities in a way that we can reverse the effect of the edge collapse, splitting a vertex into two, adding an edge, and adding two triangles. This operation, the inverse of the edge collapse, is called a *vertex split*. Figure 7.29 shows how the edge collapse and vertex split work.

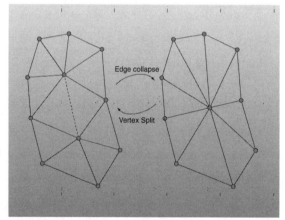

Figure 7.29:
The edge collapse and vertex split operations

To construct a progressive mesh, we take our initial mesh and iteratively remove edges using edge collapses. Each time we remove an edge, the model loses two triangles. We then save the edge collapse we performed into a stack, and continue with the new model. Eventually, we reach a point where we can no longer remove any edges. At this point we have our lowest resolution mesh and a stack of structures representing each edge that was collapsed. If we want to have a particular number of triangles for our model, all we do is apply vertex splits or edge collapses to get to the required number (plus or minus one, though, since we can only change the count by two).

During run time, most systems have three main areas of data: a stack of edge collapses, a stack of vertex splits, and the model. To apply a vertex split, we pop one off the stack, perform the requisite operations on the mesh, construct an edge collapse to invert the process, and push the newly created edge collapse onto the edge collapse stack. The reverse process applies to edge collapses.

There are a lot of cool side effects that arise from progressive meshes. For starters, they can be stored on disk efficiently. If an application is smart about how it represents vertex splits, storing the lowest resolution mesh and the sequence of vertex splits to bring it back to the highest resolution model doesn't take much more space than storing the high-resolution mesh on its lonesome.

Also, the entire mesh doesn't need to be loaded all at once. A game could load the first 400 or so triangles of each model at startup and then load more vertex splits as needed. This can save some time if the game is being loaded from disk, and a lot of time if the game is being loaded over the Internet.

Another thing to consider is that since the edge collapses happen in such a small region, many of them can be combined together, getting quick jumps from one resolution to another. Each edge collapse/vertex split can even be morphed, smoothly moving the vertices together or apart. This alleviates some of the popping effects that can occur when progressive meshes are used without any morphing. Hoppe calls these transitions *geomorphs*.

Choosing Our Edges

The secret to making a good progressive mesh is choosing the right edge to collapse during each iteration. The sequence is extremely important. If we choose our edges unwisely, our low-resolution mesh won't look anything like our high-resolution mesh.

As an extreme example, imagine we chose our edges completely at random. This can have extremely adverse effects on the way our model looks even after a few edge collapses.

> **Warning:** Obviously, we should not choose vertices completely at random. We have to take other factors into account when choosing an edge. Specifically, we have to maintain the topology of a model. We shouldn't select edges that will cause seams in our mesh (places where more than two triangles meet an edge).

Another naïve method of selecting edges would be to choose the shortest edge at each point in time. This uses the well-founded idea that smaller edges won't be as visible to the user from faraway distances, so they should be destroyed first. However, this method overlooks an important factor that must be considered in our final selection algorithm. Specifically, small details, such as the nose of a human face or the horns of a cow, must be preserved as long as possible if a good low-polygon representation of the model is to be created. We must not only take into account the length of the edge, but also how much the model will change if we remove it. Ideally, we want to pick the edge that changes the visual look of the model the least. Since this is a very fuzzy heuristic, we end up approximating it.

The opposite extreme would be to rigorously try to approximate the least-visual-change heuristic, and spend an awfully long time doing it. While this will give us the best visual model, it is less than ideal. If we can spend something like 5 percent of the processing time and get a model that looks 95 percent as good as an ultra-slow ideal method, we should use that one. We'll discuss two different edge selection algorithms.

Stan Melax's Edge Selection Algorithm

Stan Melax wrote an article for *Game Developer* magazine back in November 1998 which detailed a simple and fast cost function to compute the relative cost of contracting a vertex **v** into a vertex **u**. Since they are different operations, cost(**u**,**v**) will generally be different than cost(**v**,**u**). The alorithm's only shortcoming lies in the fact that it can only collapse one vertex onto another; it cannot take an edge and reposition the final vertex in a location to minimize the total error (as quadric error metrics can do). The cost function is:

$$\text{cost}(\mathbf{u}, \mathbf{v}) = \|\mathbf{u} - \mathbf{v}\| \times \max_{f \in Tu} \left(\min_{n \in Tuv} \left\{ (1 - f.normal \bullet n.normal) \div 2 \right\} \right)$$

where *Tu* is the set of triangles that share vertex **u**, and *Tuv* is the set of triangles that share both vertex **u** and **v**.

Quadric Error Metrics

Michael Garland and Paul Heckbert devised an edge selection algorithm in 1997 that was based on quadric error metrics (see "References" at the end of the chapter). The algorithm is not only extremely fast, its output looks very nice. I don't have the space to explain all the math needed to get this algorithm working (specifically, generic matrix inversion code), but we can go over enough to get your feet wet.

Given a particular vertex **v** and a new vertex **v'**, we want to be able to find out how much error would be introduced into the model by replacing **v** with **v'**. If we think of each vertex as being the intersection point of several planes (in particular, the planes belonging to the set of triangles that share the vertex), then we can define the error as how far the new vertex is from each plane.

This algorithm uses the squared distance. This way we can define an error function for a vertex **v** given the set of planes **p** that share the vertex as:

$$\Delta(\mathbf{v}) = \sum_{\mathbf{p} \in planes(\mathbf{v})} (\mathbf{p}^T \mathbf{v})^2$$

$$\Delta(\mathbf{v}) = \sum_{\mathbf{p} \in planes(\mathbf{v})} (\mathbf{v}^T \mathbf{p})(\mathbf{p}^T \mathbf{v})$$

$$\Delta(\mathbf{v}) = \sum_{\mathbf{p} \in planes(\mathbf{v})} \mathbf{v}^T (\mathbf{p} \mathbf{p}^T) \mathbf{v}$$

$$\Delta(\mathbf{v}) = \mathbf{v}^T \left(\sum_{\mathbf{p} \in planes(\mathbf{v})} \mathbf{K_p} \right) \mathbf{v}$$

The matrix $\mathbf{K_p}$ represents the coefficients of the plane equation $<a, b, c, d>$ for a particular plane $\mathbf{p}$ multiplied with its transpose to form a 4x4 matrix. Expanded, the multiplication becomes:

$$\mathbf{K_p} = \begin{bmatrix} a^2 & ba & ca & da \\ ab & b^2 & cb & db \\ ac & bc & c^2 & dc \\ ad & bd & cd & d^2 \end{bmatrix}$$

$\mathbf{K_p}$ is used to find the squared distance error of a vertex to the plane it represents. We sum the matrices for each plane to form the matrix $\mathbf{Q}$:

$$\mathbf{Q} = \sum_{\mathbf{p} \in planes(\mathbf{v})} \mathbf{K_p}$$

which makes the error equation:

$$\Delta(\mathbf{v}) = \mathbf{v}^T \mathbf{Q} \mathbf{v}$$

Given the matrix $\mathbf{Q}$ for each of the vertices in the model, we can find the error for taking out any particular edge in the model. Given an edge between two vertices $\mathbf{v}_1$ and $\mathbf{v}_2$, we find the ideal vertex $\mathbf{v}'$ by minimizing the function:

$$\mathbf{v}'^T (\mathbf{Q}_1 + \mathbf{Q}_2) \mathbf{v}'$$

where $\mathbf{Q}_1$ and $\mathbf{Q}_2$ are the $\mathbf{Q}$ matrices for $\mathbf{v}_1$ and $\mathbf{v}_2$.

Finding $\mathbf{v}'$ is the hard part of this algorithm. If we want to try and solve it exactly, we just want to solve the equation:

$$\begin{bmatrix} q_{11} & q_{12} & q_{13} & q_{14} \\ q_{21} & q_{22} & q_{23} & q_{24} \\ q_{31} & q_{32} & q_{33} & q_{34} \\ 0 & 0 & 0 & 1 \end{bmatrix} \mathbf{v'} = \begin{bmatrix} 0 \\ 0 \\ 0 \\ 1 \end{bmatrix}$$

where the 4x4 matrix above is $(\mathbf{Q_1}+\mathbf{Q_2})$ with the bottom row changed around. If the matrix above is invertible, then the ideal $\mathbf{v'}$ (the one that has zero error) is just:

$$\mathbf{v'} = \begin{bmatrix} q_{11} & q_{12} & q_{13} & q_{14} \\ q_{21} & q_{22} & q_{23} & q_{24} \\ q_{31} & q_{32} & q_{33} & q_{34} \\ 0 & 0 & 0 & 1 \end{bmatrix}^{-1} \begin{bmatrix} 0 \\ 0 \\ 0 \\ 1 \end{bmatrix}$$

If the matrix isn't invertible, then the easiest thing to do, short of solving the minimization problem, would be to just choose the vertex causing the least error out of the set $(\mathbf{v_1}, \mathbf{v_2}, (\mathbf{v_1}+\mathbf{v_2})/2)$. Finding out if the matrix is invertible, and inverting it, is the ugly part that I don't have space to explain fully. It isn't a terribly hard problem, given a solid background in linear algebra. A good text-book on linear algebra is listed at the end of the chapter in the "For Further Reading" section.

We compute the ideal vertex (the one that minimizes the error caused by contracting an edge) and store the error associated with that ideal vertex (since it may not be zero). When we've done this for each of the edges, the best edge to remove is the one with the least amount of error. After we collapse the cheapest edge, we re-compute the $\mathbf{Q}$ matrices and the ideal vertices for each of the vertices in the immediate neighborhood of the removed edge (since the planes have changed) and continue.

Implementing a Progressive Mesh Renderer

Due to space and time constraints, code to implement progressive meshes is not included in this text. That shouldn't scare you off, however; they're not too hard to implement. The only real trick is making them efficient.

How you implement progressive meshes depends on whether you calculate the mesh as a pre-processing step or at run time. A lot of extra information needs to be kept around during the mesh construction to make it even moderately efficient, so it might be best to write two applications. The first one would take an object, build a progressive mesh out of it, and write the progressive mesh to disk. A separate application would actually load the progressive mesh off the disk and display it. This would have a lot of advantages, most notably you could make both algorithms (construction and display) efficient in their own ways without having to make them sacrifice things for each other.

To implement a progressive mesh constructor efficiently, you'll most likely want something along the lines of the code used in the subdivision surface renderer, where each vertex knows about all the vertices around it. As edges were removed, the adjacency information would be updated to reflect the new topology of the model. This way it would be easy to find the set of vertices and triangles that would be modified when an edge is removed.

Storing the vertex splits and edge collapses can be done in several ways. One way would be to make a structure like the one in Listing 7.10.

Listing 7.10: Sample edge collapse structure

```
// can double as sVSplit
struct sECol
{
    // the 2 former locations of the vertices
    point3  locs[2];

    // where the collapsed vertex goes.
    point3  newLoc;

    // Indices of the two vertices
    int verts[2];

    // Indices of the two triangles
    int tris[2];

    // The indices of triangles that need to
    // have vertex indices swapped
    vector<int> modTris;
};
```

When it came time to perform a vertex split, you would perform the following steps:

■ Activate (via an active flag) verts[1], tris[0], and tris[1] (verts[0] is the collapsed vertex, so it's already active).

■ Move verts[0] and verts[1] to locs[0] and locs[1].

■ For each of the triangles in modTris, change any indices that point to verts[0] and change them to verts[1]. You can think of the modTris as being the set of triangles below the collapsed triangles in Figure 7.29.

Performing an edge collapse would be a similar process, just reversing everything.

Radiosity

The lighting system that Direct3D implements, the one that most of the real-time graphics community uses, is rather clunky. It's just an effort to get something that looks right, something that can pass for correct. In actuality, it isn't correct at all, and under certain conditions this can become painfully obvious. We're going to discuss a way to do lighting that is much more correct, but only handles diffuse light: radiosity lighting.

The wave/particle duality aside, light acts much like any other type of energy. It leaves a source in a particular direction; as it hits objects some of the energy is absorbed, and some is reflected back into the scene. The direction it reflects back on depends on the microscopic structure of the surface. Surfaces that appear smooth at a macroscopic level, like chalk, actually have a really rough microstructure when seen under a microscope.

The light that leaves an object may bounce off of a thousand other points in the scene before it eventually reaches our eye. In fact, only a tiny amount (generally less than a tenth of one percent) of all the energy that leaves a light ever reaches our eye. Because of this the light that reflects off of other objects affects the total lighting of the scene.

An example: When you're watching a movie at a movie theater, there is generally only one light in the scene (sans exit lights, aisle lights, etc.), and that is the movie projector. The only object that directly receives light from the movie projector is the movie screen. However, that is not the only object that receives any light. If you've ever gotten up to get popcorn, you're able to see everyone in the theater watching the movie, because light is bouncing off the screen, bouncing off of their faces, and bouncing into your eyes. The problem with the lighting models we've discussed so far is that they can't handle this. Sure, we could just turn up the ambient color to simulate the light reflecting off the screen into the theater, but that won't work; since we only want the front sides of people to be lit, it will look horridly wrong.

What we would like is to simulate the real world, and find not only the light that is emitted from light sources that hits surfaces, but also find the light that is emitted from other surfaces. We want to find the interreflection of light in our 3-D scene.

This is both good and bad (but not ugly, thankfully). The good is, the light in our scene will behave more like light we see in the real world. Light will bounce off of all the surfaces in our scene. Modeling this interreflection will give us an extremely slick-looking scene. The bad thing is, the math suddenly becomes much harder, because now all of our surfaces are interrelated. The lighting calculation must be done as a pre-calculating step, since it's far too expensive to do in real time. We save the radiosity results into the data file we use to represent geometry on disk, so any program using the data can take advantage of the time spent calculating the radiosity solution.

Aside: Radiosity isn't for everyone. While *Quake II* used it to great effect to light the worlds, *Quake III* did not. The motivation behind not using it for *Quake III* lies partially in the fact that computing the correct radiosity solution for Bezier surfaces is a bear, and radiosity doesn't give shadows as sharp as non-interreflective lighting schemes. *Quake* had a very certain look and feel because of how its shadows worked. *Quake III* went back to that.

Radiosity Foundations

We'll begin our discussion of radiosity with some basic terms that we'll use in the rest of the equations:

Table 7.1: Some basic terms used in radiosity

Radiance (or intensity)	The light (or power) coming into (or out of) an area in a given direction.
	Units: power / (area x solid angle)
Radiosity	The light leaving an area. This value can be thought of as color leaving a surface.
	Units: power / area
Radiant emitted flux density	The unit for light emission. This value can be thought of as the initial color of a surface.
	Units: power / area

Our initial scene is composed of a set of closed polygons. We subdivide our polygons into a grid of *patches*. A patch is a discrete element with a computable surface area whose radiosity (and color) remains constant across the whole surface.

The amount we subdivide our polygons decides how intricately our polygon can be lit. You can imagine the worst case of a diagonal shadow falling on a surface. If we don't subdivide enough, we'll be able to see a stepping pattern at the borders between intensity levels. Another way to think of this is drawing a scene in 320x200 versus 1600x1200. The more resolution we add, the better the output picture looks. However, the more patches we add, the more patches we need to work with, which makes our algorithm considerably slower.

Radiosity doesn't use traditional lights (like point lights or spotlights). Instead, certain patches actually emit energy (light) into the scene. This could be why a lot of the radiosity images seen in books like Foley's are offices lit by fluorescent ceiling panel lights (which are quite easy to approximate with a polygon).

Let's consider a particular patch *i* in our scene. We want to find the radiosity leaving our surface (this can be a source of confusion: Radiosity is both an algorithm and a unit!). Essentially, the radiosity leaving our surface is the color of the surface when we end up drawing it. For example, the more red energy leaving the surface, the more red light will enter our virtual eye looking at the surface, making the surface appear more red. For all of the following equations, power is equivalent to light.

$$\begin{pmatrix} \text{outgoing} \\ \text{power of} \\ \text{element } i \end{pmatrix} = \begin{pmatrix} \text{power} \\ \text{emitted by} \\ \text{element } i \end{pmatrix} + \begin{pmatrix} \text{power} \\ \text{reflected by} \\ \text{element } i \end{pmatrix}$$

We know how much power each of our surfaces emit. All the surfaces we want to use as lights emit some light; the rest of the surfaces don't emit any. All we need to know is how much is reflected by a surface. This ends up being the amount of energy the surface receives from the other surfaces, multiplied by the reflectance of the surface. Expanding the right side gives:

$$\begin{pmatrix} \text{outgoing} \\ \text{power of} \\ \text{elem. i} \end{pmatrix} = \begin{pmatrix} \text{power} \\ \text{emitted by} \\ \text{elem. i} \end{pmatrix} + \begin{pmatrix} \text{reflectance} \\ \text{of elem. i} \end{pmatrix} \times \sum_{\forall j \neq i} \begin{pmatrix} \text{outgoing} \\ \text{power} \\ \text{of elem. j} \end{pmatrix} \times \begin{pmatrix} \text{fraction of power} \\ \text{leaving elem. j that} \\ \text{arrives at elem. i} \end{pmatrix}$$

So this equation says that the energy reflected by element *i* is equal to the incoming energy times a reflectance term that says how much of the incoming energy is reflected back into the scene. To find the energy incoming to our surface, we take every other surface *j* in our scene, find out how much of the outgoing power of *j* hits *i*, and sum all of the energy terms together. You may have noticed that in order to find the outgoing power of element *i* we need the outgoing power of element *j*, and in order to find the outgoing power of element *j* we need the outgoing power of element *i*. We'll cover this soon.

Let's define some variables to represent the terms above and flesh out a mathematical equation:

Table 7.2: Variables for our radiosity equations

A_i	Area of patch *i*. (This is pretty easy to compute for quads.)
e_i	Radiant emitted flux density of patch *i*. (We are given this. Our luminous surfaces get to emit light of a certain color.)
r_i	Reflectance of patch *i*. (We're given this too. It's how much the patch reflects each color component. Essentially, this is the color of the patch when seen under bright white light.)
b_i	Radiosity of patch *i*. (This is what we want to find.)
$F_{j\text{-}i}$	Form factor from patch *j* to patch *i* (the fraction of the total radiosity leaving *j* that directly hits *i*, which we will compute later).

So if we simply rewrite the equation we have above with our defined variables we get the following radiosity equation:

$$b_i = e_i + \rho_i \sum_{j=1}^{n} b_j F_{j-i} \frac{A_j}{A_i}$$

We're going to go into the computation of the form factor later. For right now we'll just present a particular trait of the form factor called the Reciprocity Law:

$$A_i F_{ij} = A_j F_{ji}$$

This states that the form factors between sub-patches are related to the areas of each of the sub-patches. With this law we can simplify and rearrange our equation to get the following:

$$b_i = e_i + \rho_i \sum_{j=1}^{n} b_j F_{i-j} \qquad b_i - \rho_i \sum_{j=1}^{n} b_j F_{i-j} = e_i$$

By now you've probably noticed an icky problem: To find the radiosity of some surface *i* we need to know the radiosity of all of the other surfaces, presenting a circular dependency. To get around this we need to solve all of the radiosity equations simultaneously.

The way this is generally done is to take all *n* patches in our scene and compose a humongous *n* x *n* matrix, turning all of the equations above into one matrix equation.

$$\begin{bmatrix} 1-\rho_1 F_{1-1} & -\rho_1 F_{1-2} & \cdots & -\rho_1 F_{1-n} \\ -\rho_2 F_{2-1} & 1-\rho_2 F_{2-2} & \cdots & -\rho_2 F_{2-n} \\ \vdots & \vdots & \ddots & \vdots \\ -\rho_n F_{n-1} & -\rho_n F_{n-2} & \cdots & 1-\rho_n F_{n-n} \end{bmatrix} \begin{bmatrix} b_1 \\ b_2 \\ \vdots \\ b_n \end{bmatrix} = \begin{bmatrix} e_1 \\ e_2 \\ \vdots \\ e_n \end{bmatrix}$$

I could try to explain how to solve this monstrosity, but hopefully we're all getting the idea that this is the wrong way to go. Getting a good radiosity solution can require several thousand patches for even simple scenes, which will cost us tens of megabytes of memory for the *n* x *n* matrix, and forget about the processing cost of trying to solve said multi-megabyte matrix equation.

Unless we can figure out some way around this, we're up a creek. Luckily, there is a way around. In most situations, a lot of the values in the matrix will be either zero or arbitrarily small. This is called a *sparse* matrix. The amount of outgoing energy for most of these patches is really small, and will only contribute to a small subset of the surfaces. Rather than explicitly solve this large sparse matrix, we can solve it progressively, saving us a ton of memory and a ton of time.

Progressive Radiosity

The big conceptual difference between progressive radiosity and matrix radiosity is that in progressive radiosity we shoot light out from patches, instead of receiving it. Each patch has a value that represents how much energy it has to give out (ΔRadiosity, or deltaRad) that is initially set to how much energy the surface emits. Each iteration, we choose the patch that has the most energy to give out (deltaRad * the area of the patch). We then send its energy out into the scene, finding how much of it hits each surface. We add the incoming energy to the radiosity and deltaRad of each other patch. Finally, we set the deltaRad of our source patch to zero (since, at this point, it has released all of its energy) and repeat. Whenever the patch with the most energy has its energy value below a certain threshhold, we stop.

Here's pseudocode for the algorithm:

Listing 7.11: Pseudocode for the radiosity algorithm

```
For( each patch 'curr' )
    curr.radiosity = curr.emitted
    curr.deltaRad = curr.emitted
while( not done )
    source = patch with max. outgoing energy (deltaRad * area)
    if( source.deltaRad < threshold )
        done = true
    For( each patch 'dest' != source )
        deltaRad = dest.reflectiveness *
                    FormFactor( dest, source )
        dest.radiosity += deltaRad
        dest.deltaRad += deltaRad
    source.deltaRad = 0
    Draw scene (if desired)
```

The Form Factor

The final piece of the puzzle is the calculation of this mysterious form factor. Again, it represents the amount of energy that leaves a sub-patch i that reaches a sub-patch j. The initial equation is not as scary as it looks. The definition of the form factor between two sub-patches i and j is:

$$F_{i-j} = \frac{1}{A_i} \int_{A_i} \int_{A_j} \frac{\cos\theta_i \cos\theta_j}{\pi r^2} v_{i-j} dA_j dA_i$$

Table 7.3 lists the meanings of the variables in this equation.

Table 7.3: Variable meanings for the form factor equation

v_{ij}	Visibility relationship between i and j; 1 if there is a line of sight between the two elements, 0 otherwise.
dA_i, dA_j	Infinitesimally small pieces of the elements i and j.
r	The length of the ray separating i and j.
θ_i and θ_j	The angle between the ray separating i and j and the normals of i and j, respectively (see Figure 7.30).

Figure 7.30 may help you visualize the relationship between some of the variables in the form factor equation.

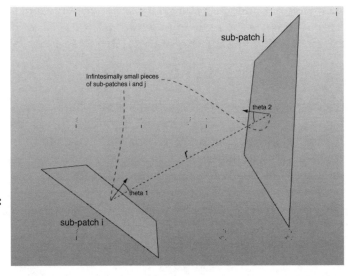

Figure 7.30: The theta and r variables visualized

Maybe you enjoy working with troublesome double integrals. I don't. I look at equations like this, think about having to write code to handle it, and run for the hills. Luckily we can give up a little bit in accuracy and get rid of those nasty integrals.

What do the integrals mean? Essentially, we want to compute the bulk of the equation an infinite amount of times for a set of infinitely small pieces of the patches, and sum them all together. Of course, doing it an infinite amount of times is unreasonable. We can do it enough so that our solution is close enough to what we would get if we had computed the integral properly. We're not even going to do it enough, though; we're just going to do it once.

What is the justification for this? Our patches are generally going to be pretty small, small to the point that the radiosity for each of the sub-patches is going to be pretty much the same. We can't get much variance in the amount of light hitting a surface when the surface is only a few inches square. Of course, there are cases where it could fail, but they most likely won't come up, and if they do that's what we get for approximating.

Instead of computing the form factor equation for a bunch of small sub-patches, we're going to just compute it once for both patches. The delta areas become the regular areas, and we compute the line-of-sight only once, using the centers of the patches. This makes our equation much nicer looking:

$$F_{i-j} = \frac{1}{A_i} \frac{\cos\theta_i \cos\theta_j}{\pi r^2} v_{i-j} A_j A_i$$

$$F_{i-j} = \frac{\cos\theta_i \cos\theta_j}{\pi r^2} v_{i-j} A_j$$

This isn't painful at all. To compute the line-of-sight, we'll just use the BSP tree code we developed in Chapter 3. Testing is quick (anywhere from $O(\lg n)$ to $O(n)$ worst case, where n is the number of polygons), and it's not dependent on the number of patches, just the number of polygons.

Application: Radiosity

With all the pieces in place, we can finally make a stab at implementing a radiosity simulator, which I have taken the liberty of doing. It loads a scene description file off the disk and progressively adds radiosity to the scene. For each frame it processes the brightest patch and then renders it. That way, as the program is running, light slowly fills the room.

The first non-commented line of the file contains the number of polygons. Listing 7.12 shows the header and the first polygon of the provided data file. The first line of the polygon has four floating-point values, the first three of which describe the energy of the surface. Most of the polygons have the energy set to black, but there are three lit polygons in the room to add light to it. The fourth component is the reflectance of the polygon. This should be an RGB triplet as well; making it just a float restricts all the surfaces to be varying shades of gray. After the polygon header there are four lines with three floats each, defining the four corners of the polygon. When the polygon is loaded, it is subdivided into a bunch of sub-patches until their area is below a constant threshold.

Listing 7.12: Sample from the radiosity data file

```
# this is a more complex data set
26
# top of the room, very reflective
0.0 0.0 0.0 0.76    ##
-10.0 10.0 -10.0
10.0 10.0 -10.0
10.0 10.0 -8.0
-10.0 10.0 -8.0
...
```

This code can only correctly deal with square polygons. Adding support for other types of polygons wouldn't be hard, but I didn't want to over-complicate the code for this program. Also, for the sake of simplicity, patches are flat shaded. Computing the right color for the patch corners is harder than you would think. The naïve solution would be to just compute the radiosity equations using the vertices instead of the centers of the patches. The problem occurs at corners. Since the point you're computing is right against the polygon next to it, it won't receive any light, and you'll get an almost black line running around the borders of all your polygons—an unacceptable artifact. There is a nifty algorithm in Foley's *Computer Graphics* in the radiosity section to compute vertex colors from patch colors; implementing it is left as an exercise for the reader.

A screen shot from the radiosity application after it has run its course (it can take a while—five minutes on my Celeron 366) appears in Figure 7.31. Some interesting snippets from the code appear in Listing 7.13.

Figure 7.31: Screen shot from radiosity calculator

Listing 7.13: Snippets from the radiosity calculator

```
bool cRadiosityCalc::LineOfSight( sPatch* a, sPatch* b )
{
    // Early-out 1: they're sitting on the same spot
    if( a->m_plane == b->m_plane )
        return false;
```

```
        // Early-out 2: b is behind a
        if( a->m_plane.TestPoint( b->m_center ) == ptBack )
            return false;

        // Early-out 3: a is behind b
        if( b->m_plane.TestPoint( a->m_center ) == ptBack )
            return false;

        // Compute the slow
        return m_tree.LineOfSight( a->m_center, b->m_center );
    }

    float cRadiosityCalc::FormFactor( sPatch *pSrc, sPatch *pDest )
    {
        float   angle1, angle2, dist, factor;
        point3  vec;

        // find vij first.  If it's 0, we can early-out.
        if( !LineOfSight( pSrc, pDest ) )
            return 0.f;

        point3 srcLoc = pSrc->m_center;
        point3 destLoc = pDest->m_center;

        vec = destLoc - srcLoc;
        dist = vec.Mag();
        vec /= dist;

        angle1 = vec * pSrc->m_plane.n;
        angle2 = -( vec * pDest->m_plane.n );

        factor = angle1 * angle2 * pDest->m_area;
        factor /= PI * dist * dist;

        return factor;
    }


    cRadiosityCalc::sPatch* cRadiosityCalc::FindBrightest()
    {
        sPatch* pBrightest = NULL;
        float brightest = 0.05f;

        float currIntensity;

        list<sPatch*>::iterator iter;

        // Blech. Linear search
        sPatch* pCurr;
        for(
            iter = m_patchList.begin();
```

```
            iter != m_patchList.end();
            iter++ )
    {
        pCurr = *iter;

        currIntensity = pCurr->m_intensity;

        if( currIntensity > brightest )
        {
            brightest = currIntensity;
            pBrightest = pCurr;
        }
    }

    // This will be NULL if nothing was bright enough
    return pBrightest;
}

bool cRadiosityCalc::CalcNextIteration()
{
    // Find the next patch that we need to
    sPatch* pSrc = FindBrightest();

    // If there was no patch, we're done.
    if( !pSrc )
    {
        DWORD diff = timeGetTime() - m_startTime;
        float time = (float)diff/1000;

        char buff[255];
        sprintf(
            buff,
            "Radiosity : Done - took %f seconds to render",
            time );
        SetWindowText( MainWindow()->GetHWnd(), buff );
        return false;  // no more to calculate
    }

    sPatch* pDest;
    list<sPatch*>::iterator iter;

    float formFactor; // form factor Fi-j
    color3 deltaRad;   // Incremental radiosity shot from src to dest

    for(
        iter = m_patchList.begin();
        iter != m_patchList.end();
        iter++ )
    {
        pDest = *iter;
```

```
        // Skip sending energy to ourself
        if( pDest == pSrc )
            continue;

        // Compute the form factor
        formFactor = FormFactor( pDest, pSrc );

        // Early out if the form factor was 0.
        if( formFactor == 0.f )
            continue;

        // Compute the energy being sent from src to dest
        deltaRad = pDest->m_reflect * pSrc->m_deltaRad * formFactor;

        // Send said energy
        pDest->m_radiosity += deltaRad;
        pDest->m_deltaRad += deltaRad;

        // Cache the new intensity.
        pDest->m_intensity =
            pDest->m_area *
            (pDest->m_deltaRad.r +
             pDest->m_deltaRad.g +
             pDest->m_deltaRad.b );

    }
    // this patch has shot out all of its engergy.
    pSrc->m_deltaRad = color3::Black;
    pSrc->m_intensity = 0.f;

    return true;
}
```

References

Foley, James D. et al. *Computer Graphics: Principles and Practice, Second Edition in C*; Addison-Wesley Publishing Co. ISBN: 0201848406.

Garland, Michael, and Paul Heckbert. "Surface Simplification Using Quadric Error Metrics." *Computer Graphics* (SIGGRAPH 1997 Proceedings).

Heckbert, Paul. "Subdivision Surfaces Reader." Contains excerpts from the SIGGRAPH 1998 course "Subdivision for Modeling and Animation."

Hoppe, Hugues. "Progressive meshes." *Computer Graphics* (SIGGRAPH 1996 Proceedings): 99-108.

Melax, Stan. "A Simple, Fast, and Effective Polygon Reduction Algorithm." *Game Developer* magazine (November 1998): 44-49.

Moller, Tomas, and Eric Haines. *Real-Time Rendering*. A K Peters Ltd, 1999. ISBN: 1568811012.

Sharp, Brian. "Subdivision Surface Theory." *Game Developer* magazine (January 2000): 34-42.

Watt, Alan H., and Mark Watt. *Advanced Animation and Rendering Techniques: Theory and Practice*. Addison-Wesley Publishing Co., 1992. ISBN: 0201544121.

Zorin, Schroder, and Sweldens. "Interpolating Subdivision for Meshes with Arbitrary Topology." *Computer Graphics* (SIGGRAPH 1996): 189-192.

For Further Reading

http://www.research.microsoft.com/~hoppe/
> Hugues Hoppe's web page at Microsoft Research. There you can find downloadable versions of all of his papers; definitely a good read if you're interested in progressive meshes.

http://www.multires.caltech.edu/teaching/courses/subdivision/
> This page is a good place to start if you want to learn more about subdivision surfaces.

http://graphics.cs.uiuc.edu/~garland/
> Michael Garland's web page at the University of Illinois at Urbana-Champaign. His papers on quadric error metrics are available online.

http://www.scs.ryerson.ca/~h2jang/gfx_c.html
> Hin Jang's web page, with discussion of lots of advanced graphics topics available online.

Bretscher, Otto. *Linear Algebra With Applications*. Prentice Hall, 1996. ISBN: 0131907298.

> If you don't have a textbook on linear algebra, you should get one. This may not be the best one on the market, but it was the one I learned the topic with.

Chapter 8

Advanced Direct3D

While I covered a lot of ground in Chapter 6, I really only scratched the surface of Direct3D's total set of functionality. While I can't hope to cover everything in this chapter (it's far too big an API), I can cover enough to get some really cool things going. By the end of this chapter, I'll have discussed everything you could ever want to know about texture mapping, along with alpha blending, multitexture effects, and the stencil buffer.

With Direct3D, there eventually comes a crest in the learning curve. At some point you know enough about the API that figuring out the rest is easy. For example, there comes a point when you've been bitten enough by setting the vertex shader parameters and zeroing out structures that you automatically do it. Hopefully, after learning the material in this chapter, you'll be over the hump. When you get there, learning the rest of the API is a breeze. It's like that parable about giving a man a fish or teaching him how to fish. This chapter is giving you a few fish, but hopefully it's also giving you a fishing pole.

Alpha Blending

Up to this point, I've been fairly dismissive of the mysterious alpha component that rides along in all of the D3DColor structures. Now, young grasshopper, you may finally learn its dark secrets. A lot of power is hidden away inside the alpha component.

Loosely, the alpha component of the RGBA quad represents the opaqueness of a surface. An alpha value of 0xFF (255) means the color is completely opaque, and an alpha value of 0x00 (0) means the color is completely transparent. Of course, the value of the alpha component is fairly meaningless unless you actually activate the alpha blending step. If you want, you can set things up a different way, such as having 0x00 (0) mean that the color is completely opaque. The meaning of alpha is dependent on how you set up the alpha blending step.

The alpha blending step is one of the last in the D3D pixel pipeline. As you rasterize primitives, each pixel that you wish to change in the frame buffer gets sent through the alpha blending step. That pixel is combined using blending factors to the pixel that is currently in the frame buffer. You can add the two pixels together, multiply them together, linearly combine them using the alpha component, and so forth. The name "alpha blending" comes from the fact that generally the blending factors used are either the alpha or the inverse of the alpha.

The Alpha Blending Equation

The equation that governs the behavior of the blending performed in Direct3D is defined as follows:

final color = source × source blend factor + destination × destination blend factor

Final color is the color that goes to the frame buffer after the blending operation. Source is the pixel you are attempting to draw to the frame buffer, generally one of the many pixels in a triangle you have told D3D to draw for you. Destination is the pixel that already exists in the frame buffer before you attempt to draw a new one. The source and destination blend factors are variables that modify how the colors are combined together. The blend factors are the components you have control over in the equation; you cannot modify the positions of any of the terms or modify the operations performed on them.

For example, say you want an alpha blending equation to do nothing—to just draw the pixel from the triangle and not consider what was already there at all (this is the default behavior of the Direct3D Rasterizer). An equation that would accomplish this would be:

final color = source × 1.0 + destination × 0.0

As you can see, the destination blending factor is 0 and the source blending factor is 1. This reduces the equation to:

final color = source

A second example would be if you wanted to multiply the source and destination components together before writing them to the frame buffer. This initially would seem difficult, as in the above equation they are only added together. However, the blending factors defined need not be constants; they can in fact be actual color components (or inverses thereof). The equation set up would be:

final color = source × 0.0 + destination × source

In this equation, the destination blend factor is set to the source color itself. Also, since the source blend factor is set to zero, the left-hand side of the equation drops away and you are left with:

final color = destination × source

A Note on Depth Ordering

Usually if you are using a blending step that changes the color already in the depth buffer, you are attempting to use a semi-transparent surface, such as a puff of smoke or a fading particle effect. For the particle to appear correctly, the value already in the depth buffer must be what you would naturally see behind the specified primitive. For this to work correctly, you need to manually sort all of the alpha-blended primitives into a back-to-front list, drawing them after you draw the rest of our scene polygons. Using qsort, the STL generic sort algorithm, or something similar using the view space z value of the first vertex of each primitive as the sorting key will generally do the trick.

Enabling Alpha Blending

Turning on alpha blending is a matter of setting a render state in the device using IDirect3DDevice8::SetRenderState. Set D3DRS_ALPHABLENDENABLE to TRUE to enable alpha blending or FALSE to disable it.

It is important that you don't enable alpha blending when you don't have to. On many cards, a penalty is suffered during rasterization if the hardware needs to read from its frame buffer. Software rendering goes spectacularly slowly when it has to perform additional blending at each pixel. Only turn on alpha blending when you are going to use it.

Blending Modes

You set the blending factors for the alpha blending step using two render states: D3DRS_SRCBLEND and D3DRS_DESTBLEND. They set up the source and destination blending factors, respectively. The second parameter for the SetRenderState call must be a member of the D3DBLEND enumeration, which defines the set of supported blending factors. Table 8.1 presents the set of values for the D3DBLEND enumeration.

> **Note:** You may see the blend factors that I was just talking about written differently in other publications. For instance, D3DRS_DESTBLEND may be written as D3DRENDERSTATE_DESTBLEND. The longer version is the way it was defined previous to DirectX 8.0, and if you try to use it you will get compile errors.

Table 8.1: Members of the D3DBLEND enumeration

D3DBLEND_ZERO	The blending factor is zero for all components: (0, 0, 0, 0)
D3DBLEND_ONE	The blending factor is set to one for all components: (1, 1, 1, 1)

D3DBLEND_SRCCOLOR	The blending factor is set to the source color:
	$(src_{red}, src_{green}, src_{blue}, src_{alpha})$
D3DBLEND_INVSRCCOLOR	The blending factor is set to the inverse of the source color:
	$(1-src_{red}, 1-src_{green}, 1-src_{blue}, 1-src_{alpha})$
D3DBLEND_SRCALPHA	The blending factor is set to the alpha of the source color:
	$(src_{alpha}, src_{alpha}, src_{alpha}, src_{alpha})$
D3DBLEND_INVSRCALPHA	The blending factor is set to the inverse of the alpha of the source color:
	$(1-src_{alpha}, 1-src_{alpha}, 1-src_{alpha}, 1-src_{alpha})$
D3DBLEND_DESTALPHA	The blending factor is set to the alpha of the destination color (this only makes sense if the frame buffer has an alpha component):
	$(dest_{alpha}, dest_{alpha}, dest_{alpha}, dest_{alpha})$
D3DBLEND_INVDESTALPHA	The blending factor is set to the inverse of the alpha of the destination color (this only makes sense if our frame buffer has an alpha component):
	$(1-dest_{alpha}, 1-dest_{alpha}, 1-dest_{alpha}, 1-dest_{alpha})$
D3DBLEND_DESTCOLOR	The blending factor is set to the destination color:
	$(dest_{red}, dest_{green}, dest_{blue}, dest_{alpha})$
D3DBLEND_INVDESTCOLOR	The blending factor is set to the inverse of the destination color:
	$(1-dest_{red}, 1-dest_{green}, 1-dest_{blue}, 1-dest_{alpha})$
D3DBLEND_SRCALPHASAT	The blending factor is the source alpha saturated against the inverse destination alpha:
	$f = min(src_{alpha}, 1-dest_{alpha})$
	$(f, f, f, 1)$
D3DBLEND_BOTHINVSRCALPHA	This state is only valid for D3DRS_SRCBLEND. It sets the source blending factor to D3DBLEND_INVSRCALPHA, and the destination blending factor to D3DBLEND_SRCALPHA.

As an example, let's say you wanted to perform the blending mode discussed above, multiplying the two components together and storing the result in the frame buffer. Code for this would look like what appears in Listing 8.1.

Listing 8.1: Enabling alpha blending

```
// turn on alpha blending
pDevice->SetRenderState( D3DRS_ALPHABLENDENABLE, TRUE );

// set our blending terms
pDevice->SetRenderState( D3DRS_SRCBLEND, D3DBLEND_ZERO );
pDevice->SetRenderState( D3DRS_DESTBLEND, D3DBLEND_SRCCOLOR );
```

The blending equation after setting these states (as long as the blending operations were supported by the device) would be:

$$result = (src_r, src_g, src_b, src_a)(0) + (dest_r, dest_g, dest_b, dest_a)(src_r, src_g, src_b, src_a)$$

There is one last thing you need to worry about, and that is determining if the blending modes we wish to use are supported by the card. This can be done by checking the primitive caps in the D3D device description. There are two member variables, SrcBlendCaps (for source blending factors) and DestBlendCaps (for destination blending factors). There is a flag for each member of the D3DBLEND enumeration. Just perform an AND with a flag to see if the blending factor you want is supported. The names are similar, following the convention that the blending factor D3DBLEND_*x* has a corresponding flag D3DPBLENDCAPS_*x*. For example, D3DPBLENDCAPS_ONE is the flag for D3DBLEND_ONE.

Now that you have alpha blending at your disposal, what can you do with it? Well, for starters, you can have semi-transparent objects. Set up your iterated alpha value to be something like 0.5 (for medium transparency). This is done by fiddling with the material settings when you draw unlit primitives, or changing the iterated alpha color in the diffuse component of lit primitives. Then set the blending mode to be SRCALPHA for the source blending factor and INVSRCALPHA for the destination blending factor. This is just scraping the surface; later in the chapter I'll explore a lot of neat effects that can be done with alpha blending. Of course, before you get there you need to learn a little bit about texture mapping.

Texture Mapping 101

It's kind of hard to think of texture mapping qualifying as advanced Direct3D material. Just about every 3-D game that has come out in the last few years has used it, so it can't be terribly complex. When drawing your 3-D objects with only a solid color (or even a solid color per vertex that is Gouraud shaded across the triangle pixels), they look rather bland and uninteresting. Objects in the real world have detail all over them, from the rings in wood grain to the red and white pattern on a brick wall.

You could simulate these types of surfaces by increasing the triangle count a few orders of magnitude, and color each triangle so it could simulate things like the pictures of letters that appear on the keys of a keyboard. This, of course, is a terrible idea! You are almost always limited by the number of triangles you can feed the card per-frame, so you cannot add the amount of triangles you need to simulate that kind of detail. There must be a better way to solve the problem.

Really, what it comes down to is that you generally have the polygon budget to represent something like a brick wall with a handful of triangles. Instead of assigning a color to the vertices, you want to paint the *picture* of a brick wall onto the mesh. Then, at least from an appreciable distance (far enough that you can't notice the bumps and cracks in the wall), the polygons will look a lot like a brick wall.

Welcome to the world of texture mapping. A *texture* is just a regular image with some restrictions on it (such as having a power-of-two width and height). The name "texture" is kind of a misnomer; it does not represent what the uninitiated think of when they hear the word texture. Instead of meaning the physical feeling of a surface (being rough, smooth, etc.), texture in this context just means a special kind of image that you can map onto a polygon.

Fundamentals

Every texture-mapped polygon in our 3-D space has a corresponding 2-D polygon in texture space. In Direct3D, the coordinates for texture space are u (the horizontal direction) and v (the vertical direction). The upper left corner of the texture is <0,0> and the bottom right corner is <1,1> regardless of the actual size of the texture; even if the texture is wider than it is tall.

Direct3D is provided with the texture coordinates for the vertices of the triangles. It then interpolates across each pixel in the triangle, finding the appropriate u,v pair, and then fetches that texture coordinate (or *texel*), and using it as the color for that pixel. Figure 8.1 shows a visual representation of what happens when you texture a primitive.

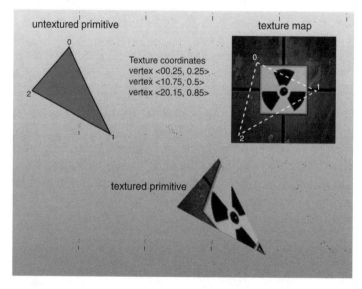

Figure 8.1: How primitives get drawn with texture coordinates

Other factors can come into play, such as the diffuse color, multiple textures, and so forth, but I'll get to this later. While you can create regular Direct3D surfaces with countless different pixel formats, only subsets of them are supported as texture formats by most hardware cards. Because of this, applications should try to use one of these formats for their textures:

- 24-bit RGB (top 8 bits for red, next 8 bits for green, lowest 8 bits for blue)
- 32-bit ARGB (top 8 bits for alpha, next 8 bits for red, next 8 bits for green, lowest 8 bits for blue)
- 32-bit RGB (top 8 bits aren't used, next 8 bits for red, next 8 bits for green, lowest 8 bits for blue)
- 16-bit RGB (top 5 bits for red, next 6 bits for green, lowest 5 bits for blue)
- 16-bit ARGB (top bit for alpha, next 5 bits for red, next 5 bits for green, lowest 5 bits for blue)
- 16-bit RGB (top 4 bits aren't used, next 4 bits for red, next 4 bits for green, lowest 4 bits for blue)
- 16-bit ARGB (top 4 bits for alpha, next 4 bits for red, next 4 bits for green, lowest 4 bits for blue)

Warning: Steer clear of 4-4-4 formats if you can (the last two in the above list). Having only 16 possible values for each of your primary colors just looks ugly if your image has any sort of color variance in it at all.

Affine Versus Perspective Mapping

To draw a primitive with a texture map, all you need to do is specify texture coordinates for each of the vertices of the primitive. How the per-pixel texture coordinates are found can be done in one of two ways, called *affine mapping* and *perspective mapping*. Affine mapping is considered old technology, and was used before there was the computing horsepower available to handle perspective mapping.

Affine mapping interpolates texture coordinates across each scanline of a triangle linearly. The u and v are interpolated the same way that r, g, and b are for Gouraud shading. Because of the simplicity (finding the delta-u and delta-v for a scanline, and then two adds per pixel to find the new u and v), affine mapping was very big in the days predating hardware acceleration.

However, betting that u and v vary linearly across a polygon is grossly incorrect. If the polygon is facing directly towards the viewer, then yes, u and v will vary linearly in relation to the pixels. However, if the polygon is on an angle, there is perspective distortion that prevents this from being true. The Playstation renders its triangles using affine rendering, and this can be really visible, especially when 1/z varies a lot over the space of a triangle. A good example is angled triangles near the camera, such as the ones at the bottom of the screen in racing games.

Perspective mapping, otherwise known as *perspective-correct* mapping, varies u and v correctly across the polygon, correcting for perspective distortion. The short mathematical answer is that while u and v do not vary linearly across a scanline, u/z, v/z, and 1/z do. If you interpolate all three of those values, you can find u and v by dividing u/z and v/z by 1/z. A division-per-pixel with a software renderer is impossible to do in real time, or at least it was back in the day, so most games found some way around it. *Quake*, for example, did the division every 16 pixels, and did a linear interpolation in between, which made the texture mapping look perfect in anything but extremely off-center polygons. With acceleration, there is no need to worry; it's just as fast as affine mapping on all modern cards.

Every accelerator you can buy these days can do perspective-correct mapping at no speed penalty compared to affine mapping, so there is really no reason to turn it off. The device has perspective texturing turned on by default, but if you really, really want to turn it off, set the render state D3DRS_TEXTUREPERSPECTIVE to FALSE.

> **Warning:** An extra incentive to use perspective-correct mapping is that not using it on certain chip sets can mess with other components that depend on w or z being interpolated correctly across the polygon, in a particular pixel fog. Some cards even ignore the texture perspective render state altogether, always rendering with perspective correction enabled.

Texture Addressing

Behavior for choosing texels at the vertices between 0 and 1 is pretty well defined, but what happens if you chose texels outside that range? How should Direct3D deal with it? This is a texture addressing problem. There are four different ways that Direct3D can do texture addressing: wrap, mirror, clamp, and border color. Each of them is described below.

Wrap

In wrap addressing mode, when a texel is selected past the end of the texture, it is wrapped around to the other side of the texture. The texel (1.3,–0.4) would be mapped to (0.3,0.6). This makes the texture repeat itself like posters on the walls of construction site, as shown in Figure 8.2.

Figure 8.2:
The wrap
addressing
mode

Care must be taken to make sure textures tile correctly when this addressing
mode is used. If not, visible seams between copies of the texture will be visible,
per the figure above.

Mirror

Mirror addressing mode flips texels outside of the (0..1) region so that it looks
as if the texture is mirrored along each axis. This addressing mode can be useful
for drawing multiple copies of a texture across a surface, even if the texture was
not designed to wrap cleanly. The texel (1.3,–0.4) would be mapped to
(0.7,0.4), as shown in Figure 8.3.

Figure 8.3:
The mirror addressing mode

Clamp

Clamp mode is useful when you only want one copy of the texture map to appear on a polygon. All texture coordinates outside the (0..1) boundary are snapped to the nearest edge so they fall within (0..1). The texel (1.3,–0.4) would be mapped to (1.0,0.0). This appears in Figure 8.4.

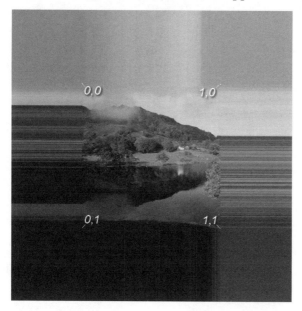

Figure 8.4:
The clamp addressing mode

Unless the texture is created with a 1-pixel boundary of a solid color around the edges, noticeable artifacts can occur, for example, the streaks in the above image.

Border Color

Border color mode actually has two stage states to worry about: one to change the state to the addressing mode and one to choose a border color. In this addressing mode, all texture coordinates outside of the (0..1) region become the border color. See Figure 8.5.

Figure 8.5: The border color addressing mode

Texture Wrapping

Texture wrapping is different from the texture addressing problem described above. Instead of deciding how texel coordinates outside the boundary of (0,1) should be mapped to the (0,1) area, it decides how to interpolate between texture coordinates. Usually, when the rasterizer needs to interpolate between two u coordinates, say 0.1 and 0.8, it interpolates horizontally across the texture map, finding a midpoint of 0.45. When wrapping is enabled, it instead interpolates in the shortest direction. This would be to actually move from 0.1 to the left, wrap past 0.0 to 1.0, then keep moving left to 0.8. The midpoint here would be 0.95.

To enable texture wrapping for each stage, you set the render state D3DRS_WRAPx, where x is the desired texture stage (from 0 to 7) to change. Until you start experimenting with multitexture, I'll only deal with stage 0. To enable wrapping for a particular direction, you include the bit for that particular direction. The u-direction bit is D3DWRAPCOORD_0, the v-direction bit is D3DWRAPCOORD_1. Figure 8.6 may help clarify what texture wrapping does.

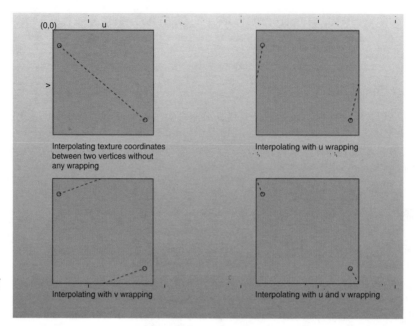

Figure 8.6:
Examples of texture wrapping

Texture Aliasing

One of the biggest problems applications that use texture mapping have to deal with is texture aliasing. Texture aliasing is a smaller part of aliasing, which is another real problem in computer graphics. Aliasing, essentially, is when your image doesn't look the way you would expect; it looks like it was generated with a computer. Texture aliasing can take many forms. If you've ever heard of moire effects, jaggies, blockies, blurries, texel swimming, or shimmering, you've heard about texture aliasing.

Why does texture aliasing occur? The short answer is because you're trying to discretely sample a signal (the texture on a polygon, being displayed on a set of pixels) that we would actually see as continuous (or as continuous as the resolution of our eyes can go). Take the example of a texture that just had a horizontal repeating sinusoidal color variation on it. If you graphed the intensity as it related to horizontal position on the screen, you would get something like Figure 8.7.

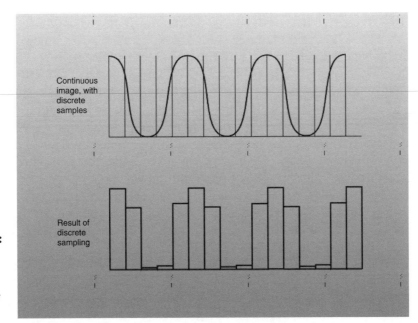

Figure 8.7:
A good result from discrete sampling of an image

Notice that even though it is being sampled discretely, the sample points follow together well, and you can fairly closely approximate the continuous signal you're seeing. Problems start occurring when the signal changes faster than the discrete samples can keep up with. Take Figure 8.8, for example.

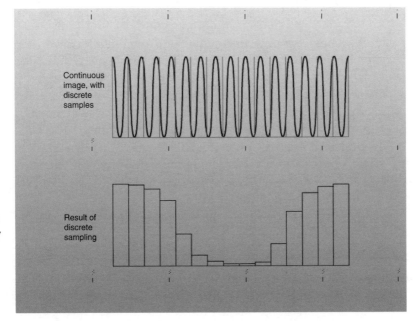

Figure 8.8:
A very, very bad result from discrete sampling of an image

In this graph, the discrete samples don't approximate the continuous signal correctly, and you get a different signal all together. As the frequency of the sine wave changes, the discrete signal you get varies widely, producing some really ugly effects. The ugly effects become even worse because the texture isn't actually a continuous signal; it's a discrete signal being sampled at a different frequency. It's easy to imagine the sine function becoming the tiniest bit wider, so that each discrete sample met up with the crest of the sine wave. This tiny difference could happen over a couple of frames of a simulation (imagine the texture slowly moving towards the camera), and the resultant image would change from a wide variation of color to solid white!

If none of this is making sense, fire up an old texture-mapped game, such as *Doom* or *Duke3D*. Watch the floors in the distance as you run around. You'll notice that the textures kind of swim around and you see lots of ugly artifacts. That's bad. That effect is what I'm talking about here.

MIP Maps

MIP mapping is a way for Direct3D to alleviate some of the aliasing that can occur by limiting the ratio of pixel size to texel size. The closer the ratio is to 1, the less texture aliasing occurs (because you're taking enough samples to approximate the signal of the texture).

 Note: MIP is short for "multum in parvo," which is Latin for "many things in a small place."

Instead of keeping just one version of a texture in memory, we keep a chain of MIP maps. The top one is the original texture. Each successive one is half the size in each direction of the previous one (if the top level is 256x256 texels, the first MIP level is 128x128, the next is 64x64, and so on, down to 1x1).

Creating MIP map surfaces can be done automatically using CreateTexture. Just create a texture with the Levels parameters set above 1.

Generating MIP levels can be done in several ways. The most common is to simply sample each 4x4 pixel square in one MIP level into one pixel of the MIP level below it, averaging the four color values. Luckily, since you're loading DDS texture files, this is done automatically.

Filtering

Filtering, or the way in which you get texels from the texture map given a u,v coordinate pair, can affect the way the final image turns out immensely. The filtering problem is divided into two separate issues: magnification and minification.

Magnification occurs when you try to map many pixels in the frame buffer to a single texel in a texture map. For example, if you were drawing a 64x64 texture onto a 400 by 400 pixel polygon, the image would suffer the torment of magnification artifacts. Bilinear filtering helps get rid of these artifacts.

Minification (I didn't make up this word) is the opposite problem—when multiple texels need to be mapped to a single pixel. If you were instead drawing that 64x64 texture onto a 10 by 10 pixel polygon, our image would instead be feeling the pain from minification. Swimming pixels such as the type discussed with the signal discussion above are tell-tale symptoms.

Most of the newer kinds of commercial hardware can use four different varieties of filtering to alleviate magnification and minification artifacts. They are point sampling, bilinear filtering, trilinear filtering, and anisotropic filtering. I'll go through and take a look at each of them.

Point Sampling

Point sampling is the simplest kind of filter. In fact, it's hard to think of it as being a filter at all. Given a floating-point (or fixed-point) u,v coordinate, the coordinates are snapped to the nearest integer and the texel at that coordinate pair is used as the final color.

Point sampling suffers from the most aliasing artifacts. If MIP mapping is used, these artifacts can be alleviated somewhat. The Playstation console uses point sampling for its texture mapping, as did the first generation of 3-D games (*Descent, Quake*). *Quake* got past some of the visual artifacts of point sampling by using MIP maps, selecting the MIP map based on distance, and point sampling out of that. However, since no filtering is done between MIP map levels, if you run towards a wall from a far-off distance, you can visually see the MIP level switch as the distance decreases. Figure 8.9 shows worst-case point sampling, a checkerboard pattern with no MIP mapping.

Figure 8.9:
Worst-case point sampling

Courtesy of Paul Heckbert

The artifacts caused by point sampling are readily visible in the distance. As the ratio between the signal and the discrete sampling changes, the output signal changes completely, giving rise to the visible banding artifacts.

Bilinear Filtering

One step up from point sampling is bilinear filtering. Instead of snapping to the nearest integer coordinate, the four nearest texels are averaged together based on the relative distances from the sampling point. The closer the ideal coordinate is to an integer coordinate, the more you weight it. For example, if you wanted a texel for the coordinate (8.15,2.75), the result would be:

Result pixel =

$(1-0.15) \times (1-0.75) \times \text{Texel}(8,2) +$

$0.15 \times (1-0.75) \times \text{Texel}(9,2) +$

$(1-0.15) \times 0.75 \times \text{Texel}(8,3) +$

$0.15 \times 0.75 \times \text{Texel}(9,3)$

Bilinear filtering can improve image quality a lot, especially if it is combined with MIP mapping. Just about all consumer-level hardware can handle bilinear filtering with MIP maps, so it is used the most often. If MIP maps aren't used, however, it only looks marginally better than point sampling, as evidenced by Figure 8.10.

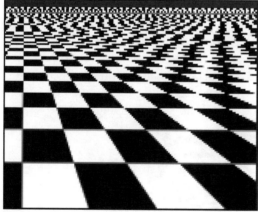

Figure 8.10: Bilinear filtering without MIP maps

Courtesy of Paul Heckbert

Many cards can implement per-pixel MIP mapping, where the correct MIP level is chosen per pixel instead of per-polygon. With bilinear filtering this can cause banding, sharp visual changes between MIP boundaries.

Trilinear Filtering

Trilinear filtering looks much better than bilinear filtering, especially as you move through a scene. Trilinear filtering is the short name for the filtering method. The long name is "trilinear MIP map interpolation." For each pixel, instead of choosing the correct MIP map to use, the two nearest MIP maps are used. Each of those MIP levels performs a bilinear filter to choose the pixel for that MIP level, and then the resultant pixels are combined together using the proximity of each MIP map to the ideal MIP level. For example, if the ideal MIP level was 4.2, then the combination would be (1 minus 0.2) multiplied by the bilinear result from MIP level 4 plus (0.2 multiplied by the bilinear result from MIP level 5). Trilinear filtering looks silky-smooth, as evidenced by Figure 8.11.

Figure 8.11:
Trilinear
filtering

Courtesy of Paul Heckbert

While many cards can do trilinear filtering (pretty much everything that came out after the Voodoo2, along with the Voodoo2 itself), most of them use the multitexture unit to do it. This is done by putting alternating MIP map levels in each texture stage, and then doing a fade filter between both stages based on the distance between MIP levels. While the card does this process transparently for you, it prevents you from using more than one stage when trilinear filtering is enabled on dual-texture cards. Cards released shortly after, such as the ATI Rage 128, and more modern cards, can handle trilinear filtering in each stage, so this restriction doesn't apply. Make sure the device has the necessary support before you try to render two trilinear textures together.

Anisotropic Filtering

A problem that arises in bilinear and trilinear filtering is that texels are sampled using square sampling. This works well if the polygon is facing directly to the viewer, but doesn't work properly if the polygons are angled sharply away from the viewer. For example, think of the point of view of a chicken crossing a road. If you could imagine each pixel as a tall, thin pyramid being shot out of the chicken's eye, when the pyramid intersected the road it wouldn't be a square at all. Figure 8.12 illustrates this concept using a circular sample region.

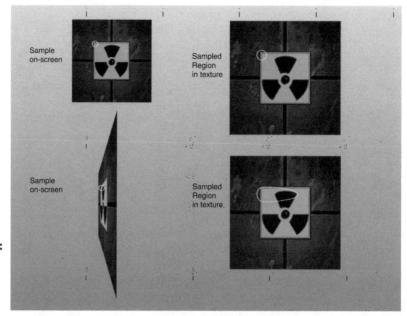

Figure 8.12:
How textures would ideally be sampled

Anisotropic filtering attempts to correct for this. It's only available on more recent cards, and can often come at a severe performance penalty. On the TNT generation of cards for example, anisotropic filtering could be done, but resulted in an 8x degradation in performance.

Performance problems or not, anisotropic filtering looks about as good as it can get, as evidenced in Figure 8.13. Just about all of the banding artifacts or blurring artifacts are gone, and the image looks more and more like a photograph taken of a real infinite checkerboard.

Figure 8.13:
Anisotropic filtering

Courtesy of Paul Heckbert

Textures in Direct3D

In Direct3D, textures are just Direct3D surfaces with a few restrictions. They almost universally need a power-of-two width and height (example: 64x128 == 2^6x2^7). This is a time-honored restriction in computer graphics. Indexing into a 2-D array is easier when the dimensions are powers-of-two; you can shift instead of multiplying. Back before dedicated hardware was doing texture mapping, this restriction made a big difference in texture mapping performance. In the future, however, this restriction will no doubt disappear.

Texture Management

Generally most scenes have many more textures than are visible at any one time. Also, all of the textures in the scene usually can't fit in the video card's texture memory. This, of course, presents a dilemma: How should an application make sure that the textures it currently needs for drawing are loaded into the video card?

To solve this problem you need a subsystem to handle texture management. Whenever you want to draw a primitive with a certain texture, the texture management subsystem makes sure that the texture is available and in memory. If it isn't, the card is uploaded and another texture is evicted from memory to make space for it.

Which texture do you evict? You can't be haphazard about it: Uploading textures is expensive and should be done as little as possible. If you know for certain that a texture won't be used for a while (say it's a special texture used in an area that you're far away from), then you can evict it, but generally such information isn't available. Instead, usually the texture that hasn't been used in the longest time, or the least recently used texture (LRU), is evicted. This system is used almost everywhere where more data is needed than places to store it (disk caches, for example). Of course, textures continue to be evicted until there is enough space to place in the desired texture.

> **Warning:** Pray that you never run into the situation where you need more texture space than is available on the card to draw a frame. Because of the way LRU works, every single texture will have to be reloaded as you render each frame, knocking your frame rates out the window.

Direct3D, thankfully, has an automatic texture management system. While it's not as fast as a more specific texture management system would be, for these purposes it's all that's needed.

To activate texture management, you must request the capability when we create the surface. When creating any resource in Direct3D, such as a surface or texture, you just have to specify the pool type as D3DPOOL_MANAGED.

The D3D managed texture manage flag instructs Direct3D to handle texture management chores. The regular texture manage flag will let the driver itself do the texture management work if it can. If it can't, the work goes to Direct3D's texture management engine.

You have no way of knowing if any of the managed textures are currently sitting in video memory; however, this information really isn't needed. You just know that whenever you try to draw with that texture, Direct3D will do what it can to make sure the texture appears in video memory.

You can't be too reckless with your newfound power, however. If you tried to draw a scene with 10 MB of textures simultaneously visible on a card with only 8 MB of texture RAM, that would mean that the texture management engine would need to download 2 MB of textures to the graphics card every frame. This can be an expensive operation, and can just murder your frame rate. In situations like this, it is a better bet to lower the resolutions of your textures, just so everything can fit on the card at once.

Direct3D lets you control the way in which managed textures are evicted. Direct3D holds on to a time stamp of when each managed texture was used, as well as a priority number for each. When Direct3D needs to remove a texture, it removes the one with the lowest priority, removing the least recently used if there is more than one candidate. You can set the priority of a texture using SetPriority(). There is also a corresponding call to get the priority called GetPriority().

```
HRESULT IDirect3DResource8::SetPriority(
  DWORD PriorityNew
);
```

dwPriority	DWORD containing the new priority value for this surface. This method only has meaning for managed texture surfaces.

Being able to use texture management makes our lives much easier. At startup we just need to load all the textures we want to use and Direct3D will take care of everything. If there are too many, the extra ones will invisibly sit in system RAM surfaces until they are used, then they'll get uploaded to the card.

Texture Loading

Just like playing sound effects in Chapter 2, in order to do anything interesting with your newly learned texture mapping skills you need to actually have some data to work with. While loading certain types of textures can be avoided by generating them algorithmically, that is beyond the scope of this book.

DDS Format

Loading the DDS (or Direct3D Surface) format couldn't be easier. The first four bytes contain a magic number that describes it as a DDS surface (0x20534444, or "DDS" in ASCII). Next is a DDSURFACEDESC2 structure describing the surface. After that are the raw data of the surface. If there are any attached surfaces (MIP maps, for example), the data for them is provided after the main surface.

DDS surfaces can be created using the DirectX Texture Tool, which comes with the SDK. It can load a BMP file (and load another into the alpha channel, if desired), generate MIP maps, and save the result as a DDS texture. You can also create compressed DDS texture files, but these aren't covered in this book. However, you don't need to worry about the intricacies of the surface format because since version 8.0 it is easy to load DDS files with the D3DXCreateTexture-FromFile() utility function.

The cTexture Class

To facilitate the loading of Direct3D textures, I'm going to create a class that wraps around a Direct3D texture object, specifically for use as a texture. The class is fairly simple, based on the Compress Direct3D sample. The source appears in Listings 8.2 (header) and 8.3 (source).

Listing 8.2: Texture.h

```
/*******************************************************************
 *         Advanced 3D Game Programming using DirectX 8.0
 * * * * * * * * * * * * * * * * * * * * * * * * * * * * * * * * *
 *    Title: Texture.h
 *    Desc: Definition of a class that represents a image
 *          that can be used as a texture map.
 *          This code borrows heavily from the 'Compress' sample
 * (C) 2001 by Peter A Walsh and Adrian Perez
 * See license.txt for modification and distribution information
 *******************************************************************/

#ifndef _TEXTURE_H
#define _TEXTURE_H

#include <ddraw.h>

#include <vector>
#include <string>

class cGraphicsLayer;

class cTexture
{
```

```
protected:

  void ReadDDSTexture( LPDIRECT3DTEXTURE8& pTexture );

  static bool m_bSupportsMipmaps;

  void BltToTextureSurface( LPDIRECT3DTEXTURE8 pTempTex );

  LPDIRECT3DTEXTURE8    m_pTexture;

  string               m_name;

  // The stage for this particular texture.
  DWORD                m_stage;

public:
  cTexture( const char* filename, DWORD stage = 0 );
  virtual ~cTexture();

  LPDIRECT3DTEXTURE8 GetTexture();

};

#endif //_TEXTURE_H
```

Listing 8.3: Texture.cpp

```
/********************************************************************
 *         Advanced 3D Game Programming using DirectX 8.0
 * * * * * * * * * * * * * * * * * * * * * * * * * * * * * * * * *
 *   Title: Texture.cpp
 *    Desc: Declaration of a class that represents a image
 *          that can be used as a texture map
 *          This code borrows heavily from the 'Compress' sample
 * (C) 2001 by Peter A Walsh and Adrian Perez
 * See license.txt for modification and distribution information
 ********************************************************************/

#include "stdafx.h"
#include "Texture.h"
#include "GraphicsLayer.h"
#include "DxHelper.h"

using std::vector;

bool cTexture::m_bSupportsMipmaps;


int GetNumberOfBits( int mask )
{
```

```
        for( int nBits = 0; mask; nBits++ )
            mask = mask & ( mask - 1 );

    return nBits;
}



HRESULT WINAPI EnumTextureFormats( DDPIXELFORMAT* pddpf, VOID* pVoid )
{

  vector<DDPIXELFORMAT>* pVec = (vector<DDPIXELFORMAT>*)pVoid;

  pVec->push_back( *pddpf );

        return DDENUMRET_OK;
}



cTexture::cTexture( const char* filename, DWORD stage )
{

  LPDIRECT3DTEXTURE8 pTempTex = 0;

  m_pTexture = 0;

  m_name = string( filename );
  m_stage = stage;

  ReadDDSTexture( pTempTex );

  BltToTextureSurface( pTempTex );

  SafeRelease( pTempTex );
}



cTexture::~cTexture()
{
  SafeRelease( m_pTexture );
}



void cTexture::ReadDDSTexture( LPDIRECT3DTEXTURE8& pTexture )
{
  HRESULT r = 0;

  r = D3DXCreateTextureFromFile(
```

```
                    Graphics()->GetDevice(),
                    m_name.c_str(),
                    &pTexture );

            if( FAILED( r ) )
            {
                throw cGameError( "Bad DDS file\n");
            }
        }


LPDIRECT3DTEXTURE8 cTexture::GetTexture()
{
    return m_pTexture;
}

void cTexture::BltToTextureSurface(LPDIRECT3DTEXTURE8 pTempTex )
{

    SafeRelease( m_pTexture );

    D3DSURFACE_DESC TexDesc;

    pTempTex->GetLevelDesc( 0, &TexDesc );
    DWORD NumLevels = pTempTex->GetLevelCount();

    D3DXCreateTexture(
            Graphics()->GetDevice(),
            TexDesc.Width,
            TexDesc.Height,
            NumLevels,
            0,
            TexDesc.Format,
            D3DPOOL_MANAGED,
            &m_pTexture );

    LPDIRECT3DSURFACE8 pSrcSurf = 0;
    LPDIRECT3DSURFACE8 pDestSurf = 0;

    for( int i = 0 ; i < NumLevels ; i++ )
    {
        m_pTexture->GetSurfaceLevel( i, &pDestSurf );
        pTempTex->GetSurfaceLevel( i, &pSrcSurf );

        D3DXLoadSurfaceFromSurface(
                pDestSurf,
                0,
                0,
                pSrcSurf,
                0,
                0,
```

```
                      D3DX_FILTER_NONE,
                      0 );

              pDestSurf->Release();
              pSrcSurf->Release();
      }

   }
```

Activating Textures

With all this talk of texture management and texture addressing, filtering, and wrapping, I still haven't described how to activate a texture for use! After creating a texture surface, filling it with image data, setting all the rendering states we want, and so forth, to actually activate it you use the SetTexture method on the Direct3D device interface.

```
HRESULT IDirect3DDevice8::SetTexture(
  DWORD Stage,
  PDIRECT3DBASETEXTURE8* pTexture
);
```

Stage	Stage for the texture. I'll be talking a lot about the texture stages in a moment. This can be an integer from 0 to 7, corresponding to the first (0) through the last (7) texture stage. If you're just activating one texture, this value should be 0.
pTexture	Pointer to the Direct3D texture to use as the current texture.

Note that SetTexture AddRef's the surface being given to it. It releases it when the texture is replaced. It can either be replaced with another texture or with NULL using SetTexture(stage, NULL). Note that it doesn't release them when the device itself is released. This is why, in cGraphicsLayer::DestroyAll(), you step through all seven stages, setting the texture to NULL to avoid a memory leak.

Once a texture has been activated, every primitive drawn will be textured. If you want to stop texturing, you must deactivate the first texture stage (which we will discuss in a moment).

Texture Mapping 202

In this day and age, regular vanilla texture mapping is not enough. There are many neat effects that you can do using multiple passes, and in this section, I'll discuss how to use multipass and multitexture effects to make textured objects that look really cool.

Multiple Textures Per Primitive

With the release of DirectX 6.0, Direct3D had the ability to support the rendering of primitives with multiple textures applied to them. The feature is supported by what are called *texture stages*.

Each texture stage can be thought of as two separate units (alpha and color), each with two arguments (such as the iterated color of the pixel, the texture at the pixel, or the result of the previous stage) and an operator combining them (such as multiplication, addition, or subtraction).

The result of stage 0 can be used in stage 1, that result can be used in stage 2, and so forth, cascading down to stage 7, the highest stage currently supported by Direct3D. All the stages don't need to be active at once, however. Whenever Direct3D encounters an inactivated stage, the current result is fed to the next stage of the rasterization pipeline. A visual representation of the texture stage cascade is shown in Figure 8.14.

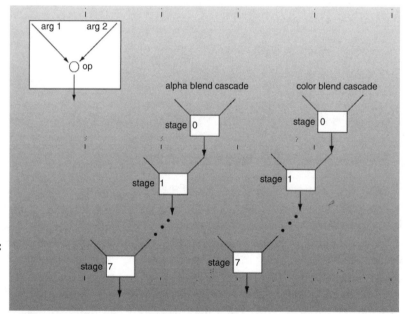

Figure 8.14: The color and alpha blending cascades

Note: The reason there are separate cascades for alpha and color is so that you can use them independently of each other. You'll see later examples where the alpha component of a texture is actually a completely different image than the color component, so being able to use it differently is a neat thing.

Be warned: You can't assume that any or all of the blending stages are available. As of this writing, the top-of-the-line graphics cards can only do four stages, and only two of them can use textures. Within the next few years cards will begin to appear that can handle all eight texture stages, but for right now, the device description should be checked to see how many stages can be used, and how many of those can use textures. There are two important member variables: MaxTextureBlendStages (how many stages can simultaneously be used) and MaxSimultaneousTextures (how many textures can be used simultaneously).

> **Warning:** Why the need for two different variables? Besides the fact that textures aren't always needed for multitexture effects, there is an important problem that the two variables help solve. On many cards, iterated color (the diffuse r, g, and b values) can only be introduced in the last stage. On these cards there is one more stage than there are possible textures, since the last stage can be used to combine the current multitexture result with the iterated diffuse color.

Multiple texture blending is a fairly complex feature, so I'll go through it step by step. Each texture stage has its own separate state independent of the other stages. That state can be set using SetTextureStageState and can be retrieved with GetTextureStageState.

```
HRESULT IDirect3DDevice8::SetTextureStageState(
  DWORD Stage,
  D3DTEXTURESTAGESTATETYPE Type,
  DWORD Value
);
```

Stage	The texture stage being changed. Valid values for this parameter are integers between 0 and 7.
Type	A member of the D3DTEXTURESTAGESTATETYPE enumeration, describing the state being changed (discussed below).
Value	New value for the state.

```
HRESULT IDirect3DDevice8::GetTextureStageState(
  DWORD Stage,
  D3DTEXTURESTAGESTATETYPE Type,
  LPDWORD pValue
);
```

Stage	The texture stage being queried. Valid values for this parameter are integers between 0 and 7.
Type	A member of the D3DTEXTURESTAGESTATETYPE enumeration, describing the state being queried (discussed below).
pValue	Pointer to data that will receive the new state.

There are a myriad of states that can be changed for each stage. The set of texture stage states is encompassed by the D3DTEXTURESTAGESTATETYPE enumeration, which is dissected in Table 8.2.

Table 8.2: Members of the D3DTEXTURESTAGESTATETYPE enumeration (D3DTSS_ prefix omitted)

COLOROP	Defines the operation done to combine COLORARG1 and COLORARG2. One of the members of the D3DTEXTUREOP enumeration, discussed below. (Default = D3DTOP_DISABLE for all stages except stage 0, which is D3DTOP_MODULATE).
COLORARG1, COLORARG2	Describes the source for the arguments in the texture color operation. The color argument can be any of the texture argument flags: • D3DTA_CURRENT The argument value is the color from the previous stage. On stage 0, this is the diffuse color. • D3DTA_DIFFUSE The argument value is the diffuse color. • D3DTA_TEXTURE The argument value is the texture color. It is recommended that this argument be used only in stage 1. • D3DTA_TFACTOR The argument value is the currently set texture factor. This is set by changing the D3DRENDERSTATE_TEXTUREFACTOR render state. • D3DTA_SPECULAR The argument value is the texture color. It is recommended that this argument be used only in stage 1. • D3DTA_ALPHAREPLICATE Additional flag, used in conjunction with one of the above. Causes the alpha component of the color to be copied to the other three color values. • D3DTA_COMPLEMENT Additional flag, used in conjunction with one of the above. Causes all components to be inverted, such that $(x = 1.0 - x)$. (Default = D3DTOP_TEXTURE)
ALPHAOP	Defines the operation done to combine ALPHAARG1 and ALPHAARG2. One of the members of the D3DTEXTUREOP enumeration, discussed below. (Default = D3DTOP_DISABLE for all stages except stage 0, which is D3DTOP_MODULATE).
ALPHAARG1, ALPHAARG2	Describes the source for the arguments in the texture alpha operation. The color argument can be any of the texture argument flags, which are supplied in the description of COLORARG1 and COLORARG2. (Default = D3DTOP_TEXTURE)

BUMPENVMAT00, BUMPENVMAT01, BUMPENVMAT10, BUMPENVMAT11	Coefficients for the bump-mapping matrix. The valid range for these values is [–8,8]. This is the mathematical way of saying that the number must be equal or greater than –8 and less than (but not equal to) 8. Bump mapping is not discussed in this text. (Default = 0)
TEXCOORDINDEX	An integer describing which set of texture coordinates to use for a particular stage (a vertex can be defined with up to eight vertices). You'll remember that back in Chapter 6 I described some vertex formats that had multiple sets of texture coordinates; this is where you can use them. If a requested index doesn't occur in the vertex, the behavior is to default to the texture coordinate (0,0). The value can also be one of the following additional flags: • D3DTSS_TCI_PASSTHRU Texture coordinates should be taken from the input index into the array of texture coordinates. This flag resolves to zero. • D3DTSS_TCI_CAMERASPACENORMAL The texture coordinates for this stage are the normal for the vertex, transformed into camera space. This is mostly useful when texture transforms are enabled. • D3DTSS_TCI_CAMERASPACEPOSITION The texture coordinates for this stage are the position for the vertex, transformed into camera space. This is mostly useful when texture transforms are enabled. • D3DTSS_TCI_CAMERASPACEREFLECTIONVECTOR The texture coordinates for this stage are the reflection vector for the vertex, transformed into camera space. This is mostly useful when texture transforms are enabled. The reflection vector is a ray that is sent from the eye point and bounced off the vertex. (Default (for all stages) = 0)
ADDRESS	Sets the texture addressing mode for a stage. Texture addressing was discussed earlier in the chapter. This state changes both the u and v addressing modes. • D3DTADDRESS_WRAP Wrap addressing mode. • D3DTADDRESS_MIRROR Mirror addressing mode. • D3DTADDRESS_CLAMP Clamp addressing mode. • D3DTADDRESS_BORDER Border color addressing mode. (Default = D3DTADDRESS_WRAP)

ADDRESSU	Sets the texture addressing mode for a stage for the u dimension only. Texture addressing was discussed earlier in the chapter. Separate addressing modes can be defined for each dimension only if the D3DPTADDRESSCAPS_INDEPENDENTUV bit is set in the dwTextureAddressCaps member of the D3DPRIMCAPS structure for the device description. • D3DTADDRESS_WRAP Wrap addressing mode. • D3DTADDRESS_MIRROR Mirror addressing mode. • D3DTADDRESS_CLAMP Clamp addressing mode. • D3DTADDRESS_BORDER Border color addressing mode. (Default = D3DTADDRESS_WRAP)
ADDRESSV	Sets the texture addressing mode for a stage for the v dimension only. Texture addressing was discussed earlier in the chapter. Separate addressing modes can be defined for each dimension only if the D3DPTADDRESSCAPS_INDEPENDENTUV bit is set in the dwTextureAddressCaps member of the D3DPRIMCAPS structure for the device description. • D3DTADDRESS_WRAP Wrap addressing mode. • D3DTADDRESS_MIRROR Mirror addressing mode. • D3DTADDRESS_CLAMP Clamp addressing mode. • D3DTADDRESS_BORDER Border color addressing mode. (Default = D3DTADDRESS_WRAP)
BORDERCOLOR	A D3DCOLOR describing the border color to be used when the D3DTADDRESS_BORDER texture addressing mode is used. (Default = 0x00000000)
MAGFILTER	Describes the filtering mode to use when texture magnification is performed. The value of this state is a member of the D3DTEXTUREMAGFILTER enumerated type, which has the following members: • D3DTEXF_POINT Sample the texel closest to the ideal texture coordinate. • D3DTEXF_LINEAR

Perform a weighted sample of the 2x2 area around the ideal texture coordinate, and use the result. This is otherwise known as bilinear filtering.

- D3DTEXF_ANISOTROPIC

Correct distortion caused by a large difference in the angle of the texture in relation to the view plane using anisotropic filtering.

(Default = D3DTEXF_POINT)

MINFILTER	Describes the filtering mode to use when texture minification is performed. The value of this state is a member of the D3DTEXTUREMINFILTER enumerated type, which has the following members: • D3DTEXF_POINT Sample the texel closest to the ideal texture coordinate. • D3DTEXF_LINEAR Perform a weighted sample of the 2x2 area around the ideal texture coordinate, and use the result. This is otherwise known as bilinear filtering. • D3DTEXF_ANISOTROPIC Correct distortion caused by a large difference in the angle of the texture in relation to the view plane using anisotropic filtering. (Default = D3DTEXF_POINT)
MIPFILTER	Describes the method that will be used to determine MIP map usage for a texture, if MIP maps are present. The value of this state is a member of the D3DTEXTUREMIPFILTER enumerated type, which has the following members: • D3DTEXF_NONE Perform no MIP mapping. Use the top-level MIP map texture in all situations. • D3DTEXF_POINT Perform nearest MIP mapping. The closest match for a MIP map is used, and minification/magnification is performed on it as needed. • D3DTEXF_LINEAR Perform MIP map interpolation. The two closest MIP maps are chosen, pixels are found in each of them, and the result is the linear combination of the two of them. Using linear here, along with linear magnification/ minification filtering is otherwise known as trilinear filtering. (Default = D3DTEXF_NONE)
MIPMAPLODBIAS	The bias value for determining the proper MIP map. Changing this value from its default of 0 can force higher or lower level MIP maps to be used, creating blurring or pixilated effects. The value is a floating-point number, so to set the state correctly, the value must be cast to a DWORD in the following way: float bias = 0.1f; // or any other value *((DWORD*)(&bias))

	(Default = 0.0)
MAXMIPLEVEL	Index of the highest MIP map to use in rendering. The default, 0, means that any MIP map can be used (0 corresponds to the top-level MIP map). Lower levels in the MIP map chain correspond to higher integers. Setting this to a non-zero value means that all MIP maps above it in the chain (all MIP levels less than the number) will not be used. This can force certain textures to appear blurry no matter what the distance.
	(Default = 0)
MAXANISOTROPY	The maximum level of anisotropy for this stage. The maximum allowable stage is described in the capability bits for the device.
	(Default = 1)
BUMPENVLSCALE, BUMPENVLOFFSET	Bump mapping texture stage states. Bump mapping is not discussed in this text.
TEXTURETRANSFORMFLAGS	Stage flags for texture transformations, discussed later in the chapter. • D3DTTFF_DISABLE Disables texture transforms for the current stage. • D3DTTFF_COUNT1 Instructs the rasterizer to expect one-dimensional texture coordinates. This is in place because it can be the case where an application takes 3-D coordinates, like the camera space position, and applies a texture transformation matrix that only cares about one of the entries. • D3DTTFF_COUNT2 Instructs the rasterizer to expect two-dimensional texture coordinates. This is in place because it is possible that an application could take 3-D coordinates, like the camera space position, and apply a texture transformation matrix that only cares about two of the entries. • D3DTTFF_COUNT3 Instructs the rasterizer to expect three-dimensional texture coordinates. • D3DTTFF_COUNT4 Instructs the rasterizer to expect four-dimensional texture coordinates. • D3DTTFF_PROJECTED All of the texture coordinates, save the last, are divided by the last element, and the last element is thrown away. For example, if we supply the flags (D3DTTFF_COUNT3|D3DTTFF_PROJECTED), the first two texture coordinates are divided by the third, the third is thrown away, and the result is passed to the rasterizer. (Default = D3DTTFF_DISABLE)

One of the most often changed texture stage states is to change the color/alpha operation performed at each stage. The set of color/alpha operations sits inside the D3DTEXTUREOP enumeration, which is presented in Table 8.3:

Table 8.3: Members of the D3DTEXTUREOP enumeration (D3DTOP_ prefix omitted)

DISABLE	Disables a stage. Once Direct3D encounters a disabled stage, the stage cascade stops and the current result is passed to the next phase of the pipeline.
SELECTARG1	Result of the stage's texture operation is the color of the first argument. Res=Arg1
SELECTARG2	Result of the stage's texture operation is the color of the second argument. Res=Arg2
MODULATE	Result of the stage's texture operation is the result of the multiplication of the arguments. Res=Arg1×Arg2
MODULATE2X	Result of the stage's texture operation is the result of the multiplication of the arguments, multiplied by 2. Res=2×(Arg1×Arg2)
MODULATE4X	Result of the stage's texture operation is the result of the multiplication of the arguments, multiplied by 4. Res=4×(Arg1×Arg2)
ADD	Result of the stage's texture operation is the result of the addition of the arguments. Res=Arg1+Arg2
ADDSIGNED	Result of the stage's texture operation is the result of the addition of the arguments biased by –0.5. This makes the range of one of the operations effectively a signed number [–0.5, 0.5]. Res=Arg1+Arg2–0.5
ADDSIGNED2X	Result of the stage's texture operation is the result of the addition of the arguments biased by –0.5 and multiplied by 2. The bias makes the range of one of the operations effectively a signed number [–0.5, 0.5]. Res=2×(Arg1+Arg2–0.5)
SUBTRACT	Result of the stage's texture operation is the result of the subtraction of the second argument from the first. Res=Arg1–Arg2
ADDSMOOTH	Result of the stage's texture operation is the result of the addition of the arguments subtracted by the product of the arguments. Res=Arg1+Arg2–Arg1×Arg2 =Arg1+Arg2(1–Arg1)
BLENDDIFFUSEALPHA, BLENDTEXTUREALPHA, BLENDFACTORALPHA, BLENDTEXTUREALPHAPM, BLENDCURRENTALPHA	Result of the stage's texture operation is the result of the linear blending of both color operations with the iterated diffuse alpha, the current iterated texture alpha, a scalar alpha factor (set with the D3DRS_TFACTOR render state), or the alpha that resulted from the previous stage.

	$Res=Arg1\times alpha+Arg2\times(1-alpha)$
PREMODULATE	For use with premodulated textures, which aren't covered in this text.
MODULATEALPHA_ADDCOLOR	Result of the stage's texture operation is the addition of the second color modulated with the first color's alpha component to the first color. This operation is only valid for color operations (not alpha operations). $Res_{RGB}=Arg1_{RGB}+Arg1_A\times Arg2_{RGB}$
MODULATECOLOR_ADDALPHA	Result of the stage's texture operation is the addition of the first argument's alpha component to the modulated first and second colors. This operation is only valid for color operations (not alpha operations). $Res_{RGB}=Arg1_{RGB}\times Arg2_{RGB}+Arg1_A$
MODULATEINVALPHA_ADDCOLOR	Result of the stage's texture operation is the addition of the second color modulated with the inverse of the first color's alpha component to the first color. This operation is only valid for color operations (not alpha operations). $Res_{RGB}=Arg1_{RGB}+(1-Arg1_A)\times Arg2_{RGB}$
MODULATEINVCOLOR_ADDALPHA	Result of the stage's texture operation is the addition of the first argument's alpha component to the modulation of the second color and the inverse of the first color. This operation is only valid for color operations (not alpha operations). $Res_{RGB}=(1-Arg1_{RGB})\times Arg2_{RGB}+Arg1_A$
BUMPENVMAP	Performs per-pixel bump mapping, using the next stage as an environment map. This operation is only valid for color operations (not alpha operations).
BUMPENVMAPLUMINANCE	Performs per-pixel bump mapping, using the next stage as an environment map. The next stage must be a luminance map. This operation is only valid for color operations (not alpha operations).
DOTPRODUCT3	Performs a dot product with the two arguments, replicating the result to all four color components. $Res_{RGBA}=Arg1_R\times Arg2_R+$ $\quad Arg1_G\times Arg2_G+$ $\quad Arg1_B\times Arg2_B$

Texture Transforms

DirectX 8.0 has a feature for texture mapping called *texture transforms*. They allow an application to specify modifiers, such as projection or matrices that get applied to texture coordinates before being used.

Each texture stage has a 4x4 texture transformation matrix associated with it. A lot of neat texture effects can be done automatically simply by fiddling with the matrix you set up. The texture coordinates that go into the matrix don't need to be four-dimensional they can be two- or even one-dimensional.

For example, let's say you want to perform a simple translation (suppose you had a texture that showed running water and you were displaying it on the clear section of a pipe). Instead of having to move the texture coordinates for the clear section of the pipe each frame, you can keep them stationary and use texture transformations. The end effect here is each frame you want to translate the coordinates horizontally to simulate movement over many frames. You would have a translation amount, which is called *du*. Just to be safe, whenever it is incremented it past 1.0, it would be wrapped around back to 0.0 to prevent overflow. Strange things can happen if the magnitude of the texture coordinates are too large. Setting up the matrix to do this would yield:

$$\begin{bmatrix} 1 & 0 & 0 & 0 \\ 0 & 1 & 0 & 0 \\ du & 0 & 1 & 0 \\ 0 & 0 & 0 & 1 \end{bmatrix}$$ Before the vertex texture coordinates are used to fetch texels from the image, the texture matrix first multiplies them for their stage. Of course, if the texture coordinate is only two-dimensional (u,v coordinates), it's padded with 1s to make the multiplication valid.

To set the texture transform matrix for a particular stage, you call IDirect3DDevice8::SetTransform using the constants D3DTS_ TEXTURE0 (for the first stage) through D3DTS_TEXTURE7 (for the last stage) in the first state type parameter.

To actually enable texture transforms, only one more step of work needs to be done. You set the texture stage state D3DTSS_TEXTURETRANSFORMFLAGS to inform it of how many of the resultant texture coordinates should be passed to the rasterizer. To disable the texture transformation, set this to D3DTTFF_DISABLE. For two-dimensional texture coordinates, set it to D3DTTFF_COUNT2. If you're doing something like projected textures (not covered in this text), you would like to perform a perspective division on the texture coordinates we receive. To do this, set this to D3DTTFF_COUNT3|D3DTTFF_ PROJECTED. This instructs the texture transform engine to take the three texture coordinates resulting from the texture transform and divide the first two by the third. If you set up the matrix correctly this will perform your perspective divide.

The cool thing is you can use things besides the specified texture coordinates with the texture transforms. You can change the D3DTSS_TEXCOORDINDEX texture stage state to use the view space position, view space normal, or view space reflection vector (all 3-D values) as texture coordinates. I'll use this fact later to do spherical environment mapping.

Effects Using Multiple Textures

Most modern games now use multiple textures per primitive for a variety of effects. While there are many more possible kinds of effects than can be described here, I'm going to run through the most common ones and show how to implement them using both multiple textures per pass and multiple passes.

The way you combine textures and the way you make the textures defines the kind of effect you end up with. Using multitexture is preferred. Since you only draw the primitive once, it ends up being faster than multipass. Multipass involves drawing each of the separate phases of the effect one at a time. Generally you change the texture, change the alpha blending effects, and redraw the primitive. The new pass will be combined with the previous pass pixel-by-pixel. Figure 8.15 may help explain the kinds of things I'm trying to do. Using multitexture, you would set the first stage to texture A, the second stage to texture B, and then set the operation in texture B to either add, multiply, or subtract the pixels. Using multipass, you would draw texture A first, then change the alpha blending steps to add or multiply the pixels together (you can't subtract), and then draw the polygon again using texture B.

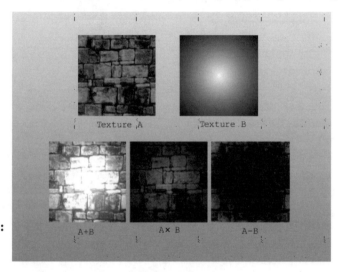

Figure 8.15:
Combining
textures

Light Maps (a.k.a. Dark Maps)

Light mapping is practically a standard feature for first-person shooters these days. It allows the diffuse color of a polygon to change non-linearly across the face of a polygon. This is used to create effects like colored lights and shadows.

Using a light-map creation system (usually something like a radiosity calculator, which I created in Chapter 7), texture maps that contain just lighting information are calculated for all of the surfaces in the scene. Since usually the light map doesn't change per-pixel nearly as much as the texture map, a lower-resolution texture is used for the light map. *Quake*-style games use about 16^2 texels of light map for each texel of texture map. The base map is just the picture that would appear on the wall if everything were fully and evenly lit, like wallpaper. The light map is modulated with the base map. That way areas that get a lot of light (which appear white in the light map) appear as they would in the fully lit world (since the base map pixel times white(1) resolves to the base map). As the light map gets darker, the result appears darker. Since a light map can only darken the base map, not lighten it, sometimes the effect is referred to as "dark mapping."

When you go to draw the polygon, you can do it in several ways. First I'll discuss the multitexture way. Using light maps with multitexture is done with two texture stages. The first texture stage can be either the base map or the light map, and the second is the other texture. You only need to worry about the color stages, too; the alpha stages aren't needed. Listing 8.4 shows sample code for setting this up.

Listing 8.4: Sample code for setting up light mapping using multitexture

```
//pDevice is a valid LPDIRECT3DDEVICE8 object
//pBase is the base texture
//pLightMap is the light map

pDevice->SetTextureStageState( 0, COLORARG1, D3DTA_TEXTURE );
pDevice->SetTextureStageState( 0, COLOROP, D3DTOP_SELECTARG1 );
pDevice->SetTexture( 0, pBase );

pDevice->SetTextureStageState( 1, COLORARG1, D3DTA_TEXTURE );
pDevice->SetTextureStageState( 1, COLORARG2, D3DTA_CURRENT );
pDevice->SetTextureStageState( 1, COLOROP, D3DTOP_MODULATE );
pDevice->SetTexture( 1, pLightMap );

// draw polygon
```

Note that the texture is put into argument 1. Some cards depend on this being the case so you should make a habit of it.

The effect using multipass rendering is similar to the above. You render the polygon twice, the first with no alpha blending and the base map, the second with the light map texture. The alpha blending done on the second stage should mimic the modulate color operation used in the multitexture rendering. Code to do it appears in Listing 8.5.

Listing 8.5: Sample code for setting up light mapping using multipass

```
//pDevice is a valid LPDIRECT3DDEVICE8 object
//pBase is the base texture
//pLightMap is the light map

pDevice->SetTextureStageState( 0, COLORARG1, D3DTA_TEXTURE );
pDevice->SetTextureStageState( 0, COLOROP, D3DTOP_SELECTARG1 );
pDevice->SetRenderState( D3DRS_ALPHABLENDENABLE, FALSE );
pDevice->SetTexture( 0, pBase );

// draw polygon

pDevice->SetRenderState( D3DRS_ALPHABLENDENABLE, TRUE );
pDevice->SetRenderState( D3DRS_SRCBLEND, D3DBLEND_ZERO );
pDevice->SetRenderState( D3DRS_DESTBLEND, D3DBLEND_SRCCOLOR );
```

```
pDevice->SetTexture( 0, pLightMap );

// draw polygon
```

The visual flair that you get from light mapping is amazing. Following is a prime example from *Quake III: Arena*. The first, Figure 8.16, is rendered without light maps. The image looks bland and uninteresting. Figure 8.17 shows the same scene with light mapping enabled. The difference, I'm sure you'll agree, is amazing.

Figure 8.16:
Quake III: Arena, sans light maps

Courtesy of id Software

Figure 8.17:
Quake III: Arena, with light maps

Courtesy of id Software

Environment Maps

Environment mapping was one of the first cool effects people used texture maps with. The concept is quite simple: You want a polygon to be able to reflect back the scene, as if it were a mirror or shiny surface like chrome. There are two primary ways to do it that Direct3D supports: spherical environment maps and cubic environment maps.

Spherical Environment Maps

Spherical environment maps are one of those classic horrible hacks that happens to look really good in practice. It isn't a perfect effect, but it's more than good enough for most purposes.

The environment mapping maps each vertex into a u,v pair in the spherical environment map. Once you have the locations in the sphere map for each vertex, you texture map as normal. The sphere map is called that because the actual picture looks like the scene pictured on a sphere. Real photos are taken with a 180-degree field of view camera lens, or using a ray-tracer to prerender the sphere map. Rendering a texture like this is complex enough that it is infeasible to try to do it in real time; it must be done as a preprocessing step. An example of a sphere map texture appears in Figure 8.18.

Figure 8.18:
A texture map for use with spherical environment mapping

Courtesy of nVidia Corporation

The region outside of the circle in the above image is black, but it can be any color; you're never actually going to be addressing from those coordinates, as you'll see in a moment.

Once you have the spherical texture map, the only task left to do is generate the texture coordinates for each vertex. Here comes the trick that runs the algorithm:

The normal for each vertex, when transformed to view space, will vary along each direction from –1 to 1. What if you took just the x and y components and mapped them to (0,1)? You could use the following equation:

$$u = \frac{n_x + 1}{2}$$

$$v = \frac{n_y + 1}{2}$$

You know that the radius of the 2-D vector $<n_x, n_y>$ will vary between 0 (when z is 1.0 and the normal is facing directly towards the viewer) and 1 (when z is 0.0 and the normal is perpendicular to the viewer). When n_x and n_y are 0, you'll get a u,v pair of <0.5, 0.5>. This is exactly what was wanted: the vertex whose normal is pointing directly towards us should reflect the point directly behind us (the point in the center of the sphere map). The vertices along the edges (with radius 1.0) should reflect the regions on the edge of the sphere map. This is exactly what happens.

As evidenced by Figure 8.19, this environment mapping method can have really nice looking results.

Figure 8.19:
In some cases, spherical environment mapping looks great.

Courtesy of nVidia Corporation

One caveat of this rendering method is that the sphere map must remain the same, even if the camera moves. Because of this, it often isn't useful to reflect certain types of scenes; it's best suited for bland scenery like starscapes.

There are some mechanisms used to attempt to interpolate correct positions for the spherical environment map while the camera is moving, but they are far from perfect. They suffer from precision issues; while texels in the center of the sphere map correspond to relatively small changes in normal direction, along the edges there are big changes, and an infinite change when you reach the edge of the circle. This causes some noticeable artifacts, as evidenced in Figure 8.20. Again, these artifacts only pop up if you try to find the sphere map location while the camera is moving. If you always use the same sphere map, none of this happens.

Figure 8.20: Spherical environment mapping can have warping artifacts

Courtesy of nVidia Corporation

Cubic Environment Maps

With DirectX 8.0, Microsoft added support for cubic environments to Direct3D. Cubic environment maps have been used in high-end graphics workstations for some time, and they have a lot of advantages over spherical environment maps.

The big advantage is cubic environment maps don't suffer from the warping artifacts that plague spherical environment maps. You can move around an object, and it will correctly reflect the correct portion of the scene. Also, they're much easier to make, and in fact can be made in real time (producing accurate real-time reflections).

A cubic environment map is actually a complex Direct3D texture with six different square textures, one facing in each direction. They are:

- Map 0 : +X direction (+Y up, –Z right)
- Map 1 : –X direction (+Y up, +Z right)
- Map 2 : +Y direction (–Z up, –X right)
- Map 3 : –Y direction (+Z up, –X right)
- Map 4 : +Z direction (+Y up, +X right)
- Map 5 : –Z direction (+Y up, +X right)

The six environment maps that are used in the images for this section appear in Figure 8.21 below.

Figure 8.21:
The six pieces of a cubic environment map

Courtesy of nVidia Corporation

How do you actually use this environment map to get texture coordinates for each of the vertices? The first step is to find the reflection vector for each vertex. You can think of a particle flying out of the camera and hitting the vertex. The surface at the vertex has a normal provided by the vertex normal, and the particle bounces off of the vertex back off into the scene. The direction it bounces off in is the reflection vector, and it's a function of the camera to vertex direction and vertex normal. The equation to find the reflection vector **r** is:

$$\mathbf{d} = \frac{\mathbf{v} - \mathbf{c}}{\|\mathbf{v} - \mathbf{c}\|}$$

$$\mathbf{r} = 2 \times (\mathbf{d} \bullet \mathbf{n})\mathbf{n} - \mathbf{d}$$

where **r** is the desired reflection vector, **v** is the vertex location, **c** is the camera location, and **n** is the vertex normal. The **d** vector is the normalized direction vector pointing from the camera to the vertex.

Given the reflection vector, finding the right texel in the cubic environment map isn't that hard. First, you find which component of the three has the greatest magnitude (let's assume it's the x component). This determines which environment map you want to use. So if the absolute value of the x component was the greatest and the x component was also negative, you would want to use the –X direction cubic map (map 1). The other two components, y and z in this example, are used to index into the map. We scale them from the [–1,1] range to the [0,1] range. Finally you use z to choose the u value and y to choose the v value.

Luckily Direct3D does the above so you don't have to worry about it. There are some truly icky cases that arise, like when the three vertices of a triangle all choose coordinates out of different maps. There is some interesting literature out on the web as to how hardware does this, but it's far too ugly to cover here.

The sphere you saw being spherically environment mapped earlier appears with cubic environment mapping in Figure 8.22. Notice that all of the artifacts are gone and the sphere looks pretty much perfect.

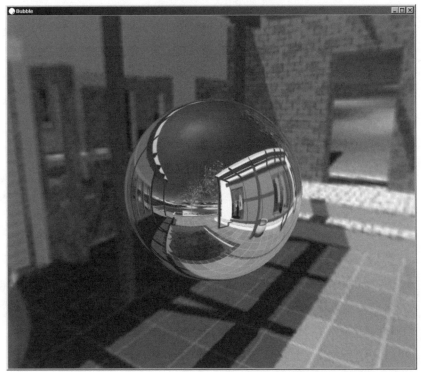

Figure 8.22:
Sweet, sweet cubic environment mapping

Courtesy of nVidia Corporation

Checking to see if a device supports cubic environment mapping is fairly simple given its device description. Have a look at *DirectX 8.0 C++ Documentation/*

DirectX Graphics/Using DirectX Graphics/Techniques and Special Effects/Environment Mapping/Cubic Environment Mapping.

Once you have your cubic environment maps set up, to activate the feature all you need is to select the texture and set up the texture processing caps to generate the reflection vector for you. Code to do this appears in Listing 8.6.

Listing 8.6: Activating cubic environment mapping

```
// pCubeTex is our cubic environment map
// pDevice is our LPDIRECT3DDEVICE8 interface pointer

// Since our texture coordinates are automatically generated,
// we don't need to include any in the vertices
DWORD dwFVF = D3DFVF_XYZ | D3DFVF_NORMAL;

pDevice->SetTextureStageState(
    0,
    D3DTSS_TEXCOORDINDEX,
    D3DTSS_TCI_CAMERASPACEREFLECTIONVECTOR );

pDevice->SetTexture( 0, pCubeTex );

// Draw our object
...
```

Specular Maps

The types of lighting you can approximate with multitexture isn't limited to diffuse color. Specular highlights can also be done using multitexture. It can do neat things that specular highlights done per-vertex cannot, like having highlights in the middle of a polygon.

A specular map is usually an environment map like the kind used in spherical environment mapping that approximates the reflective view of the lights in our scene from the viewpoint of an object's location. Then you just perform normal spherical (or cubic) environment mapping to get the specular highlights.

The added advantage of doing things this way is that some special processing can be done on the specular map to do some neat effects. For example, after creating the environment map, you could perform a blur filter on it to make the highlights a little softer. This would approximate a slightly matte specular surface.

Detail Maps

A problem that arises with many textures is that the camera generally is allowed to get too close to them. Take, for example, Figure 8.23. From a standard viewing distance (15 or 20 feet away), this texture would look perfectly normal on an 8- to 10-foot tall wall.

Figure 8.23:
An example
wall texture

However, a free-moving camera can move anywhere it likes. If you position the camera to be only a few inches away from the wall, you get something looking like Figure 8.24. With point sampling, we get large, ugly, blocky texels. With bilinear or trilinear filtering the problem is even worse: You get a blurry mess.

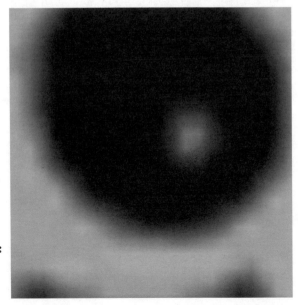

Figure 8.24:
Getting too
close to our
wall texture

This problem gets really bad in things like flight simulators. The source art for the ground is designed to be viewed from a distance of 30,000 feet above the ground. When the plane is dipping close to the ground, it's almost impossible to correctly gauge distance, there isn't any detail to help you gauge how far off the ground it is, resulting in a bad mark against the visual experience.

A bad solution is to just use bigger textures. This is bad for several reasons; most of them tied to the memory requirements that larger textures bring. You can use larger textures in the scene, but then you need to page to system RAM more, load times are longer, etc. This entire headache, and all you get is improved visual experience for an anomalous occurrence anyway; most of the user's time won't be spent six inches away from a wall.

What this problem boils down to is the designed signal of an image. Most textures are designed to encode low-frequency signals, the kind that changes over several inches. The general color and shape of an image are examples of low-frequency signals.

The real world, however, has high-frequency signals in addition to these low-frequency signals. These are the little details that you notice when you look closely at a surface, the kind that change over fractions of an inch. The bumps and cracks in asphalt, the grit in granite, and the tiny grains in a piece of wood are all good examples of high-frequency signals.

While you could hypothetically make all of the textures 4096 texels on a side and record all of the high-frequency data, you don't need to. The high-frequency image data is generally really repetitive. If you make it tile correctly, all you need to do is repeat it across the surface. It should be combined with the base map, adding detail to it (making areas darker or lighter).

Figure 8.25 has the detail map that you'll use in the application coming up in a little bit. The histogram of the image is tightly centered around solid gray (127,127,127). You'll see why in a moment. Also, it's designed without lots of sharp visual distinctions across the surface, so any details quickly fade away with MIP level increases.

Figure 8.25:
The detail map used in this example

If you tile the high-frequency detail map across the low-frequency base map, you can eliminate the blurry artifacts encountered before. As an added bonus, after you get far enough away from a surface, the MIP level for the detail map will be solid gray so you can actually turn it off, if you'd like, for faraway surfaces. Doing this improves the performance penalty on non-multitexture hardware since you don't need to do an extra pass for the detail map for every polygon on the screen, only the ones that will benefit from it. Figure 8.26 shows the base map with the detail map applied.

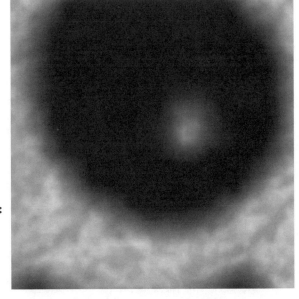

Figure 8.26:
The base map combined with the detail map

There are two primary ways to implement detail maps. Actually, there are three methods, but two of them are very closely related. Which one to use depends on the hardware configuration of the machine running the code.

The preferred, ideal, use-this-if-it's-available way to implement detail maps is using the ADDSIGNED blending mode. To recap, the equation for the ADDSIGNED blending mode is:

$$Res = Arg1 + Arg2 - 0.5$$

This essentially does an addition, having one of the textures have signed color values ($-127..128$) instead of the unsigned values ($0..255$) that you're used to. Black corresponds to -127, white corresponds to 128, and solid gray corresponds to 0. If the second texture map is a solid gray image (like the detail map at a low MIP map level), the result of the blend is just the other texture.

The way ADDSIGNED works is that lighter-gray texels in the detail map will brighten the base map, and darker-gray texels will darken it. This is exactly what you want. Source code to set it up using multitexture appears in Listing 8.7. One important difference with the light map code is you usually define a second pair of texture coordinates that wrap over the texture map multiple times (for example, u would vary from 0..1 in the base map, 0..8 in the detail map).

Listing 8.7: Sample code for setting up detail mapping using multitexture

```
//pDevice is a valid LPDIRECT3DDEVICE8 object
//pBase is the base texture
//pDetailMap is the detail map

pDevice->SetTextureStageState( 0, D3DTSS_COLORARG1, D3DTA_TEXTURE );
pDevice->SetTextureStageState( 0, D3DTSS_COLOROP, D3DTOP_SELECTARG1 );
// use the low-frequency texture coordinates
pDevice->SetTextureStageState( 0, D3DTSS_TEXCOORDINDEX, 0 );
pDevice->SetTexture( 0, pBase );

pDevice->SetTextureStageState( 1, D3DTSS_COLORARG1, D3DTA_TEXTURE );
pDevice->SetTextureStageState( 1, D3DTSS_COLORARG2, D3DTA_CURRENT );
pDevice->SetTextureStageState( 1, D3DTSS_COLOROP, D3DTOP_ADDSIGNED );
// use the high-frequency texture coordinates
pDevice->SetTextureStageState( 1, D3DTSS_TEXCOORDINDEX, 1 );
pDevice->SetTexture( 1, pDetailMap );

// draw polygon
```

If the ADDSIGNED blending mode isn't available on the hardware you're running on, don't despair; there are other options. Well, actually just two, and they're almost the same. The first backup option is to use the MODULATE2X blending mode. To recap, the equation for this blending mode is:

$$Res = 2 \times Arg1 \times Arg2$$

Looking at the equation, realize that if arg2 (the detail map) is 0.5 or solid gray, then the equation will resolve to arg1 (the base map). Also, if arg2 is a lighter gray, arg1 will be brighter; if arg2 is darker, arg1 will be darker, just like ADDSIGNED. MODULATE2X is also supported by more hardware devices than ADDSIGNED. To handle mod2x rendering, just use the same code in Listing 8.7, replacing D3DTOP_ADDSIGNED with D3DTOP_MODULATE2X. The only problem is that the modulate2x blending mode tends to wash out colors a little, so it is less ideal than ADDSIGNED. It'll do the job well enough, however, when ADDSIGNED isn't supported.

What do you do if you can't add detail maps in the same pass as our base map? What if the hardware you're designing for only has two stages, and the second stage is already taken up by light map rendering? You can do detail rendering multipass. All you need to do is mimic what MODULATE2X does in multitexture with an alpha blending step.

Let's take the original equation above, and move pieces of it around:

$$Res = 2 \times Arg1 \times Arg2$$
$$Res = Arg1 \times Arg2 + Arg1 \times Arg2$$
$$Res = Arg1 \times Arg2 + Arg2 \times Arg1$$
$$Res = dest \times source + source \times dest$$

You draw the scene once with the base map, then draw it again with the detail map. The *dest* color will be the base map color, and the *source* color will be the detail map color. All you need to do is have the source blending factor be the destination color, and the destination blending factor be the source color. This blending operation isn't supported on all hardware; so again, you should check the device description to make sure you can do it.

Coding up a multipass detail map renderer is fairly simple; it's very similar to the light map renderer I discussed earlier in the chapter. Source code to set it up appears in Listing 8.8.

Listing 8.8: Sample code for setting up detail mapping using multipass

```
//pDevice is a valid LPDIRECT3DDEVICE8 object
//pBase is the base texture
//pDetailMap is the detail map

pDevice->SetTextureStageState( 0, D3DTSS_COLORARG1, D3DTA_TEXTURE );
pDevice->SetTextureStageState( 0, D3DTSS_COLOROP, D3DTOP_SELECTARG1 );
// use the low-frequency texture coordinates
pDevice->SetTextureStageState( 0, D3DTSS_TEXCOORDINDEX, 0 );
pDevice->SetRenderState( D3DRENDERSTATE_ALPHABLENDENABLE, FALSE );
pDevice->SetTexture( 0, pBase );
```

```
// draw polygon

pDevice->SetRenderState( D3DRS_ALPHABLENDENABLE, TRUE );
pDevice->SetRenderState( D3DRS_SRCBLEND, D3DBLEND_DESTCOLOR );
pDevice->SetRenderState( D3DRS_DESTBLEND, D3DBLEND_SRCCOLOR );
// use the high-frequency texture coordinates
pDevice->SetTextureStageState( 0, D3DTSS_TEXCOORDINDEX, 1 );
pDevice->SetTexture( 0, pDetailMap );

// draw polygon
```

Application: Detail

To show off the texture loading code I set up earlier in the chapter and explain detail textures, I threw together a simple application that shows the base map/detail map combo used throughout this section. The application uses the new version of the gamelib library (which has texture support). A screen shot from the application appears in Figure 8.27.

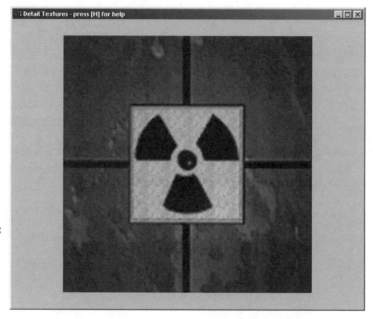

Figure 8.27: Screen shot from the detail texturing application

There are two main pieces of code that are important for this application: the device checking code and the actual code to draw the unit. The rest is essentially initialization and upkeep, and won't be listed here for brevity. See Listing 8.9 for the source code.

Listing 8.9: Device checking code for the Detail sample

```
bool CheckCaps()
{
  D3DCAPS8 DevCaps;

  Graphics()->GetDevice()->GetDeviceCaps( &DevCaps );

  m_bCanDoMultitexture = false;
  if( DevCaps.MaxSimultaneousTextures > 1 )
  {
      m_bCanDoMultitexture = true;
  }

  m_bCanDoAddSigned = false;
  if( DevCaps.TextureOpCaps & D3DTEXOPCAPS_ADDSIGNED )
  {
      m_bCanDoAddSigned = true;
  }

  if( !(DevCaps.TextureOpCaps & D3DTEXOPCAPS_MODULATE2X) )
  {
      // the device can't do mod 2x.  If we also can't do add signed,
      // we have no way to do the multitexture.
      if( !m_bCanDoAddSigned )
      {
          // turn off multitexture and just go with the one detail texture
          m_bCanDoMultitexture = false;
      }
  }

  bool bSrcColor = DevCaps.SrcBlendCaps & D3DPBLENDCAPS_SRCCOLOR;
  bool bDestColor = DevCaps.SrcBlendCaps & D3DPBLENDCAPS_DESTCOLOR;
  if( !m_bCanDoMultitexture && !(bSrcColor && bDestColor) )
  {
      // device couldn't do the alpha blending we wanted.
      return false;
  }

  return true;
}
```

Glow Maps

Glow maps are useful for creating objects that have glowing parts that glow independently of the base map. Examples of this are things like LEDs on a tactical unit, buttons on a weapon or other unit, and the lights on a building or space ship. The same scenery during the daytime could look completely different at night with the addition of a few glow maps.

To implement it you use a texture map that is mostly black, with lighter areas representing things that will glow on the final image. What you want is the glow map to have no effect on the base map except in glowing areas, so you can't use the modulate blending mode. Instead you can use the addition blending mode, D3DTOP_ADD. Listing 8.10 has the source code to do it.

Listing 8.10: Sample code for setting up glow mapping using multitexture

```
//pDevice is a valid LPDIRECT3DDEVICE8 object
//pBase is the base texture
//pGlowMap is the glow map

pDevice->SetTextureStageState( 0, COLORARG1, D3DTA_TEXTURE );
pDevice->SetTextureStageState( 0, COLOROP, D3DTOP_SELECTARG1 );
pDevice->SetTexture( 0, pBase );

pDevice->SetTextureStageState( 1, COLORARG1, D3DTA_TEXTURE );
pDevice->SetTextureStageState( 1, COLORARG2, D3DTA_CURRENT );
pDevice->SetTextureStageState( 1, COLOROP, D3DTOP_ADD );
pDevice->SetTexture( 1, pGlowMap );

// draw polygon
```

The additive blending mode can also be approximated with multipass rendering when either the blending mode isn't available or the extra stage is being used by something else. You just set the source blending factor to 1.0 and the destination blend factor to 1.0. See Listing 8.11 for the source code.

Listing 8.11: Sample code for setting up glow mapping using multipass

```
// pDevice is a valid LPDIRECT3DDEVICE8 object
// pBase is the base texture
// pDetailMap is the glowmap

pDevice->SetTextureStageState( 0, COLORARG1, D3DTA_TEXTURE );
pDevice->SetTextureStageState( 0, COLOROP, D3DTOP_SELECTARG1 );
pDevice->SetRenderState( D3DRS_ALPHABLENDENABLE, FALSE );
pDevice->SetTexture( 0, pBase );

// draw polygon

pDevice->SetRenderState( D3DRS_ALPHABLENDENABLE, TRUE );
pDevice->SetRenderState( D3DRS_SRCBLEND, D3DBLEND_ONE );
pDevice->SetRenderState( D3DRS_DESTBLEND, D3DBLEND_ONE );
pDevice->SetTexture( 0, pGlowMap );

// draw polygon
```

The one danger of using glow maps is you can easily saturate the image if you use a bad choice of texture. Saturation occurs when the result of the blending step is greater than 1.0. The value is clamped down to 1.0 of course, but this causes the image to look too bright. If the base map is too bright, consider using darker shades of color for glowing areas of the glow map.

Gloss Maps

Gloss maps are one of the cooler effects that can be done with multitexture, in my opinion. Any other effect you can do (like environment maps or specular maps) can look cooler if you also use gloss maps.

Gloss maps themselves don't do much; they are combined with another multitexture operation. The gloss map controls how much another effect shows through on a surface. For example, let's suppose you're designing a racing car game. The texture map for the car includes everything except the wheels (which are different objects, connected to the parent object). When you go to draw the car, you put an environment map on it, showing some sort of city scene or lighting that is rushing by (see *San Francisco Rush* by Atari for an example of this).

One small issue that can crop up using this method is the fact that the entire surface of the car (windshield, hood, bumper, etc.) reflects the environment map the same amount. *SFR* got around this by using a different map for the windshield, but there is another way to go about it: using a gloss map on the car. The gloss map is brighter in areas that should reflect the environment map more, and darker in areas where it should reflect it less. So, in this example, the area that would cover the windshield would be fairly bright, almost white. The body of the car would be a lighter gray, where the non-reflective bumpers would be dark, almost black. Figure 8.28 shows how you combine the base map, gloss map, and specular/environment map to make a gloss mapped image.

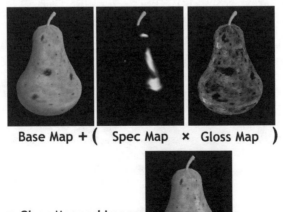

Base Map + (Spec Map × Gloss Map)

= Gloss Mapped Image

Figure 8.28: The separate pieces of gloss mapping in action

Pear images courtesy of Jason L. Mitchell, ATI Research, Inc.

You can do some amazing effects with this. For example, let's say you're driving through a mud puddle, and mud splatters up on the car. You could use a special mud texture and blit some streaks of mud on top of the base car texture map around the wheels, to show that it had just gone through mud. You could <u>also</u> blit the same mud effects to the gloss map, painting black texels instead of mud-colored texels. That way, whatever regions of the car had mud on them would not reflect the environment map, which is exactly the kind of effect wanted.

The way it works is, you perform a first pass with the base map modulated by the diffuse color to get the regular vanilla texture mapped model we all know and love. Then you perform a second pass that has two textures (the environment map and the gloss map) modulated together. The modulation allows the light areas of the gloss map to cause the environment map to come out more than in dark areas. The result of the modulation is blended with the frame buffer destination color using an addition blend (source factor = 1, dest factor = 1).

Source code to implement gloss mapping appears in Listing 8.12.

Listing 8.12: Sample code for setting up gloss mapping

```
// pDevice is a valid LPDIRECT3DDEVICE8 object
// pBase is the base texture
// pSpecularMap is the spec map
// pGlossMap is the gloss map

// Pass 1: base map modulated with diffuse color
pDevice->SetTextureStageState( 0, COLORARG1, D3DTA_TEXTURE );

pDevice->SetTextureStageState( 0, COLOROP, D3DTOP_SELECTARG1 );

pDevice->SetTextureStageState( 1, COLORARG1, D3DTA_DIFFUSE );
pDevice->SetTextureStageState( 1, COLORARG2, D3DTA_CURRENT );
pDevice->SetTextureStageState( 1, COLOROP, D3DTOP_MODULATE );

pDevice->SetRenderState( D3DRS_ALPHABLENDENABLE, FALSE );
pDevice->SetTexture( 0, pBase );

// draw polygon

// Pass 2: spec map modulated with gloss map.
// not included: code to set up spec-mapped texture coordinates

pDevice->SetTextureStageState( 0, COLORARG1, D3DTA_TEXTURE );
pDevice->SetTextureStageState( 0, COLOROP, D3DTOP_SELECTARG1 );

pDevice->SetTextureStageState( 1, COLORARG1, D3DTA_TEXTURE );
pDevice->SetTextureStageState( 1, COLORARG2, D3DTA_CURRENT );
pDevice->SetTextureStageState( 1, COLOROP, D3DTOP_MODULATE );
```

```
pDevice->SetTexture( 0, pSpecMap );
pDevice->SetTexture( 1, pGlossMap );

pDevice->SetRenderState( D3DRS_ALPHABLENDENABLE, TRUE );
pDevice->SetRenderState( D3DRS_SRCBLEND, D3DBLEND_ONE );
pDevice->SetRenderState( D3DRS_DESTBLEND, D3DBLEND_ONE );

// draw polygon
```

Other Effects

There are a myriad of other multitexture effects that are possible given the set of blending operations provided by Direct3D. To do a certain effect, all you need to do is dream it up; chances are there's a way to do it using multitexture. To showcase that concept, I'm going to throw together the blending modes I've discussed thus far into a menagerie of multitexture!

Application: MultiTex

To show off some multipass and multitexture effects, I threw together an application that shows an object resembling the earth with six total passes that can each be toggled on and off. Some of the code in this application is based off of the bumpearth DX SDK sample, specifically the code to generate the sphere. Also, the base texture map is from the SDK.

When you first start the application, it loads all the textures and starts running with just the base map modulated with the diffuse color. There is one mostly white (but a little yellow) directional light in the scene to mimic the sun.

Pass 1: Base Map

The first pass, which is the only one displayed when the program starts up, is the base pass. It just modulates the base texture map (a picture of the earth, which appears in Figure 8.29) with the diffuse color coming in from the sun directional light, making Figure 8.30.

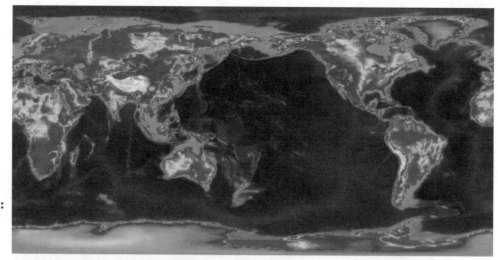

Figure 8.29:
The first
pass texture
map

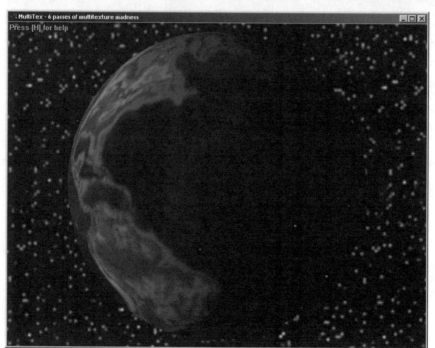

Figure 8.30:
The base
pass all by
itself

The code to draw the base pass appears in Listing 8.13.

Listing 8.13: Code to draw the base pass

```
void cMultiTexApp::DoBasePass()
{
  LPDIRECT3DDEVICE8 pDevice = Graphics()->GetDevice();
```

```
/**
 * first pass should modulate with the diffuse color
 */
pDevice->SetTexture( 0, m_pTextures[0]->GetTexture() );
SetColorStage( 0, D3DTA_TEXTURE, D3DTA_CURRENT, D3DTOP_MODULATE );

/**
 * first pass doesn't use alpha blending.
 */
pDevice->SetRenderState( D3DRS_ALPHABLENDENABLE, FALSE );

    sMaterial mat(
    0.f,
    color3(0.8f,0.8f,0.8f),
    color3(0.0f,0.0f,0.0f),
    color3(0.0f,0.0f,0.0f) );
    pDevice->SetMaterial(&mat);

pDevice->DrawPrimitiveUP(
    D3DPT_TRIANGLESTRIP,
    m_earthVerts.size() - 2,
    &m_earthVerts[0],
    sizeof( sMTVertex ) );

}
```

Pass 2: Detail Map

The second pass, activated by pressing the 2 key, enables detail mapping. A higher-frequency set of texture coordinates is generated for the second pair of texture coordinates, and the texture map in Figure 8.31 is used for the detail map.

Figure 8.31:
The second pass texture map

Using MODULATE2X style alpha blending, the detail pass is combined with the base pass to accomplish the desired detail effect, which appears in Figure 8.32.

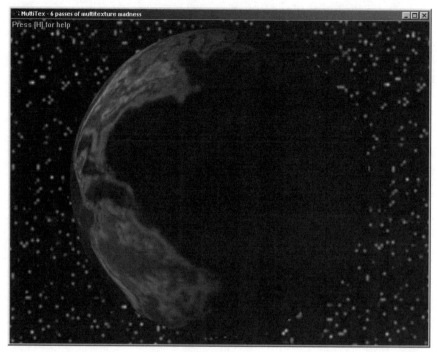

Figure 8.32:
The base
pass plus the
detail pass

The code to draw the detail pass appears in Listing 8.14.

Listing 8.14: Code to draw the detail pass

```
void cMultiTexApp::DoDetailPass()
{
  LPDIRECT3DDEVICE8 pDevice = Graphics()->GetDevice();

  /**
   * set up modulate 2x style alpha blending
   */
  pDevice->SetRenderState( D3DRS_ALPHABLENDENABLE, TRUE );
  pDevice->SetRenderState( D3DRS_SRCBLEND, D3DBLEND_DESTCOLOR );
  pDevice->SetRenderState( D3DRS_DESTBLEND, D3DBLEND_SRCCOLOR );

  /**
   * first stage is the detail map
   */
  pDevice->SetTexture( 0, m_pTextures[2]->GetTexture() );
  SetColorStage( 0, D3DTA_TEXTURE, D3DTA_CURRENT, D3DTOP_SELECTARG1 );

  /**
   * The detail map needs the second pair of coordinates
   */
  pDevice->SetTextureStageState(0, D3DTSS_TEXCOORDINDEX, 1 );
```

```
pDevice->DrawPrimitiveUP(
    D3DPT_TRIANGLESTRIP,
    m_earthVerts.size() - 2,
    &m_earthVerts[0],
    sizeof( sMTVertex ) );

/**
 * Restore the texture coordinates
 */
pDevice->SetTextureStageState(0, D3DTSS_TEXCOORDINDEX, 0 );
pDevice->SetTextureStageState(1, D3DTSS_TEXCOORDINDEX, 1 );
}
```

Pass 3: Glow Map

Third is the glow pass. It's activated with the 3 key. For this pass, I wanted to simulate the city lights that appear when the earth is shrouded in darkness. I wanted to simulate millions of little lights, rather than have blotchy areas that were lit. Finally, I wanted the lights to gradually disappear as light shined on them, since most city lights aren't on during the day.

This pass was accomplished using two simultaneous textures. The first texture, which appears in Figure 8.33, provided kind of a gross concept of which areas were populated and which weren't. Lighter areas on the texture map would receive more city lights than darker areas, so I tried my best to approximate where there would be city lights (for example, coastal regions are much more populated than, say, the Sahara desert, so they are brighter).

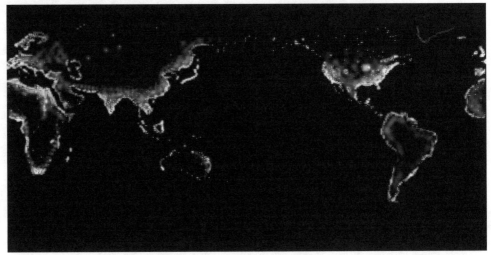

Figure 8.33: The first texture of the third pass

The second stage of the glow pass has a noise texture of pixels from gray to white. It uses the same higher-frequency texture coordinates used by the detail pass. The texture is modulated with the first stage texture, so that black areas appear as black and white areas appear as a random speckling of pixels, to simulate city lights. The noise map appears in Figure 8.34.

Figure 8.34: The second texture of the third pass

The result of the modulation is combined with the frame buffer using additive blending (both source and destination blending factors set to D3DBLEND_ONE). This produces Figure 8.35.

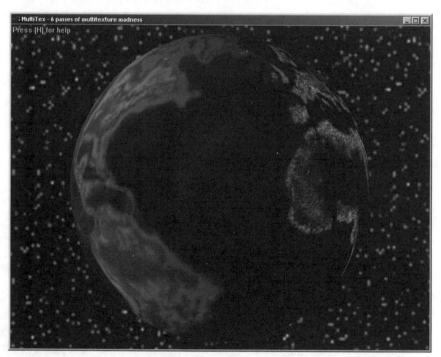

Figure 8.35: The base pass plus the glow pass

The code to draw the glow pass appears in Listing 8.15.

Listing 8.15: Code to draw the glow pass

```
void cMultiTexApp::DoGlowPass()
{
  LPDIRECT3DDEVICE8 pDevice = Graphics()->GetDevice();

  /**
```

```
 * glow map the glow map mask gets modulated with the
 * inverse diffuse color, that way it fades as light
 * hits it.
 */
pDevice->SetTexture( 0, m_pTextures[1]->GetTexture() );
SetColorStage(
     0,
     D3DTA_TEXTURE,
     D3DTA_DIFFUSE | D3DTA_COMPLEMENT,
     D3DTOP_MODULATE );

/**
 * The second pass is the noise map, to give the
 * illusion of millions of little lights.  just
 * modulate with whatever made it through the
 * first pass
 */
pDevice->SetTexture( 1, m_pTextures[4]->GetTexture() );
pDevice->SetTextureStageState(1, D3DTSS_TEXCOORDINDEX, 1 );
SetColorStage(
     1,
     D3DTA_TEXTURE,
     D3DTA_CURRENT,
     D3DTOP_MODULATE );


/**
 * set up add style blending
 */
pDevice->SetRenderState( D3DRS_ALPHABLENDENABLE, TRUE );
pDevice->SetRenderState( D3DRS_SRCBLEND, D3DBLEND_ONE );
pDevice->SetRenderState( D3DRS_DESTBLEND, D3DBLEND_ONE );

/**
 * Turn up diffuse all the way to accentuate the
 * effect
 */
  sMaterial mat(
     0.f,
     color3(1.0f,1.0f,1.0f),
     color3(0.0f,0.0f,0.0f),
     color3(0.0f,0.0f,0.0f) );
  pDevice->SetMaterial(&mat);

/**
 * The second light is to help accentuate the light hitting the earth.
 * This helps the little lights fade away as they hit sunlight.
 */
pDevice->LightEnable(1, TRUE);
```

```
pDevice->DrawPrimitiveUP(
    D3DPT_TRIANGLESTRIP,
    m_earthVerts.size() - 2,
    &m_earthVerts[0],
    sizeof( sMTVertex ) );

/**
 * Restore the basic state
 */
pDevice->SetTextureStageState(1, D3DTSS_COLOROP ,D3DTOP_DISABLE );
pDevice->SetTextureStageState(1, D3DTSS_TEXCOORDINDEX, 0 );
pDevice->LightEnable(1, FALSE);

}
```

Pass 4: Environment Map

The fourth pass uses texture transforms to do spherical environment mapping. A texture transformation matrix multiplies the camera space normal vector, and the first two components are used to index into the environment map. The map itself is the coffee shop texture given in the environment mapping section before. The texture transformation equation that is used appears below:

$$\begin{bmatrix} n_x & n_y & n_z & 1 \end{bmatrix} \begin{bmatrix} 0.5 & 0 & 0 & 0 \\ 0 & 0.5 & 0 & 0 \\ 0 & 0 & 1 & 0 \\ 0.5 & 0.5 & 0 & 1 \end{bmatrix} = \begin{bmatrix} \dfrac{n_x+1}{2} & \dfrac{n_y+1}{2} & n_z & 1 \end{bmatrix}$$

The environment map is combined using alpha blending with the same map I'll use in the glow map pass (so that the envy map reflects more on the water) and is also modulated by the inverse diffuse color (so that the envy map reflects more during the night). The result appears in Figure 8.36.

Figure 8.36:
Base pass
plus environ-
ment map-
ping pass

The code to draw the environment mapping pass appears in Listing 8.16.

Listing 8.16: Code to do environment mapping

```
void cMultiTexApp::DoEnvyPass()
{
  LPDIRECT3DDEVICE8 pDevice = Graphics()->GetDevice();

  /**
   * The first color pass is just the inverse diffuse color.
   * the first alpha pass takes the earth mask used in
   * the gloss pass.  This will be modulated with the
   * final color before being alpha blended onto the
   * frame buffer.
   */
  pDevice->SetTexture( 0, m_pTextures[1]->GetTexture() );
  SetColorStage(
       0,
       D3DTA_DIFFUSE | D3DTA_COMPLEMENT,
       D3DTA_CURRENT,
       D3DTOP_SELECTARG1 );

  SetAlphaStage(
       0,
       D3DTA_TEXTURE,
       D3DTA_CURRENT,
```

```
            D3DTOP_SELECTARG1 );

/**
 * The second pass is the envy map.  Sure, a nice
 * star pattern would have worked, but using the
 * coffeeshop texturemap really points out that
 * the envymapping is working correctly.
 */
pDevice->SetTexture( 1, m_pTextures[5]->GetTexture() );
SetColorStage(
     1,
     D3DTA_TEXTURE,
     D3DTA_CURRENT,
     D3DTOP_MODULATE );

/**
 * Set up texture transformations.
 */
pDevice->SetTextureStageState(1, D3DTSS_TEXCOORDINDEX,
D3DTSS_TCI_CAMERASPACENORMAL  );
 pDevice->SetTextureStageState(1, D3DTSS_TEXTURETRANSFORMFLAGS,
D3DTTFF_COUNT2);

/**
 * Set up the environment mapping matrix.
 * This performs the calculation we want:
 * u=n_x/2 + 0.5
 * v=-n_y/2 + 0.5
 */
matrix4 texMat;
texMat.MakeIdent();
texMat._11 = 0.5;
texMat._41 = 0.5;
texMat._22 = -0.5;
texMat._42 = 0.5;
pDevice->SetTransform( D3DTS_TEXTURE1, (D3DMATRIX*)&texMat );

/**
 * Reflect lots of the diffuse light again
 */
     sMaterial mat(
     0.f,
     color3(1.0f,1.0f,1.0f),
     color3(0.0f,0.0f,0.0f),
     color3(0.0f,0.0f,0.0f) );
     pDevice->SetMaterial(&mat);

// Turn on that extra light we used in the glow pass too.
pDevice->LightEnable(1, TRUE);

/**
```

```
 * set up add style blending
 */
pDevice->SetRenderState( D3DRS_ALPHABLENDENABLE, TRUE );
pDevice->SetRenderState( D3DRS_SRCBLEND, D3DBLEND_SRCALPHA );
pDevice->SetRenderState( D3DRS_DESTBLEND, D3DBLEND_ONE );


pDevice->DrawPrimitiveUP(
    D3DPT_TRIANGLESTRIP,
    m_earthVerts.size() - 2,
    &m_earthVerts[0],
    sizeof( sMTVertex ) );

/**
 * Fix up all of our esoteric states
 */
pDevice->SetTextureStageState(1, D3DTSS_TEXTURETRANSFORMFLAGS,
D3DTTFF_DISABLE);
 pDevice->SetTextureStageState(1, D3DTSS_COLOROP ,D3DTOP_DISABLE );
 pDevice->SetTextureStageState(1, D3DTSS_TEXCOORDINDEX, 0 );
 pDevice->LightEnable(1, FALSE);
}
```

Pass 5: Gloss Map

The fifth pass, which performs gloss mapping, uses two textures. The first texture is the gloss map, and it appears in Figure 8.37. To save texture space, this image hides in the alpha component of the glow map texture. This is why I used the source alpha in the blending step: It essentially performs a modulation for you (the alpha, holding the gloss value, is modulated with the specular value).

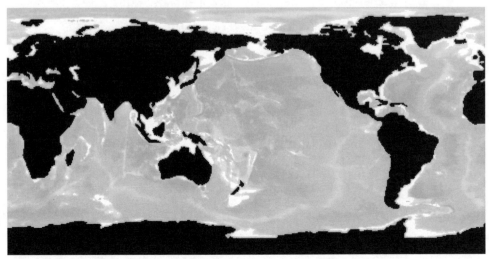

Figure 8.37:
The gloss
map texture

To create the specular value, I used spherical environment mapping with a texture with a bright spot in the upper-left corner. The original version of this application just used the interpolated specular value.

The result of the operation is that you get really shiny looking water, especially at coastal regions, while the land doesn't reflect specularities at all. The image showing this appears in Figure 8.38.

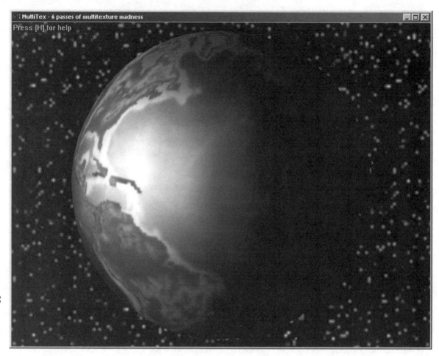

Figure 8.38:
The base
pass plus the
gloss pass

The code to draw the gloss pass appears in Listing 8.17.

Listing 8.17: Code to draw the gloss pass

```
void cMultiTexApp::DoGlossPass()
{
  LPDIRECT3DDEVICE8 pDevice = Graphics()->GetDevice();

  /**
    * The first color pass is just the diffuse color.
    * the first alpha pass uses the gloss map texture.
    * This will be modulated with the
    * final color before being alpha blended onto the
    * frame buffer.
    */
  pDevice->SetTexture( 0, m_pTextures[1]->GetTexture() );
  SetColorStage(
      0,
      D3DTA_DIFFUSE,
```

```
        D3DTA_CURRENT,
        D3DTOP_SELECTARG1 );

SetAlphaStage(
    0,
    D3DTA_TEXTURE,
    D3DTA_CURRENT,
    D3DTOP_SELECTARG1 );

/**
 * The second pass is the specular map.  It isn't even
 * close to being correct, but it looks good enough.
 */
pDevice->SetTexture( 1, m_pTextures[6]->GetTexture() );
SetColorStage(
    1,
    D3DTA_TEXTURE,
    D3DTA_CURRENT,
    D3DTOP_SELECTARG1 );

/**
 * Set up texture transformations.
 */
pDevice->SetTextureStageState(1, D3DTSS_TEXCOORDINDEX,
D3DTSS_TCI_CAMERASPACENORMAL  );
pDevice->SetTextureStageState(1, D3DTSS_TEXTURETRANSFORMFLAGS,
D3DTTFF_COUNT2);

/**
 * Set up the environment mapping matrix.
 * This performs the calculation we want:
 * u=n_x/2 + 0.5
 * v=-n_y/2 + 0.5
 */
matrix4 texMat;
texMat.MakeIdent();
texMat._11 = 0.5;
texMat._41 = 0.5;
texMat._22 = -0.5;
texMat._42 = 0.5;
pDevice->SetTransform( D3DTS_TEXTURE1, (D3DMATRIX*)&texMat );

/**
 * Reflect lots of the diffuse light again
 */
    sMaterial mat(
    0.f,
    color3(1.0f,1.0f,1.0f),
    color3(0.0f,0.0f,0.0f),
    color3(0.0f,0.0f,0.0f) );
```

```
                    pDevice->SetMaterial(&mat);

        // Turn on that extra light we used in the glow pass too.
        pDevice->LightEnable(1, TRUE);

        /**
         * set up add style blending
         */
        pDevice->SetRenderState( D3DRS_ALPHABLENDENABLE, TRUE );
        pDevice->SetRenderState( D3DRS_SRCBLEND, D3DBLEND_SRCALPHA );
        pDevice->SetRenderState( D3DRS_DESTBLEND, D3DBLEND_ONE );

        pDevice->DrawPrimitiveUP(
            D3DPT_TRIANGLESTRIP,
            m_earthVerts.size() - 2,
            &m_earthVerts[0],
            sizeof( sMTVertex ) );

        /**
         * Fix up all of our esoteric states
         */
        pDevice->SetTextureStageState(1, D3DTSS_TEXTURETRANSFORMFLAGS,
        D3DTTFF_DISABLE);
         pDevice->SetTextureStageState(1, D3DTSS_COLOROP ,D3DTOP_DISABLE );
         pDevice->SetTextureStageState(1, D3DTSS_TEXCOORDINDEX, 0 );
         pDevice->LightEnable(1, FALSE);
        }
```

Pass 6: Cloud Map

The final pass tries to simulate cloud cover on the earth. The cloud map hides in the alpha component of the base texture. It's modulated with the diffuse color using alpha blending, and combined with the background using (SRCALPHA: INVSRCALPHA) blending. The cloud map appears in Figure 8.39.

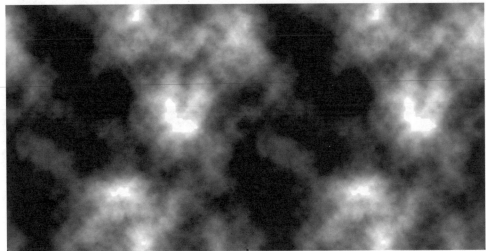

Figure 8.39:
The cloud
map

The result of the pass when applied to the base map appears in Figure 8.40.

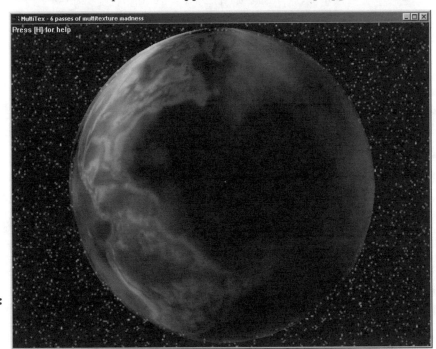

Figure 8.40:
Base pass
plus cloud
pass

The code to draw the cloud pass appears in Listing 8.18.

Listing 8.18: Code to draw the cloud pass

```
void cMultiTexApp::DoCloudPass()
{
```

```
LPDIRECT3DDEVICE8 pDevice = Graphics()->GetDevice();

pDevice->SetTexture( 0, m_pTextures[0]->GetTexture() );

SetColorStage(
    0,
    D3DTA_TEXTURE,
    D3DTA_DIFFUSE,
    D3DTOP_SELECTARG2 );

SetAlphaStage(
    0,
    D3DTA_TEXTURE,
    D3DTA_DIFFUSE,
    D3DTOP_SELECTARG1 );


/**
 * Reflect lots of the diffuse light again
 */
    sMaterial mat(
    0.f,
    color3(1.0f,1.0f,1.0f),
    color3(0.0f,0.0f,0.0f),
    color3(0.3f,0.3f,0.3f) );
    pDevice->SetMaterial(&mat);

/**
 * Alpha blending modulates with source color, so
 * the brighter the texture is the more it is seen.
 */
pDevice->SetRenderState( D3DRS_ALPHABLENDENABLE, TRUE );
pDevice->SetRenderState( D3DRS_SRCBLEND, D3DBLEND_SRCALPHA );
pDevice->SetRenderState( D3DRS_DESTBLEND, D3DBLEND_INVSRCALPHA );


pDevice->DrawPrimitiveUP(
    D3DPT_TRIANGLESTRIP,
    m_cloudVerts.size() - 2,
    &m_cloudVerts[0],
    sizeof( sMTVertex ) );
}
```

Putting Them All Together

Figure 8.41 has all six passes combined together into a composite image. When viewed on a good card this looks quite nice.

Figure 8.41:
All six passes

One important piece of code that we need to worry about is the device checking code. It goes through and checks for the needed capabilities of each pass. If the effects aren't available, the app doesn't let you activate them. The code to check device capabilities appears in Listing 8.19.

Listing 8.19: Device confirmation code

```
bool cMultiTexApp::CheckCaps()
{
  // certain base functionality is assumed, like MODULATE
  // and SELECTARGx

  m_bCanDoBasePass = true; // lord help us if can't do the base pass.
  m_bCanDoDetailPass = false;
  m_bCanDoGlowPass = false;
  m_bCanDoGlossPass = false;
  m_bCanDoEnvyPass = false;
  m_bCanDoCloudPass = false;

  D3DCAPS8 DevCaps;

  Graphics()->GetDevice()->GetDeviceCaps( &DevCaps );
```

```
bool bCanDoMultitexture = (DevCaps.MaxSimultaneousTextures >= 2);
bool bCanDoMod2x = (DevCaps.TextureOpCaps & D3DTEXOPCAPS_MODULATE2X)? true :
false;


/**
 * check detail mapping
 */
if( (DevCaps.SrcBlendCaps & D3DPBLENDCAPS_DESTCOLOR) &&
     (DevCaps.DestBlendCaps & D3DPBLENDCAPS_SRCCOLOR) )
{
    m_bCanDoDetailPass = true;
}


/**
 * check glow mapping
 */
if( bCanDoMultitexture &&
     (DevCaps.SrcBlendCaps & D3DPBLENDCAPS_ONE) &&
     (DevCaps.DestBlendCaps & D3DPBLENDCAPS_ONE) )
{
    m_bCanDoGlowPass = true;
}


/**
 * check envy mapping
 */
if( (DevCaps.VertexProcessingCaps & D3DVTXPCAPS_TEXGEN ) &&
     (DevCaps.SrcBlendCaps & D3DPBLENDCAPS_SRCCOLOR) &&
     (DevCaps.DestBlendCaps & D3DPBLENDCAPS_ONE) )
{
    m_bCanDoEnvyPass = true;
}


/**
 * check gloss mapping
 */
if( bCanDoMod2x &&
     (DevCaps.SrcBlendCaps & D3DPBLENDCAPS_ONE) &&
     (DevCaps.DestBlendCaps & D3DPBLENDCAPS_ONE) )
{
    m_bCanDoGlossPass = true;
}


/**
 * check cloud mapping
 */
if( (DevCaps.SrcBlendCaps & D3DPBLENDCAPS_SRCCOLOR) &&
     (DevCaps.DestBlendCaps & D3DPBLENDCAPS_INVSRCCOLOR) )
{
    m_bCanDoCloudPass = true;
```

```
   }

   return true;
}
```

Using the Stencil Buffer

I promised back in Chapter 6 that I would talk about stencil buffers more, and here we are. While they've been in high-end SGI hardware for quite some time now, it's only been recently that they've started to crop up on consumer hardware. They allow you to perform a lot of nifty effects easily that otherwise would be extremely difficult/slow, if not impossible.

The stencil buffer is yet another buffer for your application (you already have the frame buffer, back buffer, and the z-buffer). It's never its own buffer; rather, it always piggybacks a few bits of the z-buffer. Generally, when stenciling is desired, you set up a 16-bit z-buffer (15 bits of depth, one bit of stencil) or a 32-bit z-buffer (24 bits of depth, 8 bits of stencil). You can clear it to a default value using IDirect3DDevice8::Clear just like you did with the back buffer and the z-buffer.

Here's the way it works: Before a pixel is tested against the z-buffer, it's tested against the stencil buffer. The stencil for a pixel is defined by the stencil reference value (which is set with one of the device render states). They are compared using a D3DCMPFUNC just like the z-buffer. It should be noted that before the reference value and the stencil buffer value are compared, they are both AND'ed by the stencil mask. The equation for the stencil test step is:

```
(StencilRef & StencilMask) CompFunc (StencilBufferValue & StencilMask)
```

What happens as a result of the comparison is defined by a bunch of other render states. There are three possible cases that can occur, and you can modify what happens to the stencil buffer for each of them. The three cases are:

■ The stencil test fails.

■ The stencil test succeeds, but then the z test fails.

■ Both the stencil test and the z test succeed.

What happens when you get to one of these three cases is defined by setting render states to a member of the D3DSTENCILOP enumeration, which is listed in Table 8.4.

Table 8.4: Values for the D3DSTENCILOP enumeration

D3DSTENCILOP_KEEP	Do not change the value in the stencil buffer.
D3DSTENCILOP_ZERO	Set the entry in the stencil buffer to 0.
D3DSTENCILOP_REPLACE	Set the entry in the stencil buffer to the reference value.

D3DSTENCILOP_INCRSAT	Increment the stencil buffer entry, clamping it to the maximum value—8-bit stencil buffers have a maximum value of 255, 1-bit stencil buffers have a maximum value of 1.
D3DSTENCILOP_DECRSAT	Decrement the stencil buffer entry, clamping it to 0.
D3DSTENCILOP_INVERT	Invert the bits in the stencil buffer entry.
D3DSTENCILOP_INCR	Increment the stencil buffer entry, wrapping to 0 if it goes past the maximum value.
D3DSTENCILOP_DECR	Decrement the stencil buffer entry, wrapping to the maximum value if it goes past 0.

The actual render states you have to set to muck with the stencil buffer appear in Table 8.5.

Table 8.5: Stencil buffer render states (D3DRS_ prefix ommited)

STENCILENABLE	Set this state to TRUE to enable stenciling. (default = FALSE)
STENCILFAIL	Operation to perform if the stencil test fails. Member of the D3DSTENCILOP enumeration, described above. (default = D3DSTENCILOP_KEEP)
STENCILZFAIL	Operation to perform if the stencil test succeeds but then the z-test fails. Member of the D3DSTENCILOP enumeration, described above. (default = D3DSTENCILOP_KEEP)
STENCILPASS	Operation to perform if both the stencil test and z-test succeed. Member of the D3DSTENCILOP enumeration, described above. (default = D3DSTENCILOP_KEEP)
STENCILFUNC	Sets the stencil comparison test function. The value must be one of the members of the D3DCMPFUNC enumeration, discussed in Chapter 6. (default = D3DCMP_ALWAYS)
STENCILREF	Sets the integer reference value that stencil pixels are tested against when stencil buffering is enabled. (default = 0)
STENCILMASK	Mask applied to both the current and reference stencil values before the stencil test is performed. (default = 0xFFFFFFFF)
STENCILWRITEMASK	Write mask applied to stencil values before they are written to the stencil buffer. (default = 0xFFFFFFFF)

Also, as a refresher, Table 8.6 has the D3DCMPFUNC enumeration, which holds the possible comparison functions we can set D3DRS_STENCILFUNC to.

Table 8.6: Values for the D3DCMPFUNC enumeration

D3DCMP_NEVER	Always fails the test.
D3DCMP_LESS	Passes if the tested pixel is less than the current pixel.
D3DCMP_EQUAL	Passes if the tested pixel is equal to the current pixel.
D3DCMP_LESSEQUAL	Passes if the tested pixel is less than or equal to the current pixel.
D3DCMP_GREATER	Passes if the tested pixel is greater than the current pixel.
D3DCMP_NOTEQUAL	Passes if the tested pixel is not equal to the current pixel.
D3DCMP_GREATEREQUAL	Passes if the tested pixel is greater than or equal to the current pixel.
D3DCMP_ALWAYS	Always passes the test.

Overdraw Counter

One simple use of stencil buffers is to implement an overdraw counter. The bounding factor in most graphics applications (especially games like *Quake III: Arena/Unreal Tournament*) is the fill-rate of the card. Very few games implement anywhere near exact visibility for their scenes, so many pixels on the screen will be drawn two, three, five, or more times. If you draw <u>every</u> pixel five times and you're running at a high resolution, the application will be completely bound by how fast the card can draw the pixels to the frame buffer.

You can use stencil buffers to help you figure out how much overdraw you're doing when rendering a given scene. Initially you clear the stencil buffer to zero. The stencil comparison function is set to always accept pixels. Then the stencil operations for both PASS and ZFAIL are set to increment the value in the stencil buffer.

Then, after you render your frame, you lock the z-buffer and average together all of the stencil values in the buffer. Of course, this is going to be a really slow operation; calculating the overdraw level is something to be done during development only!

Sample code that would set up the stencil buffer to handle an overdraw counter appears in Listing 8.20.

Listing 8.20: Sample code to set up the stencil buffer for an overdraw counter

```
// pDevice is a valid Direct3D Device

// Turn on stenciling
pDevice->SetRenderState( D3DRS_STENCILENABLE, TRUE );

// Set the function to always pass.
pDevice->SetRenderState( D3DRS_STENCILFUNC, D3DCMP_ALWAYS );
pDevice->SetRenderState( D3DRS_STENCILREF, 0 );
pDevice->SetRenderState( D3DRS_STENCILMASK, -1 );

// Always increment the stencil value
```

```
pDevice->SetRenderState(
    D3DRS_STENCILZFAIL,
    D3DSTENCILOP_INCR );
pDevice->SetRenderState(
    D3DRS_STENCILPASS,
    D3DSTENCILOP_INCR );
```

Dissolves and Wipes

Another use for stencil buffers is to block out certain regions of an image. You can use this to do film-like transitions between scenes, such as wiping left to right from one image to another.

To implement it, you have a polygon that grows frame to frame, eventually enveloping the entire screen. You initially clear out the stencil buffer to zero. The wipe polygon doesn't draw anything to the frame buffer (use an alpha of 0 and the alpha-testing render states to prevent anything from being drawn), but it sets the stencil pixels it covers to 1. The old scene should be rendered on all the stencil pixels marked with a 0 (the ones that weren't covered by the wipe polygon) and the new scene should be rendered on all the pixels with a stencil value of 1. When the wipe polygon grows to the point that it's completely covering the frame buffer, you can stop rendering the first scene (since it's completely invisible now). Sample source code to set up a wipe effect appears in Listing 8.21.

Listing 8.21: Sample code to set up the stencil buffer for a wipe

```
// Stencil is initially cleared to 0.
// pDevice is a valid Direct3D Device pointer

// Set up stencil states for the wipe polygon
pDevice->SetRenderState( D3DRS_STENCILENABLE, TRUE );
pDevice->SetRenderState( D3DRS_STENCILFUNC, D3DCMP_ALWAYS );
pDevice->SetRenderState( D3DRS_STENCILPASS,D3DSTENCILOP_INCR);
pDevice->SetRenderState( D3DRS_ALPHAFUNC, D3DCMP_NEVER );
pDevice->SetRenderState( D3DRS_ALPHATESTENABLE, TRUE );

// Render the wipe polygon
...

pDevice->SetRenderState( D3DRS_ALPHAFUNC, D3DCMP_ALWAYS );
pDevice->SetRenderState( D3DRS_ALPHATESTENABLE, FALSE );
pDevice->SetRenderState( D3DRS_STENCILFUNC, D3DCMP_EQUAL );
pDevice->SetRenderState( D3DRS_STENCILPASS,D3DSTENCILOP_KEEP);
pDevice->SetRenderState( D3DRS_STENCILREF, 0 );

// Render the old scene
...
```

```
pDevice->SetRenderState( D3DS_STENCILREF, 1 );

// Render the new scene
...
```

Stencil Shadows and Stencil Mirrors

While there isn't enough space to discuss stencil shadows and mirrors, they are a really nifty use of stencil buffers. See the "For Further Reading" section at the end of the chapter for some resources on the topic.

Validating Device Capabilities with ValidateDevice()

While hardware manufacturers are exceeding our expectations with hardware performance every day, there is yet to be a perfect Direct3D hardware device. By perfect I mean one that completely implements the entire Direct3D feature set. Most cards, for example, can only draw two or three textures simultaneously. By the time you read this book there should be cards available that can draw four textures simultaneously, but Direct3D can support up to eight.

Because of this, you should become accustomed to checking the capabilities of the device before doing anything really tricky by using the device description structure. This way you can transparently degrade your rendering is to support less able cards (for example, only enabling cubic environment mapping if the device supports it).

Unfortunately, this sometimes isn't enough to make sure an application works correctly. All too often, a card can only do a certain feature when a certain other feature is disabled.

A common example: Many cards on the market (most of them since Voodoo2) have been able to do trilinear filtering on texture maps. The capability bits of the device description say so. However, they do it using a trick. Since the device can support multiple textures, they transparently place the MIP maps of a texture into alternating texture stages. That way, the blending step done between MIP maps can be done just by using alpha to blend between the two texture maps.

There is, of course, a problem with this method: If the second texture stage is filled up with half of the MIP map levels for the first texture, you can't put your own textures in there. So while most multitexture cards can draw multiple textures at the same time, and also support trilinear MIP mapping, they can't do both of them at the same time. Luckily, cards since the ATI Rage 128 are being released that can perform trilinear filtering in each stage separately.

Unfortunately, using just the device description there is no way to anticipate problems like this. This was one of the primary complaints with Direct3D before version 6.0. When version 6.0 came out, there was a new function to help people fix this sort of problem.

The function is IDirect3DDevice8::ValidateDevice. It examines the state of the device (render states, texture stage states, and the currently set textures) and lets you know if the device is capable of rendering it in one pass. If it is not, it will give you a fairly helpful error code, along with giving you an idea of how many passes it will take to correctly render primitives with the desired configuration.

```
HRESULT IDirect3DDevice8::ValidateDevice(
  LPDWORD pNumPasses
);
```

lpNumPasses	Pointer to a DWORD that will be filled with the number of passes the desired configuration will take in.

Table 8.7 lists some of the error codes that can result from using this function.

Table 8.7: The useful error codes that ValidateDevice can return

D3DERR_CONFLICTINGTEXTUREFILTER	Some of the current texture filters currently set cannot be used together.
D3DERR_CONFLICTINGTEXTUREPALETTE	The current textures cannot be used together. This generally results from some multitexture hardware that requires simultaneous paletted textures to use the same palette.
D3DERR_TOOMANYOPERATIONS	More texture filtering operations are being requested than are supported by the driver.
D3DERR_UNSUPPORTEDALPHAARG	One of the alpha arguments being used in the texture blend stages is not supported.
D3DERR_UNSUPPORTEDALPHAOPERATION	One of the alpha operations being used in the texture blend stages is not supported.
D3DERR_UNSUPPORTEDCOLORARG	One of the color arguments being used in the texture blend stages is not supported.
D3DERR_UNSUPPORTEDCOLOROPERATION	One of the color operations being used in the texture blend stages is not supported.
D3DERR_UNSUPPORTEDFACTORVALUE	The texture factor value is not supported by the driver.
D3DERR_UNSUPPORTEDTEXTUREFILTER	One of the currently set texture filters is not supported.
D3DERR_WRONGTEXTUREFORMAT	The pixel format for one of the textures is not supported by the device with the currently set blending modes (or with the other textures).

There are a few guidelines that you should follow if you want to increase the chances of a desired rendering setup to validate correctly:

■ There are cards (for example, ATI cards, although there are most likely others) that are designed to anticipate any texture argument to appear in the first argument of a texture stage. Only put D3DTA_TEXTURE into the D3DTSS_COLORARG1 and D3DTSS_ALPHAARG1 texture stage states.

■ Using iterated color arguments (like D3DTA_DIFFUSE or D3DTA_SPECULAR) often are only valid in the last texture stage. If you want to do light mapping with diffuse shading, for example, use three stages: The first selects the base texture, the second modulates the light map, and the third modulates the diffuse color.

■ Don't use both D3DTA_TFACTOR and D3DTA_DIFFUSE, as many cards don't support this.

■ Don't use trilinear filtering with multiple textures unless you absolutely need to. If you really, really need it, consider rendering each texture with its own pass. This, of course, limits the types of texture blending you can perform, but it's more likely to be supported by the hardware.

For Further Reading

Abrash, Michael. *Michael Abrash's Graphics Programming Black Book, Special Edition*. The Coriolis Group, 1997. ISBN: 1576101746.

While this book is currently out of print, you can still find it at most bookstores. This book has a mind-boggling 1,200 pages of amazing optimization concepts, rasterization of textured polygons, and a lot of really meaty information about the inner workings of the *Quake* engine.

Kilgard, Mark J. "Improving Shadows and Reflections via the Stencil Buffer." Available at www.nvidia.com.

This document gives some really interesting uses of the stencil buffer that are too involved to discuss here. A copy of the document appears on the companion CD.

Chapter 9

Scene Management

Sometimes I wish I was in an industry that moved a little slower. Imagine the car industry—if car manufacturers had to move at the speed that computers have to move at, cars would be traveling at supersonic speeds, flying, and driving themselves. Luckily for them this isn't the case. Large strides in most industries happen over years, not days.

The computer industry is an entirely different matter. Users are always clamoring for more—bigger bad guys, more complex physics and AI, higher resolution textures, and so forth. If a game doesn't provide what the users want, it won't be what users buy.

Aside: In fact, it's quickly becoming the case that the programmers aren't the ones running the fastest to keep up. For many artists, creating a texture twice as detailed takes more than twice as long to make. The same thing goes for models and worlds. Content creation, within the next few years, will become the bottleneck for games. It took a team of artists years to create the relatively small house players wandered around in *The 7th Guest*, and it won't be long until cards can handle worlds like that in real time. In fact they probably could these days.

The Scene Management Problem

An extremely large problem that every game has to deal with is managing its world on a per-frame basis. The problem as a whole is called *scene management*. It has many different facets: managing the per-frame polygon count, keeping the $O(n^2)$ physics and AI algorithms in check, and managing the network throughput, among others.

As an example, suppose you're writing a first-person style game, where the world is a large research facility with a scientist you must find. The research facility might be tremendously large, with a hundred rooms or more, and hallways connecting them. Each room has dozens of objects, most with hundreds of triangles. All in all, the entire world could have upwards of two or three million triangles in it.

There are a number of issues that you need to deal with to handle this world. For starters, how do you draw it? Early naïve systems would have no structure to the world at all, just a list of two million triangles. There is no choice but to draw the entire two million triangle list. This is pretty ridiculous, as almost all of the polygons drawn won't end up contributing pixels to the final image. In most cases, we'll be standing in one room. If the door is closed, all of the visible polygons belong to the room you're in, and you'll end up drawing less than 1% of the total polygon count. The only way you'll be able to draw the world at interactive frame rates is to somehow chop away polygons that you know won't be visible. Drawing 1% versus drawing 100% of the polygons can mean the difference between 30 frames per second and 3 seconds per frame!

There's an even worse example: collision detection. Whenever an object (such as our fearless player) moves in the world, you must make sure it hasn't hit any other objects. The brute force algorithm involves us taking each object and checking it for a collision. True, for most of the several thousand objects in the scene, you will quickly reject them with a trivial bounding box or bounding sphere test. However, you still need to perform all multi-thousand tests, however quick and trivial they may be, for each object that moves! The time complexity of this algorithm, $O(n^2)$, will completely devour any processor power you have, and the frame rate will slow to a crawl.

The idea of doing this is completely ridiculous. If an object is situated in a room, you should test against the dozens of objects in the room, not the thousands of objects in the whole world! As you reduce n (the number of objects each object must test against for collisions), the physics code speed increases quadratically!

The same issues that plague collision detection also attack the networking code. As characters move around the scene, their movements must be broadcast to all the other clients, so they can keep an accurate picture of the world. However, each client couldn't care less about where things that they can't see are moving. Rather than knowing where each of the thousands of scene objects are, it just wants to know about the ones that are relevant to it.

There needs to be a system of scene management. You have to be smart about which parts of the scene you choose to render, which sets of objects we perform tests against, and so forth, to keep the running time of the application in check. Ideally the size of the total scene shouldn't matter; as long as there is RAM to hold it all you can increase the size of the worlds without bounds while keeping all of the ugly algorithms running at about the same speed.

Solutions to the Scene Management Problem

I'll go over a few different systems that can be used to manage different types of scenes. I'll end up using one of them (portal rendering) to write a game at the end of this chapter, so I'll obviously be going in-depth on that one the most. The other ones we'll hopefully cover enough that you'll be able to implement them on your own.

Quadtrees/Octrees

Quadtrees are a classic form of spatial partitioning, and are used in scene management algorithms for many systems where the spatial data can be usefully boiled down to two dimensions. The most prevalent example of this is games that take place over terrain, like *Myth* or *Tribes*. While objects have a particular height value, the space of possible height values is much less than either of the lateral dimensions. You can take advantage of this and use the two lateral dimensions to classify the relations of the objects.

The scene is initially bounded on all sides by a bounding square. The recursive algorithm proceeds as follows: If there is more than one object in the bounding square, the square is divided into four smaller squares, or subnodes. The subnodes are associated with their parent node in the form of a tree with either four or zero children at each node (hence the name *quadtree*). When an object is bridging a boundary between two nodes, both nodes contain a handle to the object. This continues until all the nodes have either one or zero objects in them, or some maximum depth level is reached. Figure 9.1 shows how you would turn a scene into a quadtree.

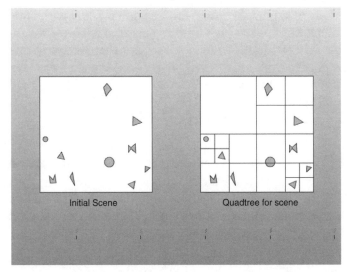

Initial Scene   Quadtree for scene

Figure 9.1:
Sample
quadtree

The advantage that quadtrees give lies in hierarchical culling. To illustrate, consider the case of drawing the world. Imagine that the total scene is very large, covering many square miles; much more than the viewer could ever see. When you go to draw the scene, you test the four subnodes of the quadtree root against the visible region from the current viewpoint. If one of the subnodes does not sit in the visible region, you know that none of its children do either. You can trivially cull that subnode and everything below it. If any part of the subnode is in the visible region, you recurse on the four children of that subnode. When we reach a leaf, you draw all of the objects inside it. This gives you a pleasingly quick way to cull out large portions of the database during rendering.

As objects move around, they may exit the current node they are in. At this point the quadtree should be recomputed. This way the tree always has the least amount of nodes necessary to represent the data. Alternatively, the tree can be constructed independently of the objects, blindly subdivided to a certain depth. Then as objects move, the code finds out the set of leaves that the bounding sphere for the object sits in.

Doing interobject collisions this way can be done really quickly using a tree such as this. The only objects that some particular object could possibly intersect with must also be in one of the same leaves that said particular object is in. To do an object intersection test, you get the list of leaves an object is sitting in, and then get the list of objects that are sitting in each of those leaves. That set of objects is the space of possible collision candidates. The space of candidates you end up with will be considerably smaller than the total number of objects. Also, if you keep the size of the leaves constant you can increase the size of the total scene almost without bound. Each of these algorithms will take about the same time to run as long as the relative proximity of objects remains the same relative to the area of the leaves.

Octrees are very similar to quadtrees, except you deal with cubes instead of squares and divide the space along all three axes, making eight subregions. Each node has eight subnodes instead of the four that we see in quadtrees. Octrees perform very well in games like 3-D space sim such as *Homeworld*, where there are many objects in the scene, but very few of them are likely candidates for collisions.

Portal Rendering

Portal rendering is a really effective way to handle scene management for indoor environments. It's the method I'll use in the game I write at the end of this chapter. It's also used in many games and public domain engines (like *Crystal Space*). Besides being effective for what it tries to do, portal rendering is intuitive and easy to implement.

Imagine you are standing in a room. This room turns out to be a bit on the sparse side; in fact there is absolutely nothing in it. The only thing in the room for us to look at is a doorway, leading into another equally empty and uninteresting room. The doorway is jumping on the minimalist bandwagon, so it happens to not have a door in it. There is an unobstructed view into the next room. Also, for the sake of discussion, assume that the walls between the rooms are made of a new space age construction material that is infinitely thin.

Now draw the room you're standing in. You have some sort of data structure that represents the room, with a list of the polygons that define the walls, floors, and ceiling. Eventually this data structure will be called a cell. You also have a special invisible polygon that covers the doorway. This special polygon is a portal.

After you have drawn the room you are in, the entire frame buffer will be filled in except for the doorway. You know for a fact that the other room, the one you can see through the doorway, is entirely behind the room you are standing in. The only pixels left to even consider when drawing the next room are the ones seen through the doorway.

Instead of blindly drawing the next room and letting the z-buffer take care of it, you can constrain the renderer, telling it to only draw the pixels that haven't been touched yet. I'll discuss the constraining part in a moment, but for right now I intuitively know that the pixels that haven't been drawn yet are the pixels in the doorway. That way, you don't waste time drawing triangles that would be obstructed by the z-buffer and not drawn anyway; you only draw pixels that will end up making it onto the screen. The bound for many applications is the fill rate of the card: how fast it can draw pixels on the screen. The fewer pixels you have it draw, the faster the application has the potential to be. An extra advantage comes from the fact that the fewer triangles you process, the less strain we put on the transformation and lighting pipeline.

This algorithm is recursive. For example, say that the second room has another doorway on the opposite wall, looking into a third room. When you finish drawing the second room, the only pixels left will be the ones that lay inside the next doorway. Once again constrain the drawing to only take place inside that doorway and then draw the next room.

Portal Rendering Concepts

A scene rendered using portal rendering must be put together in a certain way. In essence, you compose your scene out of a set of rooms that are all connected by doorways. The rooms, which I'll call *cells*, can have any number of polygons, as long as the cells themselves remain convex. Each cell represents empty space, and all of the polygons in the cell face inwards. They can be connected to any number of other cells, and the boundary locations become the portals. You can think of two adjacent cells (call them A and B) having two portals that connect them. One belongs to A and points to B as the neighbor, and the other that belongs to B and points to A as the neighbor. The two portals must be exactly the same except for vertex ordering and normal orientation. If this is not the case, portal rendering will not work correctly. To help illustrate the point, consider a standard scene of polygons, as shown in Figure 9.2.

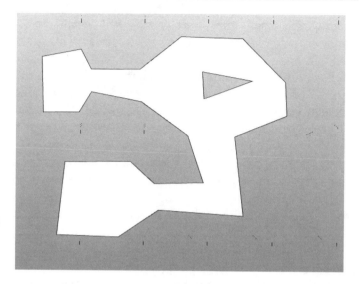

Figure 9.2:
A regular scene of polygons

This scene is of a few angular rooms, seen from a top-down view. The white area shows the region you can move around in. As you have it set up now, there is no spatial relationship set up for this scene. You can draw the world using the z-buffer and not have to worry about anything, but you'll have to suffer through all the scene management problems detailed above.

Instead, how about turning the scene into something you can portal render with. I'll discuss later how you can take an arbitrary polygonal scene and decompose it into a bunch of convex cells, but for right now assume that I have a black box that can do it for you. It might come up with a composition like the one that appears in Figure 9.3.

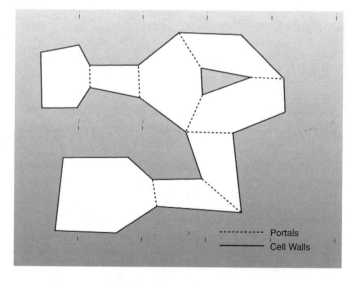

Figure 9.3:
The scene divided into eight cells

Now you have divided the scene into eight distinct convex rooms, all connected together with portals. Even without the rendering efficiency of having zero overdraw, this data representation is useful in many ways. Since the cells are convex, you can quickly perform a test between the bounding sphere of an object and the cells in the world to find out which cell(s) an object is touching (it may be situated in a portal such that it is sitting in more than one cell). All you do is perform a plane-sphere test with each polygon and portal of the cell. If the sphere is completely behind any of the planes (remember that the normals all point into the cell), then you know that the sphere isn't touching the cell at all.

If you know the space of cells an object exists in, then suddenly the scene becomes much more manageable. When you want to do any processing on an object that needs to be tested against other objects (for example, checking for collisions), you don't need to check all the objects in the scene; you just need to check the objects that are in each of the cells that the target object is in. Even if the world has a hundred thousand cells and a hundred thousand objects wandering around those cells, the hard algorithms will only need to be run with an extremely small subset of that total set; there might only be 10 or so other objects in the cell(s) a target object is currently in. You can imagine how much faster this makes things.

The extra bonus that you get with cell-based worlds of course lies in portal rendering, which allows you to efficiently find the exact set of cells that are visible from that viewpoint. Even better, you can find the exact set of polygons visible from that viewpoint.

To generate this visibility data, I use what I'll call a viewing cone. A viewing cone is an *n*-sided pyramid that extends infinitely forward, with all the sides meeting together in world space at the location of the viewer. The sides bound the visible region of space that can be seen from the camera. Before you do any portal rendering, the sides of the cone represent the sides of the screen; anything outside the cone will be outside the screen and shouldn't be drawn. Note that when you're rendering, the viewing cone has two extra conceptual polygons that lop off the tip of the cone (everything in front of the near z-plane is not drawn) and the bottom of the cone (everything behind the far z-plane is not drawn). You must ignore these two planes for right now; portal rendering won't work correctly if you don't.

Aside: A pyramid with the top and bottom chopped off is called a frustum.

Given the viewing cone, clipping a polygon against it is fairly easy. You perform a polygon-plane clipping operation with the polygon and each of the planes of the cone. If at any time we completely cull the polygon, we know that it is invisible and we can stop processing it.

To use this functionality, we'll make a class called cViewCone. It can be constructed from a viewer location and a polygon (which can be extracted from a portal in our scene), or from a viewer location and the projection information (width, height, field of view). It clips polygons with Clip(), returning true if some part of the polygon was inside the viewing cone (and false otherwise). Also an output polygon is filled with the inside fragment, if one was there. The source for cViewCone appears in Listings 9.1 (header) and 9.2 (source).

Listing 9.1: ViewCone.h

```
/*****************************************************************
 *          Advanced 3-D Game Programming using DirectX 8.0
 * * * * * * * * * * * * * * * * * * * * * * * * * * * * * * * *
 *    Title: ViewCone.h
 *     Desc: code to handle n-sided viewing cones
 *           (for portal rendering)
 * copyright (c) 2001 Peter A Walsh and by Adrian Perez
 * See license.txt for modification and distribution information
 *****************************************************************/

#ifndef _FRUSTUM_H
#define _FRUSTUM_H

#include "..\math3d\point3.h"
#include "..\math3d\plane3.h"

#define MAX_PLANES 32

class cViewCone
{
    plane3  m_planes[MAX_PLANES];
    int     m_nPlanes;
    point3  m_camLoc;

    /**
     * We need this functionality twice, encapsulate it
     */
    void GenFromPoly(
        const point3& camLoc,
        const polygon< point3 >& in );

public:

    /**
     * Default constructor
     */
    cViewCone();

    /**
     * Construct a frustum from an inputted polygon. The polygon
     * is assumed to wind clockwise from the point of view of the
     * camera
     */
    cViewCone( const point3& camLoc, const polygon< point3 >& in );
```

```
    /**
     * Construct a frustum from the viewport data.  uses the
     * data to construct a cameraspace polygon,
     * back-transforms it to worldspace, then constructs a
     * frustum out of it.
     */
    cViewCone( float fov, int width, int height, matrix4& viewMat );

    /**
     * Clip a polygon to the frustum.
     * true if there was anything left
     */
    bool Clip(
        const polygon<point3>& in,
        polygon<point3>* out );

    /**
     * Get the center point of a frustum
     * this is needed when we create frustums
     * from other frustums
     */
    const point3& GetLoc()
    {
        return m_camLoc;
    }

};


#endif // _FRUSTUM_H
```

Listing 9.2: ViewCone.cpp

```
/********************************************************************
 *          Advanced 3-D Game Programming using DirectX 8.0
 * * * * * * * * * * * * * * * * * * * * * * * * * * * * * * * * * *
 *    Title: ViewCone.cpp
 *     Desc: code to handle n-sided viewing cones
 *           (for portal rendering)
 * (C) 2001 by Peter A Walsh and Adrian Perez
 * See license.txt for modification and distribution information
 ********************************************************************/

#include "stdafx.h"
#include <assert.h>

#include <algorithm> // for swap()

#include "ViewCone.h"
```

```
using namespace std;

cViewCone::cViewCone()
: m_nPlanes( 0 )
, m_camLoc( point3::Zero )
{
    // Do nothing
}

cViewCone::cViewCone(
    const point3& camLoc,
    const polygon< point3 >& in )
{
    assert( in.nElem );
    assert( in.pList );
    GenFromPoly( camLoc, in );
}

cViewCone::cViewCone(
    float fov, int width, int height,
    matrix4& viewMat )
{
    /**
     * This function is kind of a magic trick, as it tries to
     * invert the projection matrix.  If you stare at the way
     * we make projection matrices for long enough this should
     * make sense.
     */
    float aspect = ((float)height) / width;

    float z = 10;

    float w =  aspect * (float)( cos(fov/2)/sin(fov/2) );
    float h =   1.0f  * (float)( cos(fov/2)/sin(fov/2) );

    float x0 = -z/w;
    float x1 = z/w;
    float y0 = z/h;
    float y1 = -z/h;

    /**
     * Construct a clockwise camera-space polygon
     */
    polygon<point3> poly(4);
    poly.nElem = 4;
    poly.pList[0] = point3( x0, y0,z); // top-left
    poly.pList[1] = point3( x1, y0,z); // top-right
    poly.pList[2] = point3( x1, y1,z); // bottom-right
    poly.pList[3] = point3( x0, y1,z); // bottom-left

    /**
```

```
        * Create a camspace->worldspace transform
        */
    matrix4 camMatInv = matrix4::Inverse( viewMat );

    /**
     * Convert it to worldspace
     */
    poly.pList[0] = poly.pList[0] * camMatInv;
    poly.pList[1] = poly.pList[1] * camMatInv;
    poly.pList[2] = poly.pList[2] * camMatInv;
    poly.pList[3] = poly.pList[3] * camMatInv;

    /**
     * Generate the frustum
     */
    GenFromPoly( camMatInv.GetLoc(), poly );

}

void cViewCone::GenFromPoly(
    const point3& camLoc,
    const polygon< point3 >& in )
{
    int i;
    m_camLoc = camLoc;
    m_nPlanes = 0;
    for( i=0; i< in.nElem; i++ )
    {
        /**
         * Plane 'i' contains the camera location and the 'ith'
         * edge around the polygon
         */
        m_planes[ m_nPlanes++ ] = plane3(
            camLoc,
            in.pList[(i+1)%in.nElem],
            in.pList[i] );
    }
}

bool cViewCone::Clip( const polygon<point3>& in, polygon<point3>* out )
{
    /**
     * Temporary polygons.  This isn't thread safe
     */
    static polygon<point3> a(32), b(32);
    polygon<point3>* pSrc = &a;
    polygon<point3>* pDest = &b;

    int i;

    /**
```

```
 * Copy the input polygon to a.
 */
a.nElem = in.nElem;
for( i=0; i<a.nElem; i++ )
{
    a.pList[i] = in.pList[i];
}

/**
 * Iteratively clip the polygon
 */
for( i=0; i<m_nPlanes; i++ )
{
    if( !m_planes[i].Clip( *pSrc, pDest ) )
    {
        /**
         * Faliure
         */
        return false;
    }
    std::swap( pSrc, pDest );
}

/**
 * If we make it here, we have a polygon that survived.
 * Copy it to out.
 */
out->nElem = pSrc->nElem;
for( i=0; i<pSrc->nElem; i++ )
{
    out->pList[i] = pSrc->pList[i];
}

/**
 * Success
 */
return true;
}
```

You can perform portal rendering in one of two ways, depending on the fill rate of the hardware you're running on and the speed of the host processor. The two methods are *exact* portal rendering and *approximative* portal rendering.

Exact Portal Rendering

To render a portal scene using exact portal rendering, you use a simple recursive algorithm. Each cell has a list of polygons, a list of portals, and a visited bit. Each portal has a pointer to the cell adjacent to it. You start the algorithm knowing where the camera is situated, where it's pointing, and which cell it is sitting in. From this, along with other information like the height, width, and field of view of the camera, you can determine the initial viewing cone that represents the entire viewable area on the screen. Also, you clear the valid bit for all the cells in the scene.

You draw all of the visible regions of the cell's polygons (the visible regions are found by clipping the polygons against the current viewing cone. Also, you set the visited bit to true. Then you walk the list of portals for the cell. If the cell on the other side hasn't been visited, you try to clip the portal against the viewing cone. If a valid portal fragment results from the operation, you have the area of the portal that was visible from the current viewing cone. Take the resulting portal fragment and use it to generate a new viewing cone. Finally, you recurse into the cell adjacent to the portal in question using the new viewing cone. You repeat this process until there are no new cells to traverse into. Pseudocode to do this appears in Listing 9.3.

Listing 9.3: Pseudocode for exact portal rendering

```
void DrawSceneExact
    for( all cells )
        cell.visited = false
    currCell = cell camera is in
    currCone = viewing cone of camera
    currCell.visited = true
    VisitCell( currCell, currCone )

void VisitCell( cell, viewCone )
    for( each polygon in cell )
        polygon fragment = viewCone.clip( current polygon )
        if( polygon fragment is valid )
            draw( polygon fragment )
    for( each portal )
        portal fragment = viewCone.clip( current portal )
        if( portal fragment is valid )
            if( !portal.otherCell.visited )
                portal.otherCell.visited = true
                newCone = viewing cone of portal fragment
                VisitCell( portal.otherCell, newCone )
```

I haven't talked about how to handle rendering objects (such as enemies, players, ammo boxes, and so forth) that would be sitting in these cells. It's almost impossible to guarantee zero overdraw if you have to draw objects that are in cells. Luckily, there is the z-buffer so you don't need to worry; you just draw the objects for a particular cell when you recurse into it. Handling objects without a depth buffer can get hairy pretty quickly; be happy you have it.

Approximative Portal Rendering

As the fill rate of cards keeps increasing, it's becoming less and less troublesome to just throw up your hands and draw some triangles that won't be seen. The situation is definitely much better than it was a few years ago, when software rasterizers were so slow that you wouldn't even think of wasting time drawing pixels you would never see. Also, since the triangle rate is increasing so rapidly it's quickly getting to the point where the time you spend clipping off invisible regions of a triangle takes longer than it would to just draw the triangle and let the hardware sort any problems out.

In approximative portal rendering, you only spend time clipping portals. Objects in the cells and the triangles making up the cell boundaries are either trivially rejected or drawn. When you want to draw an object, you test the bounding sphere against the frustum. If the sphere is completely outside the frustum, you know that it's completely obscured by the cells you've already drawn, so you don't draw the object. If any part of it is visible, you just draw the entire object, no questions asked. While you do spend time drawing invisible triangles (since part of the object may be obscured) you make up for it since you can draw the object without any special processing using one big DrawIndexedPrimitive or something similar. The same is true for portal polygons. You can try to trivially reject polygons in the cell and save some rendering time, or just blindly draw all of them when you enter the cell.

Another plus when you go with an approximative portal rendering scheme is that the cells don't need to be strictly convex; they can have any number of concavities in them and still render correctly if a z-buffer is used. Remember, however, that things like containment tests become untrivial when you go with concave cells; you can generally use something like a BSP tree for each cell to get around these problems.

Portal Effects

Assuming that all of the portals and cells are in a fixed location in 3-D, there isn't anything terribly interesting that we you do with portal rendering. However, that's a restriction you don't necessarily need to put on yourself. There are a few nifty effects that can be done almost for free with a portal rendering engine, two of which I'll cover here: mirrors and teleporters.

Mirrors

Portals can be used to create mirrors that reflect the scene back onto you. Using them is much easier when you're using exact portal rendering (clipping all drawn polygons to the boundaries of the viewing cone for the cell the polygons are in); when they're used with approximative portal rendering a little more work needs to be done.

Mirrors can be implemented with a special portal that contains a transformation matrix and a pointer back to the parent cell. When this portal is reached, the viewing cone is transformed by the portal's transformation matrix. You then continue the recursive portal algorithm, drawing the cell we're in again with the new transformation matrix that will make it seem as if we are looking through a mirror.

> **Warning:** Note that you should be careful when using multiple mirrors in a scene. If two mirrors can see each other, it is possible to infinitely recurse between both portals until the stack overflows. This can be avoided by keeping track of how many times you have recursed into a mirror portal and stopping after some number of iterations.

To implement mirrors you need two pieces of information: How do you create the mirror transformation matrix, and how do you transform the viewing cone by that matrix? I'll answer each of these questions separately.

Before you can try to make the mirror transformation matrix, you need an intuitive understanding of what the transformation should do. When you transform the viewing cone by the matrix, you will essentially be flipping it over the mirror such that it is sitting in world space exactly opposite where it was before. Figure 9.4 shows what is happening.

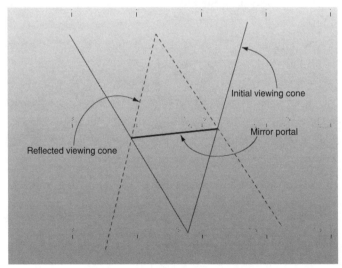

Figure 9.4:
2-D example of view cone reflection

For comprehension's sake, let's give the mirror its own local coordinate space. To define it, you need the **n**, **o**, **a**, and **p** vectors to put the matrix together (see Chapter 3). The **p** vector is any point on the mirror; you can just use the first vertex of the portal polygon. The **a** vector is the normal of the portal polygon (so in the local coordinate space, the mirror is situated at the origin in the x-y plane). The **n** vector is found by crossing **a** with any vector that isn't parallel to it (let's just use the up direction, <0,1,0>) and normalizing the result. Given **n** and **a**, **o** is just the normalized cross product of the two. Altogether this becomes:

$$\mathbf{a} = \text{mirror}_{normal}$$

$$\mathbf{n} = \overline{\mathbf{a} \times \langle 0,1,0 \rangle}$$

$$\mathbf{o} = \overline{\mathbf{a} \times \mathbf{n}}$$

$$\mathbf{T}_{mirror} = \begin{bmatrix} - & \mathbf{n} & - & 0 \\ - & \mathbf{o} & - & 0 \\ - & \mathbf{a} & - & 0 \\ - & \mathbf{p} & - & 1 \end{bmatrix}$$

Warning: The cross product is undefined when the two vectors are parallel, so if the mirror is on the floor or ceiling you should use a different vector rather than <0,1,0>. <1,0,0> will suffice.

However, a transformation matrix that converts points local to the mirror to world space isn't terribly useful by itself. To actually make the mirror transformation matrix you need to do a bit more work. The final transformation needs to perform the following steps:

■ Transform world space vertices to the mirror's local coordinate space. This can be accomplished by multiplying the vertices by $\mathbf{T}_{mirror}^{-1}$.

■ Flip the local space vertices over the x-y plane. This can be accomplished by using a scaling transformation that scales by 1 in the x and y directions and –1 in the z direction (see Chapter 3). We'll call this transformation $\mathbf{T}_{reflect}$.

■ Finally, transform the reflected local space vertices back to world space. This can be accomplished by multiplying the vertices by $\mathbf{T}_{mirror}$.

Given these three steps you can compose the final transformation matrix, $\mathbf{M}_{mirror}$.

$$\mathbf{M}_{mirror} = \mathbf{T}_{mirror}^{-1} \mathbf{T}_{reflect} \mathbf{T}_{mirror}$$

Given $\mathbf{M}_{mirror}$, how do you apply the transformation to the viewing cone, which is just a single point and a set of planes? I haven't discussed how to apply transformations to planes yet, but now seems like a great time. There is a real way to do it, given the plane defined as a 1x4 matrix:

$$\mathbf{n} = \begin{bmatrix} a & b & c & d \end{bmatrix}$$

$$\mathbf{n}' = \mathbf{n}(\mathbf{M}^{-1})^{T}$$

If you don't like that there's a slightly more intuitive way that requires you to do a tiny bit more work. The problem with transforming normals by a transformation matrix is that you don't want them to be translated, just rotated. If you translated them they wouldn't be normal-length anymore, and wouldn't correctly represent a normal for anything. If you just zero-out the translation component of $\mathbf{M}_{mirror}$, ($\mathbf{M}_{14}$, $\mathbf{M}_{24}$, and $\mathbf{M}_{34}$), and multiply it by the normal component of the plane, it will be correctly transformed. Alternatively you can just do a 1x4 times 4x4 operation, making the first vector [a,b,c,0].

> **Warning:** This trick only works for rigid-body transforms (ones composed solely of rotations, translations, and reflections).

So you create two transformation matrices, one for transforming regular vectors and one for transforming normals. You multiply the view cone location by the vector transformation matrix, and multiply each of the normals in the view cone planes by the normal transformation matrix. Finally, recompute the *d* components for each of the planes by taking the negative dot product of the transformed normal and the transformed view cone location (since the location is sitting on each of the planes in the view cone).

You should postpone rendering through a mirror portal until you have finished with all of the regular portals. When you go to draw a mirror portal, you clone the viewing cone and transform it by $\mathbf{M}_{mirror}$. Then you reset all of the visited bits, and continue the algorithm in the cell that owned the portal. This is done for all of the mirrors visited. Each time you find one, you add it to a mirror queue of mirror portals left to process.

You must be careful if you are using approximative portal rendering and you try to use mirrors. If you draw cells behind the portal, the polygons will interfere with each other because of z-buffer issues. Technically, what you see in a mirror is a flat image, and should always occlude things it is in front of. The way you are rendering a mirror (as a regular portal walk) it has depth and faraway things in the mirror may not occlude near things that should technically be behind it. To fix this, before you render through the mirror portal, you change the z-buffer comparison function to D3DCMP_ALWAYS and draw a screen space polygon over the portal polygon with the depth set to the maximum depth value. This essentially resets the z-buffer of the portal region so that everything drawn through the mirror portal will occlude anything drawn behind it. I recommend you use exact portal rendering if you want to do mirrors or translocators, which I'll discuss next.

Translocators and Non-Euclidean Movement

One of the coolest effects you can do with portal rendering is create non-Euclidean spaces to explore. One effect is having a doorway floating in the middle of a room that leads to a different area; you can see the different area through the door as you move around it. Another effect is having a small structure with a door, and upon entering the structure you realize there is much more space inside of it than could be possible given the dimensions of the structure from the outside. Imagine a small cube with a small door that opens into a giant amphitheater. Neither of these effects is possible in the real world, making them all the neater to have in a game.

You perform this trick in a way similar to the way you did mirrors, with a special transformation matrix you apply to the viewing cone when you descend through the portal. Instead of a mirror portal which points back to the cell it belongs to, a translocator portal points to a cell that can be anywhere in the scene. There are two portals that are the same size (but not necessarily the same orientation), a source portal and a destination portal. When you look through the source portal, the view is seen as if you were looking through the destination portal. Figure 9.5 may help explain this.

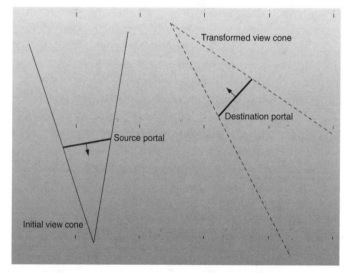

Figure 9.5: 2-D representation of the translocator transformation

To create the transformation matrix to transform the view cone so that it appears to be looking through the destination portal, you compute local coordinate space matrices for both portals using the same **n**, **o**, **a**, and **p** vectors we used in the mirrors section. This gives you two matrices, $\mathbf{T}_{source}$ and $\mathbf{T}_{dest}$. Then to compute $\mathbf{M}_{translocator}$, you do the following steps:

■ Transform the vectors from world space to the local coordinate space of the source matrix (multiply them by $\mathbf{T}_{source}^{-1}$).

■ Take the local space vectors and transform them back into world space, but use the destination transformation matrix ($\mathbf{T}_{dest}$).

Given these steps you can compose the final transformation matrix:

$$\mathbf{M}_{translocator} = \mathbf{T}_{source}^{-1}\mathbf{T}_{destination}$$

The rendering process for translocators is identical to rendering mirrors and has the same caveats when approximative portal rendering is used.

Portal Generation

Portal generation, or finding the set of convex cells and interconnecting portals given an arbitrary set of polygons, is a fairly difficult problem. The algorithm I'm going to describe is too complex to fully describe here; it would take much more space than can be allotted. However, it should lead you in the generally right direction if you wish to implement it. David Black originally introduced me to this algorithm.

The first step is to create a leafy BSP of the data set. Leafy BSPs are built differently than node BSPs (the kind discussed in Chapter 3). Instead of storing polygons and planes at the nodes, only planes are stored. Leaves contain lists of polygons. During construction, you take the array of polygons and attempt to find a plane from the set of polygon planes that divides the set into two non-zero sets. Coplanar polygons are put into the side that they face, so if the normal to the polygon is the same as the plane normal, it is considered in front of the plane. Trying to find a splitter will fail if and only if the set of polygons forms a convex cell. If this happens, the set of polygons becomes a leaf; otherwise the plane is used to divide the set into two pieces, and the algorithm recurses on both pieces. An example of tree construction on a simple 12-polygon 2-D data set appears in Figure 9.6.

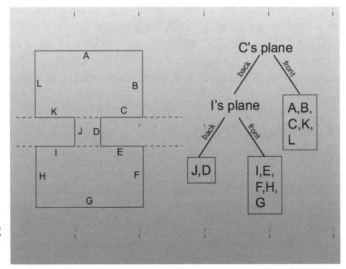

Figure 9.6: Constructing a leafy BSP tree

The leaves of the tree will become the cells of the data set, and the nodes will become the portals. To find the portal polygon given the plane at a node, you first build a polygon that lies in the plane but extends out in all directions past the boundaries of the data set.

This isn't hideously difficult. You keep track of a *universe box*, a cube that is big enough to enclose the entire data set. You look at the plane normal to find the polygon in the universe box that is the most parallel to it. Each of the four vertices of that universe box polygon are projected into the plane. You then drop that polygon through the tree, clipping it against the cells that it sits in. After some careful clipping work (you need to clip against other polygons in the same plane, polygons in adjacent cells, etc.), you get a polygon that isn't obscured by any of the geometry polygons. This becomes a *portal polygon*.

After you do this for each of the splitting planes, you have a set of cells and a set of portal polygons, but no association between them. Generating the associations between cells and portals is fairly involved, unfortunately. The sides of a cell may be defined by planes far away, so it's difficult to match up a portal polygon with a cell that it is abutting. Making the problem worse is the fact that some portal polygons may be too big, spanning across several adjacent cells. In this case you would need to split the cell up.

On top of all that, once you get through this mess and are left with the set of cells and portals, you'll almost definitely have way too many cells and way too many portals. Combining cells isn't easy. You could just merge cells only if the new cell they formed was convex, but this will also give you a less-than-ideal solution: you may need to merge together three or more cells together to get a nice big convex cell, but you wouldn't be able to reach that cell if you couldn't find pairs of cells out of the set that formed convex cells.

Because of problems like this, many engines just leave the process of portal cell generation up to the artists. If you're using approximative portal rendering the artists can place portals fairly judiciously and end up with concave cells, leaving them just in things like doorways between rooms and whatnot. *Quake II* used something like this to help culling scenes behind closed doors; area portals would be covering doors and scenes behind them would only be traversed if the doors weren't closed.

Precalculated Portal Rendering (PVS)

Up to this point I have discussed the usage of portal rendering to find the set of visible cells from a certain point in space. This way you can dynamically find the exact set of visible cells you can see from a certain viewpoint. However, you shouldn't forget one of the fundamental optimization concepts in computer programming: Why generate something dynamically if you can precalculate it?

How do you precalculate the set of visible cells from a given viewpoint? The scene has a near infinite number of possible viewpoints, and calculating the set of visible cells for each of them would be a nightmare. If you want to be able to precalculate anything, you need to cut down the space of entries or cut down the number of positions for which you need to precalculate.

What if you just considered each cell as a whole? If you found the set of all the cells that were visible from <u>any</u> point in the cell, you could just save that.

Each of the n cells would have a bit vector with n entries. If bit i in the bit vector is true, then cell i is visible from the current cell.

This technique of precalculating the set of visible cells for each cell was pioneered by Seth Teller in his 1992 thesis. The data associated with each cell is called the Potentially Visible Set, or PVS for short. It has since been used in *Quake*, *Quake II*, and just about every other first-person shooter under the sun.

Doing this, of course, forces you to give up exact visibility. The set of visible cells from all points inside a cell will almost definitely be more than the set of visible cells from one particular point inside the cell, so you may end up drawing some cells that are totally obscured from the camera. However, what you lose in fill-rate, you gain in processing time. You don't need to do any expensive frustum generation or cell traversal; you simply step through the bit vector of the particular cell and draw all the cells whose bits are set.

Advantages/Disadvantages

The big reason this system is a win is because it offloads work from the processor to the hardware. True, you'll end up drawing more polygons than you have to, but it won't be that much more. The extra cost in triangle processing and fill rate is more than made up for since you don't need to do any frustum generation or polygon clipping.

However, using this system forces you to give up some freedom. The time it takes to compute the PVS is fairly substantial, due to the complexity of the algorithm. This prevents you from having your cells move around; they must remain static. This, however, is forgivable in most cases; the geometry that defines walls and floors shouldn't be moving around anyway.

Implementation Details

I can't possibly hope to cover the material required to implement PVS rendering; Seth Teller spends 150 pages doing it in his thesis. However, I can give a sweeping overview of the pieces of code involved.

The first step is to generate a cell and portal data set, using something like the algorithm discussed earlier. It's especially important to keep your cell count down, since you have an n^2 memory cost to hold the PVS data (where n is the number of cells). Because of this, most systems use the concept of detail polygons when computing the cells. Detail polygons are things like torches or computer terminals—things that don't really define the structural boundaries of a scene but just introduce concavities. Those polygons generally are not considered until the PVS table is calculated. Then they are just added to the cells they belong to. This causes the cells to be concave, but the visibility information will still remain the same so we're all good.

Once you have the set of portals and cells, you iteratively step through each cell and find the set of visible cells from it. To do this, you do something similar to the frustum generation we did earlier in the chapter, but instead of a viewing cone coming out of a point, you generate a solid that represents what is viewable from all points inside the solid. An algorithm to do this (called *portal stabbing*) is given in Seth Teller's thesis. Also, the source code to QV (the application that performs this operation for the *Quake* engine) is available online.

When finished, and you have the PVS vector for each of the cells, rendering is easy. You can easily find out which cell the viewer is in (since each of the cells is convex). Given that cell, you step through the bit vector for that cell. If bit *i* is set, you draw cell *i* and let the z-buffer sort it out.

Application: Mobots Attack!

Mobots Attack! was a collaborative effort between Adrian Perez and Dan Royer, the author of Chapter 5. Their intent was to make an extremely simple client-server game that would provide a starting point for your own 3-D game project. As such, it is severely lacking in some areas but fairly functional in others. There is only one level and it was crafted entirely by hand. Physics support is extremely lacking, as is the user interface. However, it has a fairly robust networking model that allows players to connect to a server, wander about, and shoot rockets at each other.

The objective of the game wasn't to make something glitzy. It doesn't use radiosity, AI opponents, multitexture, or any of the multi-resolution modeling techniques we discussed in Chapter 7. However, adding any of these things wouldn't be terribly difficult. Hopefully, adding cool features to an existing project will prove more fruitful for you than trying to write the entire project yourself. Making a project that was easy to add to was the goal of this game. I'll quickly cover some of the concepts that make this project work.

Interobject Communication

One of the biggest problems in getting a project of this size to work in any sort of reasonable way is interobject communication. For example, when an object hits a wall, some amount of communication needs to go on between the object and the wall so that the object stops moving. When a rocket hits an object, the rocket needs to inform the object that it must lose some of its hit points. When a piece of code wants to print debugging info, it needs to tell the application object to handle it.

Things get even worse. When the client moves, it needs some way to tell the server that its object has moved. But how would it do that? It's not like it can just dereference a pointer and change the position manually; the server could be in a completely different continent.

To take care of this, a messaging system for objects to communicate with each other was implemented. Every object that wanted to communicate needed to implement an interface called iGameObject, the definition of which appears in Listing 9.4:

Listing 9.4: The iGameObject interface

```
typedef uint msgRet;

interface iGameObject
{
public:
    virtual objID GetID() = 0;
    virtual void SetID( objID id ) = 0;

    virtual msgRet ProcMsg( const sMsg& msg ) = 0;
};
```

An objID is an int masquerading as two shorts. The high short defines the class of object that the ID corresponds to, and the low short is the individual instance of that object. Each object in the game has a different objID, and that ID is the same across all the machines playing a game (the server and each of the clients). The code that runs the objID appears in Listing 9.5.

Listing 9.5: objID code

```
typedef uint objID;

inline objID MakeID( ushort segment, ushort offset )
{
    return (((uint)segment)<<16) | ((uint)offset);
}

inline ushort GetIDSegment( objID id )
{
    return (ushort)(id>>16);
}

inline ushort GetIDOffset( objID id )
{
    return (ushort)(id & 0xFFFF);
}

/**
 * These segments define the types of objects
 */
const ushort c_sysSegment    = 0;   // System object
const ushort c_cellSegment   = 1;   // Cell object
const ushort c_playerSegment = 2;   // Player object
const ushort c_spawnSegment  = 3;   // Spawning object
const ushort c_projSegment   = 4;   // Projectile object
const ushort c_paraSegment   = 5;   // Parametric object
const ushort c_tempSegment   = 6;   // Temp object
```

All object communication is done by passing messages around. In the same way you would send a message to a window to have it change its screen position in Windows, you send a message to an object to have it perform a certain task. The message structure holds onto the destination object (an objID), the type of the message (which is a member of the eMsgType enumeration), and then some extra data that has a different meaning for each of the messages. The sMsg structure appears in Listing 9.6.

Listing 9.6: Pseudocode for exact portal rendering

```
struct sMsg
{
    eMsgType      m_type;
    objID         m_dest;
    union
    {
        struct
        {
            point3 m_pt;
        };
        struct
        {
            plane3 m_plane;
        };
        struct
        {
            color3 m_col;
        };
        struct
        {
            int m_i[4];
        };
        struct
        {
            float m_f[4];
        };
        struct
        {
            void* m_pData;
        };
    };

    sMsg( eMsgType type = msgForceDword, objID dest = 0 )
    : m_type( type )
    , m_dest( dest )
    {
    }

    sMsg( eMsgType type, objID dest, float f )
    : m_type( type )
```

```
  , m_dest( dest )
  {
      m_f[0] = f;
  }

  sMsg( eMsgType type, objID dest, int i )
  : m_type( type )
  , m_dest( dest )
  {
      m_i[0] = i;
  }

  sMsg( eMsgType type, objID dest, const point3& pt )
  : m_type( type )
  , m_dest( dest )
  , m_pt(pt)
  {
  }

  sMsg( eMsgType type, objID dest, const plane3& plane )
  : m_type( type )
  , m_dest( dest )
  , m_plane(plane)
  {
  }

  sMsg( eMsgType type, objID dest, void* pData )
  : m_type( type )
  , m_dest( dest )
  , m_pData( pData )
  {
  }
};
```

When an object is created, it registers itself with a singleton object called the message daemon (cMsgDaemon). The registering process simply adds an entry into a map that associates a particular ID with a pointer to an object. Typically what happens is when an object is created, a message will be broadcast to the other connected machines telling them to make the object as well and providing it with the ID to use in the object creation. The cMsgDaemon class appears in Listing 9.7.

Listing 9.7: Code for the message daemon

```
class cMsgDaemon
{
    map< objID, iGameObject* > m_objectMap;
```

```
                    static cMsgDaemon* m_pGlobalMsgDaemon;

        public:
            cMsgDaemon();
            ~cMsgDaemon();

            static cMsgDaemon* GetMsgDaemon()
            {
                // Accessor to the singleton
                if( !m_pGlobalMsgDaemon )
                {
                    m_pGlobalMsgDaemon = new cMsgDaemon;
                }
                return m_pGlobalMsgDaemon;
            }

            void RegObject( objID id, iGameObject* pObj );
            void UnRegObject( objID id );

            iGameObject* Get( int id )
            {
                return m_objectMap[id];
            }

            /**
             * Deliver this message to the destination
             * marked in msg.m_dest.  Throws an exception
             * if no such object exists.
             */
            uint DeliverMessage( const sMsg& msg );
        };
```

When one object wants to send a message to another object, it just needs to fill out an sMsg structure and then call cMsgDaemon::DeliverMessage (or a nicer-looking wrapper use function SendMessage). In some areas of code, rather than ferry a slew of messages back and forth, a local-scope pointer to an object corresponding to an ID can be acquired with cMsgDaemon::Get and then member functions can be called.

Network Communication

The networking model this game has is remarkably simple. There is no client-side prediction and no extrapolation. While this makes for choppy gameplay, hopefully it should make it easier to understand. The messaging model implemented here was strongly based on an article written by Mason McCuskey for *GameDev.net* called "Why pluggable factories rock my multiplayer world."

Here's the essential problem pluggable factories try to solve. Messages arrive to you as datagrams, essentially just buffers full of bits. Those bits represent a message that was sent to you from another client. The first byte (or short, if there are a whole lot of messages) is an ID tag that describes what the message is (a tag of 0x07, for example, may be the tag for a message describing the new position of an object that moved). Using the ID tag, you can figure out what the rest of the data is.

How do you figure out what the rest of the data is? One way would be to just have a massive switch statement with a case label for each message tag that will take the rest of the data and construct a useful message. While that would work, it isn't the right thing to do, OOP-wise. Higher-level code (that is, the code that constructs the network messages) needs to know details about lower-level code (that is, each of the message IDs and to what each of them correspond).

Pluggable factories allow you to get around this. Each message has a class that describes it. Every message derives from a common base class called cNetMessage, which appears in Listing 9.8.

Listing 9.8: Code for the cNetMessage class

```
/**
 * Generic Message
 * Every message class derives from this one.
 */
class cNetMessage
{
public:
    cNetMessage()
    {
    }

    ~cNetMessage()
    {
    }

    /**
     * Write out a bitstream to be sent over
     * the wire that encapsulates the data of
     * the message.
     */
    virtual int SerializeTo( uchar* pOutput )
    {
        return 0;
    }

    /**
     * Take a bitstream as input (coming in over
     * the wire) and convert it into a message
```

```
    */
    virtual void SerializeFrom( uchar *pFromData, int datasize )
    {
    }

    /**
     * This is called on a newly constructed message.
     * The message in essence executes itself.  This
     * works because of the objID system; the message
     * object can communicate it's desired changes to
     * the other objects in the system.
     */
    virtual void Exec() = 0;

    netID GetFrom()
    {
        return m_from;
    }
    netID GetTo()
    {
        return m_to;
    }

    void SetFrom( netID id )
    {
      m_from = id;
    }

    void SetTo( netID id )
    {
      m_to = id;
    }

protected:

    netID m_from;
    netID m_to;
};
```

Every derived NetMessage class has a sister class that is the maker for that particular class type. For example, the login request message class cNM_LoginRequest has a sister maker class called cNM_LoginRequestMaker. The maker class's responsibility is to create instances of its class type. The maker registers itself with a map in the maker parent class. The map associates those first-byte IDs with a pointer to a maker object. When a message comes off the wire, a piece of code looks up the ID in the map, gets the maker pointer, and then tells the maker to create a message object. All the maker does is create a new instance of its sister net message class, call SerializeFrom on it with the incoming data, and then return the instance of the class.

Once a message is created, its Exec() method is called. This is where the message does any work it needs to do. For example, when the cNM_Login-Request is executed (this happens on the server when a client attempts to connect), the message tells the server (using the interobject messaging system discussed previously) to create the player with the given name that was supplied. This will in turn create new messages, like an acknowledgment message notifying the client that it has logged in.

Code Structure

There are six projects in the game workspace. Three of them you've seen before: math3D, netLib, and gameLib. The other three are gameServer, gameClient, and gameCommon. gameCommon just eases the compile times; it has all the code that is common to both the client and the server.

The server is a Win32 dialog app. It doesn't link any of the DirectX headers in, so it should be able to run on any machine with a network card. All of the render code is pretty much divorced from everything else and put into the client library. The gameClient derives from cApplication just like every other sample app in the book.

The companion CD contains documentation to help you get the game up and running on your machine; the client can connect to the local host, so a server and a client can both run on the same machine.

For Further Reading

Abrash, Michael. Michael Abrash's Graphics Programming Black Book, Special Edition. The Coriolis Group, 1997. ISBN: 1576101746.

The last few chapters of this gem discuss the PVS system used in the *Quake* engine. This book is currently out of print.

Teller, Seth. Visibility Computations in Densely Occluded Polyhedral Environments. U.C. Berkeley, 1992.

Seth Teller's Ph.D. thesis. Contains a thorough discussion (150 pages worth) on PVS style rendering. It's available on his web site: http://graphics.lcs.mit.edu/~seth/.

Closing Thoughts

I've covered a lot of ground in this text. Hopefully, it has all been lucid and the steps taken haven't been too big. If you've made it to this point you should have enough knowledge to be able to implement a fairly complex game.

More importantly, you hopefully have acquired enough knowledge about 3-D graphics and game programming that learning new things will come easily. Once you make it over the big hump, you start to see all the fundamental concepts that interconnect just about all of the driving concepts and algorithms.

Appendix

An STL Primer

The world has two kinds of people in it. People who love the STL and use it every day, and people who have never learned the STL. If you're one of the latter, this appendix will hopefully help you get started.

The Standard Template Library is a set of classes and functions that help coders use basic containers (like linked lists and dynamic arrays) and basic algorithms (like sorting). It was officially introduced into the C++ library by the ANSI/ISO C++ Standards Committee in July 1994. Almost all C++ compilers (and all of the popular ones) implement the STL fairly well, while some implementations are better than others (the SGI implementation is one of the better ones; it does a few things much more efficiently than the Visual C++ implementation).

Almost all of the classes in the STL are template classes. This makes them usable with any type of object or class, and they are also compiled entirely as inline, making them extremely fast.

Templates

A quick explanation of templates: They allow you to define a generic piece of code that will work with any type of data, be it ints, floats, or classes.

The canonical example is Swap. Normally, if you want to swap integers in one place and swap floats in another, you write something like Listing A.1.

Listing A.1: Non-template code

```
void SwapInt( int &a, int &b )
{
    int temp = a;
    a = b;
    b = temp;
}

void SwapFloat( float &a, float &b )
{
    float temp = a;
    a = b;
    b = temp;
}
```

This is tolerable as long as you're only swapping around these two types, but what if you start swapping other things? You would end up with 10 or 15 different Swap functions in some file. The worst part is they're all exactly the same, except for the three tokens that declare the type. Let's make Swap a template function. Its source is in Listing A.2.

Listing A.2: Template code

```
template < class swapType >
void Swap( swapType &a, swapType &b )
{
    swapType temp = a;
    a = b;
    b = temp;
}
```

Here's how it works. You use the templated Swap function like you would any other. When the compiler encounters a place that you use the function, it checks the types that you're using, and makes sure they're valid (both the same, since you use T for both a and b). Then it makes a custom piece of code specifically for the two types you're using and compiles it inline. A way to think of it is the compiler does a find-replace, switching all instances of swapType (or whatever you name your template types; most people use T) to the types of the two variables you pass into swap. Because of this, the only penalty for using templates is during compilation; using them at run time is just as fast as using custom functions. There's also a small penalty since using everything inline can increase your code size. However for a large part this point is moot—most STL functions are short enough that the code actually ends up being smaller. Inlining the code for small functions takes less space than saving/restoring the stack frame.

Of course, even writing your own templated Swap() function is kind of dumb, as the STL library has its own function (swap())... but it serves as a good example. Templated classes are syntactically a little different, but we'll get to those in a moment.

Containers

STL implements a set of basic containers to simplify most programming tasks; I used them everywhere in the text. While there are several more, Table A.1 lists the most popular ones.

Table A.1: The basic container classes

vector	Dynamic array class. You append entries on the end (using push_back()) and then can access them using standard array notation (via an overloaded [] operator). When the array needs more space, it internally allocates a bigger block of memory, copies the data over (explicitly, not bitwise), and releases the old one. Inserting data anywhere but the back is slow, as all the other entries need to be moved back one slot in memory.
deque	DeQueue class. Essentially a dynamic array of dynamic arrays. The data doesn't sit linear in memory, but you get array-style lookups really quickly, and can append to the front or the back quickly.
list	Doubly linked list class. Inserting and removing anywhere is cheap, but you can't randomly access things; you can only iterate forward or backard.
slist	Singly linked list class. Inserting to the front is quick, to the back is extremely slow. You shouldn't need to use this, since list is sufficiently fast for most code that would be using a linked list anyway.
map	This is used in a few places in the code; it is an associative container that lets you look up entries given a key. An example would be telephone numbers. You would make a map like so: map<string, int> numMap; and be able to say things like: numMap["joe"] = 5553298;
stack	A simple stack class.
queue	A simple queue class.
string	A vector of characters, with a lot of useful string operations implemented.

Let's look at some sample code. Listing A.3 creates a vector template class of integers, adds some elements, and then asserts both.

Listing A.3: Template sample code

```
#include <list>
#include <vector>
#include <string>

using namespace std;

void main()
{
    // Create a vector and add some numbers
    vector<int> intVec;
    intVec.push_back(5);
    intVec.push_back(10);
    assert( intVec[0] == 5 );
```

```
        assert( intVec.size() == 2 );
}
```

Notice two things: The headers for STL aren't post-fixed by .h, and the code uses the Using keyword, which you may not have seen before. Namespaces essentially are blocks of functions, classes, and variables that sit in their own namespace (in this case, the namespace std). That way all of STL doesn't cloud the global namespace with all of its types (you may want to define your own class called string, for example). Putting the Using keyword at the top of a .cpp file declares that we want the entire std namespace to be introduced into the global namespace so we can just say vector<int>. If we don't do that, we would need to specify the namespace we were referring to, so we would put std::vector<int>.

Iterators

Accessing individual elements of a vector is pretty straightforward; it's, in essence, an array (just a dynamic one) so we can use the same bracket-style syntax we use to access regular arrays. What about lists? Random access in a list is extremely inefficient, so it would be bad to allow the bracket operator to be used to access random elements. Accessing elements in other containers, like maps, makes even less intuitive sense. To remedy these problems, STL uses an iterator interface to access elements in all the containers the same way.

Iterators are classes that each container defines that represent elements in the container. Iterators have two important methods: dereference and increment. Dereference accesses the element to which the iterator is currently pointing. Incrementing an iterator just moves it such that it points to the next element in the container.

For vectors of a type T, the iterator is just an alias to a pointer to a T. Incrementing a pointer will move to the next element in the array, and dereferencing will access the data. Linked lists use an actual class, where increment does something like (currNode = currNode->pNext) and dereference does something like (return currNode->data).

In order to make it work swimmingly, containers define two important iterators, begin and end. The begin iterator points to the first element in the container (vec[0] for vectors, head.pNext for lists). The end iterator points to one-past-the-last element in the container; the first non-valid element (vec[size] for vectors, tail for lists). In other words, when our iterator is pointing to end, we're done. Listing A.4 gives some sample code for using iterators.

Listing A.4: Using iterators

```
#include <list>
#include <vector>
#include <string>

using namespace std;

class cFoo
{
    ...
public:
    void DoSomething();
}

void main()
{
    vector< cFoo > fooVec;

    // Fill fooVec with some stuff
    ...

    // Create an iterator
    vector<cFoo>::iterator iter;

    // Iterate over all the elements in fooVec.
    for( iter = fooVec.begin();
         iter != fooVec.end();
         iter++ )
    {
        (*iter).DoSomething();
    }
}
```

You should realize that the picture is much richer than this. There are actually several different types of iterators (forward only iterators, random iterators, bidirectional iterators). I'm just trying to provide enough information to get your feet wet.

Why are iterators so cool? They provide a standard way to access the elements in a container. This is used extensively by the STL generic algorithms. As a first example, consider the generic algorithm for_each. It accepts three inputs: an iterator pointing to the first element we want to touch, an iterator pointing to the-one-after-the-last element, and a functor. We'll get to functors in a second. The functor is, as far as we care right now, a function called on each element in the container. Look at Listing A.5.

Listing A.5: A cleaned-up version of for_each

```
// for_each.  Apply a function to every element of a range.
template <class iterator, class functor >
functor for_each( iterator curr,  iterator last, functor f)
{
    for ( ; curr != last; ++curr)
    {
        f(*curr);
    }
    return f;
}
```

This code will work with any kind of iterator, be it a list iterator or a vector iterator. So you can run the generic function (or any of the other several dozen generic functions and algorithms) on any container. Pretty sweet, huh?

Functors

The last thing we'll talk about in this short run through the STL are functors. They are used by many of the generic algorithms and functions (like for_each, discussed above). They are classes that implement the parentheses operator. This allows them to mimic the behavior of a regular function, but they can do neat things like save function state (via member variables).

Chapter 6 uses a functor to search through a list of z-buffer formats for a good match using the generic algorithm find_if. The algorithm runs the functor on each element in the container until either it runs out of elements or the functor returns true for one of the elements (in this case, the particular z-buffer format we wish to use). See the source code for Chapter 6 to get an idea of how functors work.

STL Resources

That should be enough information to get you into the basics of the STL. With what you know you should be able to understand the code in the book that uses it. Everything else you can learn off the web. These two sites have plenty of information on the STL, and there are a bunch of good books on the market.

http://www.sgi.com/tech/STL/

http://www.cs.rpi.edu/~musser/stl-html

Index

2-D
   animation, 369
   Cartesian coordinate system, 126
   graphics, 40-55
3-D
   animation, 369
   points, graphing, 126-128
32-bit color, 42

A
ACKs, processing, 294-299
action steering, 220
AddACKMessage(), 294-295
addition, vector, 132-134
AddPacket(), 281-282
AddRef(), 30-31
addressing, texture, 448-451
AdjustWindowRect(), 17
affine mapping, 447
AI, 219-220
   issues with, 220
   pattern-based, 222-223
   rule-based, 245-246
   scripted, 223
alpha, 42, 186, 441
alpha blending, 441-442
   enabling, 443-444
   equation, 442
ambient light, 188
amplitude, 95
AND, 249-250
animation, 369-371
   2-D, 369
   3-D, 369
   bone-based, 370
anistropic filtering, 457-458
API, 2

application programming interface, *see* API
approximating subdivision, 404
approximative portal rendering, 534
artificial intelligence, *see* AI
Assign(), 130
axis-angle rotations, 177-179
   matrix, 177-179

B
back buffer, 44
back-face culling, 152-153
Bernstein polynomial, 382-383
Bezier curves, 380-382
   calculating, 382-387
   cubic, 380-382
   drawing, 391-392
Bezier surfaces, 392-393
   example application, 393-399
big endian, 263-264
bilinear filtering, 456
binary trees, *see* BSP trees
bit block transfer, *see* blit
blending modes, 443-445
blit, 49
blitting, 49-50
bone-based animation, 370
border color addressing, 451
bounding boxes, 183
bounding spheres, 183
   creating, 184-185
b-rep, 141
BSP trees, 197-199
   algorithms, 204-206
   creating, 199-204, 206-217
b-spline, 399
b-spline curves, 399-400
   example application, 400-401

buffers,
    back, 44
    changing format of primary, 107-111
    execute, 344
    in DirectSound, 97
    primary, 97
    secondary, 97
    stencil, 328-329
    vertex, 329-331

C
C++ class, 11
cApplication, 23, 26-28
    modifying, 69-70, 94, 117-118
cells, 525
cGraphicsLayer, 57
    modifying, 356
chasing algorithm, 221
clamp addressing, 450-451
class encapsulation, 23-29
Cleanup(), 273-274
client area, 4
client-server configuration, 266
ClientToScreen(), 16
Clip(), 156
clipper, 55
clipping, 153-158, 339
collision detection, 183-184
color, representing, 186
    on computers, 41-42
color3, 186
color4 structure, 186-188
COM, 30-32
Component Object Model, *see* COM
concave polygons, 141
continuity, 381-382
control points, 380
convex polygons, 141
cooperative levels, 78-79
    setting, 106-107
coordinate space, left-handed, 126
coordinate system, 126
CreateDevice(), 66-67
CreateVertexBuffer(), 330
CreateWindow(), 11-13
cross product, 139-140

cSound, 111-117
cSoundLayer, 105
cTexture, 461-465
cubic Bezier curves, 380-382
cubic environment maps, 481-484
    initializing, 484
culling, *see* back-face culling
curves,
    Bezier, 380-382
    b-spline, 399-400
    drawing, 391-392
    subdividing, 402-403
cWindow, 23-26

D
D3D example application, 357-368
D3DBLEND enumeration, 443-444
D3DCAPS8 structure, 314-317
D3DCMPFUNC enumeration, 321, 515
D3DCOLOR conversion macros, 322
D3DCOLOR structure, 322
D3DCOLORVALUE structure, 322-323
D3DFOGMODE enumeration, 343-344
D3DLIGHT8 structure, 332-333
D3DMATERIAL8 structure, 336-337
D3DMATRIX structure, 324
D3DPRESENT_PARAMETERS structure, 64-66
D3DSTENCILOP enumeration, 513-514
D3DSURFACE_DESC structure, 46-49
D3DTEXTUREOP enumeration, 473-474
D3DTEXTURESTAGESTATETYPE enumeration, 468-472
D3DTRANSFORMSTATETYPE enumeration, 339
D3DVECTOR structure, 323-324
D3DVIEWPORT8 structure, 339-340
D3DXLoadSurfaceFromSurface(), 50-52
dark mapping, 476
data access,
    buffered, 75
    immediate, 75
data, reducing, 304-305
depth issues, 324-325
depth ordering, 443
depth, creating, 325-328
detail maps, 484-490

example application, 490-491
device capabilities,
    determining, 314-317
    validating, 517-519
device render states, setting, 318-321
device states, receiving, 75-76
device types, 312-314
devices, 74
    cooperative levels of, 78-79
    creating, 66-67
diffuse light, 189
Dijkstra's algorithm, 232-235
DIMOUSESTATE structure, 76
Direct3D, 38-40
    device, 309-310
    device object, 54
    example application, 70-73
    implementing, 57-63
    initialization, 63-69, 351-355
    object, 55-56, 309
    render states, 319-321
    shutting down, 69
    texturing, 459-461
    vertex structures, 344-347
Direct3D structures, 322-324
    creating, 56-57
Direct3D8 object, 310
Direct3DDevice8 object, 310-311
Direct3DX library, 357
DirectDraw, 38-39
DirectInput, 73
    devices, 74-79
    implementing, 80-94
    keyboard constants, 76-78
    using, 73
DirectInput object, 79
    creating, 79
directional lights, 191-192
DirectSound, 94-100
    buffers, 97
    example application, 118-123
    implementing, 105-111
    interfaces, 97
DirectSound object, creating, 105-106
DirectX, 35
    installing, 36

dissolve, 516-517
Dist(), 131
division, vector, 134-135
DNS, 265
Domain Name Server, *see* DNS
DOS, 1
dot product, 137-139
double buffering, 44
DrawIndexedPrimitive(), 349-350
DrawIndexedPrimitiveUP(), 350
DrawPrimitive(), 348
DrawPrimitiveUP(), 349
DSBUFFERDESC structure, 97-99

E
edge collapse, 422
edge selection, 423-424
    algorithms, 424-426
emissive light, 189
encapsulation, 23-29
endianness, 263-265
environment mapping, 478-484
epsilon edge, 241
equality, 135-136
error codes, 6
evading algorithm, 222
exact portal rendering, 532-533
execute buffers, 344
extrapolation, 305-307

F
filtering, 454-45
    methods, 454-458
flexible vertex format, 344-345
    flags, 345
floating-point z-buffers, *see* w-buffer
focus, 5, 79
fog, 340-341
    pixel-based, 342
    render states, 342-343
    table-based, 340, 342
    vertex-based, 341-342
form factor, 432-434
forward differencing, 387-389
    implementing, 389-391
forward kinematics, 371-373

frame buffer, 312
frequency, 95
full-screen initialization, 63-69
full-screen rendering, 55

G
game example, 542-549
genetic algorithms, 244-245
geographic independence, 302
geometry pipeline, 338-339
geomorphs, 423
GetClientRect(), 16-17
GetMaterial(), 337
GetReliableData(), 279
GetRenderState(), 319
GetStatus(), 101-102
GetTransform(), 338-339
GetViewport(), 340
gimbal lock, 177-178
globally unique identifier, *see* GUID
gloss maps, 493-495
glow maps, 491-493
Gouraud shading, 195-196
graphic effects, using stencil buffer for, 516-517
graphics layers flags, 351
GUID, 32

H
HAL, 57, 312
handle, 5-6
hardware abstraction layer, *see* HAL
hardware device, 312
hardware emulation layer, *see* HEL
HEL, 57
hierarchical culling, 523-524
hierarchical model for animation, 370
hill climbing, 244-245
homogenous coordinate, 166
host address, 264
host names, 264-265
HRESULT, 6
Hungarian notation, 2-3
HWND, 5-6

I
ICMP, 267
IDirect3D8 interface, 55-56
    acquiring, 351-352
IDirect3DSurface8 interface, 49
IK, *see* inverse kinematics
initialization, 11-14, 63-69
Internet Control Message Protocol, *see* ICMP
Internet Protocol, *see* IP
interpolating subdivision, 404
inverse kinematics, 373-376
    example application, 376-379
inverse, transformation matrix, 169
inversion, 182-183
IP, 266
IP address, 264
IUnknown interface, 30

K
kinematics,
    forward, 371-373
    inverse, 373-376

L
Lambert shading, 195
leaf-based BSP trees, 199
leafy BSP trees, 199
leaves, 198
left-handed coordinate space, 126
length, 127
libraries, 37-38
light,
    mapping, 476-478
    types, 191-194
    using, 332-336
LightEnable(), 334
lighting, 185
    models, 188-190
limit surface, 401
line segments, comparing, 206
lines, clipping, 153-154
link ping, 297
listeners, 80
little endian, 263-264
loading, 51

local coordinate space, 167
locality, testing, 205-206
lock, 44-45
Lock(), 102-103, 330-331
LockRect, 53
locomotion, 220-221
LookAt matrix, 179-181

M

Mag(), 130-131
magnification, 454-455
magnitude, 127
MagSquared(), 131
mapping, 447-448
mask, 402
materials, using, 336-338
mathematical operators, vector, 132-140
matrices, 161-172
matrix, 161, *see also* matrices
    inverse of, 182-183
    multiplication, 173-174
    operations, 161-163
matrix4 structure, 172-173
memory, 52
menu bar, 4
message pump, 11
MessageBox(), 13-14
messages, 5-7
    handling in Windows, 5-7
    processing, 5-7
    window, 17-22
MFC, 22-23
Microsoft Foundation Classes, *see* MFC
minification, 455
MIP mapping, 454
mirror addressing, 449-450
mirrors, 534-537
MMX, 314
modified butterfly method
    example application, 408-420
    subdivision scheme, 405-408
motivation, 220, 241
motor skills, 220
MTUDP classes, 279-286, 293-302
multipass, 475-476
    example application, 495-513

using to set up detail mapping, 489-490
using to set up glow mapping, 492
using to set up light mapping, 477-478
multiple texture blending, 467
multiple textures,
    example application, 495-513
    using, 475-476
multiplication, vector, 134-135
multitexture, 475-476
    example application, 495-513
    using to set up detail mapping, 488-489
    using to set up glow mapping, 492
    using to set up light mapping, 477
multitexturing, 311
multithreading, 268-270
mutex, 270-272

N

network models, 265-266
network play, implementing, 302-307
neural networks, 246-247, 249-251
    example application, 252-261
    training, 251
    using in games, 252
neuron, 247-249
NFA, 241-243
node-based BSP trees, 199
    creating, 199-200
nodes, 198
non-deterministic finite automata, *see* NFA
non-stationary subdivision scheme, 405
non-uniform subdivision scheme, 404-405
normal, 146
Normalize(), 131

O

object viewer, creating, 357-368
objects, 74, 158
    representing, 158-160
octrees, 523-524
OR, 250
origin, 126
overdraw counter, 515
    setting up stencil buffer to implement,
    515-516

P

packets, 267
painter's algorithm, 325
paletted color, 41-42
parallel lights, 191-192
patch, 379, 392-393, 429
path following, 229-230
path planning, 229-237
    example application, 237-241
pattern, 222-223
pattern-based AI, 222-223
perspective mapping, 447
perspective projection matrix, 181
perspective-correct mapping, 447-448
Phong shading, 196-197
physical controllers, 220-221
ping, 297
pitch, 45-46
pixel, 40
pixel fog, 340, 342
pixel formats, 447
plane3 structure, 147-148
planes, 146-147
    constructing, 148-149
    orienting point in, 149-151
    splitting, 151
Play(), 100-101
point lights, 192-193
point sampling, 455
POINT structure, 15-16
point3 operators, 132-140
point3 structure, 129
    functions, 130-131
points, 125-128
    3-D, 126-128
    orienting in plane, 149-151
polygon ordering, 204-205
polygon template structure, 142-143
polygons, 140-141
    clipping, 154-158
portal, 231
    effects, 534-539
    generation, 539-540
    polygon, 540
    stabbing, 542
portal rendering, 524-528

approximative, 534
exact, 532-533
precalculated, 540-542
ports, 265
PostMessage, 15
potential functions, 224-226
    example application, 227-229
Potentially Visible Set, *see* PVS
precalculated portal rendering, 540-542
prediction, 305-307
primary buffers, 97
    changing format of, 107-111
primary surface, 46
primitive types, 347-348
Process(), 228-229
ProcessIncomingACKs(), 294-295
ProcessIncomingData(), 278-279, 291-292
progressive meshes, 421-422
    constructing, 422-423
    implementing, 426-427
progressive radiosity, 432
projection matrix, creating, 354-355
protocols, 266-267
PVS, 540-542

Q

quadtrees, 523-524
QueryInterface, 31

R

radiance, 429
radiosity, 428
    calculating, 429-431
    progressive, 432
    example application, 434-438
Ramp, 314
rasterization, 310
RECT structure, 15-16
reference device 313-314
RefRast, 313
Release, 30-31
ReliableSendTo, 279, 286-293
render states,
    Direct3D, 319-321
    fog, 342-343
    stencil buffer, 514

rendering, 55
resize bars, 4
rotation transformation, 165-166, 175-177
rule-based AI, 245-246

S

scalar quantities, 125
scan line, 42-43
scene management, 521-522
scripted AI, 223
secondary buffers, 97
SendMessage, 15
SetCooperativeLevel(), 78-79, 106-107
SetLight(), 333
SetMaterial(), 337
SetRenderState(), 319
SetStreamSource(), 331
SetTransform(), 338-339
SetViewport(), 340
shading models, 194-197
socket, 265
software device, 312-313
sound, 95-96
sound buffers, working with, 100-103
sparse matrix, 431
specular highlight, 189
specular light, 189
specular maps, 484
specular reflection, 190-191
spherical environment maps, 479-481
splines, 379
Split(), 154, 157-158
spotlights, 193-194
sprites, 369
Standard Template Library, *see* STL
StartListening(), 275-276
StartSending(), 276
Startup(), 273-274
stationary subdivision scheme, 405
steering, 220
    algorithms, 221-241
stencil buffers, 328-329, 513-515
    render states, 514
    using to create effects, 516-517
    using to implement overdraw counter,
    515-516

STL, 551
    containers, 552-554
    functors, 556
    iterators, 554-556
    templates, 551-552
subdivision schemes, 404-405
    modified butterfly method, 405-408
    example application, 408-420
subdivision surfaces, 401
subtraction, vector, 132-134
surfaces, 44-45
    and memory, 52
    complex, 46
    creating Direct3D, 56-57
    drawing, 392-393
    locking, 44-45, 52-54
    primary, 46
    working with, 49-50
Sutherland-Hodgeman algorithm, 155

T

table fog, 340, 342
tagMSG structure, 5
task generation, 220
TCP, 267
tearing, 43
teleporters, *see* translocators
temporal independence, 302
texel, 446
texture, 446
    addressing, 448-451
    aliasing, 452-454
    enabling, 465
    management, 459-460
    mapping, 331-338, 445-447
    stages, 466
    transforms, 474-475
    wrapping, 451-452
ThreadProc(), 276-278
timing, 303-304
title bar, 4
transformation matrix, 535-538
transformation matrix inverse, 169
transformations, 160-161
translation transformation, 160-161, 175
translocators, 537-539

Transmission Control Protocol, *see* TCP
transmission latency ping, 297
tri template structure, 144
triangle fans, 144-145
triangle strips, 144-145
triangle subdivision scheme, 404
triangles, 143-144
trilinear filtering, 456-457
true color, 42

U
UDP, 266
    implementing, 268-302
uniform subdivision scheme, 404
unit sphere, 127
unit vector, 127
universe box, 540
Unlock(), 103
User Datagram Protocol, *see* UDP

V
vector, 125
    equality, 135-136
    length of, 127
    magnitude of, 127
    mathematical operators, 132-140
    quantities, 125
vertex buffers, 329-331
vertex fog, 340-342
vertex split, 422
vertical blank, 43
vertical retrace, 43

vertices, 158
view space, 168
viewport, creating, 354-355
Visual C++, setting up, 36-38

W
WAV files, loading, 103-104
WAVEFORMATEX structure, 99-100
w-buffer, 327-328
w-buffering, 327-328
Win32, 2
    example program, 7-11
window, 3-4
    class, 11
    handle, 5-6
    initializing, 11-14
    messages, 17-22
windowed rendering, 55
Windows, 1-2
    message handling in, 5-7
    user interface, 4
WinMain(), 9-10
wipe, 516-517
WndProc, 13, 15
world coordinate space, 167
wrap addressing, 448-449

X
XOR, 251

Z
z-buffer, 326
z-buffering, 326-327

nVIDIA.

softwaredevelopment**kit**

graphics^n

www.nvidia.com/developer

About the CD

The companion CD-ROM included with this book contains source code, the DirectX 8.0a SDK, and other material, organized into the following directories:

Applications—A 30-day evaluation version of Paint Shop Pro Anniversary Edition.

Book Code—Source code for Chapters 1-9, plus the game *Mobots Attack!*. See the Readme file in this directory for instructions on compiling the code.

DirectX 8.0a SDK—The DirectX SDK; must be installed if you want to use any of the book code.

Documents—Reading material covering such topics as multithreading, radiosity, and the *Quake II* BSP file format.

Other code—Other source code including *Descent* 1 & 2, *Quake*, and STLport.

For more information, see the Readme file on the root.

> ***Warning:*** Opening the CD package makes this book nonreturnable.